AREA HANDBOOK

for

NIGERIA

Co-Authors

Harold D. Nelson

James Mc Laughlin
Barbara J. Marvin
Philip W. Moeller
Donald P. Whitaker

Research and writing were completed July 1971

Published 1972

(This handbook supersedes the March 1964 edition)

DA Pam 550–157

916.69
N426a

Library of Congress Catalog Card Number: 77–183 909

For sale by the Superintendent of Documents, U.S. Government Printing Office

Washington, D.C. 20402–Price $3.50

Stock Number 0820–0404

FOREWORD

This volume is one of a series of handbooks prepared by Foreign Area Studies (FAS) of The American University, designed to be useful to military and other personnel who need a convenient compilation of basic facts about the social, economic, political, and military institutions and practices of various countries. The emphasis is on objective description of the nation's present society and the kinds of possible or probable changes that might be expected in the future. The handbook seeks to present as full and as balanced an integrated exposition as limitations on space and research time permit. It was compiled from information available in openly published material. An extensive bibliography is provided to permit recourse to other published sources for more detailed information. There has been no attempt to express any specific point of view or to make policy recommendations. The contents of the handbook represent the work of the authors and FAS and do not represent the official view of the United States government.

An effort has been made to make the handbook as comprehensive as possible. It can be expected, however, that the material, interpretations, and conclusions are subject to modification in the light of new information and developments. Such corrections, additions, and suggestions for factual, interpretive, or other change as readers may have will be welcomed for use in future revisions. Comments may be addressed to:

The Director
Foreign Area Studies
The American University
5010 Wisconsin Avenue, N.W.
Washington, D.C. 20016

PREFACE

Extensive political, economic, and social changes have occurred in Nigeria since the research and writing of the first edition of the *Area Handbook for Nigeria* were completed in 1961 and brief amendments were made in the second edition in 1964. A thoroughly revised third edition is presented to bring up to date the material about a country and society of continuing importance in West Africa.

The second edition was published at the beginning of an era of political crises that strained regional relationships in the country, threatened national unity, and led to a series of military coups d'etat in 1966. Attempts by the Federal Military Government (FMG) to deal with Nigeria's internal problems were interrupted by thirty months of civil war, which erupted after the secession of the eastern states as the separate and self-proclaimed Republic of Biafra. In early 1970 the secessionists were defeated by federal forces, and the FMG began a vast program of reconstruction in preparation for a return to civilian rule by a target date of 1976.

The present handbook seeks to provide a compact and objective exposition of the dominant social, political, and economic aspects of Nigerian society. It is designed to give the reader an understanding of the forces operating within the society. There remain, however, a number of gaps in information to which attention has been called.

The spelling of place names generally follows those established for West Africa by the United States Board on Geographic Names. The spelling of other proper names conforms to current usage in the country or to the most authoritative available sources.

The *Area Handbook for Nigeria* published in 1961 was prepared by a research team composed of Norman Walpole, Donald M. Bouton, Neda A. Franges, Lyman H. Legters, Jr., Edward J. McNally, Barbara Reason, and Linvill F. Watson under the chairmanship of John A. Cookson. Chapter 6, Social Systems, of the current revised edition was contributed by Dr. Charles O. Noble.

The authors wish to thank those persons in various governmental and international organizations who gave of their time, documents, and special knowledge of the country to help improve the work.

COUNTRY SUMMARY

1. COUNTRY: Republic of Nigeria; formerly British colony and protectorate of Nigeria; date of independence, October 1, 1960; became republic, October 1, 1963. Capital Lagos.

2. SIZE: 356,669 square miles.

3. TOPOGRAPHY: Five major geographic divisions consisting of low coastal zone along Gulf of Guinea; succeeded northward by area of hills and low plateaus; Niger-Benue River Valley bisecting central part of country on east-west axis; broad stepped plateau stretching to northern border with highest elevations over 4,000 feet; mountainous zone along eastern border includes country's highest point (6,700 feet).

4. CLIMATE: Tropical climatic variations governed by interaction of moist southwest monsoon, dry northeast trade winds (harmattan), and high equatorial easterlies. Mean maximum temperatures of 89°F. (south) and 95°F. (north); mean minimum temperatures of 71°F. (south) and 66°F. (north). High humidity in south throughout year, May–October in north; low humidity in north during dry season. Two rainy seasons in south (March–July and September–November) with dry interseasons; single rainy season north of Niger-Benue River Valley (April–October) and hot, dry season (November–March). Annual rainfall decreases northward; 80 inches in coastal zone (except Niger Delta, with average of over 140 inches); 20 to 30 inches in north.

5. POPULATION: Over 55 million estimated in 1971; annual growth rate, 2.4 to 2.8 percent. Heaviest concentrations in southwestern, southeastern, and northern sections separated by sparsely inhabited Middle Belt (see Glossary). One-sixth to one-fifth of population lives in urban centers of 20,000 or more. Population approximately 99.8 percent African, divided into more than 200 ethnic groups. Major groups (Hausa, Yoruba, and Ibo) constitute 58 percent of total; Edo, Fulani, Ibibio, Ijaw, Kanuri, and Tiv account for over 22 percent.

6. LANGUAGES: More than 200 indigenous languages and dialects. Principal northern language is Hausa (mother tongue of roughly 16 million people); other major languages are Ibo in southeast and Yoruba in southwest; all have scripts. English is official language used for government affairs, education, and mass

communication; classical Arabic has special religious significance in north.

7. RELIGION: Of adult population, about 44 percent are Muslims; 22 percent are Christians; and rest adhere to traditional forms. Practice of Christianity or Islam does not preclude participation in traditional rituals. Islam more widespread in north, Christianity in southeast; mixture of both in southwest.

8. ADMINISTRATIVE DIVISIONS: Twelve states divided into provinces or divisions and hundreds of smaller units known as local authorities in north and districts or counties in south. Two northern states have provinces with no divisions; four have only divisions. Local authority or county and subordinate-level units (municipalities, villages, and rural councils) are under control of popularly elected officials in some areas and traditional rulers and their advisers in others.

9. GOVERNMENT: Federal Military Government (FMG) has ruled since 1966; top policymaking body is 19-member Supreme Military Council composed of military and police officers and single civilian administrator for East Central State. Administrative body is 16-member Federal Executive Council, functioning as cabinet. Major General Yakubu Gowon, chairman of both councils, is chief of state and commander in chief of armed forces. Some constitutional principles remain in effect, but FMG governs by decree. Legislative functions vested in Supreme Military Council. Court system functions independently, as established by constitution. State governments controlled by FMG-appointed military governors, all members of Supreme Military Council.

10. JUSTICE: Federal Supreme Court at Lagos is court of final appeal, has original jurisdiction in interstate and federal-state disputes and cases involving constitutionally guaranteed fundamental rights. High Court of Justice in each of six southern states, one for all six northern states; all have wide original jurisdiction and appellate powers over lower courts. Separate Sharia Court of Appeal in north considers cases under Islamic customary law. Lower courts include magistrate courts and area courts. Legal system based on inherited British common law, parliamentary enactments, 1963 Constitution, and FMG decrees. Criminal law entirely statutory with separate penal codes for northern and southern states.

11. EDUCATION: In 1968 an estimated 3.3 million students in school through secondary level. About 3.1 million students in primary schools, and approximately 18,000 persons enrolled in technical schools. Over 30,000 in teacher training schools in 1966. Primary education free in Lagos, Mid-Western, and Western

States; cost partially subsidized in eastern and northern states. Five universities offer degree programs. Literacy rate estimated at 25 percent in Lagos area and some sections of eastern states, lower in other areas.

12. HEALTH: Major prevalent diseases include tuberculosis, parasitic infections, leprosy, malaria, dysentery, pneumonia, and other respiratory diseases. Health problems complicated by nutritional deficiencies, disease-carrying insects, water pollution, and poor sanitation practices.

13. ECONOMY: Based primarily on agriculture and mineral commodities, which provide about three-fifths of national income. Largely self-sufficient in food production, country has relied heavily on agricultural exports. Industrial activity contributes only small percentage of gross national product (GNP); centers on primary extraction and processing of consumer and export goods and includes cement factories, lumber and plywood mills, textile mills, and petroleum refinery. Large petroleum reserves offshore and in Mid-Western and Rivers States are major sources of foreign exchange. Civil war (1967–70) severely strained country's economic infrastructure and drained foreign exchange reserves. Oil exports improving balance of payments outlook, but some import restrictions and exchange controls still required in mid-1971.

14. PRINCIPAL EXPORTS: Crude oil, cocoa, groundnuts (peanuts), palm products, rubber, cotton, timber and wood products, and hides and skins.

15. PRINCIPAL IMPORTS: Machinery, transportation equipment, manufactured goods, textiles, and chemicals. Principal sources are United Kingdom, Japan, United States, and European Economic Community (EEC, the Common Market).

16. CURRENCY: Monetary unit is Nigerian pound (N£) divided into 20 Nigerian shillings; 1 Nigerian pound equals US$2.80.

17. COMMUNICATIONS: Posts and telecommunications provided by quasi-commercial organization under direction of federal Ministry of Communications. In 1969, 80,839 telephones in domestic use (about 1 per 700 inhabitants), 52 telex lines, 42 private wire telegraphs, 1,760 postal facilities. External telecommunication services to other African countries and most other parts of world. Government-owned and -operated domestic radio services; international broadcasts over Voice of Nigeria to Africa, Middle East, and Europe; expanding government-owned television service to major population centers; highly developed press publishes 21 daily and 21 weekly newspapers and numerous periodicals.

18. RAILROADS: 2,200 route-miles of track; main lines from

Lagos and Port Harcourt run northward, joining at Kaduna and proceeding through Zaria and Kano to Nguru cattle-raising area in northeast; important branch lines to Maiduguri in North Eastern State, tin-producing center of Jos, Kaura Namoda in groundnut area of northwest, and Niger River port at Baro. Pre-civil war annual rail traffic of 12 million passengers and 3 million tons of freight. Rail operations, seriously affected by war, showed some recovery in 1971.

19. INLAND WATERWAYS: Extensive system embracing Niger, Benue, and Cross rivers. Creeks and lagoons in south form continuous waterway from western border to Niger Delta.

20. PORTS: Major ports at Lagos and Port Harcourt; smaller ones at Calabar and Warri. Other minor ports at Bonny and Degema in southeast and Forcados, Burutu, Koko, and Sapele on western side of Niger Delta.

21. ROADS: In 1970 about 55,500 miles of roads, of which 9,500 miles were hard surfaced; 13,500 miles of trunk roads linked federal and state capitals, main administrative centers, and ports. Lack of maintenance and heavy use during civil war caused considerable road deterioration.

22. CIVIL AVIATION: International airports at Lagos-Ikeja and Kano; major domestic airports at Calabar, Enugu, and Port Harcourt in east, Benin City and Ibadan in west, Kaduna, Jos, Sokoto, Maiduguri, and Yola in north; numerous smaller airports. Domestic service provided by government-owned Nigerian Airways Corporation; international service by Nigerian Airways Corporation and foreign commercial carriers to other African countries, Europe, Middle East, Soviet Union, and United States.

23. INTERNATIONAL MEMBERSHIPS AND AGREEMENTS: British Commonwealth of Nations; Organization of African Unity (OAU); United Nations and its specialized agencies, including United Nations Economic Commission for Africa (ECA); Organization of Petroleum Exporting Countries (OPEC); African Development Bank; Cocoa Producers' Alliance; Inter-African Coffee Organization; Chad Basin Commission; Niger River Basin Commission; Union of National Radio and Television Organization of Africa. Articles of affiliation signed with European Economic Community, but not in effect in mid-1971. No military assistance agreements, but bilateral trade agreements with various Western countries and East European communist countries.

24. ARMED FORCES: Product of British military tradition; equipped substantially by Western countries and East European communist sources during civil war. Approximate total strength of 252,000 includes army (240,000) organized in three light infantry

divisions, one marine commando division. Air force (7,000) equipped with less than 40 combat aircraft, including Soviet ground attack jets and Italian and Czechoslovakian armed jet trainers; other planes include light transports, conventional liaison-communications aircraft, helicopters. Navy (5,000) equipped with light coastal vessels, one frigate. National police with total strength of about 30,000.

NIGERIA

TABLE OF CONTENTS

LIST OF ILLUSTRATIONS

LIST OF TABLES

Figure 1. The Federal Republic of Nigeria

CHAPTER 1

GENERAL CHARACTER OF THE SOCIETY

The Republic of Nigeria—a British colony and protectorate before independence on October 1, 1960—is the largest of the coastal states of West Africa. About 357,000 square miles in area, it lies wholly within the tropics and occupies a dominant position along the Gulf of Guinea. A nation in which English is the official language, it is surrounded by French-speaking neighbors: Dahomey to the west, Niger to the north, Chad to the northeast, and Cameroon to the east.

Nigeria is a land of great contrast, both in its physical attributes and in its cultural patterns. Its main topographic areas are distinguishable by marked variations in terrain, vegetation, and climate (see ch. 2, Physical Environment). In its extreme southern limits a palm-studded coastline more than 400 miles long is backed by a hot, humid belt of mangrove swamps succeeded northward by a broad area of tropical rain forest that merges in the country's eastern extremity with dense groves of oil palms. Above the rain forest a series of plains and broad, lofty plateaus are characterized by open woodland and savanna; they extend into the lower sections of the drier northern country, where semidesert conditions exist.

On an east-west axis, further physical variations include the deep valleys carved by the Niger and Benue rivers, which enter from opposite sides of the country, merge in the central plateau region, and course southward, forming a broad delta at the Gulf of Guinea. In the east the land rises to a low mountain range where peaks ranging to nearly 7,000 feet above sea level present a scarped edge on the border with Cameroon.

The country—Africa's most populous—is inhabited by an estimated 55 million people. Although the average density in 1970 was between 151 and 154 persons per square mile, the population was unevenly distributed, with areas of high density in the southeast, the southwest, and the central section of the north. About one-fifth of the people lived in urban centers of 20,000 or more; the rest resided in basically rural settings. Ibadan, the capital of Western State, had more than 1 million inhabitants, and approximately 700,000 resided in the federal capital of Lagos. The annual growth

1

rate of approximately 2.6 percent, continued high fertility, **and** declining mortality rates indicated that if the growth rate were unchecked, the predominantly young population probably would double in size before the end of the twentieth century (see ch. 4, Population and Labor).

According to the most recent census (1963), Nigeria is inhabited by more than 200 different ethnic groups. The Nigerian peoples fall into five broad cultural categories: the Muslim Sudanic cultures centered traditionally on northern city-states; the nomadic pastoralists scattered throughout the north; the forest and independent coastal village communities of the southeast; the former forest kingdoms of the southwest; and the many small groups of the Middle Belt (see Glossary) and those along the eastern frontier.

Although English is the official language of government, education, and the mass media, almost as many local languages and dialects are spoken as there are ethnic groups. This extraordinary variety is carried over to the local religious forms (which exist alongside Islam and Christianity) and to the diversity that characterizes sociopolitical attitudes, values, and ways of life (see ch. 6, Social Systems; ch. 11, Value Systems).

The outstanding characteristics of modern Nigerian society have been indelibly imprinted with the dominant traits of the three most populous and powerful ethnic groups—the Hausa, the Yoruba, and the Ibo, who together represent nearly 60 percent of the total population. Although no section of the country is ethnically unmixed, each of these major groups predominates in different sections. The north is the domain of the Hausa who, along with more than 1 million Fulani, represent the Muslim Sudanic culture. The west is dominated by the Yoruba, representing the forest kingdom cultures. The Ibo, characterized traditionally by independent communities, are largely concentrated in the east. Other groups range in size from small clusters of 1,000 or less to those numbering more than 1 million. The larger groups include the Tiv and the Nupe of the Middle Belt; the Ibibio, Efik, and Ijaw of the southeast; the Edo centered on the ancient royal city of Benin; and the widespread Muslim Kanuri of the northeast (see ch. 5, Ethnic Groups and Languages).

Except for the successful proselytizing activities of Islam among the Yoruba, religion to a degree also has been compartmentalized. The Hausa, the Fulani, and other peoples of the north are predominantly Muslim, whereas Christianity has made its greatest inroads among peoples of the south, particularly the Ibo and the Yoruba. The remaining groups adhere to a variety of traditional religious practices. About 44 percent of all Nigerians are

2

Muslims, and 22 percent are Christians. As rural traditionalists develop contacts with urban societies, they are gradually accepting Islam or Christianity. Nominal adherence, however, is common, and the profession of the adopted faith frequently does not preclude continued acceptance of traditional beliefs (see ch. 6, Social Systems).

Nigerian living standards vary considerably from area to area and between rural and urban environments. Those people who have had contact with European ways of life aspire to education and consumer products, neither of which are cheaply acquired. With a rising cost of living, widespread urban unemployment, and an annual per capita income equivalent to about US$80 large numbers of people do not have access to the imported goods—radios, bicycles, and automobiles—that have become symbols of status for the more affluent citizens (see ch. 7, Living Conditions).

The urban sprawl of such cities as Ibadan and Lagos, with their government buildings, modern transportation systems, and well-stocked shops, reflects in varying degrees the metropolitan atmosphere of their European model. Housing varies from multistoried modern dwellings to traditional mud huts with thatched or corrugated metal roofs. In many of the cities the flow of migrants exceeds efforts to construct housing to accommodate them. The older Muslim cities of the north are Middle Eastern in style; most of them are overcrowded and disease ridden. Few of the urban centers throughout the country have adequate sanitary facilities.

In the rural or traditional sectors of the country, conditions of life derive largely from Nigerian cultures rather than from foreign models. Life is based largely on the immediate family circle and the extended family. Housing takes the form of compounds rather than single dwellings. Most rural peoples are engaged in some form of agricultural activity, and many have little contact with the Western influences seen in the cities.

Nigeria's infant mortality rate is high, and many people suffer the effects of diseases that have not been completely controlled by the increasing but limited practice of modern medicine. Although the efforts of the federal and state governments, international health organizations, and missionaries have eradicated some of the infections that once were endemic to the area, progress is limited by a shortage of trained medical personnel and health facilities. Large numbers of Nigerians, particularly those in remote rural areas, continue to rely on traditional diagnosis and treatment in times of illness.

Archaeological discoveries indicate that the area's earliest known culture was that of the Iron Age Nok peoples, who lived above the confluence of the Niger and Benue rivers sometime between 500 B.C. and A.D. 200. The early history of peoples from whom present-day Nigerians are descended is still being developed from a variety of sources. All information, however, points to early migratory movements from other parts of the African continent, probably the north and the east. Literate recordkeeping societies in the northern part of the country trace cultural and economic ties with Islamic centers in North Africa over a complex series of trade routes several hundreds of years before European explorers arrived in the southern areas (see ch. 3, Historical Setting).

Although attempts were made by European explorers and traders to establish permanent posts along the Guinea coast as early as the fifteenth century, British commercial interests—including the slave trade—were clearly dominant by the end of the eighteenth century. During the nineteenth century the British government, impelled at first by public consternation at the atrocities of the slave trade, found itself deeply involved in the internal affairs of the coast. With the diminution of anti-imperialist sentiment in Great Britain and subsequent British participation in the race for African colonies, the area that later became independent Nigeria changed its status in 1900 from a sphere of British influence to a protectorate of the British crown.

Nigeria emerged as a geopolitical entity in 1914 when its northern and southern areas were united. By that time British administrators, traders, and missionaries had been at work, particularly in the southern area, for about 100 years, during which period the influences of Western education and other social institutions had continued to expand while portions of traditional local systems declined. In the northern sector, however, the British found it easier to rule indirectly through the Muslim emirs, whose autocratic systems were deliberately maintained and whose traditional Islamic resistance to Westernization of any kind was thereby bolstered.

Northerners have long been regarded by southern Nigerians—particularly the Ibo—as tradition bound and ultraconservative. Lines of class distinction in that area have been rigidly drawn, with ultimate authority resting in the hands of the Fulani emirs, who assumed control over the Muslim Hausa after an early nineteenth-century holy war. Personal achievement is not regarded by most Hausa inhabitants as an avenue to success because leadership and favored position have been limited traditionally to members of the ruling Fulani elite (see ch. 6, Social Systems; ch. 11, Value Systems).

Southerners, by contrast, have been more progressive because their traditional sociopolitical values have been more adaptable to

4

the process of modernization started by the British. The Ibo and other groups of the southeast have traditionally subscribed to concepts of competition, personal aggressiveness, and freedom from rigid class structure. They place great stress on individual achievement and initiative and have always been willing to engage in any type of work that offers a chance for personal advancement and a better way of life. Among the Yoruba and other peoples of the southwest, individual effort is highly regarded, but tradition and a certain amount of authoritarian stratification—the legacy of their system of kingship—provide a certain measure of restraint.

Political consciousness—a byproduct of Western education— first began to manifest itself in the 1920s in nationalist movements. Although they were united in opposition to British rule, the nationalist leaders were far from agreement as to what should ultimately replace it. They were influenced by ethnic cleavages ranging from the broad north-south and southeast-southwest divisions to hositilities among peoples within the regions themselves. The difficulties were compounded by rivalries in economic interests; religious tensions; and the insistence of such groups as the Hausa-Fulani that independence should be acquired within the framework of Nigerian culture and traditions and of such others as the Ibo, who were equally insistent on the adoption in large measure of European political systems, technology, and values (see ch. 3, Historical Setting; ch. 9, Government and Political Dynamics).

Because of the differences between the various areas of the country based on language, religion, and sociopolitical values, there are two types of nationalism in Nigeria. Modern nationalism, with a unified republic as its goal, is championed by a small number of people who are members of the new educated elite, which comes largely from the ranks of the civil service, the military officer corps, and the professions and includes politicians and students. The other nationalism pertains to loyalties owed to traditional ethnic entities or regional amalgams of related ethnic groups.

From the outset of independence the nation was faced with ethnic and regional tensions as basic mistrust grew between the slowly developing north and the more advanced south. The commoners and traditional elite of the north regarded southerners, particularly the Ibo and other peoples associated with them, as aggressive, overly concerned with achievement, proud, disdainful of northern custom, and disrespectful of established authority. In addition, the southerners aroused opposition among the northern elite because they were able to use their drive and educational superiority to capture most of the available positions in govern-

5

ment and private commerce, thus depriving the younger northerners of the few salaried positions open to them. Northerners came to fear that the Ibo were attempting to dominate the country through control of the civil service and the federal government.

In this climate of ethnic and regional antagonism, two coups d'etat occurred in 1966 within the space of six months. The first, which resulted in military government at the request of the federal cabinet, was followed by an attempt to force national unity. The objective, however, was feared or misunderstood by the various ethnic and regional interests, and further violence led to a second coup. Lieutenant Colonel Yakubu Gowon (later promoted to major general) was chosen to lead the Federal Military Government (FMG).

In an attempt to preserve the federation, General Gowon, a nontraditionalist northern Christian, abandoned the former military government's unification approach. The new FMG proposed a constitutional revision to settle Ibo fears of northern domination and to preserve the union, but the military governor of the Eastern Region, Lieutenant Colonel C.O. Ojukwu, refused anything short of autonomy for his area. On May 27, 1967, General Gowon reorganized the regions into twelve states in an attempt to balance various areas and ethnic groups. Three states were created from the Eastern Region, and three were developed in the southwest; the Northern Region became six separate states.

The move to the twelve-state system was designed to weaken the power held by the northern Hausa-Fulani and the Ibo over the smaller ethnic groups in their respective regions and to create a new basis for Nigerian political institutions—one free of the old ethnic and regional alignments and their attendant problems. The move also had the immediate aim of offering eastern non-Ibo groups their own states and thus weakening their support of the Ibo, who had begun to plan for withdrawal from the republic after the northern pogrom in 1966. The efforts of the FMG to preserve national unity failed, however, and on May 30, 1967, Colonel Ojukwu proclaimed the independence of the former Eastern Region as the separate Republic of Biafra.

On July 6, 1967, fighting broke out between the armies of Gowon and Ojukwu in a civil war that dragged on for thirty months (see ch. 15, National Security). Both sides stepped up their recruitment of men and sought military equipment and supplies from external sources in both the Western and communist blocs.

In 1968 federal troops invaded Calabar from the sea, while other units moved east to Port Harcourt and the Niger River. Federal forces soon overran the northern part of the secessionist area and compressed Biafran holdings to a narrow triangle between the towns of Enugu, Onitsha, and Owerri. Cut off from the coastal ports and isolated from outside support except by erratic aerial supply to a few makeshift airstrips, Biafran resistance faltered. A long period of stalemate followed, during which large numbers of civilians in the east died from malnutrition as the Biafran regime sought to win international support for its cause.

During the last week of 1961 federal forces launched a heavy ground and air attack against the remaining Biafran positions. Driving from the south, they captured the last Biafran stronghold at Owerri and seized the airfield at Uli shortly after Colonel Ojukwu departed by air for refuge in the Ivory Coast. On January 15, 1970, the surrender of the Biafran forces was signed in Lagos. Estimates of casualties suffered by both sides, including those who died from malnutrition, ranged from 1 million to 2 million.

Immediately after the war the Ibo and other easterners were accepted back into the federation, and wide amnesty was granted to the former supporters of secession. Under the direction of the Nigerian Red Cross, relief feeding of malnourished people in the war zone was accelerated, and projects were initiated to rebuild the areas damaged by the war, largely in East Central State. As the number of jobs and opportunities open to former secessionists expanded, conditions in the east began to improve.

The FMG's broad program of reconciliation—enunciated by General Gowon—recognizes the need for solutions to the political, economic, and social problems that had propelled Nigeria through the series of violent and divisive crises of its first decade of independence. In mid-1971, eighteen months after the end of the war, the FMG was moving forward in its primary task of expanding the national economy as a major step along its course toward the restoration of civilian rule. The war had not halted economic progress outside the battle zone in the east, but after the Biafran surrender the government was faced with the need to restore conditions in which the country's rich economic potential could be fully realized. Moreover, renewed efforts were necessary to combat the prewar problems of corruption, unemployment, and ethnic antagonism.

As a vehicle for increased national development, the FMG in 1970 initiated the Second National Development Plan covering the period up to April 1974. Under the program each of the twelve states has prepared plans for its own administrative area, which together are coordinated and integrated into the national plan by the FMG. The plan appears to be more realistic in terms of estimated resources and available foreign exchange than previous Nigerian development plans.

Economically, Nigeria appears to have a promising potential for long-term growth (see ch. 12, Character and Structure of the Economy). Although the war severely strained the economic infrastructure, the national communications system, and foreign exchange reserves, the republic's fiscal position received priority attention in the postwar period and in mid-1971 was fundamentally sound.

Agriculture and minerals—primarily petroleum—are the major sources of Nigeria's wealth (see ch. 13, Agriculture and Mining). Because of a wide range of climatic variations, nearly every product of tropical agriculture can be cultivated. This has resulted in agricultural diversification that has protected the nation from the economic dangers inherent in dependence on a single crop. Except for animal proteins, the agricultural base provides an adequate and varied basic food crop for the large population. Cocoa is the main export crop, but important revenues also come from groundnuts (peanuts), palm products, rubber, cotton, sesame, and tropical hardwoods. Potential for the expansion of agriculture is demonstrated by the fact that only 9 percent of the country's vast arable acreage is under cultivation. The agricultural economy is predominantly one of individual smallholder farms, which characteristically average between one and five acres. Handtools are employed in most cases, and little use is made of modern agricultural technology.

Although agriculture provides about half of the national income and employment for nearly 80 percent of the labor force, Nigeria is on the threshold of a transition to increased reliance on its large petroleum reserves as a source of national wealth. Most of the oil discovered by 1971 was located in Mid-Western and Rivers States, but there were also large offshore reserves. Although most of the original exploration and exploitation had been handled by foreign oil firms, the FMG in early 1971 announced the establishment of a national Nigerian oil corporation. This new organization would eventually engage in the exploration, drilling, refining, and marketing of Nigerian petroleum products. The country's position among the world's eleven largest oil producers led to its membership in the Organization of Petroleum Exporting Countries (OPEC), a group that produces 85 percent of worldwide petroleum exports.

In addition to petroleum, Nigeria's principal mineral resources include tin, columbite, iron ore, coal, limestone, lead, and zinc. Of these, only tin and columbite are exported, and hard mineral production constitutes only a small proportion of the national revenue. The existence of coal, iron ore, and limestone deposits in quantity has created interest in the possible establishment of an iron and steel industry.

Although strained and deteriorated in places by overuse and damage suffered during the war, the national transportation system is one of the most important elements of the economic infrastructure (see ch. 2, Physical Environment). Two principal ports and eight smaller ones provide support to the large import and export trade. More than 5,000 miles of navigable inland waterways assist in domestic trade activities. The 55,000 miles of roads link federal and state capitals, major administrative centers, leading towns, and ports. A 2,200-mile railway system connects the principal ports in the south with the cattle area in the northeast, the groundnut area of the northwest, the tin-producing center of the central plateau, and the oil-producing areas of the southeast. Three airports support international air service, and domestic flights link most major towns in the country.

In its efforts to deal with national economic and political problems, the government has not lost sight of Nigeria's history of ethnic and regional antagonisms. The FMG's goal of continued national unity is dependent on economic and social development, but these factors are conditional on the maintenance of public order and acceptance of governmental decisions by the Nigerian people.

Despite the success achieved in breaking up the power blocs of the former regional arrangement, there are sharp differences between the new states. These include disparities in economic resources, educational development, and technical abilities of the various population groups. To avoid the rivalries and tensions that such disparities produce, the Second National Development Plan aims at solving this underlying political problem by stressing the advancement of the less developed states, although others are not neglected.

Among different ethnic groups education is valued alternatively for its own sake and as a means of preparing for future employment and an improved standard of living. Although the country as a whole has a high proportion of university graduates by African standards, a low general rate of education persists despite rapid expansion of the educational base during the 1960s. Probably not more than 10 percent of Nigeria's total population is literate, although the rate increases to perhaps 25 percent in the Lagos area and certain sectors of the southeast (see ch. 8, Education, Public Information, and the Arts and Sciences).

The major focus of the government's efforts to expand the educational base and restructure the school system to meet national development needs has been on the ultimate provision of a primary-level education for all children of school age. Goals for this effort are being met in all areas except the north, where the historic inequality of the lower levels of education remains. Goals established for the secondary and higher educational levels are being satisfied throughout the country. The five universities stress the production of graduates with professional, technical, and administrative qualifications rather than those with degrees in the pure and applied sciences. A general teacher shortage exists throughout the educational system, but attempts are being made to reduce this problem. Literacy rates will also be increased further in the older age groups as the effects of adult education programs become more widespread.

In October 1970, on the tenth anniversary of Nigerian independence, General Gowon outlined a nine-point program for returning the country to civilian rule in 1976. Among the essential steps he proposed are a new census and a new constitution; implementation of the economic, political, and social goals of the Second National Development Plan; final settlement of the question of the number of states Nigeria should have; reorganization of the large military establishment; and the eradication of corruption from all national institutions and from society in general. Some critics of the FMG's timetable for the return to civil government feel that the nine-point program cannot be accomplished in five years; others believe that its magnitude will provide the military with an excuse to remain in power for a longer period of time.

Because of the ethnic character of prewar political parties and the unrest that their rivalry created, political activity is formally proscribed. Because all meaningful political power is concentrated in the hands of the FMG, none of the three major ethnic groups has a dominant—or even powerful—voice in the direction of governmental affairs at federal or state levels. Since the reorganization of the north into six separate states, northern political power has virtually disappeared, and the emirs' former local courts, police, and prisons—major elements of their earlier authority— have been absorbed by national institutions of law and order. Similar modifications have occurred in the former Western Region, although much of the Yoruba power base in that area has remained largely unchanged since prewar days.

The political changes in the north and in the east have effectively removed the former major contenders from places of predominance in governmental affairs. Under the new system enhanced stature has accrued to the smaller ethnic groups that formerly were dominated by the Hausa, Yoruba, and Ibo. This new force in Nigerian politics includes the Ijaw and Ibibio of the east;

10

the northern Muslim Yoruba; and the Tiv, Nupe, and other Middle Belt minorities. Together they controlled five of the twelve states in mid-1971.

In 1971, in its fifth year in power, the FMG faced a number of difficult problems in its quest for greater national unity and development. An inflationary trend, caused largely by pressures on resources that have also produced rising costs of living, had not yet been brought under control. Widespread unemployment was complicated by increased migration from rural areas to urban centers, a larger school output than the job market could accommodate, and a general shortage of technical specialties among the labor force. Many of the unemployed blamed the government for their lack of jobs. This element of the population, together with the largely idle army of about 240,000, provided a latent source of unrest.

The government has worked carefully to build close political and economic ties with its African neighbors and within the context of its membership in the British Commonwealth of Nations and the United Nations. As an active member of the Organization of African Unity (OAU) and its subsidiary committees, Nigeria strongly condemns the apartheid (statutory racial segregation) doctrine of the Republic of South Africa and supports self-determination in the Portuguese African territories and majority rule in Rhodesia. The FMG's foreign relations policies can be expected to assume even greater importance to Nigerians as a rallying point for national unity.

CHAPTER 2

PHYSICAL ENVIRONMENT

Nigeria is the easternmost of the countries that face on the Gulf of Guinea in the West African bulge. It lies entirely in the tropics, its southern edge being only a few degrees above the equator and its northern border well below the Tropic of Cancer. It is bordered on the east by the Federal Republic of Cameroon and for a very short distance in the northeast by the Republic of Chad. The northern and northwestern borders are bounded by the Republic of Niger, and the western border is bounded by the Republic of Dahomey (see fig. 1).

The country has a total area of 356,669 square miles, and its boundaries roughly form a square, excluding the great extension into the Gulf of Guinea of the Niger Delta. The greatest east-to-west distance is somewhat over 700 miles, and the north-south distance is about 650 miles. The outstanding geographic feature is the basin of the Niger and Benue rivers, running east and west through the center of the country. South of the basin the elevation is generally under 1,000 feet except for some plateau surfaces. To the north of it is a broad plateau region that occupies the country to its northern border and has elevations of 1,000 to over 4,000 feet. On the east the country is bordered by mountainous regions, in which the highest point—of 6,700 feet—is located.

High temperatures occur generally throughout the year, rarely falling below 50°F. Rains occur in all areas during certain times of the year, and the alternation of wet and dry periods determines the seasons. Humidities are usually high but drop substantially in the northern part of the country during the dry season. The amount of rainfall influences vegetation, which varies from rain forest in the south to increasingly drier savanna types in the north.

Large towns are found chiefly in the southern and northern parts of the country; few communities of any size are located in the central region. The concentrations are explained largely by historical factors that led to the development of Yoruba kingdoms in the southern forest zone and, later, trading centers along the coast and Muslim emirates in the northern savannas. Rural settlements, much the same in most of the country, consisted of nucleated villages, except in parts of the southeast and the middle Benue River valley, where the rural population lives in dispersed compounds.

The transportation system is relatively well developed, railways and main roads connecting all important centers. During the rainy season, however, heavy downpours sometimes cause considerable damage and disrupt communications. The country also has an extensive inland waterway system totaling well over 1,000 miles. All transportation systems suffered from the civil war, either directly or from overuse and lack of maintenance, and were in need of rehabilitation or reconstruction.

GEOGRAPHIC REGIONS

A number of major geographic divisions are readily distinguishable, stretching in generally east-west zones across the country. Along the lower part is a low coastal zone, representing a general continuation of the belt of low plains that extends along the entire Gulf of Guinea coast of West Africa. North of this zone lies an area of hills and low plateaus. Through the middle of the country, bisecting it from east to west, extends the great valley of the Niger and Benue rivers. North of this valley the area as far as the country's northern border is occupied by a broad plateau. Along the eastern border is found a distinct zone of mountainous country.

Within these general divisions variations occur, forming separate geographic regions (see fig. 2). At least twelve such regions have been recognized and in the southern part of the country consist of the Low Plains, the Lower Niger Valley, the Niger Delta, the Southeastern Scarplands, the Southeastern Lowlands, and the Western High Plains. In the central part is the Niger-Benue River Valley region, and in the north are the Northern High Plains, Jos Plateau, Sokoto Plains, and Chad Basin regions. The twelfth region comprises the Eastern Highlands.

Low Plains

The Low Plains lie mainly in Western and Mid-Western States. They are bordered on the Gulf of Guinea by a coastal stretch of low-lying, often swampy land interspersed with lagoons and creeks and varying up to twenty miles or more in width. The outer edge of the coastal area consists of sand spits in its western part; however, it changes to mud as the coast nears the Niger Delta. Behind the outer spits and lagoons creeks of varying size generally parallel the coast and form a continuous waterway from the border with the Republic of Dahomey on the west to the tributaries of the Niger Delta in the east.

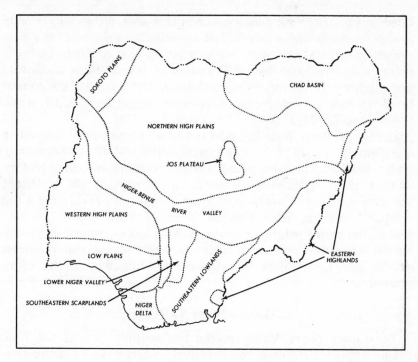

Source: Adapted from J.C. Pugh and A.E. Perry, *A Short Geography of West Africa*, London, 1960, p. 176; and Reuben K. Udo, *Geographical Regions of Nigeria*, Berkeley, 1970, inside cover and front page.

Figure 2. Geographic Regions of Nigeria

Much of the land in this coastal area is below an elevation of 50 feet; however, it rises to above 150 feet inland, and the average elevation above sea level is about 100 feet. Drainage on the mainland side of the lagoons is poor, and many smaller rivers lose themselves in the freshwater swamps that line the northern edges of the lagoons. The only major opening to the gulf from this area is at Lagos, the country's capital, located on a group of islands at the western end of Lagos Lagoon.

The plains in Western State rise gently from the lagoon and creek area northward toward the Western High Plains. In their southern part they consist of a dissected plain underlain by clay, limestone, and sandstone formations. Erosion has produced low, relatively flat-topped hills. This area is heavily forested, and its physical features are often masked by the vegetation. Elevations in this southern section are mostly below 600 feet.

The northern part is underlain by crystalline rocks, and the land has an undulating appearance. Elevations range generally from about 400 feet to 1,000 feet above sea level. Numerous isolated, steep-sided rock domes occur in this area, either singly or in groups. Some of these domes, left standing by erosion of the surrounding terrain, are quite high; a group east of Ondo includes points rising to 3,000 feet. Soil and rainfall conditions make this area highly suitable for cocoa cultivation, and as of 1971 it constituted the country's major cocoa-growing region (see ch. 13, Agriculture and Mining).

In Mid-Western State the land in the west and south consists of a low sandy coastal plain with gentle slopes and elevations mostly under 400 feet. The central and western sections contain extensive and luxuriant forest areas in protected reserves. To the northeast the terrain rises to elevations of from 750 to 1,000 feet to form the comparatively flat Ishan Plateau. Many of the rivers in this section of the plains originate in the Ishan Plateau, where they have cut deeply incised valleys. In their lower courses the valleys widen greatly and are subject to extensive flooding during the rainy season.

Lower Niger Valley

The Lower Niger Valley region lies roughly east of the Low Plains and consists of a comparatively narrow valley extending from the confluence of the Niger and Benue rivers at Lokoja southward for about 185 miles to the apex of the Niger Delta. In its upper section it comprises a number of quite narrow gorges between which lie somewhat broader stretches bordered by hills with elevations between 300 and 700 feet.

In its central section the valley widens. On the left bank there is a broad alluvial plain, which is intensively farmed during low-water periods. The section has numerous sandbanks and islands that are also farmed at certain times of the year. During the rainy season, however, the water level rises as much as thirty feet and completely inundates these features. Near Onitsha, the largest and most important port on the Niger, the river again narrows. Below this point it flows through an alluvial flood plain that stretches to the delta. Much of this area is also flooded at high water.

Niger Delta

One of the major features of the West African coastline is the Niger Delta, which projects into the Gulf of Guinea from the southern coast of Nigeria between the Bight of Benin and the Bight of Biafra. This great bulge of sedimentary material, deposited by the Niger River, stretches some 75 to 80 miles from its apex below the town of Aboh to the sea; it covers an area of about 10,000 square miles. The water of the Niger flows through this delta in a series of radial tributaries. For navigational purposes, the two most important are the Forcados and Nun rivers.

The outer edge of the delta is fringed by sand spits and ridges, varying in width from a fraction of a mile to 10 or more miles. Behind these ridges are mangrove swamps covering about 4,000 square miles, and farther inland an extensive area of freshwater swamps is found. Islands of solid ground within the delta are occupied by populated settlements. The delta is the site of large natural gas and oil deposits (see ch. 13, Agriculture and Mining).

Southeastern Scarplands

Directly to the east of the Lower Niger Valley is a highly eroded plateau area characterized by prominent scarps. The region's chief geographic features are the Udi and Igala plateaus and the Akwa-Orlu Uplands. The Udi Plateau runs from north to south; its northern end merges with the Igala Plateau, which extends from east to west. The general elevation of these plateaus is about 1,000 feet above sea level, with escarpments rising considerably higher. The scarps on the northern and eastern edges drop abruptly at various points in their 500-foot descent in elevation. The plateau surface is dotted with flat-topped and domed hills that have produced one of the country's most highly scenic landscapes. Important coal-bearing formations are exposed in these scarps.

The scarp faces of both plateaus have been deeply gullied by stream erosion; many of these gullies are nearly 300 feet deep. In the Awka-Orlu Uplands, which lie to the west of the plateaus and have nearly the same elevation, even more extensive erosion has occurred. Gullies in this area are hundreds of feet deep, and some cover more than a square mile.

The western part of the region embraces the upper valley of the Anambra River and the valley of its major tributary, the Mamu River. Much of this area is a rather featureless plain about 200 to 400 feet above sea level, which in places is heavily forested. Alluvial materials have been deposited along the rivers, as well as in the valleys of smaller tributary streams.

Southeastern Lowlands

The Southeastern Lowlands occupy the area between the Lower Niger Valley and the Niger Delta on the west, the Eastern Highlands on the east, and the Benue River valley on the north. The coastline of this region resembles that found in the Low Plains area; it is similarly fringed with sandy spits and mangrove swamps. Unlike the more westerly coastal areas, longitudinal lagoons are completely absent in this region.

The Southeastern Lowlands are divided into two subregions—an oil palm belt and the Cross River basin. The oil palm belt lies generally east and northeast of the Niger Delta. The area is underlain by the coastal plains sand formation, and its porous, leached soils are relatively infertile. The area formerly supported a high forest growth, but this was largely cut down and replaced with secondary vegetation, of which the oil palm is the dominant species.

The Cross River basin lies generally east of the scarplands and has a width in the Enugu area of about 50 miles. Extending from north to south for nearly 200 miles, the upper limit of its drainage system approaches the Benue River trough. Elevations of the low region vary from about 200 feet in the south to 500 feet in the north. Large areas are relatively flat, and land along streams and rivers becomes swampy in the rainy season.

Large parts of the basin are thinly populated. In early 1971 transportation facilities in some areas were poorly developed. Most of the basin is covered with parkland and grass. In the eastern section near the Eastern Highlands, however, heavy forests are found; patches of forest also occur at several other places in the basin.

Western High Plains

The Western High Plains, or Plateau of Yorubaland, are part of the belt of high plains that extends through West Africa. They lie between the low western coastal plains and the Niger-Benue River Valley region and are broadest in the west near the border with Dahomey, where the land has a general elevation of more than 1,000 feet. It displays a mature erosion surface surmounted by ridges of more resistant rock and numerous dome-shaped hills that project several hundred feet above the surrounding terrain. The area is covered largely with savanna parkland and grass.

The eastern section of the Western High Plains has two distinct plateau surfaces—one has an elevation of about 750 feet, and the other, of about 1,200 feet. The landscape is characterized by dome-shaped hills, some of which attain a height of 2,000 feet above sea level. Drainage throughout the Western High Plains is generally good; however, many streams disappear in the harmattan (dry) period, and holes must be dug in streambeds to obtain water.

Niger-Benue River Valley

The combined valleys of the Niger and Benue rivers form a great east-west arc approximately across the middle of the country.

The Niger River valley extends from the border with Dahomey on the west, and the Benue River valley extends from the eastern border with Cameroon. Near Lokoja in the center of the country the Benue River joins the Niger River, which changes its course at this point to flow southward to the Gulf of Guinea.

After entering the country from Dahomey the Niger River flows in a relatively open valley underlain by sedimentary rocks. Between Yelwa and Jebba the valley is characterized by open flood plains, separated by comparatively narrow, rocky stretches. In the area of Jebba the river traverses a rather narrow gorge. The gradient between Yelwa and Jebba and the harder underlying rock have produced a series of rapids and falls that limit use of the river for navigation. In the late 1960s this section of the valley was altered by construction of a dam at Kainji above Jebba. Flooding of an eighty-five-mile stretch of the valley produced Kainji Lake (see ch. 14, Industry and Trade).

Eastward from Jebba to the confluence of the two rivers at Lokoja the valley broadens; in some places it is more than 50 miles wide. At many points along this part of the river, extensive swampy plains are found. Sections of the undulating valley have elevations of about 400 feet above sea level; in other places the land consists of eroded hill country.

The Benue River valley is underlain by sedimentary formations throughout its entire length from the Cameroon frontier to the confluence at Lokoja. For most of this distance the valley is broad and in some places attains a width of about 100 miles. Terrain features vary considerably in the erosional low plains that parallel the river's course. In some sections they have an undulating, but otherwise featureless, appearance. In other areas flat-topped hills are found, and near the confluence of the two rivers they become a dissected sandstone plateau.

The Benue River's course has not been affected by harder basement rocks as in the case of the Niger River. Rapids and falls are completely absent, and navigation is affected only by shifting sandbars. During flood periods the Benue River is navigable by flat-bottomed boats to Garoua in Cameroon. Most of the river's tributaries are comparatively shallow and are characterized by sandbars and islands. Entry to the Benue River is at a low gradient, and the tributaries may have more than one channel.

Northern High Plains

The Northern High Plains comprise a broad plateau area. The large central section of the plateau extends for about 300 miles from east to west. Sometimes designated the High Plains of Hausaland, the region consists of a series of stepped plains that range from about 600 feet above sea level at the outer edge to roughly 3,000 feet in the area surrounding the Jos Plateau. Some plains' levels are separated by prominent escarpments.

The central section consists largely of undulating surfaces with occasional smooth, low ranges. At various points, however, steep-sided, domed hills project more than 1,500 feet above the surrounding countryside. Rivers and streams in these plains flow in broad, shallow valleys. Because of the low gradients, they generally contain numerous sandbars.

The Northern High Plains in the Gongola River basin east of Bauchi are highly dissected, and the rivers and streams in the basin flow through relatively deep, narrow valleys, paralleled by flat-topped hills. Much of the area is characterized by sandstone ridges.

East of the Gongola River basin lies the Biu Plateau, an area of about 2,000 square miles. The upper level of the plateau, from 2,000 to 3,000 feet, is separated from the Northern High Plains by a pronounced scarp. Inactive volcanic cones are found in the northern part of the area.

Jos Plateau

The Jos Plateau, surrounded by the south-central section of the Northern High Plains, includes distinctive features that set it aside as a separate geographic region. Covering an area of about 3,000 square miles, it is separated from the surrounding plains area by pronounced escarpments. The area's general elevation is over 4,000 feet above sea level, and hills in its eastern part attain heights of over 5,800 feet.

The plateau's cooler temperatures and difference in vegetation also set it off from the Northern High Plains. The region is the site of tin and other metals that have made the region economically important (see ch. 13, Agriculture and Mining).

Sokoto Plains

The Sokoto Plains occupy the extreme northwestern part of the country and are generally monotonous in appearance. In the western part erosion has left occasional tablelike hills that stand about 100 feet above the surrounding plain. Trenchlike stream and river valleys characterize this part. They have broad flat floors 2 or more miles in width and steep clifflike sides 100 to 200 feet high. Water in the rivers is largely seasonal and is limited chiefly to the short rainy season.

Retarded waterflow and deposits have gradually raised the height of some riverbeds to levels above the surrounding valley floor. Floods in the late 1960s were reported to be increasing, resulting in considerable damage to crops. Many of the settlements that formerly lined the valleys have retreated to the higher plains.

Chad Basin

The Chad Basin consists of a broad plains area in the northeastern part of the country. In this area the land slopes gently eastward from the Northern High Plains to Lake Chad. The region has a general elevation of about 1,000 feet above sea level and is largely featureless except for fixed dune formations in the northern section, many of which are covered with trees and grass.

Extremely low gradients affect riverflow in the region. During much of the year the flood plains are swampy areas, and the rivers disappear into them before reaching Lake Chad. During the rainy season the flat river valleys are flooded over broad areas, but water supply becomes a problem in the dry period. In this season shallow wells to underground water reservoirs, as well as artesian sources that underlie the basin, are used.

Eastern Highlands

The eastern boundary with Cameroon is characterized for about 500 miles by mountainous country. The northern part of the highlands consists of several hill groups, with high points around 3,600 feet. To the south of these are the Mandara Mountains, which extend along the border to the Benue River valley. These mountains comprise a dissected plateau with a general elevation of about 4,000 feet. Encompassing an area of some 300 miles in length with an average width of about 20 miles, they give the impression of being a collection of giant granite blocks.

The central part of the region consists of the Adamawa Highlands, a discontinuous series of mountain ranges and high plateau surfaces situated between the Benue River valley and the Donga River valley. They include the Alantika Mountains along the border and, separated in the west by a lower plains area, the Shebshi Hills. The Shebshi Hills, generally at an elevation of 3,500 feet, are a dissected plateau with highly eroded lower slopes. The highest surveyed point in the country, Vogel Peak, with an elevation of 6,700 feet above sea level, is located in these hills.

To the southwest of the Adamawa Highlands and connected with it by a narrow belt of land ranging about 4,000 feet in elevation is the Nigerian section of the Bamenda Highlands, most of which lie in Cameroon. Westward extensions of these highlands are known as the Obudu Uplands and the Oban Hills. High points in the uplands reach close to 6,000 feet. Transportation is difficult, and both of these areas are sparsely populated. They are heavily forested except for the uppermost levels of the uplands, which have grassland cover.

CLIMATE

The climate is tropical throughout the country, but considerable variation exists between the south and north. Differences in the principal weather components—temperature, humidity, and rainfall—are governed mainly by the movement and interaction of the three major airmasses that affect all of West Africa. These include the harmattan, a trade wind that originates in the Sahara region. It blows from the northeast and is hot, dry, and dust laden. The second airmass is tropical maritime and comes from the southwest across the Gulf of Guinea. It is monsoonal in character and is composed of moist, relatively cool air. The third airmass consists of the cool equatorial easterlies that are found at higher altitudes.

The movement of these airmasses over Nigeria, influenced by the movement of the sun back and forth across the equator, is accompanied by alternating periods of rain and drought that mark the seasons. The number of seasons, however, is not identical throughout the country. Above a line that runs east and west approximately north of the Niger and Benue river valleys, one rainy season and one dry season are relatively well defined.

The rainy period in this area occurs between April and October, usually starting in late April or early May along the dividing line and continuing progressively northward; the rains in the far north usually begin in June. Peak rains are experienced throughout the area usually in August. The start of the rains is often accompanied by violent storms, which may cause considerable damage. About the middle of September harmattan winds begin moving southward, bringing dry, hot days and relatively cooler nights. By the middle of October the rains have generally ceased throughout the area north of the Niger-Benue River Valley region, and the harmattan continues to dominate the weather until the start of the next rainy season.

From the Niger-Benue River Valley southward, four seasons are usually distinguishable. These consist of a long rainy season, a short period in which the rains slacken, a short period of heavier rain, and a long dry season. The start of the rainy season in the south occurs in February along the coast and moves gradually northward, reaching the Niger-Benue River Valley region in April. Heavier rains continue over the area through July. There is a decline in rainfall in August, and in some years it is particularly noticeable. Rains are again heavier from September to early November. By mid-November the harmattan usually covers the area to the coast, with the exception of the delta region and the southeast, where it becomes dominant usually in December. The dry period usually continues until February or March.

The amount of annual rainfall decreases northward from the coast. In parts of the Niger Delta and the southeast it totals over 140 inches a year. This area receives some rainfall during every month of the year, including the period of the harmattan. The southwest is drier, with Lagos averaging about 73 inches annually. A zone across the country from Lagos to the Eastern Highlands receives 80 or more inches annually. Farther inland total rainfall declines in the central part of the country to 40 or 60 inches. Within this area, the Jos Plateau, affected by its higher elevation, constitutes an island of greater precipitation registering an annual average of 60 to 80 inches. In the north rainfall declines to 20 or 30 inches annually and in parts of the extreme northeast falls below 20 inches (see fig. 3).

The northern half of the country receives less than one inch of rainfall for periods of from five to seven months during the dry season. Water shortages are often acute; local streams and wells dry up in some areas, forcing villagers to travel considerable distances to obtain needed water. The lack of water also forces cattle raisers in the north to move their herds in the dry season to better watered areas, such as the valleys of the Niger or Benue rivers.

Temperatures throughout the country are comparatively high at all times of the year, with mean maximums increasing northward from the coastal area. Mean annual maximums recorded over a period of years at different points in the south showed a range of about 86° to 89°F. In the northern savanna regions—excluding readings at places such as Jos, where higher elevation results in lower temperatures—the range is from about 92° to 95°F. The highest temperatures in the south occur in February and March during the dry season, when mean monthly maximums rise to between 91° and 94°F. In the north they occur in March and April and range between 101° and 105°F. Mean monthly maximum temperatures in the coastal area decline to about 82°F. in July and August when the rains slacken. They are lowest in the north in August at the height of the rainy season, declining to 85° or 86°F.

Mean annual minimum temperatures in the south are about 71° to 73°F. A variation of less than 2°F. occurs throughout the year. Mean annual minimum temperatures in the northern region range from about 66° to 71°F. During December and January in the dry

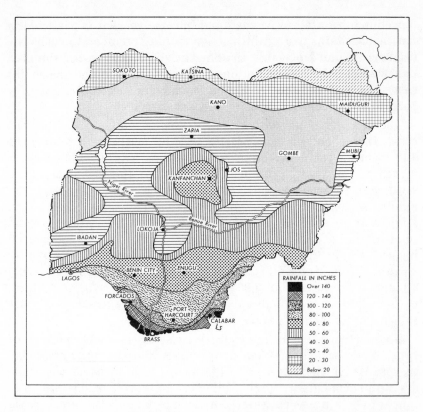

RAINFALL IN INCHES
Over 140
120 - 140
100 - 120
80 - 100
60 - 80
50 - 60
40 - 50
30 - 40
20 - 30
Below 20

Source: Adapted from Reuben K. Udo, *Geographical Regions of Nigeria*, Berkeley, 1970, p. 2.

Figure 3.   Annual Rainfall in Nigeria

season, mean monthly temperatures decline an average of about 10°F. from the annual minimum.

There is little daily variation between mean maximum and minimum temperatures in the coastal areas; the differences are usually less than 20°F. As a result, little relief is obtained at night. Because of the high humidity, the climate is generally enervating. In the north, on the other hand, the range is between 30° to 40°F., and actual readings on particular days during the harmattan season may vary as much as 70°F., with a low of less than 50°F. To a certain extent this is invigorating, but the extreme variations place a considerable strain on the population.

The humidity varies considerably in different parts of the country and at varying times of the year. High nighttime humidities are registered regularly in the coastal regions and range between 95 and 99 percent throughout the year. During the rainy season midday humidities are above 70 percent; during the dry period they range from about 60 to 70 percent. In the north the humidity during the rainy period rises to above 90 percent at night and declines to 60 or 70 percent at midday. During the harmattan both daytime and nighttime humidities are quite low. During this period wooden articles and furniture dry out and crack, and painful cracking of the skin and lips also occurs.

THE LAND

Vegetation

Seven principal types of vegetation can be distinguished: swamp forest, rain forest, derived savanna, Guinea savanna, Sudan savanna, Sahel savanna, and montane vegetation. The first six of these lie in roughly east-west zones that progress inland from the coast to the country's northern limits. The montane vegetation occurs in the Eastern Highlands (see fig. 4). The vegetation pattern resembles that found throughout West Africa and is closely related to the amount of rainfall received in different parts of the country.

The swamp forest zone consists of two subzones. One borders the Gulf of Guinea and is characterized by dense mangrove growths in areas containing brackish water. Along part of the coast this growth extends inland only a short distance; in the region of the Niger Delta, however, it has a width of from twenty to thirty miles. Behind this subzone lies a freshwater swamp forest, dominated by raffia palms and broad-leaved trees. This latter vegetation occupies the greater part of the delta; it forms a strip of varying width in the remainder of the coastal area and merges into the rain forest.

The rain forest belt extends inland for a distance of from 50 to 100 miles. In its natural state it forms a three-tiered canopy structure. The highest level of trees stands at approximately 120 feet; trees of this height are more dispersed, and their canopy is not in continuous contact, as are those of lower heights. Many of the more valuable timber trees, including ebony and various types of mahogany, are found in this group. The middle level of trees ranges from 50 feet to about 120 feet, and the lowest trees reach heights of about 50 feet. The lowest level has dense crowns that often prevent direct sunlight from reaching the forest floor.

The country's rain forest has been extensively modified by commercial exploitation and cultivation. Little of the original forest remains except in the government forest reserves, which were estimated in the mid-1960s by the Food and Agriculture Organization of the United Nations at between 6,000 and 7,000 square miles. An

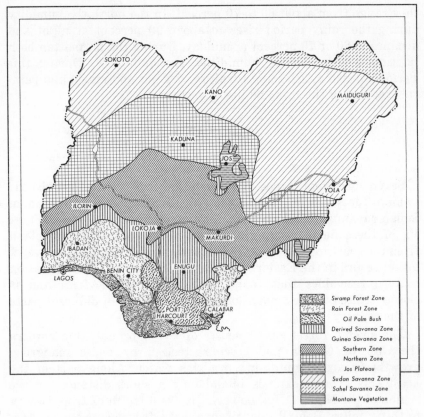

Legend:

- Swamp Forest Zone
- Rain Forest Zone
- Oil Palm Bush
- Derived Savanna Zone
- Guinea Savanna Zone
- Southern Zone
- Northern Zone
- Jos Plateau
- Sudan Savanna Zone
- Sahel Savanna Zone
- Montane Vegetation

Source: Adapted from V.A. Oyenuga, *Agriculture in Nigeria: An Intro-duction*, Rome, 1967, p. 43; and Reuben K. Udo, *Geographical Regions of Nigeria*, Berkeley, 1970, p. 4.

Figure 4. Vegetation of Nigeria

additional estimated 23,000 to 31,000 square miles outside the reserves were being progressively converted to agricultural use. In the western part of the zone large areas outside the reserves are under cocoa cultivation; a few tall trees remain standing to pro-vide shade for the shorter cocoa trees (see ch. 13, Agriculture and Mining). Other areas of rain forest have been replaced by rubber plantations and kola trees.

Northeast of the Niger Delta a large area of former rain forest has been almost completely replaced by a secondary growth domi-nated by the oil palm. Occasional patches of forest are found, but these are in less populated areas and in groves considered sacred by the local people. Farther east in the Cross River basin large areas of dense rain forest exist in the forest reserves. Some of the forest in this area outside the reserves has been replaced by cocoa, kola, and rubber plantations.

On its northern edge the former drier part of the rain forest has been replaced by a modified vegetation zone described as derived savanna. This zone varies in width from about 20 to 150 miles and stretches completely across the country from west to east. Savanna grasses and trees typical of the Guinea savanna occur throughout the zone. Rain forest trees line the banks of rivers and streams, and similar forests are found on protected rocky elevations. The derived savanna appears to have arisen largely as the result of regular burning for cultivation purposes, which killed off the less fire-resistant trees.

The area from the upper limit of the derived savanna to the northern border is occupied by savanna vegetation. This vast area, approximately 350 to 450 miles wide from south to north, is divided into Guinea, Sudan, and Sahel savanna zones. Considerable correlation appears to exist between the type of vegetation and the total amount of rainfall. The Guinea savanna receives between 40 to 60 inches of rain a year; the Sudan savanna, between 20 and 40 inches; and the Sahel savanna, less than 20 inches.

In the southern part of the Guinea savanna, grasses are five to twelve feet high, and broad-leaved trees forming woodlands may attain a height of fifty feet. In the northern Guinea savanna area, grasses are shorter, and trees are twenty to forty-five feet tall. In some places these trees form a continuous cover with little grass underneath. Fringing forests also occur along streambanks.

The flood plains of the Niger-Benue River Valley region in some areas support growths of raffia, oil palms, and fan palms. The Jos Plateau lies within the Guinea savanna zone. It receives more rainfall, however, and appears to have been covered formerly with savanna woodland. Exploitation of the woodland over a long period has resulted in its general destruction, and much of the plateau is covered with grass.

Sudan savanna vegetation covers most of the upper quarter of the country. Grasses and trees are generally shorter than in the Guinea savanna, and the country is more open. Many of the trees have slender leaves and thorns or spines on their trunks; acacias are common in this zone.

Sahel savanna vegetation is found in the extreme northeast in an area of some 7,000 square miles that receives appreciable rainfall only during three or four months of the year. The grass cover is sparse and short; trees are of the thorn type, some reaching 15 to 30 feet. In some places stands of acacia occur, from which a gum arabic is obtained. Montane vegetation is found in a few high spots in the Eastern Highlands. Woodlands occupy lower levels in this zone, and higher points have a grass cover and isolated trees.

Soils

The largest class of soils occur in the savanna areas of the country. They are well drained, reddish, and moderately to rather strongly leached, and their humus content is generally low. These soils have developed from both crystalline and sedimentary rocks and, in the northern part of the country, from the sandy deposits that cover much of that area. Their various origins have resulted in differences in fertility; soils formed from sedimentary rocks generally are less fertile than many of those derived from underlying crystalline rocks. Minerals needed by plants are usually less abundant in the sedimentary soils. Many of these same soils also have a coarser texture, through which water percolates rapidly, with consequent rapid leaching; this same characteristic is found also in those crystalline soils originating from granite and sandstone.

The soils formed by the sand deposits in the north are basically of windborne origin carried from farther north during an earlier arid geological period. They consist of light sandy northern drift soils and a Zaria soil composed of finer sand that was blown farther south. The northern drift soils have been found highly suitable for growing groundnuts, and the more compact Zaria soils have proved excellent for the growing of cotton (see ch. 13, Agriculture and Mining).

The second principal class of soils is found in the more humid rain forest area of the south. They are generally well drained and yellowish-brown in color but exhibit excessive leaching, largely because of the abundant rainfall. Those covering sedimentary formations are usually porous and sandy or sandy clay, with low fertility. Certain soils in this zone that formed on crystalline rocks are a clayey loam and possess greater water retentive capacity and fertility.

Alluvial soils are found mainly in the Niger Delta, the swamps along the coast, and in the major river valleys. Soils along the rivers and in the coastal freshwater swamps contain some organic matter and, when properly drained, are agriculturally useful. Certain soils near Lake Chad are poorly drained clays and dry sands; they are saline in character, and their production potential is generally limited.

Drainage

The dominant feature of the drainage system is the Niger River and its principal tributary, the Benue River. The Niger enters the country in the northwest after traveling some 1,800 miles through other areas of West Africa. It flows roughly southward and then eastward to the middle of the country, where it is joined by the

Benue. Turning south at this point, it empties into the Gulf of Guinea, after a total traverse within the country of approximately 730 miles through a network of tributaries in the great delta formed at its mouth. The Benue River, which rises in Cameroon, flows about 495 miles inside Nigeria, in a generally westward direction, to its confluence with the Niger River.

The Niger drains all of western Nigeria north of the Western High Plains, and the Benue drains the east-central part of the country. The most important river outside the Niger-Benue system is the Cross River in the southeast. The Cross originates in southern Cameroon and enters the country through the Eastern Highlands. Until the early part of the twentieth century this river was the principal link between the Cross River basin area and the outside world. During the period of the slave trade it was a major route for that trade (see ch. 3, Historical Setting).

The country's overall drainage pattern is somewhat complex. In the southwest a drainage divide runs from the Dahomean border eastward through the Western High Plains to the Lower Niger Valley. South of this divide the rivers flow directly into the Gulf of Guinea or its fringe lagoons; those rivers to the north are tributaries of the Niger. East of the Lower Niger Valley another divide passes through the Igala and Udi plateaus and separates the Lower Niger Valley from the Cross River basin to the east. A northern extension of this divide to the Eastern Highlands marks the divide between the basin and the Benue River system.

In the north the watershed pattern centers on the Jos Plateau. From the ground this center appears quite insignificant; the area is rather featureless and consists of an undulating, swampy plain. From it, however, radiate the major tributaries of both the Niger and Benue rivers, as well as rivers that flow in the direction of Lake Chad. Thus, to the west and southwest from headwaters on the plateau flow the Sokoto and Kaduna rivers, each for well over 300 miles before reaching the Niger. To the east, then south for a total distance of some 330 miles, the Gongola River flows to the Benue.

To the east and northeast above the Gongola River basin, the Komadugu Yobe River and its tributaries flow toward Lake Chad. This river passes through the Sahel savanna zone and loses large amounts of water to evaporation and seepage; only a trickle finally reaches the lake. In the dry season it usually contains no running water in this area but only pools of varying sizes.

Two large bodies of fresh water are found in the country. In the northeast a portion of Lake Chad lies within the country's borders; in the far western part is Kainji Lake, formed during the latter 1960s by the damming of the Niger River.

Lake Chad is subject to great seasonal variations in area and water level; these conditions result in its alternately advancing and receding over considerable distances in the flat plains area on the Nigerian side. The lake at its height, usually between December and January, may cover up to 10,000 square miles in central Africa. During the ensuing months it may diminish to less than 5,000 square miles. Depths are between 10 to 16 feet but in places may be only 4 feet or less. Little water is supplied to the lake from rivers in Nigeria; its principal source is the Chari River in the Republic of Chad.

Kainji Lake was developed as a combined hydroelectric power and river navigation project. The lake itself extends for about 85 miles in a section of the Niger River valley from Kainji to a point beyond Yelwa and has a width of from 9 to 15 miles. Filling of the lake was accomplished between August and October 1968. At maximum level it covers an area of about 480 square miles. Formation of the lake displaced some 45,000 persons who lived in 135 towns, villages and hamlets along the river. Resettlement of these individuals has been made in planned communities newly constructed along the lake or at selected spots farther inland.

Minerals

In mid-1971 the chief mineral resources included petroleum, natural gas associated with the petroleum, tin, columbite, lead, zinc, iron ore, coal, and limestone. The known petroleum deposits were located in the Niger Delta region and offshore from the delta. The principal known tin and columbite deposits were in the Jos Plateau. These consisted mainly of alluvial deposits, but some deposits were found in mineralized veins. Some columbite had also been discovered in the younger granites of the plateau area.

The principal deposits of lead and zinc, with which some silver was associated, were near Abakaliki in South Eastern State and Zurak in Benue-Plateau State. The deposits extended over a distance of some 350 miles through these states and North Eastern State. Iron ore was found in various parts of the country. Two of the larger deposits included one on the Agbaja Plateau near the confluence of the Niger and Benue rivers and one near Enugu. The Enugu deposit had an estimated 46 million long tons of reserves compared with an estimated reserve of 30 million long tons at Agbaja Plateau.

Important coal deposits existed in several places, including the area of Enugu, where 1970 estimates placed reserves at about 72 million long tons, and in Benue and Kabba provinces, where reserves were estimated at about 170 million long tons. Poorer qual-

30

ity coal was also found on the plateau to the west of Enugu, and other coal deposits were reported from Bauchi Province in North Eastern State. Deposits of lignite, estimated at 72 million long tons, were situated in Benin Province in Mid-Western State. These deposits had not been developed in mid-1971 because of the ready availability of domestic coal and oil.

Limestone was widely located, with important formations near Enugu and in the lower basin of the Gongola River. Limestone also occurred in Benin Province and in the Niger River valley northwest of Lokoja. Other deposits existed in the northwestern part of the country in Sokoto Province. Other minerals of varying importance were kaolin; monazite, thorite, tantalite, and zircon—all byproducts of tin mining on the Jos Plateau; gold, principally in alluvial occurrences; and wolframite.

Minor minerals included asbestos, beryl, topaz, diatomite, gypsum, feldspar, fluorite, graphite, ilmenite, mica, rutile, pyrochlore, and small quantities of copper and bismuth. Salt deposits were mined to some extent in Benue and Bornu provinces. Glass sands were found in the Port Harcourt area.

Wildlife

The larger wildlife includes many animals common to tropical Africa. The high forest abounds with several species of monkeys, and chimpanzees, gorillas, and the drill baboon also live in this zone. Other large animals in the forest region are dwarf antelopes, wild hogs, and elephants. In the savannas are found lions, cheetahs, hyenas, jackals, and several other predators, as well as elephants, buffaloes, and a considerable variety of antelopes. In the more northerly part of the savanna there are gazelles and the scimitar-horned oryx. The Nigerian giraffe also inhabits the savannas but reportedly has become relatively scarce. Leopards occur throughout the country.

The hippopotamus and manatee are found in the Niger and Benue rivers. Crocodiles live in all the large rivers and lakes, as do several kinds of turtles. Both poisonous and nonpoisonous snakes are numerous; they include African and royal pythons and such poisonous varieties as the black cobra, green mamba, and giant viper. Lizards and chameleons are also common.

Birds are found in great variety and include among the widespread larger species—parrots, hornbills, touracos (plantain eaters), eagles, kingfishers, herons, storks, pigeons, guinea and bush fowl, ducks, and geese. Large flocks of ibis, flamingo, marabou, and the crowned crane are found in the north, as are bustards and ostriches. Smaller birdlife is also numerous.

Many types of insects are found, including species of the tsetse fly and mosquito. Butterflies and moths, some of quite large size, occur in large numbers in the forest region. Goliath beetles up to five inches in length are also found; these are among the world's largest insects. Large scorpions also occur.

Numerous fish species inhabit the rivers; they include catfish, Nile perch, tilapia, and varieties of carp. In the lagoons are mullet, catfish, tilapia, carp, sea perch, snappers, prawns, and shrimp. Coastal and offshore salt-water fish are those common to the Gulf of Guinea. They include sardines, mackerels, breams, threadfins, and croakers. Rays, sharks, tarpon, and barracuda also occur. Crayfish are plentiful in the Niger Delta area.

Many of the larger animal species have been depleted by hunting or by the spread of agriculture and the human population. As of the late 1960s the government had established two game reserves. The first of these, set up in 1957, was the Yankari Game Reserve, about 40 miles southeast of Bauchi. This reserve covers an area of 720 square miles. The other reserve, the Borgu Game Reserve, established in 1962, covers 1,500 square miles and lies just west of Kainji Lake in Kwara State.

BOUNDARIES AND ADMINISTRATIVE DISTRICTS

Nigeria has a land frontier of over 2,500 miles and an additional 475 miles of coastline on the Gulf of Guinea. The borders shared with neighboring countries have little connection with natural features. They are the result largely of agreements between expanding colonial powers made in the late 1800s and the first part of the twentieth century (see ch. 3, Historical Setting). The 480-mile western border with Dahomey generally was established by the British and French in 1898; minor modifications were agreed upon in 1906. The alignment of the border with the Republic of Niger, which extends for 930 miles from the Niger River on the northwest—first northward and then across the northern part of the country—to a point in Lake Chad, is based on a demarcation convention between Great Britain and France in 1910.

Part of the 1,050-mile eastern border with the Republic of the Cameroon is based on agreements between the British and the Germans in the early 1900s. Another part consists of new lines drawn after the end of World War I by the British and French governments as part of the division of the former German protectorate of Kamerun into British- and French-administered United Nations mandates. A third part consists of an administrative dividing line established by the British government between northern and southern sections of its mandate. In 1961 a plebiscite was held under United Nations supervision in which northern sections of the British mandate voted to join Nigeria, while a southern part decided to unite with Cameroon. The international boundary in the south reverted to the former Anglo-German line; in the north it continued to follow that set in the post-World War I Anglo-French agreement, with the administrative line forming the boundary connecting these two lines.

In the extreme northeast, Nigeria shares a short border with the Republic of Chad. This consists of a straight line forty-seven miles long running through a part of Lake Chad. This border was also defined by agreement between the British and French governments.

At independence on October 1, 1960, the country was divided into three regions—Northern, Western, and Eastern—each containing a number of provinces, which were further subdivided into divisions, and the Federal Territory of Lagos. In 1963 the eastern two provinces of the Western Region were separated from that region and established as the new Mid-Western Region (see fig. 5). Demands for the creation of further regions continued in the mid-1960s. During the crisis immediately preceding the secession

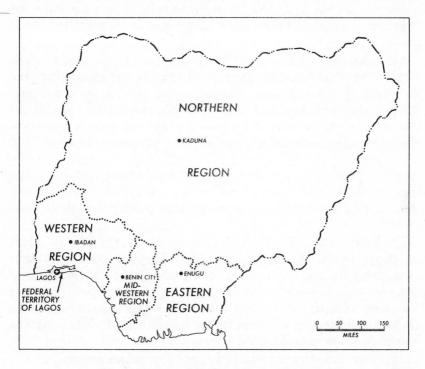

Figure 5. Principal Administrative Units of Nigeria, 1963 to 1967

of the Eastern Region, the Federal Military Government announced, on May 27, 1967, a reorganization of the four regions into twelve states. This new federal structure became effective on April 1, 1968 (see ch. 3, Historical Setting; ch. 9, Government and Political Dynamics).

In mid-1971 the twelve designated states constituted the first-order division in the country's administrative hierarchy (see fig. 1). Until 1969 they were divided into a total of thirty-one provinces and more than ninety divisions. The divisions were in turn subdivided into an undetermined number of local administrative units. During 1970, however, several states abolished their provincial organization and raised the division to the second level of administration. At least two states, while retaining provincial administrations, abolished their existing divisions. Further changes were anticipated (see ch. 9, Government and Political Dynamics).

SETTLEMENT PATTERNS

The general pattern of settlement throughout the country is the result in large part of earlier historical factors that saw the development of Muslim emirates in the northern part of the savanna zone about the beginning of the eleventh century. Somewhat later the Bini and Yoruba kingdoms were established in the southern forest zone.

Trade and cultural interests of the northern peoples led them to look to the Arab world in North Africa. At the same time, the activities of the southern kingdoms centered on the coast and flourished after the arrival of the Europeans and the expansion of the slave trade between the sixteenth and nineteenth centuries. The rather vast land area between these two zones attracted little attention (see ch. 3, Historical Setting). Thus, in mid-1971 the heaviest population concentrations were confined largely to the two zones. The broad middle belt between them, comprising about 40 percent of the country, was only sparsely inhabited and almost entirely rural in character.

Long before the advent of the Europeans, large urban centers developed in the northern part of the country around important trading points and administrative centers. Other urban-type concentrations developed in the southern forest zone; their principal locations were in the Yoruba kingdoms of the southwest. These towns were similar in appearance, consisting of closely packed houses of red mud and usually surrounded by a wall.

Many of these towns remained important urban centers in 1971. In the north they included Kano, Zaria, Katsina, and Sokoto, all the seats of historic emirates. In the south were the Yoruba centers of Ibadan, Ilorin, Ogbomosho, Oshogbo, Oyo, Ilesha, and Ife. Others were Benin City, earlier the capital of the kingdom of Benin, and in the southeast the city of Calabar. The impact of modern urban concepts, however, was everywhere apparent in the grafting on to the older nucleus of new commercial and residential zones patterned on the modern city.

New towns were also created by Europeans, first along the coast as ports and trading centers. Eventually others were formed inland, chiefly in connection with economic development. Such towns are laid out usually in a gridiron pattern and bear the definite imprint of the western city form. They include ports, such as Sapele and Port Harcourt; the towns of Enugu and Jos, both of which originated as mining centers; and the railroad junctions of Kaduna, Kanfanchan, and Minna. The capital city of Lagos, although developed from an old Yoruba town, is essentially a new town; only a small section of Lagos Island remains of the original settlement.

Despite early urbanization and a continuation of urban trends in mid-1971, a large part of the population lived in rural villages (see ch. 4, Population and Labor). The usual rural settlement pattern was the nucleated village, except in the case of some ethnic groups that lived in generally dispersed compounds or in ribbon settlements along the roads (see ch. 7, Living Conditions).

TRANSPORTATION

Railways

In 1969 the railway system, operated by the Nigerian Railway Corporation, a statutory public organization, had 2,178 route-miles of track, all 3-feet, 6-inch gauge. It included a single-track main line running north from Lagos through Ibadan and Ilorin to Jebba, where it crossed the Niger River, and northeast to Kaduna. At Kaduna it was joined by another single-track main line originating in Port Harcourt; this line passed through Enugu and crossed the Benue River at Makurdi. The combined line then proceeded to Zaria and Kano and finally to Nguru, a cattle-raising area in the far northeastern part of the country, 843 miles (six days by train) from Lagos (see fig. 6).

Branch lines of the railway ran to Maiduguri, capital of North Eastern State; the important tin-producing center of Jos; Kaura Namoda in the groundnut-growing area of northern North Western State; and Baro, a port on the north bank of the Niger River in southern North Western State.

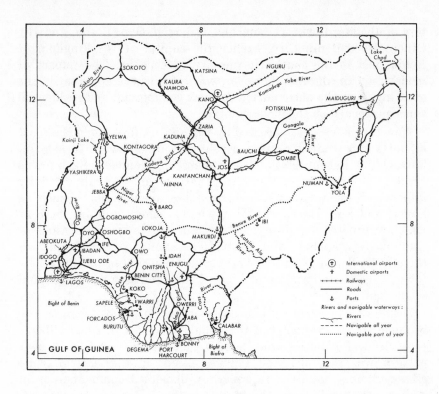

Figure 6. Transportation System of Nigeria

Rolling stock in 1968 consisted of 240 steam locomotives, 191 of which were main line, and 89 diesel locomotives, of which 72 were main-line locomotives. There were 546 passenger cars, and main-line freight cars of all types totaled 6,612, with a carrying capacity of 173,339 tons. Railway operations were seriously affected in the latter 1960s by the crisis preceding the civil war and the war itself. Train service between the railway's eastern and northern districts stopped in December 1966, and the line from Port Harcourt to the north was not reopened until September 1970.

Shortages caused by the unavailability of a large number of coaches, freight cars, and locomotives within the eastern district and the use of trains for military purposes in the area controlled by the Federal Military Government resulted in a drastic reduction of the number of trains used for civilian passenger and freight services. This was reflected in a drop in the number of passengers from 11.6 million in fiscal year 1965/66 to 6.9 million in 1967/68 and of freight tonnage from 2.9 million long tons in 1965/66 to 1.9 million long tons in 1967/68. Some recovery in passenger traffic occurred in 1968/69 and 1969/70, but freight tonnage had not increased appreciably.

The railway has been replacing steam locomotives with diesel locomotives to increase efficiency. By the mid-1960s most lines were using diesel locomotives; the principal exception was the Port Harcourt-Kanfanchan line, which used coal from the Enugu mines. Further conversion to diesels was being carried out in the early 1970s through the purchase of thirty-four additional locomotives from Japan, under a loan granted by a Japanese banking group, and sixty-four locomotives from Canada under a Canadian government loan.

Roads

In the late 1960s there were about 55,500 miles of roads throughout the country. Approximately 9,500 miles of the road network had tarred surfaces, and about 46,000 miles were surfaced either with gravel or earth. The road network was divided into three categories. The first consisted of major roads designated Trunk A. These linked the federal capital of Lagos, the twelve state capitals, certain other large towns, and the country's ports. Also included in this group were roads leading to important points in adjacent countries. Maintenance of Trunk A roads was the responsibility of the federal government.

Included in the second category were roads designated Trunk B. These connected the provincial and divisional administrative centers with various larger towns and provided access to the Trunk A roads and the railway system. Trunk B roads were maintained by the state governments.

Trunk A and Trunk B roads accounted for about 13,500 miles of the total road network. The remaining 42,000 miles of the system connected small towns and villages with one another and with the larger towns in the area. Their upkeep was the responsibility of the local authorities. In some cases financial assistance was furnished by the appropriate state government.

Major trunk roads proceeded from Lagos and Port Harcourt northward to Kano. Four others crossed the country from west to east—two above and two below the Niger-Benue River Valley region. These six roads formed the basic grid upon which the rest of the road system had been developed.

All major roads along a north-south axis must cross the Niger and Benue rivers. In mid-1971 bridges existed only at Jebba in the west, where a road crossed the Niger River, and at Makurdi in the east, where another road crossed the Benue River. Ferry service capable of handling heavily loaded vehicles was also provided at two places on the Niger and two on the Benue. Minor ferries also operated in the upper stretches of the Benue River.

The lower Niger River similarly acts as a barrier between the southwestern and southeastern parts of the country. In early 1966 a three-lane bridge was opened between Onitsha and Asaba on the lower east-west trunk road. This bridge was seriously damaged during the civil war, but it was reopened in 1970. A major ferry service existed at the confluence of the Niger and Benue rivers at Lokoja. A minor service was operated at Idah, about halfway between Onitsha and Lokoja.

Lack of proper maintenance during the war caused considerable deterioration of the country's roads. Wartime disruption of traffic between Port Harcourt and the northern areas forced the Lagos-Kano trunk roads to be used for most surface transportation between the north and south. Excessive use brought rapid deterioration of these roads. Much damage to roads also occurred in the war zone in Mid-Western, East Central, and South Eastern States. The Second National Development Plan, 1970–1974, has designated a substantial sum for road rehabilitation (see ch. 12, Character and Structure of the Economy).

In early 1967, before the start of the civil war, 87,600 motor vehicle registrations were reported—23,300 were commercial vehicles, including trucks and buses, and 64,300 were private cars and taxis. In addition, there were more than 20,000 motorcycles and motor bicycles. Some of these motor vehicles were destroyed during the war, but imports from 1967 through 1969 added more than 25,000 commercial vehicles and 21,000 private cars.

Ports and Inland Waterways

The country has two major ports—Lagos, on the western coast, and Port Harcourt, which is located on the Bonny River, forty-one miles from the mouth of the Bonny estuary in the eastern Niger Delta area. Smaller ports include Calabar, on the Calabar River in the far southeastern part of the country; Bonny, located near the mouth of the Bonny estuary, which in 1971 was being developed as a tanker terminal for crude oil export; and Degema, situated some distance up the Sambreiro River in the eastern delta. On the western side of the delta are the ports of Forcados, a crude oil terminal in the lower Forcados estuary; Burutu, thirty-eight miles up the Forcados estuary; Warri, seventy-nine miles from the Gulf of Guinea on the Warri River, which empties into the Forcados River; and farther west, some fifty miles up the Benin River, the ports of Koko and Sapele.

As of 1971 the ports of Lagos, Port Harcourt, Calabar, and

Warri formed a national system under the control and operation of the Nigerian Ports Authority, a statutory public body. The port of Lagos was able to accommodate up to thirty-one vessels and had two large floating cranes. The main berthing was at Apapa Quay, which was 5,000 feet in length and able to handle up to ten vessels, The quay area had thirty-six portal cranes, considerable transit space, and four large storage warehouses. All berths and transit storage facilities were directly served by railway sidings. Other facilities included the Customs Quay, which could handle three large vessels, and wharves for oil and coal shipment. Several buoy berths and anchorages were available, and the port had a large dockyard and a floating dock that could service vessels of up to 4,000 registered tons.

Port Harcourt is the terminus of the main railway line in the eastern part of the country and the port that handles coal mined at Enugu. It has a 3,500-foot-long quay capable of accommodating up to seven vessels, a coal conveyor berth, mooring buoys, and anchorages. The port sustained a good deal of damage during the civil war, and substantial reconstruction and rehabilitation were underway in 1971.

Calabar and Warri were private ports until December 1969, when they were taken over by the Nigerian Ports Authority. They are included in a national ocean ports development plan intended in part to relieve the congestion at Lagos and Port Harcourt.

Shipping service is provided by the government-owned Nigerian National Shipping Line; the West African Shipping Conference; and various European, Far Eastern, and North American shipping lines. The government line furnished service to West African ports and between Nigeria and Europe. In 1970 it had about thirteen ships totaling approximately 87,600 registered tons.

The country has an extensive inland waterway system embracing the Niger and Benue rivers, the Katsina Ala and Gongola tributaries of the Benue, and the Cross River. In addition, the creeks and lagoons of the southern part of the country interconnect to form a continuous waterway from the western border with the Republic of Dahomey eastward to the Niger Delta. The Niger River is navigable by large river boats throughout the year to Onitsha and for about ten months during high-water periods to Yelwa in the northwestern part of the country. Regulation of water levels in the Niger through flow control at the Kainji (Niger) Dam is expected eventually to allow continuous river traffic by larger craft. The main ports on the Niger above Onitsha include Idah, Lokoja, Baro, Jebba, and Yelwa.

The Benue River is navigable to Yola by shallow-draft boats for about three months during the high-water season. The main river ports on the Benue are at Makurdi, Ibi, Numan, and Yola. Limited navigation is also possible to the port of Garoua in Cameroon. The Cross River is navigable for some distance by small river vessels.

Air Transportation

Air services were provided at the beginning of 1971 between many of the larger cities by regularly scheduled flights of the government-owned Nigerian Airways Corporation. In addition, a number of private air taxi firms furnished transportation for companies involved in oil exploration and production in the southeast and provided limited service to various parts of the country. A number of business firms and missionary groups had their own aircraft.

Two international airports, at Lagos and Kano, handled commercial jet aircraft. Larger domestic airports in operation were located at Calabar and Port Harcourt in the southeast; Benin City and Ibadan in the southwest; and Kaduna, Jos, Maiduguri, Sokoto, and Yola in the north. The airport at Enugu, damaged during the civil war, was reopened in March 1971. Smaller airfields were also located at many places throughout the country.

International air service was furnished at the end of 1970 by Nigerian Airways Corporation and various international commercial airlines. The national airline carried passengers and cargo to Accra, Douala, and Kinshasa in Africa and to London. International airlines flying into Nigeria connected the country with Europe, the Middle East, the Soviet Union, other African countries, and the United States.

CHAPTER 3

HISTORICAL SETTING

The history of the modern Nigerian nation dates largely from 1914 when the previously distinct northern and southern Nigerian protectorates were amalgamated under British rule. Nonetheless, oral traditions of the area's various ethnic groups, documentary sources, and archaeological evidence reveal the evolution of various dynamic, interacting kingdoms within its boundaries several hundred years before the arrival of Europeans in the fifteenth century. Many of the ethnic political and social institutions in existence at that time were preserved under later British colonial rule. A number of these traditions, in modified form, continued to serve as meaningful institutions in the early period after independence in 1960.

Historical background evolves from numerous histories of the large number of ethnic groups that populate the country. It is possible, however, to trace the emergence of the various northern and southern ethnic clusters on the basis of their interaction with each other and with more distant peoples. Literate recordkeeping societies in the north were culturally and economically tied to Islamic centers of North Africa by a complex series of trade routes several hundred years before the arrival of the Europeans. Ethnic groups in the south, however, lacked written languages and depended on oral traditions for the preservation and transmittal of historical events. After the fifteenth century the orientation of these peoples was directed toward coastal contacts rather than the interior trade routes.

Trade—initially in slaves and later in commodities—served as the stimulus for European expansion in the region. Original British interests were focused on the activities of the Royal Niger Company, whose interests were commercial. It was not until the end of the nineteenth century that the European presence began to have an impact on the traditional patterns of the region. Eventually British development of the southern coastal areas increased the political prominence of ethnic groups living in that sector.

At the same time, the northern areas were separated from their traditional source of influence, and the flow of authority from north to south was reversed. Protection of its commercial interests and the desire to eliminate slavery and other practices led Great Britain to assume political administration over an increasingly larger portion of the area. By the early twentieth century it controlled nearly all of what was later to become the state of Nigeria.

The years between World War I and World War II served as an incubation period for the movement toward modern nationalism. The emerging educated leadership began to resolve some of its internal conflicts and prepared to voice its demands, first for increased participation in self-government and later for independence. These developments, however, took place against a background of continuing political factionalism that derived largely from traditional ethnic tensions. Ethnic political alignment was reinforced by the British decision to leave the country divided into three regions, each of which was dominated by a major ethnic group. These consisted of the Hausa in the north, the Yoruba in the southwest, and the Ibo in the east. Unity appeared to have been reached at the time of independence but only under a loose federal structure. Latent ethnic hostility resurfaced early in the 1960s and led to the breakdown of the constitutional system, the military coup of 1966, the secession of the Eastern Region as the separate Republic of Biafra, and thirty months of civil war.

THE PRE-EUROPEAN PERIOD

Oral traditions of many northern peoples claim Eastern points of origin—Egypt, Arabia, or even Persia. It is probable that the country was first settled by successive waves of migration from northern and eastern directions. Cultural influence radiated at least as far as the Western Sudan directly from North Africa and less directly from Egypt. Most of the contemporary ethnic groups have been settled within the country for centuries. They have evolved their own forms of social and political organization, either in comparative isolation in the south until the Europeans arrived in strength or through continuous interaction with outside influences, as in the open, freely traveled northern territories.

The first known culture in Nigerian prehistory was that of the Nok peoples. Located in an area 300 miles long and 100 miles wide above the confluence of the Niger and Benue rivers, the group existed between 500 B.C. and A.D. 200 and was an Iron Age culture. The Nok are generally believed to be the ancestors of contemporary ethnic groups in the area. They reached a cultural level that was not repeated in the country until the emergence of the Kanem-Bornu Empire in the ninth century (see ch. 8, Education, Public Information, and the Arts and Sciences).

Southern Kingdoms

The most highly organized people of the southern forest zone are the Yoruba, long the dominant group in the southwest (see ch. 6, Social Systems). Like most of their immediate neighbors, the Yoruba developed their political organization from the small, clan-like descent group of a single village with a subsistence agricultural economy into a territorially delimited state with formal hierarchies under the recognized authority of a chief. In the absence of written records the best available evidence of cultural attainment among the Yoruba is provided by an impressive scale of political organization and by discoveries of superior-quality sculpture in stone and bronze dating from the thirteenth or fourteenth century.

The two major political powers in the south were associated with the kingdoms of Oyo and Benin. Both originated in the Yoruba system, which had an initial focal point at Ife, a center that still preserves its religious significance.

Both kingdoms expanded during the fifteenth century, and the Benin kingdom exploited the firearms made available by trade with the Portuguese to achieve its greatest power in the following century at a time when it was in continuous and apparently fruitful contact with Portugal. The Oyo Empire attained its maximum extension sometime in the eighteenth century. The Benin kingdom had already declined because of the constant warfare unleashed in the attempt to procure slaves and other commodities needed for the lucrative trade. The power of the Oyo Empire during this period extended to what is now Dahomey in the west and the Hausa states in the north and encroached on the coastal ports outside its actual realm.

By the time the British arrived in force in the nineteenth century, the decline of Benin had left room for the rise of the Ijaw and the Ibo dynasties as competing centers of trade around the Niger Delta. The Yoruba-based Oyo Empire had disintegrated as well, partly as a result of internal strains and partly because of the Fulani incursions from the north. A series of successor states —Ibadan, Ijaiye, Ijebu, and the Egba state at Abeokuta—preserved the characteristic Yoruba political institution.

The fragmented political condition of the coastal areas determined the course of relations with the British after the middle of the nineteenth century. There was no single power capable of resisting gradual British incursions, and most of the existing dynasties were either founded on, or dependent upon, the European slave trade that had attracted the British initially. Competition among the indigenous systems of power ensured that the British could find allies, even when proceeding against a Nigerian chief or commercial oligarch.

To the east there had never been large-scale and complex political organization. The Efik trading oligarchy of Old Calabar was simply a more highly developed instance of the coastal authorities' reliance on trade with Europeans. Moreover, the divisions and hostilities among the local people tended to draw the British increasingly into an active political role in order to maintain conditions favorable to trade. The lack of an effective and inclusive coastal political organization also enhanced the impact of new techniques and ideas introduced by the Europeans.

The pre-European period in the history of the peoples residing in the area was notable for the transmission of external influence from north to south. Political, religious, and commercial contacts profoundly modified the lives of the northern peoples, and these influences were transmitted in attenuated form southward. The arrival of Europeans in the Gulf of Guinea signified that the traffic in ideas and techniques would eventually be reversed. Yet there was still a long interval before the imperial competition of European states imposed an artificial unity on the disparate elements of the population.

Northern Kingdoms

From the earliest times trade played a decisive role in the emergence of states in the north. Trans-Saharan routes of migration and trade had linked the Western Sudan with the Mediterranean from the time of Carthage and established the avenue of communication and influence that remained supreme until the twentieth century. From this direction migrating peoples were received into an amalgamation with the negroid groups south of the Sahara in prehistoric times. By the same route Islam later made its way south from the Mediterranean coast.

The great empires that grew up in the Western Sudan from the ninth and tenth centuries onward—Ghana, Mali, Songhai, Kanem-Bornu and others—were held together loosely and were subject to disintegration as the central military power declined. Their cultural development and economic prosperity were equal to many parts of Europe in the same period. The city of Timbuktu (now in the country of Mali) was long a center of Muslim learning and culture.

The only empire on future Nigerian territory illustrious enough in extent and duration to be compared with Mali, Songhai, and the other great Western Sudanese empires was that of Kanem-Bornu. Originating in the ninth century beyond Lake Chad, the empire of

Kanem-Bornu was an early recipient of Islamic impact. By the end of the twelfth century the empire had a Muslim king.

During the twelfth and thirteenth centuries Kanem established lasting relations with other Muslim states and began to shift its center of influence westward toward Bornu. Its authority extended well to the west, until the Hausa states of Kano and Katsina became satellites of Bornu. Continuous movement of the seat of government through the dominions was a feature of the Bornu kinship. This eased the process of shifting the center of the empire from Kanem, when these original provinces were lost during the decline of power in the fourteenth century, without destroying the dynastic basis of the state. The sixteenth century witnessed a renewal of Bornu power under the leadership of Mai Idris when a revival of Islamic fervor coincided with a broad expansion of Bornu power as far as Darfur in the east.

Thereafter, although Bornu remained a center of Islamic culture, the rulers tended to accept the status quo, substituting piety for the dynamic leadership that Mai Idris had supplied. The decline in political power lasted until the Fulani religious war at the beginning of the nineteenth century. Then Bornu, unlike the Hausa states, revived and successfully resisted the onslaught under the military guidance of a new dynastic leadership headed by an outsider, Mohammed al-Kanemi. By the end of the nineteenth century Bornu's power had declined again and could not prevail against the expanding frontiers of the European colonial powers.

The early history of the Hausa states in the northern part of the country is uncertain, but they probably date from the tenth century. The *Kano Chronicle* records the introduction of Islam by missionaries from the empire of Mali in the west, followed by the conversion of the ruling Kano dynasty in the fourteenth century. Different states assumed leading roles at various times, and Kano, Zaria, and Gobir were among the outstanding powers. Hausa territory was ringed by other powers—Bornu in the east, the great Sudanese empires in the west, and the pagan states of Nupe and Jukun in the south—and was subject to constant pressure.

At times some of the city-states were forced to pay tribute to Bornu; at other times they were overrun by western invaders. The thread of continuity was never really broken—even the conquest by the Songhai Empire involved only a loose system of tribute collection—but the Hausa states never coalesced into a major power in the region. In the eighteenth century Islam apparently declined among the Hausa states. Gobir was the dominant Hausa state of the period, and its dynasty is reputed to have conceded much to its pagan population while observing a nominal Islamic faith.

Trade with North Africa was a pivotal feature of Hausa activity, and it contributed greatly to the spread of the Hausa language as the commercial medium of West Africa. Despite the faltering observance of Islam, the Islam-based fiscal and judicial systems remained intact through the Fulani conquest. It was as self-appointed guardians of Islamic culture in Hausa territory that the Fulani launched a holy war (*jihad*).

The origins of the Fulani peoples are conjectural, but they began to enter the Hausa area from the west in peaceable fashion about the thirteenth century. One group of Islamic Fulani settled in towns and mingled freely with the Hausa, becoming a religious and educated class. The other group, pastoral Fulani, remained aloof from both Islam and the Hausa, herding cattle outside the towns. The Muslims became the vehicle of the holy war at the beginning of the nineteenth century, when religious passions congealed around a devout Muslim Fulani, Othman dan Fodio, who refused to be repressed by the ruler of the Hausa state of Gobir. Between 1804 and 1810 the Fulani overcame all the Hausa states and part of Bornu, waging religious war against fellow Muslims on the grounds that their religious practices had become debased.

The Fulani emirates thus superimposed on the Hausa states formed an empire with allegiance to the sultan of Sokoto. Although the sultanate was almost immediately divided into two parts under Sokoto and Kano, the Islamic religious revival affected primarily the locus of political authority. The structure of the Hausa states was little altered, but the various emirates soon became independent powers in the secular realm, recognizing the sultan's supremacy only in spiritual matters. Fulani conquest was extended well to the south, reaching as far as the former Yoruba province of Ilorin. This gave stimulus to the spread of Islam in that direction and formed the basis for future Yoruba irredentism. A stalemate was reached in the east, where al-Kanemi repulsed the Fulani attacks on Bornu but was unable to dislodge the new rulers in the Hausa area. In the Benue region to the southeast, Fulani influence was felt unevenly; the mid-section of the country was never absorbed in any conclusive fashion into the Fulani sphere.

ADVENT OF THE EUROPEANS

The motivation for the European era of exploration and discovery was a combination of trading interest and Christian missionary spirit. As early as the fifteenth century the Portuguese led in the attempt to circumvent the power of Islam. The campaign made steady progress along the African coast. By the end of the century the Portuguese had completed their route around Africa. At first their aim was to find a route to the riches of the Indian Ocean; eventually the incipient West African trade in ivory, slaves, and gold was of sufficient importance to interest them. They erected a permanent fortification at Elmina on the Gold Coast to protect their monopoly against encroachments by unlicensed traders of other European powers.

Spanish, French, and English ships were seen along the coast from time to time, but for the most part the Portuguese position was secure for a century. Except for a trading station established near Benin in 1486, Portuguese penetration beyond Elmina was limited. The impact on indigenous societies was still more restricted by the unhealthful nature of the Niger Delta, which discouraged permanent settlement or continuous missionary establishments. The traders confined their interest to the slave trade, which they could pursue from the islands in the Gulf of Guinea. When the trans-Atlantic slave trade finally slipped into other hands, traces of Portuguese influence on the mainland soon disappeared.

Soon after the beginning of the seventeenth century, Dutch naval power wrested from Portugal its favorable trading position. The Dutch gradually won a dominant position on the West African coast, taking over many Portuguese trading stations and assuming the leadership as a source of slaves for Spanish and English plantations in the North and South American colonies. After 1650 French and British trade competition seriously undermined the Dutch preeminence. Additional challenges came from other Europeans, such as the Danes, Swedes, and Brandenburgers.

By the eighteenth century the chief competitors in West Africa, as in Europe and North America, were France and England. The British were dominant in the Guinea coast area beginning at this time. Although the residents of the principal slave-trading towns from Lagos to Benin to Old Calabar henceforth saw diverse European traders at their ports, British policy proved decisive for the subsequent history of the coastal region.

The Slave Trade

Trade in slaves was not a European innovation in West Africa; domestic slavery was prevalent throughout the region, and slaves had long been an item in the trade with North Africa. From the sixteenth century, however, the increased demand for slaves for work on New World plantations gave new impetus to the practice. Moreover, where indigenous domestic slavery had not always been an intolerable or even necessarily permanent condition, the profitable features of slave trading with Europeans rapidly led to brutal practices. The captive was treated as a commodity at all stages of the transaction. West Africans who competed with each other for shares in the proceeds were distracted from their normal pursuits and led into ruinous warfare, which contributed largely to the downfall of the states in the forest region.

The volume of the slave trade in West Africa grew rapidly from its inception around 1500 to its peak in the eighteenth century. Reliable estimates indicate that roughly 6.3 million slaves were shipped from West African slave ports, and more than 4.5 million in the period from 1701 to 1810. Estimates of the number of Africans who died in the course of slave-raiding, while awaiting shipment, or in transit vary widely. Most estimates generally are highly inflated and fail to take into account the fact that individual samplings do not represent the record of the slave trade as a whole. Depopulation of various sections of West Africa is often cited as a major result of the slave trade. This practice, however, does not appear to have had as deleterious an effect on the Nigerian region as did the disruption of the normal economy and intersocietal relations.

British domestic pressure in the 1730s provided the initial moral impetus for the abolition of the slave trade. In 1807 both Great Britain and the United States passed legislation making the practice illegal. Denmark, Sweden, and the Netherlands expressed similar legislative prohibitions. In 1833 Great Britain outlawed slavery throughout the British Empire, but enforcement of the law proved costly and was not always successfully enforced. The Royal Navy attempted to interfere with the slave trade directly, but the trans-Atlantic trade did not end until the 1860s.

The other phase of the British campaign against the slave traffic involved the cooperation of West Africans. British agents attempted repeatedly by means of entreaty, diplomacy, and bribery to bring pressure on the chieftains and principal traders along the coast, who had grown wealthy on their monopoly of slave traffic from the interior, into relinquishing their profitable business. The combination of force and subvention, reinforced by the moral suasion of the missionary establishments, involved Great Britain increasingly in the internal affairs of the Guinea coast after the middle of the nineteenth century. These efforts were partly responsible for the British decision to assume administrative supervision of portions of the coast. Slavery, an issue prominent in British dealing with local kings and chiefs until after the establishment of the Nigerian colony, frequently involved the British in intervention against chiefs who resisted rules against slaving.

Commodity Trade

The gradual elimination of the slave trade left many British merchants with useless capital investment. It also left the local population with a major gap in its economy unless a substitute could be found. Some trade in local products—palm oil, ivory, pepper, and cloth—had existed alongside the slave trade from the era of Portuguese exploration. After 1850 palm oil seemed the most promising trade commodity. Although this trade grew to significant proportions and was worth £1 million a year to British traders in 1840, it was concentrated along the coast and failed to satisfy people in the interior who had prospered through slave raiding.

Only gradually did the local population take to the cultivation of cash crops instead of subsistence agriculture. The kind of interest that prompted Englishmen to encourage genuine economic development along the West African coast represented a profound change from the era of quick profit from slaving operations. The new interest implied permanent establishments in constant contact with the local people. Local stability and development thus became important issues to the British.

Because of the hazards of the coastal climate and the lack of any authority responsive to their interests on the mainland, European traders ordinarily moored their ships in harbors or at the mouth of the rivers on the bights of Benin and Biafra and used the ships as trading stations (see ch. 2, Physical Environment). Eventually they also moved up the rivers to such interior stations as Onitsha. After payment of variable amounts that were more in the nature of gifts than duties to the coastal chieftains or dominant commercial authorities in the trading towns, the traders could then negotiate with the native suppliers of commodities and purchase the products that would earn them a profit.

Contemporary evidence suggests that the traders were anything but civilizing agents. Many of them had adopted legal trade only as a last resort when their original slave-trading occupation had grown too hazardous. Brutal and disreputable as many of them were, they often suffered greatly from the precariousness of their position at the mercy of unpredictable coastal rulers. Accordingly, as the volume of trade increased, the British government responded to repeated requests from the traders and appointed John Beecroft, an explorer of the Niger River area and Spanish-appointed governor of the island of Fernando Po, as consul for the bights of Benin and Biafra.

Beecroft's efforts in behalf of stability and order in the coastal trading operations constituted the first step toward official British intervention. His jurisdiction extended from the area of what is now Dahomey to the Cameroons, and he relied upon the limited British naval forces for his enforcement power. He also enjoyed considerable esteem and could usually count on the support of some West Africans if he proceeded against a violator of accepted trading practices.

The growth of legitimate trade brought more reputable European merchants to the Guinea coast and led them to organize into groups. The most important one with far-reaching consequences for Nigeria was founded by Sir George Goldie in 1879 as the United Africa Company. This association of the major British firms trading on the coast became the National African Company in 1882. Four years later it received a charter from the British government granting the Royal Niger Company, as it was then renamed, wide powers of government in the Niger River region.

The terms of the charter specified the maintenance of free trade —a principle that was systematically violated as the company strengthened its monopoly and forestalled French and German trade expansion. It also enjoined the company to avoid trespassing on local religious practices or customs "except so far as may be necessary in the interests of humanity." The qualifying clause was aimed at slavery and other tribal practices, foreshadowing the qualifications applied to noninterference as a guide to official policy after the British government assumed formal colonial responsibility. Meanwhile, the company exercised quasi-governmental, quasi-judicial, and punitive powers in its area.

Inland Exploration

The Royal Niger Company represented a culmination of private interest in West African development, the final phase of private British efforts to develop a positive alternative to the destructive slave trade. Earlier aspects of such constructive interest had included the establishment of the colony of Sierra Leone as a refuge for Nigerian slaves liberated by the Royal Navy from captured slave ships, the missionary movement designed to bring Christianity along with its collateral benefits to the peoples, and programs of exploration sponsored after 1788 by the African Association.

Exploration of the Niger River region had scientific, adventurous, and commercial motivation. The chief stimulus was the curiosity aroused by the Niger River, the course and destination of which were masked from coastal travelers by the delta that divided the great river into many small outlets (see ch. 2, Physical Environment). The first expedition to achieve any success was that led by Mungo Park, an intrepid Scottish physician, who reached the Niger from the northwest in 1796 but could not proceed because of warfare in the region. After 1800 the British Colonial Office showed some interest in the possibility of trade in the West African interior and sent Park on an expedition, which cost him his life. Although he failed to reach the river's outlet at the coast because the entire expedition was wiped out by fever and misfortune, Park's journals survived and significantly advanced European knowledge of the interior.

Additional explorations by Dixon Denham and Hugh Clapperton contributed to British knowledge of the Sudan, particularly of the Fulani empire and of Bornu. The solution of the Niger River puzzle was reserved for the Lander brothers, who finally reached the Niger Delta in 1830. A high mortality rate defeated initial attempts to open trade with the interior by way of the Niger River. After the mid-1800s the use of quinine to combat malaria enabled the merchant Macgregor Laird to initiate trade up the Niger and Benue rivers. His efforts were stimulated by the detailed reports emanating from one of the last of the pioneer explorers of West Africa, Heinrich Barth. Barth, a German scholar turned explorer for the English, traveled through much of northern Nigeria, recording features of natural geography and much about the peoples and customs of the time.

In its penetrations of the interior the Royal Niger Company built on the foundations laid by the explorers. Although it proceeded along routes of trade and held its jurisdiction together by means of trade stations rather than by strict territorial delimitation, its advance toward the north was an important prelude to the territorial consolidation of Nigeria under British colonial rule at the end of the nineteenth century. Its interior station at Lokoja, at the confluence of the Niger and Benue rivers, also formed a significant link between north and south. Along with the longitudinal boundaries that emerged from the rivalry of European colonial powers, this north-south axis constituted an orientation superimposed by Europeans; it did not conform with the cultural cleavage of ethnic groups in the area.

Influence of Christian Missions

The Christian missionaries first arrived at the end of the slave trade era and were the first Europeans to establish systematic contact with the people. Their efforts were more intensive and personal but less massive in their impact than those of the traders or colonial administrators. They were confined in the 1840s to the coastal areas, starting with Abeokuta and soon spreading to Lagos and Ibadan. This early concentration of effort in Yoruba territory is reflected in the greater total impact of Christianity in this area. The Wesleyan and Church Missionary Society (Anglican) groups arrived first. Missionaries of these and other persuasions—Church of Scotland (Presbyterian), Baptist, and Roman Catholic—did not hesitate to penetrate northward as avenues of travel opened up. Their effect in the interior diminished, however, as they encountered entrenched Islam.

The Protestant denominations tended to divide the country into spheres of missionary activity to avoid competition with each other. Similarly, the Roman Catholic missionaries, arriving later in the 1900s, avoided duplication by dividing the territory among orders, of which the Holy Ghost Fathers were the most active. The proliferation of Christianity among a variety of separate religious organizations made the missionaries' task more difficult than that of the adherents of Islam. Christianity's influence, however, was enhanced by the auxiliary functions of its missions. The establishment of mission schools was of vital importance in the emergence of a small but important group of literate Nigerians, who eventually staffed government offices and founded nationalist movements. The missions also built hospitals and provided medical service as part of their self-appointed task. These activities, combined with the infusion of Western ideas and techniques, gave the missionary movement an important role in the development of modern Nigeria.

Most early missionary enterprises installed Africans in responsible positions in the religious establishments. The most famous of the early ecclesiastical figures was Samuel Adjai Crowther, an enslaved Yoruba who was liberated and educated in Sierra Leone and England before returning to his homeland in a clerical role. Eventually, Crowther became the first Nigerian bishop of the Church Missionary Society.

This was a crucial attempt to transform the European religious establishment into an indigenous instition. The effort failed, however, when Europeans came to feel that religious practices were growing too lax under Crowther's supervision, and he was succeeded by an Englishman. Nevertheless, acceptance of Christian establishments depended finally on their coming to terms with local conditions. This problem of Africanization involved the installation of increasing numbers of African clergymen, and by 1894 the Church Missionary Society, for example, had only half as many European as African clergymen in the area of the present-day Western State.

In many particulars the missionaries agreed in large measure with colonial administrators. A significant segment of the missionaries were convinced of the virtues of continued colonial tutelage, thereby reinforcing official policy. On the other hand, there were frequent disagreements between officials and clergymen above and beyond those arising from official discouragement of Christian missionary effort in the north. Colonial officials often complained that missionary influence had contributed to the uncooperative attitudes of some northern ethnic groups.

In Yoruba territory, the oldest area of missionary activity and a place where Protestantism predominated over Catholicism, the number of Christian adherents rose from about 6,000 in 1880 to more than 17,000 between 1900 and 1910 and then spurted to roughly 260,000 in 1920. In the Eastern Region, where missionary work got a late start and then became an area of Roman Catholic predominance, except in Old Calabar among the Efik, conversion was more spectacular. From 18,500 converts between 1900 and 1910 the number rose to over 500,000 by 1920, when the Ibo evinced a strong receptivity to European influence. Progress in the north, except in Lokoja and Kabba, was slow and did not start until after 1910. In 1920 there were an estimated 20,000 Christians in the middle section of the Northern Region.

ESTABLISHMENT OF BRITISH COLONIAL RULE

During the last part of the nineteenth century the British moved reluctantly and hesitatingly toward outright colonial rule. Action against the slave trade had woven a fabric of diplomatic connections, not only with other European states but also with many kings and chiefs in Nigeria. It had often dictated the application of force by the Royal Navy and by military units maintained by the Royal Niger Company as well as the use of suasion by British consular officers. Moreover, the large-scale missionary effort implied the need to protect missions and their personnel, at the same time as the missionaries were contributing to the desire to eradicate what the British considered savage customs and thus helping to justify further British intervention. Finally, the marked increase of trade and the growth of major trading enterprises, initially responsible for bringing British Foreign Office representatives to the bights of Benin and Biafra, had led to the use of private armies for protection in the areas of trade (see ch. 15, National Security).

For many years these factors were largely outweighed by general British reluctance to add a tropical dependency to the empire. The hesitation was reinforced by the fact that, because of its unhealthful climate, the area had not attracted white settlers. The prevailing sentiment, even after Lagos became a colony, was expressed in 1865 in a House of Commons report urging withdrawal from commitments on the West African coast. Colonies tended to be regarded as liabilities, especially where trading opportunities could be held open without resort to annexation.

By the end of the century the situation had changed. The depressed European economy sent the great industrial nations scurrying to find and develop new markets. For the sake of trade, Great Britain had been content with its spheres of influence until the appearance of both French and German ambitions for colonies in the 1880s.

Inevitably the colonial powers came into conflict over their respective campaigns of expansion. The Berlin Conference of 1885 was called jointly by Germany and France for the purpose of resolving conflicts of interest in Africa. The conference enunciated the principle, later known as the dual mandate, that the best interests of Africa and the world at large would be served by maintaining free access to the continent for trade and missionary endeavor and by conferring on Africa the benefits of European civilization.

The conference, however, acknowledged British claims to the area around the Niger River but stipulated that only effective occupation would suffice for future recognition of claims under international law. This ruling and the increasing pressure from France and Germany on the periphery of Nigeria hastened the establishment of British administration.

Extension of British Control

The measure of stability and pacification necessary to encourage trade and safeguard European missionaries increasingly involved the British consul at the port of Lagos in the factional strife of the surrounding Yoruba region. Ostensibly to stamp out slave trading, the Foreign Office in 1861 instructed the consul to undertake the occupation of Lagos. The Yoruba king, Dosumu, vacillated in the matter of signing a treaty of annexation, but a show of force overcame his resistance. A governor was appointed for Lagos itself until 1866, when the city was assigned to the jurisdiction of the West African Settlements, which had its headquarters in Sierra Leone. From 1874 to 1886 it was attached to the Gold Coast Colony but with its own deputy governor. In 1906, after twenty years under its own colonial governor, it was joined to the colony and protectorate of Southern Nigeria.

The history of Lagos Colony consists largely of attempts to resolve recurrent strife among the principal Yoruba cities. Ibadan was in ascendance at the time and at odds with the Egba people of Abeokuta in particular, while all of Yoruba territory was threatened from the west by the Dahomey and from the north by the Fulani in Ilorin. The governor succeeded finally in mediating the wars, aided by some of the missionaries (including the Yoruba clergyman Samuel Johnson) and, when necessary, by his Hausa troops. The outcome confirmed the British governor as the preeminent political force within the Lagos region, which had been extended some distance in both directions along the coast.

In 1885, after the Berlin Conference, Great Britain announced the establishment of the Oil Rivers Protectorate extending from the Niger Delta to Old Calabar, where the consul general had his headquarters. This official was moved there from Fernando Po to expand the limited powers that he had been exercising for over thirty years. The change in status was not immediately noticeable, except as vice consuls were stationed in the major port cities with whose kings the British had earlier signed treaties of protection. The consul continued to use and support the same kings for governing purposes as well as the mercantile courts of equity established by the traders. A constabulary force was raised and used to pacify the coastal area. In 1893 the protectorate was expanded to include the whole region from Old Calabar to Lagos and northward along the Niger River to Lokoja; the territory was designated the Niger Coast Protectorate. It remained under the jurisdiction of the British Foreign Office, in contrast to Lagos, which was under the British Colonial Office.

By 1900 the protectorate had been further extended to include almost all of the southern territory except Lagos. The expansion had been accomplished with limited violence, except in Benin where, following a treaty violation and the massacre of a visiting British party, the area was pacified and the king was exiled. This concluded the work of the protectorate, which had been constantly occupied with the difficult tasks of enforcing the restrictions on local customs abhorrent to the British and suppressing the almost ceaseless tribal strife of the region. The beginnings of orderly administration were bequeathed in 1906 to the colony and protectorate of Southern Nigeria, which included Lagos and operated under the British Colonial Office.

Although treaties had been signed at the initiative of the British consul with rulers as far north as Sokoto, in 1885, when German and French expansion threatened, administration of an official character was still confined to the coastal region. The territory from Lokoja northward and extending along the Niger and Benue rivers beyond their confluence remained under the supervision of the Royal Niger Company. As this region was dominated by the entrenched emirs, the governing functions of the company were limited. In 1900 the British government withdrew the company's charter, compensating the firm but leaving it in a strictly private, if favored, commercial position.

What had been a sphere of influence was now enclosed within formal boundaries as the protectorate of Northern Nigeria, arrived at in negotiations with the French and Germans who had gained control of all the areas to the west, north, and east. Although British control was entirely nominal, with Frederick Lugard's appointment as high commissoner in 1900, the British had finally assumed full responsibility for all of Nigeria.

The Protectorate of Northern Nigeria

During the six years of Lugard's tenure as high commissioner of Northern Nigeria, the British authorities were largely occupied with the extension of their actual control of the territory. They inherited from the Royal Niger Company a system of rather tenuous adminstration, which closely followed the Niger and Benue rivers without penetrating deeply into the interior. Their objective, however, was to pacify the entire region and obtain recognition of British protective rule by all indigenous powers. Corollaries of the primary aim were the gaining of acceptance for British concepts of efficient government and, at least ostensibly, the elimination of slave trading.

Although Lugard avoided abrogating Muslim law or the Fulani system of rulership that prevailed in most of the north, available British forces were involved in a lengthy process of military conquest and pacification. The Muslim emirates were disunited and recognized the primacy of the sultan of Sokoto only in the spiritual realm. The British campaign moved step by step in subduing local resistance and brought the emirates into line. Force was used only when peaceful measures failed. Bornu was occupied without fighting, but Kano and Sokoto had to be defeated militarily.

The fall of these major centers tended to weaken local resistance elsewhere, and by 1903 British control had been effected in most of the region; the last section, the Tiv lands, recognized British rule in 1914. British forces were thinly distributed, however, and control depended largely upon the resident officers stationed at each important city. Pacification was, therefore, a prolonged process, lasting into the twentieth century. It was impossible to foresee and prevent intermittent disorders until British rule won general acceptance from all the local powers.

Much of Great Britain's success was attributable to its determination to govern through traditional rulers. If the emirs accepted British authority, abandoned slave trading, and strove to improve their own administrations, the British were willing to confirm them in power. In some cases this meant shoring up and preserving a faltering sovereignty beyond its reasonable life expectancy. It also allowed the British to rule effectively with a limited number of personnel and small military contingents.

The principle came to be known as indirect rule. Lugard applied this system of control in Northern Nigeria and later incorporated it in theoretical elaborations designed to prove that it was the best means of realizing the dual mandate of the accessibility of Africa to European countries and the welfare of Africa as the beneficiary of European civilization.

Lugard placed great emphasis on responsible fiscal operations as a key to effective government. While adopting indigenous systems of taxation, law, and administration, his resident and district officers supervised all operations to ensure their equity and efficiency. This often entailed intervention, but it also required skilled, knowledgeable colonial officials capable of understanding each local situation. Hindsight suggests that the availability of a few such officials was essential to the workability of the system. Later evidence demonstrated that it worked best where a well-rooted tradition of political authority was at hand.

The essential features of indirect rule as developed by Lugard in the north after 1900 included recognition of the emirs as native authorities, with their power and activities left largely undisturbed. Final sovereign authority, however, rested with the governor, who could depose a local ruler. The governor used a few scattered officers throughout the territory as overseers. Depending on local conditions, they had a wide range of discretion in guiding and helping the emir to govern effectively. All orders from the governor were transmitted through the emir, not through the resident officers. Although legislative power resided in the governor, most of the activities of government stemmed from the emir and his local administration, subject to British approval.

Lugard and others of his generation did not entertain the notion of eventual independence for Nigeria and were therefore little concerned about wider political participation or more democratic procedures. In 1900 elective councils at the local government level were still in their infancy in England itself. Consequently, it seemed that indirect rule was well suited to enable the British to fulfill their obligations as trustee and guardian of the Nigerian people.

The accomplishments of Lugard and his successors in the field of economic development were limited by available revenues. From the taxes collected by the emirate officers, the British took first one-fourth and later one-half to support the services that the British colonial regime could best provide. All of these services—public health, education, agricultural development, and transportation —lagged because of limited funds. The north did not enjoy the lucrative customs duties that undergirded constructive policies in the south. The north also did not profit from the educational and medical services offered by the missionaries because Lugard discouraged Christian penetration of the Muslim areas in the belief that it would disrupt the indigenous culture. By 1906 Lugard was urging amalgamation of all three administrative regions into one colony in order to make possible the unified and uniform development of modern services. It was not until his return in 1912 as governor of both Northern and Southern Nigeria that progress in this direction could be made.

The Colony and Protectorate of Southern Nigeria

The years from 1906 to 1914, during which Southern Nigeria existed separately from the north but, with it, as a single unit of British administration, were notable for such fundamental economic improvements as road and railway building, the laying of telegraph lines, and harbor dredging. These efforts resulted from a comparative economic well-being that increasingly differentiated the south from the north. A spreading monetary base for the economy, although uneven in its impact on the south, further separated the coastal cultures from the relatively static societies of the north. The growing functions of government coincided with increasing commercial activity to advance the process of urbanization.

The Colony and Protectorate of Nigeria

Lugard's return to the area in 1912 set in motion the process of merging Northern and Southern Nigeria into one administrative entity. In 1914 unification was achieved. The principle of indirect rule was extended to the south, and economic development began to spread northward. Before any important inroads could be made on Nigerian diversity, World War I intervened. Both goods and attention were diverted to the war. Nigerians were also called upon to participate in the war effort. The Nigeria Regiment of the Royal West African Frontier Force, composed of troops from north and south, served in the campaigns against the German colonies, mainly in the Cameroons but also East Africa, and won praise for valor from its British officers.

When the war ended, attention once again turned to colonial matters. Lugard's term as governor expired in 1920, and he bequeathed to his successor a country that was enjoying unparalleled prosperity as a result of the postwar boom in commerce. Lugard had also taken steps to effect the merger and instituted a tax program along northern lines in the south during the war. The tax program was the main source of discontent and anti-British activity that marred wartime harmony.

The Nigerian Council, a deliberative group appointed by the governor and dominated by Europeans, was the device initiated to give expression to opinion from all parts of Nigeria in the form of advice to the governor. This body never awakened the interest of local chiefs, and it led a nominal existence until it was abolished in 1922.

A more successful institution was the Legislative Council. This characteristic feature of British colonial rule was instituted in Lagos in 1862 and functioned there until a legislative council was created for the entire south in 1922.

Efforts to apply indirect rule to the south meant a search for the legitimate loci of indigenous authority. This task proved comparatively easy in Yoruba areas, except for some of the detribalized newer urban areas. In the southeast, where Ibo and Ibibio traditions did not include large-scale systems of political authority, the search for acceptable local rulers was continued in vain throughout the interwar period. This shortcoming of indirect rule left the tasks of government largely in the hands of colonial officials and antagonized the Ibo in particular; their leadership of national movements in opposition to alien rulers subsequently developed. It was a type of dichotomy that was checked to some degree in Yoruba territory and to a major extent in the north by the devolution of governing functions to indigenous local rulers. To the extent that local authorities and local courts were able to manage public affairs, forces of change and resistance to alien supervision were mediated.

EMERGENCE OF NIGERIAN NATIONALISM

Nationalism began to emerge as a viable political force between World War I and World War II. Its development, however, was surrounded by fractionalism. Among the cleavages that acted as conditioning factors in the emergence of national consciousness were regional animosities. Varying hostilities existed between the north and south and between the southeast and southwest; most of the complex hostilities were based on ethnicity. Various urban centers stood in competition with each other, and conflicting economic interests and religious differences also served as sources of tension.

Variations in British policy complicated the situation and furthered internal imbalance by attempting simultaneously to preserve, sometimes artificially, the indigenous culture of an area while introducing technology and other elements of Western culture. Urban centers began to emerge, dominated by a new class of Africans who thought more in terms of the administrative unit than ethnic origins. As late as the 1930s, however, when many of the elite came from families with three generations of European education, there was a lack of dialogue and social interaction between the Africans and the British.

The forms of nationalism that grew up in this setting proceeded from diverse motivations and involved their exponents in frequent disagreement—quite apart from the discouragement all of them received from colonial rules and local authorities. Colonial governors often ridiculed any notion of nationalism in such a heterogeneous country as Nigeria. This reaction appeared to be justified at the time, but it disregarded the potent forces unleashed by the British.

Incipient nationalism, however, was equally prone to ignore the territorial entity of Nigeria and concentrated on the opposition to alien rule. This was the common denominator of the various nationalisms that originated, on the positive side, in assertions of Yoruba or, later, Ibo folk-consciousness or in racial and pan-African ideas. Sometimes the antiquity and excellence of native culture were celebrated, with the implication that European influence had been destructive. At other times emphasis was given to modernity and the capability of local people for self-government, implying that only conservative colonial rule prevented the unshackling of new forces that would rapidly carry Africa into the modern world.

At its inception the national movement as manifest in Nigeria was really neither national nor Nigerian. The ideological inspiration of the movement came from a variety of sources within the African continent and from such outside sources as the Negro Americans Marcus Garvey and W.E.B. DuBois. Nigerian students abroad joined with other African students in groups, such as the West African Students Union, founded in London in 1925 and active until 1945. The original focus was not against the colonial system but rather against the system's racial and exclusive bias. The issue was not independence but increased participation and self-determination in local issues. The focus, moreover, was not solely on Nigeria but on all of West Africa.

Many Africans had resisted the British presence in their territory even before the beginning of the nationalist movements. There were uprisings and protests, sometimes with the loss of lives, during the late nineteenth and early twentieth centuries, such as the 1895 attack on the Royal Niger Company, the tax revolts of 1895, the war protest of 1904, and the 1929 Aba riots sparked by economic grievances. All of these, however, represented instances in which local questions were at issue, and the participants identified with local ethnic groups and values rather than with a concept of emergent nationhood.

Probably the first major instances of outright rejection of European domination that were more comprehensive than mere protests against a tax measure or signs of tension arising from cultural disruption occurred at the end of the nineteenth century when several church groups broke away from their white-dominated parent bodies. Such groups seceded from Anglican, Methodist, and Baptist congregations and provided one of the few available avenues for the free expression of anticolonial attitudes.

No less important in the pre-World War I era were the newspapers, such as the *Lagos Weekly Record*, the *Nigerian Chronicle*, the *Lagos Standard*, and the *Nigerian Times*. All give limited coverage to anticolonial and early nationalist views.

The 1920s saw the range of ideas expanded from several sources but notably from the movement founded in the United States by Marcus Garvey on the basis of Negro self-assertion and the slogan "Africa for the Africans." Garvey's extremism was disavowed by most Negro leaders but had a delayed importance in West Africa.

It is impossible to say whether or not nationalist agitation, still in its infancy and highly localized, created pressure that hastened constitutional change in 1922. But the opportunity thus afforded —for the first time in British West Africa—to elect even a handful of representatives gave politically conscious Nigerians something substantial to work on. The principal figure in the agitation that ensued was Herbert Macauley, often referred to as the father of Nigerian nationalism. He spoke vitriolically through the columns of his *Lagos Daily News* and dominated the Nigerian National Democratic Party, which controlled the small arena of free political activity that existed in Lagos until 1938. The party platform called for the expansion of the party throughout Nigeria, economic and educational development, Africanization of the civil service, and local self-government for Lagos. Significantly, however, it remained almost entirely a Lagos party, since that was the only area sufficiently advanced in political awareness to support party activity.

A new period of political activity occurred in the 1930s in connection with a large number of organizations of various types, all of which became involved to greater or lesser extent in nationalist agitation. As a whole, they spread political awareness beyond the confines of Lagos and produced a generation of leaders as well as a fateful split in the forces of nationalism.

Two types of organization had little if any political motive at their inception. These were the professional or occupational organizations, which only incidentally entered the political arena, and the clan or tribal associations of persons uprooted from their cultural matrix and deposited in strange, usually urban, surroundings. The clan associations often acquired a nationalistic coloration as a consequence of the forums they offered for expression and discussion, but their effect was often to impart a Yoruba or Ibo frame of reference to political aspirations. They also prefigured and contributed largely to the regional divisions of political party strength in the postwar period.

National unity was first advocated explicitly by the civil service, labor, and youth organizations. Though not directly political in aim, the Nigerian Union of Teachers was the first important organization to spread throughout the country and to represent many ethnic groups in its leadership. More far reaching were the effects of youth organizations. The antecedents of the Nigerian Youth Movement (NYM), so christened in 1938, can be found in student associations in London, the Lagos Youth Movement, and the national education agitation sponsored by Professor Evo Ita, who was extremely nationalistic in his long campaign for improvements in Nigerian education.

The NYM brought to the fore a long list of national leaders, including H.O. Davies, Ernest Ikoli, and Nnamdi Azikiwe. Although Azikiwe has achieved the greatest fame and was long the oustanding nationalist agitator in Nigeria because of his writings and speeches, his orientation upon returning from university training in the United States was more racial than national. He betrayed much less consciousness of Nigerian goals than did Harold Laski's student, Davies. Azikiwe preferred to emphasize the African or Negro struggle against Europe and the white man.

Nevertheless, the NYM began in 1938 to express a territorial nationalism aimed at uniting all Nigerians and establishing a complete autonomy within the British Empire. Macauley's domination of elections to the Legislative Council was ended in 1938 by the NYM, which moved to establish a genuinely national network of affiliates. Three years later the promising beginning crumbled as a result of internal division. Ikoli and Azikiwe fell out and precipitated a leadership crisis in which ethnic identification proved to be a primary consideration. Azikiwe and other Ibo left the NYM in Yoruba hands. Although the leadership soon dispersed, Chief Obafemi Awolowo, who had earlier founded the Egbe Omo Oduduwa (Society of the Descendants of Oduduwa), a pan-Yoruba cultural organization, was able to regenerate the NYM during World War II as the foundation of his Action Group. Some years after the

62

war, the Action Group came to dominate the Western Region (see ch. 9, Government and Political Dynamics).

Yoruba-Ibo rivalry became a major political current in the late 1940s. An open press war existed between the *West African Pilot* of Azikiwe and the *Daily Service* of Ikoli, a Yoruba supporter. By late 1947 a movement to support Azikiwe became so radically oriented that he disavowed support for it.

The rapid growth of organized labor in the early years of World War II brought a new political force into play. During the war the number of unions grew from twelve, with less than 5,000 members, to eighty-five, with 30,000 members. The rapid proliferation of labor organizations, however, was accompaned by a fragmentation of the movement. Labor leaders lacked the experience and skill to draw the movement together. The potentially powerful role of labor as a political pressure group had still not developed in 1971.

Assessments of the effect of World War II on the nationalist movement vary. The participation of two Nigerian divisions in the Middle East and Asian campaigns provided an international experience for Nigerians for whom even domestic interaction might not otherwise have taken place. The war also left the British with an awareness of the need for a reappraisal of the Nigerian situation. The war years, moreover, brought a polarization between the older parochial leaders inclined toward gradualism and the younger intellectuals who thought in more immediate and intense terms.

The establishment of party lines on the basis of ethnicity precluded the elimination of factionalism in Nigerian politics in the post-World War II period. After the demise of the NYM the nationalist movement separated into the Hausa- and Fulani-supported Northern People's Congress (NPC), the Yoruba-supported Action Group, and the Ibo-dominated National Council of Nigeria and the Cameroons, which later became the National Council of Nigerian Citizens (NCNC). The merger of the demands of these groups in their negotiations with the British regarding the 1950 Constitution was the result of expediency rather than of growing national unity. Because of the essentially regional political alignment based on the ethnic origins of the parties, the British felt constrained to provide political outlets in a regionally based, federally structured constitution.

CONSTITUTIONAL DEVELOPMENTS

Evolutionary Stages

Before the establishment of British rule each locality had its own unwritten, customary political order (see ch. 11, Value Systems). The governing order, however, was based on a formal legal footing only among the northern Fulani emirates, where political systems were based on Islamic law.

The British introduced the modern Western concept of constitutionalism, but only gradually and unevenly as dictated by their devotion to indirect rule and the accommodation to the ethnic diversity this entailed. The keystone of the colonial regime was the governor who, as a representative of the crown, possessed full authority and responsibility. Broadly speaking, a formal constitutional order along Western lines emerged most rapidly in Lagos, the first area to assume colonial status, and least quickly in the north, where pacification was completed late and where an existing order could be absorbed, relatively intact, into the colonial system. Only in Lagos was an indigenous legislative council created at the outset as an advisory body. Its composition was largely determined by the governor, but three of its forty-six members were elected by adult male residents of Lagos.

When Northern and Southern Nigeria were amalgamated in 1914, Governor Lugard established the Nigerian Council, but the constitutive order expressly deprived the body of any actual legislative or executive authority. The governor, with his executive council of British officials, retained the pivotal constitutional position. The advisory Nigerian Council included six Africans from different parts of the country, who were appointed by the governor but who rarely attended meetings.

In actual practice the Nigerian constitutional order consisted of the interaction between the colonial administration as sovereign authority and the indigenous forms of political authority recognized and frequently assisted by the British. The system was modified, moreover, by regional differentiation, whereby the northern provinces were governed by gubernatorial decree, but the Legislative Council, as an advisory body, shared the governor's authority in Lagos Colony. The northern and southern administrations varied widely in terms of the quality of their personnel and the scope of their operations.

During his tenure as governor from 1912 to 1920, Lugard officially followed the concept of indirect rule for local affairs. This policy was continued by his successors, who stressed that the political officers would interfere as little as possible with the existing order. It was not until the administration of Donald Cameron in 1931 that the first check was made on the growing separatism that was appearing, particularly in the north. Under Cameron the system of administrative justice was abolished, and administrative reforms were effected throughout the country.

The Constitution of 1922, sometimes called the Clifford Constitution, represented an attempt to forestall Nigerian discontent. Although it left the northern provinces unaltered in their constitutional structure and operation, the Lagos Legislative Council and Lugard's moribund Nigerian Council were supplanted by a new legislative council for Lagos and the southern provinces. Although only four of the council's forty-six members were elected, for the first time the elective principle made its appearance outside Lagos, substantially altering the rough concept of representation embodied in gubernatorial appointment.

During the twenty-five years that the 1922 Constitution was in effect, it was altered only slightly, mainly by the inclusion of northern administrative departments in the total administrative structure in 1933. Nevertheless, there was mounting criticism, especially in the 1940s, of a system that curtailed local political aspirations; it was often acknowledged by British officials that constitutional advance was overdue. Nigerian opposition to this system was based not so much on a desire for self-government as on an interest in a greater participation in administration.

The Richards Constitution of 1946 was the first of a series of documents that followed each other in rapid succession and led to independence under a federal constitution in October 1960. Under the 1946 Constitution the elective principle was not extended, and effective power remained in the hands of the governor and his appointed executive council. For the first time, however, a deliberative body with a Nigerian majority could regard the whole of Nigeria as its legitimate province.

The Northern, Western, and Eastern Regions were established and vested with houses of assembly. At the discretion of the governor, these regional houses were permitted to deliberate matters of regional import and give advice to the governor. This prelude to federalism and institutional recognition of regionalism was designed to give expression to ethnic and traditional diversity. Although it fell far short of the fragmentation that a genuine ethnic breakdown would have entailed, the Richards Constitution undoubtedly intensified regionalism as an alternative to unification.

The pace of constitutional change demanded by vocal Nigerian sentiment far exceeded the original timetable. Intended to last for nine years, the Richards Constitution was superseded in only four. Governor Macpherson, who gave his name to the next constitution, was calling for popular discussion of needed revision as early as 1948. The main lines of the next constitution emerged from a general conference at Ibadan in January 1950, based on recommendations from the regions. In 1951 the Macpherson Constitution took effect.

The most important innovations of the new charter reemphasized both major strands of constitutional evolution in Nigeria—national unification and regional autonomy. By extending the elective principle and providing for a central government with ministers, the 1950 Constitution gave renewed impetus to party activity and general political participation on the national level. By providing for regional governments of similar type with legislative powers that could not necessarily be overridden by the central House of Representatives, the new document also encouraged the forces of regionalism. The concepts of political participation and self-government were gaining rapidly. The idea of national unity, so crucial in the ideological aspect of Nigerian nationalism, was increasingly subject to competing regional claims.

The Constitution of 1954 firmly established the federal principle and supplied the vehicle for the final achievement of independence. The principal governmental changes that paved the way for complete independence occurred within the framework of this constitution. The powers of the governor, still a colonial official, were substantially reduced, not so much by formal enactment as by judicious hesitation in using them as Nigerians displayed their capacities for self-government.

The parliamentary form of government stipulated ministerial responsibility to the legislature. In August 1957 Abubakar Tafawa Balewa was chosen first prime minister of the federation. For the three ensuing years the central government operated in almost complete autonomy from the British. Only matters of defense and external affairs among those reserved to the federation were withheld from its immediate competence.

The three constituent states of the federation evolved along parallel lines, but at different paces. After August 1957 both the Western and Eastern Regions were formally self-governing. Similar status was requested and received by the Northern Region two years later. There were numerous differences of detail among the three regional systems, but all adhered to parliamentary forms and enjoyed equally semiautonomous relations with the central government at Lagos.

The federation retained exclusive specified powers—such as banking, currency, external relations, shipping and navigation, defense, and others—but the regions became the decisive centers of political power within the federation. Constitutional development to this point had attempted to provide Nigeria with a staff of personnel who had extended experience and training in self-government; in the north, however, training lagged behind administrative needs. The main lines of the constitutional system were already well established before final independence.

The preparation of the federal constitution involved two constitutional conferences in London, in 1957 and 1958, as well as meetings of Nigerian leaders aimed at reaching agreement on outstanding constitutional issues. Until the second conference the Nigerian objective was to attain independence in 1959, which was later amended to April 1960. Technical internal problems and disagreements, coupled with British unwillingness to countenance undue haste, led to an agreement between Nigerians and British on the target date of October 1960.

Both conferences were attended by a delegation of Nigerians carefully chosen in preliminary discussions to represent various areas and shades of opinion. The leading delegates were Chief Awolowo for the Action Group, Azikiwe for the National Council of Nigeria and the Cameroons, Alhaji Ahmadu (Sultan of Sokoto), and Abubakar Tafawa Balewa for the NPC. The first three delegates were also the premiers of the Western, Eastern, and Northern Regions, respectively. All were supported by several party colleagues. The smaller groups, including the three Cameroon parties, were all represented by delegates, as were the regional chiefs.

By the time the second conference convened in September 1958, it was clear that certain outstanding problems would require compromise. The form and structure of government were scarcely at issue, but various questions engaged the major parties and regions in head-on conflict. These were the inclusion of a constitutional guarantee of fundamental rights, federal or regional control over the police forces, protection of minorities and the related issue of forming new regions, and the extension of universal adult suffrage to all elections.

The last issue was a bargaining point and was dropped during the conference. The other questions were resolved, for constitutional purposes at least, to the apparent satisifaction of all participants. The constitution was to be provided with an enumeration of basic human rights. A federal police force was created, but in the west and north local police forces under local control predominated. Provision was made for reopening the minority and boundary issue by parliamentary means after independence, but no changes were to be undertaken in existing arrangements until then. The effect was to smooth the path toward constitutional agreement at the price of confronting an independent Nigeria with major unresolved political problems.

Constitutional Structure

Before 1967, the federal Constitution of 1963 comprised eleven chapters, followed by a schedule of exclusive and concurrent legislative powers. It defined the territories of the federation and constituent regions, including the Federal Territory of Lagos. It established the supremacy of the federal constitution within its jurisdiction and of the regional constitutions in their respective territories so far as they did not conflict with either the federal constitution or the Nigeria Independence Act of 1960. Provision was also made for amendment of the several constitutions.

Nigerian citizenship was conferred automatically by the constitution on all persons born in the former colony or protectorate of Nigeria who were citizens of the United Kingdom and its colonies or British protected persons before October 1, 1960, provided that one parent or grandparent was born in the former colony or protectorate.

The constitution contained a lengthy chapter specifying the human and civic rights guaranteed to all citizens. The deprivation of life or liberty without due process of law was prohibited, and fair and expeditious hearings were assured. Freedom of conscience, expression, assembly, and movement was guaranteed. Property rights were protected from compulsory alienation without compensation. An emergency clause was included, however, making possible the infringement of certain guarantees of life and liberty during a period of emergency, provided the measures taken were reasonably justifiable for dealing with the situation during the period of emergency. It also provided for direct application to the courts by any person who alleged that provisions of the chapter had been contravened.

The governor general and commander in chief of the federation represented the British monarch in Nigeria and was appointed by the British monarch on the advice of the Nigerian prime minister, who was to consult the regional premiers before tendering his advice. The signature of the governor general was required on all federal bills, and the governor general could choose his prime minister among contending leaders when the choice was not clearly indicated by a parliamentary majority. The duties of the governor general, however, were largely circumscribed by the need to act with the advice of the prime minister or the Council of Ministers. His functions as commander in chief were similarly limited. Scope for the governor general to act on his own discretion was found largely in the realm of informal advice and consultation.

The Nigerian Parliament comprised the Senate and the House of Representatives. The Senate consisted of twelve senators from each region, chosen by the respective regional legislatures from the regional governor's list of nominees; four senators from the

Federal Territory of Lagos; and four senators selected by the governor general on the advice of the prime minister. The House of Representatives was composed of 305 members, one elected from each of the 305 constituencies in the country. Representatives were chosen by simple majority vote on the basis of universal adult suffrage, except in the north, where only adult males were enfranchised.

The Senate was presided over by its president, and the House, by its speaker; each was elected by the membership of his legislative house. Ministers were privileged to attend sessions of either house. Except for certain interim arrangements and for the attorney general, federal ministers were members of one house or the other, and they could vote only in the house to which they belonged. Except for the Oba of Lagos, members of Parliament could not simultaneously serve as a regional minister and as a member of a regional legislature. Explicit rules of parliamentary procedure were established.

The constitution authorized the establishment of a system of courts, headed by the Federal Supreme Court, with the chief justice and all subordinate judges enjoying independence from political interference by reason of extended tenure and the appointing authority of the Judicial Service Commission. Judicial interpretation of constitutional questions was stipulated as a province of the Federal Supreme Court whenever a lower court determined that a substantive issue of law was involved. There was also a right of appeal from decisions of the Federal Supreme Court to the Privy Council.

The order in council that contained the federal constitution also contained constitutions for the three regions of Nigeria, only slightly less detailed than the federal document. In general, the regional constitutions adhered to the same system, structurally and functionally, as the federal constitution. Aside from differences in terminology (for example, calling the regional legislative houses the houses of chiefs and the houses of assembly and using the title premier instead of prime minister), the most striking difference was in the Northern Region, where special provision brought the constitution into consonance with Muslim law and custom as to the role of women. Also in the north, Hausa and English jointly were the official languages of legislative business, although all records had to be in English.

The identical character of the several constitutions, federal and regional, was deceptive as regards actual practice. The informal elements of governmental operation and the conduct of public affairs reflected wide differences among—and within—the regions.

POSTINDEPENDENCE CRISES

On October 1, 1960, Nigeria was the sixteenth African state to achieve independence. Balewa became the first prime minister and Azikiwe was installed as governor general of the federation. During the latter half of the 1950s the various factions pressing for independence had presented an appeal for national unity that cooperation. Such hopes were short lived, however, and within two years the country experienced a series of events that eventually many expected to continue as the foundation for postindependence led to the suspension of constitutional government.

Political Disturbances in the Western Region

The first major crisis of postindependence Nigeria occurred in May 1962. The leadership of the Action Group, the chief opposition party in the federal Parliament and the ruling party in the Western Region, split during the first half of 1962 over the question of party tactics. In May, as a result of a complicated series of political maneuvers for control of the Action Group between party leader Chief Awolowo, then a member of the federal Parliament, and Western Region Premier Samuel Akintola, effective government in the region collapsed, and the regional legislature disintegrated into a rioting mob. On May 29 the federal government declared a state of emergency in the Western Region, dissolved the regional legislature, and named a federal administrator of the Western Region to serve until December 31, 1962. One of his first acts was to place many of the Action Group leaders under residence restriction or house arrest.

Akintola, who had been dismissed by the regional governor on the demand of a majority of the regional legislature shortly before the declaration of a state of emergency, was expelled from the Action Group by the radical majority under Awolowa's leadership. He immediately formed a new party, the United People's Party (UPP), which pursued a policy of collaboration with the majority parties in the federal Parliament—the NPC and the NCNC. The Action Group continued to develop a more radical policy in opposition to the government parties and demanded the rapid creation of a socialist democracy following the Ghanaian pattern.

During the aftermath of the May crisis, investigations by the emergency administration of the past activities of Awolowo and other Action Group leaders led to accusations made against them of criminal misuse of public funds and conspiracy to overthrow the Nigerian government by force. The Coker Commission was appointed by the federal government in June 1962 to investigate alleged misuse of the funds of the Western Region government statutory corporations. It found evidence that through the National Investment and Properties Corporation (NIPC), a private corporation founded by Awolowo when he was premier of the Western Region from 1954 to 1959, the Action Group had received the equivalent of US$11.2 million from the regional Marketing Board, the Developing Corporation, and other public corporations. Awolowo was sharply criticized by the commission for his role in the scandal, and several other party leaders were threatened with legal action. In March 1963 the reconstituted Western Region government took over the assets of the NIPC and pressed the legal claims against the Action Group and its leaders.

In the course of this financial investigation, police uncovered evidence linking Awolowo with a conspiracy to overthrow the government. Together with 21 other Action Group leaders, he was arrested and tried for treason in November 1962. It was charged that the conspirators had sent 200 young men to receive guerrilla training in Ghana and had smuggled into Nigeria caches of arms and ammunition in preparation for a coup d'etat scheduled for September 1962. The other leading defendant, Anthony Enahoro, a close colleague of Awolowo, was extradited from England, tried separately, and sentenced to fifteen years' imprisonment. Seventeen other defendants received sentences of from two to seven years' imprisonment; 3 were acquitted.

In the meantime, the state of emergency was lifted on schedule on December 31, 1962, and a new Western Region government was appointed by the federal government. Prime Minister Balewa, deciding that Akintola had been improperly dismissed as Western Region premier, reinstated him; Akintola formed his government around a coalition of the UPP and the NCNC. The legality of the Akintola premiership was contested by the Action Group, whose position was supported by the British Privy Council, the highest court of appeal in the Commonwealth. A quick retroactive amendment to the Western Region Constitution proscribing the means by which the regional governor had dismissed Akintola in May 1962, however, was recognized by Balewa as validating Akintola's appointment.

Creation of the Mid-Western Region

In 1962 the plan to create the new Mid-Western Region from the eastern provinces of the Western Region further complicated the country's internal administrative situation and prepared the way for unprecedented political agitation. The plan for creating the Mid-Western Region had been adopted by the federal Parliament in April 1961; it was subsequently approved by the legislatures of the Eastern and Northern Regions. In March 1962 the federal Parliament again approved the plan by a large majority. Action Group opposition to the plan was ineffective. In July 1963 a plebiscite in the proposed region overwhelmingly approved its creation. A federal administration was appointed for the new region in August, pending election of the regional legislature in early February 1964.

The creation of the Mid-Western Region reopened the question of a general reorganization of the internal structure of Nigeria. Michael Okpara, premier of the Eastern Region, and other NCNC leaders reiterated their earlier demands for the creation of a large number of smaller states in a federal system based on that of the United States. Behind this plan was their desire to break up the Northern Region, which, as set up under the British colonial administration, included over half the population of Nigeria and thus controlled a majority of the electoral districts for the federal House of Representatives.

The traditional south-north antipathy was exacerbated by the expectation—confirmed by the regional elections—that the NCNC would gain control in the new region and thus become the dominant party in the south. The effect was to eliminate the earlier three-way political split that had prevented a direct confrontation between south and north; such a confrontation was seen as a threat to the tenuous national unity.

A new political party, the Mid-West Democratic Front (MDF), was formed by the leaders of the Action Group and the UPP to contest the election with the NCNC. During the election campaign the UPP accepted the support of the NPC, a fact that the NCNC candidates stressed in their call to keep northern influence out of the new region. Many Action Group leaders also withdrew from the MDF in protest; some allied themselves with the NCNC. The NCNC won fifty-five of the sixty-five seats in the regional legislature against ten for the MDF. Dennis Osadebay became premier and formed a government whose declared policies were similar to those of the Eastern Region.

The Census Controversy

Animosity between north and south was also the motivating force behind the extraordinary sensitivity of the regional governments and political parties to the question of the 1962 census. Because all seats in the federal Parliament—and thus political power—were apportioned on the basis of regional population distribution, census taking had important political implications. The Northern Region's political strength has arisen in large measure from the results of the 1952–53 census, which had placed 54 percent of the population in that area.

Southern hopes for a favorable reapportionment of legislative seats were bolstered initially by the preliminary results of the 1962 census, which gave the south a clear population majority (see ch. 4, Population and Labor). Immediately thereafter the Northern Region submitted an increased count substantiating its right to a continued majority of parliamentary seats. In the ensuing protests political leaders agreed to a second nationwide census in 1963. Despite efforts to assure an ostensibly accurate count, initial returns indicated an impossibly high total. Further disagreement resulted in the acceptance of a scaled-down figure, but the census distribution adopted by the federal government left the existing parliamentary representation virtually unchanged.

The NCNC leaders publicly challenged the results of the 1963 census; they accused the Northern Region government of padding its figures, a claim refuted by the region's premier, Ahmadu Bello, and Prime Minister Balewa. The political parties in the Western Region split over the acceptance of the census results, with Akintola and his UPP supporting its validity.

Republican Government and the Election Crises

Despite the agitated political situation, on October 1, 1963—the third anniversary of independence—Nigeria became a republic within the British Commonwealth of Nations. The major change in its new constitution was the creation of a president as head of state in place of the governor general, who represented the British crown. Azikiwe was named in the constitution to be the first president. The president was to be elected for a five-year period by secret ballot at a joint session of the two houses of Parliament, and he could be reelected.

As a republic, Nigeria no longer recognized the judicial committee of the Privy Council in Great Britain as the highest court of appeal. This responsibility was transferred to the Nigerian Federal Supreme Court. Except for these and consequent technical changes, the constitution remained virtually unchanged from that promulgated in 1960.

Nigeria's attainment of republican status did not change its structural arrangement as a federation of regions, each dominated by a particular ethnic group and political party. Each region, moreover, had an ethnic minority linked politically with the majority group of another region. The move to republican status also did little to erase other divisions that had long separated sections of the country. Notable among these was the line that cut across regional boundaries, separating north from south.

When the southern hope of challenging the political domination of the north was diminished by the results of the 1963 census, southern politicians turned their attention to the ballot box. The first national elections since independence were scheduled for December 1964 and were to be followed by a political contest in the Western Region in 1965. The regional elections were of considerable national importance because the Western Region was the only political subdivision where the opposition had any potential for bringing about a change in the government. Both elections produced crisis situations that threatened the federation's existence.

With the loss of power of the Action Group, the composition of the federal House of Representatives shifted more heavily than before in favor of the NPC as a number of deputies shifted their allegiance to that party. As a result, the NPC claimed about two-thirds of the membership in the House and, with the support of the UPP deputies, appeared to be in an unassailable position in the federal government, even if the NCNC pulled out of the coalition.

The political picture became more confused in March 1964 when Akintola created a new political party, the Nigerian National Democratic Party (NNDP). The NNDP was intended to recreate the original Nigerian National Democratic Party that joined all Yoruba (the majority ethnic group in the Western Region). The NNDP quickly gained the adherence of a majority of the NCNC members in the Western Region legislature; on March 12 Akintola dissolved the UPP–NCNC coalition government and created a new NNDP government. Virtually all the former NCNC and UPP ministers remained in office as members of the new party. The NCNC denounced the new party as a "tool of the NPC" and allied itself with the remnants of the Action Group in the Western Region to oppose it.

In the federal elections seats in the national House of Representatives were contested by two political alliances formed by existing parties throughout the country. The Nigerian National Alliance (NNA) was led by Bello, premier of the Northern Region, and the United Progressive Grand Alliance (UPGA) was led by Okpara, premier of the Eastern Region. The northern-oriented NNA was composed of the NPC, the NNDP, and the MDF. The southern-oriented UPGA consisted of the NCNC, the Action Group, the Northern Elements Progressive Union (an opposition party formed in Hausa parts of the Northern Region), and the United Middle Belt Congress, which sought the vote of the non-Muslim areas of the north.

Regional and ethnic antagonisms provided the main issues. The NNA expected Ibo domination of the federal government and sought support from the Yoruba to prevent such an eventuality. The UPGA party workers stressed the Muslim northerner's anti-southern, antidemocratic, and anti-Christian attitudes.

The NNA's appeal was essentially to conservative modernists and was based on the advantage of power that had accrued to the dominant group. The UPGA offered a program of governmental reform, advocated more purposeful domestic planning, and supported more forceful pan-Africanism in its foreign policy pronouncements. The southern alliance proposed to split the republic into a number of small states similar to the former colonial provinces; this plan was based on the UPGA assumption that such an arrangement would strengthen the federal government. The basic appeal of the UPGA lay in its obvious intention to rid the government of domination by northerners.

Before the balloting began, the UPGA charged that the NNA was engaging in unconstitutional electoral practices and announced that it would boycott the election. The boycott was effective in the Eastern Region, where polling places did not open, and in other scattered areas as well. In January 1965 the results of the election were announced, despite UPGA protests that many citizens had been unable to vote. The northern coalition won an overwhelming majority of the contested seats in the north and the west. After a lengthy delay President Azikiwe agreed to call upon Prime Minister Balewa to form a new government, with membership of the cabinet drawn from all political parties. In the special elections to fill the seats in the Eastern Region, the NCNC candidates were again successful, taking the NNA's 197 seats and adding them to the UPGA's 105. Balewa formed a second government with multiparty representation, but he placed all executive power in the hands of the three parties ruling in each region. This had the effect of reinforcing regionalism at the expense of national unity.

After the UPGA losses in the federal elections, the southern politicans looked forward to the November 1965 contests in the Western Region as a possible means of gaining political power in the national Parliament. If the UPGA could win control of the Western Region, it foresaw the possibility that it could control the three regions in the south and the Federal Territory of Lagos. Such a position would not have threatened the northern control of the federal House of Representatives, but it would have given the southerners a majority in the Senate and thus provide them with leverage over national legislation.

The NNDP candidates were declared the winners by an overwhelming majority. Charges of widespread electoral irregularities and unorthodox practices led to public outcries and resulted in a marked decline in the people's respect for local authority. Acts of violence became rife; soldiers in armored cars patrolled the streets; and riot police were employed to disperse angry crowds of people with tear gas. Popular disillusionment with the federal government, already well-advanced after the federal elections, became even more widespread.

Four weeks after the election in the Western Region the official death toll was placed at 46, but the official figures were seldom believed by the people. Violence continued, and in January 1966 the *Nigerian Tribune* estimated that more than 500 people were known to have been killed and 1,000 injured since the elections. Later estimates suggested that more than 2,000 people were killed in the Western Region between August 1965 and January 1966.

Coup d'Etat and Civil War

Disorders throughout the country grew steadily worse, and there was strong pressure on Balewa to act to avert a national calamity. The prime minister procrastinated, and on January 15, 1966, a small group of progressive army officers, largely Ibo, attempted to seize power. They assassinated Balewa, the premiers of the Northern and Western Regions, and a number of other political and military figures. The coup leaders were not motivated by tribal animosities but by a desire for a stronger and more progressive government. The coup ultimately failed, however, because of the efforts of Ibo Major General J.T.U. Aguiyi-Ironsi, commander of the army.

President Azikiwe was in a London hospital when the coup attempt was staged. Because the cabinet was unable to deal decisively with the chaotic situation, it accepted General Ironsi's offer to assume control and to form a national military government. He suspended the federal and regional executives and legislative bodies, and outlawed all political parties. The Federal Military Government (FMG) then initiated plans to reform and strengthen the country's administration as the prelude to a return to constitutional rule by civil authorities.

The FMG under General Ironsi quickly lost support in the north. Its action to strengthen the national government at the expense of the regions opened the FMG to accusations of favoring the Ibo. Northerners generally saw similarities between the program of the FMG and that of the NCNC; they also recalled that most of the coup victims had been northerners. Attempts by the FMG to combine the regional and federal civil services led to widespread resentment in the north. The Hausa felt that they would lose positions and power in competition with the aggressive Ibo and other educated southerners in a unitary state (see ch. 9, Government and Political Dynamics; ch. 11, Value Systems).

On July 29, 1966, a countercoup was mounted by a group of northern army officers. General Ironsi was killed, and a military government was established under the leadership of Lieutenant Colonel Yakubu Gowon (who was later promoted to major general). The FMG, with general support of the armed forces, ruled by military decree. Shortly after the countercoup an estimated 10,000 to 30,000 Ibo who had settled in the Northern Region were killed in another, greater series of widespread acts of violence. The FMG intervened, and more than 1 million Ibo fled to the Eastern Region.

Throughout the remainder of 1966 and into early 1967, the FMG attempted to convene a constituent assembly for revision of the constitution and thus make possible a return to civil government. The Eastern Region, however, insisted on maintaining a weak central government; the military governor refused to accept anything less than total autonomy for his region. At all of the many meetings held to negotiate these matters, there were frequent differences of interpretation of the previous agreements reached. The situation rapidly deteriorated.

On May 27, 1967, the Consultative Assembly of the Eastern Region gave its military governor, Lieutenant Colonel C.O. Ojukwu, a mandate to declare the region a sovereign republic to be known thereafter as Biafra. The FMG responded by declaring a state of emergency and issued a decree abolishing the regions and dividing the country into twelve states. On May 30 Colonel Ojukwu formally announced the secession of the Eastern Region; General Gowon declared the move an act of open rebellion. On July 6, 1967, federal troops began an attack on the self-proclaimed Republic of Biafra in the opening phase of a protracted civil war (see ch. 9, Government and Political Dynamics; ch. 15, National Security).

CHAPTER 4

POPULATION AND LABOR

Nigeria, with a population variously estimated at between 54 million and 64 million persons at the beginning of 1971, was the most populous country in Africa and among the top ten or twelve countries in population size in the world. Its people were generally youthful—over 43 percent were estimated to be under fifteen years of age—and they possessed a high fertility rate. The estimated 2.4 to 2.8 percent annual rate of growth, which appeared to be rising as mortality decreased, indicated that, despite deaths occasioned by the civil war, the population would probably double before the end of the twentieth century.

Population distribution was characterized by areas of high density in the southeast and southwest and another area in the north-central part of the country. Areas in the Middle Belt (see Glossary) separating the north and the south were generally less heavily inhabited. Urban centers have existed in the north and the southwest for hundreds of years. A steady migration to these and the more recently founded towns occurred during the 1960s. By 1971 perhaps one-fifth to one-sixth of the population lived in urban communities of 20,000 persons or more.

The labor force in 1970 constituted about two-fifths of the total population; over 98 percent of this force was gainfully employed. A majority of persons were engaged in agriculture, most of which was of the peasant farm type carried out by the family unit. About one-eighth of those gainfully employed were in petty trade —which was dominated by women—and commerce.

Almost 1.4 million individuals worked for wages, but only half of them were found in the modern sector of the economy. This sector was growing; however, in 1971 the vast majority of new entrants to the labor force continued to be absorbed into the traditional agricultural sector.

Unemployment was a growing problem, particularly in the cities, a fact that may have possible political implications (see ch. 15, National Security). It involved largely young persons and those with limited education. In contrast, despite increased output of graduates from institutions of higher learning, shortages of qualified Nigerians existed at the higher occupational levels. This situation had resulted in the employment of foreigners in many top-level positions. The government had a policy of Nigerianization of both civil service and private enterprise staffs. Some progress was achieved during the 1960s, but the civil war had reduced —at least temporarily as of early 1971—the free movement of trained persons between different parts of the country. As a result, some increased employment of foreigners in certain positions was a possibility.

Labor unions have existed since the early 1900s and include both civil service and private enterprise employees. The total number covered was uncertain, but perhaps half of the individuals working for wages in 1971 were members of a union. The labor movement throughout much of its history has been characterized by factionalism and ideological differences among its leaders that have resulted in a varying number of competing central labor organizations. Mergers have occurred from time to time, only to be followed by a new split. The most recent alliance was formed in late 1970 and was still effective in mid-1971.

POPULATION

Estimates of the Office of Population of the United States Agency for International Development (AID) and the Center for Population Studies at the University of Ibadan indicated a total population in mid-1970 of probably between 54 million and 55 million persons. National censuses have been taken regularly at approximately ten-year intervals since 1911, with the exception of 1941, when none was conducted because of World War II conditions. Censuses taken before World War II, however, involved very little actual counting of individuals except in some municipal areas. The totals published were essentially only estimates obtained from tax and other records.

The first comprehensive census was carried out during 1952 and 1953—the count was not made simultaneously but was conducted at different times during this period in different parts of the country. The final results reported a total population of some 30.4 million persons (see table 1). Subsequent analyses by demographers, however, have indicated that an undercount probably occurred, which has been estimated by the Center for Population Studies at about 11.7 percent.

The succeeding decennial census was undertaken during a two-week period in May 1962; this was the first conducted after independence. The 1952–53 census had shown that many people connected census taking with taxation and avoided being counted.

Table 1. Nigeria, Population and Average Number of Persons Per Square Mile, Selected Years

Administrative division	Population			Average number of persons per square mile		
	1952–53 Census	Mid-1962 Estimate [1]	1963 Census	1952–53	Mid-1962	1963
Northern Region_____	16,840,479	22,027,096	29,808,658	60	78	106
Eastern Region_____	7,217,829	12,332,046	12,394,464	245	418	420
Western Region_____	4,595,801	8,157,554	10,265,848	151	268	337
Mid-Western Region_____	(1,492,116[2])	(2,365,091[2])	2,535,839	100	158	170
Federal Territory of Lagos_____	271,800	450,392	665,246	10,066	16,681	24,639
Total__	30,418,025	45,332,179	55,670,055	85	127	156

[1] As estimated by the Center for Population Studies University of Ibadan.
[2] Mid-Western Region not established until 1963; population breakdown shown for comparison.

Source: Adapted from John C. Caldwell and Chukuka Okonjo (eds.), *The Population of Tropical Africa*, New York, 1968, pp. 78–96; and Republic of Nigeria, Federal Office of Statistics, *Population Census of Nigeria, 1963*, III, (Combined National Figures, Provisional), Lagos, 1968, pp. 52–57.

Others had also done the same for various superstitious reasons. A national campaign was therefore prepared in early May 1962 to educate the population on the value of the forthcoming census. Unfortunately, the demographic aspects of the census were not the only things emphasized. Politicians throughout the country stressed the connection between the number counted and parliamentary representation, as well as the financial advantages for area development of a large local population.

Many persons managed to be counted more than once. Others were counted in more than one place—for instance, as members of their father's family, in the area where they worked, and in the place where they had built their house. The census was to be by head count, but there was substantial evidence that many enumerators obtained their figures chiefly from heads of families.

Early unofficial results showed that the Northern Region no longer held a majority of the total population, with consequent political implications (see ch. 3, Historical Setting). A supplementary count was immediately undertaken by this region, which turned up an additional 9 million persons reportedly missed in the

81

first count. Subsequent unofficial figures set the overall population at 53.2 million—30.2 million in the Northern Region, 12.5 million in the Eastern Region, and 10.5 million in the Western Region.

Charges of falsification were voiced generally and finally led to an agreement in February 1963 among the federal and regional prime ministers to nullify the count and hold a new census. The National Census Board was set up by the federal government, and under its direction another census was carried out in early November 1963. The number of enumerators and supervisors was greatly increased, and honesty and accuracy were presumably further enhanced by the exchange of enumerators between regions. Additionally, female enumerators from the Eastern Region were sent to the Northern Region to ensure an actual headcount of many women who by Muslim custom were kept in seclusion.

The initial overall total in the 1963 census was reportedly about 60.5 million. The National Census Board refused to accept the figures for certain districts but, after rechecks, announced an official total for the country of more than 55.6 million persons. This included about 29.8 million in the Northern Region, almost 12.4 million in the Eastern Region, more than 10.2 million in the Western Region, 2.5 million in the newly established Mid-Western Region, and more than 665,000 in the Federal Territory of Lagos.

Contention again arose over the figures, but they were confirmed by the federal government. Demographers have generally rejected the results of this census as highly inflated, pointing out that, despite the probable undercount in the 1952–53 census, the indicated average annual rate of growth of 6.3 percent during the intercensal period was much too high to be acceptable. Estimates of the population in 1962 made by various demographers place it at that time between about 42 million and 45 million. The Center for Population Studies has determined a mid-1962 population of 45.3 million persons, of whom 22 million were in the Northern Region; 12.3 million, in the Eastern Region; about 8.2 million, in the Western Region; 2.4 million, in the Mid-Western Region; and 450,000, in the Federal Territory of Lagos.

The Federal Military Government (FMG) has recognized the need for an unbiased enumeration of the population. One point of the nine-point program the military government plans to accomplish before returning control to elected civilian authorities is a national census (see ch. 9, Government and Political Dynamics). As of mid-1971, however, no date had been announced for this, but census officials had indicated that the earliest possible time would be in 1973.

The 1963 census showed the population to be almost entirely indigenous. The three major ethnic groups—Hausa, Yoruba, and

Ibo—constituted 58 percent of the total; six other groups—the Edo, Fulani, Ibibio, Ijaw, Kanuri, and Tiv—accounted for more than 22 percent. Africans of non-Nigerian origin constituted less than 0.1 percent of the population; non-Africans were also less than 0.1 percent (see ch. 5, Ethnic Groups and Languages).

Regional and Rural-Urban Distribution

The population density in 1970 was probably between 151 and 154 persons per square mile, based on Office of Population estimates. The official 1963 census indicated a density of 156 persons per square mile, a number considered too high. The Center for Population Studies mid-1962 population estimate showed a density of about 127 persons per square mile. This compares with about 95 persons per square mile (corrected to reflect an estimated undercount of 11 to 12 percent) for the 1952–53 census.

The 1963 census showed that the population was quite unevenly distributed throughout the country (see fig. 7). More than 44 percent of the population lived in densities above 300 persons per square mile while occupying only 13 percent of the country's total land area. The greatest area concentration was in the Eastern Region, which averaged 420 persons per square mile. Some subdivisions of this region showed densities of more than 1,000 individuals per square mile.

Another area of higher population density was the Western Region, with 337 persons per square mile. Ibadan Province in this region, in which the city of Ibadan is located, had 736 persons per square mile. In general, the area occupied by the swamp and high forest zones in the southern part of the country had densities above the national average (see ch. 2, Physical Environment).

In the north the area of highest population concentration in 1963 was Kano Province, with 347 persons per square mile. Adjacent Katsina Province had a density of 269 persons. Otherwise, population densities in the Northern Region were generally well below the national average. The middle part of the country had much lower densities than the northern and southern parts, despite the fact that it had extensive areas of good or potentially good soil and moderately good rainfall, according to the United Nations Food and Agriculture Organization (see ch. 13, Agriculture and Mining). Slave raiding and wars, particularly during the nineteenth century, have been given as an explanation for the thin population. There is some evidence that these factors did affect density in places, but they do not appear to be the entire explanation.

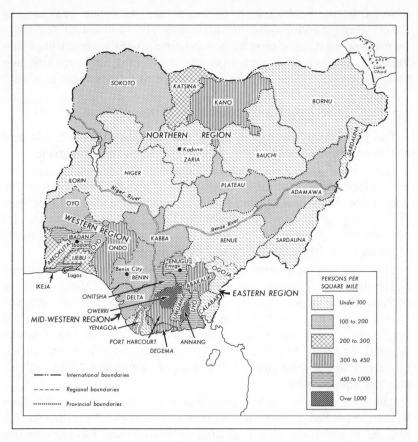

Source: Adapted from United Nations Food and Agriculture Organization, *Agricultural Development in Nigeria, 1965–1980*, Rome, 1966.

Figure 7. Population Distribution of Nigeria, 1963

The population was arbitrarily divided into urban and rural census categories based on the size of the community; the dividing line was set at 20,000 persons or more for the urban classification. On this basis approximately 9 million individuals, or about 16 percent of the population, were recorded as urban residents at the time of the 1963 census; this compared with about 11 percent in the 1952–53 census. In 1963 there were 183 urban centers listed, 23 of which had populations of more than 100,000; there were 7 urban centers with over 100,000 population at the time of the 1952–53 census. Individuals in these 23 centers accounted for some 55 percent of the total urban population. The greatest urban concentration was in the southwestern part of the country, and another area of higher urban concentration was in the north-central part.

Individuals classified as rural residents totaled 46.7 million and constituted 84 percent of the overall population in 1963. Among this group, however, many lived in rural communities of considerable size. The 1963 census listed more than 2,350 rural centers with populations ranging between 5,000 and 20,000 persons; 510 of these had populations between 10,000 and 20,000.

Urbanization and Migration

The urban population of nearly 9 million in 1963 represented an average annual growth rate from the preceding 1952–53 census of about 6 percent, compared with a roughly 2.5 percent growth rate estimated for the population as a whole. This move to urban centers took place in all parts of the country. At the time of the 1963 census the Northern Region had seventy towns of 20,000 persons or more, compared with thirteen towns of that size recorded in the 1952–53 census; this represented more than a fivefold increase. In the Western Region, and including the city of Lagos, the number of urban centers increased about threefold, from twenty-nine in the 1952–53 period to seventy-eight in 1963. In the Eastern Region the number of towns of 20,000 persons or more rose from ten to twenty-nine; in the Mid-Western Region they increased from two to six.

Some indication of the magnitude of the trend toward urbanization was shown by a rural sample survey conducted by the Federal Office of Statistics in 1965 and 1966. Covering 191 rural village areas throughout the country, the survey found a net migration rate to urban areas of over 1.3 percent, or about half the estimated rate of natural population increase. Migration tends to vary from year to year, and some overstatement may have occurred; however, the marked movement to urban centers was evident in the growth of town populations in the latter 1960s. The population of Kaduna, for instance, was estimated in 1967 to be increasing over 11 percent a year, and that of Kano, about 8 percent. In 1971 Greater Lagos as a whole was growing at an estimated rate of 11 percent a year. Areas inside the city limits were increasing about 8 percent annually, and the population in the suburbs was expanding by 20 percent a year.

People migrated to the towns for various reasons. The two most important ones brought out in the sample survey were search for employment and education. A more limited study in the Mid-Western Region in late 1965 indicated that other individuals moved to the towns because of the spread of new ideas and development of desires for the amenities found in the towns. This group, and those persons seeking an education, became generally permanent town residents. On the other hand, many who migrated strictly for economic reasons tended to keep up stronger contacts with their tribal and home village group and eventually returned to their rural environment.

The rural survey showed additionally that a majority of migrants to the towns were males. In the southern part of the country they constituted two-thirds of the net migration. In the north, although the total new migration was smaller, they made up over 72 percent. About three-quarters of all migrants were under thirty-five years old.

Age and Sex Distribution

Underlying factors, including individual lack of knowledge of exact age, made age determination difficult during the 1963 census, particularly in rural areas. The figures published for the census as a whole showed 43.1 percent of the population in the age bracket from birth through fourteen years of age. Another 54.9 percent was between fifteen and sixty-five years of age, and 2 percent was sixty-five years and older. Although the accuracy of the census has been questioned, these proportions conform generally to those found in other developing countries.

Rural totals showed 44 percent in the under-fifteen age group, and 53.8 percent in the fifteen-through-sixty-four age group; 2.2 percent were recorded as being sixty-five years of age or older. The subsequent rural sample survey conducted during 1965 and 1966 determined that 42.9 percent of the rural population was under fifteen years, 54.2 percent was from fifteen through sixty-four years of age, and 2.9 percent was sixty-five years and older. The Federal Office of Statistics, which carried out the survey, concluded despite certain reservations that these data were sufficiently reliable to consider the totals approximately a true picture of the rural age distribution throughout the country.

The urban population, on the other hand, had a considerably smaller number of persons in the group between birth and fifteen years of age, the total in 1963 being 37.3 percent. The fifteen-through-sixty-four age group constituted 61.1 percent, and those sixty-five and above constituted 1.6 percent. The large fifteen-to-sixty-four age group probably resulted from the migration of larger numbers in this group to the towns. For instance, Lagos recorded only 36.4 percent of its population in the under-fifteen age group, whereas over 62 percent was from fifteen through sixty-four years of age, and 1.2 percent was sixty-five years and older.

The sex ratio for the overall population in 1963 was recorded as 102 males for every 100 females. In urban areas a higher ratio showed almost 115 males to every 100 females. A sample survey in Lagos in 1964 showed 117.6 males to 100 females. In rural areas the 1963 census showed sex ratios almost at parity, with 99.7 males to every 100 females. The rural sample survey of 1965 and 1966, however, indicated a greater disparity; the ratio for all rural areas was 91.7 males to 100 females. The higher urban ratio was explained largely by the movement of more men to the towns. An unusual situation was the lower life expectancy among females found by the rural survey. The average life expectancy at birth for females was 36.7 years, compared with 37.2 years for males. Female death rates were found to be higher from 5 to 39 years of age, after which they tended to be lower than that of males. Female death rates were particularly high between the ages of 15 and 29, apparently because of very high mortality during pregnancy and childbirth.

Rate of Population Growth

In 1970 vital statistics were largely nonexistent except for Lagos, whose vital rates were not necessarily typical of other parts of the country. Sample surveys taken in both rural and urban areas during the 1960s showed both fertility and death rates to be generally high everywhere. The most comprehensive sample survey, conducted in rural districts in 1965 and 1966 by the Federal Office of Statistics, indicated that an average of 5.6 children were born to each woman who lived through the childbearing age. Other nongovernment surveys in urban communities generally showed equally high or higher numbers.

The rural survey revealed a death rate in the 1965–66 period of about 26.9 per 1,000 persons, and the Office of Population estimated an overall death rate in 1968 of 22 to 26 persons per 1,000 persons. The crude birth rate in both instances was estimated at about 50 per 1,000 persons, indicating an annual rate of natural increase in the population of 2.4 to 2.8 percent. If maintained this would result in a doubling of the population in approximately twenty-five to thirty years. International migration plays an insignificant part in the country's population growth.

There was little indication at the start of the 1960s of any drop in the birth rate. Gradual improvement in health facilities and conditions can be anticipated (see ch. 7, Living Conditions). This will result in lowering the comparatively high mortality rate with a consequent increase in the population growth rate. The civil war, however, had an important impact on actual growth. Because of deaths caused by the war, the increase in population in 1969 was probably negligible.

Family Planning

Surveys made during the mid-1960s showed that most women in the traditional society throughout the country considered the ideal number of children to be between six and seven. Social change was bringing some modification of this attitude. Among better educated women and families in the modern society with greater economic resources, the mean ideal number was between four and five children. There was little evidence in 1971 of any important decline in the general desire for a large family. The practice of artificial contraception was confined almost entirely to urban areas. This method of birth control was limited to a proportionally small number of families; many of these were of higher economic or educational status.

The first organized work in family planning was started in 1958 in Lagos as part of the city's maternal and child health services. The national Family Planning Council was established in 1964 with the assistance of the International Planned Parenthood Federation and other international agencies. The council had about twenty-five clinics in operation in 1970 in different parts of the country. In 1969 about 4,700 new individuals visited these clinics, more than double the number of new patients in 1968.

The universities of Lagos and Ibadan also had family planning demonstration clinics for medical and nursing students; the University of Lagos Medical School was training students, practicing physicians, and other workers in family planning techniques. Various state governments also had taken steps to promote family planning. Lagos State had made facilities available for clinics, and Western State had requested that its hospitals furnish family planning services in connection with child and maternal health care. In mid-1971, however, there was no national policy on population control, although the federal government was showing an increasing awareness of the problems likely to arise from the country's rapid population growth.

Most of the actual financing for family planning in mid-1971 came from foreign sources. The United States aid program had financed training of statisticians and students in health, vital statistics, and demography. Substantial assistance through annual grants and materials continued to be given to the Family Planning Council by the International Planned Parenthood Federation. Large grants had also been made for maternal and child health care, family planning services, and population studies by the Ford Foundation. Other organizations providing help included the Rockefeller Foundation, the Swedish International Development Authority, and a number of foreign church organizations.

MANPOWER

Labor Force

Statistics on the labor force were generally limited. In drawing up the Second National Development Plan, 1970–74, the planners estimated that the labor force constituted close to 40 percent of the total population and that in 1970 it numbered somewhat over 26 million persons. This figure was based on 1963 census data and an estimated annual growth rate of about 2.5 percent, which approximated the rate of growth of the overall population. In view of the overcount considered by many demographers to have occurred in the 1963 census, the actual size of the labor force in 1970 may have been smaller than the assumed figure.

About 43 percent of the male and 36 percent of the female population were estimated in 1970 to be in this force; 39 percent of the total population, or roughly 98 percent of the labor force, was actually employed in gainful work. Overall unemployment in the active labor force was less than 2 percent; however, the rate was much higher in urban areas, where it was about 7.6 percent compared with about 0.5 percent in rural areas.

The largest number of persons were employed in agriculture and related activities. A labor force sample survey made in 1966 and 1967 showed that 71.7 percent of those gainfully employed were in agriculture; the next largest segment, 12.9 percent, was engaged in commerce. Manufacturing and crafts accounted for 9.6 percent, and services, for 3.9 percent. Construction and transport and communications had less than 1 percent each. An earlier 1952 survey showed agriculture's share of employment at 78 percent. Employment data were sketchy, however, and data for earlier years were not necessarily comparable with more recent survey results. Other estimates surmised that between 70 and 80 percent of the labor force was engaged in agriculture during the 1960s (see ch. 13, Agriculture and Mining; ch. 12, Character and Structure of the Economy).

The industrialization and urbanization that was going on at the start of the 1970s was expected to result in a continuing small decline in the share of agriculture in the labor force. At the same time, however, the absolute number of individuals employed in agriculture would grow substantially. The modern sector in 1971 was expanding far more rapidly than the agricultural sector, but there was no indication that the employment created would be able to absorb most of the job-seeking migrants from the rural areas during the 1970s.

The labor force sample survey showed that 63.9 percent of those working were self-employed; 29.7 percent were unpaid household workers, and 0.9 percent were unpaid apprentices. More than 71 percent of these groups were engaged in, or connected with, agriculture. Only 0.3 percent of those gainfully occupied were employers, and another 5.2 percent were paid employees.

Wage Employment

About 1,385,000 persons were estimated to be working for wages in 1970, accounting for over 5 percent of all persons gainfully employed. Some 168,000 of these wage earners, or 12.2 percent, were engaged in the agricultural sector, and over 1.2 million, constituting 87.8 percent, were in nonagricultural jobs. More than half of all wage earners (an estimated 765,000 persons) were employed in medium- and large-scale establishments, which were defined as those with 10 or more employees. This group essentially comprised the modern sector of the economy. Most of the remaining 625,000 persons were found in small-scale operations fabricating a variety of products or were engaged in repair and other work. The overall wage-earning sector grew during the latter 1960s at an estimated average annual rate of about 3 percent with about 45,000 new jobs added annually. During the second development plan period the average annual growth rate was expected to rise to 7 percent, with about 100,000 jobs created annually. Of these, about 55,000 were anticipated in medium- and large-scale operations.

Occupational Skills

The 1967 labor survey showed that more than 60 percent of all gainfully occupied persons were either self-employed or working on their own account in the traditional sectors of the economy. They were largely rural residents engaged in small-scale farming, petty trading, and the various traditional handicrafts. Skills in these sectors were acquired chiefly by informal on-the-job training through knowledge and methods handed down from parents to children. In the late 1960s, however, many children attending regular schools in rural areas were reported unwilling to learn the traditional skills needed for maintenance of, and employment in, their traditional society.

In that part of the wage employment sector composed of small establishments with fewer than ten employees, the acquisition of skills was mainly through apprenticeships in which younger persons were attached to journeymen or master craftsmen. In the modern sector, consisting of about 765,000 persons in 1970 in medium-sized and larger establishments, employees at the upper levels acquired their skills through formal education. Employees at this level included senior directors, managers, and professional and technical staff members with university degrees or the equivalent. They were estimated at about 45,650 persons in 1970.

In 1970 another 126,880 employees in the modern sector on the intermediate level, including junior managers and supervisors, laboratory technicians, certain teachers, and others, had lesser educational qualifications. Skilled workers in various trades, acquired usually through technical courses, totaled 217,300, and office employees numbered an additional 102,350. Unskilled workers numbered 221,480, and there were 51,330 other nondifferentiated employees.

Programs to train entering employees as well as refresher and upgrading training were found at all occupational levels in the modern sector. Employees in the higher occupational levels were frequently sponsored by the government and private establishments for training either at Nigerian universities or abroad. A number of government and private establishments employing large numbers of workers provided organized training leading to examinations of the City and Guilds of London Institute. Occupational training was also furnished in their own schools by government agencies and state corporations, such as the Nigerian Ports Authority and the Posts and Telecommunications Corporation, and by some larger private companies. Programs ranged in duration from a few weeks to several years. In smaller firms training was generally provided on the job and was designed to fit the new employee into the organization. Some concerns in the modern sector also used the apprenticeship system.

Growth of the modern sector during the 1960s was effected in part through the use of foreign personnel to meet shortages of high-level occupational staff. At the end of the 1960s many senior positions still remained filled by foreign staff. In such positions as medical doctors, graduate teachers, estate managers, and architects, they constituted in 1970 between 30 and 40 percent of the total and overall filled about 28 percent of senior managerial and administrative jobs.

Until the late 1940s Nigerians were excluded from jobs above the level of chief clerk and were unable to gain the experience needed to fill higher positions. Nationalist pressures after World War II, however, finally brought a policy of Nigerianization, whereby no post in the civil service could be filled by a foreigner if a qualified Nigerian was available. The policy was maintained by the federal government after independence and remained in effect in 1971.

Efforts were also made during the 1960s to get private industry to replace foreign personnel with Nigerians and to give them responsibilities for whatever their qualifications fitted them. In a few cases this was done, but in others Nigerian managers represented only a front, and effective managerial control remained in foreign hands. One of the problems with respect to private firms was the lack of an enforcement system. The result was that employers decided how far and at what rate Nigerianization was effected. An agency to oversee the program was to be established during the period of the second development plan; however, this had not been set up as of mid-1971.

In an attempt to bring about effective Nigerianization of foreign firms, the government in late 1969 introduced the stipulation that in the new oil leases Nigerians must hold 75 percent of the managerial, professional, and supervisory positions in each operation within ten years after granting of the lease. At the end of 1970 it was also announced that all foreign firms starting businesses in the country must be prepared to train Nigerian personnel for eventual assumption of the principal managerial jobs.

Entry of foreign staff at the beginning of 1971 was controlled by a quota arranged between the country's immigration authorities and concerned ministries. Early in the year it was reported that quotas had been reduced and that permanent residence permits were no longer being given. A closer check was also being made on qualifications, although needed specialists were welcomed and there was no evidence that Nigerianization, at least in the higher occupational levels, was being carried out for its own sake. Unemployment, however, was resulting in increasing pressures for the replacement of non-Nigerians in lower level occupations, particularly in the distributive trades (see ch. 14, Industry and Trade).

SEASONAL AND MIGRATORY LABOR

Details on seasonal and longer term migration were generally lacking. During the dry harmattan season in the north considerable numbers of persons were known to migrate to work in more favorable food-producing areas, returning home when the rainy period began. The cattle-raising Fulani in the north also moved periodically during the dry season to better watered areas in the Niger-Benue River Valley.

Before the civil war many Ibo in the densely populated areas in the eastern part of the country migrated seasonally to work on farms in the Western and Mid-Western Regions and as laborers to timber-producing areas in the south. More permanent migrations involving large numbers of Ibo occurred after independence and, until 1966, numerous Ibo were found in the commercial and administrative centers throughout the country. Civil disturbances in the north in 1966 resulted in more than 1 million Ibo returning to their home areas. Many Ibo in the former Western and Mid-Western Regions reacted similarly just before and during the civil war from 1967 to 1970. Some Ibo outmigration has occurred since the war's end, but the numbers involved were unknown. Semipermanent migrants from the Yoruba, Hausa, and other ethnic groups, however, were found in varying numbers in other ethnic areas in 1971 (see ch. 5, Ethnic Groups and Languages).

UNEMPLOYMENT

Unemployment and underemployment constituted a serious problem during the 1960s and continued to do so in early 1971. Only limited statistical information was available; however, a survey conducted by the National Manpower Board in 1963 had showed an average unemployment rate of 14 percent in twenty-seven towns covered in the survey. Another labor force sample survey taken in 1966 and 1967 indicated that about 8 percent of all persons between fifteen and fifty-five years of age in urban communities were unemployed. Of those unemployed, 70 percent were between the ages of fifteen and twenty-three; 59 percent of all unemployed comprised individuals who had completed primary school but were below the School Certificate level (see ch. 8, Education, Public Information, and the Arts and Sciences). Many individuals in the small-industry and service sectors were known to be only marginally employed and not receiving regular wages. They included a large number who had gone to urban areas seeking higher wage employment and, although not finding it, still did not want to return to the rural setting.

Substantial increases in employment in the public sector were expected during the Second National Development Plan period from 1970 to 1974, resulting from needed expansion of the government machinery and lifting of restrictions on government employment during the civil war. There was little evidence as of early 1971, however, that the unemployment situation in general would be materially ameliorated since the labor market was being flooded annually by about 600,000 primary school leavers and dropouts, of whom only about 70,000 found openings in secondary schools.

During the period of the second development plan the government intended to expand and intensify existing vocational and apprenticeship schemes designed to impart skills more likely to result in employment. The plan also contained funds to establish the National Youth Service Corps. The chief immediate purpose of the corps was to remove young persons in the fifteen-to-twenty-three age group from the labor market and to provide them with training in a variety of useful skills under actual working conditions. Thus, members of the corps were to be used on projects to build bridges, schools, dispensaries, and roads, thereby acquiring skills in such areas as carpentry, bricklaying, welding, and motor vehicle and equipment use and repair. Other projects would impart such skills as shoemaking and pottery making and skills in electrical work.

The Ministry of Information and Labor in 1971 had a number of employment offices in operation in different parts of the country. Under the second development plan it was reconstructing several damaged offices in the war area and, because of increased industrial and government activities, extending or modifying offices at Kano, Kaduna, Jos, Ilorin, and Warri. Thirteen new offices and labor exchanges were planned for areas having larger populations. Nine of these were to be located in the northern part of the country—at Sokoto, Maiduguri, Katsina, Zaria, Lokoja, Gombe, Minna, Makurdi, and Yola. The remaining four were in South Eastern State—at Calabar, Port Harcourt, Ogoja, and Uyo.

An area of especially heavy unemployment in early 1971 was East Central State. The economic stagnation that followed the end of the civil war affected the reopening of factories, and because of economic situations many small enterprises had not yet begun to hire employees. A large number of former civil service employees, many in senior grades, also remained without jobs (see ch. 12, Character and Structure of the Economy).

WAGES, HOURS, AND WORKING CONDITIONS

There was no statutorily established minimum wage for the entire country in 1970. Minimum wages existed, however, for government workers in the unskilled, semiskilled, and artisan categories, based upon agreement reached with joint union representatives after a 1964 general strike. The provisions of this agreement were also accepted by various private employers. In other cases, minimum wages have been established through action of government-appointed wage boards in trades and industries where wages were very low or where workers were not sufficiently well organized to conduct effective collective bargaining. The recommendations of these boards were statutorily enforceable, and the concerned trade or industry was required under penalty to accept the decision.

Minimum wages for government workers in these labor categories in 1970 were set at different rates in different regions of the country. The highest minimums were in the Lagos area; they were the equivalent of US$1.08 a day for unskilled workers and

US$1.29 for semiskilled workers. The lowest minimums were in the north, where they approximated the equivalent of US$0.70 a day for unskilled workers and US$1.00 a day for skilled workers. The south and certain urban and mining areas in the north had minimums intermediate between these. Artisans were paid the same rates throughout the country and, depending on grade, received the equivalent of US$1.40 to US$3.05 daily.

In 1970 salaries for positions in government service, such as clerks, typists, and secretaries, started at the equivalent of US$374 a year; depending on training, length of service, and advancement, pay levels rose to nearly US$2,000 a year. Persons in administrative positions of essentially a managerial nature had salaries ranging from US$1,100 to US$3,802. Technicians, who included persons not holding higher degrees, received salaries ranging from US$1,142 to US$3,802, while individuals in administrative positions involving policymaking and professional staff were paid on a scale from US$1,728 to US$4,536. Starting salaries for various staff categories in this group, however, occasionally were higher depending upon the type of position.

The highest level of the civil service, including the government's senior staff, received the equivalent of US$4,147 to US$9,360 annually in 1970. In addition, all regular government employees were accorded fringe benefits; the type and amount of these varied with job category. Salaries paid to foreign personnel in senior posts were on the same scale as for Nigerians; however, a supplemental amount equivalent to 10 or 20 percent of the base salary was usually added.

Private industry has tended to follow the government pay scales but may make considerable adjustments for competence and skill. Wage increases in the private sector above the minimums were usually set by negotiated agreements between the union and employer, whereas salary increases in the public sector have been generally determined by government-appointed commissions. During 1970 pressures from government employees led to establishment of the Wages and Salaries Review Commission, headed by Chief Simeon Adebo. At the end of December 1970 the commission recommended an interim cost-of-living allowance backdated to April 1970; this was the equivalent of US$4.80 a month (or US$0.22 a day for persons employed on a daily basis) for workers making less than US$1,200 a year. The recommendation was accepted by the government.

In January 1971 the federal commissioner of information and labor recommended to private sector employers that a similar increase be given, less any cost-of-living raises that had been made since the wage determinations of 1964. Many employers did this, but large numbers of workers had expected the full amount, and in early 1971 the resultant unrest was heightened by union demands for a general wage increase. In an effort to quiet the situation, the government in February 1971 requested the private sector to pay the full increase without regard to any earlier adjustments.

General conditions of service were contained in the Labor Code Act, but this chiefly concerned workers paid less than the equivalent of US$180 a year. In some cases conditions of service were specified in agreements negotiated between the unions and employees. Hours of work for government employees in early 1971 were forty a week for clerical and administrative staff and forty-four for technical and manual workers. In industry, hours of work were up to forty-eight for all categories. Overtime at increased rates was paid by both government and industry for work on weekdays, Sundays, and holidays.

Vacation leave with full pay after a certain period of service was specified for certain industries by cabinet order; the length of leave varied according to position. Similar leave with pay was given government employees, the amount depending upon the salary scale. Sick leave of up to seven days with full pay in a six-month period was also specified in the Labor Code Act for workers hired without a written contract. In certain industries workers under written contract were entitled to similar leave on the basis of cabinet orders. In other cases, employers were expected, but not legally required, to give similar sick leave. In government a liberal policy entitled employees to up to six months' sick leave with full pay in any twelve-month period and another six months on half-pay within any four-year period or less.

Two other legislative measures providing additional protection for workers included the Factories Act, which established minimum conditions of health, safety, and welfare for factory workers, and the Workmen's Compensation Act, which governed compensation by employers to employees injured in job-related accidents, including incapacity or death occasioned by certain diseases, such as tuberculosis. The amount of compensation was based upon worker earnings and kind of injury.

LABOR ORGANIZATIONS AND LABOR RELATIONS

Unions

Unions have been in existence since 1912, when workers of various government institutions, which then constituted the majority of wage-paying enterprises, formed the Southern Nigerian Civil Service Union. This union—renamed the Nigerian Union of

Civil Servants in 1914 when the protectorates of Northern and Southern Nigeria were merged—was the chief workers' organization until 1931. Its membership was generally limited, however, to higher level employees, although the interests of all employees were statedly a matter of concern.

Lack of active representation by the union led to formation in the latter 1910s of a separate association by clerical workers of the Nigerian Railway Corporation, and in 1921 railway artisans and technicians formed the Mechanics Union, which carried out the earliest recorded strike. Wage reductions and economy measures brought on by the worldwide depression that began in 1929 led to more militant worker attitudes and in part resulted in formation in 1931 of the country's second significant labor union, the Railway Workers Union, by manual workers and other nonclerical employees. That same year the Nigerian Union of Teachers was formed; this included not only government employees but also teachers from the private sector.

Unionization in general, however, progressed slowly during the 1930s. In part this was probably because of lack of competent leadership and of political consciousness on the part of the workers. Another significant reason appears to have been lack of legal protection for union members until passage of the Trades Union Ordinance in 1938. The ordinance, which became effective in April 1939, legalized unions and specified the rights and privileges of members, as well as the conditions under which a union could operate.

Under the ordinance, the requirement for collective bargaining with an employer or industrial action was prior registration. The first unions registered in 1940; numbering 14 in all, they had a total membership of over 4,600 members. By 1950 the total had increased to 144 unions with more than 144,000 members. Growth was steady during the 1950s and the first half of the 1960s. In 1966, the year before the outbreak of civil war, there were 625 registered unions with a reported membership of almost 491,000 individuals. The number of unions registered in 1970 was unknown. Membership claims of over 800,000 were made, but the figure appeared much too high.

Federation of the country's labor movement began in 1941 with formation of the African Civil Servants Technical Workers Union. This organization was open, however, only to unions of workers in the civil service. Workers in private firms first began organizing in 1941. In 1942 a new central body, the Federated Trades Unions of Nigeria, was established that encompassed both private and civil service unions. Renamed the Trades Union Congress of Nigeria in 1943, this organization maintained its paramount position until 1948, when an internal split over affiliation with the political National Council of Nigeria and the Cameroons (later known as the National Council of Nigerian Citizens) resulted in the withdrawal of various member unions and the formation in 1949 of the rival Nigerian National Federation of Labor (see ch. 9, Government and Political Dynamics).

This internal struggle was not looked upon with favor by many of the unions, and a majority, including the largest unions, adopted a position of neutrality. The result was an effort to compromise, and in 1950 formation of a single, new central body, the Nigerian Labor Congress (NLC), occurred. Shortly thereafter, NLC leaders attempted to affiliate it with the World Federation of Trade Unions (WFTU), which is dominated by the East European communist bloc. Strong opposition arose from other union leaders who favored affiliation with the Western-oriented International Confederation of Free Trade Unions (ICFTU). The issue, which continued as a disruptive force even to 1970, had so weakened NLC solidarity by early 1951 that NLC virtually ceased to have any influence as a central labor organization.

Unity in the labor movement was once again achieved in 1953 with the joint founding of the All-Nigerian Trade Union Federation. Dissension within continued, however, the top leadership being accused of WFTU orientation. Finally, in 1956 several major unions that looked to ICFTU for international leadership broke away and established the National Council of Trade Unions of Nigeria. Two years later another agreement once more united the factions in a new body, the Trade Union Congress of Nigeria (TUCN).

The subsequent history of the central labor movement to late 1970 was generally one of fragmentation and factionalism. In 1959 TUCN affiliated with ICFTU, whereupon it was accused by opponents of betraying workers' interests, and a splinter body, the Nigerian Trade Union Congress (NTUC), was formed. Three years later the two central organizations, after extended negotiations, joined in the United Labor Congress (ULC). The merger, however, was short lived. Members of ULC voted to join ICFTU, and rival leaders once more withdrew and formed the Independent Unity Labor Congress (IULC). Before the end of 1962 another splinter group withdrew from ULC and formed a third central labor body, the Nigerian Workers Council (NWC). In 1963 a split within IULC produced a fourth organization, the Labor Unity Front (LUF).

Substantial rises in the cost of living generated demands for wage increases by labor unions throughout the country during 1963. Finally agreed upon the need for combined action, leaders of the four central bodies formed the Joint Action Committee in 1964 to present a united front to employers and the government on wage and salary demands. Factionalism and ideological differences soon reasserted themselves, however, and the committee, after attaining its goals, broke up in 1965.

Events following the killing of Ibo in the Northern Region in 1966, among whom were many union members, led to a further split within ULC. In an apparent attempt to maintain its favored position with the federal government, ULC offered only limited support to demands for compensation by union members in the Eastern Region. This brought on a withdrawal of ULC's eastern affiliates and the formation in that area of the Biafran Trade Union Confederation. This body functioned during the civil war period in support of the breakaway regime.

The end of the war in January 1970 saw an increase in labor militancy and an apparent recognition by labor leaders of the advantages to be gained in wage and other demands from a united front similar to the Joint Action Committee of 1964. This resulted in the formation in October 1970 of the United Committee of Central Labor Organizations (UCCLO), which in mid-1971 was still functioning as the coordinating body for the four central labor organizations. The four, however, continued to operate independently with respect to internal matters, international affiliations, and maintenance of ideological position.

Collective Bargaining and Industrial Disputes

The country's industrial relations system has developed in accordance with the concept of free, voluntary negotiation and collective bargaining in which the settling of terms and conditions of service in the private sector is effected through mutually agreed worker-employer machinery. The government's long-term attitude has been that solution of industrial relations problems can ordinarily best be solved by those parties directly concerned. This attitude was reflected in the general tenor of the Trade Disputes (Arbitration and Inquiry) Act of June 1958, which until mid-1968 permitted the government to intervene where the negotiating machinery had broken down and submit a labor dispute to arbitration only with the consent of the parties involved.

The need for greater industrial peace during the civil war led, after consultation by the Federal Military Government with various worker and employer organizations, to the promulgation in 1968 of the Trade Disputes (Emergency Provisions) Decree Number 21, which suspended the existing 1958 act. The decree, which became effective on June 1, 1968, continued to recognize the fundamental right of workers and employers to industrial action but introduced a provision allowing the commissioner of labor to refer an industrial dispute to compulsory arbitration.

Under the decree parties to a collective agreement were required to deposit a copy of the agreement with the commissioner of labor within a specified time. In case an industrial dispute arose and was not settled through the voluntary negotiating machinery within seven days and if either side wished to continue the dispute, the commissioner of labor was to be notified in writing and given details of the efforts to reach agreement. The commissioner was then empowered to appoint a conciliator, refer the dispute to a board of inquiry, or refer it to arbitration by an arbitration tribunal.

After notification of the dispute, it became illegal for workers to strike or for the employer to lock out his employees. Moreover, the terms or awards decided for settlement of the dispute could be confirmed by the commissioner of labor; they were then binding upon both parties. A chief purpose of this decree was reportedly to emphasize a more purposeful approach to collective bargaining and reduce the intransigencies often exhibited by employers and the more powerful unions. The decree was expected also to help the small house unions, which usually had little influence in decision-making in their industries.

As the war progressed the government and the central labor organizations continued to emphasize the need for industrial peace. In general, the advice appears to have been heeded by many workers. Industrial action did not cease, however, and the number of industrial disputes reported in 1969 showed a considerable increase over 1968, that is, 190 in 1969 compared with 133 in 1968. Included were strikes by civil service employees demanding wage increases.

In December 1969 the Federal Military Government promulgated the Trade Disputes (Emergency Provisions) (Amendment) Decree Number 53. The decree, effective for one year beginning December 12, 1969, prohibited under severe penalties any strikes or lockouts or the threatening or incitement of a strike or lockout. The news media were prohibited from dramatizing or presenting news in a way likely to cause industrial unrest. The decree also authorized detention and indefinite custody of anyone concerned with, or suspected of instigating, acts prejudicial to industrial peace.

Despite the ban on strikes, a number of work stoppages, slowdowns, and demonstrations occurred during 1970, and the provisions of the decree were applied in several cases. In December 1970 the decree was extended for an additional year. Unrest among workers in all sectors rose, however, in the latter part of 1970 in connection with demands for wage increases. A commission appointed in late 1970 recommended cost-of-living raises for workers in the public sector. This was followed by demands from the private sector for similar awards and led to some rather large strikes and work stoppages in early 1971. In February 1971 the Federal Military Government detained the president and secretary general of NTUC on undetermined charges. This led also to large demonstrations and threats of strikes from unions affiliated with NTUC.

Relations with International Labor Organizations

The largest central labor body in mid-1971, the United Labor Congress (ULC), was pro-Western in outlook and affiliated with the International Confederation of Free Trade Unions (ICFTU). The United States-based African-American Labor Center has provided regular financial support to ULC, including funds for the joint founding of the Trade Union Institute for Economic and Social Development in Lagos in 1966. This institution provides a residential labor education program for ULC officers and those of affiliated unions. Also generally Western leaning was the Nigerian Workers Council (NWC). Considered by some to be closer to a Western-type labor union organization, NWC was affiliated with the Brussels-based World Confederation of Labor (formerly the International Federation of Christian Trade Unions).

The leadership in the remaining two central labor organizations was considered leftist oriented. The Nigerian Trade Union Congress was affiliated to the World Federation of Trade, which was dominated by the East European communist bloc and reportedly was receiving supporting funds from the Soviet Union. Soviet funds also reportedly financed the construction of a new printing plant for the NTUC daily publication *Advance*. The Labor Unity Front (LUF), constituted chiefly of several larger, loosely grouped unions, including some composed of public service workers, had no apparent connections with any international labor body as of mid-1971. Its leadership, however, included individuals with strong leftist leanings.

Nigeria is a member of the International Labor Organization (ILO), and ILO maintains an area office in Lagos. Three other international labor bodies also maintained offices in Lagos as of 1971. These included the African Regional Organization of ICFTU; Africa Trade Union Confederation; and International Federation of Petroleum and Chemical Workers, the headquarters of which is located in the United States.

CHAPTER 5

ETHNIC GROUPS AND LANGUAGES

The 1963 Nigerian census recognized the existence of more than 200 ethnic groups ranging from clusters of fewer than 1,000 members to three nations of 9 million or more. With few exceptions, the population is negroid. Physical variations are generally not sufficient to permit individuals to be identified as a member of a specific ethnic group; primary distinctions are based on language, religion, customs, and history. The country's ethnic complexity results from the mixture of cultures, language stocks, and religions of West and Central Africa that have occurred within its borders. Some major ethnic groups are linguistically, religiously, and culturally more closely related to neighboring groups outside the country than to each other.

The country's ethnic groups are classified generally into five broad cultural types. These consist of: the Muslim Sudanic cultures, centered on earlier northern city-states; the diversified forest and coastal cultures of the southeast, based on independent communities; the forest kingdoms in the southwest; the nomadic pastoralists scattered throughout the north; and numerous small, less developed groups in the Middle Belt (see Glossary) along the Niger and Benue river valleys and along the eastern border area, where they withdrew during past centuries to escape from the influences of more powerful neighbors.

Each of the first three cultural varieties is represented by one of the major ethnic groups: the Hausa in the north, the Ibo (or Igbo) in the southeast, and the Yoruba in the southwest (see fig. 8). Although population figures—particularly the results of the 1963 census—are of questionable reliability, these three groups are each generally believed to number over 9 million persons (see ch. 4, Population and Labor). They are concentrated in regions separated from one another by areas that are sparsely settled by numerous smaller ethnic groups. There may be as many as six other groups that number more than 1 million each. With the Hausa, Ibo, and Yoruba, these groups comprise about 80 percent of the total population of the country.

The major distinction between ethnic groups is generally lin-

103

guistic. There are nearly as many languages as groups, and no single language is understood by more than one-third of the population. Most people, even in the remotest areas, speak more than one language, including one of the several that serve as lingua francas. The most widely spoken language is Hausa, the mother tongue of an estimated 16 million persons in the north. The Yoruba and Ibo languages play a similar role in the west and east. In addition to serving as the main language of education, English is the official language of the federal government and most state governments. Most printed matter appears in English, which has its greatest expression among young, educated southerners. Large numbers of less educated peoples in the south speak a distinctive English-based dialect known as Wes Cos (West Coast).

The more than 100 indigenous languages have been classified by linquists into four separate stocks and thirteen major subdivisions. Such a division does not, however, indicate degrees of mutual intelligibility. Instead, it reflects the fact that numerous waves of intra-African migration began or ended within the country's boundaries, providing differing cultural and linguistic bases from which contemporary inhabitants and languages have developed.

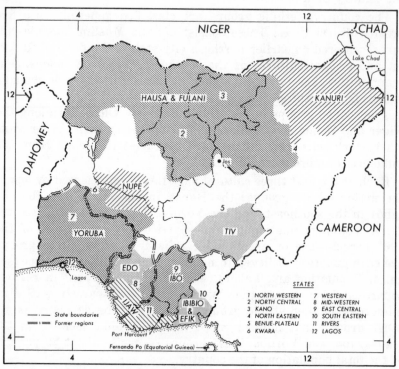

Source: Adapted from James L. Gibbs, *Peoples of Africa*, New York, 1965.

Figure 8. Major Ethnic Divisions of Nigeria

104

Until the first half of the twentieth century, when they were brought together by a common British colonial policy and improved communications, many communities were unaware of the existence of any but their near neighbors and the larger, more aggressive groups who engaged in wars and slave-raiding activities. The larger groups, in turn, were often fragmented to such an extent that they were not conscious of belonging to a single ethnic community.

The Ibo particularly have been splintered into independent and often hostile communities, differentiated in dialect and details of religious practice. The Yoruba remembered the common history of their earlier empires and retained a common reverence for the *oni* (priest-king) of Ife as their religious leader. For centuries before the British entered the area, many Yoruba communities were independent under local kings, who often waged war with one another. The people who identify themselves as Hausa are of a number of different origins. The sources of Hausa identity as an enthic group are limited largely to the uniting influence of the Muslim religion and the Hausa language. Smaller ethnic groups, on the other hand, are often fiercely proud of their differences from their neighbors.

British colonial policy tended to enlarge and reinforce ethnic consciousness, particularly of the Hausa, the Ibo, and the Yoruba. After World War II the country was regionalized into three semi-autonomous political units, in each of which one of the three chief ethnic groups formed a majority. This contributed to the sense of ethnic competition for control of the government by the three major groups and made the minority groups more aware of their subordination to their larger neighbors (see ch. 9, Government and Political Dynamics).

In the past, Nigerian ethnic groups distinguished themselves to some degree by dress, distinctive scar patterns cut during childhood, speech, and other distinctive traits of behavior. The practice of ethnically distinctive scarification has begun to die out, but as late as the 1950s almost half of the rural youths were still scarred. In the towns dress distinctions are changing to European styles or a common national costume (see ch. 7, Living Conditions). Differences of language and customs persist, but imported ideas and local innovations sometimes override ethnic lines, and the functions of older cultural distinctions have gradually changed.

MAJOR ETHNIC GROUPS

The Hausa, Ibo, and Yoruba, together comprising over half of the total population, are the largest ethnic groups in Nigeria.

Each predominates in one of the three regions that were organized by the British colonial administrators in recognition of the ethnic complexity of the country. The Ibo cluster, northeast of the Niger Delta, represents the densest concentration of population in West Africa. The Yoruba are more numerous than all other groups west of the Niger River. There are densely populated clusters of Hausa around the old towns and Katsina, Kano, and Zaria and a lesser one along the Sokoto River in the far northwest.

The Ibo and Yoruba peoples in their respective homelands are separated by the wide, relatively sparsely populated zone west of the lower Niger River valley; both peoples are remote from the Hausa area, separated by the country's ethnically diverse Middle Belt. These separations in space correspond to pronounced differences in traditional character among the three groups. Both Yoruba and Hausa show closer, longstanding cultural similarities to major groups outside Nigeria than they do to the Ibo or to each other.

Other important ethnic groups are the Tiv in the Benue River valley, the Anang and Ibibio east of the Niger Delta, the Ijaw in the Niger Delta, the Ido around ancient Benin, the Nupe in the lower Kaduna River valley, the pastoral Fulani scattered through the north, and the Kanuri around Lake Chad. The population of six of these eight groups exceeds 1 million each.

Hausa

The largest ethnic group is the Hausa. The Hausa proper numbered 11.6 million in the 1963 census. They are of mixed origins and have little consciousness of their ethnic unity. The primary unifying factors are the Hausa language and the Islamic religion. Because the language is used widely as a lingua franca throughout northern Nigeria and the neighboring Republic of Niger and because Islam is the religion of many non-Hausa-speaking Nigerians, the outlines of the group are blurred. The difficulty of establishing a precise definition of the Hausa is increased by the tendency of some groups who share ethnic origin, language, and religion with the main body of Hausa to distinguish themselves by other names (see ch. 11, Value Systems).

The original Hausa speakers in the northern sections of the country were the Habe. An aggressive people, they raided their weaker southern and western neighbors for slaves. Gradually, many of these peoples were absorbed into the Hausa culture, became Hausa speakers, and eventually were indistinguishable from their conquerors.

The Fulani entered into the Hausa area gradually from the

north and the west, beginning in the fifteenth century. The Fulani, of a strongly orthodox Muslim inclination, settled in the Hausa cities, intermarried with the Hausa, and adopted their language. In the early nineteenth century the Fulani rose up in a *jihad* (holy war—see Glossary) and conquered their hosts. The resulting Muslim Hausa-Fulani culture and political structure became the chief uniting factor among the Hausa peoples.

The Hausa language and culture have been established for 1,000 years around dominant urban centers along the northern edge of the sub-Saharan zone. These city-states, heavily influenced by Islam for at least six centuries and with a long-developed written history and literature, still have a strong awareness of cultural ties to the rest of the Sudan region of West Africa and to the Muslim world (see ch. 3, Historical Setting). Their contacts with the Nigerian coastal areas were indirect or nonexistent until the twentieth century.

The bulk of the Hausa are peasant farmers living in villages surrounding one of the Hausa capitals (see ch. 6, Social Systems). Large numbers of these peasants are also part-time craftsmen and traders. As full-time traders, Hausa are conspicuous in many parts of West and Central Africa, from Sierra Leone to the Congo River.

For many years the rulers of Hausa states harassed the less advanced peoples situated nearby or farther southward in the Middle Belt. Until the early twentieth century a long-sustained process of raids and enslavement continuously augmented the Hausa-speaking population at the expense of many weaker ethnic groups.

Self-awareness of the mixed origins of Hausa ethnic identity persists to some degree, especially with regard to certain localities. The Hausa of Katsina, for example, recognize the mixed origin of the Hausa of Zaria. Since the days of the earliest chronicles, the Zaria realm was a Hausa wedge thrust southward among non-Hausa peoples, and the city of Zaria was recognized as the hub of the slave-procurement traffic (see ch. 3, Historical Setting). The Hausa of Katsina often call the Hausa of Zaria "Gwari," the name of a nearby ethnic group known to have supplied numerous slaves, whose descendants are now Muslim Hausa speakers. Within the nominally Hausa population, however, former ethnic distinctions have been transmuted into class distinctions or are reflected in variations on Muslim orthodoxy.

The Hausa feeling of distinctiveness is weaker than the group consciousness of non-Muslim peoples because they are dominated by a proselytizing faith of universal claims that, in principle, transcend all boundaries of ancestry or place of birth. On the other hand, they lump together as pagans many peoples, such as the Ibo and Tiv, without regard for the important ethnic distinctions between them.

Some Hausa speakers do not use the ethnic name but proudly assert a more specific designation because of their successful resistance to Fulani conquest. These groups include the Kabbawa of Argungu and Sokoto Province, who are further distinguished (as are certain other sectors of the Hausa population) by their maintenance of conspicuous pre-Muslim religious practices.

The largest group of Nigerian peoples, therefore, has the vaguest limits and the most fluid composition. It is primarily an acquired culture rather than an ethnic division and is in contact with other diverse peoples, who are still contributing to its makeup.

Although the Hausa color term, *turawa* (white people), is applied to Europeans, the more usual Hausa term for them has been *nasarawa* (Christians), showing once again the Hausa preoccupation with religious distinction as a means of identification. Generally the Hausa had displayed cordial relations with the British colonial government. Their overt hostility has been reserved for non-Muslim migrants—Ibo, Yoruba, and Ibibio—from the coastal areas.

Ibo

The Ibo, who approximate 9.2 million, have an obscure past, partly because they have never been unified. Until the twentieth century they were divided among roughly 200 sovereign and relatively isolated communities based on kinship ties. These communities varied in size of population from several hundred to 10,000 or 20,000, each possessing different customs and, often, different dialects. These ethnic clusters resembled each other, however, in their broad cultural outlines.

On the other hand, cumulative differences in details and even in major features are so great across the length and breadth of the whole Ibo territory that there are greater cultural contrasts between some distant Ibo localities than between Ibo and quite separate neighboring ethnic groups. One reason for this diversity is the previous lack of any widespread network of communication, in addition to the absence of any central overall Ibo authority. Certain neighboring communities were chronically at war with each other, sometimes despite recognized kinship links.

Partly because of the fluidity of the Ibo social structure and partly because of the paucity of a material culture, the Ibo have been particularly susceptible to foreign influences. Various Ibo sectors of the west, south, and east have clearly borrowed from their non-Ibo neighbors, whom they know better than other, more distant Ibo groups. In the Ibo areas west of the Niger River can be seen the influence of the Benin kingdom, to which these Ibo were subordinate for several centuries. At the southeast, near the Cross River, Ibo and Ibibio customs converge.

European penetration of the Ibo area was comparatively late, but the mission schools and other new opportunities brought by Europeans were more eagerly received there than anywhere else in the country. After an initial suspicious resistance to Western ways, the Ibo rapidly adopted Westernization and became the most thoroughly Westernized of the larger ethnic groups. This Westernization trend became more complete because few of the younger Ibo had vested interests in the past; educated Ibo often revealed a sharp, embarrassed impatience with former customary practices.

Traditional Ibo culture in all its variety from one small group to the next still persists throughout large sectors of the countryside, but Western influences have been introduced in all areas as a result of the development of a cash economy based on growing oil palm. Literacy in English and an awareness of expanded modern horizons accompanied economic contacts with Europeans. The culture changed rapidly in Onitsha and Port Harcourt, in the new towns along the railroad, such as Aba and Enugu, and in Lagos, where literate Ibo migrated in significant numbers.

The Ibo became the most geographically mobile of the major Nigerian peoples. Densely confined to an agriculturally poor area with maximum need to expand or disperse geographically to diversify their economic role, they left their home area by the hundreds of thousands, either seasonally or semipermanently, for work and advancement in more favorable surroundings.

Until the civil war in the late 1960s, Ibo migrants were among the laborers, clerks, and new professional men of the predominantly Yoruba territory of western Nigeria; their presence was similar in non-Ibo districts throughout the east. This was of greatest significance in Lagos, the center of federal government affairs and overseas contacts. Although Lagos was fundamentally a Yoruba town, about 11 percent of its population consisted of more or less permanent Ibo migrants; this percentage included the most important Ibo personalities on the national scene. Lagos was also vigorously invaded by Ibo entrepreneurs.

Along with other southerners, such as the Yoruba, Ibibio, and Ijaw, the Ibo settled at every important commercial town in the Northern Region. The Ibo were predominant in the *sabon gari*

(Hausa term meaning new town), which was a separate development for modern commerce. In *sabon gari* residences of culturally alien migrants were located alongside the traditional walled towns of the Muslims.

In the north the Ibo arrived later than the Yoruba migrants but by the mid-1960s were far more numerous. The Ibo genrally bore the brunt of Muslim resentment and violence that was directed against educated southerners who held government jobs in the northern cities (see ch. 9, Government and Political Dynamics).

Yoruba

The Yoruba is the one major ethnic group with a long pervasive cultural homogeneity that is specifically its own. The traditional Yoruba economy combines subsistence farming with a considerable development of crafts and commercial activity in a series of sizable urban centers. According to the 1963 census, 4.1 million of the 11.3 million Yoruba lived in cities of over 20,000 population. The Yoruba lands in 1970 included at least thirteen cities with populations of more than 100,000, including the capital city of Lagos. In contrast, the more heavily populated Ibo lands contained only three such cities. The Yoruba's high urbanization reflects an ancient tradition of urban capitals for the rulers and a compact settlement pattern throughout the countryside. These patterns underlay the nineteenth-century consolidation of many distinct village populations into heavy quasi-urban agglomerations for military-defense purposes (see ch. 6, Social Systems).

During the nineteenth century the old Yoruba kingdoms and their successor fragments were alternately aggressive slave raiders and the targets of conquest and enslavement by others. The various kingdoms or city-states maintained a religious unity under the recognized preeminence of the ruler of Ife, the sacred mythical site of the pagan Yoruba origin. Respect for the *oni* of Ife still helps to bind the Yoruba together, even though great numbers have become Muslims or Christians. Among Yoruba converts, Islam is alleged to be much more secular in flavor and more tolerant of other faiths than is Islam among the Hausa. This has permitted Yoruba ethnic unity to persist vigorously in spite of religious cleavages.

Relations with the Yoruba's nearest neighbors, the Fon of Dahomey, have been on an approximately equal footing, although both had long been hostile. Nineteenth-century Fon conquests account for the international boundary separating a Yoruba minority in Dahomey from those in western Nigeria. To the east and

110

southeast, the Benin territory, with a different language (Edo) and divergent customs, was nevertheless originally an extension of the Yoruba political system. As a feudal state it gained its independence and for a long time exerted its own power at Yoruba expense, with suzerainty over Lagos. Cultural affiliation between the two ethnic groups, Yoruba and Edo, remains manifest in the Ogboni (their joint religious and political secret society), in artistic styles, and in types of dwellings.

In the north the Yoruba suffered heavy political encroachment in the loss of their Ilorin sector to Fulani control. The subordinate class position of the Yoruba population in the north has long been resented by most Yoruba. Friction between the Yoruba and the Fulani dynasty at Ilorin was partly expressed in the colonial period in agitation to detach the Yoruba-speaking area from the Northern Region and create a separate state. It contributed to the overall tension between the Yoruba and the Hausa leaders of the north.

The Yoruba, although chauvinistic and strongly opinionated regarding the superiority of their culture and institutions, are said to be less aggressive, less direct in manner, and more easy-going than the Ibo. As migrants in the far north, they shared the general reputation of southerners for zealous ambitiousness, contrasting with the outwardly placid and formal Hausa. The Yoruba were not as hated as the Ibo because of their smaller numbers and their outward adherence to Islamic mores. The Yoruba are apt to label the Ibo as uncouth and the Hausa as dull or overconservative. Many Yoruba associate the Hausa in general with the groups of Hausa traders who dominate the cattle and kola nut marketing between the regions and who are distrusted by the Yoruba.

Much of the Yoruba's early role in the country's political development was the result of their experience, particularly near Lagos, in dealing with Europeans and European culture over many generations. The western railroad through Yoruba territory was built a generation earlier than the eastern line through Ibo country and had more influence from the outset because it connected existing towns. Missions also were established earlier in the west than in most of the east. Generally, the Yoruba assumed an early lead in the ferment of the south as a whole, reflecting the primacy of Lagos as the colonial capital.

Other Large Ethnic Groups

Fulani

The Fulani ethnic group, sometimes called the Fulbe or Peul, is

111

usually described in terms of its separate existence and pastoral way of life. Actually the group includes two very different ethnic types, both of which are called Fulani. The sedentary and nomadic Fulani were already differentiated when they entered Nigeria in the fifteenth century. The sedentary Fulani, who are preponderant in numbers, are found mostly in Hausa territory where they form a part of the joint Hausa-Fulani society.

Fulani, numbering 4.8 million in 1963, comprise a dominant class, with privileged entrée to the whole range of prestigious government posts of traditional character, while commonly still retaining their original role as *mallams* (Koranic scholars and teachers). Although they are Hausa by language and custom, the sedentary Fulani nevertheless retain their old ethnic label as a claim to class privilege. Thus the designation "Hausa-Fulani" is used for the totality of Hausa speakers in those states that, in strictly political terms, have been "Fulani emirates" for 150 years. The politically dominant sedentary Fulani differ only slightly, if at all, from other Hausa speakers in their physical appearance.

The Fulfulde-speaking pastoral Fulani are important for their association with the early nineteenth-century *jihad*, the establishment of the still-existing emirates with settled Fulani rulers, and their economic role as cattle breeders for the country (see ch. 3, Historical Setting). The exact relationship of the pastoralists with leaders and followers of the *jihad* is not clear. The nomadic pastoralists differ from the sedentary Fulani in a whole range of cultural matters, particularly their adoption of cattle as the center of life, language, marriage customs, and the role of women.

Nomadic Fulani women make butter and are the characteristic vendors of dairy products throughout the north. This commercial contact with non-Fulani customers is almost the only regular relationship that these seasonally migratory bands have with outsiders. They keep their contacts with towns and state authorities to a minimum in their anxiety to maintain their freedom and to avoid paying taxes on their cattle. A third, separate concentration of Fulfulde-speaking Fulani live along the Nigeria-Cameroon border in the area adjacent to the Benue River valley.

The pastoral Fulani is the only group that shows any marked racial contrast with others. They are lean, with narrower noses, thinner lips, and straighter profiles than other Nigerians. Because their skin color is often a good deal lighter, the Hausa term them red men; the white designation is reserved for the Tuareg, North African Arabs, or Europeans. Because their features are sometimes strikingly Mediterranean, there has been much speculation about trans-Saharan or other Near Eastern origins. They are al-

112

leged to be proud of their distinctive appearance and to avoid intermarriage with more negroid peoples.

The sedentary Fulani are entirely or almost entirely negroid in physique. The direct forbears of the present Fulani dynasties and ruling classes of the states they conquered in the ninteenth-century *jihad* seem to have been more negroid originally. They shared this similarity with the Fulfulde-speaking Tukulor of the lower Senegal River area, who were apparently the source from which all other Fulani throughout West Africa derived their language.

The nomadic pastoral Fulani overlap the borders of Nigeria more decisively than do any other ethnic group. The great majority are located in other West African teritories, as far as Senegal to the west and well into the interior of Cameroon to the east. Religiously, these Muslim pastoralists are so indifferent that Hausa-Fulani often contemptuously call them pagans.

Tiv

The Tiv, numbering about 1.4 million in 1963, occupy a large block of territory in the middle Benue River valley, mainly south of the river. They long had a special reputation as a crude, fierce, and unapproachable people. Although the Tiv are active hunters, they are primarily cultivators, combining the southern root crops with northern grains and sesame (benniseed), a cash crop peculiarly their own in Nigeria.

The Tiv social structure is unstratified. Especially warlike and given to feuding among their many segments, they did not all come into peaceful agreement with the British until 1914. The Tiv, like the Ibo, baffled British exponents of indirect rule who could not find chiefs through whom they could exert control. The Tiv are of interest because of their numbers and their strategic location within the underpopulated zone, which includes the Benue River valley. Because of the special status given them by the British, the Tiv have just begun to enter the mainstream of Nigerian development as an important group. There is some friction between the Tiv and the Ibo over borderland for expanding agricultural settlement. There also is considerable Tiv resentment of any attempts of outsiders, particularly the Hausa, to exert control over them.

Ibibio and Anang

The 2 million Ibibio of the southeastern coast share many cultural features with the Ibo (especially those Ibo who are their immediate neighbors), although the two languages are fundamentally distinct. Both cultures feature the cycle of four days for

113

markets and cult observances and the prominence of women in local trade. The comparable role of women in neighboring Ibo and Ibibio communities was shown by their joint participation in the 1929 Aba riots, called the Women's War, as a protest against certain local British policies. Nevertheless, in the post-World War II era there was considerable hostility toward Ibo immigrants in Ibibio communities, and sentiment for partitioning the Eastern Region along a new boundary to match the language line began early. The supposedly gentler Ibibio temperament contrasts with the harsher vigor of the Ibo.

The Ibibio background resembles that of the Ibo in its lack of a centralized coordinating authority. Their self-conscious unity as a distinctive people is fragile. Their Anang (western) section prefers not to use the generic Ibibio label, and its 675,000 people are therefore listed separately in reports of the 1963 census. Similarly, the closely related Efik people of Calabar, numbering 160,000 in 1963, are inclined to consider themselves superior to the Ibibio. They disdain the Ibibio ethnic label because of pride over the distinctive local history of Calabar, the use of Efik as the written form of the Ibibio language, and its use by the non-Ibibio as a common language.

The old slave port of Calabar, basically an Efik town, reveals a mixture of other ethnic elements and the effects of Westernization to such a degree that it forms a minor parallel to Lagos, at the opposite corner of the country's coastline. It has been the entering wedge for Christian missions that spread up the Cross River and made the commercial orbit of Calabar the most thoroughly Christianized sector in the country.

Ijaw

The Ijaw, numbering about 1 million along and within the coastline of the Niger Delta, are fundamentally fishermen, swimmers, and boatmen who are thoroughly adapted to the distinctive environment of the delta creeks and vast mangrove swamps. For centuries before the decline of the slave trade, Ijaw towns, such as Brass and Bonny, exploited their strategic coastal location to profit as middlemen in the export of slaves from the interior and the import of European goods. Their prosperity declined in the late nineteenth century after European commercial firms fought fierce Ijaw resistance to penetrate past the Niger Delta. In contemporary times they have contributed a minor contingent of Western-educated clerks, professional men, and politicans to the mixed communities of Ibo and others at such modern centers as Lagos.

114

The Ijaw had long been interested in the proposal for creation of the separate Rivers State, to partition the Eastern Region on essentially ethnic lines as they resented Ibo domination in eastern regional politics. Most of the country's important oil reserves are in Ijaw, not Ibo, portions of the former Eastern Region. The reformed federal system of 1967, however, still left the Ijaw divided between Rivers State and Mid-Western State (see ch. 9, Government and Political Dynamics).

Edo

The Edo-speaking group, whose population is estimated at nearly 1 million, cannot be rigidly defined. Its core is the old royal town of Benin (known as Edo in the Edo or Bini language), around which are a series of peoples who acknowledge cultural similarities and allegiance but lack an accepted common ethnic name. A subgroup, usually identified by its own separate name, is the Urhobo or Sobo; this element numbers an additional 639,000 persons who live south of Benin, partly in the Niger Delta. The western Ibo share much of the common Edo culture except for language. There are cultural overlaps in several directions, especially with the Yoruba.

Benin became known to Europeans early in their period of exploration. The area in modern times, however, is comparatively a conservative backwater, partly because of the ethnic pride of the Edo and partly because of their location outside the mainstream of modern developments (see ch. 3, Historical Setting). Local religious cults persist more strongly among the Edo than among either the Yoruba neighbors to the west or the Ijaw and the Ibo farther east.

Edo agitation in 1963 led to the creation of the separate Mid-Western Region, the first success for those who opposed the strongly divisive three-region federal structure. The creation of the Mid-Western Region separated the Yoruba and the non-Yoruba groups of the Western Region from which it was carved. The resulting administrative entity was one in which the Edo shared power and population with the Ijaw, the western Ibo, and others. A few Edo have been prominent in national movements, particularly Anthony Enahoro, former editor of the *West African Pilot*, whose career of shifting party allegiance shows the uncomfortably intermediate positions of the Edo midwest area.

Nupe

The Nupe, numbering more than 650,000 in the lower Kaduna

River valley and along part of the Niger River, are an old kingdom that once resembled that of the Yoruba states. It was already largely Islamized before the Fulani conquest of the nineteenth century and the accession of Fulani rulers. The ruling class is a contingent of nominally Fulani people. As with the sedentary Fulani associated with the Hausa farther north, they have fully adopted the language and general culture of their subjects, have intermarried with them, and are said to be indistinguishable from other Nupe.

The Nupe do not have an especially dynamic role in modern Nigeria in spite of their strategic location astride the national road, rail, and river network (see ch. 2, Physical Environment). Moreover, they have the reputation of being rather apathetic. One careful observer who has made a thorough study of Nupe society attributes this trait to especially corrupt and oppressive emirate politics. The economy of the Nupe rests on a combination of southern root crops and northern grain crops, as in the case of the Tiv, but includes a fairly impressive range of traditional crafts, such as glass manufacture and brass work.

Kanuri

The 2.2 million Kanuri reside in the extreme northeastern corner of the country. They are, like the Hausa-Fulani, ethnically mixed and strongly Muslim and have had a dominant role in relation to varous smaller ethnic groups. They are both the rulers and peasants of the Bornu Empire, which has had a long history paralleling that of the Hausa states. Its historical realm lay partly outside Nigeria, to the north of Lake Chad. Its former slave-hunting grounds among non-Kanuri groups extended still farther into the swampy river valleys that drain into Lake Chad from the southeast. An Arab invasion in the 1800s and the history of partitions among colonial powers further complicated ethnic relations in the Kanuri sphere of influence.

The Fulani *jihad* failed in its efforts to penetrate the Bornu Empire, and the Kanuri take special pride in the history of this area as a distinct political entry. There are still distinctions of Muslim practices between Hausa-speaking and Kanuri-speaking people; for instance, the Kanuri do not usually seclude their women. The Hausa, therefore, tend to regard them as lax and semipagan. The Kanuri emirate structure closely resembles that of the Hausa, but there is less intraclass tension, as all inhabitants belong to the same ethnic and clan groups. Nevertheless, relations between the two major sectors of northern Islam are generally

116

friendly, and the Kanuri and Hausa adopt a common attitude toward non-Muslims from the south. Many Kanuri (called Beri-Beri in Hausa) are settled among the Hausa and have intermarried with them.

NON-NIGERIAN GROUPS

The terms *European* and *expatriate* are used by English-speaking Nigerians and by the government in an ethnic sense to contrast white residents of the country with Nigerians or other Africans. To Nigerians the term *European* generally includes Americans. According to the 1963 census, the major portion of resident Europeans were British, who comprised about 15,000 of the 47,000 non-Africans in the country.

The history of the minor European settlement is that of maritime international trade, the British colonial regime, Christian missions, and generally of implanted Western civilization. Their influence in bringing about changes in the social system was shared with the continually growing number of Western-educated Nigerians.

Except for missionaries, Europeans are concentrated at a few urban centers, such as Lagos, Kano, and Jos. The missionaries usually have not associated intimately with other non-Nigerians. Conversely, they had closer, more thorough contact with African life, especially in outlying areas. Approximately 5,000 Asians and Middle Easterners, mainly Lebanese but often labeled Syrians, are engaged in trade and have an urban distribution resembling that of the Europeans.

MODERN ETHNIC TRENDS

After World War II the British recognized the growing demands for political independence pressed by a small group of educated southern Nigerians, particularly the Ibo and Yoruba nationalists who gained a large and growing following. In 1946 the British administrators promulgated a constitution intended to prepare the way for gradual autonomy for a united Nigeria, but it also recognized the ethnic diversity of the country by the establishment of strong regional governmental units. Each region was controlled by the predominant ethnic group within its boundaries.

One result of this development was the reinforcement of ethnic rivalries by direct political competition. Political and economic disputes became identified with ethnic antipathies, which led to riots, exemplified by those at Kano in 1953, against other ethnic groups. The Hausa were particularly sensitive to the differences between themselves and the southerners. As the need for a large educated corps of administrative officers became more apparent with the growth of self-government, the Hausa's general lack of formal education was seen as a serious handicap. Southerners, particularly the Ibo, rushed northward to fill the positions and quickly asserted their superiority through education and aggressiveness. The government of the Northern Region took steps to limit the numbers of southerners in its administration, although this required the retention of British administrators.

In the governments of the Eastern and Western Regions Nigerians pressed to gain complete control of the administration by replacing British administrators as quickly as possible. Both governments—Ibo in the east and Yoruba in the west—were parochial in preserving leading positions for people of the ethnic group that controlled the government. This was particularly true of the Yoruba. Neither group made any effort to secure fair representation in the administrations for minority ethnic groups, although formal barriers generally were not placed in the way of their entry and advancement.

Similarly, groups other than the Ibo and the Yoruba were unable to compete on an equal basis for civil service posts. Like the Hausa, they did not have the educational background; like the Edo, Ijaw, and Ibibio in the southern regions, they did not have the political strength to demand equal representation. Because governmental and paragovernmental organizations controlled more than half of the country's wage-paying jobs, such exclusions became a major popular issue and increased intra-ethnic tensions and demands for alterations in the federal-regional system (see ch. 9, Government and Political Dynamics).

LANGUAGES

No single language is understood by a majority of the population. Hausa, the mother tongue of approximately 16 million persons and the major auxiliary language in most of the north, is best known. It is followed by Ibo and Yoruba, languages of the second and third largest ethnic groups, and English, the imported language of the former colonial power. English has hardly any base as a mother tongue among Nigerians, but it is understood to some extent by many millions of the country's inhabitants. It has its greatest impact among young educated southerners.

The use of English as a supplementary language has been expanding along with the accelerated access to schooling. It is the main medium of literacy and publications; it dominates in specialized modern sectors of the country's life and serves as the sole official language of the federal and southern state governments. English and Hausa share official status in some northern states.

More than 100 other languages are spoken as mother tongues by members of the country's various other ethnic groups. Each serves as the normal medium of communication within a group's home territory. Nigerians are keenly aware of the language and dialect differences that are practical barriers to communication and test or badges of social identity.

The main official test of one ethnic group's distinctness from another is the difference in their languages. Usually the variation is so pronounced that knowledge of one is not adequate for an understanding of the other. The Yoruba are distinguished clearly from the Ibo, the Edo, or the Nupe by this language variation; but there are borderline cases, such as Igala, where both the ethnic separateness from the Yoruba and the status of the speech—as a language lacking mutual intelligibility with Yoruba—have been disputed.

The main subdivisions within each ethnic group are marked by contrasts of dialect; differences in pronunciation and vocabulary do not prevent communication but may hamper it. Yoruba has ten to twelve such dialects in addition to Oyo, which is used in schools, publications, and radio broadcasts, and is gradually being accepted as standard Yoruba. In the other languages one dialect is usually acknowledged as dominant; thus the Kano dialect is standard Hausa for official use.

Several widely spoken languages, such as Ibo, have been written in more than one important dialect and lack a single generally acknowledged standard. Official efforts to make one of the artificial syntheses of the several Ibo dialects the standard for all Ibo people still encountered considerable popular opposition in the early 1960s. Members of each ethnic group are alert both to dialects as evidence of specific local affiliations and to the use of other languages as the mark of alien ethnic groups.

The problem of language barriers to communication is lessened by a high frequency of bilingualism among those living close to each ethnic border. If people do not understand one another's mother tongue, a third language generally known in their area is commonly used as a lingua franca. Hausa is the main example of a language that has been learned by large numbers for whom it is not a mother tongue but who use it for trade or other dealings with strangers. Although a majority of the northern population can understand Hausa, language barriers still separate parts of that region from each other and from the south, where English is the only supplementary language used at nearly all major crossroads.

Along the eastern border in a broad strip from Lake Chad to the Gulf of Guinea, where the richest profusion of languages is concentrated, neither Hausa nor English is well known. A version of pidgin English known as Wes Cos is spoken by about 2 million persons living in the southeastern coastal area. Farther north a series of other key languages—Efik, Jukun, and Kanuri—serve as the lingua franca.

English and classical Arabic are of special significance because of their official or religious use and the links they provide between Nigeria and other parts of the world. Both are learned at school rather than at home and are associated with literacy in roman and in arabic script, respectively.

Knowledge of English is scarce among older adults in most places any distance from the coast. It is most common among the school-age population in the southern half of the country and especially in the major towns where both Western-style schools and enterprises are concentrated.

Among Muslims, who make up 45 percent of the population, classical Arabic has unique prestige as the language of the Koran and of the Muslim legal tradition. It is well known only by some of the *mallams* and judges in the major emirates. The Shuwa Arabic spoken near the Lake Chad area is virtually a separate language. A more widespread result of exposure to Koranic schooling is the familiarity with the arabic alphabet and its use in reading and writing Hausa.

The arabic script used in the north is of a distinctive Sudanic style, similar to that used in northwest Africa and introduced by way of Timbuktu around the fourteenth century. Intimately associated with the conservative Muslim tradition, this script has not commonly been adopted for printing, but it is the form of writing typically used by the northern Muslim elite. People who are able to read arabic script far outnumber those who can read Hausa in roman print.

Although the far north has had its Western Sudan Muslim literate tradition for many centuries, most of the Nigerian peoples could not write until the arrival of Western influences (see ch. 3, Historical Setting). Christian missionaries pioneered in providing written expression for previously unwritten languages, primarily for religious purposes but also for general education.

The various Nigerian governments have given their sponsorship and financial help to the development of printed materials using the roman alphabet and beginning primary school instruction in the local languages. For each separate language certain modified letters have been added to the alphabet, where needed, for additional distinctive sounds. Missionary or other research and teaching agencies have not always been in agreement on details of writing methods for a given language, but since the 1950s the governments have brought about a uniform system of writing and printing for use with all vernaculars.

In the schools the usual policy has been to teach reading and writing in the local language and then in English, after the alphabet and its use are familiar. In adult education programs, literacy in the local languages has been promoted. Thus the roman alphabet is familiar to many primary school pupils and some adults, who may or may not become literate in English.

Publications in English exceed all vernacular publications combined, but vernacular publications are increasing in number, especially through cheap booklets and periodicals produced in some thirty languages by government agencies for the benefit of the newly literate (see ch. 8, Education, Public Information, and the Arts and Sciences). The roman alphabet has always been used for the printed Hausa version of official documents in the north, and a Hausa newspaper in roman type was first published in 1939.

The only fairly abundant vernacular publishing is in Yoruba. The Ibo and other southerners, whose levels of literacy match the Yoruba, publish little in their own languages and read more often in English.

Linguistic Stocks

The profusion of languages in the country provides a rich sampling of the basic linguistic stocks that extend throughout the African continent. One comprehensive linguistic survey has classified the languages by degrees of similarity reflecting common origins.

The mother tongues of Nigerian peoples fall into three independent African language stocks: Afro-Asiatic, Niger-Congo, and Sudanic. Sometimes Indo-European is added as a fourth basic stock. The three African language stocks are so thoroughly divergent from each other in basic vocabulary that it is difficult to trace them to a common root.

Regardless of the stock they represent, most Nigerian languages reveal a striking feature of significant tone. In each one, words are distinguished from one another partly by raising or lowering syllables to a different musical pitch; the number of significant levels usually are two or three and rarely more. In Ibo the word *akwa*, with the pitch rising from the first to the second syllable, means "egg"; with falling pitch, it means "bed"; and with a high pitch on both syllables, it means "to cry."

It is possible in each of these tonal languages for a certain repertory of phrases to be indicated on drums, trumpets, or other musical instruments. This possibility has been exploited traditionally for ceremonial or emergency drum "talking" and signaling. A few other phonetic features that appear frequently in the majority of the languages include the use of syllables with consonant combinations, such as *gb*, *nk*, and *mb*, before a vowel.

Afro-Asiatic

Three substocks of the Afro-Asiatic language stock (also known as Hamito-Semitic) are found in Nigeria. These are Chadic, Semitic, and Berber. Chadic, used entirely south of the Sahara, has been used much longer in Nigeria than the other two. Its tonal character contrasts with the nontonal Semitic and Berber languages.

The Chadic substock consists of Hausa and a large number of less important languages spoken farther southeast, some of them among hill peoples of the Jos Plateau and its vicinity, some around the hills of the Cameroon border, and others extending beyond Lake Chad. Of this language substock, only Hausa has been of great historical or contemporary importance.

The Semitic substock is represented by Arabic, of which one dialect is spoken by the pastoral Shuwa Arabs near Lake Chad. Other dialects are spoken among the small numbers of North African and Syrian immigrants. The literary Arabic associated with formal Koranic study is a different form and is recited in ritual rather than spoken generally.

The Berber substock is represented by Tamashek, the language of the Tuareg, who dwell mainly much farther north in the Saharan oases but who have had close historic relationships with Hausa states. The number of Tamashek speakers in Nigeria is uncertain but is probably quite small; most of those who claim Tuareg ethnic identity now use Hausa as their mother tongue.

Niger-Congo

The Niger-Congo language stock comprises a vast assemblage of languages covering most of black Africa from Senegal to Natal. All seven of its substocks are represented in Nigeria: Kwa, Ijaw, Benue-Niger, Adamawa-Eastern, Voltaic, Mandingo, and Atlantic.

122

The Kwa substock includes Ibo, Yoruba, Edo, Nupe, and a few others, grouped rather compactly in areas flanking most of the lower Niger River and extending westward as far as the Ivory Coast. The Ibo, the Yoruba, and their Kwa relatives are supposed to be more extensively tonal in character than are most other substocks of Niger-Congo. Ijaw is a substock consisting of a single language with strongly distinctive dialects and is used in most of the Niger Delta.

The Benue-Niger substock is of great importance for Africa as a whole because the Bantu languages belong to it. In Nigeria it is represented by Ibibio, Tiv, Jukun and Birom, and a large number of minor languages spoken in the Cross River region, the hilly eastern border areas, the Benue River valley, the Jos Plateau, and scattered areas near the western border. In earlier times languages of this substock apparently were spoken in more of the eastern and north-central parts of the area than they are now, but they were displaced or submerged by others. Ibibio is most well known in its Efik dialect, which is used by other Ibibio as the written form and which was also adopted as a trade language by minor ethnic groups of the Cross River region. Jukun also has some slight use as a common auxiliary language in its own neighborhood by the Benue River, reflecting the past importance of a wider Jukun kingdom in the east.

The Adamawa-Eastern substock includes several minor languages of the eastern border areas. The Voltaic and Mandingo substocks are of minor importance, although both cover enormous areas west of Nigeria where they include important languages of historically powerful kingdoms. They include the languages of the Borgu state, now spoken mostly in Dahomey; and Bussa, spoken mainly in the territory of the small but once fairly important Bussa state on the Niger (see ch. 3, Historical Setting). The area in Nigeria's Ilorin Province, where both of these stubstocks are located, is sparsely populated and out of the mainstream of modern Nigerian life.

The Atlantic substock, whose member languages are primarily spoken in or near Senegal, is represented in northern Nigeria by Fulfulde, which has a number of variant names. It is the language of the Fulani nomads and certain settled related communities. Fulfulde, like its Atlantic relatives, is nontonal.

Sudanic

The Sudanic language stock embraces two historically significant Nigerian languages of different substocks, Kanuri and Songhai. They are associated with the traditions of the Bornu and

123

Songhai empires, flanking the Hausa language area to the east and west.

The Songhai substock consists of a single language, Songhai, spoken for nearly a thousand miles along the banks of the Niger River upstream from Nigeria's western border; inside the country it is spoken along the border and in a few other parts of western Sokoto and Niger provinces. The more common of the two Songhai dialects is called Zarma. Songhai speakers, like the speakers of Mandingo and Voltaic languages in the same western border zone, are significant mainly as links with their non-Nigerian linguistic and ethnic relatives.

The Saharan substock is much more important in Nigeria because of Kanuri, the language of the ancient Bornu state (see ch. 3, Historical Setting). Several other Saharan languages are spoken in Bornu Province, linking it linguistically with much larger non-Nigerian areas to the north and east and extending into the desert and as far as the Nile basin. The languages of this group, including Kanuri, have been directly influenced by the spoken Arabic of their close neighbors, the Shuwa Arabs.

Major Auxiliary Languages

The country's languages may be ranked roughly in numbers of speakers according to the size of the corresponding ethnic groups. Some have an augmented importance because of their auxiliary use between people who speak different mother tongues. The main examples, in addition to English, are Hausa, Kanuri, and Fulfulde in the north and Efik and Wes Cos in the southeast. Each of the last four serves to counteract the unusually great diversity of speech forms that occurs all along the eastern edge of the country. Hausa has spread more vigorously into the other main region of greatest speech diversity, the Jos Plateau. Hausa, Kanuri, and Fulfulde serve areas in which English is especially limited and overlap the national borders to the north and northeast in the republics of Niger and Chad and to the east in Cameroon.

Hausa, Kanuri, and Fulfulde dominate and serve as auxiliary languages in three separate northern zones. Hausa serves in this manner in all the areas from the northwestern border down to the Niger-Benue confluence and across the Jos Plateau. Similarly, Kanuri is predominant in Bornu Province to the northeast; Fulfulde is preeminent around the upper course of the Benue River and generally in Adamawa Province. In each instance, the dominance of the key language amid a variety of other tongues reflects the coordinating role of the key ethnic group among weaker and less numerous groups.

The ancient Hausa city-states have exerted linguistic influence over their primarily non-Hausa-speaking neighbors for many centuries through the spread of commercial contacts and direct subjugation. Hausa enjoys prestige as the speech of a sophisticated urban culture, and among the Nupe, for instance, Hausa and Arabic words and phrases may be inserted in conversation to give a more elegant flavor to the home language.

Among people who have become Muslims much more recently than the Hausa, the prestige of Hausa speech is associated with the role of Hausa religious teachers in furthering the religion. For most Nigerians, Hausa is the only language other than Arabic that is known to be written in the same script as the Koran.

Hausa was the only Nigerian language that British colonial officials were required to learn and use. This policy helped to spread its influence at a faster and more widespread rate than had been reached previously. Both deliberately and inadvertently, British policy favored the spread of Hausa ahead of, or instead of, the spread of English. Knowledge of English has begun to grow more vigorously in the north, but Hausa remains paramount.

On a smaller scale, the Kanuri language dominates its neighbors because of the political influence and cultural prestige of the Bornu rulers. Like Hausa, it has been written for centuries in arabic script.

Effects on Social Relations

The ethnic groups are distinguishable from one another more by language than by any other cultural feature. In most cases the mother tongue alone has been a good guide to how people classify themselves and one another in encounters with members of other ethnic groups. There are exceptions, as with the social classes among the Hausa speakers, or the Efik and Anang, who are linguistically distinguished only by dialect from other Ibibio. Although most adult males learn to speak languages of ethnic groups other than their own, ethnic pride and antipathies or political and commercial dominance sometimes make the process unilateral; the prouder or more advantageously situated group expects strangers to learn its language, but it often does not reciprocate. Those whose mother tongue is Hausa are descended mainly from non-Hausa who learned the Hausa language as a second tongue and then virtually abandoned their own mother tongues under pressure from the dominant Hausa culture.

The Yoruba are said to be less willing to learn the Ibo language than the Ibo are to learn the Yoruba tongue. The Ibo are immigrants into Yoruba territory. The Yoruba seldom go to Ibo lands;

they are inclined to scorn the Ibo language, which they associate with an inferior background. A common Yoruba epithet is *koko koko*, meaning either Ibo specifically or any African who does not understand the Yoruba language. It is a fighting taunt in Lagos.

Wherever a language is well established as a common auxiliary language, the political or commercial dominance of its original speakers is indicated. Accordingly, Hausa is widely spoken not only because it is the mother tongue of 11 million people but also because Hausa states and traders have long played dominant roles in relation to less developed peoples. The spread of Hausa accelerated because it was used as the language of administration by the British in non-Hausa northern districts. One exception to the custom that the ruler's language prevails is found among the Fulani, who came in the early nineteenth century to dominate the Hausa but abandoned their own language in favor of Hausa.

Among the peoples directly bordering on the Hausa states, those of Bornu Province in North Eastern State show the least interest in learning the Hausa language. Kanuri, their own common language and, to some extent, a vehicle of literacy, is linked to the proud traditions of the ancient Bornu Empire.

Within each ethnic group, local subdivisions are marked by lesser differences in speech than between groups. The number of dialects may be few, each one spoken by a relatively large number of people. In some groups, however, a large number of dialects divide the people into many small subgroups, depending on local conditions, ethnic history, and how closely the people interact with one another.

Dialect differentiation is extremely slight among the Tiv of the Benue River valley, who have expanded rapidly from a small nucleus. They have retained a strong consciousness of their common origin despite frequent intragroup feuds. Dialects are more clearly pronounced in the Hausa language, which has ten times the number of speakers spread over a much wider territory for a much longer time.

Each of the several main Hausa dialects is spoken fairly uniformly by people varying in number from hundreds of thousands to more than a million. The degree of uniformity in each Hausa dialect reflects the political and economic unity of each Hausa state around its traditional urban nucleus at a royal capital. The reasonable degree of mutual intelligibility among the dialects reflects the close ties and flow of communication among Hausa states. The same is true on a smaller scale for the Yoruba language.

The much sharper splintering of the Ibo language into a large number of dialects corresponds to the great profusion of small

126

local Ibo groupings. Each of these has been traditionally self-governing and has been separated from close neighbors by suspicion and frequent local wars. All share a general lack of regular communication with other Ibo groups outside a narrow orbit. A result of jealousies between Ibo localities was the persistent reluctance to accept a single dialect as the standard for schools and publications. An officially accepted orthography was not devised until 1961. The Ibo and their neighbors, the Ibibo, present the most prominent instances of acute dialect differentiation, which seems to have contributed to the rapid growth in the use of English among both peoples.

Because all traditional social systems stress separate areas of specialized activity for the sexes, the speech of women usually differs to some degree from that of men. Almost everywhere, except among Christians, male and female adults have separate religious lives, with corresponding differences in vocabulary, some of which may be secrets for initiates of one sex. More generally, the vocabulary for details of ordinary daily life diverge somewhat according to sex. In certain languages, such as Fulfulde, there are also noticeable sex differences in grammar and pronunciation.

Throughout the country men tend to have more abundant and varied contacts with strangers and therefore possess greater knowledge of additional languages. A higher percentage of men have some schooling, and they know relatively more English and are far more likely to be literate than the women in their families (see ch. 8, Education, Public Information, and the Arts and Sciences).

Within any local community or family, language skills are apt to vary greatly with age levels. Adults, particularly males, acquire more versatility in mastering the languages of neighboring ethnic groups. In recent years the younger adult males have migrated to distant places and have learned languages unknown to those who remained at home.

The young children and adolescents are far more literate and better acquainted with English than are their elders because of the rapid spread of formal education. The contrast between illiterate, non-English-speaking parents and their literate offspring who know English will gradually move into the upper age brackets. Meanwhile, schoolchildren or young adults often serve as interpreters for their elders and translate orally into the mother tongue from newspapers or other English-language printed matter.

There is more literacy and knowledge of English in the towns than in the rural hinterlands. Similarly, townsmen are likely to have wider knowledge of other African languages, which they learn to use in their contacts and dealings with the urban migrants of many other ethnic groups. The greatest linguistic versatility is found in such towns as Lagos, Onitsha, Jos, and Kano or among those migrants who have lived in a number of such ethnically mixed urban settings.

Language difference usually has not been a political issue. There have been suggestions that the people should select an African language for official use throughout the country. This approach has not received significant governmental support because the choice of any one major language would antagonize the other major ethnic groups. The great majority of people in the southern half of the country believe in the practicality of maintaining and expanding the use of English.

As a nationalistic gesture, many Nigerians have ceased to use personal names of British or missionary origin and have adopted names of purely African flavor. Thus Benjamin Nnamdi Azikiwe, first president of Nigeria, used only his latter two names and gave purely Ibo names to his children. The policy of vernacular teaching in the lower grades has at times been challenged in favor of an earlier use of English, but the question has been more technical than political.

There is some interest in developing French as a subject in the schools because of the importance of French in all of the countries that surround Nigeria. Nigerians have studied and learned other European languages when required in courses of higher education abroad.

Official use of French by the republics of Dahomey, Niger, Chad, and Cameroon poses language barriers on the bureaucratic level at all land frontiers. Although most Africans know neither French nor English, Western-educated African elites and Europeans find that the barrier poses some practical problems. It probably matters least along the northern frontier, where there is little knowledge of European languages. The British regime supported the official use of Hausa on the northern border, and practically all the people on both sides of the border are Hausa speaking (or Kanuri speaking in the northeast). Because most of the international boundaries cut through ethnic groups, informal communication in local mother tongues usually transcends the frontiers.

CHAPTER 6

SOCIAL SYSTEMS

Many Nigerians have had contact with Western culture and have adopted a number of its elements; the traditional cultures, however, remain very much a part of the present and play a decided role in the country's social systems. The various ethnic peoples have a strong sense of identity for their own group. Overlaying the various traditional social systems is a life style introduced in some areas of the country by the British scarcely a generation ago. The objects associated with this way of life—from tractors to educational systems—have been adopted generally as the economic means of the people allow. Traditional values, however, derive largely from Nigerian cultures rather than from European models (see ch. 11, Value Systems).

Nigerians are a culturally diverse people, and few general statements about their social structure can be made. Social organizations range from simple groups of interconnected families with little political superstructure to highly elaborate city-states. Certain traditional institutions, however, are common to a number of ethnic groups. In all ethnic groups the family is important, and in most it forms the basic unit of the social structure.

Kingship and hereditary rank are found in two areas of the country: the Hausa northern states and the western section occupied by the Yoruba. Kingship is still important, particularly in the north, where the royal tradition is supported by strong religious ties. The central government can function more efficiently than the kings in the purely secular realm, however, and in many areas the institution is being absorbed into the modern secular government. Although slavery is no longer permitted, almost everywhere the social status of the descendants of slaves has been affected by this earlier practice. Forms of social mobility have similarities in many areas, including membership in title societies or other associations that confer prestige, European-style higher education, and the holding of public office. All of these in some way involve the acquisition and wise expenditure of wealth.

Guild-like professional groups are important in some areas, particularly those occupied by the Hausa and the Yoruba. Voluntary associations that provide various aspects of mutual support have gained in power and importance as the movement of workers to faraway cities has increased.

Religion has broad social dimensions alongside its spiritual value. The interplay between the indigenous traditional religions and the foreign imports—Islam and, later, Christianity—has created a vastly complex range of beliefs and practices.

THE ELITE CULTURE

During the colonial era the British maintained a high degree of social separation from the Nigerians. Government officials and members of business firms made up the greater part of the European presence, and they were largely situated in the cities. In the cities also were to be found the European-style houses, the automobiles, the clubs, and the shops that formed the model and goal of the young educated African's aspirations. After World War II, because of the advance of educational levels and in anticipation of ultimate national independence, Africans began to enter the ranks of the governmental administration. Although the economic level of these persons was roughly the same as that of the Europeans whom they were replacing, the two groups mingled very little socially.

Within the colonial community missionaries were respected, but few were integrated in the governing group. The missionaries, moreover, did not form a unified group because they came from various national backgrounds and represented a number of often rivalrous Christian communities. Their personal contacts with African cultures and their role as educators, however, brought them closer to the people than most government officials were able to come. The people respected them for their learning and looked on them sympathetically, despite the contradictions between Christian teachings and ethnic traditions at many points.

Because the climate was regarded as inhospitable by Europeans, there was no influx of white settlers into the country. Largely because of this, the traditional ways of the ethnic groups were never threatened by Europeans and their culture, and traditional cultures remained vitally operative.

The culture built up by the former colonial elite in Nigeria was one of sojourners. All the members had goals of home leave and ultimate retirement somewhere away from Nigeria. This pattern also has strongly persisted with the educated African elite who replaced the British. A large proportion of the inhabitants of the modern African cities, or of the modern areas of the old cities, regard themselves as temporary residents with no deep emotional investment in the life of the city.

130

Despite the observable differences between the modern Nigerians of the cities and traditionally oriented rural people, the ethnic ties are still strong and deep seated between members of the elite and their home areas. The homogeneity of the educated elite is still more a matter of appearance than a social reality. Many educated persons living in the cities plan to retire to the region of Nigeria where they were born.

Because the Christian mission schools were the source of Western education in the country, the greater proportion of the members of the educated elite are Christian. Since the Christian missions were largely excluded from the Muslim north, the greater part of the educated class comes from the southern groups, notably the Yoruba and the Ibo. It was largely from these tribes that the replacements came for the departing British civil servants.

TRADITIONAL PATTERNS

All of the major institutions of the traditional cultures, with the possible exception of the kingship, continue in the modern period. It is not possible to describe these institutions as they function in each of the 200 or more ethnic groups that make up the people of the country, but three groups—the Hausa in the north, the Yoruba in the southwest, and the Ibo in the southeast—because of their preponderant numbers and influence in the country, supply examples of the kinds of customs commonly encountered.

Family

A number of family relationship patterns are widely found, such as respect for age, the high value set on having children, sharply differentiated roles for the sexes, bridewealth (see Glossary) payments, and polygyny. Most traditions stress descent through the male line, but the male lineage (see Glossary) of an individual's mother often has as great importance as that of his father. In non-Muslim areas the male links, reckoned through many generations, serve to join cousins into extensive lineages that are the basic traditional sources of an individual's social identity. The Muslim societies of the north differ in the degree of their adoption of Islamic family principles, many of which differ from the traditional African forms. Generally the importance of the lineage groups is reduced. The accent on male dominance is greater than among non-Muslims, and women are secluded to a greater extent.

Kinship forms the basis for many ties, obligations, and rights in traditional societies. Groups bound by common ancestry from the principal or exclusive basis for the organization of social life, land tenure, political roles, and even religion in many of the local traditions. The compact household of one male family head with his wife or wives and their young children may be an important practical unit in its own right, but typically it is regarded as a minor or subordinate part of the much more extensive lineage group founded on descent through the male line from an ancestor several generations back. Such lineages make up the basic unit of the Yoruba cities, for example, and a single-walled lineage compound may house a thousand individuals related through common descent. Kinship ties have relatively the greatest range and significance in small societies of the eastern Middle Belt (see Glossary) of the southeast. Among the Muslims of the north, where land tenure, religion, and civic relationships are not systematically organized along kinship lines, extended lineage ties are not maintained except among the aristocracy, whose privileged status does rest in part on genealogy.

Marriage is regarded primarily as the means of acquiring children. Fertility is of paramount value; sterility is dreaded and may be used as a ground for divorce. Marriages often are relatively unstable. The tie between husband and wife commonly is much weaker than the tie between either parent, particularly the mother, and the offspring. Celibacy is virtually unknown and is almost invariably the result of physical or mental disability. In some instances women of high modern education have priced themselves out of a traditional marriage and have difficulty finding a husband of equal status, but such individuals are in a small minority. Traditionally, marriage for girls takes place a few years after puberty; boys usually marry later.

Three forms of marriage coexist in the country. Indigenous marriage customs permitting unlimited polygyny and based on the payment of bridewealth are common to many groups. Muslim marriage customs limiting polygyny to four wives predominate in the north. Christian monogamous marriages are found mostly in the south. Monogamy as a secular Western institution is practiced in some degree even among educated non-Christians, but monogamy of any sort is not generally popular and, except among Christians, is rarely the ideal. The government has established a marriage ordinance, based on English common law, under which a couple may solemnize their marriage before a Christian minister or a civil registrar and which then requires them to observe European marriage customs. Marriages under this ordinance are not common because of the restrictions it places on plural marriages and easy divorce.

The mission churches' doctrinal requirement of monogamy is a chronic source of controversy and tension. Some of their adherents practice polygamy more or less openly despite the clergy's disapproval. Many of the smaller independent churches fully acknowledge polygamy as honorable and attempt to vindicate the traditional African custom by calling on Old Testament Biblical authority.

In marriage relationships, the formal principle of male dominance in the household persists throughout the country; actually, however, women in all three major areas have some degree of personal and economic independence. Trade is open to women in all areas, and some of them have gained great wealth from it, even by European standards. In the Muslim north women sell their craftwork at the markets, and their husbands must sometimes borrow money from them to run the household or to pay taxes.

Traditional marriage in all areas is a dignified institution surrounded by an involved etiquette, but in the southern groups this formality is coupled with warmth and affection. Divorce is possible for either sex, and cold, unsatisfying relationships are dissolved. Among the Hausa in the north the situation is different, the marriage relation being controlled by restraints and formal avoidance. A husband and wife may not call each other by their first names; they also must avoid their first child, who is frequently adopted by the paternal grandparents. Sometimes this avoidance, based on shame felt for sexual relations, extends even to the second and third child. By Muslim law only the husband is allowed to divorce; thus a dissatisfied Hausa wife often has to rely on a traditional religious cult to help her obtain a divorce.

The modern monogamous marriage is common only among the elite in the cities as a preferred—as distinguished from a temporary and transitional—form. In the cities both husband and wife, away from parents and village, independently cultivate a number of friendships that amount to adopted families.

Educated men still generally prefer women of a lower educational level than their own with whom their traditional male dominance is reinforced by modern educational superiority. Only rarely is a marriage of two highly educated equals to be found.

Although modern marriages in the cities could be free from the interference and scrutiny of the lineage members, both husband and wife nevertheless actually prefer to maintain strong ties with their parents and hometowns by means of visits on the holidays and frequent exchange of letters and word-of-mouth greeting from friends who happen to be traveling between the relatives. Almost without exception a young city couple plans to return to their home village at the time of their retirement.

Most of the non-Muslim traditional groups of Nigeria resemble each other in several important general characteristics of the family relationship systems. Some aspects of family relationship vary in stress and importance from group to group, and there are also wide differences of details. All groups subordinate youth to age, assign the two sexes to sharply distinct realms of activity, tend to separate the married couple as a public unit, and require a substantial bridewealth payment to be made by the husband to his bride's family in return for his rights over all children she may produce and occasionally for services she will render his household. This bridewealth is not a purchase of the wife as a chattel and, beyond the specific delimitations at the time of payment, it gives the husband no rights over his wife.

Kinship ties remain most conservative in form in areas where neither Islam nor Christianity has supplanted the indigenous religion because kinship and the pagan religions are logically interlocked with each other and with the whole heritage of custom. Ceremonies are held to propitiate spirits of recently deceased relatives and of various ancestors as remote as the lineage founders, extending as far back as fourteen generations.

Members of a specific household show obedience and deference to the household head similar in kind, though milder in degree, to the propitiatory reverence for dead ancestors. No really clear boundary distinguishes kinship among the living from the religious ties between living and dead. The spirits lend their authority to each family head, who is the formal intermediary offering prayers and sacrifices while he lives and who will become the object of a cult when he dies.

The emphasis on spiritual continuity with past generations is linked to the relation between men and land. It is the lineage, including the ancestors and those as yet unborn, that owns the land. An individual is awarded the use of the land according to his needs from the lineage head. A man has the rights to the crops he raises and, if he plants kola nut or oil palm trees, he usually has the rights over them. Since women leave home customarily at the time of their marriage, they do not have landholdings, but they usually have rights over the produce of any land they work. Ideally, land is gained through inheritance, but is possible to lease lands from persons of a different lineage. In Ibo areas land can be bought after a brief ceremony of appeasement of the ancestors and the sacrifice of a goat in their honor. The sacrifice is considered a desperate and shameful measure and is not publicly admitted.

Bridewealth payments, formerly made in commodities, were in 1971 made almost entirely in cash. The rates have been variously inflated, raising the occasional complaint that parents are primarily concerned for financial profit from their daughters' marriages.

Other relationships in the family take their cue from that of the household head. Age outranks youth, and male outranks female. Accordingly, within any one household the person of highest rank is usually a very old man, and the person of lowest rank is often a very young girl. The etiquette that governs this vertical hierarchy of rank is clear and definite, and an individual always has a sense of place with either his superiors or his inferiors.

The relationship of peers is less clear and is often a source of confusion and anxiety. Thus in the case of co-wives of a single husband, their primary rank with respect to the community is largely derived from their husband's rank, but between themselves problems may arise. Traditionally, the first wife married is the senior wife of the household and in some areas is the only woman who is called mother by all the children of the household. If the age difference between the senior and the junior wives is great enough, conflicts usually are minimal; the younger accepts the authority of the elder from long conditioning. If they are more nearly the same age, and thus more nearly peers, tensions are likely to be greater. In the same way, among the Ibo the relations between boys of widely different ages is likely to be smooth, but boys of nearly the same age sometimes fight until the dominance of one has been proved.

One traditional institution exists alongside the family and in some instances substitutes for it. This is the relationship of the special friend. Special friendships begin early in life, often in childhood and growing out of fights between boys. Special friendships are always contracted between members of the same sex. Among the Yoruba, for example, the special friend is recognized only slowly as two men grow to trust each other with their most intimate secrets. Such a friendship is regarded as closer and more dependable than a man's relation with his mother. This relationship is expressed through daily visits and talks.

This friend is entrusted with a man's burial wishes and instructions for dividing his property after his death. This apparently reduces tensions and arguments among a man's relatives, who will be his heirs. They seek out the friend to determine their kinsman's wishes in these matters at his death. Special friendship is a lifelong affair, and it is difficult to replace a deceased friend with another. Such a choice is made with great care and testing of the new prospective friend. In the north a similar, though less deep, relationship exists. The northern special friend is allowed access to the parts of the Muslim's house usually open only to family members.

Social Stratification

Each individual's sense of place in the world and his relation to his fellows reflect the precepts of traditional systems of social stratification. In a country with as many diverse traditions as Nigeria, the systems of social stratification are varied.

In each of the three major ethnic groups social mobility is possible. The degree to which social mobility is possible, however, varies with the rigidity of the group. The Yoruba in the southwest, for example, have developed a style of life in cities and are the most intensely urbanized of all African people. Most of the people living in the traditional Yoruba cities are farmers who commute to their farms, which may extend fifteen to twenty miles out from the city.

Traditionally, Yoruba life was a world of settled ranks in which everyone knew his place, but it had certain features that protected it from rigidity and provided for considerable mobility. Most Yoruba cities were presided over by kings who claimed descent from one of the sixteen sons of Odua, the Yoruba god of creation. Their claim to common origin does not imply common social structure, and there are numerous variations to be found in Yoruba kingship. Usually a king ruled not only his city and its lands but also a number of smaller towns around it, and the size of his kingdom depended on his power.

Below the king were a number of officers. In the city of Ife, for example, shortly before independence the king ruled the capital through a group of town chiefs who presided over each of the wards of the city. Each ward was in turn divided into precincts, which were in turn divided into walled compounds, each housing the members of a single lineage. The numbers of these lineage groups could range from a few hundred to over a thousand. At a certain point a large compound would divide, so that a number of compounds in the city represented the same lineage.

Aside from the town chiefs who served as representatives of the people to the king, a number of palace chiefs resided at the king's palace. These palace chiefs were spokesmen for the king and were often the first people to know his feelings on any given matter. Because of the special privileges granted to this group, many wealthy men sought to enter into it; although the palace chiefs technically derived from a single group of people, it was possible to be initiated into the group in return for a considerable payment.

An important job of the palace chiefs was to serve as spokesmen for the king to the outlying towns of the city. The palace chiefs served as the main link between the rulers of the towns, whose hierarchy somewhat resembled that of the city, and the king. The sons of palace chiefs assumed lesser roles as palace functionaries, as police and bodyguards of the king, and as judges of the court.

All offices, even that of king, were elective and depended on the support of a broad base of the people. Each functionary was chosen from among the eligibles of a clan that had hereditary right to the office. At Ife the king was chosen from a clan of over 5,000 members. Many Yoruba cities had some formal arrangement to allow for more than one eligible candidate for kingship. The king of Ife was chosen from one of four rotating "houses" within the larger lineage.

Once a king was elected, he went into seclusion in his palace and was not seen by his people. Because of this seclusion, no Yoruba king ever saw another monarch until 1925, when the first gathering of ruling Yoruba kings occurred. Thereafter, seclusion was practiced less and less; the king of Ife became the first governor of the former Western Region.

A king, although regarded in some ways as divine, could be deposed if he became unpopular. The deposed king was then expected to commit suicide; if he did not, he could be killed by cult leaders.

Ultimately the Yoruba social order, although it was divinely established and heavily hierarchical, nevertheless made it impossible for one class to monopolize all privileges and high ranks. An ambitious man could move upward in the social scale, at least obtaining any titles or privileges to which his lineage was entitled. Wealth was important, for generosity and popularity with the people were difficult for a poor man to achieve.

Although the priests of the many Yoruba religious cults are feared for their supernatural powers and have the capacity to refuse certain rites for the community, they nevertheless have low prestige and have no voice in the traditional councils. They are often poor.

The emirs of the cities of Hausa country in the north occupy their position not through divine descent but rather as descendants of the soldiers of the Fulani warrior and religious leader Othman dan Fodio, who conquered the Hausa early in the nineteenth century during a *jihad* (holy war—see Glossary) against them in order to purify their Muslim faith.

Social stratification, as every other aspect of Hausa life, is suffused with an Islamic coloring. The ruling class derives largely from the Fulani conquerors and, although these ruling Fulani have long since adopted the Hausa language and have intermarried with them, the association between the two groups remains one of rulers and the ruled. Moreover, the Fulani regard themselves as purer Muslims than their Hausa subjects.

Within this framework a further breakdown is made on the basis of occupational specialists. Ruling is regarded not as something apart but rather as the highest occupational specialty. Then, in order, come Koranic learning; large-scale trading; and special skills, such as dyeing, metalworking, or weaving. Butchers and praise-singing poets are ranked at the bottom. These occupational skills are particularly appropriate to the stratification of a relatively stable society, such as the Hausa, because most skills are passed on from father to son.

Below these strata of the Muslim Hausa are the pagan Hausa, who live in scattered villages and still follow a traditional worship of nature spirits. They farm and have few occupational specialists. Descendants of slaves have a low position, although in the nineteenth century some emirs themselves were descendants of concubines.

There is no single dynastic representative who must be chosen as emir. Some communities have alternating dynasties, and others have two houses within a single dynasty. Any qualified individual from a dynastic line might be chosen, the qualifications of the eligible individuals being reviewed by a council of men learned in the Koran. Hausa culture strongly encourages the individual to accept the status into which he was born.

The social stratification among the Ibo is not based on pride of ancient descent, like the Yoruba, or on militant piety, like the Hausa. Each Ibo man, family, or village must prove its worth before all other Ibo. This proving of worth is an immensely important theme in Ibo culture.

There is no tradition of a central political authority among the Ibo to lend strength to a formal system of social stratification. The Ibo have conflicting opinions about their origins and believe that the past is not as important a source of order in human society as the present. The Ibo philosophy of stratification is that status may be bargained for and achieved. They are highly concerned with rank, the more so because they believe that a man takes his rank with him into the next world.

The traditional social structure consisted of freeborn men and slaves. Since the passing of slavery as an institution, all men have assumed equal rights, including the right of access to a higher status. Some ways of achieving enhanced status are individual and bring about personal prestige, and others result in a shared prestige of the individual's home community.

In the past a man could gain prestige by buying expensive initiations into the societies or into the medicine society. This road to prestige is still followed occasionally, even by the educated when they retire to their hometowns after after having achieved a degree of prosperity in the cities. In more recent times, however, other means of using wealth for prestige have arisen. Along with taking title, an Ibo man of wealth is expected to own a fine house in the country, provide money for school fees and college tuition for his relatives, and give generously to his town's development fund.

Prestige for the community in the past was gained by having a large market, a famous oracle, or a special important product, such as salt. In modern times this status competition among communities has shifted its goals to schools, piped water, electricity, and medical centers. Big markets have maintained their prestige. Community prestige can also be gained through education of native sons, and education funds are maintained for sending deserving scholars to British, continental European, or United States colleges.

The philosophy of gaining prestige through improvement is called "getting up" by the Ibo. "Getting up" is a major source of concern to each village; its accomplishment through cooperative means, such as the education and development funds, is a major source of village solidarity.

The immense energy and industry of the Ibo have given them an ambivalent status to other members of the elite. On the one hand, they are admired for being modern and industrious; on the other, they are looked down on for their willingness to perform any job, even those of low status in other tribal areas. As a result, they provide strong competition for the available good jobs. Because Ibo areas generally have been economically poor and their populations have been large, many Ibo are to be found on all economic levels in all parts of the country. To the local people they have been regarded as foreigners and, as such, are not overly well liked. In the Muslim north before 1966, they were also stigmatized as pagans. This ambivalence toward the Ibo helped to set the stage of the period of crisis that culminated in civil war.

Slavery

Until the twentieth century the main type of hereditary ranking found in nearly all the traditional societies was that between the free and the enslaved. People were commonly kidnapped and taken as slaves into another society or degraded by their own people and sold away into slavery as penalty for debt or a serious breach of custom. The contrast of civic rights, work obligations, and style of living between slave and freeman was not always severe, and slaves were even adopted as kinsmen by their masters. In most places the possible assimilation of slaves into free lineages was gradual over successive generations, and some permanent stigma was apt to remain attached to known slave descent. Free status with full civic rights in one's community of residence was usually dependent on having been born there as an unquestioned descendant from its founder or founders through one of its free lineages.

Slave raiding, the enslavement of free persons for any reason, and trade in slaves were prohibited and stopped in each area as it came under effective British occupation (see ch. 3, Historical Setting). All children born after April 1, 1900, were declared to be free. The relations between existing slaves and their owners, however, were allowed to continue indefinitely, on the assumption that wholesale liberation would cause more harm than good by interrupting the agricultural economy. In the south slaves could legally be forced to return to their owners until 1914. In the north those slaves who wished to claim freedom could do so by registering at a British court, but comparatively few took up this formal option. Throughout the colonial period in the generally conservative Muslim north, descendants of slaves were still dominated economically by the descendants of former slaveowners, who controlled the land. Although the bond no longer has legal standing, in many parts of rural Nigeria, particularly in the north, former slaves and their descendants often give homage and unpaid service to the families of their former owners, who can control land for farming. Economic pressures, conservative local attitudes, and custom, rather than formal law, keep these strata distinct and their relations in line with the traditional model.

In some areas there was more than one rank below that of the freeborn. A type of indenturing or pawning was possible whereby a freeborn man could pledge himself and his services in return for a certain amount of money. Among the Ibo, for example, such a man lost part of his freeborn rights and could not engage in certain ritual activities until he had redeemed himself. Nevertheless, it was regarded as an honorable, if extreme, act and was even thought praiseworthy when a young man pawned himself in order to gain bridewealth to pay for a wife. This form of pawning oneself into a less than free status is still going on, although its practice is dwindling.

Another form of slavery among the Ibo was the cult slaves, who were dedicated by their master to one of the Ibo gods. This was usually done after a series of misfortunes or illness drove an individual or a whole lineage to consult an oracle regarding the cause of the trouble. When the oracle announced that it was caused by their sins, they could offer a slave as a scapegoat to the offended god for relief of the trouble. The cult slaves were thus living monuments to Ibo shame and, as such, were hated. At the same time no one dared to harm them because they were considered to be protected by their god and indeed served an indispensable role as priests of the deity. In their priestly functions they did not gain prestige, as did the freeborn priests, and the cult slaves were ranked even lower than ordinary slaves. They lived apart from other people, near the markets, whereas ordinary slaves shared much the same accommodations and food as their masters. The descendants of cult slaves still have about the same status; although they were among some of the first individuals in Iboland to be Christianized and some have gone on to become the wealthiest men in the area, they remain despised and feared.

Status of Women

Polygyny is practiced primarily to obtain children. Aside from childbearing and the household activities that attend the bringing up of children, a woman's time in a polygynous household is largely her own. She has more leisure than a monogamous wife has, and this leisure time can be spent to cultivate her own personal status in the community. Any money that she receives from working in her own spare time is her own, and she may spend it as she chooses. There is often bickering among co-wives, but this does not usually last long; if a woman finds her position intolerable in such a situation, she can leave and divorce her husband. In any fairly peaceful household the cooperation between co-wives outweighs the discord.

The bridewealth payment does not purchase the woman but rather claims the rights to her children for the husband, for otherwise they would revert to the wife's family. To be a fully paid wife is a source of prestige, similar to the possession of a large engagement ring in Western society. There are abuses of the bridewealth institution, and some families are more concerned for the money they receive than for their daughter's happiness, but these cases are limited. A daughter would promptly leave an intolerable marriage situation, and the bridewealth would have to be returned. The return of the bridewealth tends to slow down the divorce proceedings and gives both parties a chance to reconsider, but it does not deter divorce. It is common for a Nigerian woman to be divorced several times in her life.

In the south a woman's rank depends in part on her father's rank; later her husband's rank will give her a certain position in the community. In effect, however, a woman is part of two ranking systems: that of the man's world and that of the woman's world. In the man's world the base for all rank is a formal, paid marriage. Beyond this, to be considered highly she must be fertile, producing healthy children and caring for them well; she must also be industrious and clever at trading. Her relative seniority among co-wives is important, the first wife having great prestige from her position.

In the world of women these same traits are important, but they have a different stress. A woman's industry and shrewdness in the marketplace outweigh all the other considerations. To have prestige among other women, a woman must be clever and reasonably honest, and above all she must be successful in amassing wealth.

Among the Yoruba the elective office of "mother of the market" is an office of high prestige that is given only to a successful woman who can adjudicate quarrels and keep the peace in the market. Among the Ibo a successful woman, as her business empire expands, may herself pay bridewealth for a "wife" who can serve as combined secretary and babysitter. Such a "wife" is allowed a lover, but the children of the relationship belong to the female "husband." Such a marriage confers prestige on the successful woman because it requires considerable means to achieve.

In the Muslim north the situation is different. Women are ideally secluded in the house. They are also legal minors. Only the wealthy are able to live up to the Muslim ideals. The common people make considerable accommodation to Hausa custom, and a woman's place is tolerable, although it does not have the individual freedom of the southern marriage. In one respect the northern women are at an advantage. They do not work in the fields and can accordingly devote their full time to craftwork. These products are sold in the markets, but the more elaborate and profitable trading is the province of the men.

Women are technically lacking in rank in the north, in that they ideally have no social position outside the home. Within the home the first wife outranks the junior wives, but there is little of the woman's world outside the home where her status is defined in relation to other women. The sole exception to this is the traditional Bori religious cult, in which women achieve a temporary importance to other cult members through spirit possession.

Institutions of the north have been less affected by independence than those in other parts of the country, and this is true of the status of women. In the south many women receive some degree of Western education, but few do so in the north. At the time of independence suffrage was granted to the women of the south, but the conservative Muslim leaders in the north would not allow it.

Professional and Occupational Groups

Among the Yoruba the traditional crafts include weaving, dyeing, ironworking, brasscasting, woodcarving, leatherworking, and pottery making. There are also fishing, divining, drumming, and the compounding of medicines and spells. These are all surrounded by trade secrets and are passed on from father to son. Recent crafts have been introduced since the arrival of the Europeans, including the tailoring of men's clothing, shoemaking, carpentry, and building. These specialties are more open to the apprenticeship system than are the traditional ones and are organized much like the medieval guilds.

Women too have specialties, but their primary occupation remains trade. They also make pottery and engage in spinning, dyeing, and weaving of a cloth appropriate for women's garments. Women also work as dressmakers for other women and for children.

In the north the occupational specialties form the basis for social stratification, and membership in the craft groups is rigidly restricted. Men's crafts and specialties are extensive and varied and include hunting, fishing, building, tanning, weaving, dyeing, woodworking, blacksmithing, tailoring, and other skills. Many artisans have a high degree of expertise. Hausa leatherwork was traded widely and during the Renaissance made its way into Europe from Morocco where it came to be known as Moroccan leather rather than by its real place of origin.

Some crafts may be practiced together. For example, the specialty of Koranic scholar, although of high rank, may properly be practiced with the specialty of silk embroidery without any loss of dignity. Other specialties are ranked low but may still be highly remunerative. Butchers, for example, are placed on the lowest social stratum, but they often gain considerable wealth because their services are much in demand. No market is likely to be successful unless a supply of meat is available.

Women's specialties are less varied. They produce sweets and other foods for snacks; they may do some weaving and pottery making; they raise goats and chickens for sale; and they sell small items, such as thread and cigarettes, at the markets. Prostitutes also form a guild and are of social importance in their support of the Bori cult.

The high degree of specialization makes a web of interdependence for all the members of a Hausa city, from the highest rank to the lowest. Within each narrowly circumscribed form of work, however, there is little place for the play of personal initiative.

Craft specialties were not of great traditional importance to the Ibo. Each large lineage group was more or less responsible for its own needs, and only a few individuals, such as some cult leaders and keepers of oracles, could be said to have been truly specialized.

In modern times, however, the whole range of European specialties, from surgery to automobile repair, has been taken up, but within the framework of Western secular training and free of the hereditary or guild concepts of the Yoruba and the Hausa. The freedom from traditional restraints to take on any job that is profitable has been important in the development of the Ibo, but at the same time it has not made them liked by their more traditionally inhibited countrymen.

Voluntary Associations

Voluntary associations range in type from informal groups of members of the same lineage who band together in a faraway city for mutual support to large organizations similar to Western fraternal orders and labor unions. The modern educated Nigerians have accepted international organizations, such as the Rotary Clubs, in a manner similar to the indigenous associations. Many organizations of the same type are found throughout West Africa; over the years many have started chapters in other countries, wherever migrant workers meet to keep their ethnic traditions alive. There are hundreds of large and small associations in any large town.

In general these associations seem to have developed to fill the needs of an individual that cannot be met by the resources of his family or lineage. This lack can develop for two reasons: on one hand, a family may not have the resources such as cash to meet a member's needs; on the other hand, the family may be too far away from an individual to provide needed help, as is the case with persons who have left their home area to work in the cities.

The types of voluntary associations can be observed relevant to these two kinds of needs. There are home organizations whose members come from the immediate community, and there are extraterritorial organizations that serve an individual's needs in a foreign community or serve to keep his ties with his home village. In this latter situation, the home community may need the help of the expatriate rather than the reverse. The same organization may serve in a number of ways.

The home organizations are probably best exemplified by the Yoruba. On the simplest level are the clubs that grow out of play groups. Both boys and girls form such groups but only with those of their own sex. In most cases the group continues with the same members; since their members are about the same age, these associations have some similarities to age-grading. Members attend the feasting connected with major ritual observances of other members, parading about town after a professional drummer on these occasions. For an adult man, the number of individuals in such a group is an index of his relative influence and importance.

The clubs are probably of greatest importance to adolescents, and their strongest adherents are to be found in that age group. Meetings are held regularly and are accompanied by drinking and eating. An individual feels free to tell his troubles to his clubmates even before he relates them to his lineage members. His attendance at his club meetings takes precedence over the lineage meetings. In most instances an individual receives support from his clubmates, but in the case of serious transgression of Yoruba ways he may be punished. Such punishments are even more dreaded than those meted out by his own lineage. Expulsion from the club, the ultimate punishment, is regarded as a disaster. In his later years a man may switch his allegiance to another club as his interests change, but club loyalty remains an important item in a person's life.

In recent years Christian clubs have been formed in which the members meet to discuss the Bible. In most respects the format remains the same, and persons of similar age and sex make up a given group.

Play associations are also to be found among the Hausa, but they do not develop into lifelong groups. Members drop out at the time of marriage. The activities of the Hausa clubs are centered on playing at carrying on village life. The same officers are elected and the same discussions are held as in the adult world.

The *esusu* organization of the Yoruba is economically oriented. Members of a group pay a fixed sum at a set time. Both the amount and frequency of payment must be agreed on by all the members of the group. At each meeting the entire amount is given to one of the members in rotation. This gift supplies a means of short-term saving for luxuries or for the purchase of goods for trading and also builds up group solidarity and friendships. The size of each chapter is limited because there is a long interval between jackpots if the group is too large. Similar clubs, called contribution clubs, are to be found among the Ibo. These have a greater socializing function in that the recipient of the money is expected to use part of it to treat the others to palm wine.

Yoruba market women band together in unions to control the supply and price of the goods they sell. Each section of the market with goods over which the women have charge is supervised by a woman union official. Thus yams, flour, cloth, and various other wares are all controlled in this way. These unions are as much concerned with keeping down the dissension and bickering that arise when undue competition develops among the women as they are with controlling prices. These unions thus are not simply economic but are known by the people to be important for social control as well. Cooperatives on the European model have also been developed; one such women's group, a weaving cooperative, claims 80,000 members. It operates a clinic for children and conducts literacy classes for women.

The Ibo have probably fostered the greatest development among the extraterritorial associations. The Ibo tribal unions have spread to other ethnic groups that have large numbers of members living as foreign workers in cities away from their home area. These associations were originally developed by the Ibo to protect themselves from the hostility of the peoples in the north and west, where they had gone to work as policemen, traders, and laborers. In contemporary society these organizations help new arrivals over their period of adjustment away from home; give moral and even financial support; and keep the language, culture, and values of the people alive in a foreign setting.

Another Ibo organization of similar goals is the improvement union, which usually draws its members from the same hometown and has a close relation with it. Improvement unions are formed by Ibo and others even when they are in their own ethnic region and simply away from their homes. These groups are of great service to their hometowns in that the town members, often of the educated class, can serve as spokesmen of the new ways, explaining the modern changes that are taking place in an atmosphere of mutual trust. This allows even the remote Ibo towns a degree of modernity that many other less fortunate groups do not possess.

The improvement unions are also of immense value in helping the community to "get up." Contributions for building funds for schools and hospitals are regularly made by the improvement unions; education funds for hometown students who are in need are also maintained by them. Members of the improvement unions make regular trips back home on the holidays at Easter or Christmas, thus maintaining a face-to-face contact with the home group. In mid-1971 it was not known whether the same dynamism that set up the network of social relations throughout the Ibo area and did much to promote its vitality could revitalize that area again after the losses incurred in the civil war.

RELIGION

Religion has an important impact on the social structure. In some of the smaller, more segmented groups, religious activity is almost purely a family affair with little or no social involvement beyond that grouping. In other groups, such as those in the Islamic north, however, religion is the basis of the social structure.

Religion is not only a means of relating men to the supernatural but also a social matter; the secular contemporary world is not separated from an afterworld, but there is a living interpenetration of the two. Each exists on different planes, but both are a real part of the present. The social structure extends up to a life after death, and both worlds are understandable only in this light.

Religious beliefs and sentiment are lively throughout the country. The converts to Christianity and Islam have amalgamated many aspects of the indigenous religions into their adopted ways, and adherents of indigenous religions for their part have felt free to add Christian and Muslim elements.

Islam holds almost exclusive sway in the provinces along the northern border, known to Nigerian Muslims as the Holy North, and has substantial footholds southward as far as the coast in the extreme southwest. Christianity's greatest strength is along the coast, primarily in the extreme southeast; it is influential in pockets northward through central and eastern sections of the Middle Belt.

The indigenous so-called pagan cults still prevail in the eastern Middle Belt and in scattered rural areas throughout the country, wherever people are most isolated from urban contacts. Almost everywhere, as urban connections develop, adherents of these beliefs are gradually accepting some elements of Christianity or Islam.

Traditional Religious Forms

Indigenous religious traditions continue to exert their influence on belief and behavior because of their intimate association in people's minds with their birthplace and kinship group. Each of the peoples in Nigeria has its own distinct religious traditions tied to sacred spots in the homeland.

Beyond these local traditions and differences, which vary from village to village, taken as a whole the traditional religious beliefs of the whole country have a number of broad similarities: a remote but basically benevolent high god; below him, a populous pantheon of lesser gods who have frequent interactions with men and whose numbers constantly increase as new gods are recognized; below them, various classes of spirits who inhabit the countryside; and lower still—and closest to men—the spirits of the ancestors. Each region has its favored means of communication, of getting in touch with these beings, but they all include cult groups and either professional or part-time priestly intermediaries.

The Yoruba have the most formally elaborated pantheon and also the most numerous; estimates vary between 400 and 600 gods. Some of them are worshiped throughout the Yoruba area, and

147

others are purely local deities. Presiding over them is the high god Olorun. According to Yoruba belief, he is interested in the welfare of the people but, like the king, he is remote. Shrines are not set up to him, and prayers and sacrifices are not offered to him directly.

Below Olorun are the lesser gods, who once lived on earth but later became divine. One of them, Eshu, serves as messenger of the high god and bears sacrifices to him. For this reason offerings intended for the high god are placed at the shrines of his messenger. Although he serves the high god faithfully, he is something of a trickster to men and is even responsible for killing them in accidents. He also serves the other gods as their messenger when they wish to do good things for men. Even though the Yoruba have their own individual cult of their special deities, they often pray to Eshu not to harm them. Ifa, the god of divination, is recognized as the scribe of the Yoruba gods. He is the friend of Eshu and, like him, serves as messenger of Olorun. Odua is regarded as the creator of the earth and of all Yoruba. The Yoruba kings consider themselves direct descendants of Odua. Shango is the Yoruba god of thunder, whose attributed powers include the ability to kill people by hurtling thunderbolts at them. Persons believed to be possessed by his spirit are recognized by their ability to perform magic tricks. Shango cult meetings are particularly dramatic.

The cult of the various gods is more important among the Yoruba than the cult of the ancestors. Each person has a god who is a special protector and helper. Usually this is the same god his father worshiped, although the god of the mother may be important too. Husbands of wives perform certain rituals for each other's gods, but usually each person's worship is a private matter. It is possible to change one's cult. In the event of a series of misfortunes, when obviously divine protection is not operative, an individual may consult the Ifa oracle to determine the cause. It may be necessary to make amends to one's deity for some offense, or a change of deities may be recommended. A more dramatic occasion for change occurs in cases of spirit possession. The possessed individual must change his cult to the god who is believed to have caused his affliction in order to be relieved of his torment. Such gods are spoken of as "riding" their devotee.

The Ibo pantheon too is numerous, but the relationships of the gods are different. In Iboland the gods are more democratic toward each other. The attitude of the people is also less propitiatory and has an air of bargaining about it. If a suppliant's prayers are not answered, he may resort to threats to stop all sacrifices so that the god will starve to death.

Like the Yoruba, the Ibo recognize a high god who is also remote. The central divine figure is Ala, the mother and protector of all Ibo, and her cult is found among them everywhere.

Among both the Ibo and the Yoruba, religion serves as a socially unifying force but in different ways. Among the Yoruba, cult activity is basically individual; however, because of the descent principle operative in the choice of cult, a whole lineage may have the same cult, and that group is drawn together in their common worship. Outside the lineage, an individual's personal cult provides times for special festivals to which clubmates may be invited, creating greater solidarity with a nonlineage group. The king's cult provides for all the people and, in a way, is the rationale for his rule over them. When he fails to obtain for the people the protection they need, they can call on other cult priests to help in eliminating the king, thus permitting religion to serve even the purposes of social change.

Among the Ibo the cult of Ala draws the people together in the assurance that she is the mother of them all. Individual cults are important, as they are among the Yoruba, but the cult of the earth mother has a strong unifying force that has no parallel among the Yoruba. Whereas among the Yoruba the cult priests are usually persons of little wealth and low prestige, the Ibo regard the role of priest to the earth mother as a great privilege. Only freeborn men are eligible for that office.

The use of divination is widespread. Among the Ibo before the arrival of the British, there were a number of famous shrine oracles. These were often in remote places and were calculated to strike awe in the hearts of their clients. The oracle priests had followers in many parts of Ibo country who also served as an intelligence service. These oracle priests are no longer important. Among the Yoruba, on the other hand, the Ifa divination device is widely consulted by Christians and Muslims, as well as by pagans. Figures are derived by the practitioner for his client, and each has special verses attached that are then applied to the client's problem. These are 256 figures with four orders of verses attached to them so that the number of possible answers to a question total over 1,000. Aside from a formidable memory, the practitioner needs a high degree of interpretive skill. There is sufficient sophistication about the system so that it is consulted by many of the educated class, as well as the traditional people.

The traditional religion of the northern Hausa has largely gone underground. From all that can be gathered from the non-Muslim Hausa who still practice it, the traditional religion of the area consisted of the worship of nature spirits called Bori. Although the majority of the Hausa have become Muslim, the Bori spirits are still believed to be present as evil spirits. As with the Yoruba gods, the Bori spirits are attributed the power to gain followers by possessing them. Belief in Bori possessions entails a great deal of emotionalism, and it is largely women who are thought to be the targets of these spirits. In the often stifling seclusion of the Muslim household, the possession and its dramatic seizures provide an outlet for the women, who as legal minors are denied an active role in the Islamic religion. The Bori cult is supported mainly by the Hausa women, and its leadership is in the hands of the prostitutes' guild. The Bori spirits are as rigidly structured hierarchically as the Hausa emirates themselves. The attributes of each possessing spirit are known, and his presence is recognizable to believers in the form of behavior it forces on the possessed woman.

The Bori cult has an important social function in assisting women to obtain a divorce. Under Muslim law men may divorce their spouses by a simple verbal formula, but divorce for women is is more difficult, contrary to the general African custom. A woman desiring a divorce may seek refuge with the Bori cult leader or with her parents; she then seeks out a judge who considers her case. The Bori refuge is the more dramatic because of its association with fallen women.

Below the gods in the pagan societies are the ancestors. They form a living presence in the lives of most Africans, but the modes of interrelation with them are based on the etiquette of interaction with living family members, and it is a dubious matter to term this interaction ancestor cult. There is rarely any worship involved.

Communication with the ancestors is rarely an individual matter but is usually undertaken through the oracles. The Ibo have a deeper involvement with their ancestors than the Yoruba and the Hausa. Both the Yoruba and the Ibo believe in reincarnation, and the belief is not always relinquished when an individual is converted to Christianity. Reincarnation usually is thought to occur within one's own lineage.

Islam

Islam is a system of faith that forms the core of an extensive body of institutions, customs, and attitudes considered by its followers to be based on divine authority. Islam was founded in Arabia during the seventh century by the Prophet Muhammad, whose sacred book, the Koran, is supplemented by later Arabic writings embodying traditions of his sayings and extensive interpretative commentaries on the basic texts. Especially important

150

among these interpretations is the system of religious law, the *sharia*, which forms the basis for the duties in this life of the pious Muslim.

Islamic institutions are strongest in the old urban centers and among the ruling strata of the extreme north from Sokoto to Bornu, an area regarded as the Holy North by the Muslims. Islam was first introduced in this area about a thousand years ago and by the end of the nineteenth century had been established as the exclusive basis of state authority. The Muslim sectors of Nigerian society are conscious of belonging to the world of Islam centering on Mecca but on the whole are not well informed about distant Muslim countries.

The Arabic language of the Koran and other canonical writings, including legal treatises regarded as sacred, is usually translated just orally into the vernacular. Most Nigerian Muslims know only imperfectly the verbal formulas of prayer in Arabic. A few literates have learned by heart the initial passages of the Koran, but only an extremely small minority, with several years of education in Arabic, know the Koran well enough to understand the texts.

Islam came to the Western Sudan from the Middle East by way of the Maghrib, the block of northwestern Africa from Tripoli across to Morocco. The caravan traffic across the Sahara brought the Maghribi version of Islam to the Senegal and upper Niger River regions, where it took on a distinctive Sudanese stamp; by the fourteenth century it was transmitted eastward to Hausa country. A separate stream of North African Muslim influence came more directly across the desert to the Kanem kingdom east of Lake Chad, whose rulers, nominally converted in the twelfth century, eventually placed their capital in Bornu (west of Lake Chad), the Kanuri-speaking sector of Nigeria.

Muslim doctrine lists five fundamental pious duties, the Five Pillars of Islam: profession of faith, regular prayers, almsgiving, the yearly fast, and the pilgrimage. A sixth, a *jihad*, is sometimes ranked with them.

The profession of faith is the verbal statement, "There is no god but God, and Muhammad is his Prophet." In Nigeria generally the first part is often stated alone.

Prayers are accompanied by a series of body movements and formal positions oriented toward Mecca, performed five times a day—at dawn, twice during the afternoon, at dusk, and once later in the evening. Ritual washing of certain parts of the body is required before prayer. The greatest emphasis is given to the Friday midday prayer, at which a reading takes place in the mosque or prayer enclosure and a sermon is usually given by the prayer leader.

Almsgiving includes obligatory payment of annual taxes assessed by the emir's officials and also voluntary contributions, such as food, given to *mallams* (Koranic scholars and teachers) and students. Fasting requires abstention from all food and drink and wordly pleasures between dawn and dusk each day throughout the month of Ramadan, the month preceding the two main Muslim festivals (in Hausa, Karamar Salla and Babbar Salla).

The pilgrimage to Mecca is recommended for all Muslims. A returned pilgrim bears the honored titled Alhaji. In Nigeria only the prosperous, who increasingly travel by air, or the extremely pious, usually advanced in age, perform this obligation and gain the honor, yet Nigerian pilgrims overwhelmingly outnumber those from other West African Muslim areas.

The *jihad* may be invoked by acknowledged leaders of great piety for the defense of the faith in danger from infidels and heathens. The two clear examples in Nigerian territory were at the beginning of the nineteenth century, when a *jihad* was declared by Othman dan Fodio against the Hausa states because of their rulers' impiety, and at the beginning of the twentieth century, when it was invoked by his heirs at Sokoto against the British invaders.

In many areas of the country where the body is not traditionally covered in public, one of the initial signs of conversion to Islam is the adoption by males of the loose Muslim tunic and a turban cloth wound about the head. Amulets, small leather cases containing Arabic—usually Koranic—inscriptions, are tied to various parts of the body to ward off diseases and ensure good fortune.

The religious prohibitions against some foods, especially pork, and against alcoholic beverages are variously observed. The general ban on alcohol is applied more strictly against millet beer, because of its association with pagan rites, than against other forms.

Christianity

Nearly all known denominations are represented among Nigeria's Christians. Christians predominate among the English-speaking literates and are drawn mainly from the younger age levels of ethnic groups near the coast, particularly the Ibo, the Ibibio, and the Yoruba, who are oriented toward Western-style enterprise. Only one ethnic group, the Ibibio of the extreme southeast, has a preponderance of Christians over non-Christians. Nearly half the Ibo and a slightly smaller proportion of the Yoruba are Christian. These three groups account for the great majority of all Nigerian Christians.

The largest church is the Anglican, and its greatest strength is among the Yoruba and northern Ibo. The next largest are: Roman Catholic, with its greatest numbers among the Ibo; Methodist among the Yoruba and southern Ibo; Baptist among the Yoruba; and Presbyterian among the Ibibio. Smaller mission denominations include the Qua Iboe Mission, Church of the Brethren, Christian Reformed, Salvation Army, Lutheran, Dutch Reformed, Evangelical United Brethren, Sudan Interior Mission, Assemblies of God, Seventh-Day Adventists, Church of God, and Jehovah's Witnesses.

The number of African denominations without foreign affiliation is much larger, ranging between thirty and forty, but none approaches any of the five larger foreign-affiliated churches in size of membership and influence. Their most prevalent common feature is the acknowledgment of a church member's right to have more than one wife. Characteristic emphases among the small sects are faith healing; baptism by immersion; a large degree of congregational participation in services; the belief in the visitation of the Holy Spirit, which may throw members into a trance and enable them to speak with many tongues; and the use of African rhythmic instruments and dance to accompany hymns and prayers. They share with the more conventional larger churches a concern for the souls of the dead, emphasizing memorial services. In doctrine they follow the Bible texts primarily but may add from Muslim or pagan sources and from the mystic experiences of their own leaders.

Christianity was first introduced in the western Niger Delta by Portuguese Roman Catholic priests who visited the kingdom of Benin from the late fifteenth to the late eighteenth centuries. Churches were built, and some partial conversions were made during the period; after direct Portuguese contacts were withdrawn, however, the religious impressions left by their missionaries weakened and disappeared except for a few specific symbols.

The oldest nuclei for permanent Christian growth were formed in the early nineteenth century among the Yoruba by small groups of Christian ex-slaves repatriated from Brazil and other parts of the Americas. At Lagos and Abeokuta they appealed for clergymen to be sent from Europe or the United States; the calls were answered by British, continental European, and American religious bodies, which sent both white and black missionaries. The most celebrated black missionary was Samuel Adjai Crowther, a Yoruba who returned from Sierra Leone and was founder and, for many years, bishop of the Anglican diocese of the lower Niger River region. Ministers and teachers from Sierra Leone did a large share of the early Protestant mission work, and their descendants remained prominent in Nigerian Christian communities in 1971.

By the middle of the nineteenth century the British Methodist Church, the Church Missionary Society (Anglican), the American Baptists, and the Church of Scotland (Presbyterian) were all represented in southern Nigeria. It was not until 1868 that the first Roman Catholic mission since that of the Portuguese, the Society of African Missions, entered Lagos. By the mid-twentieth century thirteen Protestant organizations, several of them interdenominational federations, and five Roman Catholic orders were conducting Nigerian missions, mostly emphasizing projects recently opened up in the Middle Belt or even farther north. The older centers near the coast to a large degree had been transformed officially into self-maintaining churches and had become Nigerianized.

Missionary influence has been effective in various aspects of Nigerian culture, including such changes as the adoption of Western clothing and the partial acceptance of monogamy. Some of the changes for which missionaries are mainly responsible have been limited to their Christian converts, but others who were more humanitarian than strictly religious in character have affected much larger numbers (see ch. 7, Living Conditions; ch. 8, Education, Public Information, and the Arts and Sciences).

CHAPTER 7

LIVING CONDITIONS

Current statistical information on living conditions was generally lacking in mid-1971. Countrywide surveys were initiated in the early 1960s, but information covering the period after 1967 was largely limited to a particular urban area and was not necessarily reflective of the country as a whole. The civil war from 1967 to 1970 not only affected the living conditions of millions of people but also made collection of definitive data virtually impossible. Although it is widely recognized that starvation and other health problems were evident in the war areas, reliable figures for the numbers who died as a result of the war probably will never be known.

By 1971 health officials claimed that the living conditions in the civil-war torn areas had generally returned to prewar levels and in some cases been improved over those of the earlier era. Despite the official end of the emergency, however, protein malnutrition in the war-affected areas in 1970 was believed to be a continuing major concern. Minor epidemics of tuberculosis and hepatitis were reported in 1971.

Nigerian births and deaths are often not recorded, and the precise cause of death in rural areas is seldom known. Tuberculosis, parasitic diseases, leprosy, malaria, measles, dysentery, and other debilitating diseases are common; together with pneumonia and other respiratory diseases, they are the most common causes of death. Infant and child mortality is high, and estimates indicate that in the early 1960s about 50 percent of all live-born infants died before the age of five. Such deaths have usually resulted from malaria, measles, or pneumonia, aggravated by the malnutrition from which many Nigerian children suffer. Miscarriages and still-births are common because pregnant women suffer from malnutrition and are unaware of modern sanitary procedures and preventive medical practices. Estimates of life expectancy ranged from thirty to fifty years, but these were based on inexact and sporadic samplings.

Missionaries and missionary societies introduced modern medicine to Nigeria. The first hospital was established in 1912 at Ilesha by the Wesleyan Methodist Missionary Society, and for twenty years thereafter missionaries were almost alone in the fight against disease. Since the end of World War II the World Health Organization (WHO) and the United Nations Children's Fund (UNICEF) have been among those agencies that have provided much financial and technical aid for the elimination of disease and the raising of health standards. There is still a serious shortage of specialists, however, although the country has institutions equipped to train all types of medical personnel. The facilites are new and small, and the graduates are young, inexperienced, and too few.

Since the end of World War II medical science has done much to lessen the incidence and severity of the prevalent diseases that are characteristic of tropical areas. The gradual extension of pure water supplies and sanitation facilities and the development of a more intelligent attitude concerning diet are contributing toward the lessening of infection and are slowly raising the general standard of health.

The government has included substantial allocations for health and social welfare projects in its Second National Development Plan, 1970–74. The federal government maintains a coordinating function in such matters, and the state governments are responsible for local operations. Social welfare programs in 1971 remained generally limited to those employed by the government or by large business firms. The government was engaged in a survey of the indigent and planned to rehabilitate and resettle these groups in rural development projects.

Government interest in national health included cooperation in regional African health programs as well as with international agencies, particularly those interested in communicable diseases. To help combat shortages of drugs, the federal government in 1971 had entered into an agreement with Hungary for the establishment of a new drug factory in Nigeria. The government has also shown interest in adopting the use of prefabricated health facilities to relieve a nationwide need.

STANDARD OF LIVING

Any attempt to determine a desirable standard of living for Nigeria confronts the difficulty of finding a common economic unit around which to evaluate income and expenditures. Social organization is so complex and varied that it is nearly impossible to apply a set of standard criteria for the determination of a household unit. Studies made since World War II have used such a variety of criteria that it is impossible to make valid comparisons for the entire country. Economic surveys that might produce statistics usable in determining standards of living generally have not been made. The most recent statistics available showed a per capita gross domestic product (GDP) equal to the equivalent of about US$80.

Calculations based on the differences in percentages of consumption expenditure for families of various income levels in Lagos indicated that, as annual income increased, expenditure on food decreased; fuel and light expenditures remained about the same; and all other areas of spending increased. Expenditure on clothing increased at a rate comparable to the rise in total household expenditure.

In the past, consumer habits were dictated by local production and small-scale trading with neighboring areas. As contacts with Europeans increased, the pattern of consumer habits changed accordingly. In 1971 the Nigerian who had come in contact with European ways of life aspired to education and consumer products, neither of which could be cheaply acquired. Imported cloth, bicycles, radios, and patent medicines are important as status symbols. The demand for automobiles is growing, particularly among the young wage earners.

Consumers also are demanding a greater variety of goods and services. In the towns the emergent middle class of civil servants, professionals, office and factory workers, and entrepreneurs wants and buys frozen, canned, and packaged foodstuffs, electrical appliances, and quality clothing in a relatively diversified price range.

The maintenance of a system of social obligations involving elaborate gifts and considerable consumption of food and drink at feasts and ceremonies is important among most Nigerians. Beer, both imported and domestic, and imported liquors, although much more expensive, are rapidly replacing home-produced palm wine.

HOUSING AND SANITATION

Diverse materials and techniques are used in the construction of housing. Mud and wattle or adobe brick walls with thatched or corrugated metal roofs contrast with modern garden apartments and bungalows. Traditionally in the rural areas each family usually constructed and maintained its own dwelling, which most frequently consisted of several huts arranged into a compound. The number of huts depended on the size of the family. Cooking was often done in the yard, and one room of the compound was sometimes reserved for washing and bathing. Except in certain highly elevated cooler areas, the major function of housing has been privacy and protection from the tropical climate. In such a climate both ventilation and water shedding are important architectural features.

By 1967 several trends in rural housing were discernible. Previously, rural settlement was scattered and transient, but it was increasingly being concentrated along roads enabling the rural population to profit from new market patterns tied to road transport. Housing forms suited to low-density, cluster family groups were being put aside for urban forms designed for higher density, self-contained family groups. Through a series of stages, materials of nonlocal manufacture and urban use were being adopted. The practice of each homeowner building his own structure individually or with the help of friends was giving way to the employment of tradesmen and small-scale contractors.

Housing in urban areas varies from many-stored reinforced concrete dwellings to mud huts with thatched or corrugated roofs. As opportunities for earning wages increase, there is more migration to the urban areas, and carefully planned housing for the migrants cannot keep up with the flow, especially into Lagos. Much of the population of Lagos lives in a labyrinth of tin-roofed houses on narrow, twisting alleys, which have open sewers. The old cities of the north are overcrowded and disease ridden and lack sewage facilities and roads. Other cities, established in more recent times for administrative or industrial purposes, show evidences of town planning in the European manner and are relatively healthier and less congested.

Traditionally, homes were owned not by individuals but by extended families and took the form of compounds rather than single dwellings. In urban areas, however, individual homeownership is increasing, and the growing urban working class is showing a marked preference for single-family housing, either individually owned or rented. Homeownership as an investment is also becoming popular; affluent city dwellers and farmers, for example, buy houses in towns and turn them into rooming or apartment houses. For the individual who wants a home in the city for his conjugal family, however, housing is expensive and difficult to find. Provision of housing or a housing allowance is often used as inducement to attract qualified people to certain jobs.

Under the First National Development Plan (1962–68) town and country planning did not play a prominent role. At the regional government levels housing corporations were established, but their activities were limited largely to the construction of middle-class housing developments in the former regional capitals. The federal government through the Lagos Executive Development Board began limited urban renewal in Lagos. Slums were demolished in certain areas of the city, but they were replaced with shops and office buildings. Actual federal and regional expenditures did not reach more than 65 and 47 percent, respectively, of the plan allocation.

Under the Second National Development Plan about N£19 million (1 Nigerian pound equals US$2.80) were allocated for town and country planning. Of this, about 28 percent is to come from federal funds, and the remainder, from state funds. The majority of funding will not cover actual project construction but will be used for surveys, planning schemes, and the establishment of planning facilities. Grants are also provided for other projects, such as the regrouping of villages and hamlets, at a total value of N£250,000.

Under the second plan the federal and state governments will expand credit facilities for housing construction through loans to building societies, housing corporations, and various staff-housing programs. To ease the shortage of critical supplies, the government will facilitate imports of building materials. It will also continue to promote domestic manufacture of cement and other construction material.

Since World War II electrification has progressed rapidly, especially in the large towns of every state. Rural electrification has begun in Western State and probably in other states, although data were not readily available in 1971. The cost of electricity is expensive and beyond the reach of modest householders. Sometimes it is erratic, and some institutions have their own generators for emergencies. Kerosine is generally used for lighting and cooking and may be used for refrigeration. Heating is not required because of the warm climate.

Many of the prevalent diseases are attributable to unsanitary conditions. Water polluted with human and animal waste is frequently used for laundering, bathing, and even drinking. Food is sold and stored in the open, exposed to dust and flies, which breed in open latrines and unprotected waste disposal sites. In the towns, overcrowded housing and the lack of adequate water and disposal facilities are a menace to health. The slaughter of animals and the sale of meat, milk, and other food products are inspected by local health authorities in the large towns, but in rural areas such inspection is not common.

Under the First National Development Plan funds were provided for initial study of the costs of a sewage disposal system for Lagos. Additional research was provided under the Second National Development Plan for Lagos, as was preliminary survey funding for Ibadan. In mid-1971, however, the country lacked any modern urban sewage disposal system. The general method of waste disposal in rural areas was by open pit latrines and by latrine buckets that were collected by public employees at night and emptied into shallow trenches or pits. In some coastal areas waste was dumped into creeks or rivers, and in other places it was used as fertilizer. Septic-tank installations had become increasingly common with higher income households in urban areas, and most public buildings in urban areas were serviced by them.

Water is available from wells, springs, and streams. In the south high annual rainfall and a close network of rivers and streams provide an abundant water supply throughout the year. In the north, however, particularly in the northeast, a prolonged dry season can cause a serious water shortage. For this reason the government is concentrating upon drilling deep wells as a continuous source of water in the more arid areas.

By the mid-1960s piped water was available in nineteen major cities. It was not always in adequate supply and was not always safe to drink from the tap. Of the nineteen systems, only about 40 percent were listed as fed by known sources. Only in Lagos, Onitsha, and Abakaliki was the water adequately treated. Under the Second National Development Plan N£51,696,000 were allocated for water supply development. About 28 percent of the allocation was for development of the Ibadan and Lagos sewage systems; most of the allocation was for hydrological surveys, equipment for waterworks, well drilling, and treatment equipment.

DIET AND NUTRITION

In the early 1960s the supply of food was generally adequate except in times of drought when temporary local shortages sometimes occurred, usually as a result of inefficient distribution. Major food imports during the mid-1960s were fish, sugar, and milk (see ch. 14, Industry and Trade). Malnutrition was most often the result of both an unbalanced diet and a deficiency in calories. In 1966, however, the average daily caloric intake was 2,170, which represented a decrease over earlier years. The average caloric intake during the civil war dropped, but reliable estimates of the decrease were not available.

The main foods are millet, sorghum, yams, cassava, beans, maize (corn), and rice. Food consumption can be divided broadly into two nutritional areas, with grains being the staple food in the north and root crops the staple food in the south (see ch. 13, Agriculture and Mining). In the north grains and other dry food products are often ground into flour and eaten in the form of gruel or mush. Sour milk, okra, and leafy vegetables, such as spinach and sorrel, are often combined with the flour or eaten separately. The protein content of the diet generally meets the standard requirements, but it is mostly vegetable protein.

The principal deficiency in the diet in the north is the low intake of vitamins A and C, which reduces resistance to several types of infection. The shortage of vitamin A leads to eye diseases, and shortage of vitamin C, to scurvy. A greater consumption of palm oil, which could easily be imported from the south, would alleviate the storage of vitamin A, but the average northerner cannot afford to buy it. Vitamin C deficiency is being gradually reduced through the success of the government agriculturalists in persuading farmers to grow more leafy vegetables and citrus fruits.

In the south, particularly in the forest region, the staple foods are such root crops as yams and cassava, usually dried, ground, and eaten as a mush with palm oil. Because of the high consumption of palm oil, the intake of vitamins A and C in the south is above the normal requirement. The low intake of protein, 20 to 25 percent below the satisfactory level, reduces the energy of adults and has particularly debilitating effects on pregnant and lactating women. The root crops are very low in protein content. Meat consumption in the south is even lower than in the north because the tsetse fly hinders the raising of cattle. The main sources of protein in the south are fish from the coastal creeks and some cattle imported from the north and from the republics of Niger and Mali. The authorities are attempting to raise the protein intake by urging the consumption of more fish and the inclusion of peanut flour in the daily diet.

Children in both the north and the south rarely receive an equitable share of the available food. The men, by custom, have principal title to food, and women and children eat what remains. In the north malnutrition tends to retard the growth of children; in the south the protein deficiencies result in a high mortality rate below the age of five and in disease of the liver, which may be fatal later. Surveys in Lagos in the late 1960s indicated that malnutrition was prevalent, even in urban areas, and was not a function of income but of education. Children suffering from malnutrition also were more likely to suffer from diarrhea, respiratory diseases, and intestinal parasites.

There are no widespread prejudices against the eating of animal products. Little meat is eaten because it is not available or because the price is too high. Sometimes children are discouraged from eating meat or eggs on the grounds that they will probably not be able to afford them later in life. Many Nigerians allege that the price of meat is kept artificially high by the operations of cattle-marketing rings that have the effect of lowering prices to the producer and raising prices to the consumer.

Both the federal and state governments have taken an active interest in food and nutrition. In addition to studies of nutritional habits, most of which are confined to urban or small village areas, the government and university centers are sponsoring education programs on proper food habits. School lunch programs and milk programs are funded heavily by international agencies.

HEALTH

Prevalent Diseases

The most recent statistics for diseases treated were those of a Lagos health center in 1968. Diagnoses were understated in fewer than half of the cases handled. About 13 percent of all cases involved persons suffering from infective and parasitic diseases. Diseases of the skin and muscular-skeletal diseases represented 9.3 percent of all cases. Diseases of the digestive system represented 6.2 percent, and respiratory disease constituted 4.6 percent.

The most recent nationwide statistics for reported deaths throughout the country may reflect the national pattern in the late 1960s, but they did not include all deaths because many deaths are unreported. The two major killers were pneumonia and measles, at 24.8 percent and 21.6 percent, respectively. Malaria was the cause of 11 percent of all deaths, and smallpox was responsible for 11.8 percent. Other causes of death were tetanus (9.5 percent), meningitis (6.7 percent), dysentery (4.2 percent), and tuberculosis (3.9 percent).

The most recent urban figures for deaths caused by disease were limited to Lagos. The major cause of death in 1967 was malaria, at 19 percent. Infective and parasitic diseases accounted for almost 18 percent of all deaths. Measles was the cause of about 10 percent of all deaths. Between 5 and 8 percent of all deaths were caused by cancer, anemias, vascular lesions affecting the nervous system, meningitis, heart disease, and hypertension with no recorded history of heart disease.

A comparison of urban and countrywide statistics clearly indicated that measles was more prevalent as a cause of death in urban areas. This may reflect lower levels of nutrition and sanitation in urban areas, the use of different categories in enumerating diseases, or an insufficient base for one of the surveys. Comparison of both sets of data with the 1950s and 1960s would indicate at least partial efficacy of programs designed to reduce the prevalence of infective, epidemic, and parasitic diseases. One of the most striking reductions was in Guinea worm infestation in urban areas.

Measles is a serious disease among children under five years of age. Nigerian children usually develop more severe symptoms and complications than are usually associated with the disease in Europe and the United States. The disease is particularly debilitating for children already suffering from malnutrition, and respiratory problems often follow, not infrequently causing death. In 1966 there was a substantial rise in cases compared to those in 1964. Statistics for the country as a whole indicate that in rural areas the disease has a definite seasonal (dry) and biennial distribution. In urban areas the disease appears endemic at all times.

Surveys for Lagos showed an estimated 40,000 cases of measles in 1966. About 36 percent of all cases occurred among children before their first birthday, and 60 percent of the cases were among children less than eighteen months of age. This heavy concentration of cases was higher than in rural areas. The greater exposure through the practice of carrying babies on the mother's back as she attends the market and other social gatherings in urban areas may explain the prevalence of the disease among the urban young.

By the late 1960s vaccination programs had begun in the country under cooperation with the West African Regional Smallpox Eradication and Measles Control Program. The United States Agency for International Development (AID) was financing the cost of technical immunization expenses. The Nigerian government and WHO were providing medical personnel and covering local costs. In most cases both smallpox and measles vaccines were administered simultaneously. In Lagos itself 90 percent of the target population had been immunized, and the program's efficiency in 1968 was estimated at 97 percent. Programs throughout the country indicated varying rates of successful immunization. The major target for vaccinations continued to be children under five years of age. By 1970 the incidence for measles in many vaccinated areas had fallen by as much as 60 to 80 percent of that reported for unvaccinated areas.

The joint program also has been successful in reducing the incidence of smallpox in treated areas. In Western State, for example, in August 1968, after fourteen months in operation, teams had vaccinated about 10.4 million persons, or roughly 92 percent of the state's total population, with smallpox vaccine. During the first three months of 1968 there were only 17 cases of smallpox reported, in contrast to 173 cases during the same period of the previous year. By mid-1968 the occurrence of smallpox had dropped to 2 cases a month, mainly among migrants.

Malaria, a mosquito-borne fever, is the chief cause of death in Lagos and the third highest in the country as a whole. For most African adults malaria is a relatively mild disease because resistance has been either inherited or built up during childhood. Non-Africans and African children are highly susceptible and are likely to contract the infection in an acute and dangerous form.

Government control efforts have included larval and residual spraying, drainage, and vegetation clearing. Several projects were launched during the 1960s in cooperation with WHO and UNICEF.

Leprosy is most prevalent in the northern and eastern portions of the country. Projections from the early 1960s indicated that the rate of infection for the whole country was 15 per 1,000 population but reached as high as 60 per 1,000 in certain areas. There were an estimated 500,000 lepers in the country in the early 1960s; most were being treated at medical centers. The more serious cases were being treated in leper settlements run by various Christian missions. The major part of their operation was financed by Nigerian government and international agency grants. Preliminary statistics in 1970 indicated an increase in the incidence of leprosy, possibly a result of disruption of patient care during the civil war. At that time there were 2 leprosariums, 30 village settlements, and 150 treatment centers for lepers. Discussion in late 1970 centered on discontinuing isolated treatment and initiating village rehabilitation.

Before 1967 there were no recorded cases of cholera. After an initial outbreak in Guinea, the disease also appeared in Nigeria. By July 1970 cholera diagnosis and treatment centers had been established by WHO, and emergency shipments of vaccine helped to offset the initial danger. Incidence of the disease was still existent in the spring of 1971, and the Nigerian army had been called upon in certain areas to help clean out refuse areas that might be possible breeding sources for the disease.

Such diseases as the various dysenteries and parasitic diseases, which are seldom fatal but seriously debilitating, are widespread. Their high incidence reflects the low standard of public health as most are transmitted through polluted water. Both bacillary and amebic dysentery occur, but the relative and absolute incidence of the two forms is unknown. Hookworm infection is widespread, with reported infection ranges of 15 to 30 percent in various areas. Roundworm infection exists, and several kinds of tapeworms are found in northern parts of the country. Guinea worms affect 10 percent of the population in some urban areas; although this parasitic condition has been greatly reduced in urban areas, it remains a disabling disease throughout the country. Another waterborne parasitic disease, schistosomiasis, is transmitted by host snails in water. It is a serious problem in some areas and has been a target of government eradication programs.

Venereal disease of all types occurs, gonorrhea being the most prevalent. Since only those with the most severe cases register for treatment, the extent of these infections is unknown. The incidence of venereal disease in rural areas seems to be on the decline, possibly as a result of the extensive use of penicillin in the treatment of yaws.

Sleeping sickness, carried by the tsetse fly, is a major problem. Some 80 percent of the country in the early 1960s was infested with the fly, which breeds in the dense bush alongside bodies of water. The disease is most prevalent in the north and contributes to sparsity of population in the Middle Belt (see Glossary). Sleeping sickness may be dormant in a person for many years, sapping his energy and lowering his resistance to other diseases, but when it emerges quick death is certain. Large-scale clearing of infested bush and the resettlement of people from affected areas have reduced the incidence in recent years. In addition, deaths from sleeping sickness have been reduced by the activities of mobile field units, which treat victims in the early stages, when it is curable.

Tuberculosis is also a major problem, particularly in Lagos and other crowded urban centers. Active detection and treatment programs are in progress with the help of WHO and UNICEF; free chest X-rays and treatment are available at mobile units in various parts of the country.

The incidence of blindness is high, particularly in the north. The major causes are various parasitic infections caused by contact with polluted water, insect bites, trachoma and, to a lesser degree, congenital syphilis. Statistics were unavailable in the early 1970s, but in the early 1960s there were an estimated 320,000 blind persons in the country. Of these, 10 percent were children under the age of eighteen.

In May 1969 the country sponsored a week-long seminar in Lagos at which representatives of nineteen African nations were in attendance. Under the auspices of WHO and AID, the major focus of the seminar was on smallpox and measles control. Nigeria was also active in organizations of professionals and was instrumental in the formation of the Association of Psychiatrists in Africa.

Traditional Treatment

In the mid-1960s it was estimated that the majority of the population relied on traditional treatment and that those who had come to accept modern medicine were largely members of the educated classes in urban areas where medical facilities were accessible. There was little evidence in 1971 to suggest that there had been any major change. Those in rural areas who do seek medical help often do so only as a last resort, and those relying on modern medicine frequently insist on receiving injections or medications that they assume to be cure-alls.

Although the expense and inaccessibility of modern treatment are responsible for much of the continued reliance on traditional cures, the main reason is a common belief that illness and death are caused by supernatural forces that can only be countered by other supernatural forces. Traditional medical practitioners are usually persons believed to possess magical powers, and their cures include the use of fetishes and amulets, which are carried on the person or displayed prominently in the home, herbal potions or salves, and incense burning. Bleeding to let out the poison is a common practice, as is rubbing herbs into an incision or inserting leaves, roots, or bark for which curative properties are claimed. Ceremonial bathing is prescribed for epilepsy, paralysis, and alcoholism. Direct applications of herbs are used to treat eye and ear problems as well as headaches. Sores, muscular complaints, and varicose veins are treated with smears from roots. Impotence is often treated with herb potions using whiskey as a base. Other remedies exist for bronchial and venereal diseases. The infection and severe pain that may result are believed essential to the cure. The religious rites of some ethnic groups prescribe various medications on auspicious occasions for totally healthy individuals in order to prepare them for an important or difficult endeavor.

Native doctors generally fall into two categories—witch doctors and herbalists—but it is often difficult to distinguish between them. Witch doctors rely for their cures on the supernatural and on their knowledge of the social relationships in their villages. They are usually priest-doctors occupying places of great prestige and power in the community. Herbalists dispense medications based on what they consider to be scientific theories. Their status in the community is that of a skilled technician, trained in the medicinal properties of herbs. Many of the formulas used in preparing cures are secret and are passed on only to initiated persons.

In the Muslim north, the *mallam* (Koranic scholar and teacher) is usually the traditional doctor. His cures include amulets carried on the person or displayed prominently in the home, herbal potions or salves, and potions prepared from the ink washed from a written formula or religious slogan taken from the Koran. The Yoruba believe in a smallpox god—Shopona—to whom temples and a priesthood are dedicated. Sometimes the priests have survived certain diseases and therefore are assumed to be endowed with special powers.

The medicinal value of traditional remedies varies. In many cases they are harmful and may result in severe infections and death. Bush tea, made from a wild plant that grows in some parts of the country and used as a cure for numerous maladies, is found to induce a liver disease that is fatal to one-third of those stricken. A few traditional practices, however, have been shown to be useful.

The Nigerian's susceptibility to the claims of magical cures makes him an excellent target for manufacturers of patent medicines. Many of the traditional witch doctors or medicine men have become small-scale druggists and dispense patent medicines— sometimes even legitimate drugs—either outright or as part of their magical cures.

Modern Medical Services

Before 1967 both the federal and regional governments exercised definite authority in matters of health within the areas under their respective administrative control. Since the creation of states in 1967, each state has taken direct responsibility for health matters in the area under its control. Functions maintained by the federal government include overseeing standards of practice in medicine and related professions, the training of health personnel, health legislation, various advisory and inspectorate services; medical certification, laboratory and chemical services, communicable disease control, international cooperation programs, and internal coordination programs. The various state programs place major emphasis on curative services and the establishment and enlargement of facilities.

Under the Second National Development Plan the total public sector allocation for health programs was listed at N£53,811,000. About 19 percent of the total allocation was to be provided by the federal government, and the remainder was to come from state funds. The main focus of the federal health programs was in epidemic control, training, and research; about 80 percent of the federal allocation was to be for the expansion of hospital teaching facilities. Interest also was evidenced in support of the manufacture and quality control of drugs. New chemical laboratory facilities were scheduled.

Specific policies outlined in the plan included the restoration of health facilities and services destroyed or damaged during the civil war, the expansion of existing facilities, and the reorganization of hospital services. Programs for the maintenance of environmental sanitation were to be expanded, as were programs designed to control communicable diseases. The development of medical manpower was to be aided through the provision of appropriate training programs and facilities. Research facilities were to be developed.

The outbreak of the civil war in 1967 created a special administrative situation, particularly in regard to relief operations for the war-torn areas that had been held by the Biafran forces during the war. Various arrangements were used before 1969, when the Nigerian Red Cross assumed responsibility for channeling international contributions into the area. Emergency medical relief was provided through the Nigerian Red Cross by voluntary teams including the Christian Council of Nigeria, the Catholic Secretariat of Nigeria, the International Union for Child Welfare, the Save the Children Fund, and UNICEF. The number of individuals treated per month during 1969 and 1970 ranged from 20,000 to 40,000, and more than N£2 million were expended.

In addition to providing medical assistance, these groups also furnished food to persons whose means of livelihood had been disrupted by the war. The number of individuals fed by the relief program each month varied from about 500,000 in late 1969 to roughly 2.5 million in early 1970. At that time milk was being provided on a daily basis for 2 million children. In May 1970 plans were initiated to transfer the responsibility for emergency relief operations to the individual state governments.

The majority of those affected by the civil war were in East Central State, which by June 1970 had spent N£3.5 million on the rehabilitation of its inhabitants. Refugee camps for war victims were gradually closed down, and the East Central State Rehabilitation Commission established a committee to coordinate the activities of the voluntary agencies still in operation. After the phase-out of the work of the Nigerian Red Cross, equipment and supplies were transferred to the state agency. Included in the transfer were several medical vehicles, electric power generators, and limited stocks of drugs. The voluntary agencies were expected to continue their role in local rehabilitation under state guidance as long as necessary.

By 1971 health conditions in the war-torn areas were generally reported to have returned to prewar levels, and relief programs of the voluntary agencies had turned to rehabilitation. General feeding had been discontinued, but selective food programs, such as those for workers and schoolchildren, continued. Emergency medical facilities were being converted into clinics.

In 1971 there was a severe shortage of medical personnel of all kinds. Because of this shortage, many medical personnel were often required to perform tasks for which they had no training. On the other hand, many who were highly qualified had to spend valuable time and effort on routine tasks for which no one else had been trained. The major cause of this shortage was the limited number of graduate and training facilities existing in the country.

In early 1971 government officials estimated that there were between 2,400 and 3,000 doctors in the country, about 60 percent of whom were Nigerian. There were an estimated 2,000 rural health workers. The most recent statistics for medical and health personnel employed by the government were limited to Lagos and dated from 1966. At that time there were 174 physicians and surgeons and 30 senior specialists. There were 38 dental personnel, 134 nursing personnel, 546 inspectors and technical specialists, and a subordinate staff of about 1,000. The only countrywide statistics for medical personnel employed in government service dated from 1964. They showed 565 physicians, 36 dentists, 355 pharmacists, 1,600 fully qualified nurses, 330 malaria field officers, 73 leprosy control officers, and about 2,000 technicians, assistants, and supervisory personnel.

In order to relieve the shortage of medical personnel in the country the federal government has established a national committee to recruit doctors from abroad. By early 1969 the program had achieved moderate success; the Soviet Union, Poland, Yugoslavia, and India had agreed to assist in providing doctors for practice in Nigeria.

In the 1960s there were medical training programs at the Ahmadu Bello University in Zaria, at the University of Ibadan, and at the University of Lagos, and pharmacy training was offered at the University of Ife. In 1967 there were 868 students enrolled in these programs. Of these, 42 were enrolled in nursing, and 165 were enrolled in pharmacy. A breakdown of the remaining students was not available. Graduates for the same year included 52 in medicine and 35 in pharmacy. Courses in nursing and midwifery were also offered.

Under the Second National Development Plan N£8 million were allocated for the expansion of the medical schools in Ibadan, Lagos, and Zaria. The completed expansion of the Ibadan school will provide 150 to 200 doctors annually. About N£750,000 were allocated for the expansion of federal training schools in radiography, laboratory technology, dental hygiene, dental technology, physiotherapy, and dispensary training. All of the state budgets under the plan provided allocations for medical training.

A major problem faced by health officials in 1971 was the standard of management of most hospitals; within a decade well-equipped hospitals had seriously deteriorated. The situation was complicated by the destruction of health facilities during the civil war and the attempt to move from facilities designed to serve a limited segment of the population to those available to the general public.

The most recent statistical information on health facilities dated from 1967, when there was a total of 2,897 medical installations in the country. About 71 percent of these were state or local government institutions. There were 258 general hospitals and nursing homes, 47 infectious disease hospitals, 1,274 dispensaries, 42 leprosy settlements, 35 special hospitals, and 1,141 maternity centers, clinics, and rural health centers. The total number of beds in these facilities was about 27,000.

PUBLIC WELFARE

Traditional Measures

The notion of the responsibilities of kinship often extends to entire ethnic or religious groups, and in these contexts welfare assistance has traditionally been given. At the lowest level an individual is expected to turn to members of his family for financial aid and advice. In the family compound, or housing areas, resources are pooled, and the members who do not contribute material assistance perform various tasks for the household. In the villages it is easy for this mutual assistance to operate; it is also easy in the larger kinship units of lineage and clan, but in the cities it becomes inoperative because few of the members are present. People from the same province, district, or town frequently form a voluntary association in which the members act as though they share kinship responsibilities although, in fact, they may not be related.

Tribal associations were originally formed between the two world wars by the Ibo and other migrants from eastern Nigeria for self-protection in a hostile atmosphere when they went to work in the towns of the west and north. Later, home branches of the tribal associations abroad were established, and every union of the same tribe combined to form a group, such as the Ibo State Union. Such groups keep alive the individual's tie to his lineage by perpetuating its songs, history, language, and beliefs. The activities of the associations include the support of jobless or ill members and the assumption of responsibility for the funeral and repatriation of the family of a member who dies. Money is also collected for improvements in the home town of the union and for scholarships. The state unions have attained influence beyond the original objectives, especially in the field of education.

Impetus for the formation of traditional group associations has also come from those remaining at home rather than from those villagers residing elsewhere. These are improvement associations that are formed on a lineage, clan, village, village group, divisional, or tribal basis and that carry out economic, educational, political, social, and general improvement activities. Within the

170

associations a loan system is often developed to make money accessible for trade, farming, title taking, and other activities. Another means by which provision is made for meeting emergencies is the formation of a savings or contribution club within an economic or kinship group.

Two traditional welfare forms exist in addition to family institutions. Among the Muslims, almsgiving is a religious duty, and the solicitation of alms is expected. Also, a patron-client relationship may be formed. The Nigerian concept of a client is generally one who, because he does not have locally recognized kin, is helpless and in need of financial or other aid from a patron. Sometimes a person may even break kinship in order to become a client of a patron of an ethnic group other than his own for the financial advantages it presents. By 1971, however, many of these traditional forms had been eroded and transformed (see ch. 6, Social Systems).

Government Programs

Before 1961 an ordinance provided for workmen's compensation; both civil servants and those employed in certain commercial enterprises were enrolled in pension plans. The first nationwide social security provision came into effect in 1961. It provided for a provident fund plan with lump sum benefits. The plan applied to all employees of firms with ten or more workers. Casual workers were excluded, but alien workers could be covered by reciprocal agreements in effect with their home government. A special pension system existed for public employees. The program was under the administration of the federal Ministry of Labor and Social Welfare until 1967, when the National Provident Fund was placed directly under the Federal Executive Council.

The insured pays 5 percent of his earnings, and the employer contributes 5 percent of his firm's payroll. Retirement is at age fifty-five or at any age after two years of unemployment. Payment at the time of retirement, death, or invalidity is a lump sum equal to total employee and employer contributions paid since 1961 plus accrued interest.

Sickness and maternity compensation was technically provided for the first time in 1961 but did not come into effect until several years later. Benefits were available to all those eligible for social security coverage but were payable only after one year of contribution. Benefits paid were deducted from the amount of credit in the worker's account. Medical benefits were not provided directly, but free medical care was available in public dispensaries and hospitals.

Work injury compensation was first provided in 1942. All employees earning N£800 a year or less were eligible. Agricultural employees of firms employing less than ten workers, casual workers, most public employees, and persons engaged in family labor were excluded. Employers paid the whole cost through direct provision of benefits or insurance premiums. There was no minimum qualifying period. Temporary disability brought two-thirds of earnings, with a maximum of N£20 a month. Total disability brought a lump sum of fifty-four months' earnings minus the temporary disability benefits paid; the total did not exceed N£1,600 but was not less than N£300. Payments were made for partial disability and for constant attendance. Other monetary supplements included limited medical payments and survivor grants.

Several contributory retirement and insurance programs were available on a voluntary basis for those employed by government agencies and large industrial or commercial enterprises. The employee's contribution was usually either matched or approximated by the employer and was made through payroll deductions. Voluntary schemes had met with limited success. A number of enterprises had discontinued these after a trial period because the number of employees taking advantage of the plans was too small to warrant the time and expense needed to administer them.

Federal responsibility for social welfare was under the jurisdiction of the Ministry of Labor and Social Welfare until 1967, when it became the responsibility of a division of the Ministry of Labor. Each of the regions had divergent social welfare administrative structures and, after 1967 and the establishment of twelve states, attempts were made to create more parallel structures.

The concern of the Social Welfare Division covered a wide range of social services. Its concern with youth included juvenile probation services, juvenile courts, day care centers, delinquency services, and remand homes. Its concern with community development included community centers and organizations, adult literacy and education programs, and the organization of voluntary services.

There were several programs in the country in the late 1960s offering training in social service. A two-year program in adult education was offered at the University of Ibadan. A one-year preservice and inservice training program in community development was available at the Shasha River Community Development Training Center. Various short courses lasting from two to ten weeks and incorporating inservice training were provided by state governments.

Under the Second National Development Plan N£11,974,000

were allocated for social welfare, community development, and cooperatives. Slightly over 25 percent of the funds were to be federally funded, and the remainder was to be provided by the states. Governmental social welfare activities envisioned under the plan would concentrate on the restoration and expansion of social welfare activities, including the reestablishment of field offices in the war-affected areas as well as the expansion of existing facilities and opening of new facilities. A national youth corps was to be developed to provide unemployed school leavers with work opportunities on national development projects or in apprentice situations.

Private Facilities

With the exception of mutual benefit associations, private welfare activities were largely provided by religious organizations. They included the operation and maintenance of schools, hospitals, nurseries for children of working mothers, and recreation facilities for the young and the elderly. The Young Men's Christian Association (YMCA) and the Young Women's Christian Association (YWCA) were particularly active in the urban areas. Private welfare organizations were licensed by the government as voluntary societies, and their activities and budgets were periodically examined to ensure honest service.

Boy Scouts and Girl Guide associations were organized throughout the country and belonged to their respective world associations, which assisted and guided them in program development and training. Various church groups and the Salvation Army also had youth programs.

The Nigerian Red Cross originated as a branch of the British Red Cross Society. After independence it was independently incorporated and received membership in the International Red Cross. Both the federal Nigeria Society for the Blind and the Society for the Care of the Deaf helped to sponsor specialized educational programs. Other private welfare societies included the Nigeria Leprosy Relief Association, the Child-Care Social Services, the National Council of Women's Societies, and the Lagos Anti-Tuberculosis Association.

CHAPTER 8

EDUCATION, PUBLIC INFORMATION, AND THE ARTS AND SCIENCES

The country has a high proportion of university graduates compared to other African countries but a low overall level of education, despite rapid expansion of the educational base during the 1960s. The literacy rate in 1970 was estimated at 25 percent in Lagos and among some sections of the eastern states, but the estimate for the country as a whole was 10 percent. The level of literacy is being raised through adult education programs. A general shortage of teachers still existed, and a historic inequality between the educational levels of different geographical areas remained to some degree. The government's expanded educational goals and the programs being pursued by students in higher institutions of learning diverged. In general, most students prefer the humanities over technical and scientific curricula, despite the critical shortage of skilled technical specialists and the government's emphasis on scientific training.

Education was alternately valued for its own sake and as a means of preparation for future employment. The main focus of national educational policy was on the ultimate provision of formal education for every child of school age, at least through the primary level, and the creation of an adequate stock of skills needed for social and economic development. Some students were being sent abroad on fellowships, but the country had various higher education facilities, including five universities, several institutes, and a law school.

The country possesses one of the richest artistic and cultural heritages in sub-Saharan Africa. It also has produced a number of young Africans who have received international recognition for their contemporary work, particularly in literature. Traditional artistic expression was characterized by the merging and interdependence of a variety of arts and artifacts. Songs and chants, for example, were used before, during, and after the creation of a wood carving, which itself was used in a dramatization or for ceremonial purposes. The arts were an important element in the traditional social, economic, and political life of the Nigerian peoples. Many songs, dances, images, and stories were used to introduce children to the values of their parents, thus creating community cohesion. Although numerous forms of traditional artistic expression existed in 1971, these forms were increasingly becoming cut off from the former social functions.

Contemporary artists tend to experiment in several media and to follow eclectic styles. Some have been trained locally, either academically or in guilds; some have had most of their training under traditional local guilds; and others have attended schools abroad. Many hold teaching positions or earn income through part-time work but, with gradual development of a local market, an increasing number support themselves entirely by the sale of their art. Some contemporary artists incorporate traditional themes into their works, but others prefer to work mainly in styles, media, and techniques that are internationally popular.

During the 1960s the government became increasingly involved in public information activities. After the civil war its major public information objectives included the fostering of national harmony and reconciliation, the mobilization of public support for national development efforts, and the projection to the outside world of what was felt to be an accurate national image.

The country had one of the most highly developed public information systems in tropical Africa. Government controls existed either through direct ownership by the federal and state governments and public corporations under the Ministry of Information and Labor, as in the case of radio, or through regulatory acts, as in the case of the press. There was a variety of newspapers and periodicals, and several well-established firms were publishing books. The total circulation of newspapers declined during the 1960s as a result of economic reverses and consolidation, but twenty-one dailies continued to circulate in mid-1971. Africanization of the publishing field was in progress, but considerable European influence remained.

Communications facilities in 1971 were insufficient to meet national needs, but efforts to expand and improve these services were included in the Second National Development Plan, 1970–74. Although there were post offices offering full services in most of the larger towns, a majority of the facilities in other areas provided limited postal services. A shortage of telephones and limits on the system's operational efficiency posed a major communications problem.

EDUCATION

Christian missionaries introduced Western forms of education into most of the country in the mid-nineteenth century, although sporadic attempts had been made as early as the sixteenth century with the first Portuguese contacts. Until the coming of the missionaries, only the Muslim north had a formal educational system. A small number of boys attended essentially religious schools. where they studied the Koran and gained a basic literacy in arabic script. By 1913 there were some 19,000 Koranic schools with about 135,000 students.

The first mission school was founded at Badagri in the former Western Region in 1842, and by 1859 the number of mission schools had risen to fifty. The early missionary teachers were interested mainly in developing a literate population with a Christian-oriented elementary education. They adopted the British system and methods and introduced a strong bias toward classical education, paying little attention to vocational and practical training or to secondary and higher education.

The British administration in Lagos Colony first concerned itself with education in 1877, when it approved an annual grant to support mission schools. In 1886 the administration passed an education ordinance that granted the government of the colony some control over the operation of schools, but it was not until 1899 that the government founded a school. The school, an establishment for Muslims, was much needed because only Christian schools were operating in the Lagos area. By 1908 the number of government-operated schools had risen to forty. In 1909 a secondary school, King's College, modeled on the English public (United States private) school, was founded by the government to give boys a general secondary education and to train them for the civil service.

In the period between the two world wars public interest in education was heightened in the south by a gradually developing intellectual elite and by a growing national consciousness. Kinship and tribal unions, which sprang up in the main urban centers in the 1920s, played a dynamic role in the improvement of education in rural areas. Small local unions built a few primary schools in their home areas and sponsored scholarships to secondary schools; larger federated unions financed the construction of secondary schools and sent promising young men abroad for higher education. A substantial number of educated members of the elite were supported through all, or part of, their university training by their local unions.

Because of the increased public interest in educatio_i, the government began to take a more active part. During the 1930s mission schools came increasingly under the control of the colonial government through inspection and conditional financial assistance. Until 1945 religious bodies operated 99 percent of the schools and taught more than 97 percent of all pupils. Except in the Muslim north, where colonial policy excluded missionary activity, the government preferred to assist these schools financially and to supervise their standards rather than to develop an extensive school system of its own.

During the civil war the educational process was largely suspended in East Central State. All primary and secondary schools were closed from July 1967 until March 1970, as were classes at the University of Nigeria at Nsukka.

In 1971 the educational structure consisted of a very broad base of primary school students, a very small secondary school population, and a smaller postsecondary school population in relation to the whole; this was a pattern found in many African countries. The type of education most sought after was an academic, general education leading to a good position in the civil service. Technical education, critically needed to develop manpower for national development, has been neglected, and only very recently have the rapidly increasing job opportunities for technicians created a demand for such education. Once a Nigerian begins his postsecondary education, it is likely that he will continue until he has received one or more degrees. The difference in salaries for graduates and nongraduates is so great that every effort is made to complete the program.

Administration and Financing

Jurisdiction over education has been variously the responsibility of regional, state, or local governments since 1940. Federal government jurisdiction, exercised through the Ministry of Education, establishes the provision and regulation of education in Lagos; the setting of uniform basic curricula and examinations throughout the country; the setting of standards for the certification of teachers; and the maintenance of a number of institutions of higher learning, such as the University of Lagos and the University of Ibadan.

Local government authority is exercised through state education ministries, which are responsible for the establishment and operation of government schools, supervision of and financial assistance to nongovernmental schools, certification of teachers, and implementation of the basic curricula. In addition to those operated under state authority, schools may be established by voluntary agencies such as missions and by private individuals with the permission of the state ministries.

Since independence, expenditures for education have comprised an increasing share of federal and state budgets. Although the civil war disrupted plans to expand the educational program, both federal and state governments have subsequently indicated a willingness to sacrifice other projects to provide needed educational funds. The proportion of federal to state current expenditures was not readily available.

Under the Second National Development Plan the federal and state governments have coordinated financial and planning responsibilities. One of the major objectives of the plan, envisioning specific federal assistance, is the restoration and reactivation of facilities disrupted by the war. Coordinated planning is provided for all levels of the educational system and for the further development of teacher training facilities, adult education programs, and financial aid to students. In 1968 an estimated 18,000 students were enrolled in technical schools. Plans for expanding technical training emphasize the training of qualified teachers and an interchange of students between technical institutions in the various states.

Under the plan a total of N£138,893,000 (1 Nigerian pound equals US$2.80) has been allocated for the public sector capital expenditure on education. Of this amount about 65 percent is to come from state sources, and the rest, from the federal budget. About 30 percent is specified for investment in university-level education, and 24 percent is to be for primary-level schools. Secondary-level education will receive about 20 percent of the total; 10 percent will go to improved teacher training facilities; 9 percent will be devoted to technical education; and 7 percent is specified for other educational programs.

All schools are subject to periodic inspection by state government inspectors; if equipment and staff meet government standards, they retain their eligibility for financial aid. A fairly common practice in rural areas is for a community to raise funds for the construction of a school and to invite a voluntary agency to operate it with the funds received from the government.

Many of the qualifying examinations offered at various stages of education are administered independently of the regular school system by the West African Examination Council. The council, an independent body founded and authorized in 1952, issues standard, universally accepted education certificates to students in all former British West African territories.

Primary Schools

As early as 1952 the regional governments began to advocate plans for free universal primary education. Such plans had mass appeal because education was regarded by many people as the first step toward political, social, and economic development.

Plans were initiated in 1955 by the government of the Western Region for free universal compulsory education, but financial limitations eliminated the compulsory requirement. The federal government began free primary education in Lagos in 1955. The government of the Eastern Region began a similar program in 1957 but had to reinstate the requirement for fees in 1958. Under the First National Development Plan (1962–68) the establishment of free universal education was envisioned, but the goal was never attained. Plans for preschool programs were advocated but were discontinued after 1961. In 1971 primary education was free in Lagos, Mid-Western, and Western States; the cost was partially subsidized in the eastern states. The goal for primary-level enrollment under the Second National Development Plan was 50 percent of all eligible children. This goal was a 20-percent increase over 1971 enrollment figures.

Although educational programs were expanded during the 1950s, they resulted in the creation of new problems or in the complication of old ones for the 1960s. Stress was placed on training in the arts and humanities and on education for its own sake rather than on its practical and technical applications. Specialization began in the middle years of secondary school, and only a narrow range of subjects was offered. The quality of primary education deteriorated. The number of students who left school before receiving certificates had reached 63 percent for the country as a whole by 1965. Although the rate was only 12 percent in Lagos, it was as high as 73 percent in certain rural areas. As a result, there was a shortage of people with intermediate skills and an excess of those with higher level skills (see ch. 4, Population and Labor).

Attempts had been made to create greater educational equality on the primary level, but inequality of access to the secondary level (based mainly on economic factors) had proved difficult to eliminate. Aspirations stimulated by the educational process, moreover, led certain young people away from rural areas to urban centers, where they hoped to find suitable employment. Many were unable to find positions that fulfilled their expectations and were living in highly crowded urban areas, suffering privations they would not have sustained in their rural villages. Although these problems had not been solved by mid-1971, the government was aware of the need for curriculum reform and for better planning coordination.

In 1966, the latest period for which reliable countrywide statistics were available, children attended classes in 14,907 primary schools (see table 2). Although this figure indicated a 3.8-percent reduction in primary schools since 1960, it probably reflected consolidations of smaller schools. By 1968 enrollment had risen to an estimated 3.1 million pupils, or about 30 percent of all children of primary school age. Voluntary agencies—missions, private individuals, or community organizations—provided schooling for various segments of the primary age group in each of the states. Most primary-level teachers were Nigerians, and many of them had little more than a primary education themselves. The length of primary school programs has varied from area to area over the years. The course lasts six years in the eastern states and in Mid-Western State, seven years in the northern states, and eight years in Lagos State and in Western State. Most children enter primary school at the age of seven, although the age spread for entry varies from five to ten.

Classes in the lower grades are conducted in the predominant local language of the area, and English is introduced usually in the third or fourth year. In Lagos, where the mixture of various ethnic groups is common, English is the primary language of instruction; local languages are used for supplementary instruction. Other subjects taught are geography, history, arithmetic, nature study, hygiene, cooking and needlework, handicrafts, religious studies, physical education, handwriting, and drawing. A syllabus provided by the state government and keyed to a Nigerian background is followed by each school. Textbooks adapted to the Nigerian educational system have largely replaced earlier books of British origin written for British pupils. The First School

Table 2. Number of Schools, Students, and Teachers in Nigeria, Selected Years, 1960, 1966, and 1967

	Primary	Secondary	Technical	Teacher training	University
Number of Establishments:					
1960	15,499	n.a.	n.a.	n.a.	n.a.
1966	14,907	1,350	73	193	5
1967 [1]	9,043	n.a.	n.a.	n.a.	5
Number of Teachers:					
1960	96,317	6,889 [2]	359	1,496	n.a.
1966	91,049	11,664	789	1,837	1,328
1967 [1]	57,866	6,946	986	1,079	n.a.
Number of Students:					
1960	2,912,617	135,364 [2]	4,741	26,212	2,659
1966	3,025,981	211,305	15,059	30,493	9,105
1967 [1]	1,778,976	137,242	16,214	19,310	8,076 [3]

n.a.—not available.

[1] Figures (except university) represented total for only nine of the twelve states.
[2] Commercial schools included with general education.
[3] The closure of one university during this period reduced figures from slightly over 10,000.

Source: Adapted from *Statistical Yearbook, 1969*, Paris, United Nations Educational, Scientific and Cultural Organization, 1970; and Republic of Nigeria, Federal Ministry of Information, *Second National Development Plan, 1970–1974*, Lagos, 1970.

181

Leaving Certificate is awarded at the close of the program and is a prerequisite for admission to secondary schools or teacher training institutions.

Secondary Schools

Expansion on the secondary school level has not kept pace with the rapid growth of primary education, largely because there are not enough qualified teachers. In 1966 there were 1,350 secondary schools; enrollment in 1968 was estimated at 215,000 students. Most secondary schools are modeled after the British grammar schools, offering a five-year academic education leading to the West African School Certificate (WASC) examination. It consists of a series of tests in prescribed subjects, six of which must be passed to obtain the certificate, which is graded I, II, or III.

All instruction in Form I through Form V is conducted in English. Courses taught include English, literature, religious knowledge, mathematics, history, geography, general science, physics, chemistry, biology, and physical education. In addition, a school curriculum may include Latin, French, local languages, higher mathematics, agricultural science, various crafts, and home economics.

Lagos, Western, and Mid-Western States have a system of secondary modern schools with a three-year course directed toward a practical education. The schools are designed to attract students who wish a postprimary education but cannot afford the expense of attending residential secondary schools, and their curriculum includes English, history, geography, civics, arithmetic, physical education, agricultural science, child care, needlework, and cooking. A great number of girls attend these modern schools in preparation for clerical and secretarial positions; their course of study includes bookkeeping, accounting, typing, and shorthand. After completing a secondary modern school, a student may sit for the General Certificate of Education (GCE) examination administered by the West African Examination Council.

Admission to any secondary school depends upon passing an entrance examination. Most of the government schools have adopted a common entrance examination administered and graded by the West African Examination Council. The examination is conducted once a year, and candidates are advised through newspaper advertisements and public notices as to the date. All holders of the First School Leaving Certificate are eligible to sit.

All secondary schools are residential, a fact that causes much complaint among Nigerians because of the expense to parents and limitations on enrollment imposed by dormitory space. Uniforms are worn by all students while in residence, both on and off school grounds, and school colors are proudly worn by undergraduates and graduates alike. A very strong sense of loyalty to school and a competitive attitude toward other schools are developed by most secondary school students.

The Sixth Form, a British institution, is a two-year course designed to prepare the secondary school graduate for university study. Admission to the Sixth Form is open to holders of a Grade I or Grade II WASC or the equivalent GCE who have passed an entrance examination. Automatic promotion from secondary school to Sixth Form in the same school is not possible. The subjects taught in the Sixth Form are the same as those taught in the secondary schools but on a more advanced level.

At the end of two years a student is qualified to take the West African High School Certificate (WAHSC) examination, successful passage of which qualifies him for university entrance. The examination consists of two essays on general subjects and tests in three major subjects, either in the arts or the sciences. The WAHSC is awarded to candidates who pass all the tests. A candidate who passes the three major subjects but fails the general test receives a Principal Level Subjects Qualification diploma.

Higher Education

In 1971 five universities offered courses leading to degrees at various levels in the humanities and in technical fields of specialization. The oldest was the University of Ibadan, whose operation and financial support were the responsibility of the federal government. It was founded in 1948 as the University College of Ibadan (UCI), and degrees were originally awarded by the University of London through a special program of the British and Nigerian governments. In 1962 UCI became the University of Ibadan and began awarding its own degrees.

The academic departments are divided into the faculties of agriculture, forestry, and veterinary science; arts; economics and social studies; medicine; science; education; and extramural studies. In addition, there are the institutes of African studies, librarianship, and child health and the Nigerian Institute of Social and Economic Research. English is the primary language of instruction, as it is in all Nigerian universities. Courses of study leading to a bachelor's degree last three or four years, depending on the student's previous preparation. All departments offer programs leading to advanced degrees at the master's and doctorate levels. Master's degrees are usually awarded after an additional two years of study, and a doctorate degree may be obtained usually after three years.

Admission to the university is by competitive examination. Students who hold a WAHSC or a GCE (Advanced) are admitted directly into degree courses, whereas those holding a WASC or GCE (Ordinary) must first take a year or two of preliminary courses. The selection of students for any institution of higher education is made extremely difficult by the widely differing standards of the lower schools.

The University of Nigeria at Nsukka, East Central State, was opened to students in 1960 after preliminary recommendations for its establishment were made in 1955 under the joint auspices of the British Inter-University Council and the United States Agency for International Development. The institution is patterned after a United States land-grant college. It is supported largely by funds provided by the government of East Central State. Michigan State University played a prominent role in the establishment of the Nigerian institution and has continued close academic ties with it.

Academic departments are divided into the faculties of agriculture, arts, education, engineering, law, science, and social studies. Most degree programs last four years for students admitted with the WASC or its equivalent. The university does not have a program for the awarding of advanced degrees.

Ahmadu Bello University in Zaria, North Central State, was founded in 1962 on the site of the former Nigerian College of Arts, Science, and Technology. Standards of the university are intended to be equivalent to those of London University. Its academic departments consist of the faculties of arts, architecture, law, science, agriculture, engineering, and Arabic and Islamic studies. Bachelor's degrees are awarded after courses of study lasting from three to five years. The university does not award graduate-level degrees, although there were indications in 1971 that it intended to do so.

The University of Lagos was established in 1962 by an act of the federal government. Its operation and financial support remain a federal responsibility. Academic departments consist of the faculties of arts, business and social studies, law, medicine, education, engineering, and science and the Institute of Petroleum Studies. Bachelor's degrees are awarded after courses of study that vary from three to five years. There are no programs for advanced degrees. Night courses are offered by the faculties of arts, business and social studies, and law.

The University of Ife in Western State was established in 1961. It is located on a 16,000-acre campus at Ile-Ife, formerly a center of early African culture. Academic departments consist of faculties of agriculture, arts, economics and social studies, law, and science. Course work leading to a bachelor's degree lasts three years. The Institute of African Studies, which began functioning in 1963, has attracted research scholars interested in African studies from all over the world.

In 1968 an estimated 8,600 students were enrolled in universities, compared with 2,659 in 1960. It was estimated that total enrollments would have been over 10,000 had not the University of Nigeria been closed as a result of the civil war. About 12 percent of all university students were women, and about 2 percent of all students were foreign nationals, mainly Africans. Approximately 39 percent of the students were following courses of study in the humanities, education, and fine arts. About 21 percent were in law and the social sciences; another 15 percent were in the natural sciences; about 22 percent were in engineering, medicine, and agriculture; and the remaining 3 percent were following unspecified programs. In 1966 there were 1,328 teachers, giving a student-faculty ratio of about seven to one.

In 1966, the latest year for which reliable statistics were available, 1,203 persons graduated from Nigerian universities. Of this number, about 42 percent had received degrees in the humanities, education, and fine arts; about 27 percent, in law and the social sciences; 16 percent, in the natural sciences; and 15 percent, in medicine and agriculture. Large numbers of Nigerian students go abroad each year in search of higher education. Most of them go to the United Kingdom, the United States, or European countries.

The cost of higher education often is extremely high, but the practical and prestige value of a degree is so great that in order to be able to complete their studies many students borrow money at high interest rates. A variety of scholarships sponsored by the government, foundations, and private individuals is available for the more gifted, but educators still lament the number of promising students who must give up their studies because of lack of funds.

SCHOLARSHIP AND INTELLECTUAL ACTIVITY

The introduction of Western education in the nineteenth century to a selected segment of the indigenous population led to the development of a small but well-qualified intellectual community by the end of the century. Most had received their initial education from a mission school, and until the 1960s those receiving advanced degrees had studied abroad, particularly in the United Kingdom. Intellectual activity of the educated elite centered first on literary movements, which brought them some international reputation; later they became involved with nationalist activities (see ch. 9, Government and Political Dynamics). By the late 1960s there were two degree holders for every 1,000 people in the country.

In 1970 three major institutions supported research: the federal government, universities, and learned societies. In 1966 these organizations expended about N£9.7 million for some 4,000 scientists and researchers engaged in various research and experimental development programs. About 33 percent of the research was in medicine, and 30 percent was in engineering and technical fields. Other efforts were devoted to the exact and natural sciences, agriculture, and the social sciences. There were also about 7,000 technicians engaged in research projects.

The federal government operates eleven major research institutes. A number of these are devoted to agricultural research, such as the Department of Forestry Research at Ibadan, the Fish Service at Lagos, the West African Coca Research Institute at Ibadan, and the Nigerian Institute for Oil Palm Research near Benin City. Others, such as the Nigerian Institute for Trypanosomiasis at Kaduna, are active in the field of health. The Nigerian Institute of Social and Economic Research associated with the University of Ibadan provides the government with the findings of work aimed at advancing various aspects of national development. Technical assistance is made available to industry by the Institute of Industrial Research.

In 1970 there were thirteen major learned societies in the country. Typical examples were the Nigerian Economic Society, which sought the advancement of Nigerian social and economic knowledge; the Nigerian Institute of International Affairs, a nonpolitical forum for the study of international relations; and the Science Association of Nigeria, which fostered the development of science.

A number of these groups published journals and professional periodicals. Several scholarly journals were issued by the various universities and organizations such as the Historical Society of Nigeria and the Nigerian Library Association. These provided members of the intellectual community with an opportunity to publish the results of their research efforts. Nigerian research, particularly in the fields of sociology and medicine, has received recognition in a number of international journals.

The first libraries founded in the country were specialized institutions, such as the Geological Library, which was established in 1919. The first public library was established in Lagos in 1932, and by 1969 the number of such facilities had increased to twenty-five, with a total book stock of some 350,000 volumes. Eight libraries attached to colleges and universities contained a total of 424,000 volumes; the largest of these belonged to the University of

Ibadan, which alone had 250,000 volumes. In 1970 the National Library in Lagos had a collection of 40,000 books.

LITERATURE

Traditional oral literature can be classified basically according to the formality of the occasion at which it was recited. The most formal level included historical sagas and long chants that were usually presented as parts of expanded dramatic productions. These long chants were often recited by a masked leader, who intoned the narrative in a disguised voice. Frequently they were parts of an ancestor ritual; others signified the reaffirmation or transferral of an inherited office. Sometimes they reflected moral issues.

At the intermediate level there were numerous folk tales and stories told to children by their elders as evening entertainment; these forms also provided a means of social interaction and the perpetuation of traditional values. At the least formal level were proverbs and riddles, used in everyday speech to reinforce a point the speaker wished to make.

Although pictographs and ideographic scripts had been developed for several of the local languages before the arrival of the Europeans, the rudimentary forms of these scripts did not permit the production of written literature. Arabic script was used in some of the northern areas, but its use was limited to a small minority for religious and administrative purposes. After the arrival of the Europeans phonetic adaptations of roman script were developed for several of the local languages, primarily to facilitate the advance of Christianity. The small number of individuals literate in these scripts limited the development of written local literature.

Some poetry in local languages has been written. One of the major contributors has been Ikponmwosa Osemwegie, whose works appeared in 1965 in *Poems in Bini*. The book contains narrative poems that follow Western poetic forms, poems of prayer and praise that resemble traditional forms of Ibo songs, historical poems based on stories and sacred myths, and philosophical poems on Bini society.

The development of local literature in English was largely confined to the twentieth century. Most writers supported themselves by means other than their writing and were often associated with religious and academic institutions or one of the public media. The first works were historical or political in content. Included in the political works were *Liberia in World Politics* (1934) and *Renascent Africa* (1937) by Nnamdi Azikiwe, who later became prime

187

minister. Continuing in this tradition were historical-political accounts, such as the first of a two-volume autobiography by Azikiwe that was published in 1971.

The production of popular literature began in the 1940s with the rise of short, colorful stories printed in pamphlet form or published in such periodicals as *Black Orpheus* and *Odu*. Cyprian Ekwensi pioneered in this style of writing with such works as *When Love Whispers, Ikolo the Wrestler,* and *Other Ibo Tales.* The first of such writers to attract attention in Europe was Amos Tutuola. His *Palm-Wine Drinkard* drew heavily on Yoruba folk tale models and utilized colloquial language. The first novel published in English by a Nigerian and the first Nigerian work to be published outside of Africa was Ekwensi's *People of the City* (1954). It marked the entrance of the novel as a major literary form in the country.

By the late 1960s two trends had developed among Nigerian novelists. The first trend was set by the veteran novelists who had gained international recognition. They increasingly focused on urban satires that attacked corruption and social injustice. The works of Chinua Achebe, an Ibo considered by most authorities to be the foremost Nigerian novelist, included *Things Fall Apart* (1958), *No Longer at Ease* (1960), *Arrow of God* (1964), and *A Man of the People* (1966). The most recent of these reflects the collision of African and Western cultures. T. M. Aluko's works include *One Man, One Wife, One Man, One Machet,* and *Kinsman and Foreman.* His latest work was published in 1966.

The second and more recent trend to develop was among a number of younger novelists, most of whom were Ibo, who produced the early work of men such as Achebe but showed little interest in contemporary urban life and its problems. Included among these authors and their works were *Highlife for Lizards* by Onuora Nxebwu, *The Concubine* by Elechi Amadi, *The Only Son* by Jon Munoye, and *Effrru,* the first novel in English by a Nigerian woman, Flora Nwapa.

THE DRAMATIC ARTS

Early dramatic performances were basically renditions of traditional oral literature known as "masquerades" because of the use of masked dancers or carved figures carried by the performers. The most highly developed dramatic forms were found among the Yoruba and other southern peoples. Traditional Yoruba theater developed from rituals associated with ancestor cults and were refined through performance at the court of the *oba* (king). By the mid-eighteenth century professional touring groups specialized in traditional dramatic presentations in various regions.

Theatrical productions required the cooperation of four guilds, membership in which was often hereditary; the four guilds were associated with dancers, carvers, costumers, and drummers. In 1971 professional theatrical companies, such as the Agbebijo at Oshogbo, the Aiyelabola at Ibadan, and the Ajangila at Iragberi-Ede, continued the tradition of the earlier touring groups. They protected their acts through a professional association, which had its headquarters at Ibadan.

Although in 1971 there was considerable experimentation with contemporary Western theatrical forms, many theatrical presentations continued to be inspired by traditional dramatic forms. Opening and closing choruses were used, but there was little concern for the ritual aspects of traditional theater. The best-known English-language playwright in the country, Wole Sokinka, originally structured his works along Western patterns. Included were *The Swamp Dwellers*, *The Lion and the Jewel*, and *The Strong Breed*. His later works of the 1960s, *A Dance of the Forest*, *The Road*, and *Kongi's Harvest*, follow traditional forms and reintroduce an interest in the ritual aspects of the theater.

Traditionally, Yoruba theater was composed of at least three parts. It opened alternately with a chant in a high-pitched voice; a chorus praising individuals, groups, or settlements; or a sketch of a village personality or character-type. A dance, sometimes including acrobats, followed; it often had social or ritual significance. The drama that was the third section of the presentation was often the improvisation of a leader or animator. Often, but not always, the drama was followed by a reappearance of the chorus or chanter. When the performance was presented at court, a chorus was often provided by the women in residence at the palace.

The drama consisted mainly of episodes, recitations, and tableaux. There was no continuous narrative, and the sketchy plot was carried through these elements by metaphors and symbolic allusions. The resulting gaps were filled by the imagination of the viewer. The drama was usually produced outside in the round and needed no setting, since it did not attempt to depict scenes of daily life.

The actual structure and tone of traditional theater were set by the occasion for which it was presented. Some theatrical presentations were performed for entertainment, but usually they were tied to the celebration of some festival, often commemorating various deities or lineage ancestors. Comic forms often were used, and presentations were paid for by a wealthy patron to enhance his social prestige.

Festivals usually lasted from several days to several weeks and included a complex series of acts, such as the creation of masks, costumes, and other objects to be used in the festival; the sending of invitations; and various dances, songs, and rituals connecting major ethnic events. Originally they were attended by members of the local lineages and implied allegiance to a local political authority or deity. In recent times they have increased their following to include tourists, followers of Christianity and Islam, and visiting relatives who have moved to distant urban areas.

The Olosunta festival is typical of the shorter festivals. It lasts five days and is performed annually in July in honor of Ikere-Ekiti, the Yoruba god of rock, who controls fertility. Each day offers a different kind of activity and many opportunities for prayers of thanksgiving and petitions for future plenty. The spectacular Odum festival in the Niger Delta area is designed to propitiate Odum, the traditional river god. The preservation of such festivals in their traditional forms has become the concern of various organizations. Since 1967 an annual festival has been held at Ife. Designed to stimulate traditional expression, the Ife festival is sponsored by the Institute of African Studies at the University of Ife and the Ife Cultural Arts Center.

MUSIC

Music, including songs, choruses, small instrumental ensembles, and rhythmic percussion backgrounds designed to accompany dances and chants, played an important role in rural areas and has provided the bases for the development of local modern music in urban areas. Several cultural organizations in 1971 were actively seeking to stimulate the preservation of traditional forms of music, and the staff of the Nigerian Broadcasting Corporation was forming a collection of recorded traditional music.

Singing was the most developed and varied traditional musical form. Songs were sung individually, by choruses, or in combinations of the two. Singing was an inherent part of the performance of certain rituals, but often it was introduced spontaneously whenever it was felt appropriate. There were songs for groups, individual and group labor, sports, children's games, marriages, and funerals. Most ethnic groups had their own war songs, songs of praise, and lullabies.

Each region had its individual musical variations. In the south the Ibo did not have full-time musicians, and music was provided by the more talented nonprofessionals. Among the Hausa and other Muslim communities in the north music was generally provided by professional musicians, who supported themselves by their playing. They were separated into guilds according to the types of music they played. Musicians in the south obtained status from factors other than their musical performance. In the north,

190

however, musicians held social status as a group and according to the kind of music they played.

With the exception of ancient rites associated with the Bori spirit possession cult, music in the north was almost entirely secular (see ch. 6, Social Systems). Music in the south was either secular or religious and often both.

In the north there was a greater variety of musical instruments than in the south, and the use of specific types of instruments was more rigidly restricted to certain types of social occasions and ceremonies. The same restrictions applied to different melodies and drum rhythms. The more common instruments in the south included the raft zither; the thumb piano; metal gongs; cymbals; rattles; wind instruments made of gourds, wood, or animal tusks; and a variety of drums, including slit gongs and ceramic pots covered with animal membranes. In the north, in addition to similar basic instruments, there were more complicated ones, such as a flute designed to be sucked instead of blown, the *kabari* (a brass trumpet), and a fifteen- or eighteen-string instrument known as a *molo*.

Western forms of music were first encountered by Nigerians in the late nineteenth century, largely as a result of activity by Christian missionaries. Major exposure of any significant portion of the population to Western music, however, did not occur until the 1930s, when the country's first radio stations were established and people gained greater access to privately or communally owned radio receivers. Lagos became an early center for a rapidly expanding number of groups, such as the Triumph Dance Club Orchestra, which played Western musical instruments and imitated, to varying degrees, forms of Western popular music.

By the 1950s local and Western forms of popular music were merged into what became known as the Highlife style of music. This style combined traditional rhythms with progressive forms of Western jazz and obtained its name from the accelerated life associated with urban centers. Many of these earlier musical groups had completely disappeared by the late 1960s and others had risen to take their places. One of the more popular dance band leaders, I.K. Dairo, and his Blue Spots Band specialized in juju music, a variation on the Highlife tradition.

In the late 1960s several composers, such as Akin Euba, Ayo Bankole, and Fela Sowande, had composed string quartets, piano suites, and art songs totally within the Western tradition with no reference to African culture. Other composers, such as Lazarus Ekweme, attempted to fuse African and Western classical music traditions into religious masses and compositions for string instruments. Small groups, usually associated with facilities at academic centers, performed these works and Western classical music.

ARCHITECTURE

Many of the contemporary Nigerian structures reflect traditional architectural styles. The most noteworthy of these styles were contained in the early Yoruba compounds with their single-storied dwellings. The typical compound's single entrance opened into a central courtyard, which was edged by a covered terrace. Each compound provided a place for living quarters, craft work, and relaxation. Several compounds constituted a village, whose inhabitants generally were united by kinship ties.

Villages were surrounded by protective walls constructed of mud, except in swampy areas where thatch was often used. The walls were built at the onset of the dry season to facilitate their baking in the sun. Roofs varied from area to area, but all extended beyond the building to keep the walls dry. There were no windows to the outside, and the doors to the covered terrace were small. Rooms sometimes had ceilings plastered with clay to keep them cooler and dry.

The most refined architectural developments were the Yoruba palaces (afin) of the obas. They were surrounded by walls, three feet thick and eighteen feet high, that provided total privacy. The main entrance often was through a special gate that, because of the size of the structure, tunneled through to the main interior courtyard. The palace was the largest structure in the town, and the social position of lesser chiefs was indicated by the distance of their dwellings from the palace, which stood in the middle of town and faced the local market. The palaces were often quite large and included numerous smaller courtyards and compounds that housed the extended family, servants, and craftsmen in the service of the oba. Often a small forest or woodland was also enclosed for the private hunting and pleasure of the oba. Palaces at Ife and Owo in 1971 covered 20 and 109 acres, respectively. Ruins indicated the previous existence of palaces covering from 400 to 600 acres.

The interiors of the palaces were elaborately decorated. Some of the mud walls were covered with murals featuring the gods and sacred animals, and others were sculptured. Wooden roof supports were carved and painted, and some of the floors were paved with potsherds; the interiors were furnished with wall hangings and carved furniture. Statuary filled corners and served as shrines.

Although some palace compounds were still in use in 1971, both their size and state of repair had declined. Most had been abandoned for two-storied structures of concrete, brick, and timber that resembled estate houses, with glass windows or louvers and roofs of tin, tile, or other various elements. Most of the function formerly performed by the palace compound had been transferred to other structures, some of which had been erected on pieces of land carved out of decayed portions of the former palaces.

Architecture in urban areas varies widely from direct adaptations of traditional architecture to modern high-rise buildings. During the 1930s and 1940s affluent farmers profiting from a cocoa boom moved to urban areas and built two-storied concrete and masonry structures with verandas, columns, and sculptured facades. Similar in scale to the new palaces constructed by the obas, they were representative of the shift away from compound living arrangements.

During the 1950s most new structures were functional and emphasized economy of construction. During the 1960s most of the building techniques developed abroad were introduced to the country. Reinforced concrete was molded and cast to create sculptured effects based on the alternation of light and shadow. Cantilevered balconies, metal-fitted and casement-like windows, sunshields, and polished stone facings were combined in designs in both private and public construction.

Next to government buildings the major stimulus to architectural development in the country has been for school buildings, churches, and health and business facilities. Several campus sites, such as the Abdullahi Bayero College in Kano, had courtyard plans that envisioned campus expansion through the construction of additional buildings to be connected to existing structures by causeways, ramps, and covered walks. Several of the campus buildings were raised on pillars, providing shaded outdoor study and social areas. St. Paul's Church in Lagos incorporates traditional and contemporary elements; its curved walls and ceilings and carved wooden madonna and baptistry screen reflect traditional styles.

THE VISUAL ARTS

With the exception of wall paintings in some of the Yoruba palaces, there was no indigenous tradition of painting. After World War II, however, many young artists adopted this medium and, although few artists think of themselves exclusively as painters, this medium has come to displace the dominant role formerly held by sculpture in the visual arts. The two major cultural centers for artists in 1971 were Lagos and Oshogbo.

Sculpture

Sculpture, executed in a wide range of materials, including wood, terra cotta, and bronze, was the most developed of the visual arts in traditional society. Although the most developed forms were found in the southern half of the country, the earliest developments were terra cotta works of the Nok culture of central Nigeria dating between 500 B.C. and A.D. 200. Nok sculpture was coarse and heavy, but it was well fired and varied in scale from human and animal figures a few inches high to nearly life-sized human figures. Human heads were also produced with a high degree of stylization; body shapes and proportions were distorted.

Except among the Ijo there was little sculptural development after the decline of the Nok culture until the rise of the Ife culture between the twelfth and fourteenth centuries. Some authorities feel that the Ijo, who not only worked in terra cotta but also seem to be the first to work in metal, were a bridge between the Nok and the Ife cultures. It is believed that during the Ijo period, as a consequence of the expansion of Yoruba territory, terra cotta work declined, but metal casting was introduced. The Ife terra cottas resemble refined versions of Nok sculpture, with particular refinement of the heads of figures. The heads are still conical or cylindrical, but the treatment of the eyes and ears is conventional. The Ife, along with the Nok, are the only African culture south of the Sahara known to have made life-sized figures of the human form.

Excavations at Ife in 1912 uncovered life-sized bronze human heads and figures cast by a wax method. The size and condition of these castings indicated a high technical proficiency. Some of the heads had nail holes, suggesting that they may have been attached to wooden bodies. The complete figures are believed to have served ritual functions in funeral ceremonies or in ancestor cults.

A similar cultural center grew up in Benin, reaching a high point in the eighteenth century. Benin sculpture was more stylized and less naturalistic than that of Ife. The treatment was more elaborate and heavier. Any feeling for anatomy was lost, and the ritual heads of Benin represented lifeless symbols of social rank more than individual personalities. Much of the sculpture was of terra cotta, but the same examples were cast bronze animal figures and human heads.

Bronze castings found in other excavations do not seem related to either Benin or Ife culture. In 1939, for example, excavations southeast of Onitsha revealed works characterized by elaborate decoration representing insect forms. Another site at Tsoedo produced castings of varying styles and sizes, including the third largest bronze casting found south of the Sahara.

A more widespread, and also more perishable, tradition of sculpture was wood carving. Many of the surviving examples reflect elements in common with sculpture in bronze. In general, certain distinctions can be made between Yoruba and Ibo wood

194

sculpture. The works of both served religious and social functions. One of the more interesting forms of traditional sculpture still found among the Yoruba and Oyo is related to the twin cult. This cult, which fostered a reversal of a previous custom that put to death all twins at birth, revered twins as divine children capable of bringing affluence or poverty to their families, depending on how they were treated by their parents. After the death of a twin, small statues were carved and were cared for ritually by the mother or placed in small shrines where they were presented token offerings. The statues were usually dressed and adorned with jewelry and were sometimes wrapped in cloth to keep them warm.

Farther north among the Kutep in Benue-Plateau State in 1971, shrine figures were still being made of unfired clay dried in the sun. In addition to standing figures, masks were also common. Animal horns were sometimes inserted, not to make the figure represent any particular animal but to stress the beast-like character of the demon it represented.

Some traditional wood carving was still being produced in 1971. Many young sculptors had descended from generations of wood carvers or were trained by carving guilds. Some had attempted to readapt traditional styles and techniques to contemporary functions. One of the more successful and well known of these was Lamidi Fakeye, who was active in the organization of the arts and was the founder and first president of the Nigerian Society of Professional Artists. The most important of his works include the doors of the Roman Catholic Chapel at the University of Ibadan, the conference table and chairs for the Western State House of Assembly, the wooden mace for the University of Ife, and the entrance door of the United States Information Service building in Lagos.

Others have created diverse forms of more contemporary sculpture. Jacob Afolabi has executed large reliefs in concrete for walls and gates that feature figures from traditional literature in modern dress. Erhabor Emokapae, who is also a painter, has achieved interesting contrasts in his works through the use of different materials. One of the best known contemporary sculptors is Ben Osawe, who works in clay, bronze, wood, and stone. His main interest is to portray human problems and individual reactions to them. His works in ebony are particularly well known for their organic forms.

Painting and Graphics

The initial attraction of Oshogbo to young artists was the opening of a cultural center in 1964, which provided opportunities for

195

exhibits and sales. One of the better known of the Oshogbo artists paints under the name of Twins Seven-Seven. His pen and ink designs, etchings, and varnished gouaches portray traditional themes with complex interlaced patterns. Muraina Oyelami originally worked in an abstract style but has since turned to icon-like faces depicting the human condition. One of his more recent works is *Dead Bodies*, a theme taken from the civil war.

Adebisi Fabunmi has done a series of linocuts and also numerous designs for theater stages. Jacob Afolabi uses surrealistic imagery in his work with murals and concrete wall reliefs. Jimoh Buraimoh is noted for his experimental work with mosaic plaques, wall hangings, beaded prints, and paintings. Bruce Onobrakpeya, one of the better known of the Oshogbo artists, specializes in prints and etchings, using traditional mythology and imagery; he has illustrated several books by prominent authors throughout West Africa.

One of the better known Lagos artists is Jimo Akolo. His works combine natural shapes and intense colors to express abstract themes related to the dilemmas of human existence in a developing nation. Demas Nwoko is known for his colorful oils, and Uche Okeke's works are intellectualized interpretations of spirits and various mythological creatures. Other prominent artists include Collete Omogbai and Ben Enwonwu.

CRAFTS

Although they are gradually being supplanted by manufactured counterparts, a great number of handicraft items were still being produced in 1971 for household use, for storage, or for protective purposes. An example of such crafts is gourd or calabash decoration. The gourds, cut into desired shapes and dried, are fashioned into a wide variety of objects, including bowls for drinking, bottle-like water containers, medicine containers, spoons, and sunshades for babies. Two different techniques are used in decorating the dried gourds. The most widespread is pyroengraving, in which a red-hot metal tool set into a wooden handle burns lines into the surface and thus achieves contrast from the natural color of the gourd. A second technique of limited use involves the cutting of lines on the surface, into which is rubbed a mixture of peanut oil and soot.

The creation of calabash ware in the northeastern section of the country is generally done by women. In other northern areas itinerant Hausa males travel from market to market with their handiwork. Patterns vary widely and include geometric, linear, and pictorial designs. Certain variations are identified with a particular artist, and the work of earlier traditional artists is highly valued. Certain styles seem to be repeated and are passed on from generation to generation. The creation of fine quality calabash ware was still highly valued in 1971 and was one of the few ways for women to earn both cash and prestige.

Another example of artistic craftwork is provided by the beaded, conical crowns worn by the *obas* of the Yoruba. These crowns not only represented the traditional authority of the office but also were symbolic of the *oba's* quasi-divine status. Archaeological evidence suggests that beaded crowns similar to those still being made can be traced back to about the twelfth century.

MUSEUMS AND CULTURAL ORGANIZATIONS

In the late 1960s the country had fifteen museums, eight of which were affiliated with the National Museum in Lagos but located in other places in Nigeria. These institutions and five other public museums were under the control of the federal Department of Antiquities at Jos, site of the Nok archaeological finds. Among the public galleries the Benin museum specialized in antiquities and bronzes. The Jos museum included in its collection an archaeological exhibit and terra cotta sculpture; it also had zoological and botanical gardens. The Ife museum specialized in bronze and terra cotta objects from ancient Ife, and the Oron museum was noted for its ancestral carvings. The Gidan Makama Museum in Kano featured local art work.

In addition to these museums there were numerous small exhibition centers established mainly for the display of contemporary works of art and local handicrafts. These smaller centers were often sponsored by local art associations. Included in the collections were pottery, hand-blocked fabrics, bronzes, wood carvings, and raffia goods. Editions of literary works by Nigerian authors were also on sale.

In 1971 the major facilities for exhibiting contemporary painting and sculpture in Lagos were in the New Exhibition Center of the Independence Building. Opened in 1967, the gallery has 900 square feet of space; it was regarded as a temporary arrangement, however, and the construction of separate facilities was planned. The Society of Nigerian Artists and the Federal Society of Arts and Humanities had sponsored art shows in the center.

There were numerous local cultural organizations throughout the country designed to stimulate the arts. In 1960 the first Mbari Mbayo Club was founded in Ibadan as a place for local artists to exhibit their works and as a source of aid to local writers. Since then, several of these clubs have been founded throughout the country. In 1971 they had also begun to arrange cultural fairs,

197

featuring handicrafts, dances, and wood carvings of various ethnic origins.

PUBLIC INFORMATION

In 1971 the country had one of the most highly developed systems for the spread of information to the public of any country in tropical Africa. This position had resulted largely from the rapid growth of political parties before national independence until the advent of military government and the banning of political parties in 1966. Since 1966 the continued expansion and improvement of the information media has been encouraged by the Federal Military Government (FMG).

The availability of information varies, however, from area to area and is generally adequate only in the urban centers. In the cities it is possible to read several newspapers, listen to the radio and, in a growing number of cities, watch television. The press in less populous areas tends to be rather parochial, so that to be well informed a Nigerian must read two or more Lagos newspapers, most of which are not easily found outside the major cities. The government-owned radio provides increasing news coverage, but this medium of information is generally less broad in its treatment than the press. Television is still basically a medium of entertainment, despite the efforts of national and state governments to adapt it to educational purposes.

The influence of the press is restricted because of the population's limited literacy rate; the impact of radio and television is reduced in those rural areas that are without electricity. The federal and state governments, however, are spending increasing amounts of their budgets to overcome these deficiencies. In mid-1971 the spread of information by word of mouth in marketplaces and by itinerant traders still far outweighed formal means of communication in many parts of the country.

Before 1967, the constitution specified that "every person shall be entitled to freedom of expression, including freedom to hold opinions and to receive and impart ideas and information without interference." These rights, however, were subject to limitation by laws justifiable in the interest of defense, public order and safety, public morality, and public health; for the purpose of protecting the rights, reputation, and freedom of other persons; or for the purpose of regulating telephone, radio broadcasting, television, or the exhibition of films. Despite changes in the constitution, the FMG in mid-1971 continued to recognize the general principles that the document formerly applied to public information. The media, however, reflected an awareness that the government will not tolerate what it regards as "destructive criticism."

198

Under the Second National Development Plan N£10.9 million had been designated for improvement of the country's information services. About 56 percent of this amount was to come from state budgets, and the remainder, from the federal government. In addition to improvement of the radio and television broadcasting systems, the plan envisioned reorganization of the information services and the establishment of a national news agency to coordinate the collection and circulation of news about the country for both the domestic and the foreign press. Also included were the development of facilities for the dissemination of printed information and further development and maintenance of library services. The government had set aside N£75,000 in 1971 for its share of the costs of a regional training center for journalists from English-speaking countries to be established at the University of Lagos with the aid of the United Nations Educational, Scientific, and Cultural Organization (UNESCO).

The Press

The Nigerian press got an early start and played a major role in the political development of the country until 1966. The African-owned press was probably the most important medium through which nationalist ideas of educated Africans found an outlet and awakened the political consciousness of the people (see ch. 3, Historical Setting; ch. 9, Government and Political Dynamics). The initial phase of development occurred in the 1920s and 1930s. This period saw a great increase in the number of English-language newspapers and periodicals, and popular vernacular newspapers made their first appearance. A milestone in this progress was the establishment by Nnamdi Azikiwe in 1937 of the *West African Pilot*, a journal characterized by flamboyant writing and the first to attain national circulation by employing modern publication and distribution methods.

During its formative years, when it was the only mouthpiece of nationalism, the press tended to be flamboyant and often irresponsible. In later years, however, strict enforcement of libel and sedition laws and the growing number of trained journalists gradually diminished the tendency toward sensationalism. The press is regulated by the federal Newspaper Ordinance of 1917, the Publication Ordinance of 1950, the Newspaper (Amendment) Act of 1964, the Nigerian Criminal Code, and various printing press regulations. In addition to federal regulations, most of the states have their own laws governing the conduct of the press that were inherited from the former regional governments.

All newspapers must be registered, and signed copies of every issue must be deposited with the government. The name and address of both the publisher and the editor must appear in every issue. In most areas a monetary deposit must be made or a bond must be signed in order to obtain a license to publish; this provision is designed to ensure proper compensation for any abuse of the privilege of the press.

In mid-1971 there were twenty-one daily and twenty-one weekly newspapers published throughout the country (see table 3). Of the principal periodicals, fifteen were published monthly, and nine appeared quarterly. In addition, a large number of specialized periodicials and journals appeared on a less frequent basis. Most were associated with universities, chambers of commerce, professional societies, and labor organizations. The largest daily newspaper, the *Daily Times,* was published in Lagos and had a circulation of 114,000. Its weekend edition, the *Sunday Times,* was the country's largest weekly newspaper; its circulation was estimated at 240,000 copies.

Although circulation figures were incomplete, the total number of copies printed by all principal newspapers and periodicals exceeded 2 million. The number of persons reached by these publications, however, was probably at least three times the official circulation figures. Many issues were shared with other persons and were read aloud to a large number of illiterates.

The three most popular periodicals were monthly magazines with circulations of 100,000 or more. The Nigerian edition of *Drum,* a pictorial publication designed for African readers, circulated 155,000 copies and was the general favorite. *Spear* and *Flamingo* were family magazines with circulations of 110,000 and 100,000, respectively.

Most of the dailies were published in English and in tabloid format. Each edition usually averaged fewer than twenty pages in length. The front page of most dailies generally focused on domestic news. Foreign news was often on the following pages or was contained in special center sections. Editorials were sometimes placed on the front page, although a few newspapers regularly featured editorials on an inside page. Regular features included domestic news briefs written as columns aimed at geographical areas. Other features included classified advertising sections, letters to the editor, radio and television schedules, a cultural page or column, and often a number of African comic strips. Sports frequently received one or two complete pages, usually the last in each edition.

Several foreign news agencies maintained bureaus in Lagos. In 1971 these included the Associated Press (AP), Agence France-Presse, the Ghana News Agency, and Reuters. The West German Deutsche Presse Agentur and the Soviet news agency Telegraf-

Table 3. Principal Newspapers and Periodicals of Nigeria, 1971

Name of Publication	Language	Place of Publication	Circulation	Publisher or Affiliation
DAILY:				
Daily Comet	n.a.	Kano	5,000	n.a.
Daily Express	English	Lagos	n.a.	Commercial Amalgamated Printers.
Daily Telegraph	do	do	14,000	United Nigeria Press.
Daily Times	do	do	114,434	Daily Times of Nigeria.
Eastern Nigerian Guardian	do	Port Harcourt	17,000	Zik Enterprises.
Eastern Observer	n.a.	Onitsha	5,000	n.a.
Eastern States Express	n.a.	Aba	11,500	n.a.
Eastern State Express	English	Oyo	n.a.	Ikemesit Company.
Irohin Imole	Yoruba	Lagos	n.a.	Modupe Printing Press.
Middle Belt Herald	n.a.	Jos	5,000	n.a.
Midwest Echo	English	Benin City	25,000	Mid-West Echo.
Morning Post	do	Lagos	n.a.	Nigerian National Press.
New Nigerian	do	Kaduna	n.a.	Northern Nigerian Newspapers.
Nigeria Outlook	do	Enugu	35,000	Eastern Nigerian Information Service Corporation.
Nigerian Citizen	n.a.	Zaria	n.a.	n.a.
Nigerian Daily Sketch	English	Ibadan	4,600	Western State.
Nigerian Daily Standard	English and Efik	Calabar	9,000	Old Calabar Press.
Nigerian Spokesman	n.a.	Onitsha	6,000	n.a.
Nigerian Tribune	English	Ibadan	15,000	African Press.
Northern Star	n.a.	Kano	5,000	n.a.
West African Pilot	English	Lagos	47,323	Zik Enterprises.
WEEKLY:				
African Film	do	do	n.a.	Drum Publications (Nigeria).
Akedo Eko	English and Yoruba	do	5,000	n.a.

Table 3. Continued.

Name of Publication	Language	Place of Publication	Circulation	Publisher or Affiliation
Akedo-Yoruba	Yoruba	Lagos	n.a.	n.a.
Bornu People	Hausa and Kanuri	Mafoni and Maiduguri	n.a.	n.a.
Eleti-Ofe	English and Yoruba	Lagos	30,000	n.a.
Gaskiya ta fi Kwabo	Hausa	Kaduna	n.a.	New Nigerian Newspapers.
Independent	English	Ibadan	11,000	National Catholic Weekly.
Irohin Imole	Yoruba	Lagos	n.a.	Modupe Printing Press.
Irohin Yoruba	English	--- do	70,000	n.a.
Lagos Weekend	---do	---do	90,000	Daily Times of Nigeria.
Nigerian Catholic Herald	---do	---do	n.a.	St. Paul's Press Catholic Mission.
Nigerian Radio-T.V. Times	---do	---do	n.a.	Broadcast House.
Nigerian Statesman	---do	---do	14,165	Socialist.
Sporting Record	---do	---do	50,000	n.a.
Sunday Express	---do	---do	n.a.	Commercial Amalgamated Printers.
Sunday Post	---do	---do	70,000	Nigerian National Press.
Sunday Sketch	---do	Ibadan	n.a.	Western State.
Sunday Star	---do	---do	n.a.	n.a.
Sunday Times	---do	Lagos	240,000	Daily Times of Nigeria.
Truth (The Weekly Muslim)	---do	---do	n.a.	n.a.
West Africa	---do	---do	n.a.	Daily Times of Nigeria.

MONTHLY:

Name of Publication	Language	Place of Publication	Circulation	Publisher or Affiliation
Africa Magazine	---do	---do	n.a.	n.a.
Amber	---do	---do	n.a.	Investment House.
Construction in Nigeria	---do	---do	4,500	Federation of Building and Civil Engineering Contractors in Nigeria.
Drum (Nigeria Edition)	---do	---do	155,000	n.a.
Flamingo	---do	---do	100,000	n.a.
Home Studies	---do	---do	18,000	n.a.

Title	Language	Place	Circulation	Remarks
In Leisure Hours	--do--	Ibadan	n.a.	Immanuel College, Ibadan.
Jakadiya	Hausa	Kaduna	n.a.	Federal Ministry of Information.
Nigerian Businessman's Magazine	English	Lagos	n.a.	Nigeria and overseas commerce.
Nigerian Opinion	--do--	Ibadan	n.a.	Nigerian Current Affairs Society, University of Ibadan.
Radio-Vision Times	--do--	Lagos	n.a.	Western Nigeria Radiovision Service.
Spear	--do--	--do--	110,000	Family magazine.
Teacher's Monthly	--do--	Ibadan	n.a.	Federal Ministry of Education.
West Africa Link	English and French	Lagos	n.a.	Mainland Press.
Woman's World	English	--do--	15,000	n.a.
QUARTERLY:				
Insight	--do--	--do--	5,000	Contemporary Nigerian problems.
Nigeria	--do--	--do--	n.a.	Historical, cultural, and general material.
Nigeria Magazine	--do--	--do--	14,000	Do.
Nigeria Trade Journal	--do--	--do--	n.a.	Federal Ministry of Information.
Nigerian Grower and Producer	--do--	--do--	n.a.	n.a.
Nigerian Teacher	--do--	--do--	n.a.	Federal Ministry of Education.
West African Journal of Biological and Applied Chemistry	--do--	Ibadan	n.a.	University of Ibadan.
Western Nigerian Illustrated	--do--	--do--	n.a.	Western State Ministry of Information.
Yoruba Challenge	Yoruba	Lagos	65,000	Sudan Interior Mission.

n.a.—not available.

Source: Adapted from *Editor and Publisher Yearbook, 1971*, New York, 1971; and *Africa South of the Sahara, 1971*, London, 1971.

203

noye Agentstvo Sovietskovo Soyuza (TASS) maintained offices in the federal capital. Various foreign newspapers and agencies obtained information through local correspondents in the major urban centers. In 1967 a government decree was issued prohibiting all foreign news agencies from publishing or relaying information considered detrimental to the FMG. This general limitation remained in effect in 1971.

During the 1960s local news service for smaller newspapers was expanded under the West African News Service, which had correspondents throughout the country. Plans were underway in 1971 for the establishment of a national news service to benefit all newspapers. Several Nigerian newspapers had correspondents abroad, mainly in London, and an increasing number of foreign newspapers were maintaining correspondents in Lagos.

In the southern part of the country most newspapers and periodicals were published in English; a few were published in Yoruba; and some publications were basically in English with Yoruba, Ibo, and Efik sections. In the north, however, publications most frequently appeared in English and a local language, such as Hausa.

Throughout the 1960s professional journalistic standards improved. Salaries were raised, and an increasing number of journalists had been trained in journalism at one of the country's institutions of higher learning. The Nigerian Union of Journalists, formed in 1954, has done much to raise the status of the profession and has opened an occupation that was formerly confined largely to individuals of elite backgrounds to individuals from diverse social and economic backgrounds.

The press, however, continued to face a number of major problems. Printing machinery, imported mainly from Western Europe, was very expensive, and few publishers were sufficiently wealthy to buy it. Much of the press, therefore, relied on second-hand equipment. Transportation facilities were slow and unreliable in many areas, forcing the major national dailies to establish their own distribution system at great expense. Most of the better produced newspapers received capital aid from private foreign investors or from the government. Support from political parties, however, was curtailed after political parties were banned in 1966. Many newspapers led a precarious existence, and the turnover of publications printed at any one given time was high. Competition for the still-limited number of readers was intense. Independent newspapers in smaller towns suffered from growing competition with the national dailies and from the better financed local chain newspapers.

Radio and Television

Radio was an important medium of public information. Its impact as a source of news and other items of public interest had grown considerably since the early 1960s, when the medium was limited larely to the urban population. In 1971 approximately 3 million receivers were in use throughout the country. Few areas, even remote sections, were beyond the range of local radio transmitters; in addition, inhabitants of cities and towns had access to a large number of receivers located in such public places as bars, hotels, and schools.

Radio broadcasting in 1971 was the joint responsibility of the federal and state governments. The national network, the Nigerian Broadcasting Corporation (NBC), originated as a government service but became a statutory public corporation with its own charter in 1957. In 1961 the NBC was placed under the supervision of the federal Ministry of Information and Labor, which is responsible for NBC policy and for the appointment of the corporation's board of directors.

Main studios of the NBC, located in Broadcast House in the federal capital, broadcast the National Program service over one mediumwave and four shortwave transmitters in English, Hausa, Ibo, Yoruba, Efik, and Ijaw. In addition, the NBC broadcasts programs in English and appropriate local languages from separate mediumwave and shortwave transmitters in six states. The Western State Program originates from Ibadan; the Mid-Western State Program, from Benin City; the North Central State Program, from Kaduna; the North Eastern State Program, from Maiduguri; the East Central State Program, from Enugu; and the South Eastern State Program, from Calabar. Part of the daily broadcast time is devoted to programs relayed from Lagos, and the rest is given to programs originating from each state studio. Transmitter power ranges from 0.25 to 100 kilowatts (see table 4).

In addition to its domestic service, the NBC provides an external service, the Voice of Nigeria, to countries in Africa, the Middle East, and northern and southern Europe. Its programs feature music, news, and panel discussions and are broadcast in French, Arabic, Hausa, and English; further language diversification was planned. Experimental transmissions in the late 1960s included programs directed toward Western Europe and North America.

The NBC service is supplemented by commercial broadcasting networks in Western and North Central States, which also provide limited television broadcasts in their respective states. Western Nigeria Radiovision Service in Ibadan is owned by the Western State government. Radio Television Kaduna, in the capital of

205

Table 4. Radio Stations in Nigeria, 1971 [1]

Location	Frequency (in kilohertz)[2]	Peak power (in kilowatts)	Type of service
Mediumwave:			
Lagos	1088	10	National Program.[3]
Ibadan	1358	10	Western State Program.
	1397	0.25	Do.
	656	10	Commercial service of Western Nigeria Radiovision Service.
Benin City	638	5	Mid-Western State Program.
	1397	0.25	Do.
Kaduna	1416	1	North Central State Program.
	1397	0.25	Do.
	593	250	Commercial service of Radio Television Kaduna.
Maiduguri	1376	1	North Eastern State Program.
	1397	0.25	Do.
Enugu	1320	10	East Central State Program.
	1397	0.25	Do.
Calabar	1397	0.25	South Eastern State Program.
Shortwave:			
Lagos	3986	100	National Program.[3]
	4990	20	Do.
	7255	10	Do.
	9690	100	Do.
	7275	100	Voice of Nigeria external service.
	11770	100	Do.
	15120	100	Do.
	15185	100	Do.
	15200	100	Do.
Ibadan	3204	10	Western State Program.
	7285	1	Do.
	6050	10	Commercial service of Western Nigeria Radiovision Service.
Benin City	4932	10	Mid-Western State Program.
Kaduna	3396	10	North Central State Program.
	6175	20	Do.
	6090	10	Commercial service of Radio Television Kaduna.
	9570	10	Do.
	11965	10	Do.
Maiduguri	6140	10	North Eastern State Program.
Enugu	6025	10	East Central State Program.
Calabar	6145	10	South Eastern State Program.

[1] All AM (amplitude modulation).
[2] One kilohertz equals one kilocycle.
[3] Nigerian Broadcasting Corporation.

Source: Adapted from *World Radio-TV Handbook, 1971* (Ed., J. M. Frost.), Hvidovre, Denmark, n.d.

North Central State, is organized and operated under a similar arrangement.

All radio networks have a great variety in program content, which is geared to meet the demands of three distinct types of audience: a small group of educated, English-speaking listeners; a larger group of listeners who have completed a primary school education and who understand simple English and local languages; and a very large group of listeners who understand only the local vernacular. Limited educational broadcasts begun in the 1960s were gaining in importance for a fourth group comprising students in the nation's schools.

Television was inaugurated in October 1959 when Western Nigeria Television Service (WNTV) became the first network to televise in Africa. Originally owned jointly by the government of the former Western Region and a British firm, the station in 1971 was owned and operated solely by the Western State government. A similar television service, Radio Television Kaduna (RKTV), is owned by the North Central State government and operates from a broadcasting studio in Kaduna. A third service is provided by NBC Television (NTS), a subsidiary of the federal NBC.

WNTV and RKTV are operated under identical arrangements with the respective state broadcasting services. Both state networks as well as NTS derive their income from advertising and from sharing the revenues of the radio networks with which they are affiliated. WNTV operates two transmitters, one at Ibadan and one near Lagos. RKTV operates transmitters at Kaduna, Kano, and Zaria. The NTS transmitters are at Lagos and Ibadan. The Second National Development Plan envisions an extension of television service to the eastern states and other states in the north.

The average daily transmission time is 5 hours; approximately 1½ hours are devoted to a special school program, and the remaining hours are for entertainment. The evening program relies heavily on taped television programs produced in the United States and the United Kingdom but also includes locally developed news, panel discussions, and special features on aspects of Nigerian life or culture.

The FMG and the governments of Western and North Central States have stated that the basic objective of their television services is to provide a medium for promoting rapidly growing educational programs, to arouse interest in community development and, in general, to inform the people of governmental activities. In mid-1971, however, its importance as a medium of public information remained limited; a total of about 75,000 sets were available throughout the entire country. Television receivers were expensive and beyond the economic means of most of the population. A large number of sets have been purchased by the various governments for installation in hospitals, schools, reading rooms, and town halls. Commercial establishments, such as bars and hotels, provided receivers for customers.

Films

The importance of films as an information medium is growing, particularly in rural areas, where mobile units attract large audiences. Recognition of this fact by the federal and state governments is demonstrated by continued expansion of the government film units. Each government has its own film unit under the jurisdiction of the Ministry of Information, which prepares documentary, educational, and other films for showing by mobile units in small towns and villages. Films shown by mobile units often reach areas where no other organized information service is available.

Full-length features are shown in commercial theaters in the larger towns and cities. In the late 1960s Nigeria had seventy-two motion picture theaters, with a total seating capacity of 67,292. Sixty-seven of these were equipped to show 35-millimeter films; the remaining five could show 16-millimeter films. The country also had three drive-in theaters.

Most full-length film features are imported for commercial showing from the United Kingdom, the United States, India, Switzerland, France, and the United Arab Republic (Egypt). In the late 1960s the federal government began to experiment with the production of full-length films, one of which utilized the subject of population control as a subtheme. A number of film showings are made available to Nigerian audiences by the United States Information Service, the British Council, religious organizations, and private business firms.

Books

In 1960 publishing in the country was an infant industry, and most book printing was contracted to publishing houses in the United Kingdom. By 1970, however, there were nine major publishers in the country, including the Government Press, which was operated by the Ministry of Information and Labor. Most large state publishing was done in Lagos. African Universities Press, an associate of Pilgrim House, specialized in educational and general books on Africa. Both Oxford University Press and the Macmillan Company had Nigerian branches. The Gaskiya Corporation in Kaduna was owned by the six states of northern Nigeria. Two other companies, the Nigerian National Press and the Daily Times of

Nigeria, were engaged in publishing books, periodicals, and pamphlets as well as a number of newspapers.

In addition to these major publishing houses, there were numerous small-scale printing establishments in Lagos, Ibadan, and other urban areas throughout the country. Their products included pamphlets and some books as well as other informational materials. There were also small-scale religious press facilities; a rapid expansion of university publication facilities occurred during the 1960s.

In 1968 the scope of Nigerian publishing included 1,004 different book titles. About 74 percent were devoted to the social sciences; 5 percent, to the arts; and 3 percent, to religious subjects. About 5 million books were printed in 1968. This total included 110,000 copies of 22 different schoolbooks designed for Nigerian students. A number of translations of books originally written in foreign languages were published in the country, of which about 40 percent were religious works.

POSTS AND TELECOMMUNICATIONS

Communications services are provided by the federal government through its Ministry of Communications. In an effort to increase the efficiency of its communications elements, the FMG in 1968 converted its Post and Telecommunications Department (PTD) into a quasi-commercial operation to be guided by profit considerations in its operations and development. The retention of PTD personnel under civil service regulations, however, had counterbalanced many of the desired benefits that had resulted from conversion of the PTD. Resolution of this problem was under consideration in mid-1971.

In the late 1960s there were 1,760 postal facilities throughout the country, but only 20 percent offered complete postal services. The number of telephones in domestic use in 1969 totaled 80,839 installed instruments. This number, which had doubled since 1960, represented approximately 1 telephone per 700 population. The country had 52 working telex lines and 42 private wire telegraphs.

External communication facilities are provided largely by Nigerian External Telecommunications (NET), established in 1963 to replace the Cable and Wireless Corporation. NET is owned jointly by the former commercial organization and the federal government. In addition to cable services, NET operates an international telex and radiotelephone service, a radiophoto service, a telegraph service, and a ship-to-shore telephone network. The federal government has expressed interest ultimately in assuming complete ownership of NET. In 1971 the FMG owned 51 percent of the firm's common stock.

Under the Second National Development Plan N£42.6 million had been designated for communications services; about 95 percent had been scheduled for investment in posts and telecommunications. Government plans placed a high priority on rehabilitation of facilities damaged during the civil war as well as improvement and expansion of external telecommunication facilities. About N£3.4 million were provided for construction of a satellite telecommunication receiving station at Lanlate, which will eventually have coaxial cables for transmission and reception of television signals via satellite.

CHAPTER 9

GOVERNMENT AND POLITICAL DYNAMICS

The basic political forces and problems that faced the country in 1971 were the same as those that had confronted it continuously since the period before independence. The country's greatest need was to weld together a unified national entity from disparate groupings whose members retained primary loyalties to smaller units and whose leaders saw these ethnic and other divisions as an advantage to themselves or their followers. A ban on political activity in 1971, which had been in effect for more than four years, made it difficult to analyze properly the changes that had taken place in the period since 1966. This was particularly true of those changes resulting from the civil war—the real, if temporary, destruction of Ibo political strength and the replacement of the four regions by twelve states. The structure of government was also in a state of change and consolidation in 1971 and could only be understood in relation to post-1966 political developments.

The major force in internal affairs has long been the unequal rate of development of the component ethnic groups. Because of economic, educational, or cultural advantages or unequal political and numerical strengths, some groups have been able to exert control over the various levels of government. Other less advantaged groups resent this because it allows the dominant ones to obtain a disproportionate share of the largess of government resources in the form of public works, schools, and jobs—all important considerations in a country in which the government controls a major portion of the limited economy.

The primary political divisions until 1967 were between traditionalist Muslim forces, particularly the Hausa-Fulani who dominated the politics of the former Northern Region, where over half the country's population resided, and the modernizing peoples of the southern tier. In the south political power was primarily in the hands of the two largest ethnic groups, the Ibo in the east and the Yoruba in the west (see ch. 5, Ethnic Groups and Languages).

Although the general problems of the society remained the same, the alignment of ethnic and regional forces had been altered radically by the thirty months of civil war (known as the Biafran war outside Nigeria) and the redivision of the country into twelve states. The conflict had all but destroyed the political power of the Ibo, although the federal government had treated them with compassion after the war.

Rearrangement of the internal political structure had altered the earlier pattern of Hausa-Fulani domination over the northern half of the country and reduced their control to the northernmost third. The changes had weakened the rigid control formerly exercised by the forces of traditionalism. The political strength of the Yoruba, the only major group not affected by the reorganization and the war, had already been weakened by political factionalism.

A major new consideration for the country's political future had become apparent. The smaller ethnic groups had achieved a degree of political power for the first time and controlled five of the twelve states, but great diversity existed within these groups. Many among them demanded a further devolution of power through the creation of still more states so that other ethnic groups might have control over their own futures. The part to be played by these new divisions remained largely uncertain in 1971. The decision of the Federal Military Government (FMG) to retain power in its own hands until 1976 had given the new states five more years to develop administrative effectiveness without the pressure of political contests.

Revelations of corruption in politics as well as violence in elections effectively had destroyed all public support for parliamentary democracy and led directly to the 1966 military coup, which had as its main aim the eradication of corruption. Nevertheless, despite efforts of the FMG, the continued burden of nepotism and corruption was a factor of grave importance for political stability in 1971. Other major factors included the grievances of city workers caught between a very low wage rate and a rapidly rising cost of living, the flight of younger rural people to the city out of boredom with village life, and the continual high level of unemployment that resulted from the large-scale output of the school system (see ch. 4, Population and Labor). The permanently unemployed, who grew in number every year, placed the blame for their condition on the government. They provided a permanent recruiting ground for those seeking to create national unrest, as did the largely idle army, which in 1971 had over twenty times its prewar strength.

ETHNICITY AND REGIONALISM IN POLITICS

The major lasting force in the country's political dynamics is interethnic tensions caused by differences in values and outlook and by clashes of interest. The most important tensions are less the result of historic ethnic differences or traditional animosities than of the mutually reinforcing geographic, economic, political, and religious differences that have been created largely in the twentieth century along ethnic and regional lines (see ch. 5, Ethnic Groups and Languages; ch. 11, Value Systems).

At the beginning of the twentieth century the major ethnic groups had little contact with one another, other than isolated encounters. In addition, the Hausa-Fulani, the Yoruba, and the Ibo were plagued by strong internal political division and, in some cases, by linguistic, social, cultural, and other divisions. Only the peace, unity, communication, and education that had been brought about during the colonial era allowed the often diverse segments of the larger ethnic groups to draw themselves together in terms of their underlying similarities.

Steps taken under colonial rule increased the reasons for the major groups to compete with each other for power and wealth. The differences in the rates of education, modernization, and economic development among the various groups resulted in part from the unequal capacity of peoples of the different cultures to make use of the new opportunities offered them by nationhood and modernization. Some, notably those of the emirates, proved too tradition bound to prepare themselves to compete in sufficient numbers for key positions in trade, in industry, and in government services. Others, chiefly the Ibo, many Yoruba, and other southern groups, proved eager to take advantage of these new opportunities.

Because of their ability to accept new ideas and opportunities, the southerners assumed a disproportionate control over the position of wealth and power, a fact that became more apparent to the northerners after the attainment of self-government. The Hausa were particularly resentful of the Ibo, whose educational training, aggressiveness, and willingness to work outside their own region enabled them to hold many of the higher posts in the north, including some in local government. Their resentment was intensified by the clash of the two divergent cultures.

Cultural differences and jealousies were given a new scale on which to operate in the 1950s. The gradual granting of self-government at national and regional levels created a new competition for political control. Until then, nationalist politics had been primarily the domain of a small element of the educated southerners and were given little attention by a majority of people, even by those who were literate. Even then, political divisions had fallen along ethnic lines, as evidenced in the 1940s by splits in the first important political party, the Nigerian Youth Movement (NYM).

The southern elite was most interested in modernization that would bring benefits and education to the masses. In the north the traditional aristocracy gradually became interested in modernization but not in change that might lead to challenges to their position of control over the dominant political party, the local government authorities, and the local courts. Anything that might bring control by the central government continued to be regarded as a challenge to this order; new ideas and opportunities for the lower classes thus threatened the status of the aristocracy. The northern elite's dislike of educated southerners in their midst before the civil war stemmed in good part from the concern that southern concepts of democratically elected local governments might prove attractive to Hausa commoners.

The political differences between the Ibo and the Yoruba, on the other hand, were primarily the result of competition for political and economic power. Both groups supported modernization and were led by elites whose status resulted from educational attainments. They were divided only by minimal differences in attitude and the desire to achieve power for themselves and their followers. Since the 1940s the strategy of the political competitors had allowed this competition to assume the aspects of an ethnic division. Conflict for office thus extended into the civil service, the state corporations, and even university faculty appointments. In the years of crisis between independence and 1967 the practice of seeking ethnic support in personal conflicts had disastrous results.

Political divisions assumed ethnic proportions in the south, largely because there were no class, religious, or economic lines along which to divide. Political leaders therefore turned to the only available group structures to develop support. After the British began to withdraw, these ethno-political divisions became more acute as their leaders controlled patronage over the main sources of limited employment opportunities: government jobs, government funds for local development, market permits, trade licenses, government contracts, and access to prized scholarships for higher education.

If the railway corporation, for example, came under the control of an Ibo chairman, it was automatically assumed that every job would go to an Ibo. If control of the Ministry of Education was given to a Yoruba, it was expected that he would placate his Yoruba constituents by assuring that a predominant share of scholarships went to Yoruba candidates. In an economy with a hundred qualified applicants for every post, great resentment was generated by the general selection of relatives, the affluent, or those who were ethnically aligned with the appointing authority.

The modernized elite contained the main center of national agitation and force for linking the nation together. Yet even this elite was always ready to divide into ethnic components under the force of social pressure and the desire to use patronage for personal advancement or to favor relatives.

The minority ethnic groups, some numbering more than 2 million, sought their share of the national and regional government largess. Unlike the animosities between the three major groups, their often hostile attitudes toward the major group dominant in their region were formed by traditional attitudes, historic animosities, and discriminatory treatment, as well as cultural and religious differences. The level of antagonism between the three dominant groups and the important minor groups varied considerably. The minorities originally incorporated in the Western Region achieved a major victory in 1963 when their own Mid-Western Region was created to contain the non-Yoruba residents. The eastern minority groups often have been portrayed as persecuted by, and hostile to, the Ibo, who constituted 60 to 70 percent of the regional population; sociopolitical surveys in the mid-1960s, however, revealed that most Ibibio, for example, willingly supported the Ibo-led regional government.

In the north the Kanuri were closely aligned with the Hausa-Fulani and received a considerable share of the high political posts. The Nupe generally were politically and economically apathetic under their Fulani rulers. The Tiv, the Yoruba of the Ilorin emirate, and the other Middle Belt (see Glossary) people were generally those must opposed to domination by a major group. Despite this opposition, however, they did not align themselves with the political parties of the south as certain advantages accrued to them in their separate status.

The civil service of the Northern Region was dominated by people from the Middle Belt who were more able to adjust to modern concepts and more willing to accept education. The Yoruba of the Kabba area were particularly strong in the government service. Thus, despite the fact that their values and attitudes linked them to the southerners and left them opposed to the Hausa-Fulani ideas, Middle Belt groups held a vested interest in maintaining regional or local autonomy because they did not have the educational strength to compete with the southerners in a unitary civil service.

POLITICAL SIGNIFICANCE OF RELIGION

Throughout Nigeria traditional governing authority has had a religious foundation. The rulers in a number of societies have been sacred kings, members of secret societies, or priestly elders—all embodying and using authority from the unseen world of gods and ancestor spirits. Local law and custom, especially regarding marriage and land rights enforced by these rulers, are thought of as originating from sanctified ancestors and gods whom it would be a sacrilege to disobey (see ch. 6, Social Systems).

In the Muslim north tribal law and rulership have been largely supplanted by Islamic institutions that give an alternative form of expression to the underlying general tradition that religion and government must somehow be linked together. Law is based on the Koran and other Islamic texts, and no sharp distinction is possible between jurisprudence and theology. Emirs claim homage and obedience because of their descent from venerated Muslim leaders who were exemplars of piety and militancy against the less orthodox.

In northern Nigeria the British colonial government took careful account of the Muslim religious factor and avoided any appearappearance of challenge to the Islamic faith in order to keep from inflaming resistance to British rule and to maintain political stability in those areas. As Muslim emirs settled more and more into their role as reliable agents of indirect rule, British policymakers in the far north were content to sustain the status quo in religious matters. They barred Christian missionaries, leaving an uncontested field for the Koranic schools, and the limited government efforts in education were completely harmonized with Islamic institutions.

In 1971 Muslims throughout the country were divided into memberships of two orders, the Tijaniyya and the Kadiriyya. These organizations often parallel existing, or stimulated new, personal and political differences, but they had no direct political involvement.

In the south, although some of the local political authorities were used earlier as vehicles of British indirect rule, particularly in the Yoruba areas, their traditional religious rationale was undermined and weakened by Christian missions and Western education. An overlap between local and Western patterns developed, including frequently a double allegiance to indigenous and Christian religious viewpoints and the related issue of double allegiance to the sacred rulership of the Yoruba kings or their counterparts in other ethnic groups and to modern electoral processes and legal concepts. Reverence for the traditional kingship helps to explain, for instance, why the *oni* (priest-king) of Ife, the major Yoruba religious head, was so prominent as a sponsor of the Action Group and was made the first African governor of the Western Region. Much of the local intensity of controversies between factions and parties in the Western Region during the 1960s had to do with maintaining the authority of such representatives of tradition.

In the southeast Ibo and other traditions of sacred authority linked minutely divided control by councils of elders with vast numbers of localized ancestor cults. Christian mission education and church adherence, which affected the southeast more extensively than any other part of Nigeria, have reinforced the inclination to democratic values, which the nature of indigenous cults already fostered.

As internal migration has increased, Nigerians have been brought into conflict with local customs contrary to their own and for which they recognize no sacred legitimacy. Migrants to the southwest often resent and ridicule the Yoruba kings in a way that seems sacrilegious to the Yoruba. The casual attitudes of Ibo, Yoruba, and other Christian migrants from the south toward the emirs and the Muslim proprieties have provoked resentment against them as impious intruders in the north, where homage to emirs is inculcated as a Muslim duty.

The nationalist ideology at independence had included a strain of criticisim against white missionaries and major Christian churches, which remained clearly under foreign influence. They were accused of inculcating a subservient mentality and opposing constitutional progress. The overwhelming majority of nationalists, however, were Christians who continued to adhere to these churches. The apparently close ties of the Ibo to the Roman Catholic Church during the civil war considerably weakened that body's position with the political authorities in the postwar era. A portion of intra-Ibo political dynamics revolved around membership in different Christian churches.

OTHER PRESSURE AND INTEREST GROUPS

Lobbying and pressure groups fall into several categories: economic and vocational (including labor union) groups; ethnic associations (which often appear as sectional interests); intellectual societies and institutions; and the vested interests of the possessors of power and influence, most notably the country's diverse civil services. Constituents of each category may be found espousing either change or the status quo, depending on the nature of the problem. Until 1966 most groups were affiliated with, or directly supported, a particular party, although some operated independently. The growing complexity of the Nigerian economy and the increasing numbers of young educated Nigerians have tended to give added weight to economic and intellectual interests.

Certain centers of opinion stand out above others, either because of existing influence, putative future importance, or the comprehensiveness of their programs for Nigerian policy. Groups that have already acquired a measure of power, such as the traditional authorities or the higher level civil servants, tend to resist change out of fear that it may threaten their status. Thus, the northern emirs espouse only those changes that will protect the north against competiton from the south. Although the emirs alone cannot be considered a pressure group, along with their obedient officials they form one of the country's most powerful political factors.

Similarly, the higher civil servants are not prone to encourage aspirants who wish to share their lofty status; hence, they wish to preserve the peaks of privilege against leveling tendencies. Nigerian civil servants play a preponderant role in directing the machinery of government. Whenever they do discover a bond of common interest, they are likely to be in a position to translate their desires into demands. In the economic field the same is generally true of Nigeria's handful of wealthy extrepreneurs and traders, many of whom have exploited their strategic positions to mold public policy to their advantage.

Members of the lower levels of the bureaucracy, on the other hand, generally have represented a highly insistent advocacy of change. Their discontent has arisen from impatience at having to climb the ladder of promotion by slow steps. They have remained a major source of demands for increasing the number of states because new political units offered them increased opportunities for promotion in a proliferating bureaucracy. This vocational group has tended, at the same time, to represent the impatient and radical outlook of young intellectuals. Similarly, the major ethnic group dominant in a particular state tends to maintain the status quo, whereas minority groups within that state agitate for a change in boundaries or guarantees of autonomy.

POLITICAL PARTIES BEFORE 1966

Many of the country's political leaders in the early 1960s were among the pioneers in the nationalist movement that began in the 1920s. They carried the country from colonial status, in which political activity by Nigerians was restricted to local affairs under the watchful eye of the British colonial government, to full self-government in a system formally based on Western parliamentary principles. Because the operations of party politics and the formulation of national policy are understood by a very small sector of the population, however, Nigeria's political life was, in effect, guided by the small educated elite rather than by the general public.

After the crises of the 1960s, critics accused many members of the elite of failing to carry out efforts to educate the people to participate in political life and of failing to represent the public

218

interest. These accusations ignored questions of whether centrifugal forces created by the ethnic diversity of the country could be reduced or controlled to the extent necessary to maintain national unity. During the early post-World II period a strong current of opinion among Nigerian leaders that was fostered by the British favored strengthening regional powers at the expense of developing central government. For a time it even appeared possible that either the Western Region or the Northern Region might secede from the federation. On the other hand, the Eastern Region was the home ground of the strongest supporters of a united Nigeria. At the time of independence in October 1960 sentiment for national unity appeared strong, but there was much doubt about how deep this sentiment ran and whether it could withstand the divisive forces of ethnic and regional loyalties.

Early Political Groupings

The origin of the Nigerian parties is found in the politics of Lagos in the period after World War I. The first genuine political party was the Nigerian National Democratic Party, founded in 1922 by Herbert Macauley. The stimulus to such political organization was provided by the opportunity of contesting elections for three Lagos seats in the new Legislative Council.

The party succeeded in dominating the elections to the Legislative Council from 1923 to 1938. In addition to giving Nigerian nationalism a rallying point in the person of Macauley, the pioneer party afforded a training ground for many young political leaders.

The 1920s and 1930s were marked by a proliferation of semipolitical organizations, most of which had some place in the awakening of Nigerian nationalism. They formed the background for the postwar political party system that appeared after World War II.

Three main types of groups formed in the 1920s. One set of associations consisted of professional and vocational societies, such as the Nigerian Law Association, launched in 1923, and the Nigerian Produce Traders' Association, led by Chief Obafemi Awolowo, later leader of a major opposition party. These groups were paralleled by the labor unions, which also were in the process of formation in the 1920s and 1930s.

The second type of voluntary association that developed in the late 1920s was the kinship organization or tribal union. These organizations were primarily urban phenomena growing out of the presence of large numbers of newcomers in the newer cities. Alienated by the inhospitable urban environment and drawn together by ties to their ethnic homelands, as well as by the impulse toward mutual aid and protection, the alien city dwellers first formed local associations and then extended these into federations covering whole regions. The Ibibio ethnic group established the first federation involving all of their brethren throughout the country and including home branches. By the end of World War II the major ethnic groups had formed associations, such as the Ibo Federal Union and the Egbe Omo Oduduwa (Society of the Descendants of Oduduwa), a Yoruba cultural movement. They played an important role in generating ethnically based political parties.

The third type of organization, which was less homogeneous, included a variety of literary and student groupings but was more pointedly political. As vehicles for intellectuals—the segment of the population most conscious of political issues in a long-range national or international context—the most influential of these organizations became the vanguard of nationalism in the period before World War II.

The first party of lasting impact was the Nigerian Youth Movement (NYM), the flowering of which coincided—by no means accidentally—with the return of Nnamdi Azikiwe from the United States and H.O. Davies from England. They mobilized for the first time a large number of educated Nigerians with an articulated political purpose and furnished the movement with a press in which to enunciate their aims. The NYM charter called for the "development of a united nation out of the conglomeration of peoples who inhabit Nigeria" and inclusion in the British Commonwealth of Nations as a dominion.

In 1938 the NYM registered an important success by defeating Macauley's party in the election to the Lagos Legislative Council seats and embarked simultaneously on a campaign of expansion into all parts of Nigeria. The NYM broke up in 1941 over an internal factional quarrel with pronounced ethnic overtones. The result was that the Ibo members, including Azikiwe, left the organization; the rump of the NYM remained under Yoruba control thereafter and eventually formed one of the bases for the Action Group. The organizational demise, however, did not diminish the force of nationalist thinking that the NYM had so effectively advanced.

The experience of war further ripened the nationalist movement, partly through the intensification of grievances that wartime exigencies could not solve and partly by giving many Nigerians their first experience of life in other parts of the country and abroad. In the postwar period the nationalist struggle was carried on by a developing political party network.

The National Council of Nigerian Citizens

Nigeria's first national political party was the National Council of Nigerian Citizens (NCNC), founded in August 1944 as the National Council of Nigeria and the Cameroons. Nnamdi Azikiwe encouraged a group of students from the Nigerian Union of Students to call a conference of all major Nigerian organizations in Lagos to "weld the heterogeneous masses of Nigeria into one solid block." The aged Herbert Macauley was elected president of this group, and Azikiwe became general secretary. The new party's purposes were stated in its constitution as democratic self-government for all of Nigeria as a member of the British Commonwealth.

From its inception until 1952 the party membership was based on affiliated organizations. Its affiliates included labor unions, social groups, political parties, professional associations, and over 100 tribal unions. These afforded unusual opportunities for political education in already existing constituencies. Most labor unions did not become affiliated, however; neither did the NYM, which was still in the hands of Yoruba leaders unattracted to Azikiwe's banner. Leadership rested firmly with Azikiwe during most of the preindependence period, in part because of the highly vocal nationalist newspapers that he owned and his personal stature as a nationalist herald but mainly because of his towering personality.

The NCNC after independence was unable to advance its cause as an all-Nigerian party and came to rely instead on an Ibo base supplemented by alliances with minority parties. Either as affiliates or allies, a large number of small parties linked themselves with the NCNC. Its most important ally in the north was the Northern Elements Progressive Union (NEPU). Some members of the Middle Belt opposition to the Northern People's Congress (NPC) also helped give NCNC a role, albeit a limited one, in northern politics. The importance attached to the NEPU was attested to by the inclusion of its leader in the NCNC executive. The NCNC itself also had some voting strength in northern cities, nearly all of it among southern migrants, but not enough to give it a significant representation in the Northern Region House of Assembly in its own name. The most remarkable feature of the alignment was the fact that the NCNC through the NEPU served as the opposition party to the ruling NPC in the north but was simultaneously part of the governing coalition at the federal level with the NPC.

The possibility of capturing a majority of western votes, as it had done between 1947 and 1950, was the NCNC's only hope to obtain a parliamentary majority and, hence, to become the governing party at the federal level. It supported the creation of more states with provincial status as a step toward the unitary national administration it had always favored.

The Action Group

The Action Group (AG) arose as a reaction against Ibo control of the NCNC and as a vehicle for Yoruba nationalism. The AG shared in the Westernized political practices of the southern part of the country and also benefited from political spadework done between 1944 and 1950 by the NCNC. Its pattern of organization and platform bore noticeable resemblance to its predecessor in the political arena. As a movement initially designed to exploit the federal arrangement to attain regional power, however, the AG found itself, with rare exceptions, in the role of the NCNC's competitor on the local and national levels.

The AG was the creation of its leader, Chief Obafemi Awolowo. As general secretary of the Yoruba cultural organization, Egbe Omo Oduduwa, and as a leader of the cocoa traders' association, Awolowo was well placed to initiate a new party. The Yoruba group was heir of a generation of flourishing cultural consciousness, and the traders' association represented the comparative economic advancement of the west over the rest of Nigeria. Awolowo, therefore, had little difficulty in appealing to broad segments of the Yoruba population; his problem was rather to prevent the AG from being stigmatized as a "tribal" group. The new party was formally inaugurated in March 1951. Despite efforts to enlist non-Yoruba support—efforts that were not entirely unsuccessful—the Yoruba nationalism that had stimulated the party initially could hardly be concealed.

Another obstacle to the development of the AG was the animosity between segments of the Yoruba community, the best example of which was the opposition to Awolowo personally by the natives of Ibadan because he belonged to the traditionally disliked Ijebu segment of the Yoruba. Despite the difficulties, the AG rapidly developed an effective organization. Its program reflected greater planning and was more idologically oriented than the NCNC. The party exploited—as had never before been done in Nigeria—the usefulness of strong, streamlined organizational structure combined with modern, sometimes flamboyant, electioneering techniques.

Collegial leadership did not prevent Awolowo from embodying the AG in the eyes of most followers. Although he did not have the compelling personality of Azikiwe, Awolowo proved to be a vigorous and tenacious competitor and a formidable debater. Some of his leading lieutenants were: Chief Samuel Akintola, his successor as party president when he went to the federal Parliament and later his rival for preeminence in the Western Region; the *oni* of Ife, a good example of the traditional ruler who could be enlisted in an ethnic cause and become effective in modern political activity; and Chief Rotimi Williams.

Like its eastern opponent, the AG emphasized different aspects of its program at different times. The consolidation of its position in the Western Region required Yoruba pride in culture and advancement along with hostility toward the aggressive Ibo in the NCNC. When ethnic factors receded before the desire to expand within or beyond the Western Region, appeals were based on minority grievances and nationalist goals.

Although AG dominance of its home region was always less secure than that of the other two major parties, it at first made notable advances in the other regions. The AG was a consistent supporter of minority group demands for autonomous states in the federation and even supported the severance of a midwest state from its own region, assuming that comparable alterations would be made elsewhere. The AG continued to support a species of Yoruba irredentism vis-à-vis the Ilorin and Kabba divisions in the Northern Region, which were heavily populated by Yoruba, as well as the separatist movements in the Eastern Region, which called for the creation of a Calabar-Ogoja-Rivers state and the drive for a Middle Belt state.

Northern People's Congress

The Northern People's Congress (NPC) did not grow out of a nationalist anti-British striving for an independent Nigeria. Instead, it was originated by the very limited number of educated northerners who obtained the support of the traditionalists to form a political party to serve as a counterbalance to the southern political parties. The most powerful figure in the party, the Sardauna of Sokoto, Ahmadu Bello, was the holder of one of the most important traditional offices and an aspirant to the post of sultan of Sokoto, the most powerful office in the Fulani kingdom. Bello was a particularly controversial figure, but his attitudes and those of the NPC generally were identical. Although he was often described by outsiders as a feudal conservative, his primary political interest was the preservation of the northern society from southern influence and control. He was fully willing to utilize any means, including the acceptance of educational and economic changes, to strengthen the north. In particular, he and the NPC sought to control the national government to protect their own society.

The old structure of authority in the Northern Region centered on the emir and his feudal staff. This system, supported by a religious faith in which obedience is the mark of the devout, did not welcome change. Most of the stimulus for improving efficiency and alleviating its more arbitrary features came from the British. The small contingent of northerners who had experienced education abroad after World War II, a group that included both the later prime minister Abubakar Tafawa Balewa and the future political dissident Aminu Kano, was allied with the British in its desire to introduce change into the emirates. The support by traditional authorities for limited modernization was motivated by the fear of southerners—either of their unsettling presence in the north or of their equally upsetting example in improving conditions in the south.

The net result was to leave the forces of moderation allied with those favoring the prevailing structure of rule, all of them opposed to ideas and forces emanating from the south. Whatever internal weaknesses existed—unexpressed peasant disaffection or potential rivalry between the Islamic factions—were concealed. The door was barred to the outright dissidents. A few genuine Nigerian nationalists and those peoples of the Middle Belt whose acceptance of Islam had always been uneven and who plainly resented domination by the Hausa-Fulani ruling faction were relegated to small parties or separatist movements on the periphery of the dominant party. In 1950 Aminu Kano, who had been instrumental in founding the NPC, broke away to form one such party, the NEPU, because of the limited NPC objectives and what he regarded as a vain hope that traditional rulers could be brought to change their views through persuasion.

The rise of the NPC represented a political awakening in the sense of a northern desire to protect its regional integrity against the south and its stake in the emerging territorial state of Nigeria, but it did not represent a change in the locus of power. The NPC strongly represented the interests of the traditional order in the preindependence deliberations. The only apparent disharmony within the NPC at the time related to the realization by moderates, such as Balewa, that only overcoming political and economic backwardness, which constituted a threat to the foundations of traditional authority, would protect the north against the more advanced south.

The success of the NPC in elections was outstanding, both for the Northern Region House of Assembly and the federal House of Representatives. In the regional House of Assembly the NPC majorities were always safe; in the federal House of Representatives the northern delegation was consistently NPC dominated. Its success was virtually guaranteed by the fact that its membership was drawn not from any mass base but from the local government and emirate officials, who had access to the major available means of communication and to the repressive traditional powers.

The constitution of the NPC placed great emphasis on the integrity and interest of the north, its traditions, religion, and social order. Support for the nation occupied a secondary place. A lack of interest in extending the NPC beyond northern borders corresponded to the heavy regional interest.

Minor Parties

The smaller parties fell into several types or classes: full-scale parties with their own organizations and, at least potentially, programs with nationwide relevance; splinter parties originating from the split of a major party; parties of minority peoples that were usually just the political aspect of an ethnic association seeking to represent their minorities in a regional assembly; and parties or movements in support of a new state.

Before 1967 Nigeria had a plethora of minor parties, most of them created for a single purpose and ordinarily short lived. Either their original purpose was fulfilled or, more commonly, they allied themselves with a major party that adopted the minor party's aims into its own program and eventually absorbed the whole party. The striving of the major parties for a geographical broadening of their influence led to whole networks of alliances, which were also attractive to the minor parties as means of gaining strength for their main objective. It was often impossible to tell whether a minor party was still independent, had an understanding with another party, was allied with it, or was absorbed by it. Also, since small parties had financial and organizational problems without much electoral compensation, they arose and then disappeared rapidly, often without eliminating the grievance that created the party in the first place.

The NEPU was the most important small independent party. Originally an offshoot of the NPC, it demonstrated a considerable permanence and strength. Close alliance with the NCNC did not deprive the NEPU of independence, since its opposition status in the north was its own accomplishment and the NCNC alliance was a liability in winning northern seats.

The president of the NEPU was Aminu Kano (also first vice president of the NCNC), who initiated the split from the NPC. The NEPU was particularly insistent on national unity, as against the separatist tenor of the NPC, and on the need for basic change in the northern system of authority. Beyond those points, its tendency was to serve as a collection point for grievances of all minority peoples in the north.

The other minor party with pretensions to independent status was the Dynamic Party, founded in Ibadan in 1955 and associated with the ideological extremism of Chike Obi, a lecturer in mathematics at the University College of Ibadan. The party propaganda featured Dynamic Collectivism and the tight totalitarian discipline of fascist models. The Dynamic Party disappeared in the late 1950s, but in 1971 its doctrines continued to have an impact and to serve as a potential rallying point for disaffected Nigerians, including some military officers. Its doctrines were less influential than the socialist philosophy expounded by Awolowo in his writings, which were accepted by large numbers among the educated younger Yoruba.

The function of ethnic minority parties was to represent the special interests of an ethnic group or collection of neighboring groups. The size of their legislative delegations, when they elected anyone to a regional assembly, was never large enough to be effective, but they served as a means of public expression for special concerns. These parties often relied chiefly upon the tribal unions for organizational continuity as well as electoral support. They were generally the object of major party attention before elections, at which time either a dominant party from another region or the opposition party from their own region offered support or an alliance. Ethnic minority parties that distinguished themselves in some way included the Igbirra Tribal Union, located in Kabba Province; the Idoma Sate Union; the Bornu Youth Movement; and several components of the Middle Belt movement, including the Birom Progressive Union, the Ilorin Youth League, and the Tiv Progressive Union.

New State Movements

After independence there were three major movements, one in each region, advocating the formation of new states. This separatist sentiment was directed against regionally dominant ethnic groups, and it generally enlisted the support of several minorities and their parties in each case. The attitudes of major parties toward the formation of new states fluctuated widely. The NCNC espoused self-determination for ethnic minorities but in accordance with its advocacy of a unitary rather than a federal state; the AG also supported such movements, as well as the campaign to restore Yoruba areas of the north (Ilorin) to the west, as an advocate of a multistate federal Nigeria; the NPC steadfastly opposed any Northern Region separatism, preferring to win over (with some success) segments of the Middle Belt movement. The NEPU generally supported the Middle Belt movement.

Mid-Western State was proposed in order to separate from the

Western Region the whole tract of territory adjacent to the Niger River. The movement was motivated by Edo, Urhobo, and western Ibo ethnic sentiment and was supplemented by Ijaw separatism, which wanted to belong not to Mid-Western State but to the proposed Calabar-Ogoja-Rivers state with other Ijaw across the Niger River.

The Calabar-Ogoja-Rivers proposal was supported in the Eastern Region by anti-Ibo ethnic elements that wanted it to cover the whole coastline from Calabar to the Niger River, thus enclosing the Ibo area. Ibo areas within the proposed state resisted inclusion. The Ibibio, Efik, and Ijaw ethnic groups provided the backbone of the Calabar-Ogoja-Rivers state movement.

The most extensive revision sought was the separation from the Hausa-Fulani areas of domination in the north of a vast Middle Belt extending from the west to the eastern border and incorporating approximately the southern half of the Northern Region along the Niger and Benue rivers. The proposal was supported by nearly all of the many ethnic groups of the area out of resentment against the powerful emirates. The United Middle Belt Congress, the federation of political parties attempting to further the movement, was not united, however. Its divergent factions could not agree, and prospects of separation were dimmed by the varying success of the NPC in reconciling parts of the United Middle Belt Congress to the continuance of existing boundaries.

POLITICS IN THE CRISIS YEARS (1963–66)

During the first three years of independence the federal government was controlled by a parliamentary and cabinet alignment of the NPC and the NCNC, despite the strongly conflicting natures of the parties and the NCNC's support for the NPC's opponents in northern election campaigns. Although an alignment of the AG and the NCNC delegations was called for by the AG leaders, it held no attraction for the NCNC as long as the NPC controlled a majority of the seats in Parliament.

Within the regions the NPC domination of the north and the NCNC control of the east and, later, of the midwest remained largely unchallenged. AG control in the west, however, was weakened and toppled because of challenges from within Yoruba society. This loss of stability in one of its regions gradually weakened the political structure of the whole country.

Division along ideological lines within Yoruba political ranks began as early as 1961. The party rift widened in 1962. Western Region Premier Akintola and his followers, ejected from the AG, formed a new party, the United People's Party (UPP) (see ch. 3, Historical Setting).

AG party leader Awolowo and his followers adopted radical language that called for a democratic socialist stage, while Akintola attempted to prevent the loss of support by more conservative and traditional elements. Awolowo was opposed to participation in a unity government with ministers from all three parties; AG financial backers were opposed to the support of opposition parties in other regions, which they regarded as fruitless efforts. The radical language in Awolowo's political pronouncements was not found in his earlier published opinions; rather, he adopted this new stance as a bid for the support of the educated young men in all four regions whose expectations were frustrated by unemployment and the rising cost of living. This, he felt, was the only way to create an interregional political party and national unity.

Other major factors in the AG–UPP split included the inherent divisions within Yoruba society. The AG represented the voice of the educated, younger, and more radical Yoruba; the UPP represented the established order and business interests. Awolowo and his AG drew its support from a portion of the Yoruba lands centered in the Ijebu city-state, whose inhabitants were traditional rivals of the people of Ibadan, a group that included most of the uneducated Yoruba Muslims. The new party remained in control of the government of the Western Region until 1966, allying itself first with the NCNC and later with the NPC (see ch. 3, Historical Setting).

Another element was the willingness of local leaders to change sides in order to exploit the advantages of ties with the party in power. One observer in Ibadan at the time of the split recorded a typical sequence of political activity by a group of ward leaders in a single morning. They met with Awolowo to pledge their loyalty; hurried to a reception for Akintola; returned to their ward to hoist the AG banner on their office; and then sat down inside to arrange for the establishment of a UPP branch office.

Because Akintola favored better relations with the NPC, he received federal backing to retain control of the government. Awolowo and the AG were investigated by a special commission, which revealed that funds belonging to government-owned and controlled corporations had been used to finance AG political campaigns. Shortly afterward, Awolowo and a number of his key followers were charged with plotting the overthrow of the government with arms and training received in Ghana. Upon conviction, Awolowo was sentenced to ten years in prison (see ch. 3, Historical Setting).

In addition to removing the AG leaders from the active political scene, the trial severely weakened popular faith in the political and judicial systems. It also revealed the extent to which violence was

228

a factor in Nigerian politics and the direct links that existed between political activity and financial gains. It further revealed that the parties in power at the regional level made frequent use of local officials—whether traditional, appointed, or elected—during elections. These officials could be coerced into influencing their followers or into hindering the opposition's campaign by the regional government's threats to withdraw supporting funds or recognition or to investigate corrupt practices.

Political abuses were widespread, including intimidation of opponents, diversion of public funds to party use, placement of party supporters in local government jobs, and manipulation of elections. Popular disillusionment was further engendered by the failure of the politicians to produce the tangible benefits they promised the people at election time, particularly more jobs, food, and material goods and increased local development. Those in urban areas observed that, while the rising cost of living made them poorer, the political leaders were growing richer and more powerful. Public support for democratic political promises was also weakened by the controversy over the census, which revealed vast manipulation of returns by regional politicians who hoped to alter the balance of representation in the federal Parliament that was to be reapportioned according to population distribution (see ch. 3, Historical Setting; ch. 4, Population and Labor).

One of the most significant results of the drama in the Western Region was the destruction of the relatively simple political structure of Nigeria. In the immediate postindependence period the Northern Region was controlled by the NPC; the Eastern Region, by the NCNC; and the Western Region, by the AG (which had at first been a moderate party standing between the more radical NCNC and the conservative NPC). The federal government was a coalition of the traditionalist NPC and the modernist NCNC in which the NPC had the greater power because the Northern Region, with 54 percent of the population, held a large plurality of seats—45 percent—in the federal House of Representatives. The AG appeared destined to be in permanent opposition. The virtual demise of the AG in the federal Parliament, as a result of the Awolowo affair and the creation of the UPP Western Region government, fundamentally changed the political complex at the national level.

By early 1964 the federal Parliament did not have a recognized opposition party and was led by a government composed of the ruling parties of all four regions. The strength of the coalition's major opponent, the AG, was considerably reduced, even in its Western Region stronghold. The positions of the NPC in the north and the NCNC in the east remained unchallenged. The federal coalition government's position had been strengthened in other respects as well. The NCNC had gained firm control of the government of the Mid-Western Region. The Western Region was ruled by a new party, the Nigerian National Democratic Party (NNDP), formed by Akintola to replace his UPP with a party attractive to all Yoruba. It met with immediate success in attracting away Yoruba members of the NCNC, although on the national level its platform called for an alliance with the NCNC in the coalition government.

This apparent calm was deceiving as the basic divisions of the country remained unaltered. Despite their relatively long duration, the interparty alliances between the traditionalist-dominated north and the progressive south were only temporary arrangements. The north continued to fear that the southerners, particularly the NCNC and the AG, would form a grouping with the limited number of northern progressives and take power in the federal Parliament. The NPC leaders believed southern control a danger to the north and viewed it as a disaster in regard to their control of their own society. Southern leaders believed that only through such unity could they bring about improvements in the country. Awolowo, for example, wrote in 1963 that democracy and progress in the country could only be brought about if the AG and the NCNC were able to combine to remove the deadweight of the north. The two parties remained divided, however, by conflicts of personalities and desires for power.

Despite growing popular disenchantment with the political situation, the first major protests against government policies came from the labor unions and were motivated by economic complaints, particularly the failure of wage increases to match the fast-rising cost of living. The potential power of the unions was crippled, however, by ineffective leadership and inability to unite (see ch. 4, Population and Labor).

Labor union divisions were neither political nor ideological but, rather, splits over issues of personality and tactics. Even after their notable success in the general strike of May and June 1964, in which 800,000 persons left their jobs, the unions failed to translate their potential power into political effectiveness. The strikes were at least partially motivated by a desire to protest the failings of the politicians. The strike negotiations, which the federal prime minister at first refused to sanction, were eventually a victory for the unions.

The 1964 Elections

In 1964 the federal parliamentary elections—the first since independence—were contested by two political alliances. The Nigerian National Alliance (NNA) was composed of the NPC, the dominant party in the north; the NNDP, the party in office in the west; and opposition parties in the midwest and east. It was opposed by the United Progressive Grand Alliance (UPGA) of the major southern parties. The UPGA had elicited the support of two northern allies, the NEPU and the United Middle Belt Congress.

The NNA adopted a stance in campaigning at the national level that reflected the views of the northern political elite. It also incorporated an appeal to nonmembers based on the benefits to be gained from associating with the party in power. The UPGA offered a reformist program to improve the conditions of the workers and the poor through moderate socialism and a planned economy without denying opportunity to private enterprise. It also returned to demands for dividing the country into a number of small states along the lines of the existing ethnically based provinces. Its intentions were to end Hausa-Fulani domination over the Middle Belt, to lessen the north's domination of the federal government, to strengthen the political position of the smaller ethnic groups at the expense of the three major groups dominating the regions and, thus, to strengthen national unity.

UPGA members, convinced that they would win if the elections were held in an atmosphere free from interference by the ruling parties in the north and west, spent most of their campaign efforts on denouncing what they regarded as plans of the NNA to rig the elections in those two areas. For the first time, the term *secession* was associated with the east. The NNA suggested that the Eastern Region might try to secede if the UPGA lost the elections, an accusation rigorously denied by regional premier and party leader Michael Okpara.

The federal elections of 1964 and the subsequent elections in the Western Region involved widespread violence and open violations of the electoral laws and provided little representative voice for the people. Popular protests reflected the almost universal disillusionment with democratic processes. Violence and protest over the Western Region election results continued unabated for six months; an estimated 2,000 persons were killed (see ch. 3, Historical Setting).

By January 1966 a military intervention was expected by all sides; the only unanswered question was the direction from which it would come. Prime Minister Balewa was urged to use federal military and police power to end the chaos in the west by declaring a state of emergency. He declined to do so, apparently under pressure from his own party and its NNDP allies, including Western Region Premier Akintola, around whom most of the violence revolved. The intervention, when it did come, came from an unexpected quarter and resulted not only in an end to political violence in the west but also in the death of Balewa, Akintola, and others and an end to the existing political order throughout the country.

Coup d'Etat and Military Rule

Even after the coup d'etat of January 1966 had ended, its origins and objectives remained unclear. There was some speculation that more than one group had been planning separate insurrections. What was clear was that the coup was led by a group of army majors, most of whom were from the Eastern and Mid-Western Regions, and that their planned actions included the seizure and probably the execution of political figures throughout the country. They were motivated by a desire to put an end to the chaos in the west and to bring about government reforms. In their only public proclamation before the revolt was stopped short of its ultimate goals by the actions of the army commander, one of the group's leaders proclaimed the suspension of the constitution and the division of the regions into a number of provinces and promised strong penalties for political corruption at every level.

The expressed attitudes of the men who planned the coup were based on ideals that appealed to the younger men in all regions of the country, particularly the educated and urbanized elements who had been best able to observe the problems of the earlier government. Despite their failure to achieve power, their policies were largely adopted by the Federal Military Government (FMG) formed under Major General J.T.U. Aguiyi-Ironsi (see ch. 3, Historical Setting).

Although political parties were forbidden, the politicians and the regional attitudes remained. Northern opinion, even in the emirates, was particularly divided over the outcome of the January coup. The rebellion's leaders were almost automatically viewed as enemies of the north because they were progressive easterners; moreover, they had executed a number of northern leaders but few easterners. On the other hand, the leaders of the rebellion had been frustrated in their bid for power by a fellow Ibo, General Ironsi, who had appointed a number of northerners to important posts. These included a popular Fulani officer, Major Hassan Katsina, who became the military governor of the Northern Region. Major Katsina, the son of a powerful emir, had given tacit support to the coup.

Even the deaths of some northerners had been viewed with mixed feelings. The Sardauna of Sokoto was not widely liked, and many were pleased with his death. Some in the traditional order were gratified because they had aligned themselves with his rivals for eventual succession to the sultanate; others, because he represented Fulani domination over the other northern peoples.

To General Ironsi and his advisers the solution of Nigeria's political, economic, and development problems required a unitary form of government, which they felt would wipe out the rigid adherence to regionalism that had become the country's foremost political problem. Unification had broad support among many people. For ethnic minority groups in both the north and the south it brought the chance for freedom from control by a larger group. For southerners it offered the opportunity to use their educational superiority, competitiveness, and drive to advance to the additional high posts in a unified civil service. The northern regional and local governments had barred their civil service posts to southerners since the early 1950s, preferring to keep British colonial officers in their posts rather than open them to southern Nigerians. Both the Yoruba and the Ibo also believed that unification would improve the status of southern traders and company employees in the north.

The concept of national unity appealed generally to all members of the modernized elite. Although they were few in number, their influence was substantial, particularly among General Ironsi's advisers. Members of the elite group also filled the top ranks of both the federal and southern civil services and the army, which were the most unified organizations in the country.

In carrying out the changes necessitated by the FMG program, General Ironsi was not always sensitive to the nuances of regional politics. In the north unification was regarded with consternation bordering on fear. Regionalism's chief appeal in the north had been its protection against domination by the more educated and aggressive southerners. In the north, even more than in the comparatively rich south, the government provided the major source of employment.

Northerners were aware that in open competition with southerners their own lack of educational opportunities and experience in modern society would mean that they would be deprived of many posts. The Hausa-Fulani and other Islamic traditionalists also feared that the influx of southerners would introduce into the sociopolitical order new ideas and values that would effectively challenge those of traditional society. The upper classes in a rigidly stratified society were particularly fearful that democratic ideals of government would be introduced, leading the peasant majority to challenge the domination of their Fulani rulers and Hausa lords.

Although the social and political values of the Middle Belt peoples were closer to those of the southerners than to the Hausa-Fulani, unification of the civil service represented a threat to their job opportunities. The educational opportunities in mission schools had enabled them to surpass the peoples of the emirates but had not been equal to those educational opportunities available to the people in the south.

Northern animosity was also stirred by a number of incidents that occurred in the first half of 1966. These included the government's failure to prosecute those responsible for the execution of northern leaders in the January coup; General Ironsi's vulnerability to accusations of favoritism to the Ibo; and the attitudes of triumph openly displayed by many Ibo residing in the north.

On May 24, 1966, General Ironsi issued a decree altering the constitutional structure of government to assure prompt national unification. The decree contained a number of accommodations to regional interests, including protection for northerners from southern competition in the civil service, but popular reaction in the north was violent. Within a week, under the urging of disgruntled civil servants, politicians, and others who had lost economic and political advantages with the change of government, the Hausa-Fulani in the northern cities carried out a pogrom against the local Ibo, killing several hundred of them.

Attempts by the Ironsi government to reduce tension met with only partial success. The continuing fear among northerners that they would lose power in a centralized, Ibo-dominated state led directly to a second coup on July 29, 1966. More than 200 soldiers from the Eastern and Mid-Western Regions were killed by northern troops in what was apparently a delayed reaction to the killing of three senior northern officers in the January coup.

Those involved in the second coup were militarily successful but, unlike the leaders of the January coup, they lacked plans for future developments. Many of their supporters demanded that the Northern Region secede from the country, taking the Western Region with it and leaving the Eastern and Mid-Western Regions as a rump Nigeria.

The void in leadership was quickly filled by the ranking northern officer remaining after the January coup, Lieutenant Colonel Yakubu Gowon, a Christian from the Middle Belt. As army chief of staff, he negotiated a settlement with the rebellious soldiers, who insisted that he assume the position of leadership of the FMG. The northern political and traditional leaders then reversed their support for secession, partly in reaction to changes in power within the FMG and partly out of fear that their new nation would not be economically viable if deprived of a share in the rich new oil revenues of the Eastern Region.

In September and October 1966 northern political and traditional leaders initiated a new pogrom against easterners in the north in a drive to crush all Ibo power. Deaths were estimated at 10,000 to 30,000, and more than 1 million people fled from the north into the Eastern Region. The division of the army into eastern and northern elements after the killings made it impossible for regional military leaders to find a continuing basis for national unity.

The Eastern Region's military governor, Lieutenant Colonel C.O. Ojukwu, was under considerable pressure from those who felt that the country could never be reunited and that the Eastern Region, with its oil revenues and with or without the Mid-Western Region, should withdraw as a separate political entity. The only question left undecided was the form of ties, if any, that might be allowed to remain between the Eastern Region and the rest of Nigeria.

Gowon, Ojukwu, and the other regional government leaders met under the sponsorship of the Ghana military government at Aburi, Ghana, in January 1967. Despite some apparent agreement on the terms of separation, amounting to a loose confederation, the results of the meeting were unsuccessful. The tentative agreements reached by the military officers were strongly criticized by the federal civil servants upon Gowon's return to Lagos, and the government declined to accept them. Faced with increasing signs that the east would withdraw entirely from the federation, the FMG largely adhered to the Aburi agreements in a decree of March 31, 1967, but the Ojukwu government rejected this effort and announced that it would retain all revenues collected in the region in reparation for the costs of resettling the refugees from the north. This announcement, however, did not affect the revenues for the oilfields, which were paid directly by the oil companies to the federal government.

The strains within the country had begun to spread by April 1967. Awolowo, who had been released from jail after the coups, had again assumed leadership of the more aggressive labor and intellectual elements in the west. He demanded the removal of all northern troops garrisoned in the west, a move that had not been carried out earlier because there were so few Yoruba in the army's ranks. He announced that if the east seceded the west would feel free to follow, as the country was no longer a workable unit. Awolowo's announcement was followed by demands of the Mid-Western Region's governor that his state be considered a neutral territory in any ensuing conflict.

Faced with these additional threats of disaffection, the leaders of the north—the first to threaten secession—now called for the creation of a multistate country and offered to sacrifice regional unity for the federation, an offer that had been the east's earliest demand. The Yoruba leaders accepted this offer, as the Ibo leaders had been eager to do earlier. The FMG then agreed to withdraw federal troops from the western areas.

The eastern leaders were no longer willing to turn back. Despite the fact that the new offers met their earliest demands, the Eastern Region Consultative Assembly voted on May 26 to secede. Gowon announced a state of emergency and the division of the country into twelve states, with the Eastern Region divided in such a way as to deprive the Ibo heartland of its control over the oilfields and access to the sea as well as the support of other eastern ethnic groups. On May 30 Ojukwu announced that the east had seceded and established itself as the independent Republic of Biafra.

The Biafrans felt that they had not withdrawn from Nigeria but rather were expelled by the other groups, who feared Ibo control of the country because of their energy, talent, and educational advantages. The secession was depicted as a move to preserve Ibo lives that was taken only after all other efforts to obtain just treatment and safeguards for their personal and economic life had failed. In press relations with the foreign news media Biafran leaders depicted themselves as Christians in defensive action against the Muslims of the north.

The central issue in Ibo relations with the rest of Nigeria was the 1966 pogrom in the north. Biafran leaders maintained that the action resulted in the deaths of 30,0000 Ibo and that it was carried out at the urging of government broadcasting stations with the help of the army's northern troops. To these casualties were added an estimated 2 million easterners who died during the war in the fighting or of malnutrition. Easterners were led to believe that any food that might be delivered to them through Nigerian lines would have been poisoned as part of an alleged program of genocide aimed at them. They also believed that, if the Nigerians won, the FMG would at least carry out a campaign of cultural genocide by killing all of the Ibo intellectual and political elite, destroying the eastern educational system, and bringing the Ibo back into the federation as laborers without having to accept them as competitors.

POLITICAL IMPACT OF THE CIVIL WAR

The extensive and successful use made of propaganda opportunities by the Biafran leaders to gain international support for their secession effort obscured political opinion in the former Eastern Region during the period of the civil war. The effect of the war on Ibo opinion was significant, but defeat and the subsequent fair treatment at the hands of the FMG make their wartime attitudes no longer a relevant political consideration. Major bitterness toward the Ibo apparently developed among other Eastern Region peoples as a result of the wartime hardships they suffered; many of these ethnic minorities regarded the war as one for which the Ibo alone were responsible.

Victory by federal Nigerian forces over those of the Biafran secessionists was achieved in January 1970 after thirty months of civil war (see ch. 1, General Character of the Society). It was followed by major efforts under Gowon's close direction to treat the Ibo as fellow countrymen rather than as conquered enemies, and the FMG immediately undertook a program designed to reintegrate them into a unified Nigeria. A general amnesty announced at the war's end was extended to all Ibo remaining in the country, and steps were taken to demonstrate that the amnesty was meaningful. An Ibo official who had remained loyal to the federal government was named administrator for East Central State; his all-Ibo cabinet included eight members who had supported the secessionists.

The FMG granted East Central State the necessary funds to cover its operating expenses until its own economy was restored. Government employment was given to as many Ibo as possible, and steps were taken to free individual assets that had been seized by the federal or regional governments. Although they had openly supported the rebellion, a number of prominent Ibo officials were appointed to high posts in the civil service. By the end of 1970 Gowon had gained popular acceptance and support among the Ibo of the eastern states.

In the postwar era all significant political power remained concentrated in the hands of the FMG; none of the three major ethnic groups had a powerful voice in the executive element of the government. In addition, the redivision of the former Northern Region into six separate states left the north without its former political power. Only the Yoruba power base retained its prewar characteristics. The chief effect of changes in the north and the east was the creation of a new force in Nigerian politics; a major share of political power and an important voice in the executive were given to the smaller ethnic groups, particularly the Ijaw and the Ibibio from the east, the northern Muslim Yoruba, and the Tiv, the Nupe, and other Middle Belt peoples.

Some observers felt that changes in the former Northern Region may have had a greater impact on the country's future political dynamics than the civil war had produced. Certainly the breaking away of the two Middle Belt states from Hausa-Fulani domination introduced a permanent factor in future relations. The other four states of the north also appeared in mid-1971 to have accepted the division of the country into twelve or more states as a permanent arrangement. In the areas traditionally dominated by emirates of the Hause-Fulani type, the position of the traditional authorities had been permanently weakened by military rule, particularly by the replacement of the emirs' council by local councils in which the remaining traditional authorities had only a single vote.

According to some observers, former Hausa hatred of the Ibo has been replaced by new tensions between the Hausa-Fulani and the Yoruba who entered the north in large numbers to replace the Ibo after 1966. Since then, the northerners have come to regard the Yoruba in somewhat the same manner in which they had earlier looked upon the Ibo. The Yoruba are feared by the northern traditional leaders as a threatening source of new ideas. The Yoruba—less aggressive, more used to giving deference to royal traditions, and often themselves Muslims—are not in such obvious conflict with Hausa society as were the Ibo, however.

Political differences in the west again reached violent proportions in 1969 over the issue of taxes; 400 persons were arrested, and 200 were killed in the second half of the year. Elimination of corrupt practices continued to receive major attention from the FMG. In 1971 conflict had again arisen between the followers of Awolowo and his opponents, who were attempting to force the FMG to divide Western State in order to provide new government job opportunities.

POSTWAR RECONSTRUCTION GOALS

In October 1970 General Gowon announced that the FMG intended to stay in power and had set 1976 as the target year for the completion of its political program and the return of Nigeria to elected civil government. In announcing the target date, the military chief of state outlined a nine-point program that the FMG officials felt must be completed before relinquishing federal control. Included were the reorganization of the armed forces; implementation of a national development plan and repair of the damage and neglect brought about by the civil war; eradication of corruption in national life; settlement of the question of creating more states; preparation and adoption of a new constitution; introduction of a new formula for allocating revenue; conducting of a national population census; organization of genuinely national political parties; and organization of electoral processes and installation of popularly elected governments at federal and state levels.

Criticism of the six-year target was widespread. Some of the points were so broad or involved such marked social changes that many people could not imagine their being carried out even in a much longer period. Some Nigerians concluded therefore that the military leaders would retain power permanently. The reactions of the civilian politicians were particularly negative. They saw themselves deprived of their opportunities for a return to power or, in the case of the leaders of the new states, a first taste of it. Awolowo knew that he would be too old to campaign effectively in 1976, and the traditional-minded northerners feared the effect of military rule in eroding their control of society in the emirates. The resulting reduction of confidence in the FMG contributed to a loss of the morale needed to accomplish the large tasks at hand.

In mid-1971 the army was the major political force in the country. Its strength had grown from about 10,000 in 1967 to approximately 250,000 to combat the Biafran insurgency. Although its size had been reduced to about 240,000 in 1971, its use was confined mainly to limited participation in civic action, a task its officers were somewhat reluctant to expand (see ch. 15, National Security). Widespread unemployment and the dangers involved in discharging large numbers of soldiers without jobs made rapid demobilization undesirable. Nigerian political and ethnic factionalism had not yet publicly surfaced in the postwar army. The army's leaders found it necessary to spend an increased portion of the national budget on the military establishment.

THE GOVERNMENTAL STRUCTURE

From independence until 1966 the federal government was at the apex of a pyramidal governmental structure. Just below the top were the regional governments, followed in descending order by the provinces within each region, divisions, or Native Authorities, and districts. At the bottom there were the organs of city, township, and village government.

The structure of the federal and regional governments was modeled after the British parliamentary system; each consisted of a two-house parliament, a responsible executive, and an independent judiciary. In each of the regional legislatures the lower house, called the House of Assembly, was elected by universal adult suffrage (in the Northern Region only adult males could vote); and the upper house, or Senate, was composed of traditional local leaders. Certain entrenched clauses of the constitution guaranteed civil and other rights.

The establishment of the republic in 1963 after three years of sovereignty did not cause any major practical change in the constitutional system (se ch. 3, Historical Setting). The president replaced the British crown as the symbol of national authority and the governor general as head of state, but real power remained in the hands of Parliament and the prime minister, who was the head of government. The transition was further minimized by the constitution's specification of Nnamdi Azikiwe, the governor general, as the republic's first president. Except for the loss of the right to appeal decisions of the Federal Supreme Court to the Judicial Committee of the British Privy Council, the rest of the constitution remained virtually unchanged.

Certain other legislation in the 1961–64 period, however, had the effect of threatening the independence of the judiciary and of bringing the office of the public prosecutor under greater political control. In 1964 a press law was passed; it was designed not so much to limit the actions of the country's independent newspapers as to reduce the tendency of journalists to inflame public opinion (see ch. 8, Education, Public Information, and the Arts and Sciences).

After the coup d'etat of January 15, 1966, the military leaders suspended the offices of the president, the prime minister, and the Council of Ministers and closed Parliament, vesting all legislative and executive powers in the FMG. The first decree of the FMG replaced the executive and legislative branches of the four regional governments with appointed officers of the military or police acting as regional military governors and functioning directly under the FMG.

The ministries at both the federal and regional levels continued to function, under the supervision of their permanent secretaries, who were ranking civil servants. On March 17, 1967, the FMG issued its Constitution (Suppression and Modification) Decree, which vested all legislative and executive power in the Supreme Military Council, whose chairman was the chief of state.

In May 1967 the Supreme Military Council issued a decree creating twelve smaller states in place of the four larger regions. The secession attempt by the leaders of the Eastern Region in mid-1967 and the subsequent 2½ years of civil war brought the actual implementation of many parts of the decree to a near standstill. The reorganization of the country along state lines thus was still new in 1971; state governmental structures were in a process of further development, with only broad and inconsistent patterns revealed.

In 1971 the head of government, Major General Yakubu Gowon, served as chairman of both the Supreme Military Council, which acted as the country's executive body, and the Federal Executive Council, which served as the cabinet. He was also commander in chief of the armed forces. The Federal Executive Council was composed of both military officers and civilians, drawn largely from the ranks of the political leadership and the technocracy.

In addition to General Gowon, members of the Supreme Military Council included the commanders of the navy and the air force, the chiefs of staff of the armed forces and the Supreme Headquarters, the country's two ranking police officials, eleven state military governors, and the civilian administrator of East Central State.

In mid-1971 the Federal Executive Council was composed of General Gowon and fifteen other commissioners. The additional military officers were members of the Federal Executive Council and the Supreme Military Council: the commander of the navy, Rear Admiral J.E.A. Wey, who served as commissioner of establishment (civil service structure); and the inspector general of police, Alhaji Kam Selem, who served as commissioner of internal affairs. The other ministries were those of external affairs, finance, transport, communications, health, justice, economic development, information and labor, education, works and housing, mines and power, trade and industry, and agriculture and natural resources. Awolowo was finance commissioner until July 1971 but resigned in protest against FMG policies.

In mid-1971 similar structure of government was repeated at the state level. Each governor, except the governor of Lagos State, had a cabinet composed of civilian commissioners, each of whom was responsible for a ministry; some ministries were composed of more than one department. In Lagos State the civilian commissioners were charged with areas of responsibility; ministries did not exist since in the capital most services were provided by the federal ministries. In North Eastern State, which had limited resources, the cabinet was limited to five ministries; the other ten states had ten or more ministries.

In the absence of a national legislature, the FMG ruled by decree. The concurrence of the state military governors, however, was required on certain matters before a decree could be issued. This restriction applied to all decrees that related to the territorial integrity of a state, national economic policy, the civil service, public security, and the entrenched clauses of the 1963 Constitution. The creation of new states was to be treated as an entrenched clause. Appointments to the higher ranks of the civil service were the prerogative of the Supreme Military Council, acting with the advice of the Public Service Commission. The Supreme Military Council had the power to override state legislation if it conflicted with federal laws.

Organization of Government Departments

The organization of ministries was not generally altered by the events of the 1966–70 period. In larger ministries the senior official was assisted by one or more appointed officials at the junior-minister level. The ranking civil servant within each ministry was the permanent secretary, who served both as the head of the department's civil service establishment and as the chief adviser to the minister. The deputy permanent secretary often was in charge of a ministry's general administration section. Other sections were headed by a deputy secretary, assisted by a senior assistant secretary and various assistant secretaries.

Considerable difference existed between ministries dealing with administrative matters and those responsible for technical affairs. In the technical ministries the permanent secretary and his deputy usually directed the general administrative section. On an equal level, one or more directors of technical services were responsible for ministerial operations. Although even in the technical ministries the permanent secretary was the minister's chief adviser, the directors of technical services might report directly to the minister. The permanent secretary was also the director of the ministry's civil service element and decided on the promotion, transfer, and discipline of junior officers.

In line with the British concepts accepted from the colonial order, the permanent secretaries were almost always drawn from that portion of the civil service known as the administrative class and were generalists chosen for their academic degrees rather than professionals with experience and technical qualifications. Considerable friction was sometimes generated among the professionals because of this general bar to their advancement to the highest level.

In addition to the ministerial structure at both the federal and state levels were a number of autonomous public corporations, which were founded and funded by the government. These were not staffed by civil servants or necessarily under ministerial control, but they always operated under the ultimate direction and supervision of the appropriate ministry. Until the establishment of the FMG, the appropriate minister or the Council of Ministers appointed the members of the board of directors. Many of the major scandals involving the misuse of public funds during the 1960–66 period involved the manipulation of public corporations for the benefit of political parties and their leaders.

Corporation appointments were also used to satisfy the demands of political patronage. The top posts were generally filled by leaders of the winning party who were unable to secure an elected office. Because of the coalition form of government found at federal and regional levels, the ministers of different parties were able to appoint directors to the boards for which they were responsible. Given the ethnic nature of party support, this generally meant that all posts in a particular corporation would be filled by one ethnic group. The Nigerian Railway Corporation, for example, became completely Ibo staffed, so that even the track workers in the far northwest were Ibo.

The FMG dissolved these boards and replaced them with members drawn from the civil service and the corporation staffs themselves to ensure technical competence. Since 1966, however, many posts again have been gradually filled with political appointees.

The Twelve-State System

The main purpose of the FMG in announcing the creation of twelve states to replace the four regions in 1967 was to lessen the support for secession in the Eastern Region. They felt that the separation of South Eastern State and Rivers State with majorities composed of Ibibio and Ijaw would weaken the Ojukwu government's political viability, particularly as the Ibo heartland would be left without any direct access to the sea and would be deprived of half of the region's oil revenues. At the same time fragmentation of the Northern Region was expected to lessen the Ibo's determination to withdraw from the federation by destroying the ability of their Hausa-Fulani enemies to exert control over the national government.

The new administrative divisions also were expected to make national unity more attractive to the Yoruba by strengthening their position in comparison to that of the Hausa-Fulani; because the new system of states included a state for the Yoruba of Kabba Province, it effectively liberated the northern Yoruba from a hundred years of Fulani domination. In addition to weakening the position of the major group, the new division strengthened the hand of the smaller ethnic groups by both giving them status in federal affairs and making them a counterweight to the former three-way division of power. In addition, the strengthened position of the Middle Belt peoples corresponded to their disproportionate position in the FMG and the army, particularly in the absence of the Ibo.

The Northern Region was divided into six states, and the Eastern Region was made into four. With one exception, the new states were created out of the existing provincial system: Abakaliki Province was divided between East Central State and South Eastern State. Apart from the designation of the Lagos capital district as a separate state, the boundaries of the Western and Mid-Western Regions remained unaltered. Kano Province became Kano State. All other states were composed of from two to four former provinces. Although two provinces of the Middle Belt were linked with Hausa and Fulani provinces in the new alignment, the important minor groups in each were linked to the north by Fulani rule, the Islamic religion, and the emirate form of government.

The Northern Region accepted its division into six states without protest, despite its earlier opposition. In part, this resulted from the FMG's relative strength in comparison with earlier civilian governments. Acceptance also was motivated by the fact that people were weary of the successive crises, less fearful of Ibo control, and apprehensive that the former leaders would return to power if reforms failed.

The decree announcing creation of the state system also created an interim administration council for the north that was to arrange the procedures by which the changes were to occur. Included were arrangements for central institutions that could not be readily divided, such as the local government training center and the High Court. The council was composed of the six state military governors, three other military officials, and the permanent secretaries of the regional ministries.

Conflicts arose over many aspects of the division of institutional services and materials as well as boundaries and capitals. A key factor in ethnic animosities was the issue of control over the federal and regional civil services. Points of conflict included the number of civil service posts to be assigned to each and the posting of civil servants from the former regional service to states other than their own. After 1967 separate civil services were formed at the federal level and within each state. Gradually the major issue again became the contest for jobs, with clamors both for a larger share of posts and demands for the apportionment of state positions along district or ethnic lines.

As the state system began to operate, new problems arose. The military governors had little experience in public administration or politics. Because of the general lack of other qualified staff, they were forced to appoint as the commissioners in charge of state ministries men who either were associated with the former political order or who did not have the requisite experience. In addition, the civil service had become demoralized by the changes and had difficulty establishing a loyalty to the new states. The movement and realignment provided an inlet for renewed political influences on the supposedly impartial civil servants.

Preoccupied with the issue of secession by the former Eastern Region, the federal government became the target of animosity generated by its failure to deal decisively with the problems of the northern states. Little guidance was given for the formulation of attitudes governing relationships between the military governors and their administrative organs, between the various states, and between the states and the federal ministries.

Despite these difficulties, by 1971 the system had been accepted, and the states were carrying out marked improvements in health, education, public services, and local government. Moreover, the system had provided a real voice for the ethnic minorities whose desires for political power had no outlet of consequence in the regional structure.

In mid-1971 threats to the stability of the state system were confined largely to the demand for jobs in the government service. Many had expressed a desire for an ethnic or geographical apportionment of all government posts. More serious was the growing demand for additional new states created along ethnic lines to provide jobs, patronage, and power for local political authorities.

Local Government

Administrative units below the state level varied from area to area as the system was changing in the 1969–71 period. In general, the states were subdivided in descending order into provinces, divisions, districts, and local authority units. In 1970 four of the northern states abolished their provinces in favor of divisions as the first subordinate level of administrative organization. In turn, the two northern states that had retained provinces had abolished their subordinate divisions. In the west units below provinces were called districts; until 1967 the corresponding unit in the east was the county.

In the north a division was generally composed of a single subordinate body called a local authority; no equivalent unit existed in the south. Some northern divisions contained two or three such units of government that functioned under divisional supervision. The provinces without divisions were composed of as few as one or as many as eight local authorities. Local authorities generally corresponded to a traditional emirate.

Subordinate to the units at the local authority level were units variously called district, village, and urban or town councils. In rural areas of the north a few units at this level were labeled outer councils. The number of local government units under a local authority varied from as few as 1 to as many as 250.

In general, the local authorities functioned under one of four different kinds of executive: chief in council, chief and council, council, or appointed administrator. The appointed administrator system, which was employed by the state government only in unstable circumstances, was common in the 1969–71 period since a large number of councils had been abolished because of corrupt practices. The chief and council form was found mainly in the most conservative areas of the north and is gradually being abolished. This form of government left all decisionmaking in the hands of the chief or the emir, who was assisted by a council often composed of the leader's traditional advisers.

The chief or emir remained the central executive figure in the chief and council form of government, but he might not act against the recommendation of the majority of his council members. The most advanced form was the council, which functioned under a chairman and arrived at decisions by majority vote. Although it was intended that a portion—preferably the majority—of all councils should be chosen by the people, the FMG's ban on all political activity barred elections, and those elected councillors who had been in office before the 1966 revolution had been removed as part of the political restrictions. Council members, therefore, were generally all appointed by the state military governor on the recommendation of the divisional administrator. In fact, however, many held office as a result of their position in the traditional order.

In mid-1971 all local authority units varied greatly in geographical size, population, and resources. The Bornu Local Authority was larger than all but three of the states. The Kano Local Authority has a population of 5 million and a budget of N£2.5 million (1 Nigerian pound equals US$2.80), but some local authority units were as small as 100 square miles and had revenues under N£20,000.

Some local authorities were actually amalgamations of smaller units that previously had local authority status. In this case the form of government was almost always a council. Its chairmanship was rotated among the chiefs of the subordinate former local authorities that continued to exist in an attenuated form, generally called administrative areas. The local authority work was carried out by its own employees, who were not members of either the state or federal civil services. Policy guidance was provided to the heads of local authority departments by councillors or committees of councillors charged with responsibility for the affairs of a department or group of departments. The committee members were not all members of the councils.

Under British rule and during the first five years of independence, the primary responsibility of the local authorities (or Native Authorities as they were called until 1966) was the preservation of law and order (see ch. 15, National Security). Since the mid-1960s the local authorities had been given increasing responsibility for fulfilling the expanding demands for economic and social welfare. Primary responsibility included the operation of a number of primary schools, local public health and veterinary services, population registration, local welfare services, secondary roads, markets, and agricultural extension services. The extent and range of these efforts varied greatly with the needs and revenues of each area.

In each state executive and administrative supervision of the local authorities were exercised by the State Ministry of Local Government through its ranking local official, the divisions officer. Their finances were supervised by the appropriate state ministry, such as those responsible for matters of health, education, or public works. About half of the local authority budget covers staff salaries, which were set by the state government. The state also approved appointments to senior posts within the local authority system.

The local authorities supervised and partially financed operations of the district, village, or other local subordinate government. These units varied from British-style town councils to traditional local chiefs. Most such units were district councils, which were required to have an elected majority. Separate legislation exists for urban centers that were granted municipal status and came directly under divisional or provincial control.

The Court System

In mid-1971 the highest court of the land, the Federal Supreme Court of Nigeria, was composed of the chief justice and eight other justices. The court might be constituted with as few as three and as many as nine justices hearing a case. It had exclusive primary jurisdiction in disputes between the federal government and the states or between the states. It had special jurisdiction over substantive questions of constitutional interpretations, including those concerning the violations of guaranteed fundamental rights. Under the 1960 and 1963 constitutions the Federal Supreme Court was granted the power of judicial review to pass on the constitutionality of acts of the federal government and laws passed by the federal Parliament. The changes brought about by the partial suspension of the consitution and the creation of a new class of legislation—decree law—had left review powers of the court largely inoperative; the decrees were above the constitution and thus beyond the court's jurisdiction.

The appellate functions of the Federal Supreme Court included hearing of appeals from decisions of the state High Courts of Justice and the Sharia Court of Appeal, which dealt with cases under Islamic personal law in the northern states. Appeals from the High Courts might be made on all matters involving questions of law or constitutionality or any decisions resulting in the death penalty. In Western State the Court of Appeal, on a level just below that of the Federal Supreme Court, had powers similar to the appeals function of the Federal Supreme Court.

The separate High Court established in each southern state and the single High Court for the six northern states function both as courts of first instance and as appeals courts. As the superior first court of record they had unlimited jurisdiction in most civil and criminal matters. The areas of exception were their lack of jurisdiction in the north over cases involving Islamic personal law, which included such matters as marriage, divorce, succession, and guardianship. They heard appeals that had been decided under non-Muslim customary law by an appropriate area court. Appeals of cases tried under Islamic law were heard by the Sharia Court of Appeal. In general cases, the High Court heard appeals directly from all levels of lower (magistrate, district, and area) courts. Cases in the High Courts were heard before a single judge, unless an appeal was involved, in which case two or more judges must hear the case.

The next level of courts included both magistrate courts with criminal jurisdiction and district courts with jurisdiction over civil cases. Primary jurisdiction was determined by the maximum assessable penalties. Both magistrate and district courts included four different types; primary jurisdiction in each was again determined by the sentencing levels each was allowed. Both magistrate and district courts were designed to hear cases involving Europeans or persons from other parts of Nigeria who did not come under the jurisdiction of local customary law courts.

Until 1967 control over local courts (then called Native Courts) was in the hands of the Native Authorities. By 1970 these lowest echelon courts had been reorganized and renamed area courts, under the direct control of the state governments. These courts tried cases involving persons subject to a particular body of customary law as sanctioned by legislation (see ch. 15, National Security). They, therefore, had primary jurisdiction over most of the cases presented for judicial decision. Area courts consisted of three or four levels, depending on the maximum penalty assessable. Upper area courts often had unlimited jurisdiction except in homicide cases, which must be heard by the High Court. Upper area courts might hear appeals from a lower area court. In 1969 one upper area court existed in each province. All area courts had both criminal and civil jurisdiction.

In order to combat the rising incidence of violent crime, the FMG in August 1970 decreed the creation of robbery and firearms tribunals, which heard cases involving armed robbery. The tribunals in each state were composed of three judges, two of whom must be military or police officers. Mandatory death sentences in cases of convictions could not be appealed to the regular courts.

CHAPTER 10

FOREIGN RELATIONS

The principal features of the publicly stated foreign policy of the Federal Military Government (FMG) in mid-1971 were the strong desire to avoid foreign entanglements, particularly those that might tie the country to either of the major power blocs, and an equally strong feeling for African unity that was accompanied by an uncompromising determination to see southern Africa rid of its colonial and minority white regimes. There was evidence that the FMG considered continued membership in the British Commonwealth of Nations to be desirable, and it continued to maintain a strong belief in, and support for, the United Nations (UN).

Nonalignment as the official policy has resulted in friendly relations with both the West and the East, with Communist China, and with both sides in the conflict between the Arab states and Israel. Despite the government's nonaligned position, however, the country's leaders tended to favor the West, with which many had intimate cultural, educational, and social connections.

Since independence in 1960 Nigeria has played an influential role in the development of, and direction taken by, the African unity movement. It has consistently maintained a moderate stance, the chief tenets of which are that all states on the continent are equal, regardless of size; the sovereignty of each, except those dominated by colonial and minority white regimes, must be respected; and there must be no interference by any state in the internal affairs of other states. At the same time it strongly supports functional integration, especially along regional lines; in this regard, Nigeria has long urged the establishment of a West African common market.

The FMG was highly anagonistic toward South African racial policies and the regimes in Rhodesia and the Portuguese colonies. In mid-1971 Major General Yakubu Gowon, chairman of the Supreme Military Council, was firmly committed to effecting a change—by force if necessary—that would give the black majorities in those areas representation and authority commensurate with their numbers. He also continued steadfastly to reject the dialogue with South Africa proposed by a number of other African leaders.

Despite some strains in relations with Great Britain at mid-1971, brought on largely by British plans to supply arms to South Africa, ties between the two countries remained firm. Some calls for withdrawal from the Commonwealth were heard in unofficial circles in Nigeria, but this probability seemed relatively remote. The FMG's attitude toward the United States was both friendly and critical, influenced on the one hand by such factors as United States aid and visits of various leaders to the United States and on the other hand by continued large-scale United States economic relations with South Africa.

Contacts with the communist world grew during the latter 1960s, and there were indications of possible further expansion during the 1970 decade. Except among essentially leftist groups and individuals, however, the primary interests appeared to be trade, technical aid, and investment funds for economic development (see ch. 12, Character and Structure of the Economy).

The alienation that developed between the FMG and the governments of Gabon, Ivory Coast, Tanzania, and Zambia in 1968 because of their recognition of the secessionist Biafran regime was ended in 1970. By mid-1971 the strained relations with France, which furnished substantial aid to the seccessionists, also appeared to be improving.

MAJOR ELEMENTS OF FOREIGN POLICY

In mid-1971 the country's primary interests in international affairs were centered on Africa and the Organization of African Unity (OAU). The FMG was strongly committed to the elimination of colonialism, imperialism, and racism on the African continent. To this end the FMG was providing continuing financial support through the Liberation Committee of the OAU—of which Nigeria was a member—for assistance to freedom fighers in African countries under foreign and white domination. The FMG was also reported in late 1970 to have promised some of the surplus civil war arms and ammunition stock for distribution to these groups through the Liberation Committee of the OAU.

International relations outside Africa were characterized by a policy of nonalignment, with Nigerian self-interest and integrity as the apparent chief determinants in specific policy decisions. This policy was a longstanding one, dating from the nonaligned position adopted by the country's first national government formed by a coalition of the Northern People's Congress (NPC) and the National Council of Nigerian Citizens (NCNC) after the 1959 preindependence election (see ch. 3, Historical Setting; ch. 9, Government and Political Dynamics).

During the period of civilian government in the 1960s the great reliance on Western aid—including acceptance of some US$225 million in assistance from the United States—and the preponderance of trade with the West appeared to belie the professed nonaligned position. Certain other actions taken during this time, however, gave every indication that the country's leaders were making foreign policy decisions on an independent basis. Examples included the breaking of diplomatic relations with France in 1961 over French nuclear tests in the Sahara and the abrogation of the Anglo-Nigerian Defense Pact in 1962. This pact, signed in November 1960 after Nigerian independence, was opposed by some domestic leaders and also by some other African states on the grounds that it impaired Nigeria's freedom of action and created the impression that it had become a member of the North Atlantic Treaty Organization (NATO). Nigeria also accorded diplomatic recognition to the Soviet Union and other communist-bloc nations during this period, removed restrictions on the entry of communist writings and propaganda materials, and pushed the development of trade with communist countries (see ch. 14, Industry and Trade).

The country's nonaligned policy was continued by the FMG. The desire to act independently appears to have been further strengthened by events during the civil war, such as French support for the secessionists, Western relief flights to Biafra from Portuguese territory, and relief efforts in Biafra by Western church groups, all of which were looked upon as foreign powers meddling in Nigerian affairs. There was also disillusionment over the refusal by Great Britain and several other Western powers to supply aircraft and other heavy military weapons to federal forces. As if to demonstrate the value of independent action, these arms were successfully obtained from the Soviet Union. Moreover, they were secured reportedly on a strictly cash basis, with no political strings attached.

Since the end of the civil war Nigerian leaders have, on a number of occasions, reiterated strongly the government's continued commitment to nonalignment and its intention not to become the satellite of any other state. In this connection the need for economic assistance from the major powers has been pointed out. The government has clearly stated, however, that this aid must be aimed solely at wholesome development of the economy, of a kind that will lead to stabilization of political freedoms as Nigerians conceive of them. Participation of the United States and the Soviet Union in this aid was considered essential but, as General Gowon cautioned in a statement on the subject during 1970, efforts by either great power to establish areas of influence would be rejected and self-defeating.

Another important element in foreign relations throughout the 1960s and in 1970 was the matter of the country's association with the Commonwealth. Mutual ties and interests with other Commonwealth members remained strong during this period. In this regard General Gowon, in a major policy speech on October 1, 1970, on Nigeria's tenth independence anniversary noted that the country continued to value this Commonwealth association. British arms sales to South Africa in early 1971, however, produced strong reactions in Nigeria, and there was some talk of quitting the Commonwealth if Great Britain persisted in this policy.

REGIONAL AND PAN-AFRICAN RELATIONS

Pan-Africanism

The government since independence has actively fostered the growth of economic, social, and political cooperation among African states. One of its first major roles in the pan-African movement was that of sponsor of the Monrovia Conference held in May 1961 in Liberia to consider the question of African unity. This conference was, in part, in response to a similar conference held in Casablanca, Morocco, in January 1961 and attended by representatives from Ghana, Guinea, Mali, Morocco, and the United Arab Republic (UAR). From this meeting emerged the Casablanca Charter, a document proposing eventual African political unification based on a proposed merging of national sovereignties, the development of a common ideology, and the formation of a single continental African unit.

The concepts embodied in the Casablanca Charter were strongly rejected by Nigerian government leaders, as well as by various other states attending the Monrovia Conference, who favored maintenance of individual state sovereignty and a more functional approach to African unity. The Monrovia Charter adopted by the conference called for unity without integration and nonacceptance of any individual country's leadership. Other important points included cooperation throughout Africa based on tolerance, state equality, noninterference in the internal affairs of other states, and condemnation of subversion abetted by other African states. Former Nigerian Prime Minister Abubakar Tafawa Balewa appears to have played an instrumental part in the formulation and adoption of this charter.

In a new effort at unity the Nigerian government called for another conference to be held in Lagos in January 1962. Members of the Casablanca group were also invited, but none attended. This conference drew up a new charter of the Inter-African and Malagasy Organization, which reaffirmed the Monrovia Charter; it did not refer to political integration. It emphasized economic, cultural, social, political, and diplomatic cooperation and offered proposals leading to the formation of a permanent organization. This charter, which in essence embodied the Nigerian position, was never implemented but was important because it served as the model for the charter of the OAU, signed in Addis Ababa, Ethiopia, in May 1963, which finally brought the divergent groups together into one body.

Nigeria assumed a positive role in the activities of the OAU from its beginning. For instance, with OAU approval, it supplied troops and police to Tanzania in 1964 during the crisis that followed the army mutiny in that country early that year. It also held membership on various commitees, including the Liberation Committee, which was established under the resolution on decolonization, also adopted at the 1963 Addis Ababa meeting. This committee furnishes both financial and diplomatic assistance to the various liberation movements attempting to overthrow by force the white minority governments in Rhodesia and South Africa and the colonial regimes in the Portuguese-held territories. In 1971 Nigeria was one of the few members of the OAU who were meeting their financial obligations to the Liberation Committee.

Despite its usually strong support for the OAU, the FMG looked with disfavor on OAU expressions of concern over the Nigerian civil war. The Nigerian government considered the war strictly an internal matter, and it felt that even a discussion of it by the OAU was a violation of the OAU charter's provisions against interference in the internal affairs of member states. The OAU statement of support for the Nigerian government's position on national unity, contained in a resolution adopted by the heads of state at the OAU conference at Kinshasa in the Democratic Republic of the Congo in September 1967, assuaged the feelings of the FMG to some extent. Efforts to bring about peace carried out by the OAU in 1968 and 1969, however, were unsuccessful. With the conclusion of the war in January 1970, the FMG's participation in OAU activities returned essentially to normal. In December 1970 Lagos was the site of an emergency meeting of the OAU Council of Ministers convened to consider the attack upon Guinea, reportedly by Portuguese forces, in November 1970.

Relations with Independent States

In mid-1971 the country enjoyed quite friendly relations with the neighboring states of Dahomey, Niger, Cameroon, Chad, and Equatorial Guinea (which attained independence in late 1968).

Some problems related to border demarcations existed, but these were in the process of mutually agreeable solution and did not constitute serious disputes. Relations with Dahomey, which had cooled during the civil war because of International Red Cross flights to Biafra that originated in Cotonou, were greatly improved when General Gowon visited Dahomey in August 1970, and a treaty of friendship was signed between the two countries. Important points included the relaxation of Nigerian immigration and customs regulations. This treaty was to continue in force indefinitely.

The close cultural affinities between the Hausa-Fulani populations of Nigeria and Niger have resulted in continuous harmonious relations between the two nations, including economic and technical assistance agreements (see ch. 5, Ethnic Groups and Languages). General Gowon visited the country in early 1971; during his visit agreement was reached on the establishment of a new joint commission that will further cooperation in a wide range of activities, including economic and cultural affairs, education, agriculture, transportation, customs, and other areas of mutual interest. Nigeria serves as a major transit route for Niger's imports and exports (see ch. 12, Character and Structure of the Economy).

Relations with Cameroon were also good as of mid-1971. During the early 1960s considerable friction had existed between the two countries over the division of the former British Cameroons Mandate (see ch. 2, Physical Environment). The results of the determining plebiscite, held in 1961 under UN supervision, were contested by Cameroon and taken to the International Court of Justice, which rejected the issue in 1963. In that year a bilateral agreement on cooperation and trade was signed. Boundary clashes continued, but in 1965 agreement to establish a permanent boundary was reached; efforts to implement the agreement were still in process in mid-1971. General Gowon made an official visit to Cameroon in April 1971, and the two countries agreed to establish a permanent consultative committee to ensure implementation and updating of all existing agreements between the two nations.

Amicable relations also existed in mid-1971 with Chad. Nigeria —with Chad, Cameroon, and Niger—was a member of the Chad Basin Commission, which was established in 1964 to promote projects of mutual interest and to develop uniform navigation regulations and transportation on Lake Chad. In April 1971 Nigeria and Chad signed a three-year trade agreement intended to eliminate discriminatory practices and to provide for use of port and transit facilities. Landlocked Chad had indicated interest in greater use of Nigerian transportation facilities for its imports and exports, particularly through Maiduguri, the terminus in 1971 of the northeast line of the Nigerian Railway Corporation (see ch. 2, Physical Environment).

Relations with other English-speaking countries of West Africa, including Ghana, The Gambia, and Sierra Leone, were influenced to some extent by common cultural ties that had developed among the elite groups in each country during the British colonial period. Many close personal relationships were formed during the time, notably among Nigerian and Ghanaian military officers who had attended the former Royal West African Frontier Force officer training center at Teshie, near Accra. Some senior officers of the two countries also were together at Sandhurst and other schools in Great Britain. On the basis of such personal ties, the leadership of the former Ghanaian military government used its good offices to convene a meeting of Nigerian military governors at Aburi, Ghana, in January 1967 in an effort to solve the crisis that preceded the Nigerian civil war (see ch. 9, Government and Political Dynamics).

Despite such ties, however, relations between Nigeria and Ghana have not always been smooth, particularly during the latter part of the regime of Kwame Nkrumah, when Ghana was accused of harboring Nigerian subversives. Relations improved greatly after the 1966 military coup in Ghana, and the Ghanaian government gave full support to the FMG during the civil war. Friction between the two countries again developed in 1969 and 1970 over measures taken by Ghana to reduce the number of aliens in that country. This resulted in the departure of large numbers of Nigerians, many of whom had to leave property behind. Improvement of relations was discussed by General Gowon and Ghanaian Prime Minister K.A. Busia at the OAU summit conference in Addis Ababa in September 1970. Agreement was reached on a commission to evaluate the property in question, and resolution of the problem appeared to have been achieved in early 1971. Ghana's high commissioner in Lagos, who had created considerable ill will by his strong support of his government's action, was replaced.

Relations with The Gambia were cordial, and General Gowon made a state visit in February 1971 during the anniversary of Gambian independence. A treaty of friendship was signed, granting citizens of both nations the reciprocal rights of residence, property ownership, travel, and participation in trade and industry. Nigeria also agreed to increase the amount of its technical assistance and training facilities.

Relations with the remaining independent African states at mid-1971 were mostly friendly. Better understanding was promoted by visits of General Gowon during the latter half of 1970 and first half of 1971 to a number of these states, including Algeria, Kenya, Mauritania, Senegal, Sudan, and the United Arab Republic (Egypt). During September 1970 a reconciliation took place between General Gowon and the leaders of Gabon, Ivory Coast, Tanzania, and Zambia, states with whom relations had been broken in 1968 because of their recognition of secessionist Biafra. Diplomatic relations, however, had not actually been restored as of mid-1971, although agreement on an early exchange of envoys with Tanzania was reported in June 1971.

Another measure to strengthen friendly relations was the reinstatement in June 1971 of bilateral travel agreements with Cameroon, Chad, Dahomey, Guinea, Ivory Coast, Morocco, Niger, and Togo. Under the agreements, nationals of these countries were not required to obtain visas before entering Nigeria. The agreements, which originally went into effect in 1964, were suspended during the civil war. Persons seeking work, however, were still required to conform to national immigration regulations.

Nigeria was a firm advocate of West African regional economic cooperation, although in mid-1971 little real progress toward this goal was visible. Most of the region's economies were actually in direct competition, their major export products being much the same and sold largely in the European markets. At the same time, marked differences in customs duties, import regulations, and currency restrictions had encouraged smuggling, which resulted in the loss of important revenues to many West African governments. A West African economic group was attractive to Nigeria as a potential market for products it expected eventually to produce through planned industrial expansion (see ch. 14, Industry and Trade). Membership in such a group, moreover, might permit more freedom of movement by Nigeria's large and fast-growing labor force, among countries belonging to the group (see ch. 4, Population and Labor).

Economic integration in West Africa has developed slowly, although interest in it dates back to the early 1960s and before. In part this was because of the strong opposition during the first half of the 1960s by Nkrumah, who looked upon the formation of regional groups as detrimental to the advancement of his concept of a politically united Africa. After his ouster in 1966, however, the Economic Commission for Africa (ECA) of the UN conducted studies aimed at developing regional cooperation. These studies showed potentialities for increasing the very limited trade then being conducted among the West African states and generated a renewed interest in development of a West African common market. As a result, twelve West African countries, including Nigeria, in April 1967 signed the Articles of Association of the West African Common Market. This document represented a transitional agreement on means of cooperation. One year later, in April 1968, at Monrovia, a West African regional group was formally established. A protocol signed at the time declared that the purpose of the group was economic integration. A general resolution and program of action were also adopted on measures needed to bring about cooperation in the development of agriculture, industry, regional infrastructure, power, and other common areas of interest.

Nigeria and nine other West African states, including The Gambia, Ghana, Guinea, Liberia, Mauritania, Mali, Senegal, Sierra Leone, and Upper Volta, signed the agreement. A draft treaty establishing a West African economic community composed of these ten countries was to have been discussed during 1969, but in mid-1971 the community still had not been formed. General Gowon, however, was known to favor strongly the formation of the community; reportedly he took advantage of the presence of the presidents of The Gambia, Liberia, Senegal, and Upper Volta at Nigeria's tenth independence anniversary celebration on October 1, 1970, to push for renewed effort on the program.

Attitude Toward South Africa

The country's official position on South Africa as of 1971 was an adamant opposition to apartheid, rejection of any form of dialogue with the South African government until the apartheid doctrine is renounced, and active support of any movement designed to bring about the downfall of the white minority regime in that country. The Nigerian government's reaction to South African policies and events stemming from them has remained quite forceful since the period just before independence.

In March 1960, for example, after the killing of unarmed Africans by police at Sharpeville in South Africa, the Nigerian minister of commerce informed Parliament that no South African would be employed by the Nigerian government. Subsequent to independence the Nigerian prime minister played a major role in the attack upon South African racial attitudes at the March 1961 conference of Commonwealth prime ministers that preceded South Africa's withdrawal from the organization. In April 1961 a total ban was placed on trade with South Africa, and during the remaining part of the year other strong domestic and international actions were taken or supported against the country.

Through the mid-1960s the former civilian government continued to reject any type of cooperation with South Africa, and this stance has been maintained by the FMG. The Nigerian civil war was publicized by South Africa as an indication that black Africans were incapable of governing themselves. General Gowon reportedly believed that South Africa had indirectly helped the secessionists during the war and considered that country a particular enemy of Nigeria (see ch. 15, National Security).

The FMG remained especially firm in its opposition to proposals for more active relations with South Africa made by leaders of several African states, including President Felix Houphouet-Boigny of Ivory Coast and Prime Minister Busia of Ghana. The proposal was termed futile by General Gowon unless South Africa abrogated its apartheid policy and first undertook with the Africans inside the country a dialogue that would restore to them their human dignity. If this occurred, according to General Gowon, relaxed relations with the rest of black Africa would follow easily.

ATTITUDES TOWARD THE ARAB-ISRAELI DISPUTE

The government's longstanding policy of maintaining friendly relations with any state exhibiting friendship toward Nigeria has been applied since independence to both sides in the Arab-Israeli dispute, despite the country's large Muslim population, whose sympathies lie with the Arab nations (see ch. 6, Social Systems; ch. 11, Value Systems). Thus, in mid-1971, although Nigeria did not have diplomatic representation in Israel, a fully accredited Israeli mission headed by an ambassador was stationed in Lagos.

The federal government established economic and cultural ties with Israel even before independence. One of its earliest foreign loans was obtained in 1961 from that country. Objections to the loan were raised by the Northern Region, but they were brushed aside by Prime Minister Balewa, who was a Muslim from the Northern Region. At the same time the governments of the Eastern and Western Regions made special efforts to establish relations with Israel, which was visited by the two regional premiers. In 1964 Israeli Foreign Minister Golda Meir visited Nigeria. The federal government's approach to the situation, and that generally shown by the succeeding military governments, was stated on this occasion by President Nnamdi Azikiwe, who declared that his country had not inherited the prejudices of others and would deal with all friendly nations.

The FMG officially adopted a neutral position after the outbreak of the Arab-Israeli hostilities in June 1967 and appears to have held a generally neutral position since then. In 1970 General Gowon visited Egypt and thanked that country for its support during the civil war. (Egyptian pilots reportedly flew the jet combat aircraft furnished to Nigeria by the Soviet Union.) At that time and on a number of later occasions, General Gowon also expressed support for the peaceful efforts of Egypt to effect the withdrawal of Israeli forces from occupied Egyptian territory.

The leftist leadership of the Nigerian Trades Union Congress, affiliated to the Soviet-bloc-dominated World Federation of Trade Unions, has called upon Nigerian workers to denounce "Israeli aggression." Official attacks upon Israel, however, have been avoided, and Israeli representatives in Nigeria have been accorded equal treatment with those from the Arab states. The Israeli ambassador, along with other diplomatic representatives, was invited by the commissioner of external affairs to be an observer at the emergency OAU conference in Lagos in December 1970 after the attempted invasion of Guinea. Objections to his presence were raised by the Arab states but were vigorously rejected by Nigerian officials as interference in Nigerian internal affairs. The Arab states then threatened certain actions that would have amounted to an affront to General Gowon, and the Israeli ambassador withdrew.

RELATIONS WITH GREAT BRITAIN AND THE COMMONWEALTH

Despite occasional disagreements, the basic relations between Nigeria and Great Britain were generally cordial throughout the 1960s and in the beginning of the 1970s. Educational ties, use of a common national language, and the continued employment both in government and private enterprise of a substantial number of British nationals tended to preserve the bonds between the two countries. After independence great reliance was also placed on British trade and investment funds; in 1971 these still constituted an important element linking the countries, despite Nigerian efforts to expand its trade with other states that began in the late 1960s (see ch. 14, Industry and Trade). Another traditional bond existed between the military establishments of the two countries. Nigerian military forces had been developed and supplied largely by the British, and many senior officers serving in 1971 had received their training in Great Britain (see ch. 15, National Security).

The fundamental points of disagreement in the 1960s and early 1970s concerned British handling of the Rhodesian demand for full sovereignty and its continued close relationships with South Africa. After Rhodesia's unilateral declaration of independence in 1965, the OAU called on all of its members to break relations with the United Kingdom, and this was done by a number of states. Although it kept up its strong criticism of British actions, the Nigerian government rejected the move, giving as reasons both the effect this would have on the country and its belief that a break was unlikely to contribute to the goal of majority rule in Rhodesia.

In mid-1971 the Rhodesian situation still constituted a point of Nigerian contention with Great Britain. The principal disagreement, however, was over British arms sales to South Africa. This subject came to the forefront in July 1970 when the British government announced plans to provide South Africa with a limited category of military supplies. Strong opposition was voiced not only by Nigeria but also by various other members of the Commonwealth and partly as a result of such objections sales were not made during the second half of 1970. This question and the subject of Indian Ocean defense, a major reason given by Great Britain for resuming arms deliveries to South Africa, were hotly debated at the conference of Commonwealth prime ministers at Singapore in January 1971. Serious dissension arose, and peace was restored only when the matter was finally referred to an investigative committee formed largely at the suggestion of Nigerian Commissioner of External Affairs Okoi Arikpo.

In February 1971, even before the first meeting of the investigative committee, the British government again announced plans for the transfer of some military equipment to South Africa. The FMG reacted by withdrawing from the committee and threatening to take retaliatory measures. Government officials mentioned the possibility of economic sanctions; at the end of June 1971 no specific actions had been reported, and official comments were restrained.

Nigeria joined the Commonwealth as an independent member in 1960, an action that had the full support of all major political parties at the time; it continued as an independent member when it became a republic in 1963 (see ch. 3, Historical Setting). It has benefited from the association through inter-Commonwealth trade preferences and from monetary and technical aid received from such members as the United Kingdom, Canada, and Australia. In mid-1971 the FMG appeared still committed to Commonwealth membership. Some voices demanding withdrawal have been heard, including the *New Nigerian,* a daily newspaper jointly financed by the six northern states. In 1970 the newspaper's opposition to continued association was generated by possible British arms sales to South Africa. In mid-1971 the newspaper again repeated its demand for withdrawal, this time in connection with Great Britain's contemplated entry into the European Economic Community (EEC, the Common Market). The *New Nigerian* expressed concern for the possible detrimental effects such a move might have on other Commonwealth members.

RELATIONS WITH OTHER STATES

Although the country held firmly to nonalignment in 1971, its leaders still looked more to the West because of training and inclination. Thus, despite the great changes during the 1960s, the growth of nationalism, and a sincere effort to practice real nonalignment, underlying attitudes remained much the same as at independence. Commissioner of External Affairs Arikpo has stated that the country in 1971 was nonaligned, but in a pro-Western manner.

United States

Nigeria's relations with the United States have, in general, been good and appear to have been favorably influenced, at least in part, by continuing United States cooperation in the country's plan for economic development and social advancement (see ch. 12, Character and Structure of the Economy). After the start of the civil war the FMG sought unsuccessfully to obtain military supplies from the United States; the lack of success, however, did not seem to affect relations materially. The United States actually refrained from any political or military involvement during the war and continued to recognize the FMG, respecting the sentiment of the large majority of African states. Some friction occurred in 1968, however, when it was reported that a number of United States cargo planes would be furnished for relief flights to secessionist forces from Fernando Po and Sao Tome. The Nigerian government asserted that this would encourage continued resistance and thus prolong the war.

Continued United States trade with South Africa—although the United States maintains an arms embargo against that country—and continued relations with Portugal have been the cause of considerable criticism in Nigeria, from both the government and private individuals. In the course of a conference of United States and African leaders in March 1971 at the Institute of International Affairs in Lagos, General Gowon voiced strong objection to the support given economically and in other ways to the foreign minority regimes in southern Africa by certain countries. A subsequent radio comment criticized alleged United States financial participation in construction of the Cabora-Bassa Dam in Mozambique, which eventually will supply electric power to the countries in southern Africa whose administrations are viewed unfavorably by the FMG.

East European Countries

In mid-1971 Nigeria maintained diplomatic relations with most of the communist countries in Europe, except the German Democratic Republic (East Germany) and Albania, with whom contacts were minimal or nonexistent. The earliest relations after independence were with the Soviet Union, and the Soviet ambassador presented his credentials in Lagos in December 1961. The first Nigerian ambassador, however, did not go to Moscow until two years later.

Criticisms were voiced by pro-Soviet elements in the country over the delay in opening the Moscow embassy. The Nigerian government's reply and statements by progovernment statesmen were indicative of the country's basic attitudes toward the two major power blocs. The government pointed out that Nigeria was a democracy and that it had advocated democratic principles and institutions for more than a 100 years; despite its nonaligned position, its ties were Western oriented. It was, however, not opposed to the East European nations, and friendship and trade would eventually be increased.

The first steps to improve economic relations with communist-bloc states were taken in mid-1961 when a Nigerian mission went to Moscow to discuss increased economic ties. Agreement was reached on an eventual trade and cultural pact. At the same time the Soviet Union tentatively agreed to provide certain types of agricultural aid and to establish training centers for personnel in agriculture and industry. An economic agreement, however, did not finally occur until July 1963. This provided for most-favored-nation treatment in respect to all trade and shipping with an automatic annual renewal; the pact continued in force throughout the 1960s.

The first trade pact signed with an East European nation, however, was with Czechoslovakia in September 1961. The terms of this agreement were effective for two years and also contained an automatic renewal clause. A year later, in September 1962, a five-year trade pact was signed with Bulgaria. During the first half of the 1960s, however, efforts by the communist-bloc countries to expand their relations with Nigeria generally met with limited success. Credit was offered by Czechoslovakia, Yugoslavia, and Poland, and at different times the Soviet Union repeated offers of aid. Within the country various Nigerian individuals as well as organizations, including the Soviet-oriented Nigerian Trade Union Congress, urged the Soviet Union and other communist-bloc states to offer as much aid to Nigeria as they had to other Africa countries. Little resulted from this, however, as control of the federal government was largely in the hands of northern politicians who apparently harbored deep suspicions of Soviet intentions. These men did not actually reject the proffered help, but they made few moves to accept the offers.

The change of government occasioned by the 1966 coups brought little modification in underlying attitudes. Although professedly nonaligned, the officers who took over were British trained and somewhat more favorably disposed toward the West. It was reported in early 1967, however, that loans from communist countries would be accepted. The situation was altered materially after the outbreak of the civil war in 1967, when the government found it necessary to turn to the Soviet Union for the arms it desired. The quick Soviet response brought a warming of relations between the two countries. The long-stalled cultural pact was signed in August 1967, and in 1968 a general agreement on technical and economic cooperation was concluded. During 1969 the Soviet Union was asked to conduct a feasibility survey, under the terms of this general agreement, for establishment of a planned national iron and steel complex; the survey was still underway in mid-1971 (see ch. 12, Character and Structure of the Economy; ch. 14, Industry and Trade).

During 1969 the Soviet airline, Aeroflot, began regular commercial service to Lagos, and various Soviet cultural performances and exhibitions were presented in different parts of the country. This atmosphere of friendliness continued after the end of the civil war. An expanded cultural agreement was negotiated in April 1970; the trade pact between the two countries was extended for another five years in May 1970; and in June 1970 an agreement was signed on a joint geologic program within Nigeria. During 1970 well over 100 scholarships to the Soviet Union were offered to Nigerian students, and a number of politicians were invited on expense-paid trips to Moscow.

Other significant events during this time involving relations with the East European communist countries included renewal in March 1969 of the 1962 trade agreement with Bulgaria, which had lapsed in 1968; and an agreement on economic, technical, cultural, and financial cooperation with that country was concluded in November 1970. A two-year trade agreement with Hungary was signed in October 1969, and a five-year pact with Romania was developed in July 1970. A further agreement on economic cooperation was signed with Romania in May 1971, calling for cooperation not only in economic matters but also in science and technology and providing for the exchange of advisers and experts. An East German delegation visited Lagos in mid-1969 with the apparent intent of discussing establishment of a trade mission. Nigeria showed little interest and as of mid-1971 still did not have any formal relations with East Germany.

Despite the general improvement of relations with the East European communist countries that was apparent in 1971, the amount of trade with those countries was still relatively small; imports accounted for only about 3 to 4 percent of total imports (see ch. 14, Industry and Trade). Nigerian interest in diversifying economic relations, however, indicated the possibility of an increase, if wanted items could be supplied. Although the Soviet Union's position apparently had improved markedly as a result of its help during the civil war, there were no signs that Soviet assistance had achieved any special influence with the Nigerian government.

People's Republic of China

Again in keeping with the nonalignment policy, Nigeria has maintained a relatively consistent attitude of friendliness toward the People's Republic of China (Communist China). At independence in 1960 the Nigerian government indicated that it would work for the admission of Communist China to the UN. Nonetheless, in 1961 when the issue came to a vote in a measure that would have excluded the Republic of China (Nationalist China), Nigeria abstained, suggesting it would be better to seat both Chinas. Subsequent abstentions also occurred in 1962 and 1963.

Direct contact between the two countries was established soon after Nigerian independence. In April 1961, apparently upon the initiative of Communist China, a Chinese mission arrived in Lagos to discuss the opening of diplomatic relations and the establishment of economic and cultural ties. A large Nigerian economic delegation visited Peking in June 1961, and a joint communique was issued in that city announcing agreement on the mutual value of diplomatic relations and trade and cultural contacts. The Nigerian government, however, failed to pursue these initial steps, and throughout the 1960s recognition was extended neither to Communist China nor to Nationalist China.

The Nigerian position during most of this time, however, was expressed in early 1964 by the minister of external affairs, who told the federal Parliament that Nigeria recognized that Communist China represented the bulk of China. During the mid-1960s Nigeria continued to support admission of mainland China to the UN. Some deterioration in relations between the two countries seems to have occurred during the Nigerian civil war as the result of Communist China's apparently sympathetic attitude toward the Biafran secessionists. In September 1968, for example, the Chinese Communist New China News Agency carried a long article considered favorable to the Biafrans; later that year Nigeria abstained in the UN vote on the China question.

In 1969 and 1970, however, the government again supported Communist China for admission to the UN. In early 1971 unpublicized negotiations for mutual recognition appeared to have started in Cairo between the Chinese Communist and Nigerian ambassadors to Egypt. A decision to enter into diplomatic relations was announced in an official press release on February 10, 1971, in Lagos. The release noted that the Nigerian government recognized the government of Communist China as the sole legal government representing the entire Chinese nation. The agreement called for mutual nonaggression, noninterference in each other's internal affairs, and respect for sovereignty and territorial integrity. Concerning the recognition, the Nigerian commissioner of external affairs stated that it did not in any way represent a move against the West but was rather a positive example of the country's policy of nonalignment into which normal, friendly relations with mainland China fitted naturally.

France

Relations with France were characterized between 1961 and 1971 by two periods of serious disagreement. In early January 1961, only a few months after independence, the French ambassador and his staff were ordered out of Nigeria as a sign of the government's displeasure over French atomic tests in the Sahara in late December 1960. French shipping and aircraft were also barred from use of Nigerian ports and airfields. This ban was removed in May 1961, however, because of the resultant detrimental effects upon the development plans of neighboring Dahomey, Niger, and Chad. Supplies for these nations were furnished by France and reached them through Nigerian transportation channels. Diplomatic relations, however, were not reestablished until more than four years later, in late 1965.

The second major estrangement began during the civil war and arose from French support of the Biafran regime. Although this did not result in a direct diplomatic break, the effects on relationships with France were still apparent in mid-1971. In 1968 high officials of the French government expressed open backing for the Biafrans. This was given added weight by President Charles de Gaulle in a statement, amounting to de facto recognition, in which he said that France was helping Biafra to the limits of its abilities; the reason it had not recognized Biafra was because this was considered strictly an African matter. He stated further that the French government felt the conflict had to be resolved on the basis of the right of a people to self-determination and that accepted international procedures should be used.

French government spokemen reported that France's aid to

Biafra consisted of substantial quantities of relief and medical supplies but denied that any arms had been sent. Despite the denials, however, there were reports of arms deliveries made through Gabon and Ivory Coast, both of which recognized the Biafran regime. The FMG regarded the French action as unwarranted interference in Nigeria's internal affairs. Moreover, members of the FMG voiced their belief that France had acted to prolong the war in the interests of French oil operations and exploration in the former Biafran territory (see ch. 13, Agriculture and Mining).

At the end of the war General Gowon stated that Nigeria would continue friendly relations with France if the latter wished. Despite this assurance, however, there was evidence in 1970 and early 1971 of continued Nigerian coolness toward France. This was indicated in a plea made in early 1971 by the French ambassador for restoration of solid, effective relations between the two countries. The FMG withheld its permission for renewal of French oil operations until 1971, long after other foreign oil companies had resumed operations in Nigeria. The Nigerian delay was regarded as retaliation against France for its wartime support of the secessionists. Some improvement in relations, however, may be indicated by a visit to France by the chief of staff of the Nigerian army in June 1971.

THE FOREIGN SERVICE AND DIPLOMATIC TIES

Foreign relations are handled through the Ministry of External Affairs under the direction of an appointed political commissioner, who in mid-1971 was Commissioner of External Affairs Okoi Arikpo. Arikpo, who held a number of political positions in the 1950s before independence, took over his post as commissioner of external affairs in September 1968 after serving as the commissioner of trade in the FMG in 1967 and 1968. He was considered a strong Nationalist.

The commissioner was assisted by a career staff headed by a permanent secretary. This staff was divided into administrative, protocol, research, political, overseas, communications, and accounts divisions. There were also units concerned specifically with Euro-American, Asian, and African affairs.

Nigeria had operating embassies in twenty-one other African countries as of early 1971. Included were five high commissions in member countries of the Commonwealth, including The Gambia, Ghana, Kenya, Sierra Leone, and Uganda. Relations with two other Commonwealth members, Tanzania and Zambia, and with Gabon and Ivory Coast were broken in 1968 when they recognized the Biafran secessionist regime. In June 1971 the Nigerian government had agreed to the resumption of diplomatic relations with Tanzania but had not done so with the other three countries. Official representation also existed in two additional African countries through accredited nonresident ambassadors. A consulate was also maintained at Buea in western Cameroon, which had been British mandated territory linked to Nigeria until 1961 (see ch. 2, Physical Environment). Another consulate functioned at Port Sudan on the Red Sea in Sudan. This consulate serviced chiefly Nigerian Muslim pilgrims traveling to and from Mecca by land.

Embassies were maintained in eight West European countries. The high commission in Great Britain also had area offices in Edinburgh and Liverpool. In the Federal Republic of Germany (West Germany), in addition to the embassy in Bonn, a consulate was maintained in Hamburg. Two embassies were located in Eastern Europe: one in the Soviet Union and the other in Poland.

In the Western Hemisphere high commissions were located in Canada, Guyana, and Trinidad and Tobago, and embassies were maintained in the United States and Brazil. There was also a consulate general in New York. A permanent mission was stationed at the United Nations in New York, and another in Geneva handled the country's relations with United Nations agencies and headquarters in that city. In 1970 interest existed in further expansion of diplomatic representation. The approach was generally realistic, however, and the opening of new embassies was based primarily on consideration of trade or other factors of practical value to Nigeria.

Most overseas offices had staffs of moderate size. The Office of the High Commissioner in London, however, was comparatively large, in part the result of the strong cultural ties with the United Kingdom. The Office of the High Commissioner included a military division, a recruitment division concerned in part with obtaining expatriate personnel for positions in Nigeria, and a student's division that handled matters concerned with the large number of Nigerians studying in the United Kingdom.

Over sixty foreign diplomatic missions were stationed in Lagos as of mid-1971. Nineteen were from African countries; fourteen represented West European nations; and seven were from Eastern Europe, including Yugoslavia. Of the East European communist-bloc countries only East Germany and Albania were not represented. Various contacts had occurred between Nigeria and East Germany, but diplomatic relations had not been established between them as of mid-1971 (see ch. 15, National Security). There were also seven Middle Eastern embassies, including one representing Israel, and nine from Asia, including Australia. Among

267

the Asian countries was Communist China, which was recognized by Nigeria in early 1971; its embassy was opened in Lagos in April 1971. Six countries from the Western Hemisphere also had embassies, including the United States, Canada, and four South American nations. In addition to their embassies in Lagos, nine countries maintained consulates at other points in the country, including Calabar, Kaduna, Kano, and Ibadan; three of these consulates were honorary. Cyprus, Greece, and Iceland, which did not have embassies, maintained consulates in Lagos; those of Cyprus and Iceland, however, were honorary.

A number of United Nations specialized agencies had regular representatives in the country. The area offices of the International Labor Organization (ILO), the United Nations Children's Fund (UNICEF), and the World Health Organization (WHO) were located in Lagos.

INTERNATIONAL ORGANIZATIONS

Nigeria applied for entry to the UN at independence and a few days later, on October 7, 1960, was admitted as that body's ninety-ninth member. Since then the country has become affiliated with all the UN specialized agencies; as of 1971 it was also a contracting party to the General Agreement on Tariff's and Trade of the UN. During 1966 and 1967 Nigeria served as a nonpermanent member of the Security Council of the UN. Throughout the 1960s and beginning of the 1970s it also served as a member of various councils and boards of the UN specialized agencies. A number of Nigerians have held important positions in various UN bodies; in mid-1971 the best known perhaps was Simeon Adebo, who had the rank of under secretary general.

The country supported the UN fully since its admission. One of its earliest positive acts was to furnish troops in late 1960 for the UN force in the Congo (see ch. 15, National Security). Its military units there actually formed the backbone of that force, and they continued to help police the Congo after most other UN units had been withdrawn.

Other international organizations of which Nigeria was a member included the African Development Bank, Cocoa Producers' Alliance (with headquarters in Lagos), and Inter-African Coffee Organization. It was a member of the four-nation Chad Basin Commission, established in 1964 to promote economic development in that area, and of the Niger River Basin Commission—made up of the states through which the river flows—which is charged with harmonizing development along the river so that it will fit in with individual state development plans. The country was also a member of the ECA of the UN and of the Union of National Radio and

268

Television Organizations of Africa, a body designed to promote the exchange of radio and television programs among its members.

On July 12, 1971, the country became the eleventh member of the Organization of Petroleum Exporting Companies (OPEC). OPEC acts as a policy-coordinating body for its member states, which in 1971 were producing about 85 percent of the world's petroleum exports. The Nigerian government radio network in Lagos noting Nigeria's entry into OPEC, stated that the country would benefit from the experience of the older members.

CHAPTER 11

VALUE SYSTEMS

Nigeria's problems in the postindependence era have largely revolved around clashes between adherents of conflicting values. In many cases the conflict has been occasioned by major differences in the value systems of various ethnic groups. In others the source of conflict lies in the difference between modernists and traditionalists, a difference that cuts across ethnic boundaries, although it affects some ethnic groups more than others.

The combination of the two conflicts in values brought about the crisis that led to the civil war of the late 1960s. The young officers who carried out the coup of January 1966 were motivated by modern ideas of social justice and a specific impatience with the existing government's failure to force the pace of development, to end corruption, and to improve the conditions of life for the Nigerian masses. Coincidentally, these officers were nearly all from ethnic groups of the Eastern and Mid-Western Regions, where traditionalist sentiment was weakest, and most were Ibo. The countercoup of July 1966 was brought about by northern traditionalists, who feared that changes would be brought about in the social order of their Muslim emirates. Their leaders succeeded in stirring up a pogrom against the many easterners residing in the north who were despised primarily as a result of differences in their social and religious behavior (see ch. 9, Government and Political Dynamics).

Although the concept of a united federal republic has the apparent support of the majority of the politically informed population, only a small number of Nigerians—even among the modernized elite—see the country as the object of their primary political attachment. Rather, nearly all people pay primary fealty to some much smaller unit, usually a traditional ethnic entity or, at most, a regional amalgam of related ethnic units. For many, this may not necessarily conflict with the broader concept of nation. It does, however, make it impossible to impute any single set of social or political values to Nigerians as a whole.

The sociopolitical values of the different ethnic groups diverge radically, running the gamut from those that derive from adherence to the rigid caste structure and the powerful emirs of the far north to those consonant with governments run by meetings of all adult citizens. Even within individual ethnic groups, great differences exist between the forms of society in different areas. For example, the social mobility of commoners varies greatly among the traditional 13 Hausa states, and the more than 200 independent Ibo village groupings include monarchial governments as well as those conducted by town meetings. Nevertheless, the great majority of the people hold values broadly characteristic of one of three sets of values: that which prevails among the Islamic emirates of the Hausa-Fulani, Kanuri, and Nupe; that of the city-states of the Yoruba and the culturally related peoples of the midwest; and that generally prevailing among the villages of the Ibo, the Ibibio, and other peoples of the Niger Delta and the former Eastern Region (see ch. 6, Social Systems).

Most of the other peoples who do not fit into one of these broad categories are found in the buffer zone separating the emirates from the southern part of the country. These Middle Belt (see Glossary) peoples include the Birom, Jarawa, Kantab, Idoma, and Tiv. Of these, only the Tiv number more than 500,000.

To the traditional ethnic divisions in the society must be added the growing number among the educated elite who have, in widely varying degrees, broken their ties to the traditional order (see ch. 6, Social Systems). Also in varying degrees, they have adapted to their needs the social and political values brought to the country by contacts with Europe and North America.

The adherence of groups already separated by ethnic differences to varying sets of values has the impact of creating ideological barriers between major elements of the society. The Ibo and most of their fellow easterners come from societies that have traditionally subscribed to a concept of individualism, competition, personal aggressiveness, and freedom from rigid class differences. The origins of political power among the Ibo are reflected by their homily that "no one knows the womb that bears the chief," indicative of the open nature of their society in which any man may become the leader by displaying superior ability (see ch. 6, Social Systems.)

The Yoruba value system places high regard on individual effort but within a formally stratified political order. Among the Yoruba only the kingship itself is hereditary and, although commoners are not in a position to challenge the kings' chiefly supporters, the commoners are the ones who elect members of their compound or village to the chieftainships.

Among the Hausa and their associates in the far north the lines of class distinction are, in general, rigidly drawn; political control is exercised by a hierarchical court structure, and ultimate power generally lies in the hands of an ethnically distinguishable elite, the Fulani. Leadership among the Hausa is primarily based on inherited position rather than on personal achievement, and little room exists for personal upward mobility in either the sociopolitical or the economic order.

The divisions characteristic of Nigeria have been accentuated by the closer contacts that are possible in the modern state and have been reinforced by the spread of Christianity in the south. The colonial government provided additional support for the ethnic divisions by linking ethnic divisions with regional boundaries. In the 1950s and 1960s politicians hardened these lines by successfully linking political party divisions with these ethnoreligious and geographic groupings (see ch. 9, Government and Political Dynamics).

THE YORUBA AND ASSOCIATED GROUPS

There are substantial differences between the Yoruba and other groups to which they are historically and culturally related. In addition, variations within the Yoruba groups, as within all major groups in the country, are sometimes larger than the differences between elements of the group and neighbors of a different ethnic origin. In the Yoruba political order a majority of the city-states are ruled by an elected king chosen by the ward chiefs from a hereditary line, but some Yoruba states are ruled in other ways, including elected councils of chiefs. Underlying these distinctions, however, is a common adherence to a largely similar set of values.

In 1971 modern ideas and education had not yet created a strong attachment to Nigerian nationalism, but they had stimulated a more limited growth of attachments beyond the parochial level. The younger Yoruba, like the Ibo, were gradually being drawn into a homogeneous cultural block composed of all Yoruba subgroups, a movement that has had distinct political implications.

The Yoruba are remarkably conscious of their various histories, even though these are largely unwritten. They take great pride in their city-states and capital cities. Those with kings look upon their monarch as a figure without whom their city would disintegrate because no other figure commands the loyalty of the various resident ethnic units. His wealth and pomp are regarded as signs of the prosperity of the city and of its inhabitants.

Prosperity is the goal sought by most men, who expect to achieve it by hard work, good health, astute trading, and the help of many sons. Wealth traditionally has been used for conspicuous consumption, particularly for new homes, clothes, and the support of several wives to produce more children. In the modern order, efforts to obtain modern conveniences, automobiles, and higher education for children have partially replaced the earlier goals. Saving wealth rather than spending it conspicuously and generously is looked upon unfavorably by the Yoruba.

A wealthy man often prefers to use his money to seek political office, with notable degrees of success in modern party politics. Wealth brings prestige and, generally, popularity. Most wealthy men use their money and connections to assist others, thus reinforcing the willingness of others to do business with them and to support their candidacy.

The primary association of any Yoruba is with his compound, which is the home and social unit comprising any number of people who acknowledge links of common ancestry. The bond of membership in the same compound cuts across all economic distinctions. The social norms require all members, rich and poor, to live within the compound and not to look to other men of wealth or power for association but to their fellow compound members (see ch. 6, Social Systems).

Regardless of the form of government in their city-states, the Yoruba spend most of their lives in the largely egalitarian lineage compounds. The compounds are governed by meetings in which all adult males have a voice. All men have the right to an equal share of the agricultural lands, which are owned by the compounds rather than by the state or individuals.

Every man also has the right to contest the few available political offices within the compound, although wealth and popularity usually play a major part. Compound chiefs are elected, but their duties are limited to representing the compound in dealings with other groups and the king. Internal decisionmaking is by popular acclamation at meetings under the chairmanship of a member who is senior in age rather than in power or wealth.

Most individuals accept their group's interests as their own. The most important interest is to assure that the group retains its size or grows in order to achieve a position of strength in contests with other groups over land or political power. Dissension within the compounds is deplored, as it might cause withdrawal from the compound, formation of a new and competitive unit, or even departure from the city. To avoid forcing the losing elements in dispute settlements into such a position, much effort is directed at gaining the agreement of both sides; decisions are rarely rendered unless they had been unanimously accepted. Every effort is made to ensure that the losing group does not feel isolated or punished and to avoid implications that the social values of the losers are different or weaker than those of the winner.

The Yoruba attach great importance to living in a town, a

tradition that stems from the town's ability to serve as a rallying point in case of external attack and as the center of the culture's social and political life. Since the town traditionally is also the center of a farming district and most of its residents are farmers, this does not imply a rejection of agriculture as a way of life. People or tribes who do not reside in cities are derided as "bush people," a commonly used pejorative in 1971.

Yoruba women have a considerable degree of economic independence. Although a woman must remain overtly deferential to her husband, a wife's position is determined more by her own business skill and her club memberships than by her husband's position. Husbands do not have a right to a wife's earnings. Many women thus are able to become wealthier than their husbands, although a man does not appreciate being reminded of his wife's success. Divorce is accepted, and a woman's social standing is not jeopardized by her lack of a husband.

Most men aspire to more than one wife because they desire many sons. A great stigma attaches to childless women. Fathers expect to be regarded as a distant, authoritarian figure by their children. Since any older person must be respected by a child and may inflict punishments, youths often stand in awe of older brothers. It is believed that children can succeed only through hard work and obedience to their father and that these values can be inculcated only by strict punishment, including severe beatings.

PEOPLES OF THE EASTERN STATES

Most of the values often attributed to the Ibo are identical with those of the majority of the peoples of the eastern states. The non-Ibo easterners have often been neglected in studies of the region, and as a result the Ibo alone are often described as the most independent and achievement-minded Nigerians. The Ibibio, the Efik, and other related peoples, however, have proved similarly oriented toward personal initiative, development, and work.

Eastern society has always been open to the acceptance of new cultural forms and ideas. Its members were quick to adapt to the value system of their colonial rulers and sought to gain power and authority by copying British methods. They accepted Christianity and European education because these practices were seen as the keys to success in the new order. The success that had always been the objective of the Ibo was later sought through posts in the civil service and British companies, control of interregional trade, commercial agricultural production, and the amassing of European-style goods. A major new avenue of prestige was sending children through school, eventually to British or American universities. The development of nationalist political forces provided the ultimate goal—the achievement of prominence and power in a political structure beyond the confines of the tribal or ethnic region.

The Ibo and other easterners place great emphasis on individual achievement and initiative. They believe that all human, cultural, or supernatural restraints can be overcome. Observers cite certain aspects of the traditional culture as the reasons for the Ibo's desire and ability to advance. These include equality of opportunity, the importance of individual initiative and achievement, competition in every sphere of life, preoccupation with material concerns, acceptance of change, willingness to innovate, participation in politics, and pragmatism or a marketplace orientation to life.

Their competitiveness and drive are not brought on by economic necessity or inherent energy but by a value system that attaches great importance to competitiveness in all fields and self-improvement for individuals and groups. Success in all fields is widely sought, and distinction in any one of them is considered as good as in another. The Ibo are well known among other Nigerians for their willingness to do almost any type of work, no matter how dirty or menial.

The Ibo see themselves as self-assertive, highly verbal, and able to set and strive for clear goals. According to a survey of Ibo attitudes, 98 percent believe that a man who gets money finds happiness, and 95 percent believe that a hard-working man is a good man. Ibo place a high value on the social forms of hospitality. Traditionally, they also valued an agricultural occupation and, through it, an attachment to the land. A sharp division of labor between the sexes is practiced, but women are granted a considerable degree of equality. Great admiration is given to the self-made man, and stress is placed on physical health and strength.

The Ibo world is based on a democratic structure and a belief that society must give all its citizens an equal opportunity to achieve success. Leadership must be achieved by personal abilities and hard work rather than through inheritance and must be constantly validated to be retained. Men are respected if they are aggressive, skilled orators and able organizers. For the Ibo, long-term goals are realized through the process of change. The Ibo ability to accept innovation is based largely on an attitude that favors anything that improves the status of the individual and the community.

A man gains prestige by accumulating capital, traditionally through his agricultural skills and through his ability to obtain the financial backing of others as a result of personal prestige and effective social control. Great effort is expected and exerted to amass personal wealth, which is used to finance further advancement or is conspicuously consumed. Until very recent times a man demonstrated success by holding great feasts for large numbers of people or purchasing a title by paying a high initiation fee to one of the title-granting clubs (see ch. 6, Social Systems).

The ideal of cooperation is a basic aspect of the culture. Although the Ibo honor individualism, they also maintain a strong attachment to the family, the kinship group, and the village. Helping one's home settlement or area to improve its position is virtually an obsession with most Ibo. Because individual success reflects honor on the group, major community effort and personal sacrifice in support of an outstanding member are commonplace.

The highest value is placed on education; families and, sometimes even a whole village, will sacrifice heavily to provide an outstanding child with the best possible academic training. A child's success reflects on all the members of the group, and he, in turn, is expected to use his enhanced status to support the group's interests. A major motivation for success is the desire to be remembered by descendants for contributions to the wealth and well-being of the family or the lineage.

Interest in improving one's own village has made the Ibo highly responsive in all self-development programs, and every village has sought to build whatever modern facility the central government allowed. For the great majority, good government is synonymous with good roads, schools, maternity clinics, and post offices because of the status they bestow on a village. In the Ibo system of values, local and national politics are intimately connected with such outward signs of modern progress.

The Ibo have brought into national politics the techniques of group leadership and the need for consensus, which were required by custom in village deliberations and in the settlement of disputes. Traditional court judgments rarely provided a definite victory for one of the litigants but rather sought a compromise in which both sides were reconciled to their losses.

Mutual dependence and cooperation are the organizing principles of eastern social relationships. Because equality is a basic ideal, domination by a few powerful men usually is deeply resented. All relationships are viewed as contractual. To remain strong, relationships must be mutually beneficial and offer the possibility of give-and-take.

The Ibo view the world as a marketplace and desire above all to make a profit in bargaining with others (see ch. 6, Social Systems). Although everyone is expected to be motivated by self-interest, the man who helps others to improve their positions commands prestige, respect and, in some cases, obedience.

The need to get along with others is of major concern, but most Ibo believe that it is good to speak out freely, even if it hurts to do so. Frankness thus is a desirable trait. On the other hand, secretiveness is regarded as contemptible. Everyone is expected to live an open life, even in such matters as interpersonal disputes, financial affairs, and sex. To be willing to criticize others and to expose evil-doing is an admired trait of leadership. The major deterrent to crime is not the fear of being found guilty by a court of law but rather the shame that would be felt in the presence of other members of the group.

The Ibo and other eastern peoples traditionally have regarded marriage as the accepted status for all adults; celibacy has been viewed as unnatural and, at times, immoral. As a social institution, marriage has served primarily as the accepted way of producing children, who are highly regarded. The eldest son is a figure of high family esteem.

In traditional groups polygamy was a prized symbol of status. Often a first wife financed her husband's bridewealth payments for a second wife in order to enhance his prestige and her own position as head wife. In modern society ownership of an automobile has largely replaced the second wife as a status symbol.

A woman may be accorded a high social status because of her husband's accomplishments, her children's achievements, her ability as a trader, or her own position of leadership in a women's society. Some women thus attain higher social rank than their husbands. Widows or divorced women who establish their own compounds are granted a degree of equality with men, particularly if they have paid bridewealth to hire other women to serve them.

Despite their rural background and strong ties to village origins, the Ibo find urban life stimulating and rewarding. They sometimes refer to those of their group who still live in rural areas as "primitive" or "bush people." Many educated Ibo, while retaining family ties, have rejected their agricultural background so thoroughly that they prefer poverty in the city to the relative comfort of life on the farm.

THE NORTHERN KINGDOMS

The social orders of the Hausa-Fulani and other northern peoples governed by Islamic emirates, such as the Kanuri and the Nupe, are associated with generally similar sociopolitical values and attitudes. These are based on two interlocking concepts: the supremacy of Islam in all affairs and the highly structured political order with supreme administrative power vested in the emir. Among all except the Kanuri, this includes the acceptance of an exclusive ethnic minority as the legitimate ruling group (see ch. 6, Social Systems).

278

In the tightly structured emirates the commoners and most of the elite remain immersed in the traditional order and are loyal to their existing values, little recognizing the changes brought about by the colonial or postcolonial eras. The changes in the organization of local government since 1966 have left most of the traditional structures intact. The influence of the relatively few educated men on social attitudes has been very limited. The number of secondary school students in the capital cities had grown considerably by the mid-1960s, but most were of southern or Middle Belt origin. New ideas were rejected because there were few educated men to work for their acceptance and because the commoners had expected change to be instituted by traditional leaders, who generally were the most conservative element of the society.

Few commoners are aware of the political entities beyond their districts. For many commoners and members of the elite, the withdrawal of the British at the time of Nigerian independence was neither sought nor fully understood.

The highest political ideal is an orderly society in which ties of discipline and respect modeled on family relationships remain unchallenged. Attitudes toward other Nigerians have been conditioned by a belief that southerners and Middle Belt people are crude pagans who do not have orderly societies or demonstrate respect for the established order. The Northern People's Congress, a political party controlled by the emirs, conducted successful campaigns by stressing that the opposition party was under the control of outsiders from the south. The southerners were portrayed as a force opposed to children's obedience to their parents. The northern commoners were willing to believe such claims because southerners with whom they had contact in the north had values that conflicted radically with their own, particularly those regarding respect for the traditional authorities (see ch. 9, Government and Political Dynamics).

Although the Yoruba also filled jobs in competition with the northerners, they were able to blend with the emirate peoples in a number of ways that reduced tensions. Many were Muslims; they dressed in traditional style, treated their women as inferiors, and were organized along compound lines. The Yoruba expressed respect for traditional authorities because they were able to equate their own rule by kings (obas) with the rule of the emirs.

The dominant attachment in Hausa life is to the Islamic faith, the impact of which is felt in everything from political structure to architectural style. A Hausa who has attained wealth usually prefers a trip to Mecca or increased gifts to the mallams (Koranic scholars and teachers) to modern symbols of status, such as an automobile. Despite the government's efforts to use the roman alphabet for the Hausa language, many prefer the arabic script because it conforms to the letters of the Koran.

Islam and clientage provide the bonds that cut across the northern class distinctions based on occupational castes. By formal Islamic concept, all men are brothers; although they may be predestined to rank higher or lower in the earthly order, they are ultimately equal in the eyes of God. Northern social values also stress patient fortitude in the face of adversity, particularly since life's occurrences are seen as predestined by God. Other virtues include self-control, industry, thrift, and pride in workmanship.

Among the emirate peoples social status is based primarily on membership in the numerous hereditary occupational groupings. The people accept this elaborate stratification as the proper basis for society. In terms of prestige the society is divided into three strata: the rulers, the administrators, and the commoners. It is accepted that one must be born into, or in some cases marry into, the ruling class. It is also expected that an individual's relative position in that class will change. The administrator class is also hereditary, but its members are commoners rather than nobles. Others may aspire to rise into its ranks, although only a limited number do so.

Within the ranks of commoners, the greatest honor and deference are accorded to the *mallams*, particularly to one's own religious teacher. Some *mallams* are members of the ruling and administrator classes. Next to Islamic scholarship, the highest regard is paid to successful traders, particularly to those with membership in the fraternity of long-distance traders.

The income-earning potential of an occupation does not necessarily determine a man's social status, nor is wealth an expected reward for hard work. Generally, high status is concomitant with political office, which is expected to provide its incumbent with the opportunity for personal gain. Some low-ranked occupations, such as butchering and metalworking, are quite profitable, and poor commoners are sometimes willing to accept low status for the chance of lucrative activity.

Success is a desirable goal, but the lack of opportunities is recognized and accepted. Those who take advantage of the few opportunities open to them are not only accepted but also admired. Except for becoming a *mallam*, only two ways of advancement are open to most people. The first is to become apprenticed to a man of a higher occupational category; the second is through the institution of clientage.

From birth the people are taught to accept the burden of obedience to all senior individuals from elder brothers to the emirs, the inevitability of fate as predestined by God, and the occupational and social order into which they were born. They learn to accept the lack of rights that applies to women, the young, and those of the lower social ranks. They learn the need for obseqious behavior toward superiors and are taught to expect advancement only through clientage. They are even taught to accept the burden of hostile relations between parent and child. The strength that these values have in society is reflected in what often appears to outsiders as the unnatural rigidity of family relationships, one of which requires that parents reject and avoid all contact with their first-born child, who must be adopted by others to survive.

The family is regarded as the model for all political relations. The most important element of such relationships is the interplay of discipline and respect between father and son. Like the father, the political leader is expected to provide his client with protection, security, and a place in the social order as well as the chance for advancement. The client in turn is expected to appear obedient, subservient, and completely loyal at all times. A part of this relationship is a pattern called shame avoidance, which requires both parties to be subdued and self-controlled. Ideally the junior person speaks only when spoken to and does not eat in the senior's presence, and both remain rigidly formal. A man avoids speaking directly to his superior, is brief, affects an abject attitude, and agrees with everything the superior says.

Being ordered to do menial tasks by a patron or superior is not viewed as demeaning because the relationship is socially acceptable and because it gives the subservient individual the chance to rise in his master's esteem. The subordinate may in turn have the opportunity to serve as master to those further down the scale in social standing, age, or wealth.

Successful clientage involves early training in subordination, an ability for political intrigue, and opportunistic choice of patrons. Despite the high regard for the ability to appear loyal, no opprobrium is entailed in changing patrons; a man who rises through clever and timely changes of loyalty is admired for his skills. Residence in a city, particularly in a capital city, carries prestige. For the Hausa, one advantage of city life is the greater opportunity it provides for changing patrons to a client's advantage.

To a Western observer the etiquette used in relationships between client and patron often appears to be obsequious and demeaning, but to the Hausa it is natural. As a parallel to the even more demanding etiquette of relations between father and son, it is a social nicety and not a burden of class inferiority. Great emphasis is placed on the enjoyment of such formalities.

Those men who can afford to do so attach great importance to maintaining their *mutumci* (manhood or self-respect). They limit their clientship to the seeking of political assistance and advice. Those who wish to rise in the sociopolitical structure, however, must necessarily forego this value in part.

In the Hausa-Fulani concept all men are considered minors until they establish compounds of their own. The head of a compound is regarded as the father, protector, and spokesman of all who reside there. The recognized compound head is the only one who may make his voice heard by the government. A man may admit without shame that he will never be able to reach a recognized state of maturity because he cannot afford to establish his own compound.

The role of Hausa women is severely limited in all matters (see ch. 6, Social Systems). Juridically they are considered minors. Married women are generally not allowed outside the women's compounds, and such tasks as shopping are done by children, servants, or old women. An adult woman without a husband, whether single, divorced, or widowed, has very low status in the society. Parents are greatly shamed if they are unable to find a husband for their daughter within a short time after she reaches marriageable age.

THE MIDDLE BELT TIV

The value system of the Tiv cannot be considered typical of the roughly 9 million people of the Middle Belt, but they are the largest group in that area. An examination of their values indicates that Middle Belt groups may have attitudes quite different from those of the major groupings.

Only the deference paid to age prevents the Tiv society from being completely egalitarian, and even this deference is much more limited than that prevailing in other Nigerian societies (see ch. 6, Social Systems). The Tiv, who do not allow any formal positions of leadership to exist in their society, place severe limits on the efforts of individuals to assume ad hoc positions as leaders. In any circumstance in which a leader is recruited—for example, as a spokesman to deal with an outside force—such assignments include the clear understanding that the individual leadership is tolerated rather than expected. Any attempt by an individual to assume a leadership role regularly brings him into difficulty with other members of his group. Considerable effort is directed by his lineage to deflating the position of such a man in order to prevent his rising above the others.

The Tiv view as a danger to their society and as a challenge to their social and political traditions any man's attempt to become more than influential or prominent. Even prominent men who do not attempt to exert control are considered dangerous because the Tiv expect that such men may use their power to strengthen themselves at the expense of their community.

The Tiv concept of the highest good is service undertaken for the benefit of the whole community rather than for personal gain. To be self-seeking is a particular evil. The Tiv deplore displays of temper or haste; quiet determination and strength of conviction are respected, as are sincerity and integrity. Men who are known for intrigue and bribery are deprecated and may even be labeled witches.

All adult males have an equal right to be heard in all councils, including the courts. They enjoy being involved in arguments and legal disputes and have succeeded in displaying a remarkable degree of cohesion and lobbying ability in modern politics.

Their political success has been a consequence of their own high degree of ethnic consciousness and the considerable fear of their warrior ability by outsiders. Although the Tiv are not linked together by any political structures and are often in conflict with each other, they are able to coalesce in the face of any external threat and to present a united front to outsiders. During the colonial era they consistently rejected all efforts by the British to impose a political order that conflicted with their egalitarian ideals. This rejection was again made clear in the extensive rioting that occurred at independence in 1960 and again in 1964 to force the removal of appointed chiefs.

The Tiv are very sensitive in relations with outsiders, particularly other Africans rather than foreigners. Their egalitarianism, practicality, and lack of superstition bring their values into conflict with others. This is particularly true of their relations with the Hausa-Fulani, who dominated the politics and administration of the former Northern Region and whose caste society and attitude toward authority were at odds with Tiv concepts of class and leadership.

ATTITUDES OF THE EDUCATED ELITE

The members of Nigeria's educated elite have been subject to the influence of several conflicting sets of values, deriving in part from their ethnic background and in part from the impact of Western ideas and ideals. Many of the educated were born into ethnic groups characterized by rigid systems of social stratification. In these systems the rightful exercise of political power was linked to status by birth. Some of the principles and practices introduced by the British supported the traditional pattern; some were in conflict with the pattern and with each other. Thus the

British tended to support the traditional patterns of authority in the north, but they also gave superior positions and status to those with higher education and wealth. The emphasis on education gave priority to achievement, but for many Nigerians the acquisition of the appropriate credentials (degrees and diplomas) meant that they and they alone were fit to rule, a notion more compatible with some of the older political systems and values than with the notions of popular rule and parliamentary democracy also introduced by the British. For many educated Nigerians there is a clear conflict between their sense that only they have a right to make political decisions and their persistent belief that a popularly elected and democratically functioning parliamentary system is the most desirable form of government.

Members of the elite are particularly sensitive to observed or imagined criticisms by Westerners that Africa lacked civilization before the colonial era, that Africans are inherently incapable of ruling themselves democratically, and that they lack the ability to adapt technical and administrative skills to their existing situations. In self-defense they seek out elements in traditional societies that presaged democratic control and stress the superiority of the traditional extended-family system in providing psychological and social welfare over the fragmented and isolationist system they observe in developed countries. They place the blame for many or all of their country's problems on the impact of colonial practices, particularly those that strengthened ethnic divisions or weakened public morality.

The great majority of the modernized elite is attached to the concepts and ideals of democratic forms of government. The announced decision of the Federal Military Government (FMG) in 1971 to postpone a return to civilian rule until 1976 came as a direct challenge to their accepted set of political values, but most appeared willing to grant priority over their desire for an elected government to the need for establishing national stability, lessening ethnic animosity, ending corruption, and beginning the downward and outward spread of economic development. They were willing to support the FMG as long as its actions portended success in those directions (see ch. 9, Government and Political Dynamics).

Despite their association with modern Western ideas, strong bonds continue to exist between members of the modernized elite and the traditional orders from which they came. A university graduate in the city is likely to maintain the friendship of uneducated brothers, a home in his native village for future retirement, and continued involvement in local and tribal associations. He is also likely to retain cultural perceptions that may prevent his utilizing fully Western or modern concepts in his work or that may lead him to transform those ideas and methods into an amalgam based upon, but different from, the modern and traditional originals. For example, educated men, having been shown that a certain disease has been caused by a virus, will fully comprehend the scientific explanation offered them. At the same time, however, they may still demand to know who picked them out for the viral attack, concluding that an enemy did it through magic or poison. Many powerful men, not all in the traditional order, retain religious leaders or magicians as close confidants because they attribute to them the ability to prevent such black magic attacks (see ch. 6, Social System).

Generally, educated persons not born there ignore the local affairs of the city in which they reside, preferring to devote their political energies to the affairs of their areas of origin, no matter how far removed they may be in time and space. They prefer supporting village development efforts to becoming involved in the affairs of the cities. Politics and local development are left exclusively in the hands of those native to the city, who have made few successful efforts to draw on the talents of the educated residents.

Western political and socioeconomic values have been institutionalized by the educated persons in power at the national level. These persons have accepted such values because the ideas are associated with the superior technology of the modern world. They have also accepted, as their own, Western patterns of education and consumption. They effectively form a remote part of the social and cultural order to which they have become acclimatized through their educational process, linking them in many ways more closely with the British than with the masses of their countrymen.

The most highly educated portion of the elite is torn between two cultures and attempts to appear superior to both. In dealing with Europeans, these members of the elite insist on the superiority of the African personality and ancient African cultures. With less educated Africans, they stress benefits, including class privileges, that derive from their European associations.

The primary political and economic goal of many of the elite is in maintaining and improving their own positions, particularly because they consider that the prospects of raising the positions of the masses are very slight. Thus, the first aim of the new graduate or student leaving before graduation generally is to find a secure and well-paying position in the civil service or in a major private or public corporation. He is interested, however, in using the wealth and influence not only for his own benefit but also for the improvement of his home community. For example, many members of the educated elite spend as much as one-fifth of their income on financing the education of relatives. The concept of involvement with, and sacrifice for, the betterment of a wider area, including the nation, comes last.

Most Nigerians are willing to work very hard to achieve wealth and status, but they also expect a successful man to refrain from any work resembling manual labor. A major prerogative of high rank in a family or in society is the right to have others perform all necessary manual labor.

High status requires the projection of an image of a "big man," including the conspicuous display of luxury goods, leisure, generosity, and personal power over subordinates. The superior, whether husband, teacher, father, or political leader, displays authority by requiring inferiors to perform all menial tasks, even those he could easily do himself. Even the most eduated men expect unqualified deference and unquestioned obedience from their subordinates. In their view high status requires the ability to get people to work and to obey unhesitatingly. This attitude is accompanied by a general abhorrence of manual labor as something below the dignity of one who has attained the status of an educated person. Such an attitude is in direct conflict with the Western value of work that is inculcated by schooling, and more educated officials at higher levels tend to subordinate the traditional to this modern value.

Despite this attitude toward inferiors, members of the upper elements of the modern elite have not developed a sense that they constitute an exclusive class. In part this is so because of the strength of ties to the traditional order across educational and income lines, because of their own rejection of the old class distinctions, and because of the open nature of the new society (see ch. 6, Social Systems).

It was not until it became possible for political leaders to gain important office in the late 1950s that the members of the elite began to attach any prestige to political work. Gradually, ranking political figures were accepted as the social and cultural pacesetters of society. In 1971 the elite was almost entirely in bureaucratic employment in the civil service, public corporations, or large, expatriate commercial firms. Their status depended upon their educational qualifications and, as a result, they attached their highest values in the modern order to education. In a survey among the Ibo, for example, 80 percent stated that they would be most likely to use a financial windfall to finance educational advancement for their children.

Although the upper elements of the elite do not consider themselves part of a closed group, most civil servants consider themselves an educated, Westernized new class in advance of the society as a whole. They are strongly oriented toward their fellow civil servants and others of the educated class. They are also politically minded and eager to use their connections and wealth to advance to posts of greater authority, pay, and prestige. In their efforts they are supported by relatives, friends, and clients, all of whom expect to receve a future return for their support.

All relationships, whether political, social, or simply administrative, are affected by the traditional culture, in which all relationships are part of the complex network of family, clan, and ethnic group ties. This has two effects: it makes people expect to see one of their own group in any post with which they deal, and it causes them to regard a political leader in terms at least analogous to the holder of a traditional post.

In the emirates, for example, traditional offices had fiefs assigned to them, which were to produce income for a person as a reward for filling the office. Stewards on these fiefs collected taxes, supplies, and labor forces on their master's behalf. These stewards in turn drew reimbursement for their work by retaining a portion of all taxes and by accepting gifts from favor seekers, including a percentage of gifts intended to influence the decisions of their master. Commoners appointed to such posts as tax collectors or public works and construction supervisors similarly expected to keep a portion of the income or to solicit gifts from favor seekers. A similar situation prevailed among other ethnic groups.

Although the British paid all officials above the level of ward leaders during the colonial era, many officeholders regarded the salaries as a replacement only for that portion of the collected taxes that traditionally they would have been allowed to retain as compensation from their employer. They continued to expect and receive the other half of their income in the form of gifts and payments from subordinates and the public. Such payments were regarded as recompense for granting requests and favors, even though these acts involved the performance of official duties. New officeseekers expected to pay such a gift in return for assistance in obtaining a civil service appointment. Civil servants expected to pay for promotions, and the general public expected to pay for small administrative services by government officials.

Thus, although in the modern order they are paid a salary to perform such services, public officials are still regarded analogously as the holders of traditional offices, and the suppliants requesting favors still expect to compensate their benefactors in the traditional manner. Protests over the payment of such "dash" money, as the payments are termed in the south, are voiced only when the level or number of payments demanded become exorbitant. Such complaints generally are not made in the north.

What appears as bribery to Westerners thus is regarded by Nigerians as a legitimate act of recognition due a superior or as a traditional method of obtaining favors. Even if the law, the government's anticorruption campaigns, and his own education create an attitude of opposition to it, a lower level public official often feels constrained to seek gifts from his clients and from the general public with whom he deals. Such acts are necessary to pay his superior for favors on his own behalf or for his subordinates. If he does not accept gifts, he will be unable to give gifts and thus will be unable to obtain the support he needs to do the job for which he is responsible.

IMPACT OF SOCIAL UNREST, 1966-71

In mid-1971 information was not available to permit accurate judgment of the impact on values and attitudes of the changes affecting the country in the period since 1965. Significant changes, however, were believed to have been brought about in some elements of the population by the introduction of military rule with its efforts at nation-building, by further economic expansion, by changes in the local government structure, by the expansion of the civil service and the armed forces, and particularly by the impact of the war. Although the changes had not yet been surveyed, in one way at least they appeared to have reinforced the differences in the development of acceptance of change, for it was again the emirates that were least affected by the need to accept changes in outlook and the eastern peoples who were most affected.

The impact of the events from 1966 to 1971 was most acute among the Ibo. They, and to a lesser extent their neighbors, were affected by the creation of new loyalties to the self-proclaimed Republic of Biafra and by an increase in animosity toward other Nigerian peoples, particularly toward those of the northern emirates with whom they were most at odds. The Ibo were also affected by the blows to their pride dealt by the defeat and loss of power in the country as a whole, by the loss of their leaders, and by the impact of wartime destruction, hunger, and death. The impact was heightened by the fact that these peoples were particularly proud of their own independence of outlook, leadership ability, judgment, and material and intellectual accomplishments.

During the war years the Yoruba were seemingly occupied to a great extent with their own interests. The lack of any changes in the social, political, and educational structures in the emirates left little reason to believe that any significant changes in values or attitudes had taken place. The political changes, however, had considerable significance for the future of the Middle Belt peoples, who were given their first taste of political power and large-scale opportunities to rise in the ranks of the civil service and the expanded army. Changes were beginning in their social and political attitudes resulting from more education, wider contacts, their improving economic opportunities, and their more widely recognized economic potential.

CHAPTER 12

CHARACTER AND STRUCTURE OF THE ECONOMY

In mid-1971 the country was still engaged in the task of reconstruction and rehabilitation from the material ravages of civil war. It had embarked upon the restoration of political stability and the pursuit of a degree of unity and effective administration that might permit better coordinated progress in economic development and balanced growth. As recovery and development proceeded, the economy would still derive its basic character from smallholder farming, internal trade, and the export of agricultural raw materials, but the structure of modern production and public revenue was on the threshold of transition to a pattern in which petroleum export would play a rapidly increasing role, and industry would continue its gradual but perceptible expansion.

Unpaid subsistence activity still occupied much of the population. In the mid-1960s only 5 percent of those gainfully employed were working for wages; some 64 percent were self-employed; and 31 percent were unpaid family workers (see ch. 4, Population and Labor). As educational opportunities expanded and urban migration increased, unemployment and underemployment became increasingly conspicuous problems. The real share of economic activity devoted to subsistence production was not known, but its imputed value had been tentatively estimated at about 30 percent of the country's gross domestic product (GDP) and 60 percent of agricultural output. Few, if any, pockets of self-sufficiency remained in the countryside; a complex and long-established system of market organization linked most rural villages as well as urban communities. About 25 percent of agricultural output was thought to be traded internally, and 15 percent, exported. Domestic cash sales of farm produce had expanded notably since World War II, but the growth of peasant commercial response to export incentives went back to the beginning of the twentieth century (see ch. 13, Agriculture and Mining).

After World War II, when the government-operated marketing boards took over the marketing of agricultural exports, the monopoly of foreign export trading houses was broken. The federal and regional (state since 1968) governments subsequently siphoned off much of the income from agricultural export for use in government consumption and capital expenditure for development (see ch. 13, Agriculture and Mining). Since independence the Nigerian government has also been gradually increasing its control of the banking sector and, through the taxation of foreign companies in mining and other sectors, has augmented the country's share of the income from gross domestic product. In 1971 a new increase was negotiated in the government's share of petroleum earnings, which were expected to furnish growing resources of foreign exchange and development financing throughout much of the 1970s.

Despite the extension of domestic government control and gradual, but growing, progess in the Nigerianization of management and entrepreneurship in banking, commerce, and manufacture, the economy remains heavily dependent on the level of activity in the foreign-oriented sectors. Imports of foods are limited; except for animal proteins and luxury foods, the country is largely self-sufficient in basic foodstuffs. Progress has also been made in the substitution of domestic manufactures for imports of textiles, footwear, clothing, beverages, tobacco, and a number of other consumer goods. The manufacturing sector's share in domestic product has risen. The growth of industry, construction, transport, and other forms of economic development, however, has required a mounting volume of imports of capital equipment and intermediate goods (see ch. 14, Industry and Trade).

The political crisis came at a time when the government had already depleted the reserves of foreign exchange acquired during the 1950s to finance the requirements of its early development plans. The military needs of the civil war added a further heavy import burden and diverted government expenditure from the capital requirements of the economy to inflationary spending on current consumption and military materiel. War devastation interrupted exports of petroleum, curtailed exports of palm products, and disrupted a few manufactures.

The country thus prepared to enter the 1970s with negative public saving (deficit financing) from the federal and state budgets and with barely enough foreign exchange to cover the current two months' import requirements. Launching an ambitious new development plan for the 1970–74 period, the country faced a growing problem of domestic price inflation, an uncertain outlook for international commodity prices, and a shortfall of foreign private investment and official loan and grant aid.

The economy is nonetheless judged fundamentally sound by international observers. The natural environment offers a variety of resources with potential for economic growth. The variety of climate favors production of a diverse range of tropical export crops, and the ratio of agricultural and forest land to population is favorable for the country as a whole, although there are several localized zones of population pressure (see ch. 13, Agriculture and Mining). Potential power resources are good and adequately developed, and the transport network, though somewhat damaged by the civil war, has been basically well developed (see ch. 2, Physical Environment). To the preexisting range of commercially exploitable mineral resources, including coal, tin, columbite, and tantalite, the rich new petroleum discoveries have added a valuable source of income, as well as employment. Because it had the largest population in Africa, the country offered a more extensive domestic market for the development of manufacture than most developing African countries. With per capita gross domestic product equivalent to about US$80, however, the market may not be sufficiently prosperous to justify the ambitious plans for development of heavy industry in iron and steel production and petrochemicals that have been a feature of each of the succeeding economic development plans.

Along with its natural advantages, the country in mid-1971 enjoyed a precarious financial stability that was nevertheless admirable in the wake of the demands and disruptions of the civil war and reconstruction. Except in the eastern states, which were most directly affected by war devastation, the economy had emerged from the conflict with strength and resilience. Agricultural production had been well maintained, and industrial production for the country as a whole had actually expanded during the war years.

The government's monetary and fiscal policies had been stringent but sound, holding price inflation and balance of payments deficits within potentially manageable proportions despite the impact of continued deficit spending and the pressure of deferred consumer demand. Payments abroad were in arrears, but the government had avoided incurring long-term foreign debt to finance the war, had maintained a cautious attitude toward supplier credits, and was consequently in a position to attract new long-term loans on favorable terms from the international monetary organizations.

The Second National Development Plan, 1970–74, was launched during some initial administrative confusion and general uncertainty as to the outlook for generating the internal saving and external finance needed to underwrite it. Revised economic projections indicated that investment resources might well fall substantially short of target in the first year of the plan but could catch up later on. Much will depend on political developments, however, as well as the evolution of a more efficient administrative structure and a smooth working relationship between state and federal government authorities (see ch. 9, Government and Political Dynamics). The well-conceived program of expenditure recommended in the plan would require restraint and sound management on the part of state as well as federal officials if scarce resources of finance, manpower, and materiel were to be effectively allocated.

PATTERN OF GROWTH

Until the 1940s economic growth in Nigeria was fueled almost entirely by the response of traders and peasant farmers to demand and prices on external markets. This response was facilitated by the construction of major roads and railways to the port cities, but in general the role of government was limited and relatively passive.

Demand for agricultural raw materials on world markets brought important new gains in the country's exchange earnings after World War II. World market prices for the principal exports —cocoa, groundnuts (peanuts), rubber, and palm products—rose dramatically in the late 1940s and early 1950s. The official marketing boards, established in the 1940s, kept the price to the producer well below market prices, so that public revenues were rapidly increased and a large share of the export proceeds were funneled into sectors of rapid growth potential. There ensued the rapid development of economic infrastructure, the beginning of industrial development, and the growth of government participation in most sectors of the economy.

The growth of import costs lagged somewhat behind soaring export prices in the late 1940s and early 1950s, but by the mid-1950s imports of goods and services began to catch up with exports, and the large payments surpluses decreased. Whereas peasant farming, the dominant sector of economic activity, had utilized few inputs other than increased amounts of land and labor, the increasing amount of capital investment in sectors of more rapid growth required large imports of machinery, transport equipment, expertise and, eventually, intermediate materials for established industry. In time there were also the usual overseas administrative costs of a newly independent country to be met. Although per capita income in the subsistence sector and in the country as a whole remained low by international standards, rising incomes among salaried personnel and increasing urbanization expanded consumer demand for imported goods, ranging from tinned sardines to luxury cars.

In the meantime, government activity had been increasing even more dramatically than export earnings. It was supported not only by the huge agricultural marketing board surpluses but also by a new range of direct and indirect taxes imposed during the period. Between 1950 and fiscal year 1962/63 (April 1, 1962, to March 31, 1963), total revenues of central and regional governments, excluding marketing board surpluses, rose from 6.8 to 12.7 percent of gross domestic product. This fiscal achievement has been termed a remarkable example of good leadership since it was achieved without authoritarian measures. It was assisted by the decentralization of government functions that began in 1954.

The transfer of power from the central to the regional governments under the Constitution of 1954, however, also accelerated the pace of government spending. Until 1954 both private and public expenditure had lagged behind the accumulation of foreign exchange earnings. Consequently, foreign exchange reserves by 1955 had been built up to an unprecedented level equivalent to two years of current imports. Thereafter, the world market prices for Nigerian exports stagnated or declined, and after 1955 the balance of payments had a deficit on current account (see ch. 14, Industry and Trade). From the mid-1950s until the mid-1960s the government was drawing upon the previously accumulated reserves to finance imports for its development programs. Since 1955 the combined resources of the central and regional authorities have been increasingly channeled into modernizing and diversifying economic activity. The real impact of the public sector on the economic structure and its rate of growth, however, was probably not very great until the 1960s.

When the political crisis that preceded the civil war interrupted economic development in the mid-1960s, the economy was on the threshold of modernization. Domestic resources had been effectively mobilized in the context of the still-limited level of development. The foreign exchange backlog had been exhausted, however, and there was mounting criticism of the continuing transfer of financial resources from peasant agriculture to other sectors through the medium of low producer prices and large marketing board surpluses (see ch. 13, Agriculture and Mining). There was also considerable concern over urban unemployment and the steady migration from rural areas to towns, partly as a result of the agricultural income policy embodied in marketing board prices.

The emerging transition from a peasant agricultural economy to a semi-industrialized one was reflected in the changed composition of imports, which in the mid-1960s were dominated by industrial materials, machinery, and transport equipment rather than by consumer goods as in the past. Improved transport, expanded educational facilities, and mounting internal trade also reflected the trend. The Central Bank of Nigeria had been created in 1958, and banking facilities had been expanded. The growth of aggregate demand from private as well as public sources had been handled without undue inflation except during 1952 and 1953. By 1964, however, the accumulated foreign reserves were being exhausted, and there was recourse to moderate foreign borrowing and grant aid. Measures had to be taken to protect the foreign exchange position, including import duties and standby legislation for exchange control.

It was against this background of beginning financial stringency that the political crisis erupted and the new burden of war expenditure had to be met (see ch. 9, Government and Political Dynamics). Consequently, the position at the war's end in January 1970 was one of moderate financial crisis, and payments abroad were in arrears. Prices had begun to rise significantly in early 1969. Consumer prices for low-income families in major cities had risen by 12 percent in 1969 and by 13 percent in the first half of 1970 and were still rising in early 1971. Price controls had been introduced, but continuing government spending, pent-up demand from the war years, local food shortages, and the need to maintain controls on nonessential imports continued to exert pressure on the internal price level. In mid-1971 the financial crisis was not resolved but was generally regarded as temporary. The increase in petroleum production, somewhat more rapid than anticipated, and the more favorable posted price and tax arrangements for oil exports promised relief to the treasury. The World Bank Group had granted a US$80-million loan for general rehabilitation until such time as a pipeline of approved aid projects could be prepared, and the group had not closed the door on further aid negotiations.

The Nigerian national accounts are not very useful for measuring the rate of growth of the economy or the inflationary gap between aggregate demand and available resources. The sectoral composition of economic activity cannot be measured with much precision, and data on the financing of capital formation are not always comparable for a continuous number of years.

International sources appear to be in agreement, however, on rough orders of magnitude for national aggregates and general trends in the major economic indicators. Thus, the overall rate of growth from the mid-1950s to the mid-1960s appears to have equaled or slightly surpassed the rate recommended by the United Nations (UN).

Economic growth, which had been moderate in the 1950s, was accelerated during the period up to the outbreak of the civil war. From fiscal 1958/59 through 1966/67 the economy grew at an average annual rate of 5.7 percent in real terms—that is, deflated for the rise in prices. The rate of growth thus compared favorably with those of most other developing countries, but the measure of growth depended to some extent on estimates of population growth, which varied widely. Assuming a population growth rate of 2.6 percent per year, the annual growth of real per capita income would have been approximately 3 percent.

Relatively little of the favorable growth trend is attributed to the development of petroleum production. Excluding the petroleum sector, the economy still grew at an average annual rate of 4.8 percent during the period. About one-third of the growth in gross domestic product was attributable to agriculture, which contributed more than 50 percent of domestic product. The average annual growth rate in agriculture was about 4 percent and would have been higher except for a decline in food crop production for domestic consumption between crop years 1964/65 and 1966/67. Agricultural exports exerted the strongest influence on growth, increasing by about 5 percent a year, supporting the expansion of distribution and transportation, and earning more foreign exchange to finance the expansion of imports. This strong growth trend in the country's major exports was achieved in spite of the negative tax policy for agriculture followed by the government's marketing boards throughout the period (see ch. 13, Agriculture and Mining).

The civil war interrupted the economic growth trend. Gross domestic product is thought to have declined by about 6.6 percent in fiscal 1967/68 and improved by less than 1 percent in 1968/69 and by 2.6 percent in 1969/70. The average annual growth rate for 1965/66 through 1969/70 was tentatively estimated at minus 0.5 percent.

The structure of economic activity, as expressed in contribution to gross domestic product, was in the process of transition in 1970 and 1971. The proportionate contribution of agriculture was declining as commercial petroleum production grew. The contribution of agriculture, forestry, and fishing, which had been 65 to 70 percent of gross domestic product in the 1950s, dropped to about 54 percent in 1966 and 1967. During the 1970s agricultural output was expected to grow at about the same rate as population, some 2.6 percent a year. Tentative projections thus estimated that in 1970 about 14 percent of gross domestic product would be derived from petroleum and 43 percent from agiculture and that by 1973 some 19.3 percent would come from petroleum and 38 percent from agriculture.

After petroleum production, manufacturing was the fastest growing sector of the economy during the 1960s. From a very low base, it expanded at an average annual rate of 11 percent at constant prices. Its proportionate contribution to gross domestic product at current factor cost thus increased from only 4 percent in 1958 to 5.6 percent in 1963 and to 8.4 percent in 1967.

Throughout the 1960s between 13 and 14 percent of gross domestic product was attributed to the distribution trades. Between 5 and 9 percent was derived from mining; 4 to 5 percent, from construction; 3 to 5 percent, from transport and communications; and about 3.5 percent, from government.

Because gross domestic product, rather than gross national product (GNP), is consistently used in the Nigerian accounts, the amount of income accruing to residents may be somewhat inflated. Gross domestic product exceeds GNP by the amount of net factor payments made abroad. In the case of Nigeria, as of most developing countries, this is a sizable net outflow in some sectors. For petroleum, for example, it is estimated that the contribution to GNP in 1967 would have been only 2.2 percent, as compared with 3.4 percent of gross domestic product.

The push toward economic growth in the 1960s was reflected in the principal components of aggregate expenditure on national product. Between 1962 and 1968 the portion of national expenditure devoted to gross fixed capital formation increased from about 10 percent to between 13 and 16 percent, and the proportion was expected to increase still further during the period of the Second National Development Plan. Consumer expenditure fell from 86 percent to 80 percent during the same period, whereas current government consumption expenditure increased at about the same rate as total expenditure, remaining at a constant 6 percent of the total. The ratio of gross domestic product to GNP was declining as factor payments abroad, consisting chiefly of dividends and undistributed profits of foreign investors, took on a more important role.

Aggregate domestic expenditure is the sum of capital investment, both public and private, plus private consumer expenditure and government current spending. The gap between this total and domestic product was filled by a surplus of imports of goods and services—that is, a deficit on the current balance of payments with foreign countries equivalent to between 1 and 4 percent of gross domestic product. Total domestic expenditure had regularly exceeded gross domestic product since 1955. On the other hand, the savings gap to be filled by net foreign investment had somewhat diminished. Between 1964 and 1968 the ratio of domestic saving to gross investment rose from 67 percent to 86 percent. The ratio of domestic saving to gross domestic product had increased from 8.2 percent to 13.4 percent in the same period.

The Second National Development Plan for the April 1970 to

March 1974 period is the latest in a series of development plans. It sets forth the policy framework for, and the program of, the reconstruction of the war-damaged areas as well as the construction and development of the rest of the country. The plan clearly establishes postwar national objectives. It also outlines the general policy measures and programs of action that flow from the objectives, as well as the national scale of priorities. The plan is to be implemented by both federal and state governments; all public sector institutions and private sector initiatives can be interpreted as being involved in the execution of the plan. Such a plan attempts to assess the manpower, production, natural, and financial resources available in the time period. Priorities are assigned in such a way that undue strain will not be placed upon resources, which would result in inflation or the abandonment of higher priority objectives.

During the period of the Second National Development Plan, petroleum production and manufacturing are expected to be the principal growth sectors. Agricultural output is projected to rise at a slower rate than before—only about 2.4 percent a year, or roughly at the same rate as population. The plan postulates an overall growth rate increasing from less than 5 percent in the first year of the plan to about 9 percent in the last year. Investment is expected to rise to as much as 20 percent of gross domestic product, half of it from the private sector and half from government. Nearly half of the private investment is expected to come from abroad, most of it from the petroleum industry. Whether nonpetroleum foreign direct investment will be as high as projected in the early years of the plan appeared somewhat uncertain in mid-1971. Another somewhat precarious estimate is that for public saving, which is expected to furnish 70 percent of government investment during the period. This estimate was made despite the high rate of government current expenditure in the late 1960s and the avowed intention of maintaining more flexible produce prices in agriculture, which might conceivably reduce marketing board surpluses available to investment. The official inflow of capital and foreign aid during the plan period is expected to furnish about 20 percent of planned investment.

During the first two years of the plan the emphasis was to be principally on reconstruction and rehabilitation to restore productive capacity and transport facilities in the war-devastated states. Three-fourths of planned public capital expenditures during the first two years were earmarked for rehabilitation and were to require the equivalent of US$335 million in foreign exchange spending. During the first year of the plan steps were taken to improve plan administration and implementation and to get more well-conceived projects in aid channels. If executive capacity could be improved and expanded rapidly enough, it was hoped that some of the investment originally scheduled for the first year could be undertaken in the second year of the plan and that investment might continue to rise in the next two years.

PUBLIC FINANCE

The public sector includes the federal government, 12 state governments, about 20 public corporations—both federal and state—and more than 100 local authorities (see ch. 9, Government and Political Dynamics). The respective taxation powers of the federal and state governments are clearly distinguished under the constitution.

The states may levy and collect personal income taxes, sales taxes, and a variety of such other taxes as the cattle tax and the betting tax. The federal government has the exclusive power to impose and collect customs and excise duties; company taxes, including the petroleum profits tax; and mining royalties and rents. In the late 1960s the proceeds of these federally imposed taxes represented about 85 percent of total current public receipts of the state and federal governments combined. Only the proceeds of the company tax accrue in full to the federal government, however. The constitution provides that the proceeds of customs and excise duties, mining rents, and royalties be shared among the states according to a complex system of revenue allocation. This system involves both direct statutory payments to each state and payments to a distributive pool shared among the twelve states according to a prescribed formula (see table 5). Revenues collected by the federal government make up about 85 percent of total government revenues, but revenues retained by it are only about 50 percent of the total.

The allocation of fiscal revenues between the federal government and the states was a very active political issue in the 1960s. It is to be resolved by a constituent assembly that the Federal Military Government (FMG) plans to convene before 1976. A new census, planned for 1973, will affect the allocation among states of funds from the distributive pool. By that time revenues from the petroleum industry (company taxes, royalties, and rents) are expected to constitute more than 50 percent of total federal and state revenues combined; their allocation may be one of the more controversial questions to be decided. As of mid-1970 all of the company tax (petroleum profits tax) was being retained by the federal government, but 95 percent of the revenues from royalties and rents was being passed on to the states either directly or through the distributive pool account. During fiscal 1970/71 a major oil company began to pay the full profits tax for the first time, having recovered all of its allowable exploration and development costs. In 1971 the government decreed that offshore oil rights would be the property of the federal government, which could collect the royalties and rents on offshore wells.

In the meantime, some changes of an interim nature were made in the allocation of revenues in Decree No. 13 of 1970, which decreased the share of the federal government and increased the share of the states in the distributive pool by including 50 percent of excise taxes and increasing the share of fast-growing mining rents and royalties from 35 percent to 50 percent.

Under the new interim formula the states will have from 13 to 17 percent more than they received under the old formula. The old formula applied in fiscal 1968/69, for example, when 63 percent of total public revenues went to the federal government; 14 percent, to the states; 12 percent, to the local authorities; and 11 percent, to public corporations. The federal share of expenditure was lower, however—just 46 percent, compared to 28 percent by state governments, 11 percent by local authorities, and 15 percent by public corporations.

This decentralization of fiscal authority dates back to the Constitution of 1954, which instituted a federal system of government and granted greatly increased powers of taxation and spending to the regional governments. Since 1954 much of the public development effort has originated with the regional governments and their marketing boards, especially investment in feeder roads, agriculture, modern manufacturing facilities, and primary education. The first coordinated national development plan was not launched until 1962.

Direct taxes on personal income and wealth were the first form of taxation used in the country, even before the arrival of the British. The tax system was particularly well developed in the Northern Region, where the British later extended the cattle tax and introduced a head tax in the more remote villages. A head tax was introduced in the Western Region in 1916 and in the Eastern Region in the 1920s. By 1940 the system of direct taxation was well established throughout the country, and until that date direct taxes contributed nearly as much to government revenue as did the indirect forms, such as customs and excise duties.

In the years between 1940 and 1970 the fiscal structure was dominated by indirect taxes, notably levies on foreign trade. In the mid-1960s it was estimated that about 70 percent of all government revenues derived directly or indirectly from foreign trade, including that share of company and personal income tax that

Table 5. Federal Government of Nigeria, Recurrent Revenue, 1964/65 Through 1970/71 [1]

(in million Nigerian pounds) [2]

	1964/65	1965/66	1966/67	1967/68	1968/69	1969/70 [3]	1970/71 [4]
Customs and Excise Duties:							
Import	83.4	74.9	58.5	53.3	58.0	69.1	69.7
Export	14.4	15.9	14.0	15.0	14.8	19.7	22.1
Excise	13.6	21.5	36.0	24.8	28.2	38.0	54.2
Other	0.2	0.2	0.2	0.2	0.2	0.2	0.3
Subtotal	111.6	112.5	108.7	93.3	101.2	127.0	146.3
Income Taxes:							
Corporations	5.4	7.6	10.1	11.2	14.6	15.2	17.3
Individuals	2.4	2.9	3.0	4.8	0.7	0.4	0.1
Petroleum profits	0.4	1.3	2.9	6.0	2.6	11.1	57.8
Subtotal	8.2	11.8	16.0	22.0	17.9	26.7	75.2
Mining Revenues:							
Minerals	2.5	3.4	2.4	2.4	1.8	2.1	2.4
Oil	7.8	12.2	16.0	14.6	9.0	21.9	38.1
Subtotal	10.3	15.6	18.4	17.0	10.8	24.0	40.5
Miscellaneous Government Services	7.9	8.5	2.3	1.5	1.3	1.1	0.9
Interest Received	4.6	4.6	5.8	6.1	7.0	6.3	7.8
Other Revenues	4.8	5.7	8.4	5.3	7.6	2.5	3.3
TOTAL	147.4	158.7	159.6	145.2	145.8	187.6	274.0

Less Transferred to Regions (States)[5]:

Import duties	12.5	11.6	2.0	4.2	12.9	14.1	8.4
Export duties	14.7	15.9	20.4	14.3	13.5	19.7	22.0
Excise duties	6.3	7.9	11.3	12.7	5.5	19.0	27.1
Mining royalties and rents	6.4	7.6	9.2	8.0	3.4	10.8	18.2
Distributive pool	28.5	22.7	25.6	22.1	17.6	29.4	39.5
Other	0.1	n.a.	n.a.	0.1	0.1	n.a.	n.a.
TOTAL	63.7[6]	65.6	68.6	61.4	53.0	93.0	115.3
Total Retained by Federal Government	83.7	93.1	91.0	83.9	92.8	94.6	168.7[6]

n.a.—not available.
[1] Fiscal year, from April 1 through March 31.
[2] One Nigerian pound equals US$2.80.
[3] Revised estimates.
[4] Budget estimates.
[5] Includes nonstatutory appropriations.
[6] Total as in sources.

could be assumed to be derived from foreign trade. Moreover, the contribution of foreign trade to the revenue structure had not decreased, as is characteristic of developing countries with a growing domestic product. The rates of taxation had been raised since the 1930s, and the impact of taxation on foreign trade consequently has been heavier. The growth in per capita income since World War II had derived largely from agricultural exports and had increased the tax capacity of the export and import trades.

The agricultural marketing boards have played a major part in providing government revenues. Until 1955 they were directly responsible for research and development through compulsory loans and tax funds. Between 1947 and 1962 the estimated proportion of producer income from agricultural exports siphoned off by taxes and marketing board surpluses ranged between 21 and 32 percent (see ch. 13, Agriculture and Mining). This negative tax policy for agriculture resulted in a substantial transfer of income and capital investment to other sectors of the economy.

The continued heavy dependence on foreign trade made the government's revenue somewhat volatile and subject to fluctuations in the business cycle in industrial countries or to speculative movements on commodity exchanges. As long as the country was able to maintain substantial reserves of foreign exchange, the reserves operated as a cushion against such fluctuations: foreign borrowing and foreign aid later performed the same function. Since the mid-1960s, however, government revenues have been more exposed to the vicissitudes of export markets.

The growing importance of the petroleum profits tax and, to a lesser extent, of other company taxes had begun to modify the structure of federal revenues in favor of direct taxes by the beginning of the 1970s. Further growth in petroleum revenues was expected through 1976. As a result of the new price agreement concluded with the oil companies in 1971, the government's total revenue from the petroleum sector in fiscal 1971/72 was expected to be as high as N£340 million (1 Nigerian pound equals US$2.80).

Tax evasion remains somewhat common, impeding the more sophisticated evolution of the tax structure. The former Eastern Region, which introduced an income tax in fiscal 1956/57, achieved a rate of compliance rather rare in the underdeveloped world, but the incidence of taxation in the rest of the country has been uneven. Traders, shopkeepers, and truck operators are thought to be the most successful in evading their share of the tax burden. The predominance of subsistence production, inadequacy of recordkeeping, and corruptibility of tax employees are further sources of inequity. Local politics are sometimes involved in assessing the tax burden.

All these factors limit the potential for further development of direct taxation and increase the burden of indirect taxes, which in an underdeveloped context may be regressive in their relation to income. Until the 1960s the personal income taxes were also somewhat regressive, particularly in the former Northern Region, where they were levied at a flat rate. The tax system in the south was thought to be more progressive. Complex changes in rates during the 1960s, however, have made it difficult to estimate the progressiveness of the direct tax system. Evasion of indirect taxes is also common. There is a long tradition of smuggling, but the aggregate value of the trade is thought to be relatively small.

Government Expenditure

The level of government activity has increased dramatically since World War II and more notably since independence. Mounting government revenues have been spent on the accelerated development programs, the civil war requirements, an expanding civil service, and the educational structure. In fiscal 1967/68, 1968/69, and 1969/70 the budget surplus on current expenditure turned into a sizable deficit (see table 6).

During the civil war, from July 1967 to January 1970, almost all of the federal government's revenues were spent on waging the war. None of the cost was borne by the states. The total budgetary cost was thought to be about N£300 million, of which N£100 million to N£150 million was in foreign exchange. The mounting war expenditures were financed by increases in the rates and scope of taxes, by cutbacks in less essential spending and in some capital expenditure, and by increased domestic borrowing. The government apparently did not resort to borrowing abroad to finance the war.

Because of the priority accorded to military expenditure, spending on economic objectives was cut back by one-third from fiscal 1966/67 through 1968/69. Current expenditure for social and community services was reduced by 30 percent in fiscal 1968/69. Data on government capital investment expenditure are incomplete, but it has been roughly estimated that it declined by at least N£15 million a year throughout the war period. The total cumulative loss in fixed investment during the period may be estimated at a minimum of N£200 million, not counting the increase in investment that presumably would have taken place had the war not occurred.

In fiscal 1969/70 expenditures on defense and internal security had been reduced somewhat from its high of the previous year

Table 6. Consolidated Federal and Regional (State) Finances of Nigeria, 1964/65 Through 1970/71 [1]

(in million Nigerian pounds) [2]

	1964/65	1965/66	1966/67 [3]	1967/68 [3]	1968/69 [3]	1969/70 [3]	1970/71 [4]
Current Revenues:							
Federal Revenues:							
Collected by federal government	145.6	156.5	156.8	142.0	142.8	210.1	270.4
Transferred to regions (states)	60.7	65.6	68.6	61.4	53.0	91.0	115.3
Net	84.9	91.0	88.2	80.6	89.8	119.1	155.1
Regional or State Revenues:							
Collected by federal government	60.7	65.6	68.6	61.4	53.0	91.0	115.3
Collected directly	28.9	29.4	29.8	15.9	23.8	19.3	40.3
Subtotal	89.6	95.0	98.4	77.3	76.8	110.3	155.6
TOTAL	174.5	186.0	186.6	157.9	166.6	229.4	310.7
Current Expenditures:							
Federal expenditures	76.4	84.1	78.6	116.8	149.4	296.2 [5]	138.0
Defense and internal security	(22.7)	(25.1)	(23.8)	(61.8)	(91.4)	(190.5)	(55.7)
Interest on public debt	(6.7)	(8.9)	(10.7)	(12.6)	(20.6)	(n.a.)	(16.5)
Regional or state expenditures	73.2	81.7	86.6	59.0	73.2	96.2	147.9
TOTAL	149.6	165.8	165.2	175.8	222.6	392.4	285.9
Current Surplus:							
Federal government	8.5	6.9	9.6	−36.2	−59.6	−177.1	17.1
Regional or state governments	16.4	13.3	11.8	18.3	3.6	14.1	7.7
TOTAL	24.9	20.2	21.4	−17.9	−56.0	−163.0	24.7

Capital Expenditures:

Federal government	39.2	52.5	57.6	39.6	45.0	n.a.	n.a.
Investment expenditure	(31.8)	(33.9)	(28.0)	(27.6)	(20.6)	(22.4)	(n.a.)
Repayment of principal	(5.5)	(6.2)	(3.3)	(8.0)	(11.8)	(n.a.)	(n.a.)
Regional or state governments	35.2	33.1	38.3	26.1	23.7	50.3	107.9
TOTAL	74.4	85.6	95.9	65.7	68.7	n.a.	n.a.

Overall Deficit:

Internally financed	41.1	39.9	57.0	64.4	117.7	225.0	n.a.
Externally financed	8.4	25.5	17.5	19.2	7.0	10.7	n.a.
TOTAL	49.5	65.4	74.5	83.6	124.7	235.7	n.a.

n.a.—not available.
[1] Fiscal year, from April 1 through March 31.
[2] One Nigerian pound equals US$2.80.
[3] Comparability of figures for the period 1966/67 through 1969/70 is impaired by uneven and incomplete coverage of the three eastern states.
[4] Budget estimates.
[5] Includes capital expenditure other than investment expenditure.

(see table 7). For the following years the plan had projected that federal expenditures for defense and security would at first be reduced to about half of their 1969/70 level and be increased only gradually thereafter. Actually, however, there was no significant reduction in the size of the armed forces in the first year of the plan; for the second year the budget proposed a further increase in recurrent military expenditures. Demobilization had been delayed in part because of the mounting rate of unemployment in civilian life, and many troops dispersed throughout the country were to be moved from their temporary civilian accommodations to new barracks and installations. The authorities referred to defense expenditure as one of the critical problems that must be corrected or contained in succeeding years, but a solution was not in sight. The plan projections had assumed that the federal and state governments would maintain strict control over the expansion of current expenditure, so that during the 1970–74 plan period expenditure other than defense, security, and debt service would increase at an average rate of about 9 percent a year, parallel with the increase in gross domestic product at current prices.

By curbing current expenditure during the plan period, it had been hoped that the federal government could achieve a rate of public saving that would permit the expansion of capital expenditure without excessively heavy recourse to domestic and foreign borrowing. Much of the proposed capital expenditure will be for reconstruction and rehabilitation of transport facilities, power and telecommunications systems, and industrial facilities.

Financing the Deficit

Because of mounting expenditure in the late 1960s, the moderate surplus on the current budget of N£20 million to N£25 million in fiscal 1964/65 through 1966/67 gave way to a mounting current deficit that reached a high of N£163 million in fiscal 1969/70 (see table 6). The overall deficit on current plus capital account reached a high of nearly N£236 million in fiscal 1969/70. Most of this was financed by domestic borrowing, largely from the commercial banks. The overall public debt, which amounted to less than N£200 million in March 1966, more than doubled during the war years to N£472 million in March 1969. The internal public debt nearly tripled, reaching N£385 million. Under an agreement of 1958, all loans are raised by the federal government and lent by it, in turn, to the states at the same rate paid by the federal government.

The country's external public debt increased from the equivalent of about US$250 million at the end of 1963 to US$610 million at the end of 1965 and US$660 million at the end of 1969, having increased only slightly during the war years. The privately held foreign debt increased from an amount equal to about US$100 million at the end of 1963 to US$169 million at the end of 1965 and had been reduced to US$111 million at the end of 1969, not including short-term commercial credits. At the end of 1970 the country's foreign debt position remained favorable compared to that of most developing countries; however, in view of the foreign exchange situation and the outlook for domestic saving compared to investment needs, it was expected to deteriorate gradually.

The foreign debt had been contracted on relatively favorable terms: of the public segment, 40 percent was owed to organizations of the World bank Group, 50 percent was owed to bilateral donors (chiefly the United Kingdom and United States), and only 10 percent consisted of supplier credits. Debt service obligations were equivalent to only 7 or 8 percent of expected foreign exchange earnings for 1970. An effort would be made to secure future loans on similar terms, as much as 40 percent being sought from the World Bank Group. The federal and state governments were resolved to avoid the burden of excessive supplier credits.

Two classes of short-term liabilities excluded from the debt data had been built up during the crisis period, when the government blocked the remittance of dividends and profits overseas and deferred payment for imports (see ch. 14, Industry and Trade). By the end of 1970 more than N£70 million in short-term liabilities had been accumulated in this way, and further transfers were blocked during 1971. In mid-1971 the government relaxed the ban on payments.

Public saving to finance capital formation is created largely by surpluses of the federal and state current budgets, supplemented by the operating surpluses and capital reserves of the marketing boards and public corporations. During the period of the Second National Development Plan it is expected that about 57.7 percent of public sector capital investment will be financed by the current budget surpluses of federal and state governments; 13.6 percent, by the marketing boards and public corporations; 9.3 percent, by the Central Bank and other public borrowing; and 19.4 percent, by external finance. This assumes that public expenditure can be held down and that export earnings will suffice to permit sizable marketing board surpluses as well as to allow greater flexibility in producer prices (see ch. 13, Agriculture and Mining).

MONETARY SYSTEM AND POLICY

The banking system built up in the 1950s and early 1960s provided for the growing volume of usual commercial and financial

Table 7. Federal Government of Nigeria, Expenditure by Function, Selected Years, 1965/66 to 1969/70 [1]
(in million Nigerian pounds) [2]

	1965/66 Total	1967/68 Total	1968/69 Recurrent	1968/69 Capital	1968/69 Total	1969/70 [3] Recurrent	1969/70 [3] Capital	1969/70 [3] Total
Administration:								
General administration	18.7	15.1	13.0	1.4	14.4	14.3	6.3	20.6
Defense and internal security	25.1	61.8	59.3	32.1	91.4	30.9	23.7	54.6
Subtotal	43.8	76.9	72.3	33.5	105.8	45.2	30.0	75.2
Social and Community Services:								
Education	9.8	8.2	6.1	0.8	6.9	8.4	3.5	11.9
Health	6.5	6.2	3.2	n.a.	3.2	3.9	0.1	4.0
Other social and community services	3.3	1.3	0.6	0.1	0.7	0.7	0.5	1.2
Subtotal	19.6	15.7	9.9	0.9	10.8	13.0	4.1	17.1
Economic Services:								
Agriculture	4.2	1.6	2.0	1.2	3.2	2.3	5.6	7.9
Transport and communications	22.3	13.2	2.0	6.3	8.3	6.2	26.5	32.7
Construction	12.4	18.2	5.8	8.1	13.9	6.0	10.9	16.9
Other economic services	2.5	2.1	0.8	2.7	3.5	1.0	3.7	4.7
Subtotal	41.4	35.1	10.6	18.3	28.9	15.5	46.7	62.2
Transfers:								
Public debt interest	3.9	12.6	20.6	n.a.	20.6	13.6	n.a.	13.6

Pensions and gratuities	4.2	3.9	3.9	n.a.	3.9	6.3	n.a.	6.3
Other [4]	12.4	4.0	n.a.	12.6	12.6	n.a.	10.8	10.8
Subtotal	20.5	20.5	24.5	12.6	37.1	19.9	10.8	30.7
TOTAL	130.3 [5]	148.4	117.3	65.4	182.7	93.4	91.9	185.3 [5]

[1] Fiscal year, from April 1 through March 31.
[2] One Nigerian pound equals US$2.80.
[3] Budget estimates.
[4] Includes loans (net) to regions and states and financial obligations; for example, compensation payments to former civil servants and subscriptions to international organizations.
[5] Total as in sources.

transactions but was judged slightly weak by international standards in such matters as centralized credit control. The foreign-owned commercial banks remained most active in credit decisions, and in some cases they were oriented primarily toward serving the needs of the foreign business community and handling short-term transfers abroad.

To deal with the financial problems that emerged from the civil crises, a number of changes were introduced after 1966 to strengthen the banking system and the powers of the Central Bank in monetary matters. The primary objectives were to facilitate government borrowing from the banking system; to strengthen monetary and credit controls; to contain the inflationary pressures generated by the financing of government deficits; and to finance economic activity in the private sector within the limits imposed by anticyclical credit policy.

The Central Bank of Nigeria was established by an ordinance in 1958. Its original powers included the right to issue currency; to buy, sell, and rediscount treasury bills and other government securities; to deal in commercial bills and crop bills as lender of last resort; and to buy and sell foreign exchange. It was also authorized to establish and enforce liquidity ratio requirements for the commercial banks and to vary the rediscount rate.

The Central Bank of Nigeria Act was amended in September 1968 to strengthen the bank's controls over commercial bank credit extension. It also took over the function of crop financing by extending advances to the marketing boards for their purchases of export crops. The commercial banks, which had previously exercised this function in a consortium, had proved reluctant to extend enough credit for the purpose during the civil war, and shortages resulted.

The Banking Decree of 1968 consolidated all the banking legislation passed since 1952 to strengthen the stakes of commercial banks in the local economy. It provided that only a company duly incorporated in Nigeria can transact banking business in the country and tripled the amount of statutory paid-up capital required for foreign-controlled banks. It also set new requirements for the ratio of paid-up capital to deposit liabilities and for the share of annual net profits to be kept in a reserve fund.

Between 1967 and mid-1970 a series of steps were taken by the monetary authorities to facilitate government borrowing from the banking system. The Treasury Bill Act of 1962 was amended several times to increase the amount of treasury bills that could remain outstanding, and a new medium-term treasury certificate was introduced. The maximum amount of development stocks that could be held by the Central Bank was also raised.

In the early part of the 1960s, until the civil war, the government had been able to limit its borrowing from the banking sector, and the Central Bank was consequently able to pursue a monetary policy designed to reallocate credit in favor of the productive sectors of the economy. A monetary program was formulated setting guidelines for credit expansion by the banking system, keeping in view the need to maintain balance of payments equilibrium and thereby to combat inflation.

Monetary policy shifted in 1967. Effective limitations on credit expansion to the government could no longer be enforced because of the war requirements. There was also a downturn in activity in the private sector, which indicated a need for liberalization of private credit. Credit guidelines, which were removed in late 1966, were not reinstated until mid-1969. There was a general easing of monetary policy and an increased reliance on fiscal measures and import controls to limit the disequilibrium in the balance of payments. Between 1966 and 1970 monetary policy was thus characterized by a high rate of credit expansion to government; a declining rate of credit utilization by the private sector; a substantial growth in money supply and liquid assets known as near-money; a decline in foreign exchange reserves; and an accumulation of foreign liabilities. The monetary legacy of the civil war period was thus a high potential for inflation and a low level of foreign exchange reserves.

Government borrowing to finance the deficit continued throughout 1970 and into 1971. Consequently, inflationary pressure remained strong, with the money supply rising and bank liquidity increasing. Monetary guidelines called upon the commercial banks to allocate credit in such a way that the anti-inflationary policy would be reinforced. Credit increases were to be allocated primarily to industry, public utilities, and transport, with only a 10-percent increase for commerce and no increase at all for private consumption. Actually, the credit granted to productive sectors did not increase appreciably in 1970.

The budget for fiscal 1971/72 proposed that the overall ceiling for aggregate expansion of credit to the private sector be limited to an increase of only 8.4 percent over the level outstanding at the end of 1970. An exception was accorded for credit to industry, which could increase by 30 percent. Nonproductive credit was expected to fall by 33 percent.

CURRENCY

British currency was first imported in quantity in 1894 and was in general use by the end of the century. The West African Currency Board was created in 1912 to serve all territories in British West Africa; their currency was equivalent to that of Great Britain. Banknotes were introduced in 1916. When the Central Bank was established in 1958, the value of the Nigerian pound was fixed at parity to sterling. There was no provision enabling the bank to change the parity of the Nigerian pound, but this was changed in the 1962 amendment to the act, which expressed the parity of the Nigerian pound in terms of gold and provided that it could be changed by the bank. Consequently, when the British pound sterling was devalued in November 1967, the Nigerian pound remained at its previous parity of N£1 equals US$2.80.

In mid-1971 the pound was still divided into 20 shillings and 240 pence, but decimalization was scheduled for 1973. Decree No. 21 of 1971 set up the Decimal Currency Board to coordinate arrangements to ensure a smooth transition to the decimal currency system. The decree stated that the new decimal unit of currency would be called the naira and would be equivalent to one-half the 1971 Nigerian pound, that is, US$1.40. Each naira would be divided into 100 kobo.

CHAPTER 13

AGRICULTURE AND MINING

Agriculture and minerals are the primary sources of the country's wealth. Production of export crops by peasant farmers was the mainspring of economic growth from 1900 to 1965. The spectacular growth of petroleum production has since reduced the proportionate contribution of agriculture to the national product and to export earnings, but agriculture is expected to remain for several decades the mainstay of the export structure and the money economy, as well as of employment and subsistence production.

The country has an exceptionally broad agricultural base. Because of the varied climate, almost every product of tropical agriculture can be grown successfully on the land. With the exception of animal proteins, the country provides an adequate and varied basic food supply for the largest population in Africa and is one of the world's two leading exporters of cocoa, groundnuts (peanuts), and palm kernels. It also furnishes other products that are in active demand in world markets; these include rubber, cotton, palm oil, palm kernel oil, sesame, and tropical hardwoods. It is Africa's leading rubber producer.

In the early 1970s agriculture still contributed about half of the national income and provided employment for 70 or 80 percent of the labor force (see ch. 12, Character and Structure of the Economy). Agricultural commodities provided 48 to 56 percent of export income and were an important source of public revenue through the taxation of export crops, the profits of marketing boards, the cattle tax, and more general taxes. The country's past financial needs and foreign exchange requirements were met almost entirely by peasant farmers, whose earnings financed the development of infrastructure, built schools and hospitals, and supplied capital for new industry. Since the late 1960's, however, petroleum earnings have provided a growing contribution to supplement the financial resources derived from agriculture.

Average yields in agriculture are low compared with their potential because most farmers still use traditional techniques; farming implements generally consist of the hoe, the axe, and the machete. Consequently, the extent of land that can be cleared and cultivated by each family worker is limited. The average farm cultivated is between one and five acres. Family farms under crops characteristically average about two or three acres in the south and eight or ten acres in low-density areas in the north, where natural vegetation is more open and clearing less strenuous. Little use is made of manure. Mixed farming, with livestock and crops raised in complementary association, is confined to a few districts of the north, notably the closely settled farming district around Kano.

The agricultural economy is predominantly one of individual smallholders, who number about 5 million. This small-scale, non-mechanized sector is thought to provide at least 95 percent of the exports. It produces all of the food crops, 98 percent of the oil palm crops, 80 percent of rubber production, and nearly all of the cocoa, groundnut, and cotton crops. Small holdings may average about six acres in cocoa production, three acres in oil palm, and between three and ten acres in rubber.

As a result of the climate and former British colonial policy, plantation agriculture did not gain a foothold in the country until the beginnings of self-government in 1951. Since then the number of plantations has increased, and the government has launched a farm settlement program to absorb a small fraction of rural unemployment. In the mid-1960s, however, plantations and farm settlements represented less than 1 percent of the entire agricultural area, and their share in total production remained very low in 1971.

Virtually all foodstuffs consumed by the population are grown within the country. Food production has kept pace with rapid population growth. By scientific standards, however, the vast majority of Nigerians are both improperly nourished and undernourished. Only about one-fifth of the minimum animal protein requirement is supplied from domestic production and, even with imports, there is a marked deficiency of animal protein in the national diet.

As effective demand is increased and nutritional standards are improved, there will be room for considerable improvement in agricultural production. The country's climate and agricultural resources should permit a large expansion in animal numbers and productivity and higher crop acreage and yields. It is estimated that the tsetse-free areas of the north could accommodate two or three times the present number of cattle, goats, and sheep. There is room for vast improvement in milk and meat yields, milk being short even in the cattle-raising area of the north. The country's agriculture has substantial unused or underutilized capacity in both land and labor; with intensified research and development, the quality of the national diet and the health and productivity of the population could be improved.

ACTUAL AND POTENTIAL LAND USE

The abundance of arable land and its productive capacity are promising for the development of a prosperous agricultural economy. The country as a whole should not be threatened by serious food shortage within the next two or three decades, despite the rapid rate of population growth; but unless the birth rate is controlled, it may be difficult to achieve the increase in per capita income and living standards sought by the government.

The climate permits considerable diversity in the production of crops that can serve as bases for future expansion. The soils, although often poor in physical properties, are generally rich in organic matter that can be quickly decomposed into nitrates and humus. Unfortunately the natural fertility of much of the soil has been exhausted, and several areas suffer from overpopulation, notably in the eastern states and around one or two of the northern towns. Social traditions sometimes operate to inhibit the resettlement of farmers from overpopulated districts in areas of land surplus.

Of the total land area of 229 million acres, about 37 percent appears reasonably suitable for agriculture, not including areas usable as rangeland. According to estimates of the United Nations Food and Agriculture Organization (FAO), as much as 79 percent of the country could be made suitable for agriculture if modern technology were used.

According to the latest sample survey of agriculture, about 24 percent of the total land area, or 1 acre per capita, consists of arable land; this includes both fallow land and land on which crops are planted. The land rotation, or bush fallow, system in predominant use has a very high land requirement, so that at any given time about 80 percent of the arable land area lies fallow. The sample census indicated that only about 9 percent of the total land area is actually under cultivation. If agricultural land is defined as including not only arable land but also permanent grazing land, it is estimated at about 52 percent of the total land area, or 2.1 acres per capita. Less than 1 percent of the land is used for settlements and other nonagricultural purposes, and coastal swamp constitutes about 2.9 percent. Approximately 1.2 percent is reserved as forest.

STRUCTURE OF AGRICULTURAL PRODUCTION

Subsistence farming is the usual pattern in parts of the north, in much of the Middle Belt (see Glossary), and in some of the less accessible rural areas (see fig. 9). In most of the country, however, individual farmers produce enough to contribute to a sizable collective food surplus. In some areas surveys have shown that the farmers do not store and consume their own crops but prefer to sell their produce at harvesttime and purchase necessary food each day in the market. It is only in the years after World War II that domestic cash sales of farm products have exceeded the income from export crops. Urban and other nonfarm demand for foodstuffs has been growing, and an ever-increasing number of cultivators and herders are producing some marketed surplus over their own consumption requirements.

About 60 percent of the total agricultural output is subsistence production consumed at the point of origin; another 25 percent is traded internally; and about 15 percent goes for exports. Subsistence production amounts to about 30 percent of the nation's gross domestic product (GDP). The same small-scale farms that produce all or most of their own food also account for most of the

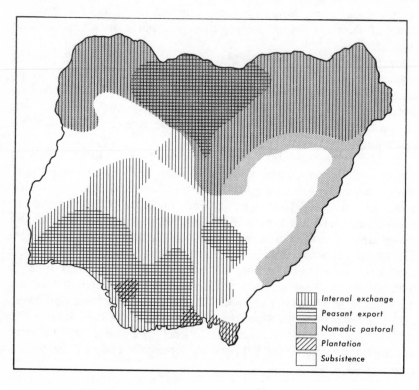

Source: Adapted from J.C. Pugh and K.M. Buchanan, *Land and People in Nigeria*, London, 1958.

Figure 9. Dominant Types of Agricultural Production in Nigeria

surplus production sold in internal markets and for most of the agricultural exports.

Most foods are produced in fairly significant variety near the point of consumption. Increasingly, however, exchange occurs not only at the village market level but also on an intervillage, inter-area, and interregional basis. Because of the pronounced structural and climatic variations among the different regions, interregional trade largely takes the place of imports of foodstuffs. The urban or densely populated rural districts of the south, in particular, are net importers in interregional trade. Beef cattle, pulses, yams, cotton, and kola nuts are the principal staples of interregional trade; cassava, maize (corn), sorghum, millet, and other crops are also produced in surplus and are sold in markets that may be close by but are sometimes hundreds of miles from the producing farms. Some commodities move great distances, as, for instance, cowpeas and cattle from the far north to the urban centers of the far south.

The regional pattern of production for internal exchange versus export still corresponds approximately to that of the early 1950s. Subsistence production is still the sole type throughout portions of the Middle Belt, although the Jos Plateau and the Benue River valley produce a number of products for internal exchange and sesame for export. It may be misleading to attempt to distinguish between a subsistence sector and a cash crop sector. One trained observer in a rural Hausa village near the northern border of North Central State remarked that any crop might happen to be sold by the grower for cash and that there are few crops that are not likely to be self-consumed. The market is commonly used instead of storage; the object is to buy grain when it is cheap and sell when prices are high, but the poorer families may be obliged to do just the opposite.

Nigeria provides a model of export development in which individual small-scale tradition-bound producers responded spontaneously and rapidly to the stimulus of external demand to produce a phenomenal expansion and diversification of crop exports after 1900. This took place without pressure from colonial authorities. In the period from 1900 to 1929 foreigners did very little to alter the technological backwardness of the economy. There was some British exploitation of mineral deposits, but the rise of exports was generated primarily by the smallholder in spontaneous response to the price and consumer goods incentives offered by foreign private trading companies, notably Great Britain's Royal Niger Company.

Before 1900 exports had consisted almost entirely of palm produce from the southeast, but before long they had become diversified nationally in cocoa, palm produce, and groundnuts, concentrated regionally in the west, east, and north, respectively. From 1900 to 1929, while traditional food output was increasing by about 10 percent, agricultural exports rose fivefold. The bulk of this production came from hundreds of thousands of small cultivators using no change in traditional techniques, apart from the introduction of the new crop varieties. It was achieved simply by increased inputs of land and labor at constant returns to scale. Productivity per man was thus increased, but until the mid-1950s productivity per acre or per man-hour scarcely improved at all.

The worldwide depression of the 1930s abruptly curtailed external demand and, just as exports were reviving, World War II brought another hiatus in world trade. Immediately after the war growth of exports was resumed. Gains in productivity began to be added, and great increases in peasant output of cotton in the north and rubber in the midwest diversified the export pattern further.

In the early 1950s the government-operated marketing boards began to siphon off an increasing share of export earnings, and the producer prices earned by peasant exporters of the board-controlled products were held down. Exports of palm products suffered, but sales of most other exports continued to show a very favorable growth rate. Their mounting earnings fueled the development effort and financed the expansion of transport and other infrastructure, and growth of industry, and the increasing diversification of the economy.

The civil war disturbed and partially destroyed the organization of smallholder subsistence production in the former Eastern and Mid-Western Regions. Agricultural trade between the east and other parts of the country was disrupted. Some transport facilities were overloaded and improperly maintained; others were destroyed or diverted to war use. Research, teaching, and extension services in the former Eastern and Mid-Western Regions were interrupted, and the advances that were being achieved in oil palm production were brought to a standstill.

The wartime losses brought about a temporary famine in the eastern provinces, necessitating relief and reconstruction measures after the war's end. Trade in palm products and other products of the former Eastern Region was greatly reduced. By early 1971, however, the flow of interregional trade had resumed, and the food markets of the east appeared well supplied. Observers still found a good deal of hidden malnutrition in the new East Central State, but there had been good recovery from the wartime ravages of kwashiorkor. The total volume of food production for the country appeared to have returned to its prewar level.

REGIONAL PATTERN OF PRODUCTION

The pattern of staple food and cash crop production conforms broadly to regional variations in climate, soils, and natural vegetation. The actual range of natural vegetation is great (see ch. 2, Physical Environment). Mangrove and swamp forests along the southern coast are succeeded by high rain forest, giving way northward to less dense forest and then to more open savanna vegetation and grassland and more arid conditions, ranging to semidesert in the far northeast.

The most crucial factor in crop production is the level and seasonal incidence of rainfall. Rainfall is abundant over much of the country, but the climate is relatively unstable. Annual rainfall and the duration of the rains decrease from south to north (see ch. 2, Physical Environment). The northern half of the country receives less than one inch of rain for periods of five to seven months during the dry season, and crops frequently suffer from the long dry periods of excessive heat. The rains do not always arrive on schedule and may aften be delayed or advanced by as much as a month, disrupting clearing and planting schedules.

The country's agricultural zones are often broadly grouped into three macroregions, which extend across most of West Africa. In Nigeria they are also sometimes used to summarize gradations in climate, culture, or population density. The macroregions are the humid south, the broad Middle Belt of transition, and the relatively arid north. In a series of studies on Nigerian rural development conducted by a consortium of United States universities in the late 1960s, these three broad regions have been further subdivided into six ecological areas (see table 8 and fig. 10).

Grains and livestock are the main food products of the arid northern third of the country. The principal staple crop is an indigenous variety of drought-resistant sorghum known in West Africa as guinea corn. This sorghum requires dry and sunny conditions; it is widely cultivated by Hausa farmers in the provinces of Kano, Bornu, Adamawa, and Sokoto (see fig. 11). Its cultivation extends southward through the Middle Belt to below the Benue River. Millet is second in importance as a staple food crop. Maize, which is cultivated primarily in the south, occurs also in scattered locations in the north where rainfall is adequate, chiefly in Kano Province. Among the crops of lesser importance, rice is grown mainly in the savanna area and to a lesser extent in the intermediate savanna and the eastern and western moist forest. In the north it is grown in the swampy areas. In the 1960s the government launched a program to increase the production of rice, which had been imported in quantity. Cowpeas, onions, peppers, sugarcane, and some fruits are also grown in the north.

Table 8. Estimated Harvested Acreage of Principal Crops in Nigeria, 1968
(in thousands of acres)

| Crop | Ecological Area* | | | | | | Total |
	1	2	3	4	5	6	
Arable Crops							
Maize (corn)	17	304	793	24	151	166	1,455
Rice	464	80	0	20	85	66	715
Millet	4,648	24	0	0	0	0	4,672
Guinea corn (sorghum)	3,741	1,611	0	0	0	0	5,352
Wheat	24	0	0	0	0	0	24
Cassava	185	530	318	90	165	229	1,517
Potato (Irish)	2	3	0	0	0	0	5
Sweet potato	6	12	0	0	0	0	18
Cocoyam	0	0	66	29	133	0	228
Yam	457	462	468	163	534	367	2,451
Cowpea	1,015	1,453	0	0	0	295	2,763
Groundnut	2,415	305	0	0	0	90	2,810
Soybean	0	0	0	0	0	154	154
Melon	13	26	90	47	106	38	320
Okra	0	0	88	30	20	18	156
Cotton	288	400	0	0	0	2	690
Tobacco	10	13	0	0	0	0	23
Total	13,285	5,223	1,823	403	1,194	1,425	23,353
Tree Crops							
Oil palm	0	0	1,050	185	2,000	800	4,035
Cocoa	0	0	1,100	43	0	0	1,143
Rubber	0	0	20	400	40	0	460
Total	0	0	2,170	628	2,040	800	5,638
TOTAL	13,285	5,223	3,993	1,031	3,234	2,225	28,991

*Ecological areas are: (1) dry savanna; (2) intermediate savanna; (3) Western moist forest; (4) Central moist forest; (5) Eastern moist forest; and (6) forest savanna mosaic.

Source: Adapted from *Strategies and Recommendations for Nigerian Rural Development 1969–1985* (Consortium for the Study of Nigerian Rural Development, Series No. 33), East Lansing, Michigan, July 1969, p. 26.

Most of the production of groundnuts and cotton is in the northern zone, which is the world's second largest producer of groundnuts. These two cash crops account for much of the zone's wealth. Hides and skins are another traditional export of the area. The former Northern Region, now divided into six states, produced about half the nation's gross national product (GNP) before commercial production of petroleum began in the south. Because of denser population, however, the per capita gross national product has always been lower in the north.

The absence of the tsetse fly in much of the northern savanna

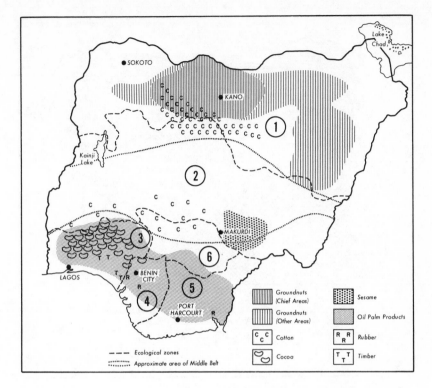

Source: Adapted from W.A. Perkins and Jasper H. Stembridge, *Nigeria: A Descriptive Geography*, Ibadan, 1966, p. 66.

Figure 10. Principal Cash Crops and Ecological Zones of Nigeria

permits the raising of substantial herds of goats, cattle, and sheep by the nomads. It is estimated that 96 percent of the country's cattle is in the six northern states, concentrated in a belt stretching from Sokoto Province eastward into the west of Bornu and south into the Jos Plateau. The most extensive herds are grazed in the provinces of Katsina, Kano, Plateau, and Bauchi. They are managed mainly by nomadic Fulani tribesmen. During the wet months of May to October, some 10 million head of cattle are grazed on the northern grasslands. During the dry months, the incidence of tsetse fly somewhat farther south is restricted to the denser vegetation, and the herders migrate southward in search of pasture and water. Some mixed farming, combining cultivation and animal husbandry on the same farm, is practiced in the north; it is not generally found elsewhere in the country.

The staple grain economy of the north and the staple root economy of the south blend in the transitional Middle Belt. The area designated as the Middle Belt by economists and physical geographers because it lies between the characteristic economies of north

323

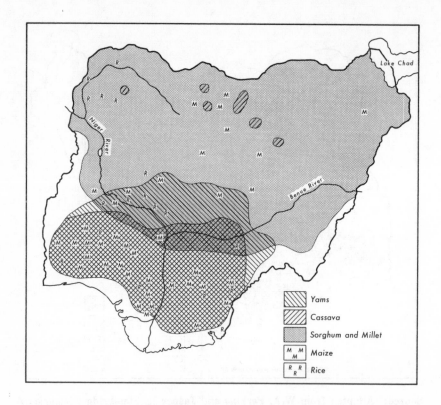

Source: Adapted from W.A. Perkins and Jasper H. Stembridge, *Nigeria: A Descriptive Geography*, Ibadan, 1966, p. 62.

Figure 11. Principal Staple Food Crops of Nigeria

and south apparently does not coincide precisely in its outlines with the Middle Belt concept used in the discussion of ethnic and political divisions (see ch. 3, Historical Setting; ch. 5, Ethnic Groups and Languages; ch. 9, Government and Political Dynamics). The economic Middle Belt is usually portrayed as extending roughly from 7°30′N to 11°N latitude (see fig. 10). Because it is fundamentally an economic rather than a geographic concept, however, its outlines may be subject to change.

In the 1960s the Middle Belt covered about two-fifths of the country's land area but contained only about one-fifth of its population. Because it is suitable for both root crops and cereals and because it has relatively sparsely populated land resources, the Middle Belt is thought to have excellent potential for future food production. It may eventually become the larder of the nation, but in the 1960s it remained the poorest and least developed sector of the country. It was largely underpopulated and, apart from a few large-scale agricultural projects, its infrastructure was poorly developed. Its principal surplus crop is yams. Other food crops include sorghum, millet, maize, rice, cassava, and beans.

The main export crop of the Middle Belt is sesame (benniseed), an important source of edible oil. It is grown by Tiv cultivators in the Benue River valley. In recent years they have been growing more soybeans in seasonal alternation with sesame. Because they are able to earn enough for their needs from the sale of soybeans, many farmers are beginning to cultivate less sesame. Cotton and indigo have also been cultivated in the valley for centuries. In the upper Benue River valley the northern grain economy prevails, and the main crops are bulrush millet and sorghum, supplemented by groundnuts, sweet potatoes, and maize. The middle and lower Benue River valleys are an important food surplus area. Cassava, millet, and rice are grown; yams are an important cash crop, shipped out by rail to the urban centers of the north and east. Besides cotton, rice, and soybeans, other cash crops of the Middle Belt include tobacco, fiber crops, coconuts, groundnuts, and sheanuts (see Glossary).

Tsetse-fly infestation of lower land prevents the keeping of productive cattle or draft animals, but a substantial dairy industry has been developed on the Jos Plateau. In the 1960s the Middle Belt's production of rice, cotton, sesame, and food crops was being expanded. In addition to the expansion of irrigated rice production, large-scale agricultural projects included the Bacita Sugar Estate and the Kainji (Niger) Dam projects.

The relatively humid and fertile southern zone has the highest per capita agricultural production. It includes most of the former Western, Mid-Western, and Eastern Regions. In the far south, the wetter parts of the freshwater swamp forest are not suitable for agriculture, and the underpopulated southeastern part of the rain forest belt around Calabar has customarily produced few crops. The rest of the south is a zone of relatively intensive agricultural exploitation.

The tree crops that are among the country's traditional export leaders are concentrated in this region: cocoa, palm produce, rubber, and kola nuts. Other cash crops include coconut, tobacco, cotton, plantains, and bananas. The staple root economy of the region relies chiefly on cassava and yams and to a lesser extent on cocoyams and sweet potatoes. Other major food crops are maize, rice, melon (for its seeds), cowpeas, okra, groundnuts, and various beans. Leafy vegetables and many types of fruit, such as pineapple, papaw, guava, citrus, and mango, are also grown in the south.

The region also produces most of the timber and fish. Because of the general prevalence of tsetse fly (except in Sardauna South), cattle cannot generally be kept. Other livestock are kept, and there are some tsetse-resistant but unproductive dwarf cattle in a few districts. Tsetse infestation also precludes the use of ox-drawn plows and thus limits the area of cultivation.

With respect to cash crops, the moist southern zone may be divided from west to east into three subzones. The western portion, in the southern part of the former Western Region, is the area of maximum cocoa production. The central portion occupies much of the former Mid-Western Region and produces most of the rubber. Maximum oil palm production is in the eastern forest zone, overlapping the three states of the former Eastern Region.

FARMING PRACTICES

The prevailing system of cultivation for annual food crops is a combination of bush fallow and mixed cropping. Bush fallow is characterized by the rotation of fields rather than of crops, with relatively short periods of cultivation and long periods of fallow. Other characteristic features of the system are clearing by fire, fertilization by wood ash, cultivation by simple hand tools, the absence of stumping, and usually the absence of draft animals or other stock. In forest regions the practice may be called forest fallow or field forest cultivation. It differs from true shifting cultivation in that fields are rotated around a fixed settlement, and the cultivator generally does not shift his place of abode, as is the practice of some tribes elsewhere in Africa.

In most farming villages there are two classes of farmland: compound land and the main or outlying farmland. Any available manure is used to permit continuous cultivation of the land within the village compound and the small kitchen gardens in the immediate vicinity. These are cropped every year. Field rotation is practiced on the main or outlying farm land, which is also usually divided into small gardens or plots. Sometimes they are found as scattered plots in the bush, but often they form a stretch of cultivated land around the village or town. A single farmer may farm several small parcels of land, often fractions of an acre, which may be widely separated.

In the 1960s bush fallow was still the predominant system used for annual food crops in most areas of the country. Among traditional cultivators, permanent or continuous cultivation was practiced for the major tree crops, such as cocoa, kola nut, oil palm, and rubber. Permanent cultivation based on the use of household manure was also practiced in the more overpopulated areas of the eastern states and in the vicinity of some of the larger towns.

On suitable soils near the larger towns of the Sudan zone, around Sokoto, Zaria, Maiduguri, Katsina, and Kano, permanent cultivation has long been the rule. In the closely settled farming zones around Kano and Katsina, a skillful system of intensive cultivation is practiced, using manure from the cities' large animal populations. Continuous cultivation within a mile or two of the farm residence is also the preferred system elsewhere among the Hausa, even where it is not necessitated by population density. For centuries the people of the Jos Plateau also practiced intensive permanent cultivation in terraces on the hills, but in the past fifty years they have abandoned the hills to practice bush fallow cultivation on the plains. Irrigated agriculture is of growing importance in the drier parts of the Middle Belt and in the far north but remains the exception to normal rain-fed farming. The popularity of commercial fertilizer is growing extremely fast, but it has been in very short supply because of foreign exchange problems. Application is confined to about 2.6 pounds per capita per year (compared to 55 pounds in the United Kingdom, for example).

Mixed cropping is the usual practice. In the high forest zone, for example, root crops, cereals, and bush crops may be interplanted so that yams, maize, cotton bushes, gourds, and pumpkins grow side by side on the same plot. The commonest root crops, such as cassava and yams, are usually planted in mounds or ridges. In the southern forest zone they are the staple crops and are interplanted with maize, rice, peppers, vegetables, and other crops.

In the northern grain economy the staples are sorghum and millet; groundnuts and sesame are subsidiary crops interplanted or rotated on the same plots. These shifting or rotational plots are lightly cultivated with a hoe, and the surrounding natural vegetation is left intact. Cultivation is usually more intensive the first year; thereafter weeds and bush may be allowed to encroach upon the clearing and, as yields diminish, the plot will be progressively abandoned. In addition to the crops produced on the rotational plots, vegetables and a variety of minor crops are raised on the small garden plots close to the settlement, which are usually under continuous cultivation.

The land requirement of bush fallow is high, because the land under crops at any one time must be multiplied by the number of years needed for soil regeneration. Thus, if it requires between three and five shifts of rotation to return to the original plot, only one-fifth of the available arable land can be under crops at one time. The system is consequently suited to areas of low or medium population density and abundant arable land. As long as these conditions prevailed throughout most of the country, the prevailing land-use system was very well adapted to the environment and the needs of the society. It was the most efficient practice available to the West African cultivator equipped only with simple hand tools and without access to modern services or supplies. Particularly in the moist lowland forest zone, long periods of bush fallow were very effective in accumulating nitrogen and other nutrients to restore the soil, and the roots of the natural bush vegetation effectively prevented erosion.

Although the country as a whole may still be described as a land surplus economy, a large proportion of its soils have had their natural fertility exhausted. There are areas where increased population density has been putting mounting pressure on the land and where inadequate periods of fallow have resulted in progressive deterioration of the land, soil depletion, erosion, and gulleying. Some areas, with initially high population densities, probably emerged from the land surplus stage quite early in the country's history. In such areas as the high-density districts of the Ibo in the east and the southern sector of the Tiv area, the bush fallow system had already begun to break down in the 1950s under the pressure of the rapidly expanding rural population. The fallow period had become dangerously short. A typical plot might be planted to yams, beans, or cassava for one year and then left to fallow for only three or four years. The enforced shortening of fallow did not permit the natural vegetation to regenerate, and over large areas the high forest was progressively replaced by grassland suitable only for rough grazing.

In the 1960s rural overpopulation was most acute in several districts of the Eastern Region where population density exceeded 800 or even 1,000 persons per square mile (see ch. 4, Population and Labor). A rural economy with a labor surplus also exists to a somewhat lesser degree in the closely settled zone of about 1,000 square miles surrounding the northern town of Kano and in densely populated rural areas of the former Northern Region southeast of Katsina and north of Zaria.

A survey by the FAO in the mid-1960s concluded that the prevailing system of bush fallow is too slow for future needs in the light of increased population densities, the growing demand for foodstuffs, and the need to improve rural incomes and living standards. The FAO recommended that permanent cultivation become the rule and that agricultural policy aim at replacing field rotation by crop rotation. The planting of leguminous crops on fallow land and the use of manure and compost were recommended by the FAO to improve the generally poor physical properties of most soils. The survey advocated the testing of high-nutrient fertilizers, the encouragement of single-crop cultivation, and the restriction of mixed-crop cultivation to a few combinations of complementary crops.

LAND TENURE

Land tenure is in a transitional stage from communal to more individualistic forms. Writers disagree as to how flexible the traditional forms are proving in the light of requirements for modernization of agriculture, expansion of production, and resettlement from overcrowded rural areas.

Studies by a consortium of United States universities in the late 1960s concluded that the various systems of land tenure, law, and social institutions were flexible enough to permit land to pass into individual ownership where it is profitable for it to do so. The many variations in tenure custom are of interest to anthropologists or students of customary law but are not of overriding significance as constraints on economic development. A report on oil palm rehabilitation in eastern Nigeria in 1967 found that progressive farmers in the east were able to acquire control over new land by purchase, rent, or other means even for the planting of oil palms, to which other observers had reported some tribal resistance. Similar observations were made among the cocoa farmers of western Nigeria. In the towns, too, individual rather than communal land ownership was gaining ground.

The consortium acknowledged, however, that the principle of inalienability of land, which is fundamental to the country's land tenure system, has been an obstacle to the resettlement of people from crowded rural areas and has made it impossible to give land to enterprising farmers without regard to their place of origin. These tenure problems were regarded essentially as subproblems of specific development projects rather than as fundamental problems calling for a program of land reform. Other Nigerian authorities on the subject, however, have seen a need for land reform to make individual transferable title to land the rule rather than the exception.

The details of tenure custom often vary from one locality to another, and there may be at least as many tenure patterns as there are ethnic groups. Most of the systems, however, have essential features in common. As in most of tropical Africa, the traditional land tenure systems tend to foster security and communal cohesiveness rather than ambition, acquisitiveness or regional mobility. They are generally characterized by highly equitable distribution among individuals or ranks within a community but there is frequent maldistribution of land between one community and another. Most are communal usufructuary systems in which rights to use land are usually held by individuals, whereas disposal rights are held by groups and exercised by traditional authorities or community elders in accordance with unwritten customary law that is in a continuous state of modification.

In northern Nigeria the application of Islamic law has tended to fragment landholdings and make tenure less communal by comparison with non-Muslim areas. In the rest of the country the communal usufructuary right to land generally has prevailed uninterrupted down to the present day. Traditional practices are well adapted to a land surplus subsistence economy, where there is little incentive to produce beyond that needed to ensure against famine in bad crop years. They do not offer much incentive to optimum exploitation of the land, which would involve introducing permanent or perennial tree crops, increasing soil fertility, or using soil conservation techniques. Where tradition is strongly entrenched, therefore, improvement of the land and of cultivation techniques may be slowed down. Conversely, in many areas of the former Eastern and Western Regions the gradual transition from a subsistence economy to a cash crop economy has been accompanied by a movement in the direction of individualized landholdings, with the farmer gaining absolute ownership. This is particularly noticeable in the cocoa area of the Yoruba.

In the 1960s in both the Eastern and Western Regions, however, problems were encountered because of resistance by traditional land-allocating authorities to further planting of tree crops. According to custom, a tree is the property of the man who plants it. The planting of large areas of trees, therefore, would eventually require the recognition of permanent individual ownership of the land on which they stand, effectively removing the land in question from the pool of resources available to members of the community for future food needs. Over large areas, particularly in the former Mid-Western Region, the elders have resisted any suggestion that further areas of land should be devoted to oil palms.

If resistance to innovation can sometimes be an obstacle to the introduction of crops, it is often a far more thorny obstruction to the introduction of farmers from alien ethnic or kinship groups or even from another village. Alienation of land to strangers tends to be regarded as a threat to the sovereignty of the group, which is bound up with the concept of inalienability of land. Each of the local sovereignties may be jealous of its land rights and unwilling to alter its pattern of tenure if this will mean accommodating outsiders. Thus communities with an excess of land coexist with communities where land is in critically short supply. Even within the north, where the population density is generally low, local sovereignties in land account for extremely high population densities in some communities.

The survival of these attitudes has posed problems in accommodation of government settlement schemes and has obliged large numbers of people from the overpopulated rural areas to migrate to the towns, thus swelling the ranks of the urban unemployed. On the other hand, the traditional systems have apparently given way at many points to the necessities of modern trends. This is evidenced by the numbers of Ibo and other outsiders who have settled to cultivate in non-Ibo areas. Moreover, land devoted to tree crops and other cash crops has been increasing everywhere. In many areas of high population density, family and community lands have become fragmented into smaller individual holdings under English forms of tenure, with land becoming a marketable asset.

In the former Eastern and Western Regions the individual cultivator is deemed to have a pledgeable, salable, and inheritable interest in the fruits of his own labor—his crops, livestock, and buildings. He may lease or sell personal lands acquired with an absolute title from another owner or from the community where such a transaction is permitted, but tribal lands held in customary tenure may not be sold absolutely except with the unanimous consent of the tribe. A majority consent is not enough. This is true for all members of the tribe, including the paramount chief and his council.

The individual may pledge his interest in communal land, and with the concurrence of the community he may lease or even sell his interest in them to someone from outside the community. A practice of some chiefs has been to grant unused tribal lands to an outsider upon the receipt of a gift that is the equivalent of the market value of the land. Migrants who desire to settle permanently and accept the political sovereignty of the landowning group usually are assigned rights of land use.

A recent observer in North Central State reported that, among the Hausa there, lip-service only is paid to the rules of Muslim inheritance; the last effective remnant of chiefly control over farm rights was abolished a few years ago; and informal sale of farms to local citizens is common, although etiquette demands that brothers or other close kin be given first refusal.

The Second National Development Plan, 1970–74, states that, because of the political nature of land tenure systems and the varying social and cultural conditions in different parts of the country, land reform is the basic responsibility of the state government. The federal government, however, will encourage the reform movement by providing funds and technical assistance as required. The plan suggests that in most southern states the solution to land tenure problems would be for the local authorities to consolidate fragmented holdings and to redistribute them into economic units suitable for tree and food crops. In most northern states the solution would be for the local authorities to exercise effective control over vacant lands and to redistribute them in more economical units.

FARM INCOMES AND GOVERNMENT POLICY

Producer prices and marketing of all the major export crops except rubber are handled by marketing boards operated by the individual states. The crops controlled by the boards include: cocoa; palm oil and palm kernels, meal, and cake; groundnuts and groundnut oil, meal, and cake; sunflower seed; sesame; soybeans; copra; and cotton and cottonseed. A few of these products are controlled only in the regions of maximum production.

Besides their price-setting and marketing functions, the boards were formerly directly responsible for certain forms of research and for development projects in the regions. In 1955 their direct development and research functions were dropped and transferred to regional governments. Since then the boards have retained in liquid form only that portion of their reserves needed within a specified period for stabilizing prices. The remainder is kept as a second line of reserve, from which they are obliged to make long-term loans to state governments for developmental purposes.

The marketing boards have responsibility for ensuring stable prices throughout the crop season, for maintaining orderly marketing, and for improving product quality. During the early years of their operation, after 1947, the marketing boards proved their value in carrying out a number of the functions for which they had been created. Besides cushioning the producer against price fluctuations, they helped to improve the position of producers and of the nation vis-a-vis the monopolistic power of the few large foreign trading firms that had controlled the trade in major export crops. They helped to restrain inflationary pressures of excess demand caused by the wartime and early postwar shortage of consumer goods. Most of all, they furnished a readily available source of government revenue at a time when the country's tax base was meager and administrative skills were largely lacking to inaugurate new and complex taxes.

The price stabilization function of the marketing boards creates a gap between the export price and producer price for any given export crop that may in theory be negative or positive. In principle, the producer price will remain below the export price in a period of high world market prices but, when export prices fall unduly, the stabilization reserve fund will be used to support producer prices at above the world market level. A portion of the export price must of course go to meet shipping and port charges and other costs; another share goes to finance the operating costs of the marketing boards. Another fraction of the marketing board "surpluses" is transferred back into agriculture as subsidies for inputs such as fertilizer and pesticides.

Since 1948, however, marketing boards have been used in practice to tax farmers by paying them less than the world market price and channeling much of the resulting "surplus" to the government for development and other needs. There was in effect a consistently negative tax policy for agriculture, resulting in a substantial transfer from the agricultural to the nonagricultural sector of the economy. Between about 1947 and 1962 estimated withdrawals through taxes and marketing board surpluses amounted to the following proportions of potential producer income: cocoa, 31.9 percent; groundnuts, 24.9 percent; palm kernels, 28.1 percent; palm oil, 21.0 percent; and cotton, 22.1 percent.

Marketing board price policy since 1948 has been subjected to considerable analysis and some criticism on several grounds. Some critics felt that export expansion was dampened by the inadequate price incentives offered to producers. The record of export growth in the ten or fifteen years extending through 1965, however, showed quite impressive compound growth rates for cotton, groundnuts, and cocoa in spite of marketing board taxes. Palm products were the exports apparently most affected by the negative price policy over the long run. Palm oil exports have stagnated since about 1950.

By dampening producer prices for particular crops, however, the marketing boards may in some cases have encouraged an unplanned or arbitrary allocation of resources of land and labor to one line of production rather than another. For example, because a substantial proportion of the earnings of oil palm exports was withheld from producers, farmers in the oil palm areas preferred to grow food crops and encouraged their kin to emigrate to other regions. Resources were diverted from oil palm production to rubber, which was not under a marketing board. At times prices were set so low that producers did not even harvest all of their palm crop. Elsewhere, the development of a money economy among the Tiv people was said to have been somewhat delayed because the marketing boards controlled the producer price of sesame, their main cash crop.

The negative export crop tax policies of the marketing boards have also been criticized for discouraging potential foreign investors in agriculture; for reducing the incentive to the introduction of new improvements, such as hybrid palms, in agricultural technology; and for holding down rural land values. Critics have also pointed out cases where marketing board surpluses were used to finance regional political parties. The Coker Commission in the Western Region in 1962 and a government white paper on the Northern Nigerian Marketing Boards and Development Corporation in 1967 found many dubious projects that had been sponsored by marketing board funds at the expense of the small peasant producers.

A more serious consequence of marketing board pricing policy in its implications for future development was the fact that income ratios moved against the farmers in favor of other classes, particularly urban workers; this encouraged the drift of rural people to the urban areas and thus contributed to the grave problem of mounting unemployment in the towns. Their price policies have also been held partly responsible for holding down the expansion of incomes and hence of effective demand among the rural people who make up 70 to 80 percent of the country's population and who in the final analysis must provide the domestic market for any future growth in the country's industrial production.

On balance, critics of the policy tend to agree that there was little alternative during the 1950s and most of the 1960s to the use of the agricultural export sector as a major source of fiscal revenue. Because of the growth of imports since the 1950s, import duties have yielded a growing return to the treasury so that the share of export earnings devoted to export taxes has actually declined, their yield remaining fairly constant. More important, the spectacular jump in petroleum exports projected for the early 1970s will make it possible to shift a major share of the collective tax burden from the peasants to the petroleum industry. This will permit a fundamental reevaluation not only of agricultural policy but also of basic decisions concerning the distribution of incomes and allocation of resource ownership among different groups within the Nigerian economy. These decisions will be crucial in their long-range effect not only on the structure of society but also on the provision of employment for the rural population, their motivations and hopes for the future, the growth of consumer demand, and the availability of financing for the development of individual peasant agriculture, which most directly affects the base of the productive pyramid.

PRINCIPAL CROPS

The principal staples of diet are millet, sorghum, yams, cassava, beans, maize, and rice. Food habits generally correspond to local production, grains forming the staple of diet in the north and root crops in the south. Demand is almost wholly satisfied by domestic production, but almost all wheat consumption and some rice consumption are met by imports. Three-fourths of the total value of food imports in 1966 and 1967 were a processed form of high-nutrition-value food: fish, wheat, milk, cream, and sugar.

To ensure that food production will continue to grow at a higher rate than population and to improve its nutritional content and meet the demand resulting from urbanization and from higher incomes, the government has resolved to intensify its agricultural research programs during the period of the Second National Development Plan, 1970–74. One objective is to introduce the use of small motor-powered implements and animal-drawn implements and carts. A national seed multiplication scheme will be established for maize, sorghum, rice, pulses, and cassava. High-yielding, early-maturing, and disease-resistant varieties of these crops have already been developed and their multiplication and distribution will be undertaken under the plan. Steps will also be taken to improve local cooperatively owned storage facilities, subsidize the formation of producers' cooperative marketing units, propagate the use of fertilizers and pesticides through reinvigorated and expanded extension services, and subsidize their supply.

The principal export crops are cocoa, groundnuts, palm oil and kernels, rubber, raw cotton, sesame, and soybeans, in that order. The main agricultural exports have increased in value at an annual rate averaging 4.6 percent from 1950 to 1966 and 3.8 percent between 1958 and 1966. This increase was achieved by utilizing previously idle capacity in land and labor, in response to generally favorable prices and in recent years with the help of improved transport facilities and technology. Some observers think that a point has been reached at which cultural and other constraints on increased utilization of land and labor must be offset by increased emphasis on price incentives, technological improvements, infrastructure, credit, and marketing. Technological improvements have increased productivity in cocoa and, to a lesser degree, in cotton and palm products. They have been most lacking in rubber and until recently in groundnut production.

Cocoa

Cocoa, the most important export crop, furnished about 19 percent of export earnings in 1969. Nigeria is the world's second largest producer after Ghana, supplying about 20 percent of the world trade (see ch. 14, Industry and Trade). About 95 percent of the crop is grown in Western State, particularly in the Oyo and Ondo districts. Small amounts are also grown in Mid-Western State and the three eastern states. In 1969 an estimated 1.2 million acres were thought to be under cocoa, mostly in smallholdings. Some 350,000 small farmers accounted for most of the production. The average yield was well over 200 pounds of dry cocoa per acre per year. Two cocoa crops are produced each year: the main crop is bought between October and March; the less abundant one, in June or July.

Cocoa is the dynamic mainspring of economic development in western Nigeria. It is believed to have been first introduced into the country in 1879 from Fernando Po, where it had been brought from Brazil around 1822. Commercial planting began in the Western Region around 1890. In the twentieth century cocoa exports have increased steadily in value from about 0.5 percent of total exports in 1900 to over 16 percent in 1938 and 21 percent in 1950; they have since maintained that level, with sharp fluctuations from year to year. World cocoa prices are the most volatile of any of the prices for the country's export crops (see ch. 14, Industry and Trade). A three-year moving average over the ten-year period from 1956–58 to 1965–67 showed that the volume of cocoa exports had grown at a compound average growth rate of about 7 percent a year.

The FAO and other development agencies foresee a favorable trend in world demand for cocoa (see ch. 14, Industry and Trade). Even though Nigeria were only to maintain its position as a world supplier, there might be an outlet for nearly 200,000 additional long tons of cocoa by 1985; with a vigorous production campaign, its share of world exports might be increased. Corrective measures would be required, however. In 1968 it was estimated that about half the country's cocoa acreage was in need of replanting. One-sixth was infested with disease, and one-third of the trees were nearing the end of their productive life cycle.

The Second National Development Plan, 1970–74, emphasized that new planting on unused land is more economical and yields a better return than rehabilitation of existing cocoa acreage because of the cost of removing old trees and other costs. With new plantings, yields as high as 850 to 1,000 pounds per acre could be reached. The government will give grants or loans as appropriate to farmers who rehabilitate their holdings or plant new acreage but will favor new acreage to the extent that suitable land can be found. It will also provide subsidies on fertilizers and pesticides and intensive extension assistance. Moreover, the plan states that the government will try to give incentive to cocoa farmers through fair and better producer prices.

An economist who interviewed 175 cocoa farmers in sixteen villages in three different farming belts in early 1968 reported that enough land appeared to be available to expand food and cocoa crops simultaneously, even with the use of old farming techniques. The limiting factor was labor, but the supply could be increased through the reduction of leisure if adequate price incentives were provided and if farmers had access to credit to hire more labor. The survey concluded that low producer prices and inadequate credit were the key bottlenecks to expanded cocoa production at that time.

Palm Products

Although oil palm production has stagnated since about 1950, Nigeria has maintained its position as the foremost exporter of palm oil and palm kernels despite increasing competition from the Far East and from the Congo (Kinshasa). The oil palm is indigenous to tropical West Africa and was introduced from there to South America and Asia during the nineteenth century. Palm oil was first exported from Nigeria to England in 1790, but exports of oil and kernels did not become commercially important until after the mid-nineteenth century. This export furnished much of the capital and enterprise from which other agricultural exports later developed.

Oil palms grow luxuriantly all through the rain forest belts of West Africa. In Nigeria their intensity of distribution is highest in the oil palm bush and along the Niger Delta from Calabar in the east to Badagri in the west. They have begun to thin out in the more western areas, where intensive cultivation of cocoa, kola nut, or food crops has developed. Their produce is of greater importance in the economy of the eastern states than in the west.

About a million people are thought to be involved in the harvesting of palm fruits from wild palm groves in the three eastern states and Mid-Western State. Harvesting is almost entirely in the hands of individuals. Oil palm plantations, both government and private, have developed greatly in recent years but still account for a very small percentage of total production.

Traditionally, harvesting of palm fruit, tapping for palm wine, and tapping of rubber trees are hereditary occupations exploited systematically for a livelihood only by specialists in the art of climbing and of extracting oil. Palm trees are usually regarded as wild, and the harvesters, who are often so-called strangers of a different tribe, pay a fee for the privilege of exploiting the palms belonging to a village. Where palms are found on family land, the head of the extended family or kin group usually contracts out the harvesting and processing, then receives a share of the oil and distributes it among the family. This practice not infrequently leads to neglect of the palms or rubber trees and to inferior methods of tapping or processing. This can be particularly damaging in rubber production. In the case of palms, it seems to operate as a disincentive to the planting of more palm trees on the family or communal land.

Before the civil war purchases of palm kernels averaged more than 400,000 long tons a year. Purchases of palm oil for export averaged about 150,000 long tons a year. During the war exports virtually ceased, and total purchases of kernels dropped to about 200,000 long tons a year because the produce was not available from the eastern states and the transport system was disrupted. Purchases of palm oil for export virtually ceased during the first two years of the war. In crop year 1970/71 the harvest of kernels was expected to increase to about 300,000 long tons, and it was thought that about 100,000 long tons of palm oil might be available for export.

The palm products industry has suffered from inadequate investment, chiefly resulting from the low producer price policy, which has not furnished adequate incentive for planting and harvesting. The wild palms are difficult to harvest and low in yield. Improved hybrid varieties, which would give a greatly improved yield under good management, have been developed by the Nigerian Institute for Oil Palm Research. They could give a very good return to smallholders. The Second National Development Plan, 1970–74, therefore, provides for better producer prices, loans, and intensive extension services to encourage the planting of new palms. It also proposes organizing farmers into producer cooperatives to replace the traditional hand-squeezing method of processing by hand hydraulic presses or oil mills.

Groundnuts

Nigeria is the second largest producer and the largest exporter of groundnuts in the world. In 1969 groundnuts represented about 11 percent of total export value. About half the country's output of groundnuts comes from Kano State, but in all four upper northern states more lives are affected by groundnut production than by any other economic activity, including nomadic pastoralism.

Between the 1956–58 and 1964–66 periods groundnut and groundnut oil exports grew at a compound annual rate of 5.2 percent. A record crop of over 1 million long tons was purchased in crop year 1966/67. At first the expansion was achieved principally by increased inputs of land and labor, but in the 1960s further increases were obtained through a program of improved seed strains, increased use of fertilizer, and expanded extension services. Limited use of bullock power has also been introduced. Because of variations in the price set for producers, groundnut purchases declined in 1967/68 but rose to around 750,000 long tons in 1970/71. The 1967/68 crop had also been affected by poor weather conditions.

The crop is produced by small peasant farmers with average plantings of between two and four acres. Cultivation on large

338

estates is unknown. Average yields are about 700 pounds of decorticated nuts per acre. It has been estimated that between 203,000 and 305,000 metric tons of groundnuts a year are consumed locally as food. They are a valuable source of proteins and other nutrients. Since local processing facilities have increased, byproducts are being increasingly used for animal feed.

The six main obstacles to expansion of groundnut exports are: the rising cost of internal transport; the consequent deterioration in quality resulting from a long period of storage; labor shortages during the planting season, especially in June; inefficient supply of requisites, especially fertilizer; the dearth of credit; and declining marketing board prices to farmers. The Second National Development Plan, 1970–74, foresees a possibility for early removal of the constraints of transport, fertilizer distribution, and producer prices. Improvement of the other three conditions would require major institutional changes, which would take longer to achieve.

Rubber

The country is now the largest rubber producer in Africa and fifth largest in the world. Annual production exceeds 70,000 long tons. About 90 percent of the rubber is grown in Mid-Western State around Benin and Sapele. There are about 450,000 acres in all under cultivation. About 98 percent of the acreage is in smallholdings, cultivated by some 100,000 producers. Most of the peasant holdings vary in size from 1 to 10 acres; some go as high as 25 acres. Production by peasants is concentrated in the Benin lowlands. Many farmers have started investing in small rubber plantations, and cultivation is expanding at the expense of food crops in areas like the Ukuani district in Aboh Division. Plantation production was discouraged under the British and first began expanding during World War II when supplies from Malaya were cut off. In the late 1960s plantations accounted for only about 20 percent of production. During the 1960s plantation production was expanded in the Calabar district of South Eastern State and in the forests of Ondo and Ijebu-Ondo in Western State.

Wild rubber trees were indigenous to the rain forests of Benin. Exports of rubber from the wild trees declined sharply between 1895 and 1900 as reckless tapping injured the trees. Thereafter a number of communal farms were established growing the indigenous tree. In 1913 a new variety was introduced from Brazil and has since completely replaced the indigenous variety in production.

Yields are low in smallholder production, averaging about 200 pounds of dry rubber per acre. The causes include the high plant density of between 200 and 500 trees per acre, poor tapping techniques that cause wastage of bark reserve, inefficient standards of maintenance, planting from unselected seedlings, low soil fertility, low fertilizer application, and poor processing methods.

In recent years the state governments have paid more attention to improvement and rehabilitation of smallholder production, encouraging the thinning of trees and planting of improved strains of seedlings. The Second National Development Plan, 1970–74, calls for further rehabilitation along these lines. The extension program will be intensified, and research will be conducted on improved varieties of seedlings. An attempt will be made to organize producers into cooperative units, with grants for tapping and processing equipment.

The FAO in its 1966 study of agricultural development in Nigeria for the 1965–80 period included a very exhaustive discussion of policies and programs for rubber development. It visualized the future world market for rubber as very favorable but emphasized that the competitive status of natural versus synthetic rubber would depend primarily on price and therefore upon efficiency of production. It therefore concluded that average yield levels of 1,000 pounds of dry rubber per acre would be a basic requirement for profitable rubber growing in Nigeria. This would require a very material increase in the share of production furnished by plantations and farm settlements as well as a radical change in long-established traditional practices of small-scale rubber farms. The expected increase would be achieved principally by ambitious planting programs in eastern Nigeria. Mid-Western State, which in 1971 contributed more than 85 percent of production, would not be able to maintain its dominant position despite extensive rehabilitation plans.

Cotton

Cotton cloth had been in use in West Africa for many centuries before the earliest European contact with the area. Kano in northern Nigeria has been a cotton market since the ninth century. The indigenous varieties of the cotton plant are no longer in cultivation, and even some of the early varieties introduced from America during the seventeenth century and later have also gone wild. Most of the cotton now cultivated in the north derives from a special improved and adapted strain of North American Allen cotton.

Cotton production has expanded rapidly since about 1950. Apart from a relatively small proportion produced in the derived savanna areas of western Nigeria, the entire crop is grown in northern Nigeria by small peasant farmers. The main cotton belt lies in the western part of the Kano region, where it overlaps the groundnut belt. Katsina Province is by far the largest cotton producer in the country. The belt also extends northwestward into Sokoto Province and southeastward into Zaria Province. Cotton does well in well-drained loam or clay-loam soils, somewhat heavier than the sandy soils needed for groundnuts. It has replaced groundnuts to some extent in the Kano region, but price differentials help to determine the relative areas planted to cotton and groundnuts from year to year. As of 1971 cotton has fit in very well with the local farming calendar in the north because it is planted in late July after the groundnuts and food crops have been planted. Harvesting begins in December, after the other crops have been harvested.

Cotton production increased at an annual compound growth rate of 9.5 percent from crop year 1949/50 to 1965/66. The increase is attributed almost entirely to increased acreage planted. In 1965 the acreage under cotton was thought to be about 1 million, compared to only a quarter of that figure twenty years earlier. Because a considerable proportion of the harvest may be consumed by the producers themselves, it is sometimes difficult to assess the annual crop. When prices are favorable, however, purchases improve. Since crop year 1965/66 purchases of cotton have risen steadily from 127,000 long tons to 240,000 long tons in 1969/70. Because it is dependent upon natural rainfall, however, cotton is subject to great annual fluctuations in yield and output. In crop year 1967/68, for example, production dropped sharply, and purchases for 1968 were only 70,000 long tons. In that year the producer price was also relatively low, and many farmers shifted acreage into food grains or other crops.

There has also been considerable expansion of industrial production of cotton textiles within the country. The cotton textile industry was founded in 1957 and by fiscal year 1966/67 was using more than 30,000 long tons of lint. Cotton textiles nonetheless remain one of the largest items on the country's list of imports (see ch. 14, Industry and Trade). Growth of the domestic industry can therefore effect an important saving in foreign exchange. Exports of raw cotton amounted to about N£3.4 million (1 Nigerian pound equals US$2.80) in 1969, and cottonseed exports were N£1 million. Planners think that exports can be maintained at about this level while raw cotton production and cotton textile production are expanding.

The cotton plants need moisture during their early growth and relatively dry weather during their ripening period. Rainfall of between thirty-five and forty-five inches a year is necessary; otherwise irrigation is required. Yields can be greatly increased with an improved supply of moisture. Early planting is important to enable the plant to benefit from the early rains. Research has indicated that there is a linear decrease in yield of about 10 percent for every week's delay after the optimum sowing date in late June. The government is therefore pressing a program for early planting; under present conditions this would often conflict with the planting of adequate food crops to sustain the farmer and his family. The rate of increase in cotton production may therefore be tied to improved and accelerated techniques for food crop production through the introduction of additional ox plows and other aids. By the mid-1960s the government's "mixed farming" project had already brought about 20,000 ox plows into use on the heavy cotton soils of the north, which are difficult to cultivate by hand.

The FAO also suggested that the use of comparatively small amounts of fertilizer and pesticides could easily increase cotton production fourfold from the level of the early 1960s. At that time Nigerian yields were considerably lower than elsewhere in Africa under comparable ecological conditions. The average yield was about 260 pounds of seed-cotton per acre. The Second National Development Plan, 1970–74, proposed a great expansion in the production of better quality cotton through a seed multiplication and distribution program as well as the guided application of fertilizers and pesticides at subsidized rates.

LIVESTOCK

Because the national diet is badly deficient in animal proteins, improvement of livestock productivity is a high-priority task of economic development. The potential for livestock production is great. Planners estimate that the tsetse free savanna lands of the north could carry double or even triple the present population of cattle, goats, and sheep. Eradication of the tsetse fly in the well-watered southern half of the country would permit further expansion of the herd and introduction of more productive breeds. With selective culling and improved breeding and range management, a tremendous improvement could be effected in milk and meat yields.

The livestock population in the late 1960s was estimated at about 11 million cattle, 7.5 million sheep, 21.5 million goats, 0.7 million pigs, and 66 million fowl. About 96 percent of the cattle are in the six northern states, but there are substantial numbers of goats, sheep, and poultry in all states. Most of the pigs are in the southern parts of the country.

Beef cattle are the main component of the country's livestock.

Because the cattle are concentrated in the extreme north where conditions are too arid for tsetse infestation, the nomadic herdsmen are forced to migrate southward during the dry season in search of water and pasture. The long treks emaciate the animals, and they are frequently exposed to the tsetse fly and die of trypanosomiasis or other diseases, such as bovine pneumonia.

The annual takeoff of cattle in relation to the total cattle population is only 7 to 10 percent, in contrast to a rate of over 28 percent in Europe and the United States. Raising the average animal to market age takes twice as long as in Europe, and when slaughtered the animals are approximately twice the age and half the carcass weight of those in Australia or the United States. Traditional customs place a low value on animal productivity and a high status value on the number of animals in the herd. There are areas of Africa no more suited to livestock production than Nigeria that have succeeded in improving the average productivity of their herds so that it more nearly approaches that achieved in other parts of the world.

The Second National Development Plan, 1970–74, states that the prime objective of policy will be the eradication of the tsetse fly, the control of epizootic diseases, and the settlement of nomadic herdsmen. More water will be provided by drilling artesian wells and constructing dams in semiarid areas, and grazing reserves will be established where nomads will be encouraged to settle and practice improved animal husbandry and mixed farming. Extension work will be directed toward pasture improvement, fodder conservation, and the feeding of protein-rich concentrates, such as cottonseed and groundnut cake. Improved animals from government livestock breeding and improvement centers will be distributed to stock owners.

Implementation of this ambitious program will probably take many years, but a start is to be made by the federal and state governments during the period of the second development plan.

GOVERNMENT PROGRAMS FOR AGRICULTURE

Nigerian farmers are perhaps less dependent upon government assistance than those of most developing or even developed countries. The national economy's capacity for dynamic growth has in the past come largely from the initiative of the peasant farmers, whose earnings have in fact financed the expansion of government and of secondary and tertiary economic activity. The farmers in turn have benefited principally from the construction of roads and railways and the search by the industrial nations and their traders for low-cost raw materials.

In the years since World War II the main thrust of government assistance to agriculture has gone into research and education. In attempting to disseminate the results of this education and research and to put agricultural improvements into practice, Nigerian governments have used three basic approaches. One involves the introduction of large-scale plantation agriculture using modern techniques and mechanization under either private or government sponsorship. This is of course a complete departure from previous practice. A second approach involves the establishment of large-scale cooperative farm settlement schemes, where the farmers must adopt a completely new way of life but where they retain individual landownership and use. The third approach, and currently the most favored, is the attempt to spread new techniques to existing farm villages without altering the villagers' basic way of life, through demonstrations, incentive schemes, subsidized supplies, and improved credit facilities.

During the 1960s the farm settlement schemes were the means favored for increasing agricultural production, providing employment for school leavers and other unemployed persons, and serving as demonstration centers for the surrounding rural areas. They were introduced in the Western Region in 1960 and adopted in the Eastern Region shortly thereafter.

The earliest settlement schemes proved impractical and costly in two respects. They took young primary and secondary school leavers from the ages of fifteen to twenty, and they sought to provide housing that would match the amenities of urban life. Later on both these features were abandoned; it was decided to recruit able-bodied adults with stable minds and family responsibilities and not to construct homes on the new plots but to let the new farmers commute to their farms from a nearby village. Eventually, however, it became evident that the farmers needed to stay with their stock and crops, and the government was obliged to build housing on the new farms.

By the mid-1960s the hoped-for demonstration effects of the settlements had not materialized. The acreage allotments had been too ambitious, and the extensive farming methods being used were not producing better crops or higher yields than those of the neighboring smallholders, whose intensive use of labor, particularly in weeding, was better suited to the humid climate.

In view of the high costs of investment, the settlement schemes also seemed to have little potential for the creation of new employment. In mid-1964 the Western Region's farm settlements employed only 1,170 settlers, and in mid-1965 those in the Eastern Region employed fewer than 2,000. Moreover, their demonstration impact on the average farmer was limited, since few could hope to afford the capital to embark on this type of farming. There were also numerous problems involving the social attitude and organization of settlers. School leavers tended to treat their training as an extension of their academic schooling and later leave to seek urban salaried jobs. Selection of experienced farmers tended to prejudice the original idea of promoting agriculture as a high-status occupation that school leavers could be proud to participate in. Those settlers most adaptable to the initial period of authoritarian direction were ill suited to the later requirement for initiative and self-reliance. A long time interval was required before the settlers began to draw income and perform productive work. All these difficulties sometimes resulted in low morale, uncooperative or resentful attitudes among settlers, factional cliquishness, and bickering.

Among the greatest difficulties were those involving the acquisition of land. The problems of compensating those who considered themselves the owners of prior rights to the land were extremely complicated, since there was no means of establishing or ascertaining these rights except by bargaining. Often it would appear that agreement had been reached but become obvious as soon as the work began that this was not so. In some places the work of clearing had to be accomplished under constant police protection for a period of months. The experience indicated that costly surveying time might best be invested in delimiting tribal areas rather than in surveying for registration of individual holdings.

In the late 1960s a consortium of United States universities compared the performance of government land settlements and public and private plantations with that of smallholders and concluded that the main thrust of the Nigerian rural development progam should be to encourage and support the efforts of private smallholders. Such programs would give higher returns for the investment required and would also have a greater impact on the average rural incomes that must form the base of future consumer demand for foodstuffs and other products of the economy.

FORESTRY AND FISHING

Forestry

Forestry and fishing together contributed an estimated 5 percent of gross domestic product in 1968. Because of the growth of petroleum exports, the proportionate importance of exports of timber and sawn wood had declined to about 1.6 percent of the value of total exports in 1969. More than 90 percent of timber and lumber exports come from the high-forest areas of Western, Mid-Western, and South Eastern States.

About one-third of the country's total land area, or about 139,000 square miles, is thought to consist of forest land. Only 10 percent, or 36,104 square miles, however, consists of permanent forest estate or forest reserves. This includes 85 square miles of mangrove swamp, 28,536 square miles of northern savanna woodland, and 7,483 square miles of southern high forest.

There are more than 100 usable tree species, but only about 30 of them were being exploited in the late 1960s. About 50 million cubic feet of industrial wood was being removed annually from the forest; about half of this was being exported, and the remainder was used domestically. Foreign exchange earnings from timber and sawn wood amounted to about N£7 million a year. A variety of tropical hardwoods is exported, including obeche, abura, sapele, agba, mansonia, afzelia, and other species. During the 1960s the forestry industry was generally stagnating. Less than 25 percent of the trees removed were being replanted.

The Second National Development Plan, 1970–74, stated that the various state governments concerned with forestry would try to increase the rate of regeneration considerably and would try to replant with fast-growing species to yield high-quality timber. Use of lesser known species would be intensified. Some species are already being used domestically for plywood and blackboards; other industrial uses will be sought. By promoting the adoption of modern techniques and equipment, the governments will try to increase the efficiency of existing forest industries. Means will be sought for better utilization of residues in fiberboard and other products. An effort will be made to increase employment in forest plantations and forest industries. There will be intensive planting of pines and other species suitable for raw material for existing and proposed paper mills and match factories.

Fishing

Planners have estimated the country's nutritional requirement for fish consumption at about 1 million long tons a year. Nigeria is the largest single consumer of fish and fish products in Africa, but there is room for a sizable increase in fish consumption and production. Before the import restrictions arising from the civil war, actual annual consumption of fish was only about 270,500 long tons. The total domestic catch was estimated at only about 120,500 long tons a year; the remaining 150,000 tons consisted of imported stockfish.

No comprehensive survey of the country's fishery resources had been completed by 1970, but the FAO made a preliminary assessment of the potential in its 1966 report on agricultural development in Nigeria from 1965 to 1980. It estimated that the maximum fish production Nigeria could hope to obtain from domestic resources (excluding shrimp fishery, fishponds, and distant-water trawling) would be between 150,000 and 300,000 long tons a year.

Of this total, 50,000 to 200,000 long tons would be derived from the Lake Chad fishery on the far northeastern border. The primitive canoe fishery practiced along the coastal banks, the lagoons, and the creeks of the Niger Delta and the brackish water fishery in the delta estuaries and the lagoons extending along the west coast to Dahomey could be expanded by the introduction of outboard motors and improved gear to yield about 50,000 long tons a year. The river fisheries could yield 20,000 long tons; the Kainji Dam, another 10,000 long tons; and the coastal trawl fishery, 10,000 long tons.

The Lake Chad fishery has already been profitably exploited by Niger, Chad, and Cameroon, but conditions on the Nigerian bank have impeded expansion. There are thought to be about 4,000 full-time fishermen and 500 seasonal migratory fishermen operating from the Nigerian side, catching about 10,000 long tons of fish a year. Because of slow transport conditions, rough handling, and insect infestation, losses after landing are thought to average as much as 40 percent of the landed weight. The fishermen set up camps on the papyrus islands in the lake and fish from canoe-shaped papyrus rafts that last only a few weeks before becoming waterlogged and useless. The thick papyrus on the Nigerian side of the lake obstructs the fishing. About 80 percent of the fishermen were using primitive gear and processing methods in the mid-1960s. Most of the catch was smoked in small bits called *banda* and shipped by numerous stages to the far southeast. Financing was secured in 1965 for construction of a good all-weather road from the lake, which was expected to take several years. The possibility of marketing the fish in the north was also being explored. Nylon nets and improved curing in cheap smoking kilns were gradually introduced in the 1960s.

The industrial shrimp (prawn) fishery along the coast was first inaugurated in 1965. It was expected to produce a yield high in export value but low in weight and would not contribute to domestic consumption. The shrimp were to be flown out in frozen form. Construction of a modern fishing terminal in Lagos was to be completed during the period of the Second National Development Plan, 1970–74, and was expected to facilitate increased landings from Nigerian, foreign, and chartered vessels. Because the rich shrimp-fishing grounds off the Niger Delta were at least twelve hours steaming time from Lagos and other ports, the shrimp were to be landed on a mother vessel with freezing facilities on board.

PETROLEUM AND MINING
Mining

The country's mineral resources have not been fully explored. Until the inland and offshore oilfields began to boom in the 1960s, commercially exploitable mineral resources were varied but not outstandingly rich (see fig. 12 and table 9). Tin ore, columbite, and tantalite production was of great strategic value but subject to fluctuations in peacetime demand; export earnings from these sources were of relatively minor significance in comparison to earnings from agricultural materials. Lead and zinc production was even smaller. The coal mines had been operated at a loss for twenty years, and the high cost of transport also affected the commerical potential of some of the other known deposits, notably iron ore. Limestone is quarried in some quantity. Minerals produced in small quantities included gold, tantalite, wolfram, monazite, and molybdenite. There are known deposits of a number of other minerals that are not commercially exploited (see ch. 2, Physical Environment).

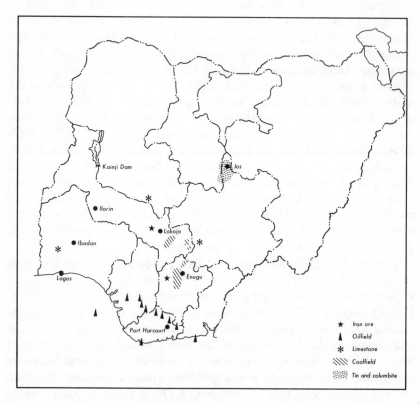

Source: Adapted from *Financial Times* [London], August 4, 1969, p. 18.

Figure 12. Principal Mineral Deposits of Nigeria

Table 9. Mineral Production in Nigeria, 1965–70 [1]

	1965	1966	1967	1968	1969	1970 [2]
Crude oil (in millions of barrels)[3]	99.4	152.4	122.5	51.9	197.2	320.0
Natural gas (in millions of cu. ft.)	79.4	101.6	91.6	51.6	145.6	n.a.
Refined tin	9.3	9.1	9.1	9.8	8.7	9.2
Columbite	2.5	2.2	1.9	1.1	1.5	1.6
Limestone	1,291.6	1,098.0	883.2	647.4	680.0	916.0
Coal	728.3	630.1	94.6	0	0	120.0
Gold (in ounces)	79.0	45.8	39.0	214.0	300.0	253.0
Marble	1.6	1.1	1.0	0.4	1.2	n.a.
Cassiterite	12.9	12.6	12.6	13.0	11.6	13.0

n.a.—not available.
[1] In thousands of long tons unless otherwise specified.
[2] Forecast.
[3] Excludes production from the eastern states for the period April 1967–September 1968. One million barrels a day equal 50 million tons a year.

By early 1971 mining and petroleum production were contributing about 44 percent of Nigeria's total export earnings and 27 percent of the government's current revenue. The Federal Military Government (FMG) had decided to establish a national prospecting and mining company, which would explore and exploit mineral deposits in the country.

In mid-1971 Nigeria joined the Organization of Petroleum Exporting Countries (OPEC), and at a subsequent meeting the organization announced that its members would seek direct ownership participation in oil concessions on their territories. The degree of participation to be sought was not specified.

Nigeria furnishes the greater part of the world supply of columbite, an ore used in the production of heat-resistant steels used in jet engines, gas turbines, and other products. Demand for columbite fluctuates widely and was further depressed in the late 1960s because of increased competition from the production of pyrochlore from Brazil and Canada. At the same time production costs in Nigeria were rising because of import duties on certain materials and increased fuel costs. Four of the thirty-eight columbite producers in the country account for about 98 percent of the output. Most columbite and some tantalite are produced in association with tin ore, but there are some companies specilizing in columbite and tantalite production. Reserves are plentiful (see ch. 2, Physical Environment).

In production of tin ore, Nigeria is first in African but only fifth in noncommunist world production, ranking well below Indonesia both as a producer and as a supplier. During World War II,

349

when Asian sources were cut off, Nigeria ranked second after Bolivia as a supplier, and price, demand, and production were far higher than they have been since. After 1960 exports were limited by quotas imposed by the International Tin Council, which operates a buffer-stock system designed to stabilize the world market price. By 1968 the price had declined considerably from its 1965 high, but it improved slightly in 1969 and still more in 1970. In December 1969 export quotas and the price ceiling were removed, but the Nigerian mines had problems in increasing production because of import restrictions on machinery and parts, a labor shortage, and the impact of tin stealing on production costs.

The latest evaluation was that, at the present cost-price ratio and rate of production, the country's known tin reserves would last until 1980; but this estimate may well be revised as past estimates have been, one of which predicted that reserves would be exhausted by 1970. There are extensive deposits of lower grade ore, which at latest estimate would not repay the cost of extraction. The mining companies had been encountering increasing cost problems in the late 1960s. Exploration and development costs have been reduced to a minimum, and the government was planning to reduce royalty payments.

Tin from the Jos Plateau was extracted, cast in local furnaces by Hausa smelters, and traded long before the colonial period. The Royal Niger Company started explorations in 1902 and began mining in 1904. The rail routes were opened after 1911, and exports increased steeply until the depression of the 1930s. In 1967 there were 101 companies, syndicates, and private individuals holding 3,505 mining leases on 257,427 acres; sixteen operators accounted for most of the acreage and 80 percent of the production. Forty percent was produced by Amalgamated Tin Mines of Nigeria, a British firm and the world's largest privately owned tin producer. Nearly all the ore produced was smelted at the Makeri Tin Smelting Company at Jos. The United Kingdom is the principal market; in 1968 it received 85 percent of its tin metal imports from Nigeria and took about two-thirds of Nigeria's exports of tin metal.

Lead and zinc are produced in the southeast at Abakaliki and Owerri, in the heart of the civil war zone, where production was completely disrupted by the war. Small quantities are also mined on the Jos Plateau.

The country's coal deposits are located around Enugu in East Central State, where mining was also disrupted by the civil war. The industry has been operating at a loss since about 1950, largely because of the heavy cost of rail transport to Port Harcourt, where it is transshipped to Lagos and shipped out again by rail to other destinations. The problem of finding markets for the coal has increased in recent years, since the railways have been converted to diesel and petroleum and gas have been widely substituted for coal. It has never been popular as a domestic fuel. In the past it has never been considered suitable for coking, but in 1969 there were plans for converting it to coke by a new process for use in a domestic steel industry. There has also been some consideration of creating a coal-tar products industry. In the late 1960s the mines were continuing in operation largely as a means of sustaining employment, though the number employed had been progressively reduced.

Coal was discovered in the Enugu area in 1909, and the first mine began operation in 1915. Since 1950 the mines have been operated by the state-owned Nigerian Coal Corporation. The four mines in operation in 1970 were Iva, Okpara, Ekulu, and Rihadu, all modern and capable of producing jointly about 80,000 long tons a month. Actual production was restricted to a considerably lower tonnage because of limited demand. There are also large reserves of coal and of lignite in northern Nigeria, which are not exploited (see ch. 2, Physical Environment).

The iron ore reserves are of rather low grade. The Soviet Union planned an iron and steel project that would use imported iron ore of higher grade in combination with the domestic ore; but in 1969 work had begun on a steelworks near Enugu, using a nearby lateritic and sandy ore body of 43 percent iron content with reserves of 46 million tons. There were plans to convert the local coal to coke by a new process. There were also plans to explore the ore reserves on the Agbaja Plateau. In November 1970 Nigeria and the Soviet Union signed a contract under which detailed geological investigations are to be carried out for richer iron ore deposits, coal, and other raw materials required for the proposed iron and steel project.

Petroleum

Before the mid-1950s the prospects for discovering oil in Nigeria were generally regarded as poor. The first search for oil was started in 1908 by a German firm, which abandoned the effort at the outbreak of World War I. The search was revived in 1938 by the consortium that later became Shell-British Petroleum (Shell-BP). After a five-year interval during World War II, exploration was intensified beginning in 1946. The first commercial discovery was made by Shell-BP in 1956 at Oloibiri in the Niger Delta (see fig. 13). In 1958 Shell-BP began exporting oil from Port Harcourt. Other international oil companies had already begun to show interest in extensive exploration in Nigeria, and the Mobil Oil Com-

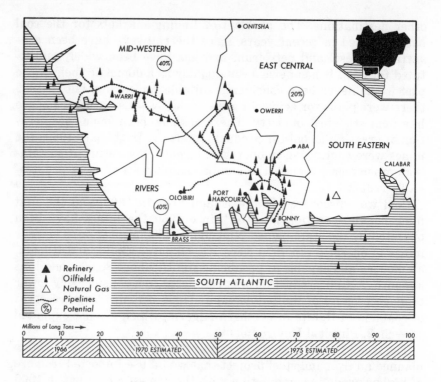

Source: Adapted from Alan Rake, "Nigeria's Oil Explosion: Who Will Become Rich?", *African Development* [London], February 1970, p. 13.

Figure 13. Location of Principal Oilfields in Nigeria, 1969

pany of the United States was particularly active during the 1950s.

The great significance to the nation of this new resource poses the usual difficult political decisions on how best to secure maximum immediate financial advantage to the nation and its people without losing the capital and expertise provided by foreign oil companies and without sacrificing competitive advantage or productive and administrative efficiency. In these circumstances there often tends to be internal political pressure for maximizing immediate production and fiscal return, whereas the marketing companies may prefer to secure a long-run competitive advantage by stabilizing supply or by offering a price advantage, as well as by seeking to minimize taxes and costs of production.

In addition, the location of the oilfields has posed sensitive problems concerning revenue sharing between the federal and state governments and the distribution of benefits among the population on a regional basis. Originally, the major onshore producing wells were located in the eastern states, although predominantly in

352

areas inhabited by minority tribes. In early 1971, however, Mid-Western State had taken the lead in oil production, and offshore production also promised to become more important.

Effective April 1, 1971, a federal decree proclaimed that all oil revenues from offshore deposits (that is, from the continental shelf including the territorial waters) would accrue to the federal government rather than to the states. These revenues include royalties, rents, taxes, and other revenues derived from exploration and prospecting.

In March 1971 the Ministry of Mines and Power announced the imminent publication of a new decree establishing a national oil corporation to engage in the exploration, mining, refining, distribution, and marketing of Nigerian oil. It was not yet entirely clear whether the corporation would be independent of the national prospecting and mining company.

A comprehensive review of oil policy was being undertaken in early 1971 after some of the other leading producing countries had obtained important concessions from the international oil companies. In April 1971 comprehensive talks were opened in Lagos between the Nigerian government and the oil companies concerning oil prices and tax and royalty rates. They followed the conclusion of the Teheran agreement of February 14, 1971, with the six Persian Gulf oil states and the Tripoli agreement of April 2, 1971, with Libya. In both agreements the supplier countries had succeeded in imposing a substantial increase in the posted price per barrel of crude oil produced. The posted price is an artificial figure that determines tax payments. In the Teheran agreement the Organization of Petroleum Exporting Countries, of which Nigeria was not then a member, had obtained an increase in tax rates to 55 percent, as well as an increase of US$0.35 a barrel in the posted price. Libya had obtained an even better concession because of the desirable low-sulfur quality of its oil and its proximity to European consumers.

On April 23, 1971, the press reported that the Nigerian government had concluded an agreement with Shell-BP on a new basic posted price of US$2.88 a barrel for crude oil exports, to be escalated after one year to US$3 a barrel. This was a substantial increase over the previous posted price and brought the price of Nigerian crude oil almost into line with that for Libyan oil. If the Suez Canal should be reopened, the Nigerian crude oil would be higher priced than that from the Persian Gulf; but in mid-1971 it enjoyed an advantage in transport costs. The five-year agreement with Shell-BP, which was expected to serve as a model for the agreements with other oil companies, also stipulates that Nigeria will receive 55 percent of the profit on future shipments, instead of the previous 50 percent.

At the same time the Nigerian government announced the conclusion of an agreement with the French concern Safrap Nigeria (see Glossary) under which the Nigerian government's participating interest in the firm would be gradually increased to 50 percent. The government had been reported as resolved to secure at least a 50-percent interest in all new oilfields as its price for granting concessions.

In early 1971 the government had announced its intention of reallocating its exploration and production concessions and was considering applications from foreign petroleum firms. In January 1971 there had been ten firms holding oil prospecting licenses or oil mining leases. They included the British firm Shell-BP; Agip Oil Company Nigeria, a Nigerian subsidiary of the Italian government firm National Fuel Agency (Ente Nazionale Idrocarburi—ENI); Safrap Nigeria, a Nigerian subsidiary jointly owned by the French government firm Society of African Oil Exploration (Société Africaine d'Exploration Pétrolière—SAFREX) and the French firm Petroleum Research and Activities Enterprise (Enterprise de Recherches et d'Activités Pétrolière—ERAP); and the United States companies Gulf Oil, Mobil Oil, Phillips Petroleum, Tennessee Nigeria (Tenneco), Union Oil, Texas Overseas Petroleum, and California Asiatic Oil.

CHAPTER 14

INDUSTRY AND TRADE

Although agriculture has provided the foundation of the country's internal economy and foreign trade, both industry and commerce have shown remarkable vitality. If mining is included in the industrial sector, the rapid growth of petroleum production dominates the structure of output and export trade. Even if mining is excluded, however, manufacturing and construction showed the most rapid rate of economic growth from 1956 to the outbreak of the civil war in 1967, and their basic strength and resilience were still more effectively demonstrated during the war, when industry outside the war-devastated zone more than made up for the loss of production in the east.

Foreign-owned firms have been more prominent in commerce and industry—particularly in mining—than in agriculture, but indigenous entrepreneurs proliferate in both sectors and are noted for their initiative and response to economic incentive. The rapid recognition of market opportunities that has characterized the country's smallholder exporters is likewise characteristic of entrepreneurs in commerce and manufacture, who have also shown a considerably greater inclination to adopt profitable innovations.

The government's program of Nigerianization in larger scale industry and commerce has made steady progress, though much remains to be done. Among developing countries, Nigeria has a relatively good supply of managerial staff and other high-level manpower, although there remains a sizable gap between requirements and availabilities, particularly in the private sector (see ch. 4, Population and Labor). In its drive for more sophisticated industrial development, the country has offered liberal incentives to private foreign investment and has encouraged the exchange of expertise and technical assistance. Although some of the heavier industries planned for the future will require large-scale government participation, private initiative (domestic and foreign) will continue to predominate in most sectors of industry and commerce.

MANUFACTURING

After petroleum production, manufacturing has been the fastest growing sector of the economy since 1960. From a very low base, it has expanded at an average annual rate of 11 percent at constant prices, increasing its contribution to gross domestic product (GDP) at current factor cost from only 4 percent in 1958 to 5.6 percent in 1963 and 8.4 percent in 1967. The country's large population, with a relatively even distribution of income, has facilitated industrialization by offering a sizable market. Because of the low per capita income, however, temporary market saturation can occur quickly when a number of manufacturers enter a field of production. The well-developed system of transport has also given the country a headstart on industrialization compared to some other developing countries. The strong incentives provided by the government for establishment or expansion of manufacturing industry have attracted valuable foreign investment to the field. Industry has taken advantage of the potential for processing existing agricultural exports and the numerous possibilities for import substitution.

Industry demonstrated its basic strength and resilience during the civil war, when overall manufacturing production grew at an annual rate of about 5 percent. Manufacturing in the eastern states had been crippled soon after the war broke out. It soon came to a complete standstill, and many plants either were damaged or deteriorated from lack of maintenance. This loss of production, together with the stringent restrictions on imports, fostered the rapid growth of manufacturing in the states outside the war zone. New capacity was added and idle capacity was utilized. Some factories introduced second and third shifts. Manufacturing production, including that in the eastern states, increased by 16 percent during the war period, or about 5 percent a year; excluding the east, it increased by 85 percent, or nearly 30 percent a year.

Spurred by the civil war, industrial development progressed rapidly during 1969 and 1970 and by 1971 was able to supply the bulk of domestic demand in many sectors. Consumer goods industries in particular had done very well. Several plants had attained an optimum international standard of size and efficiency. Most of this development during the three-year war period was undertaken by established domestic entrepreneurs, using funds generated by their existing operations. There was little investment from outside.

Available data on manufacturing and industry deal with establishments employing ten or more persons. Production in smaller scale establishments is thought to be extensive, but its exact magnitude is unknown, and it probably is not adequately represented in the statistics on origin of national product. In a 1965 rural survey the Federal Office of Statistics estimated that about 900,000 rural households may have been engaged in manufacturing activities such as food processing, palm oil extraction, and the making of textiles, clothing, mats, and metal products. Another source estimated that total employment in urban small-scale industry may have been around 100,000, which was less than those involved in rural cottage industry but greater than the number employed in establishments of ten or more. These minuscule urban enterprises tend to be concentrated where purchasing power for consumer goods is found, in the new commercial and administrative cities of the south rather than the large traditional towns of the north and west. They include unskilled producers of crude consumer goods dependent on the volume of urban immigration; skilled artisans of better quality goods in cabinetmaking, goldsmithing, and the making of leather shoes and those in motor vehicle repair; and workers in more complex, modern small-scale industry, such as baking, soft-drink bottling, and undershirt manufacture.

The Second National Development Plan, 1970–74, estimated that nonagricultural enterprises employing fewer than ten workers accounted for more than 25 percent of total employment in the economy in fiscal 1966/67. These included petty trading as well as industrial enterprises. It estimated that wage employment accounted for only about 5 percent of those gainfully occupied and that about half of wage employment in the economy was in establishments employing fewer than ten persons. These included small-scale fabricating establishments, furniture and joinery workshops, motor and bicycle repair shops, bakeries, dressmaking enterprises, retail shops, and brickyards.

In most statistical data, small-scale industrial activities are either included under "crafts" or not counted at all. As a result, the small share of national product attributed to manufacturing may be somewhat underestimated. In the estimates for the early 1950s, handicraft production accounted for a greater share of gross domestic product than modern manufacturing. By survey year 1962/63, however, modern manufacturing made up 3.5 percent of gross domestic product, and handicrafts made up only 1.9 percent; in 1967/68 the shares were 6.7 percent and 1.6 percent, respectively.

A 1961 survey in Lagos, the chief industrial center, showed that the average size of industrial establishment was 5.1 persons. About 10 percent of the Lagos establishments engaged 10 or more workers; only half of these had 10 or more paid employees, however, the others were unpaid family workers. Another survey found 2,109 small-scale manufacturing establishments in Ibadan alone. A survey conducted in fourteen towns in eastern Nigeria found 10,728 small firms employing an average of 2.7 workers each, with a fixed capital per worker of N£100 (1 Nigerian pound equals US$2.80). In areas such as these, the number, variety, and vigor of small enterprises in manufacturing, trade, and services are striking. As some of the older handicrafts die out before the onslaught of cheap mass-produced consumer goods, the proliferation of modern tools, sewing machines, and similar equipment has created many new opportunities for small-scale enterprise.

The government-established minimum standards for wages in the modern sector of private large-scale industry and government enterprise are considerably above the labor market level for small-scale enterprise. In the 1960s the average in the modern sector may have approximated a subsistence wage, and the extensive use of family labor made it possible for many wages to remain below subsistence level (see ch. 4, Population and Labor). Other inputs, such as equipment and management, are correspondingly of lower cost and quality than in the more modern and larger scale sector of manufacturing.

The Second National Development Plan notes that the very small-scale industries are particularly appealing for the purpose of creating employment because of their high ratio of employment to investment. In the context of a largely rural labor-surplus economy, a particularly large demand potential exists for the low-priced products of these enterprises. A pilot study conducted in 1965 concluded that with small additional investment, increased production and considerable additional employment could be created in selected promising enterprises that were working below capacity in such lines as shoe and leather work; furniture and woodwork; timber, pottery, ceramic, and glass manufacture; weaving; and undershirt manufacture.

In comparison to the average in industrially developed countries, the ratio of labor to capital investment in manufacturing activity in Nigeria is relatively high, but in many of the newer and more productive industries the capital ratio is so high that they offer only limited potential for absorbing unemployment. In the 1960s priority was given to the objective of increasing output rather then employment. The requirements for skilled labor are high in the modern sector, most notably in such lines of production as the manufacture of mattresses, readymade clothing, and furniture, tailoring, printing, steel rolling, motor-vehicle repair, flour milling, and petroleum refining. As Nigerian labor is trained in these requirements, foreign skilled labor can be replaced.

Modern manufacturing is broadly defined as including all establishments employing ten or more persons. There were only 464 such establishments in 1966. Even so, it was the largest manufacturing sector in black Africa. Manufacturing as a share of gross domestic product, however, was higher in the Congo (Kinshasa), Kenya, and Uganda.

There is considerable diversity in industrial production, which covers enterprises of many different types and products and processes of varying degrees of complexity. The modern sector includes highly capital-intensive enterprises, usually owned by government or foreign interests, and a variety of medium-scale processing and assembly enterprises of a more labor-intensive nature but using advanced technical processes. Among the smaller scale enterprises are some capital-intensive producers.

There are relatively few large enterprises. Of the 464 establishments reported in 1966, only 158 had 100 or more employees; 27 had 500 or more; and 7 had 1,000 or more. Within the modern sector the greatest concentration of employment was in plants employing between 200 and 499 people, or what would usually be termed medium-scale industry.

In the 1950s about half the value added in manufacturing came from the semiprocessing of primary raw materials for export, such as palm oil processing, rubber creping, sawmilling, and veneer production. In the early 1960s there began a shift in the structure of manufacturing from processing traditional primary products for export toward processing imported materials for the domestic market. This shift was later accelerated by the civil war. which brought more stringent restrictions on imports. In 1967 it had been estimated that value added by upgrading domestic agricultural and forest products accounted for only about 25 percent of the total output of manufacturing industry.

The manufacturing industries existing during the 1960s could be classified in two ways: processing of domestic materials versus import processing; or production for the domestic versus the export market (see table 10). A far greater variety of industries were engaged in production for the domestic market than for export. Of the limited range of export manufactures, many are quite close to the raw material stage; these include tin smelting, rubber processing, tanning, sawmilling, and oilseed crushing. The value added by domestic processing in these industries, however, need not be relatively low. Consumer goods based upon imported components often tend to be a more sophisticated stage of manufacture, although there are many exceptions.

According to a study made in 1960, industries with a relatively low dependence on imported inputs included leather tanning and the production of butter, beer and soft drinks, groundnut oil, and

Table 10. Principal Types of Manufacturing in Nigeria, 1960-69

Domestic material processing		Import processing	
For domestic consumption	For export	For domestic consumption	For export

Domestic material processing — For domestic consumption	Domestic material processing — For export	Import processing — For domestic consumption	Import processing — For export
Beer*	Tin smelting	Flour	Shoes*
Soft drinks*	Oil refining*	Radios	Cookies*
Cement and cement products	Fruit canning*	Milk and ice cream	
Textiles	Oilseed crushing: groundnut, palm kernel, and palm oil*	Steel products	
Oil refining*		Metal windows	
Sugar		Biscuits and bakery products	
Meat processing	Rubber processing	Vehicle assembly	
Macaroni	Tanning*	Bicycle assembly	
Butter and cheese	Sawmilling*	Sweets and confection- ery	
Furniture	Cocoa processing	Phonograph records	
Fruit canning*		Aluminum sheets	
Boatbuilding		Pharmaceuticals	
Margarine and soap		Rubber tires and accessories	
Oilseed crushing: groundnut and palm oil*		Enamelware	
Tanning*		Industrial gas (oxygen and acet- ylene)	
Sawmilling*		Oil blending	
Matches		Plastic shoes*	
Thread		Steel drums and con- tainers	
Tire retreading		Printing, stationery, and publishing	
Jute bags		Sewing machine assembly	
Cigarettes*		Undershirts	
Glass bottles		Soft drinks*	
Mattresses		Tarpaulins	
Building materials*		Umbrella assembly	
Shoes (rubber)		Beer*	
Carbon dioxide and dry ice		Toilet paper	
Tiles and concrete		Cigarettes*	
Foam rubber		Paints	
		Building materials*	
		Bitumen	
		Plastics	
		Perfumes and cos- metics	
		Car battery assembly	

*Industries listed under more than one heading.

Source: Adapted from Gerald K. Helleiner, *Peasant Agriculture, Government, and Economic Growth in Nigeria,* Homewood, Illinois, 1966.

large textiles. Those with the highest rate of dependence on imports were bicycle assembly, vehicle assembly, and the processing of bitumen, some types of footwear, perfumes, cosmetics, undershirts, and miscellaneous textiles and apparel. Value added domestically amounted to more than 50 percent of total output in the case of carbon dioxide, plastics, foam rubber, cement, ceramics, printing, publishing, beer and soft drinks, and tobacco products. On beer and soft drinks and tobacco products excise taxes probably represented an important component of value added.

In the 1960s there was some domestic manufacturing or assembly in most of the major categories of industrial production. In 1967, for example, the net contribution to gross national product,

Table 11. Value Added in Manufacturing Industry of Nigeria, 1958, 1963, and 1967
(in million Nigerian pounds)[1]

| Industry group | Value added [2] | | | 1967 | |
	1958	1963	1967	Gross output	Value added as percent of gross output
Food (including tobacco), meat, dairy products, fruits, grain, and sugar confectionery	4.76	10.77	16.02	31.07	51.56
Beverages (including soft drinks)	4.50	10.17	11.79	15.33	76.91
Vegetable oil milling	1.51	3.42	7.22	24.19	29.85
Textiles	1.76	3.99	13.68	30.24	45.24
Garments	0.04	0.09	1.02	2.41	42.32
Footwear	0.24	0.54	1.35	3.64	37.09
Furniture and fixtures	0.32	0.73	1.62	3.61	44.83
Glass products and pottery	0.01	0.02	0.05	0.46	10.87
Paints	0.16	0.36	0.59	1.34	44.03
Bricks and tiles	0.04	0.10	0.12	0.23	52.17
Cement and concrete products	1.51	3.42	3.14	5.81	54.04
Basic industrial chemicals, petroleum products, and miscellaneous chemicals	1.27	2.87	7.04	14.39	48.92
Electrical equipment	0.05	0.12	0.44	1.38	24.18
Basic metal and metal products	1.27	2.88	6.07	25.60	23.71
Motor vehicle assembly (including bicycle assembly)	0.29	0.65	0.80	8.50	9.41
Others	6.57	14.80	19.55	51.05	32.94
Crafts	16.20	20.40	22.40	n.a.	n.a.
TOTAL	40.50	75.33	112.90	219.25	39.96

n.a.—not available.
[1] One Nigerian pound equals U.S. $2.80.
[2] Net contribution to gross national product.

Source: Adapted from Republic of Nigeria, Federal Ministry of Information, Second National Development Plan, 1970–1974, Lagos, 1970, p. 142.

or value added, ranged from as low as 9 percent of gross output in motor vehicle assembly to as much as 77 percent in beverages (see table 11).

Although the tariff protection and quantitative restrictions on imports were originally intended to protect the balance of payments rather than infant industry, they have had the effect of fostering import-substitution industries at the expense of export-processing and intermediate and capital goods industries. The structure of protection also tends to favor industries with a relatively low component of value added within the country. From a development standpoint, these industries would have low priority. It has been estimated that in the 1960s only 10 percent of the value added to production in large-scale manufacturing industries actually stayed in the country; the remainder was spent on imported raw materials, intermediate goods, and machinery. In fact, the Second National Development Plan stated that most industrial activities in the country are still not manufacturing in the true sense of the term but are mere assembly industries. Very often, all the components are imported and are merely put together behind the tariff wall.

It was estimated that in 1970 about 60 percent of the production of manufacturing was for final demand and only 40 percent consisted of intermediate or capital goods. Light manufacturing and consumer goods industries predominated. Some of the consumer goods industries have done very well, notably breweries and cotton textiles, household plastics, quality wooden furniture, and paper conversion industries. The capital goods industries that had been established by 1971 were in the minority; most were fairly large establishments by Nigerian standards. In the 1960s there were in this group only cement, other building materials, sawmilling, late-stage fabrication of imported aluminum and other metals, and some vehicle assembly industries. The most successful was cement, in which the country had almost attained self-sufficiency before the civil war.

The development of industry producing for the home market until 1971 had followed the classical pattern of import substitution; planners have concluded, however, that during the period of the Second National Development Plan, 1970–74, the country should be ready to move away from the easier early phases of industrialization to the more demanding second-generation phase of basic structural change. As the country attains self-sufficiency in consumer goods, such as food, beverages, and textile fabrics, the possibilities for import substitution will become more limited. In providing incentives or capital for new industry, the government will place greater emphasis on the production of intermediate and capital goods that will increase the domestic segment of value added. The object is to increase the degree of interdependence between finished goods and domestically produced raw materials and semifinished products.

Preference will be given to industries that can induce the establishment and growth of other domestic industries, creating so-called backward linkages by buying domestically produced inputs or forward linkages by selling some or all of their output to other domestic industries for use in production, instead of exporting it or selling it as a finished product. Examples of the kind of intermediate goods that might be produced domestically are industrial yarn; pulp and paper; iron and steel tubes, rods, and structures; bottles; tins; paper and cardboard containers; industrial chemicals; artificial fibers and plastic granules; fertilizers; tanned leather for shoe and upholstery manufacture; nails; and printing ink.

In entering the production of intermediate and capital goods, the country's industry will be faced with problems of scale. The limited size of the market for such goods and the lack of technical and managerial expertise will be a greater handicap in industries of this type than in the assembly or consumer-goods industries. Location, transport costs, fuel, and other supplies will become crucial cost factors, and skilled labor requirements are likely to exceed the immediate supply.

In comparison to the average in industrially developed countries, manufacturing activity in Nigeria is relatively labor intensive, but many of the newer and more productive industries are so capital intensive as to offer only limited potential for absorbing unemployment. Priority up to 1971 had been given to the objective of increasing output rather than employment. The requirements for skilled labor are high in the modern sector, most notably in such lines as production of mattresses, readymade clothing and furniture, tailoring, printing, steel rolling, motor vehicle repair, flour milling, and petroleum refining. As Nigerian labor is trained in these requirements and foreign skilled labor can be replaced, the domestic share of industrial earnings can increase.

FOREIGN ECONOMIC RELATIONS

The country's economic development depends heavily upon its ability to purchase machinery, transport equipment, industrial inputs, and expertise from abroad, notably from the leading industrial countries. During the early part of the 1960s the country was able to finance these import requirements not only by its continuing agricultural exports but also by drawing upon the reserves of foreign exchange built up during the 1940s and early

1950s, when earnings from raw material exports had exceeded import requirements. In the early 1950s reserves had been raised to unprecedented heights. In 1955, reserves were sufficient to purchase nearly two years' worth of imports; after 1955 these reserves were used by the government for the development effort.

The civil war, however, prompted some capital flight and, with its military requirements and disruption of normal production and transport patterns, brought an abrupt worsening of the balance of payments picture. Since 1967 Nigeria has been among the many countries whose foreign exchange holdings fall precariously below the level regarded as safe by international standards, which is equivalent to at least four months' import requirements. This means that its foreign exchange position, as reflected in the balance of payments, must be closely watched by the authorities from month to month and that any undue drain on the foreign exchange holdings of the Central Bank of Nigeria must be curbed if possible, either by strengthening direct controls on imports or by taxes, controls on bank credit, and other measures designed to curb excess private purchasing power. Priorities are carefully enforced, and military and development needs take precedence.

Merchandise imports and exports are the main determinants of a country's foreign exchange position. The net annual inflow or outflow of foreign exchange reflected in the current balance of payments is also influenced, however, by receipts and payments for a range of invisible services. Of these, the most important for Nigeria have been dividends and earnings of direct investors and miscellaneous expenditures abroad by government agencies and private firms.

Capital receipts from abroad, including direct investment and private and government loans, exceed the outflow of banking funds and other capital by a very substantial margin. During the 1960s this capital surplus covered most of the deficit on goods and services. Consequently, the country's annual shortfall of foreign exchange has been kept within manageable proportions. This has been accomplished, however, only with the help of curbs on imports, private expenditure, and remittances of investment earnings that may have a dampening effect on investment and economic growth. Moreover, import controls make it difficult for the government to combat domestic price inflation, since they cut off much of the competition from low-priced imports of consumer goods.

Nigeria has been relatively fortunate along developing countries in having a range of several raw material exports in fairly strong demand on the world market. Diversification has also been growing in other sectors, and the economy has demonstrated its strength in coming through the civil war relatively unscathed (see ch. 12, Character and Structure of the Economy). During the late 1960s the rapid development of crude petroleum exports added a very valuable source of foreign exchange, much of which will accrue to the government through improved tax and price arrangements (see ch. 13, Agriculture and Mining). There was thus hope for some improvement in the level of permissible imports at least until 1976, when oil production may be expected to level off.

After the conclusion of the civil war in early 1970, the country enjoyed friendly relations with most of the leading industrial countries that constitute the principal sources of trade, aid, and capital (see ch. 10, Foreign Relations). Political considerations thus did not exert any undue restraint on normal economic exchange. Along with other developing producers of raw materials, Nigeria has been seeking lower tariffs and price stabilization arrangements for its principal export commodities but, as of mid-1971, without signal success.

Merchandise Trade

Until the mid-1950s the country's agricultural exports generally exceeded its modest import needs, which were limited by the low per capita consumer income, lack of industrialization, and agricultural inputs that were limited chiefly to land and labor. Because of the higher rate of overall growth and more rapid progress in industry since the 1950s, there have been heavy imports of capital equipment, transport materials, raw and intermediate materials for industry, and consumer goods. Commodity imports exceeded exports, resulting in a regular annual deficit on merchandise trade. In 1950 imports had been only 10.7 percent of gross domestic product; by 1960 they were 24.7 percent of gross domestic product. In 1966, for the first time since 1955, there was a commodity trade surplus, attributed to the jump in petroleum exports and to some progress in such import-substitution industries as cotton textiles. After the imposition of controls on nonessential imports, there was a continuing small trade surplus in 1969 and 1970. During the 1967–70 period, however, the overall balance of payments had deteriorated sharply.

By 1969 crude petroleum had assumed a dominating position on the list of domestic exports, far surpassing in gross customs valuation such traditional agricultural exports as cocoa beans, groundnuts, and rubber (see table 12). During this period, however, only about 44.5 percent of the gross value of oil earnings was accruing to the country, whereas the benefit of earnings from agricultural exports accrued largely to government revenue, domestic farmers, and the marketing boards. It was estimated that more than 90

Table 12. Principal Exports of Nigeria, 1965–69

Commodity	1965	1966	1967	1968	1969
Quantity (in long tons):					
Petroleum crude oil	13,020	18,945	14,774	6,890	26,867
Cocoa beans	255	190	242	206	171
Groundnuts	512	573	20	638	518
Tin metal	11	11	10	11	10
Groundnut oil	91	108	71	109	99
Palm kernels	416	394	163	159	176
Rubber	68	70	48	52	56
Timber and plywood [1]	20,106	18,896	11,598	11,353	12,133
Groundnut cake	163	133	131	171	168
Hides and skins [2]	171	163	150	144	144
Raw cotton	14	23	33	14	14
Cotton seed	70	66	63	29	42
Palm oil	150	140	16	3	8
Value (in million Nigerian pounds) [3]:					
Petroleum crude oil	68.1	92.0	72.1	37.0	136.0
Cocoa beans	42.7	28.3	54.7	51.5	52.6
Groundnuts	37.8	40.8	35.4	38.0	35.9
Tin metal	14.9	15.4	13.0	13.7	13.9
Groundnut oil	10.0	10.0	7.2	9.5	11.1
Palm kernels	26.5	22.4	7.8	10.2	9.8
Rubber	10.9	11.5	6.3	6.3	9.6
Timber and plywood	7.7	6.8	4.3	4.3	5.2
Groundnut cake	5.3	4.7	4.2	4.9	5.0
Hides and skins	4.7	5.8	4.4	4.0	4.2
Raw cotton	3.3	5.2	6.5	3.3	3.4
Cotton seed	1.8	1.9	1.9	0.9	1.0
Palm oil	13.6	11.0	1.3	0.1	0.4
TOTAL VALUE:					
Major Commodities	247.3	255.8	219.1	183.7	288.1
Other Commodities	16.2	22.9	19.0	22.8	32.0
Domestic Exports	263.5	278.7	238.1	206.5	320.1

[1] In thousand cubic feet.
[2] In thousand hundredweight.
[3] One Nigerian pound equals U.S. $2.80.

Source: Adapted from Republic of Nigeria, Federal Ministry of Information, *Second National Development Plan, 1970–1974*, Lagos, 1970, p. 23.

percent of export value consisted of raw materials or commodities in the earliest stages of processing, such as rubber, groundnut oil, and tin metal. The campaign to increase the degree of processing, and hence the value added within the country to export commodities, was still largely in the planning stage in mid-1971.

The trade and payments pattern in the years from 1967 through

1969 was somewhat distorted by the strain of civil war conditions. As a result of wartime disruption, petroleum exports were interrupted in July 1967, producing a trade deficit in the last half of the year. Net earnings of foreign exchange from petroleum dropped promptly in 1968 and by 1969 had only slightly surpassed the 1967 level. The result was thought to be a loss in foreign exchange of more than N£100 million.

Exports of palm oil from the eastern states virtually ceased after the war began. Palm kernel oil, produced in large part in the midwest, remained on the export list but slumped along with rubber and timber exports when the former Mid-Western Region was temporarily occupied by Biafran forces in 1967. These losses in agricultural and forestry exports from the war area were balanced, however, by the cutoff of imports for the east as a result of its break with the rest of the country. Moreover, agricultural exports from the areas outside the war zone actually increased slightly during the same period.

Because of war damage to the petroleum refinery at Port Harcourt, some petroleum products that were usually produced domestically had to be imported. Another N£100 million to N£150 million in foreign exchange costs is attributed to heavy imports of military materiel in advance of, and in support of, the civil war effort, which weighed heavily on the balance of payments. These purchases are not identified as such, and it is not clear whether they appear in the balance of merchandise trade as well as under government expenditures on the balance of payments.

Merchandise imports were further affected by the tightening of import and foreign exchange controls. Higher customs duties had already been imposed as early as 1954 in an effort to restrain the impact of consumer demand on the balance of payments. In August 1965 import and excise duties had been increased, and a geographical ban was imposed on some goods. The Exchange Control Act had been passed in 1962 and was designed primarily to apply to exchange with the nonsterling areas. As the balance of payments deteriorated, fairly stringent import and foreign exchange controls were introduced under the act in October 1967. The devaluation of the British pound sterling in November 1967 produced a foreign exchange loss, since the country had held part of its reserves in sterling. Because of the basic strength of the Nigerian economy, however, it was decided not to devalue the Nigerian pound. Instead, exchange controls were further strengthened in December 1967 and in early 1968, and the distinction between the sterling and nonsterling areas was removed from the Exchange Control Act.

This process of stringent but selective import restrictions was consolidated in 1969. The authorities clamped down on the use of foreign exchange for other than wartime or developmental purposes, and the government tightened its grip on the economy's financial and commercial operations. The repatriation of profits and dividends overseas by foreign businesses was deferred, and a moratorium was imposed on repayments of foreign contractor finance. Payment was delayed on commercial imports. Internal fiscal measures were designed to curb the inflationary pressure of private demand on the balance of payments, although deficit financing was being used to inflate government expenditure throughout the period (see ch. 12, Character and Structure of the Economy).

In April 1971 the government announced that most of the import restrictions necessitated by the civil war had been lifted, except for license requirements on certain foods, beverages, and secondhand clothing. Tight exchange controls were retained, however, because, despite the tremendous gain in oil exports, the balance of payments had not shown sufficient improvement to permit a full return to the former liberal exchange system. The country was still importing more goods than could be paid for by the due date. Only 40 percent of dividend earnings could be transferred abroad during fiscal 1971/72; similar rules applied to management and consultant fees, royalties, and patents; foreign nationals were permitted to transfer only 40 percent of their net taxed income or a maximum of N£3,000 per annum. Currency allowances for foreign travel were further reduced for 1971/72, and certain arrangements for deferred payment for imports of certain items were made mandatory.

Significant imports range evenly over a very extensive variety of products. Despite restrictions on nonessential imports, foodstuffs were still a significant category of imports in 1968 and 1969 (see table 13). Because of the development effort, however, the great bulk of imports fell into two broad categories: machinery and transport equipment and intermediate goods for industry. Intermediate products are listed in the Standard International Trade Classification under "Manufactures classified chiefly by material" (textile yarns and fabrics, metals and semimanufactures, paper and pulp, and others) and under "Chemicals and related products," which comprises soap, plastics, fertilizers, paints, explosives, and other goods, as well as chemical elements and compounds. The cost of imports of mineral fuels and lubricants had been greatly reduced by the output of the domestic petroleum refinery.

The United Kingdom remained the leading market for the country's exports, notably crude petroleum, cocoa beans, and tin. It had

Table 13. Imports and Exports of Nigeria by Commodity Group, 1968–70
(value in million Nigerian pounds) [1]

Standard international trade classification	Imports			Exports [2]		
	1968	1969	1970	1968	1969	1970
Mineral fuels and lubricants_____	14.5	15.6	11.0	37.5	133.0	258.0
Food and live animals (including cocoa)_____	14.2	20.9	28.8	65.7	69.9	84.4
Crude materials (inedible)_____	5.7	5.7	8.3	71.1	73.2	61.5
Manufactures classified chiefly by material_____	54.7	72.0	113.2	16.4	17.4	19.5
Animal and vegetable oils and fats_____	0.3	0.2	0.5	12.9	15.3	16.4
Machinery and transport equipment_____	59.9	73.2	149.7	0	0.8	0.5
Chemicals and related products___	22.4	30.4	44.1	0.3	0.3	0.4
Beverages and tobacco_____	1.2	0.8	2.0	0.01	0	0
Miscellaneous manufactures_____	14.0	13.4	19.7	0.1	0.3	0.2
Other_____	5.7	16.5	9.1	2.5	7.9	2.1
TOTAL_____	192.6	248.7	386.4	206.5	318.1	443.0

[1] One Nigerian pound equals U.S. $2.80.
[2] 1969 and 1970 data may include reexports; source does not specify.

Source: Adapted from *Standard Bank Review* [London], April 1971; Republic of Nigeria, Federal Office of Statistics, *Nigerian Trade Summary, December 1968*, Lagos, 1969; and Republic of Nigeria, Federal Office of Statistics, *Nigerian Trade Summary, December 1969*, Lagos, 1970.

also retained a very substantial lead over other industrial countries as a source of imports, notably motor vehicles and machinery. Imports of machinery and transport equipment from the United Kingdom in 1969, for example, totaled about N£30 million, compared to only N£12 million from the Federal Republic of Germany (West Germany), the nearest competitor, and about N£10 million from the United States.

In 1967 and 1969 the Netherlands was in second place as a market, taking chiefly crude petroleum as well as cocoa beans and cocoa butter for its active cocoa industry, but it ranked only fifth as a source of imports (see table 14). The active participation of United States oil firms in the growing petroleum industry was beginning to augment that country's role as a market for Nigerian exports by 1969. The United States was second as a market for crude petroleum but only sixth on the list of cocoa markets. As a source of imports, it was about on a par with West Germany, furnishing chiefly machinery and transport equipment, wheat, and a wide range of intermediate goods, such as steel pipe.

The six countries of the European Economic Community (Common Market) were growing in aggregate importance as trading partners, with the Netherlands and West Germany in the lead. France was the principal market for groundnuts. The lowering of Common Market tariffs on tropical raw materials, including cocoa beans and palm oil, extended to nonassociated African countries such as Nigeria, appeared to assure the continuation of this trend. In July 1966 Nigeria concluded an agreement providing for association with the Common Market. At the outbreak of the civil war, however, the agreement had not been ratified; in mid-1971 the prospect for agreement appeared uncertain. The government was concerned over the consequences for Nigerian exports of eventual British adherence to the Common Market.

Most of the exports to Eastern Europe consisted of cocoa beans to the Soviet Union, the fourth largest customer after West Germany in 1969, with a cocoa import from Nigeria of about N£8 million. None of the communist countries was a significant source of imports. The People's Republic of China (Communist China) was in the lead, furnishing goods, consisting mainly of cotton fabrics, in the amount of about N£5 million in 1969.

Trade with other African countries was insignificant in value. Imports consisted chiefly of cotton yarns and fabrics from Egypt and petroleum products from Algeria, along with a little powdered coffee from the Ivory Coast and zinc from Congo (Kinshasa). Exports were extremely limited and consisted mainly of petroleum

Table 14. Principal Trading Partners of Nigeria, 1967–69
(value in million Nigerian pounds)*

Country of origin or destination	Imports			Exports		
	1967	1968	1969	1967	1968	1969
United Kingdom	64.6	59.9	86.3	70.3	61.9	87.7
Netherlands	9.3	7.8	11.6	30.8	27.0	42.8
United States	27.8	22.3	29.3	18.5	16.0	40.0
West Germany	25.2	21.2	26.4	25.1	17.9	19.3
Italy	10.7	13.8	13.5	14.1	13.1	14.5
France	9.4	7.2	8.0	22.4	11.5	31.9
Communist China, Soviet Union, and countries of Eastern Europe	13.8	12.1	14.3	7.5	12.2	12.3
African countries	2.6	4.3	5.5	2.8	2.0	3.0
Other countries	60.1	44.0	53.8	46.6	44.9	66.6
TOTAL	223.5	192.6	248.7	238.1	206.5	318.1

*One Nigerian pound equals U.S. $2.80.
Source: Adapted from Republic of Nigeria, Federal Office of Statistics, *Nigerian Trade Summary, December 1967*, Lagos, 1968; Republic of Nigeria, Federal Office of Statistics, *Nigerian Trade Summary, December 1968*, Lagos, 1969; and Republic of Nigeria, Federal Office of Statistics, *Nigerian Trade Summary, December 1969*, Lagos, 1970.

products to Ghana and Sierra Leone, as well as shipments rejected and returned to Angola.

Balance of Payments

Despite the appearance of a surplus on the balance of merchandise trade beginning in 1966, there was a sharp deterioration in the overall balance of payments beginning in 1967 that had not been entirely reversed by the end of 1970. When it became evident that adequate foreign loans would not be forthcoming, there was recourse to draw on the country's foreign exchange reserves to finance the First National Development Plan (see ch. 12, Character and Structure of the Economy). Consequently, the flight of capital in anticipation of the civil war and the growing expenditure of foreign exchange for military purposes led to a serious drain on the country's foreign exchange reserves, amounting to the equivalent of US$105 million in the first six months of 1967. Official reserves were equal to US$122 million at the end of 1967, equivalent to less than 2½ months' current imports. Reserves were held steady in 1968 and increased slightly in 1969. By February 1971, because of improved oil exports, reserves had returned to the mid-1960s level, which was equivalent to 3 months' imports in 1970.

Details on annual net movements in the principal components of the country's foreign exchange position are reflected in its balance of payments (see table 15). The current account, representing the net flow of goods and services between the country and the rest of the world, is composed of merchandise exports and imports and of services (invisibles). The deficit on current account is offset by the balance of capital payments, private and official, and by unrequited transfers, which include such items as grant aid, private gifts, charitable contributions, missionary expenditures, emigrant remittances, and other receipts for which there is no equivalent compensation. An overall deficit on current plus capital account must be covered by monetary movements in gold and foreign exchange reserves and International Monetary Fund (IMF) balances.

The foreign transactions of the three eastern states are excluded from the balance of payments data for the years 1967–69, since they did not take place through the federal government. The balance of payments during these years was also materially affected by foreign exchange restrictions, such as the ban on remittances of investment income.

The interruption of petroleum exports in 1967 and 1968 and their resumption and increase in 1969 had the most material effect

Table 15. *Balance of Payments of Nigeria, 1966–69*
(in million Nigerian pounds) [1]

	1966		1967 [2]		1968 [2]		1969 [2]	
	Oil	Total	Oil	Total	Oil	Total	Oil	Total
Current Account:								
Exports[3]	91.9	280.8	72.0	238.8	37.0	208.4	131.0	313.3
Imports[4]	−19.5	−250.7	−17.5	−218.4	−9.9	−191.1	−11.1	−228.9
Trade Balance	72.4	30.1	54.5	−20.4	27.1	17.3	119.9	84.4
Service payments:								
Travel	−2.4	−12.5	−2.0	−10.7	−5.2	−15.7	−1.9	−12.9
Transportation and insurance	0	3.4	0	0.8	0	2.2	0	4.2
Investment income	−19.4	−74.3	−19.8	−40.4	0	−53.9	0	−55.0
Government transactions	0	2.5	0	−23.0	0	−15.5	0	−23.9
Other service payments	−36.1	−43.4	−29.5	−37.8	−23.0	−35.7	−42.9	−57.2
Service Payments (net)	−57.9	−124.3	−51.3	−111.1	−28.2	−118.6	−44.8	−144.8
Balance on current account	14.5	−94.2	3.2	−90.7	−1.1	−101.3	75.1	−60.4
Capital Account:								
Private capital (net)	28.9	66.8	45.5	51.5	29.9	79.2	−19.2	36.4
Direct investment	28.9	55.0	45.5	39.5	29.9	46.4	−19.2	7.8
Loans	0	13.0	0	9.9	0	14.4	0	−0.5
Receipts	0	0	0	12.7	0	17.2	0	3.5
Payments	0	0	0	−2.8	0	−2.8	0	−4.0
Short-term trade credit	0	−1.2	0	2.1	0	18.4	0	29.1
Official capital (net)	0	13.5	0	9.9	0	0.8	0	1.4

Loan receipts	0	24.9	0	13.6	0	7.5	0	9.4
Loan payments	0	−11.4	0	−6.8	0	−9.0	0	−10.0
Receipts of transfer payments	0	2.1	0	7.7	0	17.2	0	10.4
Capital Account (net)	28.9	82.4	45.5	69.1	29.9	97.2	−19.2	48.2
Balance on current and capital account	43.4	−11.8	48.7	−21.6	28.8	−4.1	55.9	−12.2
Net change in external reserves[5,6]		11.3		36.8		0.7		−2.2
Net errors and omissions		14.3		−12.1		7.1		16.4

[1] One Nigerian pound equals US$2.80.
[2] Excluding former Eastern Region.
[3] f.o.b. (free on board).
[4] c.i.f. (cost, insurance, and freight).
[5] Minus sign indicates increase in reserves.
[6] Including assets of federal and state governments.

Source: Adapted from Scott R. Pearson, *Petroleum and the Nigerian Economy*, Stanford, 1970.

on the current balance of payments. In the balance of payments, merchandise trade is valued exclusive of insurance and freight, and delayed payments are recorded during the year in which they occur rather than for the year in which the merchandise is delivered. Consequently, the trade balance showed a deficit in 1967. Non-oil trade showed a consistent deficit but was more than covered by oil exports in 1968 and 1969.

Despite the deferral of some payments, net investment income paid abroad remained the largest deficit item among invisible payments (services) through 1969. Most of this consisted of direct investment income—dividends and undistributed profits of foreign companies operating in Nigeria. Interest on the foreign debt produced a net outflow of only a few million pounds a year during the 1964–69 period. The country's external public debt is low and favorably structured. The substantial increase in the deficit on government transactions since 1967 may reflect military expenditures. The category "other service payments" included contractors' fees and fees for technical advice paid by resident oil companies to nonresident companies and represented a fairly substantial outflow from the oil sector during the period. Tourism and other travel expenditures made a smaller contribution, about N£9 million to N£13 million a year, to the current payments deficit.

As a result of all these factors, the balance of payments on current account showed a record deficit for the year 1968 (excluding the three eastern states). The net outflow for the non-oil sector was considerably higher in 1969, notably for merchandise imports and government transactions, but the strong gain in petroleum exports reduced the deficit on current account to N£60 million.

The inflow of private capital was curtailed in 1966 and still further in 1967. Since investment in the petroleum sector increased substantially in these two years, the reduction in direct investment in other sectors was particularly disquieting. In 1967 there was actually a net deficit of N£6 million in other direct investment. Net receipts of official capital declined steadily throughout the period. Public investment was curtailed for the duration of the civil war, and the government did not want to incur foreign indebtedness to help finance the war, relying instead on deficit budget financing.

Whereas in 1967 the authorities covered the deficit on current and capital account by drawing down foreign exchange reserves, in 1968 and 1969 much of the slack was taken up by private capital and by official grants (transfers). The apparent inflow of private foreign capital in 1968 and 1969 was deceptive; the favorable balance on this item actually represented the withholding by Nigeria of foreign exchange payments on account of commercial imports and remittances of investment income. By the end of April 1970 there was still a backlog in deferred payments for commercial imports and a backlog on income from investment. Some of this investment income was subsequently released, but by April 1971 the backlog of import payments had mounted further.

Despite the material improvement in foreign exchange reserves by mid-1971, the authorities did not feel that vigilance could be relaxed. Reserves would cover only three months' current imports; a substantial backlog of deferred import payments remained; and development needs for the Second National Development Plan would require a material increase in imports of capital equipment and intermediate goods. The dearth of foreign exchange was expected to be the most serious resource bottleneck in carrying out the provisions of the plan. In spite of the stringent import restrictions, foreign exchange budgeting, and the greatly improved export prospects, the government planners anticipated that substantial amounts of foreign assistance would be required to meet the plan's goals.

Besides the need to finance the enormous current and capital requirements of the plan, the government in 1971 faced the challenge of reducing the backlog of external payments from the war years, rebuilding some modest balance of payments holdings as a contingency reserve against the future, and maintaining the stability of the country's currency. Considerable inflationary pressure had developed during 1969 from pent-up consumer demand and the deficit spending of the war years, and beginning in early 1969 internal prices began rising significantly (se ch. 12, Character and Structure of the Economy).

The government planners and potential lenders concurred that, if the country were to obtain the private foreign capital needed for reconstruction and development, an early return to its former liberal trade and foreign exchange policies would seem to be indicated; before this could take place, however, the short-term liabilities accumulated during the war would have to be repaid, and the foreign exchange position would have to be improved. Although the outlook for petroleum earnings appeared better by mid-1971 than earlier projections had indicated, the deficit in trade in other sectors may be high, and the private capital inflow may be lower than the planners had hoped. Moreover, petroleum earnings are expected to level off after 1976, when import requirements will continue to mount. A year after the inauguration of the Second National Development Plan the external outlook thus remained highly uncertain.

Foreign Aid and Investment

With the largest population in sub-Saharan Africa, Nigeria has been one of the leading recipients of foreign aid and credits from the industrial countries and multilateral organizations. Receipts of grants and credits from the communist countries, on the other hand, have been extremely modest. Between 1954 and 1969 the country had received more than the equivalent of US$531 million from world donors and lenders. These receipts, which excluded about US$27.2 million in grants from the United Kingdom between 1950 and 1960, as well as aid from agencies of the United Nations other than the World Bank Group, averaged about US$35 million a year from 1960 through 1964, with Nigeria only tenth on the list of African recipients. After the mid-1960s, when Nigeria had drawn down its favorable foreign exchange reserves, its need for foreign assistance increased abruptly. From 1965 through 1968 loan and grant receipts from the Organization for Economic Cooperation and Development (OECD) countries and the World Bank Group averaged US$98 million a year, and Nigeria was the third leading recipient after Algeria and Congo (Kinshasa).

From the OECD countries (including the Western European countries, the United States, Canada, and Japan) receipts from 1960 through 1968 totaled the equivalent of US$273 million. Aggregate financing received from the World Bank Group as of mid-1971 came to US$367 million, including a loan of US$80 million in postwar rehabilitation approved in April 1971.

Nigeria's receipts from the group were the highest in Africa, exceeding the sizable credits extended to the Republic of South Africa during the 1950s. At the end of 1970 lending from the World Bank Group represented about 40 percent of the country's external debt. Most of the credits received from the group came from the International Bank of Reconstruction and Development (IBRD, commonly known as the World Bank); others came from the International Development Association (IDA) and the International Finance Corporation (IFC).

Combined net official receipts from the OECD countries and multilateral agencies during the 1967–69 period averaged US$101.5 million a year; of this, US$71.4 million a year was bilateral, and US$30.1 million a year was multilateral. Annual average aid receipts per capita of population totaled US$0.93 in the 1960–66 period and US$1.62 in the 1967–69 period. Among ninety-two aid recipient countries in the entire world, Nigeria ranked eighty-first in official aid receipts per capita of population in the 1967–69 period. Aid receipts from the communist countries from 1954 through 1967, totaling only US$14 million, consisted entirely of economic aid from the non-Soviet countries of Eastern Europe.

Loans and grants from foreign governments and international financial agencies had not been very significant as sources of finance during the 1950s. The International Cooperation Administration of the United States made some grants, and the IBRD made a loan of US$28 million toward the financing of the Bornu railway extension.

Most of the foreign aid received has gone into economic or social infrastructure; dams, ports, roads, and other transport facilities; education; or health. Financing for industrial or agricultural projects has relied heavily on private foreign investment and internal public saving (see ch. 12, Character and Structure of the Economy). One of the projects that received the largest amount of foreign aid during the period of the first six-year development plan was the Kainji (Niger) Dam. It absorbed some US$78 million from the IBRD, US$25 million from the Italian government, US$14 million from the United States, US$8.4 million from the United Kingdom, and US$5.6 million from the Netherlands. Other loans received since independence have been used for installation and development of ports, railway extension and materiel, water supply, and electricity development. It is difficult to make a quantitative assessment of the amount of technical assistance received, but an increasing amount has been forthcoming from such agencies as the United States Agency for International Development (AID) and the Ford Foundation and various United Nations agencies, such as the International Labor Organization (ILO), the World Health Organization (WHO), the United Nations Education, Scientific and Cultural Organization (UNESCO), and the Food and Agriculture Organization (FAO).

By 1964 the United Nations Special Fund had committed funds for aid projects worth more than US$12 million, and many others were under active consideration. The projects underway between 1960 and 1964 included the Kainji (Niger) Dam feasibility study; a fisheries survey in the former Western Region and the Sokoto River Valley soil and water resources survey, and the Federal Teacher Training College, the University of Lagos Engineering Faculty, and vocational training aid.

The First National Development Plan had been predicated on the assumption that about 50 percent of the required financing could be derived from external sources of finance, including grants, credits, and private investment. Most of these funds did not materialize, however; by the end of the plan period foreign loans had in fact amounted to only about 25 percent of realized capital investment. The political crisis preceding civil war intensified the problem by provoking capital flight and increasing the demands on available foreign exchange. During the plan, promises of aid were received from several industrial countries. The United States committed US$224 million, including capital grants, technical assistance, and Export-Import Bank loans; the United Kingdom promised more than US$28 million.

The progress report on the First National Development Plan noted that one very important lesson learned from the experience of the plan was that bilateral aid is almost invariably tied to the goods and services of the donor country and is therefore not as attractive as had been thought initially. In consequence, by the time the Second National Development Plan was launched in mid-1970 there was a greater realization that implementation of development plans must rely more and more on internal resources.

Actual utilization of aid during the first plan lagged behind commitments; there was some overspending of domestic resources on administration as a result of military requirements for the civil war, but there was an overall shortfall of about one-fifth in actual expenditure (see ch. 12, Character and Structure of the Economy).

The Second National Development Plan aims at securing about 19 percent of the financing of public investment from foreign aid and investment. This would require a minimum annual net capital inflow of about N£150 million. The prospects for securing this amount were somewhat uncertain; the administrative demands of the civil war period had interfered with project preparation, and most present-day prospective aid lenders required thorough preparation of project feasibility analyses before committing aid funds. The ambitious plans for establishment of heavy industries, such as an iron and steel complex and a petrochemical industry, were not sufficiently assured of profitable operation in the initial stages to be very attractive to private investors. The government's overall concern with, and careful management of, the foreign exchange crisis, however, appeared to have made a favorable impression on prospective official lenders. In mid-1971 a consultative group for Nigeria, composed of representatives of the World Bank Group and prospective bilateral lenders, was meeting to consider the country's aid requirements, and the finance commissioner reported that the government leaders had hopes that the conclusion would be favorable.

Except in the petroleum industry, private foreign investment has been lagging. During the 1950s direct investment by foreign firms had been an important source of finance for domestic capital formation. Although investment had been low in 1950, it reached a high in 1960 that had not been regained by the mid-1960s. At the end of 1962 total foreign investment in fixed assets in Nigeria was the equivalent of US$324.8 million, of which 74.9 percent was from the United Kingdom, 9.9 percent from the United States, 3.9 percent from continental Western Europe, and 11.3 percent from other countries.

After 1960 domestic public and private investment assumed a more important role in capital formation. The lag in foreign investment after independence was attributed to several causes: a "wait-and-see" attitude on the part of potential foreign investors; successive economic slowdowns in industrial countries; the political crisis that began in western Nigeria in May 1962; and the eventual crisis that culminated in civil war.

The commercial exploitation of the country's petroleum resources brought a revival of capital inflow for exploration and development. A 1970 source estimated that the net direct and indirect benefits of private foreign investment in petroleum had amounted to about 7 percent of precivil war national income and might be expected to increase to about 18 percent of the much larger national income in the first half of the 1970s.

Actual figures on private foreign investment in petroleum or in other sectors were not available in 1971. A rough United States government estimate of total United States investment in Nigeria through 1971 was between US$350 million and US$500 million, almost all in the petroleum industry, with a few other small, scattered plants and some bank investment.

DOMESTIC TRADE

Because of the relatively low income level of much of the population the greater part of domestic trade in consumer goods is concerned with foodstuffs (see ch. 13, Agriculture and Mining). Probably second in volume is trade in low-cost products of small-scale artisan manufacture, including such goods as baskets and mats, simple tools, handmade clothing, and cheap footwear. Imports of consumer goods grew throughout the 1960s and penetrated the markets of the interior. Such imported wares as sugar are often sold at village stores or markets in extremely small units, such as a lump or two of sugar at a time. The luxury imported foods and other goods that were imported in growing volume until the outbreak of the civil war are sold principally at the larger city shops to a clientele composed of relatively high income groups.

Except in rubber, the export trade has been taken over almost entirely by the government marketing boards, apart from the activities of their private agents in the field (see ch. 13, Agriculture and Mining). The wholesale and large-scale retail trade in imports and domestic products in the mid-1960s was dominated almost entirely by a few large foreign-owned firms that enjoyed advantages of cost and scale of operation as well as ties of ownership or traditional trade with overseas suppliers. The United Africa Company, a subsidiary of Unilever of the United Kingdom, is probably the largest wholesale and retail trading company in the country and operates large department stores called Kingsway stores in all the major cities. Other important companies are Leventis, Paterson, Zochonis, John Holt, Chellerams, Mandilas, Karaberis, and several others of equal consequence. As elsewhere in Africa, Lebanese and Greek traders as well as British firms have established large-scale commercial enterprises. In some cases these firms have established manufacturing capacity in Nigeria to produce items that they formerly imported.

Advertising is concentrated in the urban centers. Brand consciousness and brand loyalty—particularly to established British brands—were formerly acute among the urban African population but have been dissipated somewhat by increasing variety and competition. Nigerian consumers are extremely quality conscious.

Most of the itinerant traders and established traders at open-air markets in town and country are women (see ch. 6, Social Systems). Some operate on a very large scale and have their affiliates at great distances. Their distribution system is most effective and, because of the improvement in the road network since 1950, the system of "mammy wagons," or wooden-bodied trucks, is able to cover most of the southern half of the country and penetrate to the main distribution centers of the north. Interregional trade has been increasing and, because of the variety of climate and other conditions encountered within the country, interregional trade in foodstuffs and raw materials largely takes the place occupied by foreign trade in many other African countries (see ch. 13, Agriculture and Mining).

The market women and other small-scale traders are obliged to operate on a minimum of working capital, often refilling their stocks daily from wholesalers, importers, or manufacturers. The larger foreign-owned stores have long enjoyed an advantage in their readier supply of capital as well as in ownership ties, overseas contacts, and other respects. Consequently, the government has moved, as in a number of other independent African countries, to legislate Nigerianization of the distributive trades at a more rapid rate than in other sectors. In early 1971 the government announced that a new agency would be established to supervise the Nigerianization of foreign enterprises Firms that had appointed Nigerian managers as "window-dressing" were criticized, and it was stressed that in the general distributive trades, both wholesale and retail, firms would have to be turned over entirely to Nigerians, and no quota would be allowed for foreign management. The government intends to extend credits to prospective Nigerian entrepreneurs in commerce and other sectors.

Many women combine the roles of food producer, trader, and customer. Most of the market women are primarily farmers or housewives who process food in the home, and this work is far more time consuming than the trading they do. Such women may gather daily in the village or by the wayside to trade in perishable foods, but these gatherings are not usually classed as markets. Daily permanent markets occur as a rule only in the larger towns, and it is only here that a significant number of the sellers are full-time traders.

In many of the rural areas the week was traditionally reckoned on an economic basis, with the market day as the standard of reference. Even since the introduction of the seven-day week by the Europeans, the days of the week are often named for the names of the principal places in which markets are held on that day. Among the Yoruba of southwest Nigeria, where a four-day market week prevails, the markets are a method of assessing space and time. In Ado-Ekiti, for example, the first day is known as "market day," followed by "market's second day," "market's third day," and "market day is tomorrow" in the local dialect.

Anthropologists have studied the traditional market cycles in West Africa and have mapped the geographic occurrence of four-day market weeks, which extends across the southern forest zone from the Cross River through the areas inhabited by the Ibo and Yoruba people and beyond the western border to Dahomey. There is a close association between the four-day market week and the eight-day market week, which occurs only in the four-day market zone. A five-day market week is found among certain people of eastern Nigeria, including the Tiv. Three-day and six-day market weeks are more rare. The seven-day market week prevails in the north among the Hausa and is often associated with Islamization.

The periodicity of markets varies considerably from one ethnic group to the next, and a number of detailed studies of local market systems have been published. Among the Yoruba, for example, it has been found generally that, where there are fewer than fifty persons to the square mile, there will be very few periodic markets, whereas above that level of density there is a regular pattern of periodic markets, distributed at a fairly even distance of about 7.2 miles from each other. The markets are not held in the villages or population centers.

ECONOMIC ATTITUDES AND VALUES

Sociological and cultural attitudes common to most of the country's ethnic groups tend to favor the initiation of business enterprise but to impede its optimum development once the enterprise is started. The drive for wealth is impressively strong, particularly in the south (see ch. 11, Value Systems). Status considerations in the Ibo and Yoruba cultures in particular provide incentive to establish a business in trade or industry with the object of achieving wealth. Indigenous businessmen are particularly adept at recognizing and responding rapidly to economic opportunity. The search for new ways of making a profit is unremitting. Whenever one entrepreneur introduces an innovation designed to increase profit or take advantage of a new market, other entrepreneurs will rapidly follow his lead, so that returns are forced down by competitive pressure. The more successful entrepreneurs try to keep one jump ahead of the field. Instead of developing an existing business, they will often start a second or third business in a new line that has not become overcrowded. Dispersal of effort over several businesses is quite common among Nigerian entrepreneurs and often cited as a cause of inadequate followup control in management.

There seems to have been a definite improvement in the quality of entrepreneurship since the early 1950s, but observers disagree on the outlook for the future. The correlation between education and training on the one hand and efficient management on the other is very weak. The skill that appears to be most lacking is management of the ongoing concern, and it has been suggested that this is attributable not to lack of education or experience but to basic sociocultural attitudes shared by most ethnic groups.

Although status mobility through the acquisition of wealth is encouraged, once entrepreneurial position is achieved conspicuous leisure is considered a sign of superior status, and it is considered degrading for an entrepreneur or manager to concern himself with supervising the performance of subordinates. Skilled and reliable intermediate personnel are in short supply, and the ability to properly delegate authority or responsibility is also largely lacking. In surveys of individual industries, observers found that poor performance was attributable to such factors as failure to maintain equipment, inadequate coordination of raw material purchases with product orders, pilfering and embezzlement by the senior clerical staff, and absence of conscientious supervision on the job. In the baking industry, for example, three-quarters of potential profits were lost to raw material wastage, damaging of bread during baking, and extensive employee pilferage.

The entrepreneurs themselves usually cite lack of credit as the principal obstacle to success in industrial or trading enterprise. One study, however, found that the weight of the evidence pointed to lack of absorptive capacity by recipients as the main obstacle to credit utilization. The lines of production selected by indigenous entrepreneurs are usually not those requiring large amounts of capital equipment in relation to labor or output. The most successful small-scale industries have been those that are technologically simple and have a fairly low investment threshold.

Another study found that small entrepreneurs are very dependent upon the extended family for capital to establish a firm. Similarly, the resources of the extended family are usually used to finance the apprenticeship training of younger members; this, in turn, augments the supply of potential entrepreneurs. One survey found that 96 percent of the apprentices interviewed were sponsored by members of the extended family. Once a young man has received his training and established his own firm, however, the extended family will begin to draw upon his receipts for current consumption and thus operates to impede the expansion of the business through reinvestment of profits.

CHAPTER 15

NATIONAL SECURITY

In 1971 Nigeria was seeking to stabilize public order and internal security after a decade of independence in which national unity had been threatened repeatedly by violent upheavals arising from regional cutural differences, political rivalries, and ethnic antagonisms (see ch. 3, Historical Setting; ch. 9, Government and Political Dynamics). The republic was in its fifth year of military rule after a bloody coup d'etat in 1966, and its people were attempting to adjust to the social dislocation generated by nearly three years of divisive civil war.

Outside the boundaries of the closely policed urban areas, family ties and the traditional respect for group authority operated to control the conduct of much of the rural population (see ch. 11, Value Systems). Lawlessness in these areas generally was not a serious problem. A rising incidence of armed robbery in the larger towns and along major highways generally was attributed to a proliferation of weapons left over from the war and to rising unemployment. Governmental decrees had imposed severe penalties on antisocial behavior, and coordinated action by the police and the army was used to combat these threats to public order.

With national unity as its goal, the Federal Military Government (FMG) had undertaken a broad program to stabilize public order through federalization and reform of the institutions responsible for internal security. Despite changes in the constitution the FMG had retained the structure of the judiciary (see ch. 9, Government and Political Dynamics). A dual system of codified criminal law, introduced in the early 1960s to accommodate the Muslim north and the non-Muslim south, remained in effect. The codes had been reinforced by a number of decrees issued since the beginning of military rule.

Responsibility for the operation of penal institutions, which formerly was divided between national and local authorities, had been assumed by the federal government. A program of prison reform to relieve conditions of acute overcrowding and to promote inmate rehabilitation was in process.

The police system, which previously had been divided between national and regional authority, was also in the process of centralization. In mid-1971 the federal Nigeria Police Force (NPF) of about 30,000 men and women—a product of British tradition and training—was the group primarily responsible for maintaining national internal security in all twelve states. Local police personnel from the northern states and Western State were being absorbed by the NPF and were being retrained to its higher standards.

To satisfy wartime requirements, the size of the national army had been increased twentyfold between 1966 and 1970. The army's primary mission was to aid the police in maintaining internal security, and its impressive size provided ample protection against threats to the nation's territorial integrity by any of its African neighbors.

In 1971 the armed forces consisted of an army of about 240,000, a navy of about 5,000, and a developing air force of about 7,000. Supplied with substantial quantities of modern military equipment from Western and communist sources, the army—one of the strongest and most recently combat-experienced light infantry forces in Africa—was being reorganized and redistributed throughout the country. The navy, equipped with light coastal vessels, basically performed a coast guard role. The air force inventory included fewer than forty combat aircraft, including Soviet jet ground attack planes and armed trainers built in Italy and Czechoslovakia. Nigerian pilots were being trained to fly these aircraft, which had been operated during the civil war by hired foreign nationals.

The nearly 14 million men of military age made the republic's military manpower potential the largest in Africa. Those with technical abilities, however, remained in short supply. The cost of maintaining the large military establishment had been consistently high, and defense appropriations were expected to consume large segments of the federal budgets for at least several more years.

FORMS OF SOCIAL CONTROL

In 1971 the government's efforts to establish and maintain public order were based on the nationally accepted concept of supremacy of the law, particularly as it applied to criminal activity. The nation's system of criminal law was entirely statutory and based largely on two separate criminal codes. The Northern Penal Code applied to inhabitants of the six states of the former Northern Region; the Nigerian Criminal Code had universal application in the remaining six states in the south. Some customary laws dealing with criminal offenses remained in effect, but these had been incorporated into one of the two codes or were supported by separate legislation. Despite the abolition of unwritten customary criminal laws in the early 1960s, there was evidence that some were still enforced by traditional authorities in certain areas.

The Nigerian Criminal Code is generally based on the uncodified principles of English criminal law as modified to fit local conditions; a crime is punishable only by the state. Offenses are classified as felonies, misdemeanors, or simple offenses. These distinctions are based largely on the punishments attached to each offense. Felonies are acts that are declared by law to be felonies or that are punishable by death or imprisonment for at least three years. Offenses classified as misdemeanors are generally those for which imprisonment of from six months to three years may be imposed. All other transgressions are classified as simple offenses.

Specific offenses enumerated within the code are categorized as those against persons, offenses relating to property and contracts, and offenses against the state. Crimes against persons include murder, manslaughter, assault, rape, abduction, bigamy, defamation, and other acts or omissions that endanger life or health. The most important offenses against property include various forms of theft: robbery, demanding with menaces, burglary and housebreaking, obtaining by false pretenses, receiving stolen property, and fraud. Other crimes involving property include arson, malicious damage, forgery, and personation.

Offenses against the state are specified as treason, treachery, sedition, unlawful assembly, membership in unlawful societies, publication or communication of official secrets, perjury, the practice of witchcraft, and the conduct of trials by ordeal. Offenses against public morals, those against public health, and cruelty to animals similarly are classified as crimes against the state.

In addition to those offenses defined in the Criminal Code, certain other acts have been defined as criminal by separate ordinances. Under the Collective Punishment Ordinance, military governors of the southern states may impose collective fines on the inhabitants of a village or district if investigation indicates they have colluded with, harbored, rescued, or failed to prevent the escape of a criminal about whom an official public announcement has been published within the village or district. All orders made under the ordinance are final and cannot be contested through appeal to higher judicial authority.

To deal with isolated threats to public order in specific areas, the Preservation of Peace Ordinance permits state governors to prescribe periods of time during which all arms and ammunition in the possession of inhabitants (other than the security forces) must be delivered to the police. Anyone violating the proclamation may be arrested without a warrant. The cost of providing additional security forces to enforce such proclamations may be levied in the form of a collective fine against the area's inhabitants.

The Northern Penal Code is based on the Sudan Code, which was derived from the Penal Code of India and ultimately from English common law. It establishes for the northern states a single criminal code that contains nothing incompatible with Islam yet is acceptable also to the area's non-Muslims. All northern courts administer the same criminal law, and no one is liable to punishment under customary law. Punishment is imposed by all courts through reference to the Northern Penal Code or some other ordinance or written law.

Unlike the Nigerian Criminal Code, the Northern Penal Code reflects considerable deviations from the English common law of crimes, largely because of its need to reflect the principles of Islamic law for the area's Muslim inhabitants. Provocation, for example, is a mitigation of punishment in cases of homicide in the northern states but not in those of the south. Crimes under traditional Muslim law, such as adultery, drinking of alcoholic beverages, and insults to the modesty of women, are preserved in the northern code, but they are not crimes per se in southern jurisdictions. Even in the north, many of the criminal sanctions apply only to Muslims.

The Northern Penal Code does not contain references to such offenses as treason, sedition, customs violations, or counterfeiting. Statutory laws dealing with such activities have been enacted separately and appear as an addendum to the code.

Punishments for criminal acts specified in both codes generally reflect a common attitude oriented toward deterrence of criminal activity. The principles of rehabilitation and social readjustment are acknowledged in both laws through cursory provisions dealing with probation and court prerogatives in the dismissal of charges. Lack of facilities to administer a reliable probation service has generally limited its use to cases dealing with juvenile offenders.

The range of punishments in both codes includes death, imprisonment, whipping, fines, and forfeiture of property. A sentence of death may not be passed on any offender who is less than seventeen years of age or on a pregnant woman. Before the advent of military government in 1966, death sentences usually were by hanging. Since the establishment of military government, however, there has been an increased tendency to execute convicted offenders by shooting, often in public.

Corporal punishment is generally administered in the form of a specified number of strokes by a light rod, cane, or whip with a single lash. In the south, courts are empowered to order corporal punishment for males under the age of seventeen in addition to the particular punishment that the Criminal Code allows for the offense. At the court's discretion, however, corporal punishment may be substituted for other specified punishments in the cases of such offenders.

The Northern Penal Code contains many of the mandatory punishments prescribed for certain misdeeds by Islamic law. These include corporal punishment for adultery and consumption of alcoholic beverages and imprisonment for theft; imprisonment for theft is a modification of the traditional Muslim practice of cutting off the thief's hand.

INCIDENCE OF CRIME

The scope of criminal activity is not known with any reasonable degree of accuracy because the government in 1971 did not have a comprehensive system of reporting statistics on crime. Before the advent of military government in 1966, the NPF published annual reports that reflected criminal activity; they did not, however, reveal data on crime dealt with at the level of the separate local authority police. These reports were discontinued in 1966, shortly before the civil war.

Despite the lack of statistical reporting, certain trends in criminal activity are reflected in the Nigerian press, in statements by the federal commissioner of internal affairs and police, and by various new decrees issued by the military government.

In the aftermath of nearly three years of civil war and rising unemployment, the incidence of armed robbery had increased throughout the country, particularly in the eastern states that constituted the former secessionist Biafran republic. Large numbers of unemployed ex-Biafran soldiers roamed the area and subjected the population to acts of violence. Widespread proliferation of firearms occurred during the civil war. Despite efforts of the federal army and police to collect them, many were still in the hands of persons who had participated in the war. In East Central State large numbers of guns were recovered in late 1970 in a series of house-to-house searches.

The Robbery and Firearms (Special Provision) Decree was enacted by the FMG in mid-1970 to deal with the rising incidence of armed robbery. The decree provides that anyone convicted of the offense anywhere in the republic will be hanged or shot. The penalty for unarmed robbery was established at not less than twenty-one years' imprisonment. Under the decree state military governors were granted authority to establish special tribunals for the trial of accused robbers; judgments of the tribunals were not challengable in any Nigerian court. The number of persons tried by these special tribunals was unknown, but by mid-1971 at least sixteen former Biafran officers and soldiers had been publicly executed for armed robbery, murder, or acts of terrorism. All of these incidents occurred in Mid-Western State, East Central State, and Kwara State.

In other parts of the country the incidence of theft appeared to have increased since the conclusion of the war. In March 1971 the chairman of the Nigerian Ports Authority revealed that since 1970 large-scale thefts had occurred at the Lagos ports. Articles stolen included industrial machinery, automobile engines, and other materials imported for use in the country's development programs. One industrial company was reported to have lost at the port machinery worth N£25,000 (1 Nigerian pound equals US$2.80) and twenty tons of steel. The ports authority chairman announced that arrangements were underway to secure the services of an experienced British ports security officer, who would organize an antitheft squad at the Lagos ports to stop pilferage.

In early 1971 the military governor of North Eastern State issued an edict designed to combat an increasing incidence of animal thefts. The proclamation, which amends the Northern Penal Code, deals with the stealing of domestic animals, such as cattle, horses, sheep, goats, donkeys, and pigs. For convictions under the new law, offenders are to receive not less than twenty-one years in prison and twelve strokes of the cane; a fine may be imposed in addition to the two mandatory punishments.

Traffic in illegal narcotic drugs did not appear to have been a significant problem before the 1960s. In 1966 a decree by the FMG imposed severe penalities for the cultivation, sale, and use of Indian hemp (hashish), but this had little effect. To combat what it described as widespread dealing in narcotic drugs, the FMG in early 1971 was preparing a decree to limit their exportation, importation, distribution, and use. The federal commissioner of health had arranged for training courses on narcotic drug control by United Nations personnel in Lagos, and a program to educate the public on the dangers of narcotic drugs was contemplated. The police had engaged in widespread efforts to search out and destroy crops of Indian hemp, which were being grown throughout the country for markets in Nigeria and abroad.

The rate of smuggling operations was relatively high in early 1971; it was attributed generally to the government's import controls and foreign exchange restrictions and to rising prices caused by a scarcity of certain goods (see ch. 12, Character and Structure of the Economy; ch. 14, Industry and Trade). Much of the traffic in illicit imports and exports involved the transfer of merchandise across the frontiers of neighboring West African countries. In many cases goods were smuggled out of the country and sold abroad to earn foreign currency with which to pay the high prices of smuggled imports on the Nigerian market.

The range of products involved in smuggling operations was extremely varied. Cocoa was smuggled from Nigeria to Dahomey, and the Western State Marketing Board had established checkpoints near the frontier as a control measure. Many Nigerian consumers believed that imported products, even if more expensive, were better than those produced locally; this created a ready market for low-value commodities in daily use, such as canned tomato paste, an ingredient considered essential in certain Yoruba cuisine. Customs officials at the nation's seaports and airports frequently seized large quantities of marketable merchandise when searching the baggage of returning travelers. Not all smuggling was limited to low-value merchandise. In late 1970 the NPF reported that more than 100 automobiles had been illicitly imported within a period of a few weeks.

Contravention of the government's Price Control Decree was a frequent offense. In early 1971 amendments to the law conferred the powers of price inspectors on the police and gave them the right to search without a warrant premises and persons suspected of violating the decree.

THE POLICE SYSTEM

The police are the primary force responsible for the maintenance of law and order and for the detection and prevention of crime. Should the need arise, they are supported in this internal security mission by the armed forces. In mid-1971 there were two distinct types of police organization: the national Nigeria Police Force (NPF), with contingents of varying strength stationed in the republic's twelve states, and the local authority police of Western State and the six states of the north. Lagos State, Mid-Western State, and the three eastern states were policed entirely by the NPF. A program to consolidate all police forces was in progress and was expected to be completed by 1972. Total police strength, including both national and local forces, was estimated at about 30,000 men and women—a ratio of police to total population of approximately 1 to 1,800.

The powers of the NPF and those of the local government police are theoretically identical. When the forces are operating together, petty crime is usually handled by the local police, while the federal force takes charge of the investigation of more serious offenses. Because the FMG has overall responsibility for security throughout the country, it has powers in time of need to requisition the services of appropriate local government forces. Under such conditions, local forces operate directly under the supervision of the NPF.

The Nigerian public regards the police with an ambivalent attitude, mainly because of its historical origin as a military organization. The individual policeman is treated with a respect born largely of fear, since the force as a whole has a local reputation for recourse to strong-arm methods to control situations that threaten public order. The public attitude prevails despite the international acclaim accorded a contingent of nearly 400 officers and men of the NPF who served in the troubled Congo at the invitation of the United Nations. Assigned to the Léopoldville area, they worked unarmed and earned the respect of the Congolese and the United Nations forces for their efficiency, courtesy, and courage.

The national police developed from early constabularies raised to protect British personnel and their administrative and commercial interests after they assumed responsibility for the port of Lagos in 1861. These early security forces grew in size and effectiveness and, as the British expanded their operations to the interior, additional constabularies came into being along their route. In the north the Northern Nigerian Constabulary, an outgrowth of the former Royal Niger Constabulary, was formed in 1900 when the British assumed administrative responsibility for the protectorate of Northern Nigeria.

The Southern Nigerian Police was created in 1906, six years after the proclamation of the colony and protectorate of Southern Nigeria. The southern police unit absorbed the former Lagos Police Force and the Niger Coast Constabulary, which had operated in the eastern provinces. In 1930 the northern constabulary and the southern police force were merged to form the NPF, which became the federal law enforcement body.

A central theme in the development of the NPF has been the federal government's continuing effort to establish the force as the sole police authority in the country. This move was opposed for many years by traditional authorities in the north and west who recognized that integration of their forces with the NPF would remove a powerful instrument for maintaining the political status quo in their areas. Considerable opposition to amalgamation was generated also by officials of the local police, who feared that absorption by the federal force would result in greater regimentation, stricter discipline, higher standards of conduct, and the loss of certain amenities.

In 1957, during deliberations on the formulation of the Nigerian Constitution, the British appointed a minorities commission to determine safeguards for the constitutional rights of all ethnic groups after independence. The commission was aware that local police forces had been used at times to intimidate political opposition to regional governments and that opposition parties almost always consisted of ethnic minorities.

The commission did not find any evidence of improper action by the NPF, which by then was responsible for law and order in the Eastern Region and whose officers had effective control over the local police of the Western Region. In the Northern Region, however, it was shown that some of the local police had favored the Hausa-dominated Northern People's Congress, including the display of party emblems. In 1958 the commission recommended the adoption of a single national police force formed by gradual absorption of the local forces and supported financially by the central and regional governments. The resulting constitution, however, did not alter the dual law-enforcement system but merely reflected the commission's recommendations as a long-term goal of Nigerian sovereignty.

When the Mid-Western Region was created in 1963, the regional government relinquished its control over local police units, which were integrated with the NPF. After the military coup d'etat in 1966 the military government began to speed up the consolidation process, but the program was interrupted in 1967 by the civil war.

The Nigeria Police Force

The federal police are organized along British lines, are trained to British standards, and in their operations generally try to conform to British concepts of law enforcement. The force had been officered by the British for many years after its origin, but Nigerianization of its commissioned grades was begun in 1956. The task was completed in 1964 when the force received its first Nigerian commander.

The Supreme Military Council, as the national policymaking body, has the authority to appoint the senior police administrator, who has the rank of inspector general. Within the structure of the Federal Executive Council, the commissioner for internal affairs and police (who in 1971 was also the inspector general of police and a member of the Supreme Military Council) is responsible for policies and administration of the NPF. The final consolidation of the NPF and local authority police was expected to result in state representation on policy matters again being effected through a police council of the type that existed before 1966.

Headquarters of the NPF, under the command of the inspector general of police, is in the Obalende area of Lagos; its staff operations are supervised by a police commissioner. Except for special functions that come directly under the national headquarters, control of the force in the field is exercised through a series of state police commands. The headquarters of these commands, each under the supervision of a police commissioner, are in the various state capitals.

Of the various specialized departments assigned to the national headquarters, the largest is the Criminal Investigation Division (CID), which is responsible for the application of scientific methods to the prevention and detection of crime. A communications branch supervises the operation of the nationwide police radio system that links all state police commands with force headquarters. A special branch is responsible for security and countersubversive requirements. A police band provides ceremonial color and entertains at governmental functions. NPF headquarters supervises the activities of all police training schools.

The size and organizational complexity of the state police commands vary depending on the population density of the state and the need for police authority. Large commands are maintained in Lagos, North Central, Kano, Western, East Central, and South Eastern States. Police posts and stations are found in the larger urban centers, mainly on the rail lines and major highways. The distribution of the NPF has become more widespread since 1966, but most of regular police duty in the north and in Western State is performed by the local police.

The largest of the state commands is that in Lagos State. Its headquarters in the capital city's Lion Building coordinates the activities of a police laboratory, a CID training school, a division responsible for the registration of aliens, and several specialized operational groups. These include a mobile unit and a police dog unit, both at Obalende; a motor traffic division at Ijora; the Nigerian Ports Authority police at Lagos and Apapa; the Nigerian railway police at Ikeja and Shomolu; and a division of policewomen.

Because they are better trained and equipped, the state commands of the NPF usually respond to specialized cases, and all maintain CID capabilities. In addition, squadrons of the NPF mobile force in patrol vehicles equipped with radio communications are available for dispatch when needed. The NPF also generally handles all traffic assignments.

Members of the NPF wear blue uniforms with silver buttons for ceremonial occasions and khaki work uniforms of British design. They are generally unarmed except for truncheons. Many have been trained in the use of light infantry weapons, however, and are armed in emergency situations.

For many years recruitment in the NPF has produced a chronic ethnic imbalance within its ranks in relation to the composition of the entire population. In the 1960s the ratio was roughly 44 percent Ibo, 16 percent Yoruba, and nearly 17 percent Hausa. Some of the ethnic imbalance has been attributed to differences in educational standards and the fact that many northerners and westerners joined their own local police instead of the NPF. At the same time, however, the NPF has long been the sole police organization in the Ibo homelands of the east; because local recruitment is a standard practice, a large input of Ibo policemen has resulted. Nevertheless, the predominance of Ibo personnel in the federal force was a significant factor in the perennial objections of many local authorities to the consolidation of the various police forces.

To be eligible for recruitment into the NPF, male applicants must be between the ages of nineteen and twenty-five, be at least five feet, six inches in height and have a chest measurement of thirty-four inches or more, and must have passed the Standard VI Certificate of Education (approximately eighth grade). Exceptions to the educational requirements have been made in the northern states because of the generally lower levels of education in those areas. Once a month, applicants are interviewed by the state command headquarters before being permitted to take the entrance test. Those who qualify are then required to pass a physical examination before they are accepted for training.

Policewomen have become a permanent element in the NPF. Since 1955, when the women's division was founded, their numbers have increased, and they have proved invaluable in the investigations of cases involving women and juveniles. They enjoy good relations with the public.

Before being assigned to duty with the active force, each recruit must successfully complete the prescribed six-month training course at one of the two police training colleges. Recruits from the northern states go to the Northern Police College at Kaduna; those from the other states attend the Southern Police College at Ikeja.

The courses of instruction at these schools include the study of police ordinances and regulations, criminal law, laws of evidence, motor traffic ordinances, police and station duties, first aid, fingerprinting, the taking of statements, and the preparation of reports and sketches at the scene of a crime or accident. Interpretation of town ordinances and the proper methods of keeping books and records in police stations are also taught. The course covers both theoretical and practical work, including the preparation of mock cases for court presentation. An intensive physical training program includes foot drill, arms drill, parades, musketry, unarmed combat tactics, and riot control techniques. Programs of organized athletics are conducted at both colleges.

Schools offering police refresher courses have been established at Ikeja, Kaduna, and Enugu. Instruction is based on the course given at the police training colleges but are more advanced, detailed, and technical. In addition to specialized training within the force, selected senior members attend courses of instruction in the United Kingdom and the United States. Selected noncommissioned officers and constables are sent to the United Kingdom to be trained in such specialized areas as fingerprinting, handwriting analysis, and photography.

In 1971 conditions of service were sufficiently attractive to assure more applicants for enlistment than could be accommodated financially. Compared with wage levels in a civilian sector faced with growing levels of unemployment, the security offered police personnel in terms of pay and other amenities provided adequate career incentives. Basic pay was augmented by a cost-of-living allowance, and members of the force were entitled to uniforms, certain special travel allowances, and quarters allowances when on duty away from their home stations. Senior personnel occupied government quarters at modest cost; other personnel received either free quarters or a quarters allowance. Liberal annual leave with full pay was received by all but the newest recruits.

When the former Eastern Region seceded from the federation in 1967 as the self-proclaimed Republic of Biafra, about 5,000 members of the NPF in the region joined the rebel faction. As part of the FMG's policy of amnesty after the civil war, investigations of these police personnel were conducted, and most were restored to duty with the NPF. A total of 285 constables and noncommissioned officers of East Central State had been discharged as of early 1971, and investigations of the rest were continuing. Many of those restored to federal duty were posted to the three eastern states and Lagos. To assist in restoring normal operations in the east and to aid in stemming the increased incidence of crime, about 1,000 additional federal policemen were on duty throughout that area.

Local Authority Police

In mid-1970 the remaining local authority police operated in Western State and the six states of the north. In Western State they were known as the Local Government Police Force; in the northern states they were designated Native Authority Police.

Although their integration with the NPF was in progress, the FMG was proceeding cautiously to avoid local political objections and to dispel inherent suspicion that the national government was attempting to usurp traditional authority.

In the past the local police units were not noted for their effectiveness, training, or discipline, although these conditions improved after they were brought under the guidance of the federal inspector general of police in 1966 and after military governors were assigned to administer the state governments. Before these developments, however, the major problem connected with local police effectiveness was the generally uncooperative attitude of local authorities, who usually were reluctant to compromise their independence even by cooperating with the police forces of their neighbors.

Although members of the NPF were often stationed with local police in an advisory capacity in many local areas, they had no authority over the local forces. To secure their assistance, consultations with local officials were necessary but were often unsuccessful. Under usual circumstances the NPF's authority extended only to areas containing federal property or to those populated by foreign nationals unless it was asked to support the local police in other areas. The arrangement often resulted in an uneven reaction to the needs of public order.

In earlier times the organization and effectiveness of the local authority police were as varied as the political bodies to which they were responsible. Since the late 1960s, however, many local police personnel have been retrained to NPF standards and in some areas have received standarized equipment and accommodations. Federal police increasingly have begun to supervise, and in some cases to command, units of the local police. As a result, levels of organization, training, and operations have improved in certain places.

To assist with the retraining of local police personnel, the NPF has increased the intake of trainees in the federal police schools. A new police staff college was to be constructed as soon as possible with the aid of a grant provided in early 1971 by the United States. The Nigerian government has allocated N£12.86 million for training operations, equipment, and the construction of housing for the growing ranks of the new consolidated force.

THE PENAL SYSTEM

Until the period of governmental reorganization that followed the 1966 coup, the nation's prison system was a product of divided responsibility between the central government and local authorities. The federal government controlled and operated fifty-one prisons, at least two prison farms, and two reformatories. Four of these installations were in the north, and the rest were situated in the southern half of the nation, mainly in the former Western and Eastern Regions and the area around Lagos. Until 1968 the local authorities of the northern states maintained sixty-four prisons, and eight penal institutions were operated by the local government in Western State. Throughout the entire system there was a lack of standardization, and all institutions suffered from serious overcrowding.

The structure of the federal penal system and its principles of operation were established during the British colonial era. Originally all federal prisons were operated by the police, but in 1908 a separate prisons department was established in the Colony and Protectorate of Southern Nigeria. In 1938 several northern prisons were redesignated federal institutions and were placed under the supervision of the federal prisons department in Lagos. At independence the federal system was transferred intact to the Nigerian central government; the operation of local authority prisons was largely unaffected by Nigerian sovereignty.

Federal institutions are classified as convict, provincial, and divisional prisons. Those of the convict classification are of the maximum security type and retain all classes of prisoners regardless of sentence. Provincial and divisional prisons receive all classes of prisoners but retain only those whose sentences do not exceed two years' imprisonment.

Crime is not common among women; consequently, the number of female prisoners throughout the country has remained low. Female offenders with sentences of a month or more are transferred to prisons that have segregated sections for women. During their incarceration, female prisoners perform domestic work and are taught trades, such as spinning, weaving, tailoring, needlework, and mat and basket making.

Nigerian law defines a juvenile as a person between the ages of fourteen and seventeen. The courts usually do not commit juveniles to prison if it can be avoided, but there are instances where imprisonment becomes necessary because of the nature of the offense or because of the past behavior of the offender. If their sentences are long enough to warrant it, many juveniles are transferred to a special section of the Port Harcourt prison where training in trades, basic education, and physical training are provided. Upon discharge, assistance in the form of tools and money are provided, and efforts are made to find employment for the dischargee. The principle of rehabilitation has been adopted generally in the handling of juvenile offenders. It has been largely untried in other prisons except in the case of prisoners serving long sentences.

The federal prisons department operates two reformatories for offenders under the age of twenty-one. The Approved School at Enugu in East Central State was established in 1933 for the education and training of young persons who, whether or not guilty of indictable offenses, are in need of a period of training and discipline. A reformatory at Kakuri in North Central State accommodates offenders between the ages of sixteen and twenty-one. Its structure and principles of operation are modeled after the Borstal reformatory institutions in the United Kingdom and other British Commonwealth countries. In addition to receiving a general education, inmates are taught trades, such as tailoring, bricklaying, carpentry, and painting. Efforts are made to obtain employment for trainees upon discharge.

In federal prisons male and female prisoners are segregated, and those with previous convictions are separated from first offenders when space allows. All prisoners are required to work, subject only to limitations prescribed by age, sex, and physical condition. Prison labor is divided into three general categories. Industrial labor, including vocational training, involves employment in prison factories and instruction in trades and handicrafts. Domestic labor includes the preparation of food, cleaning, gardening, woodcutting, clothing repair, and laundry. Unskilled labor comprises quarrying, roadbuilding, general sanitation work, and prison upkeep.

Recent statistics on the size of the prison population have been unavailable since the early 1960s. General publication of prison department statistical reports have been discontinued, and annual statistical abstracts by the Federal Office of Statistics do not include data on institutions in the eastern states. Nonetheless, these reports do show a slightly larger number of inmates in southern states than in the north. Whether this reflects actual trends in criminal activity or merely the sentencing patterns of the different courts is not revealed.

In 1968 the FMG began to federalize all of the prisons that previously had been under the control of local authorities. In mid-1971 the process was complete, and administrative responsibility for all penal institutions was vested in the Federal Executive Council's commissioner for internal affairs and police. Headquarters of the prison department in Lagos was administered by a director of prisons, who was responsible for the policies and procedures carried out in all penal institutions. In those states where prisons existed, the department maintained state headquarters, each supervised by an assistant director of prisons.

The government's program of penal reform, which was expected to be completed by 1974, was designed to reduce the general state of overcrowding in prisons, optimize the use of prison labor, and expand the rehabilitation program for prisoners. Plans existed for the reclassification of prisons on a functional basis into remand and reception centers, industrial production prisons, industrial training institutions, and prison farms. Under the development plan, supporting services dealing with improved prison medical facilities, expanded educational and library activities, and the training of prison staffs are expected to be improved. Other features of the plan involve the establishment of units within the prison administration to deal with social welfare measures, the expansion of prison agricultural activities, and the keeping of statistical records. To upgrade the level of prison staffs, the entry qualification into the prison service was raised to Secondary IV (tenth grade). In early 1971 the government allocated N£5.6 million for the four-year program.

THE ARMED FORCES

The military establishment traces its history from the British colonial era, when it consisted solely of a modest army formed along infantry lines. Expanded largely for purposes of national prestige after independence in 1960, the army rapidly grew in size and was joined by a small navy and air force. The traditional task of the armed forces was that of aiding the police in the maintenance of internal security and of protecting the republic's territorial integrity against any external aggression.

Throughout the period of emerging nationalism that heralded and followed the country's independence, the armed forces maintained an apolitical position in a scene of rising regional competition and ethnic distrust. In 1966, when these forces threatened to divide the federal army and the republic, the military establishment became the national governing authority to preserve the country's unity. A long and costly civil war followed, but the federal forces were victorious. In 1971, after five years of divisive strife throughout the republic, the armed forces had retained their own integrity and their position as one of the country's most important national institutions.

Armed Forces and the Government

Authority for maintaining the national armed forces was contained in the federal Constitution adopted at the time of independence. When the authority of this document was abolished after the 1966 coup, many of its features, including those affecting the authorization of a national military establishment, were preserved in the Constitutional Decree issued by the Federal Military Government (FMG).

In mid-1971 the chief of state and chairman of the Supreme Military Council, Major General Yakubu Gowon, was commander in chief of the armed forces. The cabinet-level Federal Executive Council did not include a commissioner for defense; General Gowon retained the defense portfolio, although he was assisted in its administration by a permanent secretary who supervised the operation of the military headquarters. Advice concerning defense policies and operations was received from the Supreme Military Council, the nation's governing body. The council was composed of General Gowon; the chiefs of staff of the supreme headquarters and the Nigerian armed forces; the commanders of the army, navy, and air force; the inspector general of police and his deputy; the military governors of the eleven states and the civilian administrator of East Central State.

The Supreme Military Council is responsible for determining the size and composition of the military forces and for the promulgation of regulations on such matters as terms of service, promotion, retirement, resignation, and military discipline. The council is authorized to order members of the forces to any place inside or outside the country for training, duty, or employment. It appoints the commanders of the army, the navy, and the air force; these commanders are responsible for the direction, general supervision, and operations of the forces subject to the policies and general direction of the Supreme Military Council.

The military chain of command descends from the commander in chief to the Supreme Headquarters of the Armed Forces under the command of a chief of staff. Beneath his authority are the separate headquarters of the army, the navy, and the air force. For ease of coordination all are located in the Republic House in Lagos.

At the beginning of the civil war the country was divided into two military districts. The Northern Military District covered the former Northern Region; its southern counterpart included the former Western and Eastern Regions. The ethnic rivalries, which were exacerbated by political motivations of the regional governments, were a major factor in the 1966 army mutinies and the coup d'etat. The fear that private regional armies were being developed was a contributing factor in the secession of the Eastern Region in 1967. The dual system of military districts remained in mid-1971, but the announced reorganization of the armed forces was expected to result in a revision of the structure into one of smaller area commands.

In 1971 the decision to maintain the large army that was mobilized during the civil war appeared to hinge on economic and political considerations. The FMG had refrained from accepting the recommendations of economists who felt that the defense budget was more than the nation could afford. Recognizing the adverse effect that large numbers of job-seeking ex-servicemen would have on the nation's already acute unemployment situation, the FMG had conceded to a partial force reduction but not before the programs of the Second National Development Plan, 1970–74, had created job opportunities to absorb discharged military personnel. A joint planning board of federal and state officials responsible for program development met for the first time in February 1971.

From a political standpoint, the continued maintenance of a large standing army provides the FMG with a position of security during its efforts at governmental reform. Even when the FMG returns the country to civilian rule, supposedly in 1976, the military can be expected to remain as an established, if latent, political force for national unity.

The Army

The origins of the army can be traced to the mid-nineteenth century constabularies formed by the British to secure their Lagos colony and to those established somewhat later by the British charter companies (see ch. 3, Historical Setting). In 1900, when the British assumed direct authority over the area, the constabularies were recognized as strictly military units within the British-trained and led Royal West African Frontier Force (RWAFF). In 1914 the Nigeria Regiment of the RWAFF was formed.

In World War I the regiment fought against the Germans in the Cameroons and in East Africa. All concerned with these operations had praise for the determination and fortitude of the Nigerian soldier, as well as for his discipline and devotion to his British officers. The regiment's four infantry battalions received many battle awards from the British government.

During World War II three battalions of the regiment were assigned to the First West African Brigade, which fought in Ethiopia and helped defend Kenya. Nigerian army units also served with British forces in Palestine, Morocco, Sicily, and Burma. Throughout the war the conduct of Nigerian soldiers received high praise from Allied commanders, and many battle honors were awarded the regiment.

In 1958, during the preparations for independence, the regiment was transferred to the control of the Lagos government; a year later Nigeria assumed full responsibility for its own defense and internal security. In December 1960 the army provided a military force of two infantry battalions to support United Nations operations in the Congo. The last of these units was removed in 1964.

Nigerianization of the officer corps was begun in 1956. The last British battalion commander was replaced in mid-1963, and by the end of that year all battalion officers were Nigerian. All staff positions within the army headquarters were Nigerianized in 1964, and the program was completed in 1965 with the appointment of Major General J.T.U. Aguiyi-Ironsi, an Ibo, as commander of the army.

During the postindependence military development, the army maintained an apolitical attitude, mainly because of its British heritage. As a national institution, efforts have been made to assure an ethnically balanced force. Before mobilization for the civil war in 1967 enlisted personnel had been recruited on a system of regional quotas: 50 percent from the north, 25 percent from the west, and 25 percent from the east. In effect, the enlisted composition of army units did not approximate these quotas; northerners exceeded the 50 percent level, and westerners were underrepresented. Largely because of lower educational standards, most northern soldiers served as general duty troops, while those from the east and the west were assigned to technical and clerical positions.

In 1960 only 14 percent of the Nigerian officers were from the north, mainly from the Middle Belt (see Glossary). Of the total number of officers, Ibo predominated. Anxiety over this ethnic imbalance led to the federal government's imposition of a regional quota for recruiting officer cadets. Fifty percent of all recruits had to come from the north; 25 percent, from the east; and 25 percent, from the west. After introduction of the quota system, ethnic proportions among junior officers were more nearly aligned to those of the general population. In the rank of major and above, officers from the west and the east, particularly those of Ibo origin, predominated over northerners by a ratio of seven to one. This imbalance was largely the result of the system of open competition and academic qualifications that the British introduced in the 1950s and that continued until adoption of the officer quota system in 1961.

The acute ethnic and regional rivalries that characterized civilian political groupings in the 1960s soon penetrated the army and destroyed its traditional apolitical ethos (see ch. 9, Government and Political Dynamics). The army was seen by some politicians as a means to achieve political power, and attempts were made to exploit the army's ethnic imbalance. These efforts led to a revolt within the officer corps in January 1966, the killing of many senior northern officers, and the establishment of military rule. In July 1966 a second mutiny occurred. General Ironsi, leader of the military government and the senior officer of the Nigerian army, was killed.

After General Ironsi's death, the attempts of the FMG to reorganize the army and ameliorate ethnic rivalries were unsuccessful. Ibo members of the army joined their people in the Eastern Region as it seceded from the federation in 1967 and served as the cadre for the recruitment of a separate Biafran army.

In July 1967 the Nigerian army crossed into the seceded Eastern Region with a standing army of about 10,000 men. To replace Ibo servicemen who had left its ranks and to mobilize for wartime operations, the FMG soon instituted an emergency recruiting program. Qualification standards were lowered, particularly for officers, and by the end of the war in 1970 the army's size had increased to about 250,000. Similar emergency recruitment by the Biafrans resulted in an opposing force of about 50,000 officers and men.

During the civil war both sides repeatedly sought weapons, ammunition, and other military equipment from external sources. The federal army was supported with supplies obtained from sources in the United Kingdom, the Soviet Union, Egypt, East Germany, France, and Czechoslovakia. Biafran army units received equipment from suppliers in France, Portugal, Spain, and Communist China.

After the war it became evident that large-scale demobilization of the armed forces was not intended. General Gowon announced that soliders recruited by the former secessionist regime would not be reabsorbed into the Nigerian services but gave assurance that former federal officers who had fought on the Biafran side would be reinstated and assigned to federal units if investigations established their loyalty to the central government.

In 1971 army personnel strength was estimated at about 240,000 officers and men; this was expected to be reduced gradually within several years to about 150,000. The army was organized into three infantry divisions and a marine commando division. Supporting units included two reconnaissance squadrons equipped with armored cars, scout cars, and armored personnel carriers. Engineering units, ordnance companies, artillery batteries, a signals unit, and medical companies also provided support to the combat infantry units. Artillery weapons were largely of British and Soviet origin. Infantry battalions were equipped with mortars, modern rifles, and other small arms.

The army was commanded by a Nigerian brigadier, who served as chief of staff in a headquarters in Lagos. Headquarters of the divisional field forces were located at Kaduna, Ibadan, Jos, and Enugu. Together these units constituted the federal field command. Battalions that had existed before the civil war had returned to their home stations; those raised during the war had been scattered throughout the country, largely in areas where they could be housed. Accommodations for the vastly increased army forces had presented serious problems after the war, and construction of barracks and military cantonments had received high priority in the defense budget.

The personnel strength of the army has always been maintained by voluntary service. Before the war applicants had to be between the ages of 17½ and 30 years. The minimum height and weight for enlistment in the infantry, artillery, and engineers were 66 inches and 112 pounds. Normal enlistments were for 6 years of active duty, but a soldier could extend his service for 3 or 6 years at a time, depending on his qualifications and length of service. Because its standing army was twenty times its prewar size, the government suspended all army recruitment in late 1970. New enlistments were not anticipated for several years.

Before the war the army offered regular commissions for a service career and short service commissions for limited periods of duty, usually up to eight years. The regular commission was available to all officers who held a short service commission and to enlisted men and young civilians who had completed a secondary school education. Applicants for a short service commission had to be at least twenty-five years old with at least six months of active service; other applicants had to be between the ages of seventeen and twenty-five with a secondary school education. These requirements were relaxed during the war with consequent dilution of trained leaders.

All army recruit training is conducted at the Recruit Training Center at Zaria in North Central State. The regular course, lasting twenty-eight weeks, emphasizes physical fitness, drill, organized sports, and complete fluency in English. Upon completion of this training, the soldier is assigned to a unit. Advanced military training is conducted at unit level; specialist training is provided in army technical schools or abroad.

The Nigerian Military Training College at Kaduna, opened in 1960, offers courses in general military subjects for all qualified personnel of the army and gives basic training to officer cadets selected by the army, navy, and air force. In addition to field exercises and classroom training, students are required to keep themselves physically fit by participating in organized sports. The college provides specialist courses for members of all three services.

In early 1971 the FMG announced its intention to reorganize the army. Details on the scope of the program were not revealed, but it included plans to conduct a two-year project of retraining for all members of the service. Army units were being dispersed throughout the country as soon as the construction of new facilities had been completed. The program also included plans to re-equip the army with more sophisticated weapons than it had during the war.

The public's favorable attitude toward the large army has deteriorated since the end of the war. In the aftermath of victory, many soldiers had indulged in offensive acts, which the people in 1971 had not forgotten. Confiscation of private homes, school buildings, hospital wards, and other public structures for troop housing had created strained relations with many civilians who deeply resented the privileges extended to the army.

Aware of the decline in public favor, the FMG had acted to reinforce discipline within the armed forces. All army battalions had increased the size of their public relations services, which attempted to improve the army's image through the entire range of the country's mass media. To keep many of its troops occupied, the army increasingly employed them in programs of civic action, such as road and bridge building, urban sanitation, and cleanup projects.

The Navy

The navy was authorized by the Nigerian Naval Forces Ordinance of 1956 and became a statutory organization forming part of the military forces in early 1958. The original objective in establishing the naval service was to develop an antisubmarine and minesweeping force to operate off the country's coastline in time of war. During the two world wars these duties had been performed by the Nigerian Marine (coast guard); the unit was dissolved in 1956, and its officers and men were assigned to the new federal navy, which was officered originally by the British.

Over the succeeding years the navy developed in two planned phases, the first of which was confined almost exclusively to peacetime duties in territorial waters. Its responsibilities, formerly undertaken by the Nigerian Ports Authority, included the maintenance of the Eastern Protective Sea Patrol, the enforcement of customs laws, hydrographic surveying outside the port limits, the manning of naval craft, and the operation of a training school for its own personnel and those of the merchant marine.

Under the second phase of development, a small, fully equipped and trained naval force developed a wartime capability of performing mining, minesweeping, and antisubmarine operations. In addition, it protected the fishing industry, carried out rescue services, and assisted the police in the maintenance of internal security. By the end of its second phase of development, the modest naval force had expanded its personnel strength and equipment inventory. It was able to conduct port examination services, aid in the control of merchant shipping, and patrol the territorial waters. By 1966 the force had developed beyond its earlier need for British officers; its commander was a Nigerian commodore. In mid-1971 the navy was commanded by a rear admiral.

Between 1961 and 1971 the strength of the navy increased from about 500 to 5,000 officers and men. During the civil war the service maintained an effective blockade of the entire Nigerian coastline, concentrating particularly on eastern ports to prevent the delivery of supplies from abroad to the Biafran forces. It also conducted amphibious operations with units of the federal army and air force.

In its first phase of development, completed shortly before the start of the civil war, the navy was equipped with a modest number of armed coastal patrol boats acquired from the United Kingdom. The largest of these vessels was a frigate, the NNS *Nigeria,* which had been built in the Netherlands and transferred to the Nigerian government in 1959. It was equipped with antisubmarine detection gear and depth charges, as well as deck and antiaircraft guns. By 1970 the vessel inventory had been increased by a submarine chaser, several seaward defense boats, a landing craft, and a few fast armed patrol boats acquired from the Soviet Union.

Candidates for officer training must meet the same standards required of those who apply as army cadets. Those accepted for training are given six months' preliminary training at the Nigeria Military College; if qualified for further training, they attend a 2½-year course at the naval training school at Apapa. Upon graduation the cadet is commissioned a sublieutenant in the navy. Selected naval officers are sent to the United Kingdom or to the Nigerian Military Training College for specialist training.

When the navy was first authorized, the Nigerian Seaman's Training School, the HMNS *Quorra,* was transferred from the Nigerian Ports Authority to the navy. The HMNS *Challenger,* built in 1955 for use in the customs service, was converted for weapons training and also operated as a seagoing tender to the *Quorra.* Both were transferred to the Nigerian government after independence and operate as training ships out of the main naval base at Apapa near Lagos.

Naval training for enlisted men consists of three months' basic seamanship and communications training on the *Quorra.* After training the men are assigned to various elements of the navy; some are given additional training in the engineering, electrical, communications, and supply branches. Technical training beyond local capabilities is carried out in the United Kingdom. In late 1970 the chief of naval staff announced plans for the construction of a new naval training base at a site between Lagos and Mid-Western State and the hiring of expatriate instructors to assist experienced Nigerian training personnel.

The Air Force

The air force, newest of the three services, was formed shortly after independence as a training squadron. Its organization was supervised initially by a mission of the Indian air force, which was replaced in 1963 by a West German training team. Early pilot training for Nigerian cadets was conducted in Canada, West Germany, and Ethiopia, but the West Germans soon established a primary flight school at Kaduna using Italian conventional trainers. The initial goal of the program was the training of 100 Nigerian pilots, 50 ground specialists, and 10 aircraft technicians. The Italian trainers and a number of West German conventional communications and liaison aircraft were provided by the West German government at regular commercial rates.

In 1964 plans for expansion of the air force to an establishment of 1,000 men were allocated N£443,000, and additional transport aircraft were delivered from West Germany. After increasing political dissension in the Northern Region, however, the expansion was halted, and some of the training personnel were withdrawn. The training program was further diminished after the 1966 coup and was suspended at the beginning of the civil war. Most of the Ibo pilots fled to the Eastern Region.

With the outbreak of hostilities the federal air force began to improve its aircraft inventory with planes purchased abroad. When the United States, the United Kingdom, and France formally prohibited major arms shipments to either belligerent in the war, the Nigerian federal government turned to the Soviet Union. As part of an arms agreement with military authorities in Lagos, the first of several shipments of Soviet jet ground attack aircraft and Czechoslovakian armed trainers arrived at Kano airport aboard Soviet transport planes in August 1967. With them came about 200 Soviet technicians. Many were withdrawn after assembling and testing the aircraft; others remained to provide regular aircraft maintenance services. In 1968 Egypt lent the Nigerian air force several light jet bombers of Soviet design. A number of armed jet trainers were obtained from Italy, and helicopters were eventually purchased from Great Britain and France.

Because few of the trained Nigerian air force pilots were capable of flying jet aircraft, the government procured the services of mercenary pilots to conduct aerial operations against the Biafran secessionists. These included Egyptians, Rhodesians, and South Africans and eventually pilots from the German Democratic Republic (East Germany). Egyptian pilots initiated a limited program to train Nigerians in the use of the newly acquired jet aircraft, but they were replaced by East Germans in 1969.

During the war the mercenary and volunteer pilots attached to the Nigerian air force assisted Nigerian pilots in their attempts to prevent the delivery of supplies and equipment to the Biafrans from external sources. Operations were mounted in support of Nigerian ground attacks, and bombing and strafing raids were conducted against Biafran targets in the war zone. The federal air force maintained almost complete air superiority, despite Biafra's acquisition in early 1969 of several combat aircraft, as well as the services of a small group of Swedish pilots. These were used mainly in harassing raids against the federal airfields and to disrupt oil operations in Mid-Western State.

In 1971 the Nigerian air force had a personnel strength of about 7,000 men. Its aircraft inventory consisted of less than forty combat planes, several transports, liaison aircraft, and helicopters. All were of Soviet, Czechoslovakian, Italian, British, or French origin. Training missions for Nigerian pilots were again in progress at the primary flight school at Kaduna and the advanced flight school at Kano. The first nine pilots to be trained in jet aircraft in Nigeria completed their advanced course in early 1971.

Defense Costs and Manpower

From the years that heralded the approach of independence to the early 1970s, governmental agencies responsible for national defense were consistently successful in obtaining a liberal share of the nation's available revenues. Between 1959 and 1966 the recurrent cost of the military establishment averaged about 4.5 percent of the total governmental budget. This money was allocated largely to the army, and the rest was devoted to further expansion of the navy, creation of an air force, a massive program to rebuild and increase the number of troop barracks, the equipping of the new military academy, and construction of a national ordnance factory.

Despite mounting defense costs during the 1960s, there were few public protests. Moreover, demands for military expansion were frequently made in the press and in Parliament. Suggestions that the government should abandon the traditional voluntary system of military recruitment and adopt a program of compulsory military service—including the induction of women—were often expressed. A comparison of government military budgets revealed that between 1964 and 1967 military spending increased 85.4 percent.

Little information is available to reflect the actual levels of military spending during the thirty months of civil war, particularly the costs of equipment obtained from foreign sources. Various estimates place military expenditures during the period at 45 to 50 percent of the total national budget.

Efforts to reduce the size of the military burden after the war, however, had not lowered military appropriations significantly. Federal statistical reports for fiscal year 1968/69 reflected a total expenditure for defense and internal security of N£91.4 million. This represented half of the federal government's total expenditures (see ch. 12, Character and Structure of the Economy).

The level of defense spending was expected to remain high, at least through the mid-1970's, as the armed forces entered an extended program of reorganization that included the dispersal of military units throughout the country and the construction of barracks and other installations to house and support the large military establishment.

With an estimated 13,375,000 males between the ages of eighteen and forty-five in 1970, the republic's military manpower potential was the greatest of any nation in Africa. The personnel strength of the active duty military establishment equated to about 1.4 percent of all men in this military age group. The country did not have a trained or active military reserve.

Except for a generally low rate of functional literacy and a comparable level of technical skills, the quality of this vast military manpower pool was difficult to assess. Precise literacy figures for this group did not exist, but the general rate could be assumed from national estimates that placed functional literacy at about 20 percent for the entire urban population (those living in towns of 20,000 persons or more) and 2 percent for the segment classified as rural.

The country's general self-sufficiency in food products provided ample support for the expanded armed forces. The small ordnance factory at Kaduna, which had been established in the mid-1960s by a West German firm, was able to furnish limited amounts of small arms and ammunition. The government planned to expand the scope of its production before 1974 to include spare parts for military equipment.

BIBLIOGRAPHY FOR THE MARCH 1964 EDITION

Section I. Social
RECOMMENDED SOURCES

Adetoro, J.E. (ed.). *The Handbook of Education, Nigeria, 1960.* N.p.: Schools and General Publications Services, 1960.

"Africa's Greatest Artist," *Ebony,* IV, March 1949, 27–29.

Anderson, J.N.D. *Islamic Law in Africa.* London: HMSO, 1954.

Aragbabalu Omadiji. "Brecht Play at University College," *West African Review,* XXXI, May 1969, 39, 40.

Awolowo, Obafemi. *Path to Nigerian Freedom.* (With a Foreword by Margery Perham.) London: Faber and Faber, 1947.

Azikiwe, Nnamdi. *Renascent Africa.* Accra: [The Author], 1937.

Bascom, William R. "West and Central Africa." Pages 331–404 in Ralph Linton (ed.), *Most of the World: The Peoples of Africa, Latin America, and the East Today.* New York: Columbia University Press, 1949.

Bascom, William R., and Herskovits, Melville J. (eds.). *Continuity and Change in African Cultures.* Chicago: University of Chicago Press, 1959.

Beier, Ulli. *Art in Nigeria 1960.* Cambridge: Cambridge University Press, 1960.

————. "Complicated Carver," *West African Review,* XXXI, June 1960, 30, 31.

————. "Three Zaria Artists," *West African Review,* XXXI, October 1960, 37–41.

Berry, J. "Linguistic Research in West Africa," *West Africa,* July 23, 1960, 829.

Biobaku, Saburi O. *The Origin of the Yorubas.* ("Lugard Lectures," 1955.) Lagos: Federal Ministry of Information, 1960.

Bohannan, Laura, and Bohannan, Paul. *The Tiv of Central Nigeria.* ("Ethnographic Survey of Africa," Western Africa, Part 8; ed., Daryll Forde.) London: International African Institute, 1953.

Bovill, E.W. *The Golden Trade of the Moors.* London: Oxford University Press, 1958.

Bradbury, R.E. *The Benin Kingdom and the Edo-Speaking Peoples of South-Western Nigeria.* ("Ethnographic Survey of

Africa," Western Africa, Part 13, ed., Daryll Forde.) London: International African Institute, 1957.

Brinkworth, Ian. "Mud Sculpture of Benin," *West African Review*, XXXI, May 1960, 29, 30.

————. "Mystery on the Niger," *West African Review*, XXXI, April 1960, 26, 27.

Buchanan, K.M., and Pugh, J.C. *Land and People in Nigeria.* London: University of London Press, 1955.

Burns, Alan. *History of Nigeria.* (6th ed.) London: Allen and Unwin, 1955.

Coleman, James S. *Nigeria: Background to Nationalism.* Berkeley: University of California Press, 1958.

Committee on Inter-African Relations. *Report on the Press in West Africa.* Ibadan: Department of Extra-Mural Studies, University College, 1960.

Davidson, Basil, and Ademola, Adenekan (eds.). *The New West Africa.* London: Allen and Unwin, 1953.

Dike, K. Onwuka. *100 Years of British Rule in Nigeria, 1851–1951.* (2nd ed.) ("Lugard Lectures," 1956.) Lagos: Federal Ministry of Information, 1960.

————. *Trade and Politics in the Niger Delta, 1830–1885.* Oxford: Clarendon Press, 1956.

Eastern Region of Nigeria. *Commission to Enquire into the Position, Status, and Influence of Chiefs and Natural Rulers in the Eastern Region of Nigeria.* (Report by Gwilym I. Jones.) Enugu: Government Printer, 1957.

————. *Report of the Committee on Bride Price.* Enugu: Government Printer, 1955.

Elisofon, Eliot. *The Sculpture of Africa.* New York: Praeger, 1958.

English, M.C. *An Outline of Nigerian History.* London: Longmans, Green, 1960.

Ezera, Kalu. *Constitutional Developments in Nigeria.* London: Cambridge University Press, 1960.

Fage, J.D. *An Introduction to the History of West Africa.* Cambridge: Cambridge University Press, 1955.

Forde, Daryll. *The Yoruba-Speaking Peoples of South-Western Nigeria.* ("Ethnographic Survey of Africa," Western Africa, Part 4; ed., Daryll Forde.) London: International African Institute, 1951.

Forde, Daryll; Brown, Paula; and Armstrong, Robert G. *Peoples of the Niger-Benue Confluence.* ("Ethnographic Survey of Africa," Western Africa, Part 10, ed., Daryll Forde.) London: International African Institute, 1950.

Forde, Daryll, and Jones, G.I. *The Ibo and Ibibio-Speaking Peo-*

ples of South-Eastern Nigeria. ("Ethnographic Survey of Africa," Western Africa, Part 3; ed., Daryll Forde.) London: International African Institute, 1950.

Great Britain. Colonial Office. *Nigeria: Report of the Commission Appointed to Enquire into the Fears of Minorities and the Means of Allaying Them.* (Cmnd. 505.) London: HMSO, 1958.

Greenberg, Joseph H. "African Languages," *Collier's Encyclopedia,* 1959 (Prepublication manuscript).

————. *The Influence of Islam on a Sudanese Religion.* New York: Augustin, 1947.

————. *Studies in African Linguistic Classification.* New Haven: Compass, 1955.

Gunn, Harold D. *Pagan Peoples of the Central Area of Northern Nigeria.* ("Ethnographic Survey of Africa," Western Africa, Part 12; ed., Daryll Forde.) London: International African Institute, 1956.

Hailey, Lord William M. *An African Survey.* (Rev. ed. 1956.) London: Oxford University Press, 1957.

Hodgkin, Thomas. *Nationalism in Colonial Africa.* London: Frederick Muller, 1956.

————. *Nigerian Perspectives; an Historical Anthology.* ("West African History Series," ed., Gerald S. Graham.) London: Oxford University Press, 1960.

Hopen, C.E. *The Pastoral Fulbe Family in Gwandu.* London: International African Institute, 1958.

International Labor Organization. International Labor Office. *African Labour Survey.* ("Studies and Reports," New Series No. 481). Geneva: ILO, 1958.

Leith-Ross, Sylvia. *African Women: A Study of the Ibo of Nigeria.* (With a Foreword by Lord Lugard.) London: Faber and Faber, 1939.

Little, Kenneth. "The African Elite in British West Africa." Pages 263-288 in Andrew W. Lind (ed.), *Conference on Race Relations in World Perspective, Honolulu, 1954.* Honolulu: University of Hawaii Press, 1955.

Lugard, F.D. *The Dual Mandate in British Tropical Africa.* London: Blackwood, 1929.

McCall, Daniel F. "Dynamics of Urbanization in Africa." Pages 522-535 in Simon and Phoebe Ottenberg (eds.), *Cultures and Societies of Africa,* New York: Random House, 1960.

Macmillan. William Miller. *The Road to Self-Rule: A Study in Colonial Evolution.* London: Faber and Faber, 1959.

Nadel, S.F. *A Black Byzantium: The Kingdom of Nupe in Nigeria.* London: Oxford University Press, for the International African Institute, 1942.

Nigeria. *Investment in Education. Report of the Commission on Post-School Certificate and Higher Education in Nigeria.* Lagos: Ministry of Education, 1960.

————. *The Nigeria Handbook.* London: Crown Agents for the Colonies on Behalf of the Government of Nigeria, 1953.

————. Department of Statistics. *Population Census of Lagos, 1950.* Kaduna: Government Printer, 1951.

————. *Population Census of Nigeria, 1952–53.* Lagos: Census Superintendent [The Federal Government Statistician], n.d.

————. *Population Census of the Eastern Region of Nigeria, 1953.* Lagos: Census Superintendent [The Government Statistician], 1957.

————. *Population Census of the Northern Region of Nigeria, 1952.* Lagos: Census Superintendent [The Government Statistician], 1954.

————. *Population Census of the Western Region of Nigeria, 1952.* Lagos: Census Superintendent [The Government Statistician], 1956.

Nigeria Magazine (Lagos), October 1960, *passim.*

"Nutrition in Nigeria," *West African Review,* XXXI, January 1960, 65.

Parrinder, Geoffrey. "Indigenous Churches in Nigeria," *West African Review,* XXXI, September 1960, 87–93.

————. *Religion in an African City.* London: Oxford University Press, 1953.

————. "The Religious Situation in West Africa," *African Affairs,* LIX, January 1960, 38–42.

————. *West African Religion.* London: Epworth Press, 1949.

Perham, Margery. *Lugard: The Years of Authority, 1898–1945.* London: Collins, 1960.

Phillips, Arthur; Mair, Lucy; and Harries, Lyndon. *Survey of African Marriage and Family Life.* London: International African Institute, 1953.

Quinn-Young, C.T., and Herdman. T. *Geography of Nigeria.* London: Longmans, Green, 1958.

Smith, Mary F. *Baba of Karo; A Woman of the Moslem Hausa.* London: Faber and Faber, 1954.

Smith, Michael G. *Government in Zazzau, 1800–1950.* London: Oxford University Press, 1960.

Smythe, Hugh H., and Smythe, Mabel M. *The New Nigerian Elite.* Stanford: Stanford University Press, 1960.

Stenning, Derrick J. *Savannah Nomads: A Study of the Wodaabe Pastoral Fulani of Western Bornu Province, Northern Region, Nigeria.* (With a Foreward by Daryll Forde.) London: Oxford University Press, for the International African Institute, 1959.

414

Trimingham, Rev. John Spencer. *Islam in West Africa*. London: Oxford University Press, 1959.

Tutuola, Amos. *The Palm-Wine Drinkard and His Dead Palm-Wine Tapster in the Dead's Town*. London: Faber and Faber, 1952.

Ward, Ida C. *Ibo Dialects and the Development of a Common Language*. Cambridge: Heffer, 1941.

Wescott, Roger W. "Revolution in African Linguistics," *Centennial Review of Arts and Sciences*, IV, Fall 1960, 484–502.

Westermann, Diedrich. "Some Notes on the Hausa People and Their Language." Pages ix–xix in G.P. Bargery, *Hausa-English Dictionary and English-Hausa Vocabulary*, London: Oxford University Press, 1934.

Westermann, Diedrich, and Bryan, M.A. *Languages of West Africa*. ("Handbook of African Languages," Part II.) London: Oxford University Press, 1952.

Wingert, Paul S. *African Negro Sculpture, a Loan Exhibition*. (San Francisco, M.H. De Young Memorial Museum.) New York: Columbia University Press, 1948.

———. *Sculpture of Negro Africa*. New York: Columbia University Press, 1950.

Wolff, Hans. "Intelligibility and Inter-Ethnic Attitudes," *Anthropological Linguistics*, March 1959, 34–41.

———. *Nigerian Orthography*. Zaria: North Regional Adult Education Office, 1954.

World Health Organization. *Report on the World Health Situation 1954–56*. Geneva: WHO, 1959.

"Writer in Fleet Street," *West African Review*, XXXI, June 1960, 37.

OTHER SOURCES USED

Ajose, Oladele A. "Preventive Medicine and Superstition in Nigeria," *Africa* (London), XXVII, July 1957, 268–273.

"Artist from Onitsha," *West African Review*, XXXII, April 1961, 21–24.

Bane, Martin J. *Catholic Pioneers in West Africa*. Dublin: Clonmore and Reynolds, 1956.

Barclays Bank, DCO. *Nigeria: an Economic Survey*. London: Barclays Bank, DCO, 1956.

Bascom, William R. *The Sociological Role of the Yoruba Cult Group*. ("Memoir Series," No. 63.) Menasha, Wisconsin: American Anthropological Association, 1944.

Bigart, Homer. "New Medications Aiding Victims of Leprosy in Northern Nigeria," *New York Times*, February 20, 1960, 2.

————. "Nigerians Battle Sleeping Disease," *New York Times,* February 17, 1960, 15.

Biobaku, Saburi O. *The Egba and Their Neighbors, 1842–1872.* Oxford: Clarendon Press, 1957.

Blake, John William. "The Study of African History," *Transactions of the Royal Historical Society* (London), Fourth Series, XXXII, 1950, 49–69.

Boyd, William C. *Genetics and the Races of Man.* Boston: Little, Brown, 1950.

Bracker, Milton. "Nigeria Will Get Television Soon," *New York Times,* January 25, 1959.

deBriey, P. "The Productivity of African Labour," *International Labour Review,* LXXII, August-September 1955, 119–137.

British Information Service. *Nigeria: The Making of a Nation.* New York: BIS, 1960.

Cameron, Sir Donald. *My Tanganyika Service* and *Some Nigeria.* London: Allen and Unwin, 1939.

Carpenter, George W. "The Role of Christianity and Islam in Contemporary Africa." Pages 90–113 in C. Grove Haines (ed.), *Africa Today,* Baltimore: Johns Hopkins Press, 1955.

Cary, Joyce. *Britain and West Africa.* London: Longmans, Green, 1947.

Christian Council of Nigeria. *Building for Tomorrow.* Lagos: N. C. Press, 1960.

Church, Ronald James Harrison. *West Africa.* New York: Longmans, Green, 1957.

Coker, G.B.A. *Family Property Among the Yorubas.* London: Sweet and Maxwell, 1958.

Daily Service (Lagos), April 2, 4, 5, 1960, *passim.*

Davidson, Basil. *The Lost Cities of Africa.* Boston: Little, Brown, 1959.

Demographic Yearbook, 1958. New York: United Nations, 1958.

"The Development of Wage-Earning Employment in Tropical Africa," *International Labour Review,* LXXIV, September 1956, 239–258.

Dike, K. Onwuka. *Origins of the Niger Mission, 1841–1891.* Ibadan: University Press, 1957.

Dike, K. Onwuka; Arene, J.D.; Biobaku, Saburi O.; et al. *Eminent Nigerians of the Nineteenth Century.* Cambridge: Cambridge University Press, 1960.

Duerden, Dennis. "Hausa on the Air," *West Africa,* October 1, 1960, 1103.

Eastern Region of Nigeria. *Government Programme.* Enugu: Government Printer, n.d.

416

————. Department of Medical Services. *Annual Report, 1957.* Enugu: Government Printer, n.d.

Eastern Region of Nigeria. Ministry of Education. *Education in the Eastern Region, with Special Reference to Universal Primary Education.* Enugu: Ministry of Education, 1957.

Eastern Region of Nigeria Ministry of Information. *Education.* Enugu: Government Printer, 1960.

The Economist, August 20, 1960, *passim.*

Edkensi, Cyprian. "Lagos—City in a Hurry," *West African Review,* XXXI, September 1960, 14–17.

Elias, T. Olawale. *Groundwork of Nigerian Law.* London: Routledge and Kegan Paul, 1954.

Fage, J.D. *An Atlas of African History:* [London] : Edward Arnold Publishers, 1958.

Federal Nigeria (Lagos), I, June, August, October, and November 1958; II, January, March, May, July, September and December 1959; III, February, March, May, and June 1960, *passim.*

Flint, John E. *Sir George Goldie and the Making of Nigeria.* London: Oxford University Press, 1960.

Food and Agriculture Organization. *Nutrition Seminar for English-Speaking Countries and Territories in Africa South of the Sahara.* (FAO Report No. 960.) Rome: FAO, 1958.

Forde, Daryll (ed.). *Efik Traders of Old Calabar.* London: Oxford University Press, 1956.

Forde, Daryll, and Scott, Richenda. *The Native Economics of Nigeria.* ("The Economics of a Tropical Dependency," I; ed., Margery Perham.) London: Faber and Faber, 1946.

Foster, J. "Women's Teacher Training in Northern Nigeria." *Oversea Education,* XXXI, January 1960, 147–155.

Galetti, R.; Baldwin, K.D.S.; and Dina, I.O. *Nigerian Cocoa Farmers: An Economic Survey of Yoruba Cocoa Farming Families.* London: Oxford University Press, for the Nigeria Cocoa Marketing Board, 1956.

Gibb, H.A.R., and Kramers, J.H. (eds.). *Shorter Encyclopedia of Islam.* Ithaca: Cornell University Press, 1953.

Gouilly, Alphonse. *L'Islam dans l'Afrique Occidentale Francaise.* Paris: Editions Larose, 1952.

Grant, James. *A Geography of Western Nigeria.* Cambridge: Cambridge University Press, 1960.

Great Britain. Laws, Statutes, etc. *West Africa. The Nigeria (Constitution) Order in Council, 1960.* (No. 1652 of 1960.) London: HMSO, 1960.

Greenberg, Joseph H. "Islam and Clan Organization Among the Hausa," *Southwestern Journal of Anthropology,* III, Autumn 1947, 193–211.

Groves, Charles Pelham. *The Planting of Christianity in Africa.* 4 vols. London: Butterworth Press, 1948–1958.

Hallet, Robin. *The Pattern of Northern Nigeria History.* Kaduna: Northern Nigeria Ministry of Internal Affairs, 1959.

Haynes, George Edmund. *Africa: Continent of the Future.* New York and Geneva: The Association Press and the World's Committee of Young Men's Christian Associations, 1950.

"Higher Education in Nigeria," *The Guardian,* July 15, 1960, 14.

Hogben, S.J. *The Mohammedan Emirates of Northern Nigeria.* London: Oxford University Press, 1930.

Hoskins, Halford L. *European Imperialism in Africa.* ("Berkshire Studies in European History.") New York: Holt, 1930.

Howe, Russell. "Marxism Would Have to 'Adapt' in Africa," *Washington Post,* May 15, 1960.

Ibadan Grammar School, *Prospectus,* N.p.: n. pub., n.d.

Ilogu, Edmund. "The Problem of Indigenization in Nigeria," *International Review of Missions,* XLIX, April 1960, 167–182.

Inter-African Labor Institute. *The Human Factors of Productivity in Africa: A Preliminary Survey.* London: Commission for Technological Co-operation in Africa South of the Sahara, 1965.

International African Institute. *Social Implications of Industrialization and Urbanization in Africa South of the Sahara.* ("Tensions and Technology Series.") Paris: UNESCO, 1956.

International Bank for Reconstruction and Development. *The Economic Development of Nigeria.* Baltimore: Johns Hopkins University Press, 1955.

International Labor Organization. International Labor Conference, 37th Session. *Migrant Workers (Underdeveloped Countries).* (Report V [1].) Geneva: ILO, 1953.

"Inter-Territorial Migrations of Africans South of the Sahara," *International Labour Review,* LXXVI, September 1957, 292–310.

Johnston, Bruce F. *The Staple Food Economies of Western Tropical Africa.* (Food Research Institute, "Studies in Tropical Development.") Stanford: Stanford University Press, 1958.

King's College, Lagos. *Prospectus.* Lagos: Federal Government Printer, 1959.

Latourette, Kenneth Scott. *A History of the Expansion of Christianity. Vol. V: The Great Century in the Americas, Austral-Asia, and Africa, A.D. 1800–A.D. 1914.* New York: Harper, 1943.

Little, Kenneth. "The Role of Voluntary Associations in West African Urbanization," *American Anthropologist,* LIX, August 1957, 579–596.

Lloyd, P.C. "Sacred Kingship and Government Among the Yoruba," *Africa* (London), XXX, July 1960, 221–237.

Maclean, Una. "Nigeria's Blood Bank," *West African Review*, XXXI, June 1960, 47.

Man O'War Bay Training Centre. *Outward Bound to the New Nigeria*. [Report on activities from 1950–1958.] N.p.: n.pub., n.d.

Meek, Charles Kingsley. *Land Tenure and Land Administration in Nigeria and the Cameroons*. London: HMSO, 1957.

————. *Law and Authority in a Nigerian Tribe*. (With a Foreword by Lord Lugard.) London: Oxford University Press, 1937.

————. *The Northern Tribes of Nigeria*. 2 vols. London: Oxford University Press, 1925.

————. *Tribal Studies in Northern Nigeria*. 2 vols. London: Kegan Paul, Trench, Trubner, 1931.

Mellanby, Kenneth. *The Birth of Nigeria's University*. London: Methuen, 1958.

Miller, Walter. *Have We Failed in Nigeria?* London: United Society for Christian Literature, 1947.

————. *Reflections of a Pioneer*. London: Church Missionary Society, 1936.

"Minister Tells ILO of Nigeria's Plan for Enlightened Labor Laws," *Federal Nigeria* (Lagos), III, June 1959, 1, 6.

Nadel, S.F. *Nupe Religion*. London: Routledge and Kegan Paul, 1954.

"New Nigerian Press Partnership," *West Africa*, August 20, 1960, 945.

New York Times, November 8, 1959, *passim*.

Nicholson, Marjorie. "Has Trade Unionism Failed in West Africa?" *West African Review*, XXXI, May 1960, 6–9, 71.

Nigeria. *Annual Volume of the Laws of the Federation of Nigeria, 1957*. Lagos: Federal Government Printer, n.d.

————. *The Census of Nigeria, 1931*. 7 vols. London: Crown Agents, 1932–34.

————. *Final Report of the Parliamentary Committee on the Nigerianisation of the Federal Public Service*. (Sessional Paper No. 6 of 1959.) Lagos: Federal Government Printer, 1959.

————. *Matters Arising from the Final Report of the Parliamentary Committee on the Nigerianisation of the Federal Public Service. A Statement of Policy*. (Sessional Paper No. 2 of 1960.) Lagos: Federal Government Printer, 1960.

————. *Short Guide to Workmen's Compensation Ordinance*. Lagos: Federal Government Printer, 1960.

————. *Ten-Year Educational Plan*. (Sessional Paper No. 6 of 1944.) Lagos: Government Printer, n.d.

Nigeria. Department of Broadcasting. *Annual Report, 1956.* Lagos: Federal Government Printer, 1957.

Nigeria. Department of Commerce and Industries. *Handbook of Commerce and Industry in Nigeria.* (3d ed.) Lagos: Federal Department of Commerce and Industries, 1957.

Nigeria. Department of Labor. *Annual Report, 1951–52.* Lagos: Government Printer, 1953.

————. *Annual Report, 1952–53.* Lagos: Government Printer, 1954.

————. *Annual Report 1953–54.* Lagos: Government Printer, 1955.

————. *Annual Report, 1954–55.* Lagos: Government Printer, 1956.

————. *Annual Report, 1955–56.* Lagos: Government Printer, 1957.

————. *Annual Report, 1957–58.* Lagos: Federal Government Printer, 1960.

————. *Short Guide to the Factories Ordinance.* Lagos: Government Printer, 1955.

Nigeria. Department of Medical Services. *Annual Report, 1958.* Lagos: Federal Government Printer, 1960.

————. *Report of the Medical Service of the Federal Territory of Lagos for the Year 1957.* Lagos: Federal Government Printer, 1958.

————. *Report of the Medical Service of the Federal Territory of Lagos for the Year 1958.* Lagos: Federal Government Printer, n.d.

Nigeria. Department of Statistics. *Urban Consumers Surveys in Nigeria: Report on Enquiries into the Income and Expenditure Patterns of Wage-Earner Households in Lagos (1953–54), Enugu (1954–55), and Ibadan (1955).* Lagos: Federal Government Statistician, 1957.

Nigeria. Federal Education Department. *Annual Report, 1958.* Lagos: Federal Government Printer, 1959.

Nigeria. Federal Ministry of Education. *Digest of Education Statistics, 1958.* Lagos: Federal Ministry of Information, 1960.

Nigeria. Federal Ministry of Information. *Our University College.* Lagos: Federal Ministry of Information, 1960.

Nigeria. Federal Office of Statistics. *Annual Abstract of Statistics, 1960.* Lagos: Federal Government Statistician, 1960.

Nigeria. Laws, Statutes, etc. *Laws of Nigeria, 1948: Ordinances Enacted on or Before 1 January 1948.* 12 vols. Lagos: Government Printer, 1948.

————. *Mines Manual, Containing the Minerals Ordinance (cap. 134 of 1948) and Ancillary Legislation.* (8th ed.) Lagos: Federal Government Printer, 1957.

———. "Ordinance to Amend Workmen's Compensation Ordinance," *Official Gazette,* XLIV, No. 10, February 28, 1957, C51.

Nigeria. Social Welfare Department. *Annual Report, 1958–59.* Lagos: Federal Government Printer, 1960.

"Nigerian Capital of Education," *The Times British Colonies Review,* No. 33, First Quarter, 1959, 31.

Nigerian Citizen (Zaria), May 7, April 13, 16, 1960, *passim.*

Nigerian Employers' Consultative Association Newsletter, No. 5, July 1959.

"Nigerian Threat to Discipline Press for 'Destructive Criticism' Protested," *Washington Post,* January 3, 1960.

"Nigeria's Free Press," *Time,* October 17, 1960, 71.

Niven, Cyril Rex. *A Short History of Nigeria.* (7th ed. rev.) London: Longmans, Green, 1959.

Northern Region of Nigeria. *The Education Law with Amendments up to 1st April 1959.* Kaduna: Government Printer, 1959.

———. *Report on the Kano Disturbances 16th, 17th, 18th, and 19th May, 1953.* Kaduna: Government Printer, 1953.

Northern Region of Nigeria. Department of Medical Services. *Annual Report, 1954–55.* Kaduna: Government Printer, n.d.

Northern Region of Nigeria. Education Department. *Annual Summary, 1956–57.* Kaduna: Government Printer, 1959.

Northern Region of Nigeria. Information Service. *The Institute of Administration, Zaria, Northern Region.* Kaduna: Ministry for Local Government, 1960.

———. *You and Nigerian Independence.* Kaduna: Northern Nigeria Information Service. 1960.

Ojike, Mbonu. *My Africa.* London: Blandford Press, 1955.

Oliver, E.I. *Nigeria: Economic and Commercial Conditions.* ("Overseas Economic Surveys.") London: HMSO, 1957.

Ottenberg, S. "Improvement Associations Among the Afikpo Ibo," *Africa,* XXV, No. 1, 1955, 1–27.

Parrinder, Geoffrey. *The Story of Ketu: An Ancient Yoruba Kingdom.* Ibadan: University Press, 1956.

Pedler, F.J. *Economic Geography of West Africa.* New York: Longmans, Green, 1955.

———. *West Africa.* (2d ed.) ("Home Study Books," ed., Sir Ifor Evans.) New York: Methuen, 1959.

Perham, Margery. *Native Administration in Nigeria.* London: Oxford University Press, 1937.

"Planning for Welfare," *The Guardian,* July 15, 1960, 18.

Prothero, R. Mansell. "The Population Census of Northern Nigeria 1952: Problems and Results," *Population Studies,* X, November 1956, 166–183.

Rattray, Robert Sutherland. *Hausa Folk-Lore Customs, Proverbs, Etc.* 2 vols. (With a preface by R.R. Marett.) Oxford: Clarendon Press, 1913.

Rodger, F.C. *Blindness in West Africa.* London: H.K. Lewis, for the Royal Commonwealth Society for the Blind, 1959.

Rudin, Harry R. "The History of European Relations with Africa." Pages 14–30 in Calvin W. Stillman (ed.), *Africa in the Modern World.* Chicago: University of Chicago Press, 1955.

Ryan, Isobel. *Black Man's Palaver.* London: Cape, 1958.

Schwab, William B. *The Political and Social Organization of an Urban African Community.* Ann Arbor: University Microfilms, 1952.

Simmons, Donald C. "Sexual Life, Marriage, and Childhood among the Efik," *Africa,* XXX, April 1960, 153–165.

Smith, Michael G. *The Economy of Hausa Communities of Zaria.* ("Colonial Research Studies," No. 16.) [London]: HMSO, for the Colonial Office, 1955.

———. "Kagoro Political Development," *Human Organization,* XIX, Fall 1960, 137–149.

Smyke, Raymond S. "Teaching in West Africa," *Africa Special Report,* III, November 1958, 13.

Solarin, T.T. *Toward Nigeria's Moral Self-Government.* Ikenne: n.pub., 1959.

Stephens, Leslie. "Impressions of Industrial Relations in Nigeria and Ghana," *Personnel Management,* XLI, March 1959, 28–33.

Stephens, Richard W. *Population Pressures in Africa South of the Sahara.* Washington: George Washington University, 1958.

Talbot, Percy Amaury. *Peoples of Southern Nigeria.* 4 vols. London: Oxford University Press, 1926.

"TV for All," *West Africa,* September 5, 1959, 681.

"Television in Nigeria," *Nigeria Trade Journal* (Lagos), October–December 1959, 165.

Temple, Charles Lindsay (ed.). *Notes on the Tribes, Provinces, Emirates and States of the Northern Provinces of Nigeria, Compiled from Official Reports of O. Temple.* Cape Town: Argus Printing and Publishing Co., 1919.

"Treaty Concluded Between the Nigerian Government and the Government of Spanish Territories of the Gulf of Guinea for the Recruitment of Native Labourers in the Former Country to Work in the Latter Area," *Nigeria Gazette,* XXX, June 17, 1943, 303–306.

"Treaty with the Government of French West Africa at Gabon for Recruitment of Nigerian Labour," *Federal Gazette* [Nigeria Gazette], Extraordinary No. 46 of 1949, Government Notice No. 1207. Lagos: Government Printer, 1949.

United Nations. Secretariat. Bureau of Social Affairs. *International Survey of Programmes of Social Development.* New York: UN, 1959.

U.S. Department of Commerce. Bureau of Foreign Commerce. *Investment in Nigeria.* Washington: GPO, 1957.

United States Information Service. *Voice of America Radio Programs to Nigeria.* Lagos: CMS (Nigeria) Press, 1960.

Urvoy, Yves. *Histoire de l'Empire du Bornou.* ("Memoire de l'Institute Française de l'Afrique Noire," No. 7.) Paris: Larose, 1949.

Walker, Eric A. *The British Empire: Its Structure and Spirit.* London: Oxford University Press, 1943.

Warmington, W.A. *A West African Trade Union.* London: Oxford University Press, for the Nigerian Institute of Social and Economic Research, 1960.

West Africa, May 7, 14, June 25, July 16, 23, 30, September 3, 10, November 26, 1960, *passim.*

West African Pilot (Yaba), April 19, 21, May 2, 7, 11, 16, 18, 21, August 8, 1960, *passim.*

West African Review, XXXI, February 1960, *passim.*

Westermann, Diedrich, *Geschichte Afrikas: Staatenbildungen Südlich der Sahara* (History of Africa: Formation of the States South of the Sahara). Cologne: Greven-Verlag, 1952.

Western Region of Nigeria. *Western Region Development Plan 1960–65.* (Sessional Paper No. 17 of 1959.) Ibadan: Government Printer, 1959.

————. Department of Medical Services. *Annual Report, 1955.* Ibadan: Government Printer, n.d.

Western Region of Nigeria. Laws, Statutes, etc. *Western Nigeria Government Broadcasting Law, 1959.* (W.R. No. 48 of 1959.) Ibadan: Government Printer, 1959.

Western Region of Nigeria. Ministry of Home Affairs. Information Division. *Facts About Western Nigeria Post-Secondary Scholarship Awards.* [Ibadan]: Ministry of Home Affairs, 1959.

Wheare, Joan. *The Nigerian Legislative Council.* ("Studies in Colonial Legislatures," ed., Margery Perham, IV.) London: Faber and Faber, for Nuffeld College, 1950.

World Health Organization. Tuberculosis Research Office. *Tuberculosis Survey in Nigeria.* Copenhagen: WHO, December 1957.

Yaba Technical Institute. *Details of Courses Offered* [1957–58]. N.p.: n.pub., n.d.

Section II. Political
RECOMMENDED SOURCES

Almond, Gabriel A., and Coleman, James S. (eds.). *The Politics of the Developing Areas*. Princeton: Princeton University Press, 1960.

Awolowo, Obafemi. *Awo: The Autobiography of Chief Obafemi Awolowo*. London: Cambridge University Press, 1960.

Azikiwe, Nnamdi. *The Development of Political Parties in Nigeria*. London: Office of the Commissioner in the United Kingdom for the Eastern Region of Nigeria, 1957.

"Borstal System," *Encyclopaedia Britannica* (1953 ed.), III, 923.

Coke Wallis, L.G. "Nigerianization of the Public Services in Western Nigeria," *Journal of African Administration*, XII, July 1960, 144–146.

Cole, R. Taylor. "The Independence Constitution of Federal Nigeria," *The South Atlantic Quarterly*, LX, Winter 1960, 1–18.

Coleman, Jams S. *Nigeria: Background to Nationalism*. Berkeley: University of California Press, 1958.

Cowan, L. Gray. *Local Government in West Africa*. New York: Columbia University Press, 1958.

Dike, K. Onwuka. *100 Years of British Rule in Nigeria 1851–1951*. (2d ed.) ("Lugard Lectures," 1956.) Lagos: Federal Ministry of Information, 1960.

Elias, T. Olawale, *Groundwork of Nigerian Law*. London: Routledge and Kegan Paul, 1954.

Ezera, Kalu. *Constitutional Developments in Nigeria*. London: Cambridge University Press, 1960.

Great Britain. Colonial Office. *Annual Report on Nigeria, 1955*. London: HMSO, 1958.

———. *Nigeria: Report of the Commission Appointed to Enquire into the Fears of Minorities and the Means of Allaying Them*. (Cmnd. 505.) London: HMSO, 1958.

Great Britain. Laws, Statutes, etc. *West Africa. The Nigeria (Constitution) Order in Council, 1960*. (L.N. 159 of 1960.)

Hailey, Lord William M. *An African Survey*. (Rev. ed. 1956.) London: Oxford University Press, 1957.

———. *Native Administration in the British African Territories. Part IV: General Survey of the System of Native Administration*. London: HMSO, 1951.

————. *Native Administration in the British African Territories. Part III: West Africa: Nigeria, Gold Coast, Sierra Leone, Gambia.* London: HMSO, 1951.

Haynes, George Edmund. *Africa: Continent of the Future.* New York: The Association Press and the World's Committee of Young Men's Christian Associations, 1950.

Hodgkin, Thomas. *Nationalism in Colonial Africa.* London: Frederick Muller, 1956.

Kalu, Ezera. *Constitutional Developments in Nigeria.* London: Cambridge University Press, 1960.

Kitchen, Helen. "Bit-Part Africa Taking Center of the State," *Washington Post,* September 11, 1960.

Mackenzie, William James Miller, and Robinson, Kenneth (eds.). *Five Elections in Africa.* London: Oxford University Press, 1960.

Macmillan, William Miller. *The Road to Self-Rule: A Study in Colonial Evolution.* London: Faber and Faber, 1959.

Marcum, John. "The Challenge of Africa," *The New Leader,* Section 2, February 8, 1960, 5–43.

Nigeria, *Estimates, 1960–61.* Lagos: Federal Government Printer, 1960.

————. Electoral Commission. *Report of the Nigeria Federal Elections, December 1959.* Lagos: Federal Government Printer, 1960.

Nigeria. Federal Information Service. *Annual Report, 1954–55.* Lagos: Federal Government Printer, 1955.

————. *Annual Report, 1956–57.* Lagos: Federal Government Printer, 1958.

————. *Annual Report, 1957–58.* Lagos: Federal Government Printer, 1959.

————. *Annual Report, 1957.* Lagos: Federal Information Service, 1960.

————. *Annual Report, 1958–59.* Lagos: Federal Government Printer, 1960.

————. *Five Years of Broadcasting, 1951–56.* Lagos: Federal Information Service, 1956.

Nigeria. Federal Ministry of Information. *Nigeria's Constitutional Development, 1861–1960.* Lagos: Federal Ministry of Information, 1960.

————. *Our Emirates.* (Rev. ed.) Lagos: Federal Ministry of Information, 1960.

Nigeria. Federal Ministry of Research and Information. Information Division. *Achievements of the Federal Government: A Verbatim Record of an Historic Debate in the Federal House of*

Representatives on August 15, 1959. Lagos: Federal Ministry of Research and Information, 1959.

Nigeria. House of Representatives. *Second Progress Report on the Economic Programme, 1955–60.* (Sessional Paper No. 1 of 1958.) Lagos: Federal Government Printer, 1958.

Nigeria. Laws, Statutes, etc. *Borstal Institutions and Remand Centers Ordinance, 1960.* (Ordinance No. 32 of 1960.)

Nigeria. Police Force. *General Report and Survey on the Nigeria Police Force for 1958.* Lagos: Federal Government Printer, 1959.

Nigeria. Prisons Department. *Annual Report, 1958–59.* Lagos: Federal Government Printer, 1960.

————. *Report on the Treatment of Offenders, 1956–57.* Lagos: Government Printer, n.d.

Niven, Cyril Rex. *How Nigeria is Governed.* (3d. ed.) London: Longmans, Green, 1958.

Royal Institute of International Affairs. *Nigeria: The Political and Economic Background.* London: Oxford University Press, 1960.

Wheare, Joan. *The Nigerian Legislative Council.* ("Studies in Colonial Legislatures," ed., Margery Perham, IV.) London: Faber and Faber, for Nuffeld College, 1950.

Younger, Kenneth. *The Public Service in New States.* London: Oxford University Press, 1960.

OTHER SOURCES USED

Adam, Thomas R. *Government and Politics in Africa South of the Sahara.* ("Studies in Political Science.") New York: Random House, 1959.

Africa Digest, VIII, December 1960, 119.

"An African Policy for Egypt," *The Egyptian Economic and Political Review* (Cairo), August 1960, 21–44.

"African Students Blast Moscow Discrimination," *Evening Star* (Washington), September 21, 1960, A–16.

Aluko, S.A. *The Problems of Self-Government for Nigeria.* Ifracombe, Devonshire: Arthur H. Stockwell, 1955.

American Assembly. *The United States and Africa.* New York: Columbia University Press, 1958.

Anderson, J.N.D. "Relationship Between Islamic and Customary Law in Africa," *Journal of African Administration,* XII, October 1960, 228–234.

Apter, David E., and Coleman, James S. "Pan-American or Nationalism in Africa," Third Annual Conference, American Society of African Culture, June 1960 (manuscript).

Awa, E. "The Federal Election (I)," *Ibadan*, No. 8, March 1960, 4–7.

Awolowo, Obafemi. *Action Group 14-Point Programme*. Ibadan: [AG], 1959.

———. *Paths to Nigerian Freedom*. (With a Foreword by Margery Perham.) London: Faber and Faber, 1947.

Busia, Kofi A. "The Gold Coast and Nigeria on the Road to Self-Government." Pages 289–304 in C. Grove Haines (ed.), *Africa Today*, Baltimore: Johns Hopkins Press, 1955.

Cowan, L. Gray. "Democracy in West Africa," *International Journal*, XV, Summer 1960, 173–184.

Daily Express (Lagos), October 20, 1960, 1.

Daldry, L. C. "Nigeria's Federal Parliament," *African Affairs*, LIX, October 1960, 292–300.

Eastern Region of Nigeria. *The Administrative Organization of the Eastern Region*. (Eastern Region Official Document No. 3 of 1958.) Enugu: Government Printer, 1958.

———. *Approved Estimates, 1959–60*. Enugu: Government Printer, 1959.

———. *Approved Supplementary Estimates, 1959–60*. Enugu: Government Printer, 1960.

———. Information Service. *Eastern Nigeria*. Enugu: Information Service, [1956].

Features of the Northern Region of Nigeria (Kaduna), Nos. 2 and 3, June and October, 1958, *passim*.

"First Woman ASP," *Daily Service* (Lagos), August 23, 1960, 1.

Fortes, Meyer M., and Evans-Pritchard, E.E. *African Political Systems*. London: Oxford University Press, for the International African Institute of African Languages and Cultures, 1940.

Great Britain. Central Office of Information. *Nigeria Today*. London: British Information Service, 1960.

Great Britain. Colonial Office. *Report by the Nigeria Constitutional Conference held in London in May and June 1957*. (Cmnd. 207.) London: HMSO, 1958.

———. *Report by the Resumed Nigeria Constitutional Conference held in London in September and October 1958*. (Cmnd. 569.) London: HMSO, 1958.

Great Britain. Laws, Statutes, etc. *West Africa. The Nigeria (Constitution) Order in Council, 1954*. (L.N. 16 of 1959.)

Gunther, John. *Inside Africa*. New York: Harper, 1955.

Hatch, John. *Everyman's Africa*. London: Dennis Dobson, 1959.

Hodgkin, Thomas. "Nigeria's External Relations; Diplomacy in Pre-Colonial Nigeria," *West African Review*, XXX, September 1960, 18–21.

Howe, Russell. "Marxism Would have to 'Adapt' in Africa," *Washington Post*, May 15, 1960.

"Justice and Judges in Northern Nigeria," *West Africa*, No. 2206, September 12, 1959, 1.

Kitchen, Helen (ed.). *The Press in Africa*. Washington: Ruth Sloan Associates, 1956.

Mabogunje, Akin. "Nigeria and Tomorrow's Africa," *Africa South in Exile*, V, No. 1, October–December 1960, 99–107.

Munger, Edwin S. *All-African People's Conference*. (Africa: ESM–1–'59.) New York: American Universities Field Staff, 1959 (mimeo.).

Nasser, Premier Gamal Abdul. *Egypt's Liberation*. Washington: Public Affairs Press, 1955.

National Council of Nigeria and the Cameroons. *The Constitution; Rules and Regulations of the NCNC*. Yaba Estate: NCNC National Headquarters, 1960.

—————. *Manifesto of the National Council of Nigeria and the Cameroons and the Northern Elements Progressive Union Alliance for the 1959 Elections*. Yaba: NCNC, n.d.

Nigeria. *Estimates, 1959–60*. Lagos: Federal Government Printer, 1959.

—————. *First Supplementary Estimates, 1960–61*. Lagos Federal Government Printer, 1960.

—————. *The Nigeria Handbook*. London: Crown Agents for the Colonies on Behalf of the Government of Nigeria, 1953.

—————. *Views of the Government of the Federation on the Interim Report of the Committee on Nigerianization*. (Sessional Paper No. 7 of 1958.) Lagos: Government Printer, 1958.

Nigeria. Department of Statistics. *Population Census of Nigeria, 1952–53*. Lagos: Census Superintendent (Federal Government Statistician), n.d.

Nigeria. Federal Ministry of Information. *Nigeria, 1960*. Lagos: Federal Ministry of Information, for the Independence Planning Committee, 1960.

—————. *Nigeria Asks for Independence*. (A Reprint of the Debate in the Federal House of Representatives on January 14, 15, and 16, 1960.) Lagos: Federal Government Printer, 1960.

Nigeria. Laws, Statutes, etc. *Borstal Training (Lagos) Ordinance, 1960*. (Ordinance No. 28 of 1960.)

—————. *Prisons Ordinance, 1960*. (Ordinance No. 41 of 1960.)

Nigeria. Prisons Department. *Annual Report, 1939*. (Sessional Paper No. 8 of 1941.) Lagos: Government Printer, 1941.

—————. *Annual Report, 1940*. (Sessional Paper No. 17 of 1941.) Lagos: Government Printer, 1941.

———. *Annual Report, 1941*. (Sessional Paper No. 7 of 1943.) Lagos: Government Printer, 1943.

———. *Annual Report, 1942*. (Sessional Paper No. 13 of 1943.) Lagos: Government Printer, 1943.

———. *Annual Report, 1943*. (Sessional Paper No. 17 of 1944.) Lagos: Government Printer, 1944.

———. *Annual Report, 1944*. (Sessional Paper No. 11 of 1946.) Lagos: Government Printer, 1946.

"Nigeria Opposes West Africa Pact," *New York Times*, October 4, 1960, 5.

"Nigeria's New Constitution," *World Today*, X, November 1954, 463–465.

"Northern Nigerian Revolution," *West Africa*, No. 2178, January 10, 1959, 1.

Northern People's Congress. *Constitution and Rules*. Zaria: [NPC], n.d.

———. *NPC Federal Government Policy*. Kaduna: NPC, 1959.

Northern Region of Nigeria. *Approved Estimates, 1959–60*. Kaduna: Government Printer, 1959.

———. *Approved Estimates, 1960–61*. Kaduna: Government Printer, 1960.

———. *Approved First Supplementary Estimates, 1959–60*. Kaduna: Government Printer, 1959.

———. *Handbook for Native Courts*. Kaduna: Government Printer, 1957.

———. *Progress Report on the Development Finance Program, 1955–60*. Kaduna: Government Printer, 1959.

———. *Provincial Annual Reports. 1958*. Kaduna: Government Printer, 1959.

———. Information Services. *Festival of Kano, 1959*. (Text by F.O. Brice-Bennett.) (London: Northern Nigeria Information Service, 1959.

———. *Giant in the Sun: The Story of Northern Nigeria*. Kaduna: Northern Nigeria Information Service, 1959.

———. *Your Government at Work*. Kaduna: Northern Region Information Service, 1960.

Northern Region of Nigeria. Laws, Statutes, etc. *Court of Resolution Law, 1960*. (N.R. No. 17 of 1960.)

———. *Criminal Procedure Code Law, 1960*. (N.R. No. 11 of 1960.)

———. *Native Courts Law, 1956*. (N.R. No. 6 of 1956.)

———. *Native Courts (Amendment) Law, 1960*. (N.R. No. 10 of 1960.)

———. *Northern Region High Court Law, 1955*. (N.R. No. 8 of 1955.)

———. *Penal Code Law, 1959.* (N.R. No. 18 of 1959.)

———. *Sharia Court of Appeal Law, 1960.* (N.R. No. 16 of 1960).

Northern Region of Nigeria. Regional Adult Education Field Headquarters. *You and Your Country.* Zaria: n.pub., n.d.

Odenigwe, G.A. "Parliamentary Democracy in Nigeria," *West African Pilot* (Yaba), August 13, 15, 16, 1960.

Oliver, E.I. *Nigeria: Economic and Commercial Conditions.* ("Overseas Economic Surveys.") London: HMSO, 1957.

Panikkar, K.M. *The Afro-Asian States and their Problems.* New York: John Day, 1959.

Phillipson, Sydney, and Adebo, S.O. *The Nigerianization of the Civil Service: a Review of Policy and Machinery.* Lagos: Government Printer, 1954.

"Police Without Politics," *West Africa,* No. 2165, October 11, 1958, 961.

Post, K.W.J. "The Federal Election (II)," *Ibadan,* No. 8, March 1960, 7–9.

[Radio Programs], *Nigerian Citizen* (Zaria), December 7, 1960, 11.

Smith, Michael G. *Government in Zazzau, 1800–1950.* London: Oxford University Press, 1960.

———. "Kagoro Political Development," *Human Organization,* XIX, Fall 1960, 137–149.

"Statement by the Prime Minister on Foreign Policy," mimeographed statement circulated by Nigeria Office, n.d.

"TUC Suspends Mike Imoudu," *Daily Service* (Lagos), March 30, 1960, 16.

U.S. Department of Commerce. Bureau of Foreign Commerce. *Investment in Nigeria.* Washington: GPO, 1957.

"A Valuable Legacy Left by the British," *Life,* September 26, 1960, 71.

Western Region of Nigeria. *Customary Courts Manual.* Ibadan: Government Printer, post-1958.

———. *Development of the Western Region of Nigeria 1955–60.* (Sessional Paper No. 4 of 1955.) Ibadan: Government Printer, n.d.

———. *Estimates, 1959–60.* Ibadan: Government Printer, 1959

———. *Supplementary Estimates, 1959–60.* Ibadan: Government Printer, 1959.

———. *Western Region Development Plan 1960–65.* (Sessional Paper No. 17 of 1959.) Ibadan: Government Printer, 1959.

———. *White Paper on the Re-Organization of Ministries.* (Sessional Paper No. 2 of 1959.) Ibadan: Government Printer, n.d.

———. Information Services. *Forward to a New Nigeria: Speeches by Chief Obafemi Awolowo, May-June 1957.* [Ibadan] : Western Region Information Services, n.d.

Western Region of Nigeria. Laws, Statutes, etc. *High Court (Civil Procedure) Rules, 1958.* (WRLN 293 of 1958.)

————. *Magistrates' Courts (Civil Procedure) Rules, 1958.* (WRLN 292 of 1958.)

Western Region of Nigeria. Ministry of Home and Mid-West Affairs. *Towards Independence: Speeches and Statements by Chief Obafemi Awolowo, Premier of the Western Region of Nigeria.* Ibadan: Information Services Division, 1958.

White, R.V.D., *et al. Our Police Force.* ("Crownbird Series," No. 10.) Lagos: Federal Information Service, 1952.

World Almanac, 1960. New York: New York World Telegram, 1960.

Section III. Economic

RECOMMENDED SOURCES

Arnott, D.W. "Councils and Courts among the Tiv—Traditional Concepts and Alien Institutions in a Non-Moslem Tribe of Northern Nigeria," *Journal of African Law,* II, Spring 1958, 19.

Baldwin, K.D.S. *The Niger Agricultural Project.* Cambridge: Harvard University Press, 1957.

Bauer, P.T. *West African Trade.* Cambridge: Cambridge University Press, 1954.

Bower, P.A., et al. *Mining, Commerce and Finance in Nigeria.* ("The Economics of a Tropical Dependency," II; ed., Margery Perham.) London: Faber and Faber, 1948.

Buchanan, K.M., and Pugh, J.C. *Land and People in Nigeria.* London: University of London Press, 1955.

"Cattle Trade in Nigeria," *Nigeria Trade Journal* (Lagos), VIII, July-September, 1960, 88–91.

Central Bank of Nigeria, *Annual Report and Statement of Accounts for the Period Ended 31 March 1960.* Lagos: Central Bank of Nigeria, 1960.

Coleman, James S. *Nigeria: Background to Nationalism.* Berkeley: University of California Press, 1958.

Cook, Arthur Norton. *British Enterprise in Nigeria.* Philadelphia: University of Philadelphia Press, 1943.

Eastern Region of Nigeria. *Approved Estimates, 1959–60.* Enugu: Government Printer, 1959.

———. *Approved Supplementary Estimates, 1959–60.* Enugu: Government Printer, 1960.

Elias, T. Olawale. *The Nature of African Customary Law.* London: Manchester University Press, 1956.

———. *Nigerian Land Law and Custom.* London: Róutledge and Kegan Paul, 1951.

Forde, Daryll, and Scott, Richenda. *The Native Economies of Nigeria.* ("The Economics of a Tropial Dependency," I; ed., Margery Perham.) London: Faber and Faber, 1946.

Galletti, R.; Baldwin, K.D.S.; and Dina, I.O. *Nigerian Cocoa Farmers: An Economic Survey of Yoruba Cocoa Farming Families.* London: Oxford University Press, for the Nigeria Cocoa Marketing Board, 1956.

433

Great Britain. Colonial Office. *Nigeria: Report of the Fiscal Commission.* (Cmnd. 481.) London: HMSO, 1958.

———. *Nigeria: Tribunal of Inquiry by Warrant of Appointment Dated 4 August 1956.* (Cmnd. 51.) London: HMSO, 1957.

Hailey, Lord William M. *An African Survey.* (Rev. ed. 1956.) London: Oxford University Press, 1957.

———. *The Future of Customary Law in Africa.* Leiden: University of Leiden, 1956.

International Bank for Reconstruction and Development. *The Economic Development of Nigeria.* Baltimore: Johns Hopkins University Press, 1955.

"Kano, Traffic Centre of Africa;" *Nigeria Trade Journal* (Lagos), V, April–June 1957, 59–65.

Lloyd, P.C. "Family Property Among the Yoruba," *Journal of African Law,* III, Summer 1959, 105.

———. "Some Notes on Yoruba Rules of Succession and on 'Family Property'," *Journal of African Law,* III, Spring 1959, 7.

Meek, C.K. *Land Tenure and Land Administration in Nigeria and the Cameroons.* ("Colonial Research Studies," No. 22.) London: HMSO, 1957.

Moncure, Robert C. "The Agricultural Economy of Nigeria and British Cameroons." Washington: U.S. Department of Agriculture, 1960. (Unpublished manuscript.)

National Economic Council. *Economic Survey of Nigeria, 1959.* Lagos: Federal Government Printer, 1959.

Newlyn, W.T., and Rowan, D.C. *Money and Banking in British Colonial Africa.* ("Oxford Studies in African Affairs.") Oxford: Clarendon Press, 1954.

Nigeria. *Estimates, 1959–60.* Lagos: Federal Government Printer, 1959.

———. *First Supplementary Estimates, 1959–60.* Lagos: Federal Government Printer, 1959.

———. *The Nigeria Handbook.* London: Crown Agents for the Colonies on Behalf of the Government of Nigeria, 1953.

———. *Report of the Committee Appointed to Advise on Ways and Means of Fostering a Share Market in Nigeria.* Lagos: Federal Government Printer, 1959.

———. *Second Supplementary Estimates, 1959–60.* Lagos: Federal Government Printer, 1960.

———. House of Representatives. *The Economic Programme of the Government of Nigeria, 1955–60.* (Sessional Paper No. 2 of 1956.) Lagos: Federal Government Printer, 1956.

———. *Second Progress Report on the Economic Programme,*

1955–60. (Sessional Paper No. 1 of 1958.) Lagos: Federal Government Printer, 1958.

Northern Region of Nigeria. *Approved Estimates, 1959–60.* Kaduna: Government Printer, 1959.

————. *Approved First Supplementary Estimates, 1959–60.* Kaduna: Government Printer, 1959.

Okotie-Eboh, F.S. "The Stability Budget," *Nigeria Trade Journal* (Lagos), VIII, April-June 1960, 46–51.

Oliver, E.I. *Nigeria: Economic and Commercial Conditions,* ("Overseas Economic Surveys.") London: HMSO, 1957.

"Onitsha Market," *Nigeria Trade Journal* (Lagos), V, July–September 1957, 88–91.

Pedler, F.J. *Economic Geography of West Africa.* New York: Longmans, Green, 1955.

Stapleton, G. Brian. *The Wealth of Nigeria.* London: Oxford University Press, 1958.

"Ubiquitous Hausa Traders," *Nigeria Trade Journal* (Lagos), VI, January–March 1958, 15–17.

United Nations. Department of Economic Affairs, *Review of Economic Conditions in Africa.* (Supplement to *World Economic Report, 1949–50.*) New York: UN, 1951.

United Nations. Department of Economic and Social Affairs. *Economic Survey of Africa Since 1950.* New York: UN, 1959.

U.S. Department of Commerce. Bureau of Foreign Commerce. *Investment in Nigeria.* Washington: GPO, 1957.

Western Region of Nigeria. *Estimates, 1959–60.* Ibadan: Government Printer, 1959.

————. *Supplementary Estimates, 1959–60.* Ibadan: Government Printer, 1959.

OTHER SOURCES USED

"Africa and the European Common Market," *West Africa,* January 10, 1959, 41.

"African Advantages for 'The Six' over 'The Seven'," *West Africa,* April 2, 1960, 381; April 9, 1960, 403.

"Africa's Economic Parliament," *West Africa,* February 22, 1960, 245; March 5, 1960, 265.

"Banking in Nigeria," *Nigeria Trade Journal* (Lagos), Special Independence Issue, [October] 1960, 72–74.

"The Beginning of a Highly Profitable Partnership—'50–50' Oil Deed Signed," *Federal Nigeria* (Lagos), II, June 1959, 3.

"Board of Customs and Excise," *Nigeria Trade Journal* (Lagos), Special Independence Issue, [October] 1960, 11–13.

"Cement Company Makes Financial History with Stock Issue," *Federal Nigeria* (Lagos), II, February 1959, 3.

Chukwuemeka, Nwankwo. *Industrialization of Nigeria.* New York: William Frederick Press, 1952.

"Civil Aviation," *Nigeria Trade Journal* (Lagos), Special Independence Issue, [October] 1960, 28–30.

"Cocoa Processing for W. Nigeria?" *West Africa,* May 21, 1960, 581.

"Cotton Piece Goods," *Nigeria Trade Journal* (Lagos), VI, April–June 1958, 66, 67.

"Development of Inland Waterways," *Nigeria Trade Journal* (Lagos), Special Independence Issue, [October] 1960, 49–51.

"The Development of Telecommunications," *Nigeria Trade Journal* (Lagos), VI, January–March 1958, 4–9.

Eastern Region of Nigeria. *Banking Monopoly in Nigeria.* Enugu: Government Printer, 1956.

"Eurafrica," *West Africa,* May 2, 1959, 411.

"Europe's Menace to Nigeria?" *West Africa,* September 26, 1959, 761.

"Expansion of Trade Since 1950," *Nigeria Trade Journal* (Lagos), Special Independence Issue, [October] 1960, 6–8.

Eyo, E.O. *£2,000,000 of Your Money in Premier Azikiwe's Bank.* Lagos: Amalgamated Press of Nigeria, Ltd., n.d.

"First Public Issue of Shares Heavily Over-Subscribed," *Federal Nigeria* (Lagos), II, April 1959, 1.

Fortes, M. "The Impact of the War on British West Africa," *International Affairs,* XXI, April 1945, 206–219.

"Hand Sheller Transforms Nigeria's Peanut Industry," *Foreign Agriculture,* December 1959, 21.

Hazlewood, Arthur. "Federal Finance in Nigeria," *West Africa,* August 9, 1958, 751, 752.

"Is the Common Market Dangerous?" *West Africa,* June 11, 1960, 645.

"Marketing Boards," *Nigeria Trade Journal* (Lagos), Special Independence Issue, [October] 1960, 9, 10.

"Motor Vehicle Assembly in Nigeria," *Nigeria Trade Journal* (Lagos), VII, July–September 1959, 93–95.

"New Oil Source Found in Western Nigeria," *Federal Nigeria* (Lagos), II, October 1959, 2.

"Nigercem—Nigeria's New Cement Factory at Nkalagu," *Nigeria Trade Journal* (Lagos), VI, April–June 1958, 61–65.

Nigeria. Department of Commerce and Industries. *Handbook of Commerce and Industry in Nigeria.* (3d ed.) Lagos: Federal Department of Commerce and Industries, 1957.

Nigeria. Laws, Statutes, etc. *Central Bank of Nigeria Ordinance, 1958.*

Nigeria. Ministry of Commerce and Industry. *Handbook of Com-*

merce and Industry in Nigeria. (4th ed.) Lagos: Ministry of Commerce and Industry, 1960.

Nigeria. Ministry of Communications and Aviation. *Annual Report of the Post Office Savings Bank, 1957–58.* Lagos: Federal Government Printer, 1960.

Nigeria. Ministry of Labor and Social Welfare. *Report of the Cooperative Department, 1956–59.* Lagos: Federal Government Printer, 1960.

Nigeria. Office of Statistics. *Digest of Statistics,* IX, July 1960.

"Nigeria Offers Oil Industry 'Realistic' Fiscal Policy," *Federal Nigeria* (Lagos), II, March 1959, 1.

"Nigerian Oil Output Doubled," *West Africa,* May 7, 1960, 525.

"No Discriminatory Tariffs Applied by Nigeria," *Federal Nigeria* (Lagos), II, November 1959, 7.

Northern Region of Nigeria. *Preliminary Statement of the Government of the Northern Region of Nigeria on the Report of the Commissioners Appointed to Advise the Government on Devolution of Powers to Provinces.* Kaduna: Government Printer, 1957.

————. *Statement on Government Activities in the Northern Region by the Governor to Budget Meeting of the Northern Regional Legislature, 1958.* Kaduna: Government Printer, 1958.

"Oil in Commercial Quantities," *Federal Nigeria* (Lagos), II, November 1959, 3.

"The Oil Industry in Nigeria—Mobil Proceeds with its Survey in the West," *Federal Nigeria* (Lagos), II, June 1959, 6.

"Oil Palm Plantations in Nigeria," *Nigeria Trade Journal* (Lagos), VI, October–December 1958, 143–150.

"One of the World's Most Important Oil Producers," *Federal Nigeria* (Lagos), III, March 1960, 3.

"Petroleum Oils," *Nigeria Trade Journal* (Lagos), VII, October–December 1959, 142–144.

"Plans for Oil Refinery in Nigeria Being Studied," *Federal Nigeria* (Lagos), II, May 1959, 6.

"Railway Development," *Nigeria Trade Journal* (Lagos), Special Independence Issue, [October] 1960, 54, 55.

"Revising the Common Market's African Ties," *West Africa,* June 18, 1960, 695.

"Road Construction," *Nigeria Trade Journal* (Lagos), Special Independence Issue, [October] 1960, 52, 53.

Roberts, Margaret. "Budgeting for the Northern Region," *West Africa,* May 7, 1960, 513.

————. "Dividing Nigeria's Revenues," *West Africa,* October 18, 1958, 988.

————. "Federal Government Loan Over-Subscribed," *Nigeria Trade Journal* (Lagos), VII, July–September 1959, 112, 113.

————. "Nigeria's Economic Prospects: I," *West Africa,* October 3, 1959, 791.

————. "Nigeria's Economic Prospects: II," *West Africa,* October 10, 1959, 832.

————. "Nigeria's Public Accounts," *West Africa,* May 7, 1960, 522.

"Rubber Planting and Processing in the Western Region," *Nigeria Trade Journal* (Lagos), VI, April–June 1958, 54–56.

"Sea Transport," *Nigeria Trade Journal* (Lagos), Special Independence Issue, [October] 1960, 45–48.

"The Search for Oil—Assessing the Commercial Possibilities," *Nigeria Trade Journal* (Lagos), VI, January–March 1958, 19–26.

"The Search for Oil In Southern Nigeria," *Federal Nigeria* (Lagos), I, December 1958, 4, 5.

"Survey of the Mining Industry—First Half of 1959," *Nigeria Trade Journal* (Lagos), VII, October–December 1959, 151.

"Trade Statistics," *Nigeria Trade Journal* (Lagos), VII, April–June 1959, 77–81.

U.S. Department of Agriculture. Foreign Agricultural Service. *Notes on the Agricultural Economies of the Countries of Africa. II: Central and Western Africa.* Washington: USDA, 1959.

Section IV. Military
RECOMMENDED SOURCES

Burns, Alan. *History of Nigeria.* (6th ed.) London: Allen and Unwin, 1955.

Coleman, James S. *Nigeria: Background to Nationalism.* Berkeley: University of California Press, 1958.

Nigeria. *Estimates, 1960–61.* Lagos: Federal Government Printer, 1960.

———. Federal Ministry of Information. *The Royal Nigerian Military Forces.* Lagos: Federal Ministry of Information, n.d.

Nigeria. Laws, Statutes, etc. *Royal Nigerian Military Forces.* (Ordinance No. 26 of 1960.)

———. *Royal Nigerian Navy Act, 1960.*

Niven, Cyril Rex. *A Short History of Nigeria.* London: Longmans, Green, 1952.

OTHER SOURCES USED

Africa Digest, VII, June 1960, *passim.*

Cole, David Henry. *Imperial Military Geography.* London: Sifton Praed, 1950.

Cook, Arthur Norton. *British Enterprise in Nigeria.* Philadelphia: University of Pennsylvania Press, 1943.

Daily Service (Lagos), May 21, 1960.

"The Economic Programme, 1955–60—II," *Nigeria Trade Journal* (Lagos), IV, October–December 1956, 128–133.

"Federal Economic Programme," *Nigeria Trade Journal* (Lagos), VI, July–September 1958, 86–91.

Federal Nigeria (Lagos), II, March 1959, *passim.*

Federal Nigeria (Lagos), III, April 1960, *passim.*

Great Britain. *Nigeria 1955.* London: HMSO, 1958.

———. Central Office of Information. *Nigeria Today.* London: British Information Service, 1960.

Great Britain. War Office. *Report of the Committee on the Organization and Administration of Boys' Units in the Army.* (Cmnd. 9433.) London: HMSO, 1955.

"H.M.S. 'Quorra'—Nigeria's Naval Base and Training School," *Federal Nigeria* (Lagos), II, January 1959, 4, 5.

Nigeria. *Estimates, 1959–60.* Lagos: Federal Government Printer, 1959.

————. *The Nigeria Handbook*. London: Crown Agents for the Colonies on Behalf of the Government of Nigeria, 1953.

————. Federal Education Department. *Annual Report, 1958.* Lagos: Federal Government Printer, 1959.

Nigeria. Federal Information Service. *100 Facts about Nigeria.* (2d ed.) Lagos: Federal Information Service, 1957.

————. *Our Military Forces.* Lagos: Federal Information Service, n.d.

————. *Our Military Forces.* (Rev. ed.) Lagos: Federal Information Service, n.d.

Nigeria. Federal Ministry of Research and Information. Information Division. *Achievements of the Federal Government: A Verbatim Record of an Historic Debate in the Federal House of Representatives on August 15, 1959.* Lagos: Federal Ministry of Research and Information, 1959.

Nigeria. House of Representatives. *Second Progress Report on the Economic Programme, 1955–60.* (Sessional Paper No. 1 of 1958.) Lagos: Federal Government Printer, 1958.

Nigeria Trade Journal (Lagos), V, October–December 1957, *passim.*

Nigeria Year Book, 1959. Lagos: Nigerian Printing and Publishing Co., Ltd., 1959.

"Nigerian House OKs British Defense Pact," *Sunday Star* (Washington), November 20, 1960, A–6.

"Nigerianization in Military Forces," *Federal Nigeria* (Lagos), III, July 1960, 7.

"Nigerianizing Military Forces," *Federal Nigeria* (Lagos), III, August 1960, 1.

"Prime Minister Opens £250,000 Military College," *Nigerian Citizen* (Zaria), April 6, 1960, 1.

"Progress in Royal Nigeria Navy," *Federal Nigeria* (Lagos), III, August 1960, 7.

"The Royal Nigerian Navy," *West African Pilot* (Yaba), July 25, 1960, 4.

West Africa, July 26, 1958, *passim.*

West Africa, January 31, 1959, *passim.*

West Africa, May 21, 1960, *passim.*

"What's Wrong with Our Navy," *West African Pilot* (Yaba), June 14, 1960, 5.

ADDITIONAL BIBLIOGRAPHY
FOR REVISED EDITION
RECOMMENDED SOURCES

Abernathy, David B. *The Political Dilemma of Popular Education: An African Case.* Stanford: Stanford University Press, 1969.

Adedji, Joel A. "Traditional Yoruba Theater," *African Arts/Arts d'Afrique,* II, No. 1, Autumn, 1969, 60–63.

Allott, A.N. *Judicial and Legal Systems in Africa.* (2d ed.) London: Butterworth, 1970.

Ananaba, Wogu. *The Trade Union Movement in Nigeria.* New York: Africana Publishing, 1970.

Anene, Joseph C. *The International Boundaries of Nigeria, 1889–1960: The Framework of an Emergent African Nation.* New York: Humanities Press, 1970.

Anthonio, Q.B.O. "Food Consumption and Income Relationship in Nigeria Engel's Curve Function," *Bulletin of Rural Economic Sociology* [Ibadan], II, No. 1, 1966, 52–67.

Arikpo, Okoi. *Nigeria's Post-War Policy on Africa, News from Nigeria.* Washington: Embassy of Nigeria, August 1, 1970.

Armer, J. Michael. *Psychological Impact of Education in Northern Nigeria,* (African Studies Association Paper.) New York: African Studies Association, 1967.

Arnold, R.B. "Maintenance of Measles Control in Kano State Nigeria." Pages 151–155 in the *Smallpox Eradication Program Report,* IV, No. 2. (Seminar on Smallpox Eradication and Measles Control in Western and Central Africa, Part II) Atlanta: National Communicable Disease Center, January 1970.

Aujoulat, L.P. *Santé et Developpement en Afrique.* Paris: Libraire Armand Colin, 1969.

Awolowo, Obafemi. *Strategy and Tactics of the People's Republic of Nigeria.* New York: Macmillan, 1970.

Baker, Pauline. "Nigeria: The Politics of Military Rule," *Africa Report,* XVI, No. 2, February 1971, 18–27.

Bascom, William R. *Ifa Divination: Communication Between Gods and Men in West Africa.* Bloomington: Indiana University Press, 1969.

———. *The Yoruba of Southwest Nigeria.* Case Studies in Cultural Anthropology. New York: Holt, Rinehart and Winston, 1969.

Beier, Ulli. *Contemporary Art in Africa*. London: Pall Mall Press, 1968.

Beier, Ulli (ed). *Yoruba Poetry: An Anthology of Traditional Poems*. London: Cambridge University Press, 1970.

Betz, Fritz H. *Entwicklungshilfe an Afrika*. Munich: Weltforum Verlag, 1970.

Bohannan, Paul, and Dalton, George (eds.) *Markets in Africa*. Evanston: Northwestern University Press, 1961.

Boston, J.S. "The Supernatural Aspect of Disease and Therapeutics Among the Igala," *African Notes* [Ibadan], V, No. 3, January 1970, 41–46.

Bourjailly, Vance. "Epitaph for Biafra," *New York Times Magazine*, January 25, 1970, 32.

Caddwell, Joan L. "Magnesium Deficiency in Extremis," *Nutrition Today*, II, No. 3, September 1967, 14–15.

Caldwell, John C., and Okonjo, Chukuka. *The Population of Tropical Africa*. New York: Columbia University Press, 1968.

Cervenka, Zdenek. *The Organization of African Unity and Its Charter*. New York: Praeger, 1969.

Cohen, Abner. *Custom and Politics in Urban Africa*. Berkeley: University of California Press, 1969.

Cohen, Ronald. *The Kanuri of Bornu*. Case Studies in Cultural Anthropology. New York: Holt, Rinehart and Winston, 1967.

Cole, Herbert, "Art as a Verb in Iboland," *African Arts/Arts d'Afrique*, III, No. 1, Autumn 1969, 34–41.

Coleman, James S. *Nigeria: Background to Nationalism*. Berkeley: University of California Press, 1958.

Committee on Education on Human Resource Development, Nigeria Project Task Force. *Nigerian Human Resource Development and Utilization, Education and World Affairs*. (Prepared for the United States Agency for International Development.) New York: International Council for Educational Development, 1967.

Crooke, Patrick. "Rural Settlement and Housing Trends in a Developing Country: An Example in Nigeria," *International Labour Review* [Geneva], XCVI, No. 3, September 1967, 280–291.

Dunstan, Elizabeth (ed.). *Twelve Nigerian Languages*. New York: Africana Publishing, for Longmans, Green, 1969.

Education and World Affairs. Committee on Education and Human Resource Development. Nigerian Project Task Force. *Nigerian Human Resource Development and Utilization*. New York: Education and World Affairs, December 1967.

Egboh, Edmund O. "Central Trade Unionism in Nigeria

(1941–1966)," *Geneve-Afrique* [Geneva], VI, No. 2, 1967, 193–215.

Eicher, Carl K., and Liedholm, Carol. *Growth and Development of the Nigerian Economy*. East Lansing: Michigan State University Press, 1970.

Elias, T. Olawale. *The Nigerian Legal System*. London: Routledge and Kegan Paul, 1963.

Fapohinda, Olanrewaju J. "The Impact of Educational Development on Manpower Planning in Nigeria, 1945–1970: A Preliminary Assessment." (Paper presented at the Thirteenth Annual Meeting of the African Studies Association, October 21–24, 1970.) Boston: African Studies Association, 1970.

Gibbs, James L. *Peoples of Africa*. New York: Holt, Rinehart and Winston, 1965.

Güsten, Rolf. *Studies in the Staple Food Economy of Western Nigeria*. (Afrika-Studien No. 30.) New York: Humanities Press, 1968.

Gutkind, Peter C.W. "The Energy of Despair—Social Organization of the Unemployed in Two African Cities—Lagos and Nairobi," *Civilisations* [Brussels], XVII, No. 3, 1967, 186–211.

Gutteridge, William F. *The Military in African Politics*. London: Methuen, 1969.

Helleiner, Gerald K. *Peasant Agriculture, Government, and Economic Growth in Nigeria*. Homewood, Illinois: Irwin, 1966.

Hodder, B.W. "The Yoruba Rural Market." In Paul Bohannan and George Dalton (eds.), *Markets in Africa*. Evanston: Northwestern University Press, 1962.

Krapf-Askari, Eva. *Yoruba Towns and Cities: An Enquiry into the Nature of Urban Social Phenomena*. Oxford: Clarendon Press, 1969.

Kulkarni, H.M. "The Establishment of an Education Library in a Developing Region: An Experiment in Northern Nigeria," *UNESCO Bulletin for Libraries* [Rome], XXII, No. 1, January/February 1968, 26–28.

Legvold, Robert, *Soviet Policy In West Africa*. Cambridge: Harvard University Press, 1970.

Leighton, Alexander, H., et al. *Psychiatric Disorder Among the Yoruba*. Ithaca: Cornell University Press, 1963.

Levine, Robert A.; Strangemen, Eugene; and Unterberger, Leonard. *Dreams and Deeds: Achievement Motivation in Nigeria*. Chicago: University of Chicago Press, 1966.

Lewis, W. Arthur. *Reflections on Nigeria's Economic Growth*. (Organization for Economic Cooperation Development Center Studies.) Paris: OECD, 1967.

Lloyd, P.C. "Class Consciousness Among the Yoruba," In P.C.

Lloyd (ed.), *The New Elites of Tropical Africa*. London: Oxford University Press, 1966.

———. "The Yoruba of Nigeria." In James L. Gibbs, Jr. (ed.), *The Peoples of Africa*. New York: Holt, Rinehart and Winston, 1965, 547–582.

Luckham, A.R. "The Nigerian Military: Disintegration of Integration." Pages 58–77 in S.K. Panter-Brick (ed.), *Nigerian Politics and Military Rule*. London: Athlone Press, 1970.

Meisler, Stanley. "The Nigeria Which Is Not at War," *Africa Report*, XV, No. 1, January 1970, 16–18.

Melson, Robert. "Nigerian Politics and the General Strike of 1964." In Robert I. Rotberg and Ali A. Mazrvi (eds.), *Protest and Power in Black Africa*. New York: Oxford Press, 1970.

Miners, N.J. *The Nigerian Army, 1956–1966*. London: Methuen, 1971.

Morgan, W.B., and Pugh, J.C. *West Africa*. London: Methuen, 1969.

Nadel, S.F. *Nupe Religion*. Glencoe: Free Press, 1954.

Nicholson, I.F. *The Administration of Nigeria, 1900–1960, Men, Methods and Myths*. Oxford: Clarendon Press, 1969.

Nnichiri, Eninnaya. *Parasitic Disease and Urbanization in a Developing Community*. (Series: Oxford Medical Publication.) London: Oxford University Press, 1968.

Northern States of Nigeria Local Government Yearbook, 1970. (Eds., W.M. Haruna and M.W. Norris.) Zaria, Nigeria: Northern Nigeria Publishing, for Institute of Administration, Amudu Bello University, 1970.

Nwankwo, Arthur Agwuncha, and Ifejika, Samuel Ndochukwu. *Biafra: The Making of a Nation*. New York: Praeger, 1970.

Ogunlusi, Jola. "The Olosunta Festival," *African Arts/Arts d'Afrique*, II, No. 1, Autumn, 1969, 52–55.

Ojo, G.J. Afolabi, "Royal Palaces: An Index of Yoruba Traditional Culture," *Nigeria Magazine* [Lagos], XCIV, September 1967, 194–210.

Okonkwo, Cyprian O., and Naish, Michael E. *Criminal Law in Nigeria*. London: Sweet and Maxwell, 1964.

Olorunsola, Victor A. "Nigerian Cultural Nationalism," *African Forum*, III, No. 1, Summer 1967, 78–89.

Ottenberg, Phoebe. "The Afikpo Ibo of Eastern Nigeria." Pages 3–39 in James L. Gibbs, Jr. (ed.), *The Peoples of Africa*. New York: Holt, Rinehart and Winston, 1965.

Owusu, Maxwell. "Culture and Democracy in West Africa: Some Persistent Problems," *Africa Today*, XVIII, No. 1, January 1971, 68–76.

Oyenuga, V. A. *Agriculture in Nigeria: An Introduction.* Rome: Food and Agriculture Organization, 1967.

Pearson, Scott R., and Pearson, Sandra C. "Oil Boom Reshapes Nigeria's Future," *Africa Report,* XVI, No. 2, February 1971, 14–17.

Phillips, Claude S., Jr. *The Development of Nigerian Foreign Policy.* Evanston, Northwestern University Press, 1964.

Plotnicov, Leonard. *Strangers to the City: Urban Man in Jos.* Pittsburg: Pittsburg University Press, 1967.

Republic of Nigeria. Federal Ministry of Information. *Second National Development Plan, 1970–1974.* Lagos: Government Printer, 1970.

Republic of Nigeria. Federal Office of Statics. *Annual Abstract of Statistics, Nigeria, 1968.* Lagos: n.pub., 1968.

————. *Population Census of Nigeria, 1963,* III. (Combined National Figures, Provisional.) Lagos: 1968.

————. *Rural Demographic Sample Survey, 1965–1966.* Lagos: October 1968.

Schram, R. *The Development of Nigerian Health Services: Five Hundred Years of Medical History from 1460–1960.* Kampala: Makerere University College, 1968.

Schwarz, Walter. "Foreign Powers and the Nigerian War," *Africa Report,* XV, No. 2, February 1970, 12–14.

————. *Nigeria.* New York: Praeger, 1968.

Smith, Michael G. "The Hausa of Northern Nigeria." In James L. Gibbs, Jr., (ed.), *The Peoples of Africa.* New York: Holt, Rinehart and Winston, 1965, 119–155.

Standard Bank Group. *Annual Economic Review: Nigeria.* London: n.pub., June 1970.

Stenning, Derrick. "The Pastoral Fulani." In James L. Gibbs, Jr. (ed.), *The Peoples of Africa.* New York: Holt, Rinehart and Winston, 1965, 361–401.

Strategies and Recommendations for Nigerian Rural Development, 1969–1985. (Consortium for the Study of Nigerian Rural Development, Series No. 33.) East Lansing: Michigan State University, for CSNRD, 1969.

Trimingham, H. S. *A History of Islam in West Africa.* London: Oxford University Press, 1962.

Turner, H. W. *The History of an African Independent Church.* 2 vols. London: Oxford University Press, 1967.

Uchendu, Victor C. *The Igbo of Southeast Nigeria.* (Case Studies in Social Anthropology.) New York: Holt, Rinehart and Winston, 1965.

Udo, Reuben K. *Geographical Regions of Nigeria.* Berkeley: University of California Press, 1970.

445

U.S. Department of Commerce. Bureau of International Commerce. "Basic Data on the Economy of Nigeria," by James H. Ashida. *Overseas Business Reports* (OBR 68–90.) Washington: GPO, October 1968.

Whitaker, C. Sylvester, Jr. *The Politics of Tradition, Continuity and Change in Northern Nigeria, 1946–1966.* Princeton: Princeton University Press, 1970.

OTHER SOURCES USED

Aboyade, 'Bimpe. "A Preliminary Bibliography of Nigerian Languages: Hausa, Yoruba, and Igbo," *African Notes* [Ibadan], V, No. 1, October 1968.

Adalemo, I. A. "The Kainji Dam—A Resettlement," *Nigeria Magazine* [Lagos], No. 99, December 1968, 265–279.

Adam Ulekun, Ladipo. "High Level in Ministerial Organization in Nigeria and the Ivory Coast." Pages 11–42 in D. J. Murray (ed.), *Studies in Nigerian Administration.* London: Hutchinson Educational, for Institute of Administration, University of Ife, 1970.

Adedeji, Joel A. "Form and Function of Satire in Yoruba Drama," *Odu* [Ibadan], IV, No. 1, 1967, 61–72.

Adegboye, R. O. "The Need for Land Reform in Nigeria," *Nigerian Journal of Economic and Social Studies* [Ibadan], IX, No. 3, November 1967, 339–350.

Adejuwon, J. O. "Vegetation Zonation and the Distribution Ranges of Savanna Trees in Nigeria," *Nigerian Geographical Journal* [Ibadan], XII, Nos. 1 and 2, December 1969, 125–133.

Ademoyega, Wale. *The Federation of Nigeria from Earliest Times to Independence.* London: Harrap, 1962.

Adeogun, A. "African Art in Epe," *Nigeria Magazine* [Lagos], XCV, December 1967, 330–336.

Afigbo, A. E. "Efik Origin and Migration Reconsidered," *Nigeria Magazine* [Lagos], LXXXIX, December 1965, 265–280.

————. "Herbert Richmond Palmer and Indirect Rule in Eastern Nigeria, 1915–1928," *Journal of the Historical Society of Nigeria* [Ibadan], III, No. 2, December 1965, 295–312.

Africa South of the Sahara, 1971. London: Europa Publication, 1971.

African-American Labor Center, 1965–1970. New York: African-American Labor Center, n.d.

"Air Forces of the World: Part 4, the African States," *Interavia* [Geneva], XXII, No. 8, August 1967, 1305–1313.

Ajaegbu, H. I. "Recent Migrations and Settlement in the Coastal Areas of Southwestern Nigeria: The Example of Epe and Ikeja

Divisions," *Nigerian Geographical Journal* [Ibadan], XI, No. 1, June 1968, 61–78.

Ajayi, J. F. Ade. *Milestones in Nigerian History.* Ibadan: Ibadan University Press, 1962.

———. "Nineteenth Century Origins of Nigerian Nationalism," *Journal of the Historical Society of Nigeria* [Ibadan], II, No. 2, December 1961, 196–210.

Ajayi, J. F. Ade, and Smith, Robert. *Yoruba Warfare in the Nineteenth Century.* Cambridge: Cambridge University Press, 1964.

Akinjogbin, I. A. "A Chronology of Yoruba History, 1789–1840," *Odu* [Ibadan], II, No. 2, January 1966, 81–86.

———. "The Oyo Empire in the 18th Century: A Reassessment," *Journal of the Historical Society of Nigeria* [Ibadan], III, No. 3, December 1966, 449–460.

Akinola, R. A. "Urban Tradition in Yorubaland," *Nigeria Magazine* [Lagos], XCV, 1967, 344–350.

Akinsemoyin, Kunle. "Nigeria in the World of Art," *Nigeria Magazine* [Lagos], XCV, December 1967, 301–303.

Akintunde, J. O. "The Demise of Democracy in the First Republic of Nigeria: A Casual Analysis," *Odu* [Ibadan], IV, No. 1, July 1967, 3–28.

Alagoa, Ebiegberi Jo. "Dating Oral Tradition," *African Notes* [Ibadan], IV, No. 1, October 1966, 6–10.

———. "Delta Masquerades (Ijo)," *Nigeria Magazine* [Lagos], XCIII, June 1967, 145–155.

———. "Songs as Historical Data: Examples from the Niger Delta," *Research Review* [Lagos], V, No. 1, 1968, 1–16.

———. "The Use of Oral Literary Data from History Examples from Niger Delta Proverbs," *Journal of American Folklore,* LXXXI, No. 321, 235–242.

Allagoa, Lawrence. "Exhibition Centre's New Home," *Nigeria Magazine* [Lagos], XCIII, June 1967, 114–127.

Alliot, Kitt. *An African School: A Record of Experience.* New York: Cambridge University Press, 1970.

Amali, Samson O. O. *Selected Poems.* Ibadan: University Bookshop, 1968.

Ames, David. "Professionals and Amateurs: The Musicians of Zaria and Obimo," *African Arts/Arts d'Afrique,* I, No. 2, Winter 1968, 40–45.

Amos, Samuel, and Onobrakpeya, Bruce. "Tortoise in Legend," *African Arts/Arts d'Afrique,* IV, No. 1, Autumn 1970, 26–35.

Andreski, Iris (ed.). *Old Wives Tales: Stories from Ibibioland.* New York: Schocken, 1970.

Anene, Joseph C. *Southern Nigeria in Transit, 1885–1906: Theory and Practice in a Colonial Protectorate.* Cambridge: Cambridge University Press, 1966.

Arikpo, Okoi. *The Development of Modern Nigeria.* Hamondsworth: Penguin, 1967.

Armer, Michael, and Youtz, Robert. *Formal Education and Value Orientation in Kano, Northern Nigeria.* (Series: African Studies Association Paper.) Washington: ASA, 1968.

Armstrong, R. G. "Onugbo Mloko: Story in Idoma Ancestral Chant," *African Arts/Arts d'Afrique,* Summer, 1968, 8–11.

Asabia, D. O., and Adegbesan, J. O. *Idoani Past and Present: The Story of One Yoruba Kingdom.* Ibadan: Ibadan University Press, 1970.

Asanye, A. M. *Outlines of Nigerian History: A Synopsis of the History of Nigeria from the 15th Century to the Present Day.* Port Harcourt: Goodwill Press, 1959.

Awe, B. "The End of an Experiment: The Collapse of the Ibadan Empire, 1877–1893," *Journal of the Historical Society of Nigeria* [Ibadan], III, No. 2, December 1965, 221–230.

Ayandele, E.A. "How Truly Nigerian Is Our Nigerian History," *African Notes* [Ibadan], V, No. 2, January 1969, 19–35.

———. "Observations on Some Social and Economic Aspects of Slavery in Pre-Colonial Nigeria," *Nigerian Journal of Economics and Social Studies* [Ibadan], IV, No. 3, November 1967, 329–338.

Babalola, A. "The Snail and the Tortoise in Yoruba Folklore," *Nigeria Magazine* [Lagos], XCVI, March–May 1968, 38–40.

Babyemi, S. O. "Oyo Ruins," *African Notes* [Ibadan], V, No. 1, October 1968, 8–11.

Baker, Pauline H. "The Politics of Nigerian Military Rule," *Africa Report,* XVI, No. 2, February 1971, 18–21.

Balogun, D. A. "The Role of Employers' and Workers' Representatives in the Settlement of Industrial Disputes in Nigeria." Pages 140–149 in *Conciliation and Arbitration of Industrial Disputes in English-Speaking Countries of Africa.* (Labor-Management Relations Series No. 37.) Geneva: International Labor Organization, International Labor Office, 1970.

Bamgbose, Ayo. "The Form of Yoruba Proverbs," *Odu* [Ibadan], IV, No. 2, January 1968, 74–86.

———. "Yoruba Studies Today," *Odu* [Ibadan], I, April 1969, 85–100.

Barbour, K. M. "North-Eastern Nigeria—Case Study of State Formation," *Journal of Modern African Studies* [London], IX, No. 1, 1971, 49–71.

Barclay's Overseas Survey, 1970. London: Barclay's Bank D.C.O., 1970.

Bascom, William R. "The Esusu: A Credit Institution of the Yoruba," *Journal of the Royal Anthropological Society* [London], LXXXII, Part I, 1952.

Beier, Ulli, "D. O. Fagunwa: A Yoruba Novelist," *Black Orpheus* [Ibadan], XVII, June 1965, 51–56.

———. "Native Nigerian Painting," *Black Orpheus* [Ibadan], No. 19, March 1966, 51–56.

———. "Public Opinion on Lovers; Popular Nigerian Literature Sold in Onitsha Market," *Black Orpheus* [Ibadan], XIV, February 1964, 4–16.

———. "Signwriters Art in Nigeria," *Africa Arts,* IV, No. 3, Spring 1971, 22–27.

Beier, Ulli (ed.). *Political Spider.* Stories from *Black Orpheus.* African Publishing, 1969.

Ben-Amos, Daniel. "Ikponmwosa Osemwegie: A Young Bini Poet," *Nigeria Magazine* [Lagos], XCIV, September 1967, 250–252.

———. "Story Telling in Benin," *African Arts/Arts d'Afrique,* I, No. 1, Autumn 1967, 54–59.

Ben-Amos, Paula. "Cen Osawa: A Modern Nigerian Sculpture," *Nigeria Magazine* [Lagos], XCIV, September 1967, 248–250.

Bergsma, Harold M. "Tiv Proverbs As a Means of Social Control," *Africa* [London], XL, No. 2, April 1970, 151–163.

Biobaku, S. O. "The Problems of Traditional History with Special Reference to Yoruba Traditions," *Journal of the Historical Society of Nigeria* [Ibadan], I, No. 1, December 1965, 43.

"Birth Control Aid for Africa," *West Africa* [London], No. 2,794, December 26, 1970–January 1, 1971, 1513.

"Blue Print on Our Industrial Relations," *ULCN Information* [Lagos], I, Nos. 10 and 11, June/July 1968, 1–3.

Bohannan, Paul, and Bohannan, Laura. *Tiv Economy.* Evanston: Northwestern University Press, 1968.

Booth, Richard. *The Armed Forces of African States.* (Adelphi Papers, No. 67.) London: Institute for Strategic Studies, May 1970.

Borders, William. "Army in Nigeria Has Little to Do," *New York Times,* May 4, 1970, C–20.

———. "China Quietly Renewing An Active Role in Africa," *New York Times,* April 9, 1971, 1, 6.

———. "In Former Biafra," *New York Times,* January 17, 1971, C–20.

Boston, J. S. *The Igala Kingdom.* Ibadan: Oxford University Press, 1968.

———. "Oral Tradition and the History of the Igala." *Journal of African History* [London], C, No. 1, 1969, 29–43.

Bowles, Samuel. *Planning for Educational Systems in Economic Growth*. Cambridge: Harvard University Press, 1969.

Bradbury, R. E. "Continuities and Discontinuities in Precolonial and Colonial Benin Politics (1897–1951)." Pages 193–252 in I.M. Lewis (ed.), *History of Social Anthropology*. London: Tavistock, 1968.

Brass, William, et al. *The Demography of Tropical Africa*. Princeton: Princeton University Press, 1968.

Bray, Jennifer M. "The Organization of Traditional Weaving in Iseyin, Nigeria," *Africa* [London], XXXVIII, No. 3, July 1968, 270–280.

Brooks, George E. "A Note on French Influence in the Oil Rivers in the 1840's and 1860's," *Journal of the Historical Society of Nigeria* [Ibadan], III, No. 2, December 1965, 421–430.

Buchanan, K.M., and Pugh, J.C. *Land and People in Nigeria*. London: University of London Press, 1958.

———. *Land and People in Nigeria: The Human Geography of Nigeria and Its Environmental Background*. London: University of London Press, 1955.

Burns, Sir Alan. *History of Nigeria* (7th ed., rev.) London: Allen and Unwin, 1969.

Callaway, Archibald. "Expanding Nigeria's Education: Projection and Achievements Since Independence," *Nigerian Journal of Economic and Social Studies*, [Ibadan], XI, No. 2, July 1969, 191–203.

Callaway, Archibald, and Musone, A. *Financing of Education in Nigeria*. (African Research Monographs, No. 15.) Paris: United Nations Educational, Scientific and Cultural Organization, International Institute for Education Planning, 1968.

Carey, Edwin L. "Business Teacher Education in Nigeria," *Journal of Developing Areas*, July 1968, 511–517.

Carleton, David A. "The Mineral Industry of Nigeria." Pages 551–557 in *Minerals Yearbook, 1968*, IV: Area Reports, International. Washington: GPO, 1970.

Carnochan, J. "The Coming of the Fulani: A Bachama Oral Tradition," *Bulletin of the School of Oriental and African Studies*, XXX, No. 3, 1967, 622–633.

Carroll, Kevin. "Church Art and Architecture in Nigeria," *Clergy Review* [London], LIII, No. 3, March 1969, 241–248.

———. *Yoruba Religious Carving: Pagan and Christian Sculpture in Nigeria and Dahomey*. London: Chapman, 1967.

Carter, Gwendolen M. (ed.) *National Unity and Regionalism in Eight African States*. Ithaca: Cornell University Press, 1966.

Carter, Gwendolen M., et al. "Oral History in Africa," *African Studies Bulletin*, VII, No. 2, September 1965, 1–23.

Cerych, L. *The Integration of External Assistance with Educational Planning in Nigeria.* (African Research Monographs, No. 14.) Paris: United Nations Educational, Scientific and Cultural Organization, International Institute for Education Planning, 1967.

"Chad Lake." Page 227 in *Encyclopaedia Britannica,* V. Chicago: William Benton, 1969.

Chambers, Robert. *Settlement Schemes in Tropical Africa: A Study of Organizations and Development.* New York: Praeger, 1969.

"The Changing Faces of Nigerian Universities," *Ibadan,* XXIV, No. 2, February 1969, 6–18.

Cheney, Sheldon. *Sculpture of the World.* Viking Press, 1968.

Chick, John D. "Nigeria at War," *Africa Report,* LIV, No. 318, February 1968, 65–71, 113.

————. *Some Problems of Administrative Training: The Northern Nigerian Experience.* Kampala: Makerere Institute of Social Research, 1968.

"Church Art and Architecture in Nigeria," *Clergy Review* [London], LIII, No. 3, March 1968, 241–248.

Church, R. J. Harrison. "Picking Up the Pieces in a Federated Nigeria," *Geographical Magazine,* XLII, No. 6, March 1970, 453–454.

Cohen, Robin. "The Army and Trade Unions in Nigerian Politics," *Civilisations* [Brussels], XIX, No. 2, 1969, 226–230.

Cole, Robert H. *The Past and Future of Igbo Arts* (African Studies Association Paper.) Washington: ASA, 1968.

Collings, Rex. "Publishing in Africa: An Industry Emerges," *Africa Report* XV, No. 8, November 1970, 31–33.

Cook, Arthur Norton. *British Enterprise in Nigeria.* Philadelphia: University of Pennsylvania, 1927.

Coppock, J. T. "Agricultural Geography in Nigeria," *Nigerian Geographical Journal* [Ibadan], VII, No. 2, December 1964, 67–90.

Cowan, L. Gray, "Military Rule in Africa," *Survival* [London], IX, No. 1, January 1967, 9–13.

Cownie, John. *Nigerian National Income Accounts: Historical Summary and Projections to 1985.* (Consortium for the Study of Nigerian Rural Development, Series No. 14r.) East Lansing: CSNRD, August 1968.

Craig, O. "Urban Planning in Lagos," *Journal of Sociology and Health* [Lagos], II, No. 1, January 1967, 29–31.

Cramer, James. *The World's Police.* London: Cassell, 1964.

Crocker, Chester A. "External Military Assistance to Sub-Saharan Africa," *Africa Today,* XV, No. 2, April–May 1968, 15–20.

Crowder, Michael. *A Short History of Nigeria.* New York: Praeger, 1962.

———. *West Africa Under Colonial Rule.* Evanston: Northwestern University Press, 1968.

Curtin, Philip D. *The Atlanta Slave Trade: A Census.* Madison: University of Wisconsin Press, 1969.

Dade, T. O. "Parasites and Epilepsy in Nigeria," *Tropical and Geographical Medicine* [Haarlem], XXII, No. 3, September 1970, 313–322.

Dark, Philip, J. D. "Preliminary Catalogue of Benin Art and Technology: Some Problems of Material Culture Analysis," *Journal of the Royal Anthropological Society* [London], LXXXVII, No. 2, July–December 1957, 175–189.

Dathrone, O. R. "The Beginning of the West African Novel," *Nigeria Magazine* [Lagos], XCIII, June 1967, 168–170.

Davies, Oliver. *West Africa Before the Europeans: Archaeology and Prehistory.* London: Methuen, 1967.

Decalo, Samuel. "Africa and the Mid-Eastern War," *Africa Report,* XII, No. 7, October 1967, 57–61.

Dema, I. S. "Some Reflections upon the Nutritional Problems of Dense Farm Population in Parts of Nigeria." Pages 307–311 in J. C. Caldwell and C. Okonjo (eds.), *The Population of Tropical Africa.* New York: Columbia University Press, 1968.

Demographic Yearbook, 1967. New York: United Nations, 1968.

Dent, Martin J. "The Military and Politics: A Study of the Relations Between the Army and the Political Process in Nigeria." Pages 113–119 in Kenneth J. Kirkwood (ed.), St. Anthony's Papers, *African Affairs,* XXI, No. 3, London: Oxford University Press, 1969.

———. "Nigeria After the War," *World Today,* XXVI, No. 3, March 1970, 103–109.

Diejomaoh, Victor P. *Economic Development in Nigeria: Its Problems, Challenges, Prospects.* Princeton: Princeton University Press, 1965.

Dike, Kenneth Onwuka. *One Hundred Years of British Rule in Nigeria, 1851–1951.* Lagos: Federal Information Service, 1958.

Dudley, B. J. "The Military and Politics in Nigeria: Some Reflections." Pages 203–218 in Jacques Van Dorn (ed.), *Military Profession and Military Regimes: Commitments and Conflicts.* The Hague: Mouton, 1969.

Dudley, B. J. (ed.) *Nigeria 1965: Crisis and Criticism.* Ibadan: Ibadan University Press, 1966.

East, Repurt M. *Stories of Old Adamawa: A Collection of Histori-*

cal Texts in the Adamawa Dialect of Fulani with Translations and Notes. Farnborough: Gregg, 1967.

Editor and Publisher Yearbook, 1971. New York: Editor and Publisher, 1971.

Egboh, Edmund O. "The Early Years of Trade Unionism in Nigeria," *Africa Quarterly* [New Delhi], VIII, No. 1, April–June, 1968, 59–69.

———. "Trade Unions in Nigeria," *Africa Studies* [Johannesburg], XXVII, No. 1, 1968, 35–40.

Eicher, Carl K. *Research on Agricultural Development in Five English-Speaking Countries in West Africa.* New York: Agricultural Development Council, 1970.

———. "Some Problems of African Development: A West African Case Study." Pages 196–246 in Frederick S. Arkhurst (ed.), *Africa in the Seventies and Eighties.* New York: Praeger, 1970.

Ekejiuba, F. I. "Preliminary Notes on Brasswork of Eastern Nigeria," *African Notes* [Ibadan], IV, No. 2, January 1967, 11–15.

Elias, T. Olawaleo. *Nigerian Press Law.* London: Constable, 1969.

Elliott, C. "Nok Culture," *History Today* [London], May 1967, 334–339.

"Eradication Notes: Nigeria." Pages 18–19 in the *Smallpox Eradication Program Report,* II, No. 5. Atlanta: National Communicable Disease Center, October 1968.

Euba, Akin. "Music in Traditional Society," *Nigeria Magazine* [Lagos], CI, July–September 1969, 475–480.

———. "Musicology in the Context of African Culture," *Odu* [Ibadan], October 1969, 3–18.

Eyo, Ekpo. "1969 Excavations at Ile-Ife," *African Arts/Arts d'Afrique,* II, No. 1, Autumn 1969, 34–41.

———. "1969 Excavations at Ile-Ife," *African Arts/Arts d'Afrique,* III, No. 2, Winter 1970, 44–47.

Ezejiofor, G. "The Federation of Nigeria." Pages 40–107 in A. N. Allott (ed.), *Judicial and Legal Systems in Africa.* London: Butterworth, 1970.

Fage, J. D. *A History of West Africa: An Introductory Survey.* Cambridge: Cambridge University Press, 1969.

Fagg, B. *The Art of Western Africa: Tribal Masks and Sculptures.* Collins, in association with United Nations Educational, Scientific and Cultural Organization, 1967.

Fagg, William. "The African Artist (Yoruba Examples)." Pages 42–57 in Daniel P. Biebuyck (ed.), *Tradition and Creativity in Tribal Art.* Berkeley: University of California Press, 1969.

"The Fall of the Fulani Empire," *South Atlantic Quarterly,* LXVII, No. 4, Autumn, 1968.

Faniran, Adetoye, and High, Colin. "Landform Examples from Nigeria, No. 1: An Inselberg," *Nigerian Geographical Journal* [Ibadan], XII, Nos. 1 and 2, December 1969, 141–144.

Feit, Edward. "Military Coups and Political Development: Some Lessons from Ghana and Nigeria," *World Politics,* XX, No. 2, January 1968, 179–193.

Food and Agriculture Organization. *Agricultural Development in Nigeria, 1965–1980.* Rome: 1966.

Forde, Cyril Daryll. "Ward Organization Among the Yako," *Africa* [London], XX, No. 4, October 1950, 267–289.

Forde, Cyril Daryll (ed.). *Efik Trader of Older Caliber.* London: Pall Mall Press, for International African Institute, 1968.

Fresco, Edward. "A Folk Tale in the Ketu Dialect of Yoruba," *African Notes* [Ibadan], V, No. 1, October 1968, 38–41.

Fyee, C. "A Historiographical Survey of the Transatlantic Slave Trade from West Africa." Pages 1–12 in *Transatlantic Slave Trade from West Africa.* Edinburgh: Center of African Studies, University of Edinburgh, 1965.

Gailey, Harry A. *Road to Ababa: A Study of British Administrative Policy in Eastern Nigeria.* New York: New York University Press, 1970.

"Gallery Labac (Lagos)," *Nigeria Magazine* [Lagos], XCIII, June 1967, 128–133.

Gbadamosi, G. O. "The Establishment of Western Education Among Muslims in Nigeria, 1896–1926," *Journal of the Historical Society of Nigeria* [Ibadan], IV, No. 1, December 1967, 89–115.

Geary, Sir William Nevill Montgomerie. *Nigeria Under British Rule.* New York: Barnes and Noble, 1965.

Gifford, P. "Indirect Rule: Touchstone or Tombstone for Colonial Policy?" Pages 351–391 in P. Gifford and W. R. Louis (eds.). *Britain and Germany in Africa.* New Haven: Yale University Press, 1967.

Glover, P. E., and Aitchison, P. J. "Some Cases of Depopulation in Northern Nigeria," *Nigerian Field* [Bath, England], XXXV, No. 1, January 1970, 12–28.

Godfrey, E. M., and Holder, K. "The Economies of an African University," *Journal of Modern African Studies* [London], IV, No. 4, December 1966, 435–455.

Grimond, J. "Nigeria Starts Again," *Economist* [London], October 24, 1970, 1–11.

Grundy, Kenneth W. "The Negative Image of Africa's Military," *Review of Politics,* XXX, No. 4, October 1968, 428–439.

Hachten, William A. "Newspapers in Africa: Change or Decay?," *Africa Report,* XV, No. 9, December 1970, 25–26.

Hallam, W. K. R. "The Men Behind Traditions," *Nigerian Magazine* [Lagos], XCI, December 1966, 271.

Hamilton, W. B. "The Evolution of British Policy Toward Nigeria." Pages 17–41 in R. O. Tilman and T. Cole (eds.), *The Nigerian Political Scene*. Durham: Duke University, 1965.

Hance, William A. *The Geography of Modern Africa*. New York: Columbia University Press, 1964.

————. *Population, Migration, and Urbanization in Africa*. New York: Columbia University Press, 1970.

————. "The Race Between Population and Resources," *Africa Report*, XII, No. 1, January 1968, 6–12.

Hanning, Hugh. "Lessons from the Arms Race," *Africa Report*, XIII, No. 2, February 1968, 42–47.

Hanson, John W., et al. *Education, Nsukka: A Study in Institution Building Among the Modern Ibo*. East Lansing: African Studies Center, Michigan State University, 1968.

Harper, Peggy. "Dance and Drama in the North," *Nigeria Magazine* [Lagos], September 1967, 219–235.

————. "Dance in Nigeria," *Presence Africaine* [Paris], LXX, 1969, 162–171.

————. "A Festival of Nigerian Dances," *African Arts/Arts d'Afrique*, III, No. 2, Winter 1970, 48–53.

————. *Studies in Nigerian Dance*. Ibadan: Institute of African Studies, University of Ibadan, 1968.

Harris, John R. "Nigerian Enterprise in the Printing Industry," *Nigerian Journal of Economic and Social Studies* [Ibadan], X, No. 2, July 1968, 215–217.

Hartle, Donald D. "Archaeology in Eastern Nigeria," *Nigeria Magazine* [Lagos], XCIII, June 1967, 134–143.

Herrmann, Teimer. "Water Supply in Nutrition in the Humid Tropic With Special Reference to Eastern Nigeria," *Yearbook of the Association of Pacific Geographers*, XXVII, 1966, 17–27.

Heussler Robert. *The British in Northern Nigeria*. London: Oxford University Press, 1968.

Hill, Polly. "Notes on Traditional Market Authority and Market Periodicity in West Africa," *Journal of African History* [London], VII, No. 2, 1966, 295–312.

Hoagland, James. "Ibos are Still Not Nigerians," *Washington Post*, December 6, 1970, C–1.

————. "Nigeria's Vast Army Extends Power," *Washington Post*, December 11, 1970, A–28.

Hodder, B. W., and Ukwu, U. I. *Markets in West Africa*. Ibadan: Ibadan University Press, 1969.

Hoffman-Burchardi, Helmut. "Die Bevolkerungballung in Südost-

Nigerian (Biafra)," *Erdkunde* [Bonn], XXII, No. 3, September 1968, 225–238.

Hobgen, Sidney John, and Kirk-Greene, A.H.M. *The Emirates of Northern Nigeria: A Preliminary Survey of Their Historic Traditions.* London: Oxford University Press, 1966.

Holmes, Brian (ed.) *Educational Policy and the Mission Schools: Case Studies from the British Empire.* London: Routledge, 1967.

Horton, Robin. "From Fishing Village to City-State: A Social History of New Calabar." In Mary Douglas and Phyllis Kaberry (eds.), *Man in Africa.* London: Tavistock, 1969.

Hubbard, John Waddinton. *The Sobo of the Niger Delta.* Zaria: Gaskiya, 1948.

Huth, W. P. *Traditional Institutions and Land Tenure as Related to Agricultural Development Among the Ibo of Eastern Nigeria.* Madison: University of Wisconsin, 1969.

Idem, Okon. "Nigeria's Population Recorded at 55,653,000," *Africa Report,* IX, No. 3, March 1964, 15.

Ikime, Obaro. *Niger Delta Rivalry: Itsekiri-Urhobo Relations and the European Presence, 1884–1936.* New York: Humanities Press, 1969.

————. "Reconsidered Indirect Rule: The Nigerian Example," *Journal of the Historical Society of Nigeria* [Ibadan], IV, No. 3, December 1968, 421–438.

————. "The Western Ijo, 1900–1950: A Preliminary Survey," *Journal of the Historical Society of Nigeria* [Ibadan], IV, No. 1, December 1967, 65–87.

Ikomi, S. U. "The System of Settling Industrial Disputes in the Federal Republic of Nigeria". Pages 129–139 in Conciliation and Arbitration of Industrial Disputes in English-Speaking Countries of Africa. (Labor-Management Relations Series: No. 37.) Geneva: International Labor Organization, International Labor Office, 1970.

Imoagene, Stephen O. "Psycho-Social Factors in Rural-Urban Migration," *Nigerian Journal of Economic and Social Studies,* [Ibadan], IX, No. 3, November 1967, 375–386.

"Individual Country Reports: Nigeria." Pages 13–14 in the *Smallpox Eradication Program Report,* II, No. 4, Atlanta: National Communicable Disease Center, August 1968.

International Bureau of Education. "Nigeria." Pages 104–106 in *International Yearbook of Education.* Paris: United Nations Educational, Scientific and Cultural Organization.

International Labor Organization. *Employment Policy in Africa: Part I, Problems and Policies.* Geneva: International Labor Office, 1969.

Izzett, A. "Family Life Among the Yoruba, in Lagos, Nigeria," in Aidan Southall (ed.), *Social Change in Modern Africa*. London: Oxford University Press, for the International African Institute, 1961.

Jakande, L. K. *The Nigerian School Directory, 1967*. Lagos: Nigerian Economic and Social Studies Syndicate Publications (Available in the United States from International Publishing Service in New York), 1967.

Jeffreys, M. D. W. "Some Ibibio Folk-Tales," *Folklore* [London], LXXVIII, 1967, 126–136.

Jennings, J. H., and Oduah, S. O. *A Geography of the Eastern Provinces of Nigeria*. Cambridge: Cambridge University Press, 1966.

Johnston, T. O. "Height and Weight Patterns of an Urban African Population Sample in Nigeria," *Tropical and Geographical Medicine*. [Haarlem], XXII, No. 1, March 1970, 65–76.

Johnston, Bruce F. *Agriculture's Role in Nigerian Development Strategy*. Stanford: Stanford University, for Agency for International Development, September 1966.

Johnston, High Anthony Stephens. *The Fulani Empire of Sokoto*. London: Oxford University Press, 1967.

Johnston, High Anthony Stephens (ed.). *A Selection of Hausa Stories*. London: Oxford University Press, 1966.

Jones, Gwilgn Iwan. *The Trading States of the Oil Rivers: A Study of Political Development on Eastern Nigeria*. London: Oxford University Press, 1963.

July, Robert W. *The Origins of Modern African Thought: Its Development in West Africa During the Nineteenth and Twentieth Centuries*. London: Faber, 1968.

Kalous, Milan. "Some Hypotheses About the Air of Southern Nigeria," *Afrika u Ubersee* [Hamburg], LII, No. 2, March 1969, 14–24.

Keil, Charles, "Tiv Dance: A First Assessment," *African Notes* [Ibadan], IV, No. 2, January 1967, 32–35.

Kemp, Geoffrey. *Arms Traffic and Third World Conflicts*. New York: Carnegie Endowment for International Peace, March 1970.

————. *Classification of Weapons Systems and Force Designs in Less Developed Country Environments: Implications for Arms Transfer Policies*. Cambridge: Massachusetts Institute of Technology Press, February 1970.

Kennedy, Jean. "I Saw and I Was Happy: Festival at Oshogbo," *African Arts/Arts d'Afrique*, I, No. 2, Winter 1968, 8–17.

Kilby, Peter. *Industrialization in an Open Economy: Nigeria, 1945–1966*. Cambridge: Cambridge University Press, 1969.

Killam, G. P. *The Novels of Chinua Achebe.* New York: Africana Publishing, 1970.

King, A. V., and Ibrahim, Rashid. "The Song of the Rains (Hausa Poem), Metric Values in Performance," *African Language Studies* [London], No. 9, 1968, 148–155.

Kirby, P. R. "Two Curious Resonated Xylophones from Nigeria," *African Studies* [Johannesburg], XXVII, No. 3, 1968, 141–144.

Kirk-Greene, A.H.M. *Crisis and Conflict in Nigeria—A Documentary Sourcebook, 1966–1969.* London: Oxford University Press, 1971.

————. "A Hausa Literacy Renaissance," *West Africa* [London], No. 2,717, June 28, 1969, 736–737.

Klinghoffer, Arthur J. "Why the Soviet Chose Sides," *Africa Report,* XIII, No. 2, February 1968, 47–49.

Kwaghbo, Cwar, "Iee: A Local Tiv Festival," *Nigerian Field* [Bath, England], XXXIII, No. 2, April 1968, 73–75.

Last, Murray, *The Sokoto Caliphate.* New York: Humanities Press, 1967.

Law, Subu. "Contemporary Works of Art Need a Home in Nigeria," *Nigeria Magazine* [Lagos], C, April 1969, 348–355.

Lawson, Charles R. "Nigerian Drama Comes of Age," *Africa Report,* XIII, No. 5, 1968, 55.

Lee, J. M. *African Armies and Civil Order.* New York: Praeger, 1969.

Legvold, Robert. "Moscow's Changing Views of Africa's Revolutionary Regimes," *Africa Report,* XIV, Nos. 3 and 4, March–April 1969, 54–58.

Leith-Ross, Sylvia. "Notes on the Osu System Among the Ibo of Owerri Province, Nigeria," *Africa* [London], X, 1937, 206–220.

Lewis, E. A. "Protein-Calorie Malnutrition Syndrome in Adults, *Tropical and Geographical Medicine* [Haarlem], XXII, No. 3, September 1970, 371.

Lewis, John R. "The Mineral Industry of Nigeria." Pages 567–575 in *Minerals Yearbook, 1967,* IV: Area Reports International. Washington: GPO, 1969.

Lewis, L. J. *Society, Schools and Progress in Nigeria.* Oxford: Pergamon Press, 1965.

Lindfors, Bernth. *Heroes and Hero-Worship in Nigerian Chapbook Drama.* (American Educational Theater Association Paper.) New York: AETA, 1967.

————. "Nigerian Novels of 1966," *Africa Today,* XIV, No. 5, October, 1967, 27–31.

Lindsay, Kennedy. "How Biafra Pays for the War," *Venture* [London], March 1969, 26–28.

Lloyd, Peter C. "Conflict Theory and Yoruba Kingdoms." Pages

25–61 in I. M. Lewis (ed.), *History and Social Anthropology.* London: Tavistock, 1968.

―――. "Craft Organization in Yoruba Towns," *Africa* [London], XXIII, No. 1, January 1953, 30–44.

―――. "The Yoruba Town Today," *Sociological Review* [Manchester], VII, No. 1, January 1959, 45–63.

Lloyd, Peter C.; Mabogunje, A. L.; and Awe, B. (eds.). *The City of Ibadan.* London: Cambridge University Press, 1967.

Longo, L. D. *Medicine and Medical Education in Nigeria.* (Africa Studies Papers Series.) Los Angeles: African Studies Center, University of California, 1963.

McDowell, C. M. "The Breakdown of Traditional Land Tenure in Northern Nigeria." In Max Gluckman (ed.), *Ideas and Procedures in African Customary Law.* London: Oxford University Press, 1969.

McFarlane, H., et al. "Development of Immunoglobulins and Malarial Antibodies in Nigeria," *Tropical and Geographical Medicine* [Haarlem], XXII, No. 2, June 1970, 198–200.

McKenna, Joseph C. "Elements of a Nigerian Peace," *Survival* [London], XI, No. 9, September 1969, 287–293.

MacLean, C.M.U. *Sickness Behaviour Among the Yoruba* (Proceedings of the Seminar Center for African Studies, Edinburgh.) Edinburgh, SCAS, 1969, 29–42.

McQueen, Albert J. "Education and Marginality of African Youth," *Journal of Social Issues,* XXIV, No. 2, April 1968, 179–197.

―――. "Unemployment and Future Orientations of Nigerian School-Leavers," *Canadian Journal of African Studies* [Montreal], Summer 1969, 441–461.

Mabogunje, Akin L. *Urbanization in Nigeria.* New York: Africana Publishing, 1968.

Marris, Peter. *African City Life.* Kampala: Transition Books, for the University of East Africa, 1968.

Mason, Michael. "Population Density and 'Slave-Raiding'—The Case of the Middle Belt of Nigeria," *Journal of African History* [London], X, No. 4, 1969, 551–564.

Meauze, Pierce. *African Art: Sculpture.* New York: World Publishing, 1968.

Mebitaghan, I. S., and Mebitaghan, Okoh. "Concurrent Assessment of the Smallpox Eradication Programme in Mid-West State, Nigeria." Pages 97–100 in the *Smallpox Eradication Program Report,* IV, No. 2, (Seminar on Smallpox Eradication and Measles Control in Western and Central Africa, Part II.) Atlanta: National Communicable Disease Center, January 1970.

The Military Balance, 1969–1970. London: Institute for Strategic Studies, 1969.

"Million Deaths Averted by Measles Vaccine," *Medical Tribune: International Edition, Africa*, May 1970, 1.

Milner, Alan. *African Penal Systems*. New York: Praeger, 1969.

Mobolade, Timothy. "Ibeji Custom in Yorubaland," *African Arts*, IV, No. 3, Spring 1971, 14–15.

Moody, H.L.B. "Ganuwa: The Walls of Kano City," *Nigeria Magazine* [Lagos], March 1967, 19–38.

———. "A Kano Mystery: The Waika Tablet," *Nigeria Magazine* [Lagos], XCVII, June-August 1968, 62–67.

Morgab, R. W., and Dada, T. O. "Attitudes Toward Epilepsy in Two Areas of Nigeria," *Lagos Notes*, II, No. 2, December 1969, 31–40.

Morohunfula, E. A. "A Diagnosis of the Educational Backwardness of the Northern State of Nigeria," *West African Journal of Education* [Ibadan], XIII, No. 3, October 1969, 152.

Mortimer, Molly. "Nigeria." Pages 570–571 in *Britannica Book of the Year, 1970*. Chicago: Encyclopaedia Britannica, 1970.

Mountjoy, Alan B., and Embleton, Clifford. *Africa: A New Geographical Survey*. New York: Praeger, 1967.

Mueller, P., and Zevering, K. H. "Employment Promotion Through Rural Development: A Pilot Project in Western Nigeria," *International Labour Review* [Geneva], C, No. 2, August 1969, 111–130.

Murray, David J. "The Federation of Nigeria," *Current History*, LX, No. 355, March 1971, 157–163.

Nafziger, E. Wayne. "The Nigerian Footwear Business," *Journal of Modern African Studies* [London], VI, No. 4, December 1968, 531–542.

Netting, Robert. "Kofyar Building in Mud and Stone," *Expedition* (Bulletin of the University Museum of the University of Pennsylvania.) Summer 1968, 10–20.

"Nigeria." Pages 452–456 in *Ports of the World, 1970–1971*. London: Benn Brothers, n.d.

"Nigeria." Pages 499–508 in *Encyclopaedia Britannica*. XVI, Chicago: William Benton, 1970.

"Nigeria." Pages B 543–B 583 in Colin Legum and John Drysdale (eds.), *Africa Contemporary Record: Annual Survey and Documents, 1969–1970*. Exeter: Africa Research, 1970.

"Nigeria." Pages 551–577 in Colin Legum and John Drysdale (eds.), *Africa Contemporary Record: Annual Survey and Documents, 1968–1969*. London: Africa Research, 1969.

Nigeria: An Economic Survey. Lagos: Barclay's Bank D.C.O., June 1966.

"Nigeria: Civil War Ends," *Africa Research Bulletin* [London], VII, No. 1, February 15, 1970, 1642–1652.

"Nigeria Notes: Report from the East," *African Development* [London], June 1970, 9–11.

Nigeria Year Book, 1971. (Ed., John Adollo.) Lagos: Daily Times Magazine Division, 1971.

"Nigerian Airways Seek New Sky Power," *African Development* [London], August 1970, 3.

Nigerian Broadcasting Corporation. *Eminent Nigerians of the Nineteenth Century.* Cambridge: Cambridge University Press, 1960.

"Nigerian Government Nullifies Census," *Africa Report,* VIII, No. 3, March 1963, 24.

"Nigeria's China Decision Surprises Diplomats," *African Progress,* I, No. 2, April 1971, 35.

Nihart, Brooke. "Nigeria." Pages 223–224 in T. N. Dupuy (ed.), *The Almanac of World Military Power.* Dunn Loring, Virginia: T. N. Dupuy, 1970.

Niven, Sir Rex. *Nigeria.* London: Ernest Benn, 1967.

Noah, Monday Efiong. "The Nigerian Civil War and the Gullibles," *Africa Today,* XVII, No. 2, March–April 1970, 5–6.

Nwoga, D. I. *West African Verse: An Anthology.* London: Longmans, 1969.

Nzekwu, Onuora. *Wand of Noble Wood.* New York: New American Library of World Literature, Signet Edition, 1963.

Obi, Dorothy S. "The Public Library in Africa as a Communication Agency," *African Scholar,* I, No. 3, March–May 1969, 20–22.

————. "The Role of Libraries and Librarianship in the Educational, Social, and Economic Development of Africa," *African Scholar,* I, No. 4, 1970, 12–14.

Obiechina, E. N. "Growth of Written Literature in English-Speaking West Africa," *Presence Africaine* [Paris], LXVI, 1968, 58–78.

O'Connell, James. "The Scope of the Tragedy," *Africa Report,* XIII, No. 2, February 1968, 8–12.

Odugbesan, Clara. "Femininity in Yoruba Religious Art." Pages 199–211 in Mary Douglas and Phyllis Kaberry (eds.), *Man in Africa.* London: Tavistock, 1969.

Odujinrin, Wole. "Medical Needs of Postwar Nigeria." (Paper presented at Colloquium of Nigerian Student Union in the Americas.) New York: n.pub., n.d.

Odumosu, Oluwale Idowu. *The Nigerian Constitution: History and Development.* London: Sweet and Maxwell, 1963.

Ofomata, G.E.K. "Landforms on the Nsukka Plateau of Eastern

Nigeria," *Nigerian Geographical Journal* [Ibadan], X, No. 1, June 1967, 3–9.

Ogunmola, Kola. *The Palmwine Drinker: Opera After the Novel by A. Tutuola.* Ibadan. Institute of African Studies, University of Ibadan, 1968.

Ohadike, Patrick. "The Possibility of Fertility Change in Modern Africa: A West African Case," *African Social Research* [Manchester], No. 8, December 1969, 602–614.

Ojo, G. J. Afolabi. "Development of Yoruba Towns in Nigeria," *Ekistics* [Athens], XXVII, No. 161, April 1969, 243–247.

————. "Traditional Yoruba Architecture," *African Arts/Arts d'Afrique,* I, No. 3, Spring 1968, 14–17, 70–72.

————. *Yoruba Culture.* London: University of London Press, for University of Ife, 1966.

————. *Yoruba Palaces.* London: University of London Press, 1966.

Okediji, Francis O. "Public Health Promotion in Nigeria: A Sociological Viewpoint," *Ibadan,* XXVI, February 1969, 25–29.

————. "Socioeconomic Status and Differential Fertility in an African City," *Journal of Developing Areas,* XXX, No. 3, April 1969, 339–353.

Okediji, Francis O., and Aboyade, O. "Social and Economic Aspects of Environmental Sanitation in Nigeria: A Tentative Report," *Journal of Sociology and Health* [Lagos], II, No. 1, January 1967, 1–20.

Okesola, Ebun. "The Agbo Festival in Agbowa," *Nigeria Magazine* [Lagos], XCV, December 1967, 293–300.

Okin, Theophilus A. *The Urbanized Nigerian.* New York: Exposition Press, 1968.

Okoronkwo, Daniel. "The Nigeria/Biafra Crisis: A Historical View," No. 1, *African Image,* January 1969, 18–29.

Olatunbosun, Dupe. *Nigerian Government's Policies Affecting Investment in Agriculture.* (Consortium for the Study of Nigerian Rural Development, Series No. 15.) East Lansing: Michigan State University, for the CSNRD, July 1968.

Olayemi, Val. "Forms of the Song in Yoruba Folktales," *African Notes* [Ibadan], V, No. 1, October 1968, 25–32.

Olusanya, G. O. "Political Awakening in the North: A Reinterpretation," *Journal of the Historical Society of Nigeria* [Ibadan], IV, No. 1, December 1967, 125–134.

Olusanya, P. O. "The Educational Factor in Human Fertility: A Case Study of the Residents of a Suburban Area in Ibadan, Western Nigeria," *Nigerian Journal of Economic and Social Studies* [Ibadan], IX, No. 3, November 1967, 351–374.

————. "Rural-Urban Fertility Differentials in Western Nigeria,"

Population Studies [London], XXIII, No. 3, 1969, 363–378.

Oluwasanmi, J. A. *Agriculture and Nigerian Economic Development.* Ibadan: Oxford University Press, 1966.

————. "Efforts to Stem Land Exodus," *Financial Times* [London], August 4, 1969, p. 18.

Onwuejeogwu, Michael. "The Cult of the Bori Spirits Among the Hausa." Pages 279–305 in Mary Douglas and Phyllis Kaberry (eds.), *Man in Africa.* Tavistock: London, 1969.

Onyemelukwe, Clement Chukukadibia. *Problems of Industrial Planning and Management in Nigeria.* London: Longmans, Green, 1966.

Organization for Economic Cooperation and Development. *Development Assistance in 1970 Review.* Paris: OECD, 1970.

Orr, Sir Charles William James. *The Making of Northern Nigeria.* (2d ed.) London: Cass, 1965.

Osundina, Oyeniyi. *Bibliography of Nigerian Sculpture.* Lagos: University Library, 1968.

Ogunelar, Titus A. "Lamidi Fakeye: Nigerian Traditional Sculptor," *African Arts,* IV, No. 2, Winter 1971, 66–67.

Osuntokun, B. O., and Odeki, E. L. "Epilepsy in Nigerians," *Tropical and Geographical Medicine* [Haarlem], XXII, No. 1, March 1970, 3.

Osuntokun, B. O.; Singh, S. P.; and Martinson, F.D. "Deafness in Tropical Nutritional Ataxic Neuropathy," *Tropical and Geographical Medicine* [Haarlem], XXII, No. 3, September 1970, 381–387.

Ottenberg, Simon. "Ibo Oracles and Intergroup Relations," *Southwestern Journal of Anthropology,* XIV, 1958, 294–317.

————. "Ibo Receptivity to Change," Pages 130–143 in William R. Bascom and Melville J. Herskovits (eds.), *Continuity and Change in African Cultures.* Chicago: University of Chicago Press, 1959.

————. "Improvement Association Among the Afikpo Ibo," *Africa* [London], XXV, No. 1, 1955, 1–28.

————. "The Social and Administrative History of a Nigerian Township," *International Journal of Comparative Sociology* [Toronto], VII, Nos. 1 and 2, March 1966, 174–196.

Ottenberg, Simon, and Ottenberg, Phoebe. "Afikpo Markets: 1900–1960." In Paul Bohannan and George Dalton (eds.), *Markets in Africa.* Evanston: Northwestern University Press, 1961.

Oudes, Bruce. "The Press Vs. the Nigerian Government," *Africa Report,* XV, Nos. 2 and 15, February 1970, 15–18.

Owomoyela, Olyekan. "Yoruba-Language Theater Draws Inspiration from Tradition," *Africa Report,* XV, No. 1, June 1970, 32–33.

Oxford Atlas for Nigeria. London: Oxford University Press, 1968.

Ozanne, Paul. "A New Archaeological Survey of Ife," *Odu* [Ibadan], April 1969, 28–54.

Panter-Brick, S. K. (ed.) *Nigerian Politics and Military Rule: Prelude to the Civil War.* London: Athlone Press, 1970.

Paratt, J. K. "An Approach to Ife Festivals," *Nigeria Magazine* [Lagos], C, April 1969, 340–348.

Parrinder, Edward Geoffrey. *The Story of Ketu: An Ancient Yoruba Kingdom.* (2d. ed., rev.) Ibadan: Ibadan University Press, 1967.

Pearson, Scott R. *Petroleum and the Nigerian Economy.* Stanford: Stanford University Press, 1970.

Perham, Margery. "Nigeria's Civil War." Pages 1–12 in Colin Legum and John Drysdale (eds.), *African Contemporary Record: Annual Survey and Documents, 1968–1969.* London: Africa Research, 1969.

Perkins, W. A., and Stembridge, Jasper H. *Nigeria: A Descriptive Geography.* Ibadan: Oxford University Press, 1966.

Peshkin, Alan. "Education and National Integration in Nigeria," *Journal of Modern African Studies* [London], V, No. 3, October 1967, 323–334.

Pettit, Lincoln C. *The General Studies Program at the University of Nigeria: Its Origins and Development, 1960–1967.* East Lansing: African Studies Center, Michigan State University, 1969.

Pitt-Tivers, Augustus, H.L.F. *Antique Works of Art from Benin.* New York: Hacker Art Books, 1968.

"Population and Vital Statistics: Latest Available Data," *Population and Vital Statistics Report,* XXII, No. 4, October 1, 1970, 1–27.

Potholm, Christian P. "The Multiple Roles of the Police as Seen in the African Context," *Journal of Developing Areas,* III, No. 2, January 1969, 139–158.

Prest, A. R. "Public Utilities in Nigeria: Economic and Financial Aspect," *Administration* [Ibadan], II, No. 4, June 1968, 197–211.

Production Yearbook, 1969, XXII. Rome: Food and Agriculture Organization, 1970.

Prvehl, Paul O. *Fundamental Rights Under the Nigerian Constitution, 1960–1965.* (Occasional Paper No. 8.) Los Angeles: African Studies Center, University of California, 1970.

Pugh, J. C., and Perry, A. E. *A Short Geography of West Africa.* London: University of London Press, 1960.

Pullan, R. A. "The Solid Resources of West Africa." Pages 147–191 in M. F. Thomas and G. W. Whittington (eds.), *Environment and Land Use in Africa.* London: Methuen, 1969.

Radday, Harold. "Backing a Loser," *SAIS Review*, XV, No. 2, Winter 1971, 3–12.

Rake, Alan. "Nigeria's Oil Explosion: Who Will Become Rich?," *African Development* [London], February 1970, 12–13.

Rake, Alan (ed.). *Africa 69/70*. Paris: Socíeté Pressee Africaine Associée, 1969.

Republic of Nigeria. *Federal Nigeria*. XI, No. 13, Lagos: August 1967.

Republic of Nigeria. Federal Census Office. *Population Census of Nigeria, 1963: Eastern Region*, I. Lagos, 1964.

――――. *Population Census of Nigeria, 1963: Mid-Western Region*, I. Lagos, n.d.

――――. *Population Census of Nigeria, 1963: Northern Region*, I. Lagos, 1965.

――――. *Population Census of Nigeria, 1963: Western Region*, I. Lagos, n.d.

Republic of Nigeria. Federal Ministry of Information. *Estimates of the Government of the Federal Republic of Nigeria, 1968–1969*. Lagos: Printing Division, 1968.

――――. *Kainji Dam and the People*. Lagos, n.d.

Republic of Nigeria. Federal Ministry of Research and Information. *Presenting the Past: A Short Description of the Museum of Nigerian Antiquities, Traditional Art and Ethnology with a Note on the Prime Art Treasures and Their Sources of Origin*. Lagos, 1959.

Republic of Nigeria. Federal Office of Statistics. *Digest of Statistics*, XIX, No. 3. Lagos, July 1970.

――――. *Nigerian Trade Summary, December 1967*. Lagos, December 1968.

――――. *Nigerian Trade Summary, December 1968*. Lagos, December 1969.

――――. *Nigerian Trade Summary, December 1969*. Lagos, December 1970.

Republic of Nigeria. Nigerian Ports Authority. *Fourteenth Annual Report for the Year Ended 31st March 1969*. Lagos, 1970.

Republic of Nigeria. Nigerian Railway Corporation. *Report and Accounts for the Year Ended 31st March 1968*. Lagos, 1969.

Richardson, S. S., and Williams, T. H. *The Criminal Procedure Code of Northern Nigeria*. London: Sweet and Maxwell, 1963.

Rowan, Carl T. "Nigeria's Spectacular Rebound," *Reader's Digest*, LXXXXVIII, No. 590, June 1971, 156–166.

Rubin, Arnold. "Uta and Utumu: Kutep Mud Sculpture," *African Arts/Arts d'Afrique*, Spring 1968, 18–20.

Rubin, Barbara. "Calabash Decoration in North East [sic] State, Nigeria," African Arts, IV, No. 1, Autumn 1970, 20–25.

Ryder, Alan Frederich Charles. Benin and the Europeans, 1485–1897. New York: Humanities Press, 1969.

Salako, L. A. "Self Poisoning by Drugs: A Survey of Admissions," Tropical and Geographical Medicine [Haarlem], XXII, No. 4, December 1970, 397–402.

Sasnet, Martena, and Sepmeyer, Inez. Educational Systems of Africa. Berkeley: University of California Press, 1966.

Scarritt, James R. Political Change in a Traditional African Clan: Structural Functional Analysis of the Nsits of Nigeria. Denver: University of Denver, 1965.

Scharfe, Don, and Aliyu, Yahaya. "Hausa Poetry," Black Orpheus [Ibadan], XXI, April 1967, 31–36.

Schmidt, Nancy. "Nigerian Fiction and the African Oral Tradition," Journal of the New African Literature and the Arts. Spring–Fall 1968, 10–19.

Seidman, Robert B. "Law and Economic Development in Independent, English-Speaking Sub-Saharan Africa." Pages 3–74 in Thomas W. Hutchinson (ed.), Africa and Law: Developing Legal Systems in African Commonwealth Nations. Madison: University of Wisconsin Press, 1968.

Shaw, Thurstan. "Archaeology in Nigeria," Antiquity, September 1969, 187–199.

————. "The Making of the Igbo Vase," Ibadan, No. 2, February 1968, 15–20.

————. Ogbo-Ukwu: An Account of Archaeological Discoveries in Eastern Nigeria. London: Faber, for the Institute of Ibadan, 1969.

Shaw, Thurstan (ed.). Lectures on Nigerian Prehistory and Archaeology. Ibadan: Ibadan University Press, 1969.

————. "Radiocarbon Dating in Nigeria," Journal of the Historical Society of Nigeria [Ibadan], IV, No. 3, December 1968, 453–465.

Shelton, Austin J. The Articulation of Tradition and Modern Igbo Literature. (African Studies Association Paper.) Washington: ASA, 1968.

Skinner, Neil. Hausa Readings: Selections from Edgar's Tatsuniyoyi. Madison: University of Wisconsin Press, 1968.

Skinner, Neil (trans. and ed.). Hausa Tales and Traditions: An English Translation of Tatsuniyoyi in Hausa (Originally compiled by Frank Edgars with a foreword by M. G. Smith.) London: Cass, 1969.

Sklar, Richard L. *Nigerian Political Parties.* Princeton: Princeton University Press, 1963.

————. "The U.S. and the Biafran War," *Africa Report,* XLV, No. 7, November 1969, 22–23.

Smith, E. A.; Daniels, S. O.; and Foster, S. O. "Measles in Lagos." Pages 19–23 in the *Smallpox Eradication Program Report,* IV, No. 2. (Seminar on Smallpox Eradication and Measles Control in Western and Central Africa, Part II.) Atlanta: National Communicable Disease Center, 1970.

Smith, R. S. *Kingdoms of the Yoruba.* London: Methuen, 1969.

Smock, Audrey C. "The Politics of Relief," *Africa Report,* XV, No. 1, January 1970, 24–26.

Smock, Audrey C., and Smock, David R. "Cultural and Attitudinal Factors Affecting Agricultural Development in Eastern Nigeria," *Economic Development and Cultural Change,* XVIII, No. 1, Part I, October 1969, 110–124.

Smock, David R. *Conflict and Control in an African Trade Union: A Study of the Nigerian Coal Miners' Union.* Stanford: Hoover Institution Press, 1969.

Sofoluwe, G. O. "Promotive Medicine: A Boost to the Economy of Developing Countries," *Tropical and Geographical Medicine* [Haarlem], XXII, No. 2, June 1970, 250–254.

Sowande, Fela. "Nigerian Music and Musicians," *Nigeria Magazine* [Lagos], XCIV, September 1967, 253–261.

Soyinka, Wole. *Idanre, and Other Poems.* London: Methuen, 1967.

Stapleton, B. Brian. *The Wealth of Nigeria.* Ibadan: Oxford University Press, 1967.

Starkweather, Frank. *Six Igbo Wood Carvers in 1966.* (African Studies Association Paper.) Washington: ASA, 1970.

————. *Traditional Igbo Art: An Exhibit of Wood Sculpture Carved in 1965–1966.* Ann Arbor: University of Michigan Press, 1968.

Statistical Yearbook, 1969. Paris: United Nations Educational, Scientific and Cultural Organization, 1970.

Stebbins, Richard P., and Amoia, Alba Amoiz. *Political Handbook and Atlas of the World, 1970.* New York: Simon and Schuster, 1970.

Stillman, Arthur M. "Economic Cooperation in Africa," *Africa Report,* XII, No. 6, June 1967, 20–26.

Stokke, Baard R. *Soviet and Eastern European Trade and Aid in Africa.* New York: Praeger, 1967.

Tamuno, Tekena N. "The Odun Festival," *Nigeria Magazine* [Lagos], XCVII, June–August 1968, 68–76.

————. "Separatist Agitations in Nigeria Since 1914," *Journal of*

Modern African Studies [London], VIII, No. 4, December 1970, 563–584.

Technical Guide. (Descriptions of series published in the *Bulletin of Labor Statistics.*) Geneva: International Labor Office, 1968.

Theroux, Paul. "Voices Out of the Skull (An African Poetry)," *Black Orpheus* [Ibadan], XX, August 1966, 41–52.

"Thin Edge of a Soviet Wedge," *Financial Times* [London], November 21, 1968, n.p.

Third Report on the World Health Situation, 1961–1964. (Official Records of the World Health Organization.) Geneva: WHO, April 1967.

Thomas, Peter. *Poems from Nigeria.* New York: Vantage Press, 1967.

Thompson, Robert Farris. "The Sign of the Divine Kings: An Essay on Yoruba Bead-Embroidered Crowns with Veil and Bird Decorations," *African Arts/Arts d'Afrique,* III, No. 3, Spring 1970, 8–17.

––––––. "Sons of Thunder: Twin Images Among the Oyo and Other Yoruba Groups," *African Arts,* IV, No. 3, Spring 1971, 8–13.

Thornley, James F. *The Planning of Primary Education in Northern Nigeria.* (International Institute for Educational Planning.) Paris: United Nations Educational, Scientific and Cultural Organization, I.I.E.P., 1966.

"Transport System Keeps Up with the Flow of Trade," *Financial Times* [London], August 4, 1970, 18.

Tukur, M. "Establishment of State Government in Northern Nigeria," *Journal of Modern African Studies* [London], VIII, No. 1, April 1970, 128–133.

Uchendu, V. C. "Some Issues in African Land Tenure," *Tropical Agriculture* [Trinidad], XLIV, No. 2, April 1967, 91–101.

Udo, Reuben K. "Census Migrations in Nigeria," *Nigerian Geographical Journal* [Ibadan], XIII, No. 1, June 1970, 3–7.

––––––. "The Migrant Tenant Farmer of Eastern Nigeria," *Africa* [London], XXXIV, No. 4, October 1964, 326–339.

Ugokwe, J.B.C. "The Politics and Consequences of the Nigerian-Biafra War," *African Scholar,* August–November 1968, 17–21.

United Nations. Department of Economic and Social Affairs. *Progress in Land Reform: Fourth Report.* (Prepared jointly by the secretariats of the United Nations, the Food and Agriculture Organization of the United Nations, and the International Labor Organization.) New York: 1966.

United Nations Educational, Scientific and Cultural Organization. *Book Development in Africa: Problems and Perspectives.* Paris: 1969.

United Nations Educational, Scientific and Cultural Organization. United Nations Development Program. *University of Lagos College of Education, Nigeria.* (Report prepared for the government of Nigeria by UNESCO, Report Series No. 11.) Paris: 1969.

United Nations Food and Agriculture Organization. *Agricultural Development in Nigeria, 1965–1980.* Rome: 1966.

U.S. Agency for International Development. *U.S. Technical and Capital Assistance in Support of Economic Development in Nigeria, Report as of January 1, 1967.* Lagos: U.S. Agency for International Development/Nigeria, 1967.

U.S. Agency for International Development. Bureau for Technical Assistance. *Office of Population.* Population Program Assistance. Washington: October 1969.

U.S. Agency for International Development. Bureau of Program and Policy Coordination. Office of Statistics and Reports. *Africa: Economic Growth Trends.* n.pub.: January 1971.

U.S. Arms Control and Disarmament Agency. *World Military Expenditures, 1969.* Washington: GPO, 1970.

U.S. Congress. 91st, 2d Session. House of Representatives. Committee on Foreign Affairs. Subcommittee on Africa. *The Postwar Nigerian Situation.* Washington: GPO, 1970.

U.S. Department of Agriculture. Economic Research Service. Foreign Regional Analysis Division. *Nigeria's Agricultural Economy in Brief,* by Snider W. Skinner. (Foreign Agriculture Economics ERS Foreign 98.) Washington: September 1964.

U.S. Department of Commerce. Bureau of International Commerce. "Best U.S. Sales Prospects in Nigeria," *Country Market Digest.* (IMIS 71–100.) Washington: February 1971.

U.S. Department of State. *Nigeria.* Washington: GPO, March 1969.

U.S. Department of State. Bureau of Intelligence and Research. *Cameroon-Nigeria Boundary.* (International Boundary Study No. 92.) Washington: November 3, 1969.

———. *Chad-Nigeria Boundary.* (International Boundary Study No. 90.) Washington: October 1, 1969.

———. *Dahomey-Nigeria Boundary.* (International Boundary Study No. 91.) Washington: October 15, 1969.

———. *Niger-Nigeria Boundary.* (International Boundary Study No. 93.) Washington: December 15, 1969.

———. *World Strength of the Communist Party Organizations.* Washington: GPO, 1970.

U.S. Department of State. Office of the Geographer. *Africa: Civil Divisions.* (Geographic Report No. 15.) Washington: October 27, 1969.

U.S. Department of State. Bureau of Public Affairs. Office of Media Service. *Republic of Nigeria* (Series: Background Notes.) Washington: GPO, May 1969.

U.S. Embassy in Lagos. *Aviation Survey—Africa.* Lagos: December 9, 1970.

Uwechue, Raph. *Reflections on the Nigerian Civil War: A Call for Realism.* London: O.I.T.H. International Publishers, 1969.

Van de Walle, Etienne. "An Approach to the Study of Fertility in Nigeria," *Population Studies* [London], XIX, No. 1, July 1965, 5–16.

————. "Who's Who and Where in Nigeria: The Latest Available Figures on Population and Tribal Distribution," *Africa Report*, XV, No. 1, January 1970, 22–23.

Vaughn-Richards, Alan. "Future Architectural Design," *Nigeria Magazine* [Lagos], XCIII, June 1967, 107–114.

Vidal, 'Tunji. "Oriki in Traditional Yoruba Music," *African Arts/Arts d'Afrique,* III, No. 1, Autumn 1967, 56–59.

Von Lichtenbergm, F., et al. "Pathological Effects of Schistosomiasis in Ibadan," *American Journal of Tropical Medicine and Hygiene,* XX, No. 2, March 1971, 224–254.

Wade, H.W.R. (ed.) *Annual Survey of Commonwealth Law, 1968.* London: Butterworth, 1968.

Walker, Barbara K., and Warren, S. (eds.) *Nigerian Folk Tales.* New Brunswick: Rutgers University, 1961.

Walsh, A. H., and Williams B. *Urban Government in Metropolitan Lagos.* New York: Praeger, 1968.

Walter, M. W. "Length of the Rainy Season in Nigeria," *Nigerian Geographical Journal.* Ibadan, X, No. 2. December 1967, 123–138.

Walter Reed Army Institute of Research. *Federation of Nigeria.* (Health Data Publications, Series No. 20.) Washington: Walter Reed Army Medical Center, 1963.

Welch, Claude E., Jr. "Africa's New Rulers," *Africa Report,* XV, No. 2, April–May 1968, 7–11.

Welch, Claude E., Jr. (ed.) *Soldier and State in Africa.* Evanston: Northwestern University Press, 1970.

West African Directory, 1964–1965. (3d ed.) London: Thomas Skinner, 1964, 269–373.

Wilkes, James W. "Africa Builds for Health," *International Commerce,* LXXVI, No. 33, October 5, 1970, 15–23.

Willett, Frank. "Ife In Nigerian Art," *African Arts/Arts d'Afrique,* I, No. 1, Autumn 1967, 30–35.

————. *Ife in the History of West African Sculpture.* London: Thames and Hudson, 1967.

Williamson, Kay, and Timitimi, A. "A Note on Ijo Number Symbolism," *African Notes* [Ibadan], V, No. 3, January 1970, 9–16.

Wolff, Hans. "Language, Ethnic Identity and Social Change in South Nigeria," *Anthropological Linguistics,* IX, No. 3, January 1967, 18–25.

World Radio-TV Handbook, 1971. (Ed., J. M. Frost.) Hvidovre, Denmark: World Radio-TV Handbook, n.d.

Worldmark Encyclopedia of the Nations: Africa, II. (Ed., Louis Barron.) New York: Harper and Row, 1967.

Yamuno, T. N. "Governor Clifford and Representative Government," *Journal of the Historical Society of Nigeria* [Ibadan], IV, No. 1, December 1967, 117–124.

Yearbook of International Organizations, 1968–1969. Brussels: Union of International Association, 1969.

Yearbook of National Accounts Statistics, 1969, II: International Tables. New York: United Nations, 1970.

Yearbook of the United Nations, 1968. New York: United Nations, 1971.

Zolberg, Aristide R. "Military Rule and Political Development in Tropical Africa." Pages 175–202 in Jacques Van Doorn (ed.), *Military Profession and Military Regimes: Commitments and Conflicts.* The Hague: Mouton, 1969.

Zukerman, Morris E. "Nigerian Crisis: Impact on the North," *Journal of Modern African Studies* [London], VIII, No. 1, April 1970, 37–54.

(Various issues of the following periodicals were also used in the preparation of this edition: *Africa Report* [Washington], January 1960–June 1971; *Africa Research Bulletin* [London], January 1964–June 1971; *Economist* [London], 1968–1971; *Financial Times* [London], August 4, 1969; *Keesing's Contemporary Archives* [Bristol, England], January 1, 1959–January 19, 1971; *Medical Tribune: International Edition,* [Africa] [New York], October 1969–January 1971; *Labor Developments Abroad* [Washington], September 1968–March 1970; *New Nigerian* [Kaduna], March 5–27, 1971–May 7, 1971; *Quarterly Economic Review: Nigeria* [London], January 1970–January 1971; *Standard Bank Review* [London], 1969–1971; *Washington Post,* October 1970–March 1971; *West Africa* [London], September 1970–June 1971.)

GLOSSARY

Biafra—Name given to the self-proclaimed republic formed by leaders of the Eastern Region, which attempted to secede from Nigeria in mid-1967; use of the name was discontinued after secessionist troops surrendered to federal forces in January 1970, following 2½ years of civil war.

bridewealth—Money, property, or services traditionally given by, or in behalf of, a prospective husband to the bride's family.

FEC—Federal Executive Council. Nigeria's acting cabinet under military government.

FMG—Federal Military Government.

ICFTU—International Confederation of Free Trade Unions.

jihad—A religious duty imposed on believers by Muslim law for the spread of Islam; popularly known as "holy war," it is waged against unbelievers and enemies of the faith; followers may fulfill their *jihad* duty in four different ways: by the heart, the tongue, the hand, and the sword.

lineage—A group of people who can trace descent from a known common ancestor. Most Nigerian ethnic groups are patrilineal in that they trace descent through the male line. A large lineage tracing descent from a relatively remote ancestor may include smaller lineages, each of which traces descent from a less remote ancestor.

Middle Belt—An ethnic and political zone stretching from east to west across the central section of the country and consisting of more than 9 million members of minor ethnic groups, who had been unable to obtain significant political influence because of traditional dominance by the Hausa-Fulani and Kanuri emirates. As used by economists and geographers, the term does not always coincide with ethnic and political divisions but usually designates the area between the characteristic northern and southern economies; in this context the area extends roughly from 7°30′N to 11°N.

Nigerian pound (N£)—Basic unit of Nigerian currency; 1 Nigerian pound equals US$2.80.

NLC—Nigerian Labor Congress.

NPF—Nigeria Police Force.

NTUC—Nigerian Trade Union Congress.

nuclear family—A man, his wife, and their unmarried children.

NWC—Nigerian Workers Council.

Safrap Nigeria—A Nigerian subsidiary, jointly owned by the French oil companies SAFREX (Sociétè Africaine d'Exploration Pétrolière and ERAP (Enterprise de Recherches et d'Activités Pétrolière).

sheanut—Oilseed of the rough-barked tropical shea tree; sheanuts are used for the widely consumed shea butter and for fuel.

SMC—Supreme Military Council—Nigeria's executive body under military government.

UCCLO—United Committee of Central Labor Organizations.

ULC—United Labor Congress.

WFTU—World Federation of Trade Unions.

INDEX

Abakaliki Province (*see also* East Central State; South Eastern State): 160, 243

Abdullahi Bayero College: 193

Achebe, Chinua: 188

Action Group: 62–63, 70, 71, 72, 216, 220, 222–223, 227–229

Adamawa-Eastern languages: 123

Adamawa Province: 21, 84

Adebo, Simeon: 95

administrative units: xv, 32–34, 243

advertising: 207, 380

Afolabi, Jacob: 195, 196

African Development Bank: x, 268

African Studies, Institute of: 185

African unity (*see also* Organization of African Unity): 249, 252

Agbebijo theatrical company: 189

Agip Oil Company Nigeria: 354

agreements and treaties: x, 11, 32

agriculture (*see also* crops; exports): ix, 8, 186, 297, 299, 315–347; labor force, 79, 89

Aguiyi-Ironsi, J. T. U. *See* Ironsi, J. T. U. Aguiyi-

Ahmadu, Alhaji: 67

Admadu Bello University: 169, 184

air force: 386, 408–409

air transportation: 40, 263

airports: x, 40

Akintola, Samuel: 70, 71, 222, 227, 228, 230, 231, 232

Akolo, Jimo: 196

Albania: 262

Algeria: 256

alienation of land: 330

alphabets: 121

Aluko, T.M.: 188

Amadi, Elechi: 188

Anambra River: 17

Anang: 106, 114

ancestor cult: 134, 148, 150

animal husbandry (*see also* tsetse fly): 323, 342

Antiquities, Department of: 197

Arabic language: viii, 120

archeology: 192, 194, 197

architecture: 192–193

area: 1, 13

Arikpo, Okoi: 260, 261, 266

armed forces (*see also* air force, army, navy): x, 308, 386, 400–410

armed robbery: 389

army: 239, 386, 402–406

art galleries: 197

Atlantic languages: 123

Awolowo, Obafemi (*see also* Action Group): 62, 67, 70, 71, 219, 222, 228, 230, 235, 239

Azikiwe, Nnamdi: 62, 67, 70, 73, 75, 76, 128, 187, 188, 199, 220, 240, 258

Bacita Sugar Estate: 325

balance of payments: ix, 295, 298, 364, 371–375

Balewa, Abubakar Tafawa: 66, 67, 70, 71, 73, 75, 224, 231, 232, 252, 258

banking system: 309, 312–313

Bankole, Ayo: 191

Bantu languages: 123

Beecroft, John: 49

Bello, Ahmadu: 73, 74, 223

Benin kingdom: 43, 194

benniseed. *See* sesame

Benue-Niger languages: 123

Benue-Plateau State: 104

Benue River (*see also* Niger-Benue River Valley): 19, 28–29, 37

Beri-Beri. *See* Kanuri

Biafra, Republic of (*see also* civil war): 6, 77, 99, 236, 288, 396, 404

birds: 31

Birom: 123, 272

Birom Progressive Union: 226

Black Orpheus: 188

blindness: 165

Bonny: River, 38; town, 114

Borgu Game Reserve: 32

Borgu State: 123

Bori cult: 142, 143, 149–150

475

Kano: dialect, 119; Province, 83; State, 85, 104, 243, 338, 340
Kano Chronicle: 45
Kano Local Authority: 246
Kantab: 272
Kanuri: 104, 106, 116, 117; language, 123, 124, 125, 126, 202; values, 215, 272, 278
Katsina, Hassan: 232
Katsina Province: 83, 84, 341
Kenya: 256, 266
kingship and hereditary rank: 129, 136, 137, 149, 216
kinship (*see also* improvement unions): 131–132, 134, 383
Komadugu Yobe River: 29
Koran: 152
Kutep: 195
Kwa language: 122, 123
Kwara State: 104, 390

Labor and Social Welfare, Ministry of: 171, 172
labor force: 79, 89–93, 358, 363; agriculture, 315, 336; industry, 357, 359; labor code, 96, 99–100
Lagos: 3, 15, 23, 35, 38, 61, 94, 158, 160, 161, 163, 193, 357; population, 1, 85, 86, 109, 111
Lagos, Federal Territory of: 33, 81, 82
Lagos, University of: 88, 169, 184, 199
Lagos Colony: 54
Lagos State: 104, 241, 243, 391, 395
Lake Chad. *See* Chad, Lake
land rotation. *See* bush fallow system
land tenure: 134, 329–331, 344
land use: 317
languages (*see also* specific names of languages or ethnic groups): 118–128; official language, vii, 2, 69
learned societies: 186
leprosy: 164
Liberia: 257
libraries: 186
life expectancy: 155
literacy: ix, 9, 10, 175, 410
living standards: 3, 156
local government: 245; indirect rule, 56–57
local police: 391, 396–397
Lugard, Frederick: 56–58, 64

Macauley, Herbert: 61, 62, 219, 221

Macpherson Constitution: 65
magic: 138, 166, 285
malaria: 162, 163–164
Mali: 257
mallams: 280
malnutrition (*see also* diet): 155, 160
Mamu River: 17
Mandingo language: 123, 124
manufacturing: 297, 355–363
market week: 381
marketing boards: 291, 294, 299, 332–334, 379
marriage: 132–133, 135, 278
Mauritania: 256, 257
Mbari Mbayo Club: 197
measles: 162
medicine and health (*see also* diseases; malnutrition); ix, 3, 186; personnel, 156, 168; treatment, 165–169
Meir, Golda: 258
men: 86, 135, 161
Michigan State University: 184
Mid-West Democratic Front (MDF): 72, 74
Mid-Western Region (*see also* Mid-Western State): 33, 71, 85, 215, 230, 243, 393
Mid-Western State: 16, 38, 104, 115, 339, 340, 390, 391
Middle Belt: 147, 243, 323–324; ethnic groups, 79, 103, 107, 165
middle class: 157
migration (*see also* resettlement): 85, 92, 217, 254, 295
mineral resources (*see also* oil reserves): 8, 30–31, 348
Mines and Power, Ministry of: 353
mining: 298, 301, 302, 348–351
ministries: 241, 242
mission schools: 109, 131, 176, 177
missionaries, Christian: 50, 51–53, 58, 114, 120, 130, 153, 154, 155, 164
Monrovia Charter: 252
Moroccan leather: 143
Morocco: 256
motor vehicles: 38
Munoye, Jon: 188
museums: 197
music: 190–191
Muslims (*see also* Fulani; Kanuri): 4, 116, 120, 131–133, 137, 139, 142; social values, 218, 272, 288

479

480

PUBLISHED AREA HANDBOOKS

550–65	Afghanistan		550–81	Korea, North
550–98	Albania		550–41	Korea, Republic of
550–44	Algeria		550–58	Laos
550–59	Angola		550–24	Lebanon
550–73	Argentina		550–38	Liberia
550–20	Brazil		550–85	Libya
550–61	Burma		550–45	Malaysia
550–83	Burundi		550–76	Mongolia
550–50	Cambodia		550–49	Morocco
550–96	Ceylon		550–64	Mozambique
550–26	Colombia		550–88	Nicaragua
550–60	Communist China		550–94	Oceania
550–91	Congo (Brazzaville)		550–48	Pakistan
550–67	Congo (Kinshasa)		550–156	Paraguay
550–90	Costa Rica		550–92	Peripheral States of the Arabian Peninsula
550–152	Cuba		550–42	Peru
550–22	Cyprus		550–72	Philippines, Republic of
550–54	Dominican Republic		550–84	Rwanda
550–52	Ecuador		550–51	Saudi Arabia
550–150	El Salvador		550–70	Senegal
550–28	Ethiopia		550–86	Somalia
550–29	Germany		550–93	South Africa, Republic of
550–153	Ghana		550–95	Soviet Union
550–87	Greece		550–27	Sudan
550–78	Guatemala		550–47	Syria
550–82	Guyana		550–62	Tanzania
550–151	Honduras		550–53	Thailand
550–21	India		550–89	Tunisia
550–154	Indian Ocean Territories		550–80	Turkey
550–39	Indonesia		550–74	Uganda
550–68	Iran		550–43	United Arab Republic
550–31	Iraq		550–97	Uruguay
550–25	Israel		550–71	Venezuela
550–30	Japan		550–57	Vietnam, North
550–34	Jordan		550–55	Vietnam, South
550–56	Kenya		550–75	Zambia

☆U.S. GOVERNMENT PRINTING OFFICE: 1972—O 482-744 (PO 328)